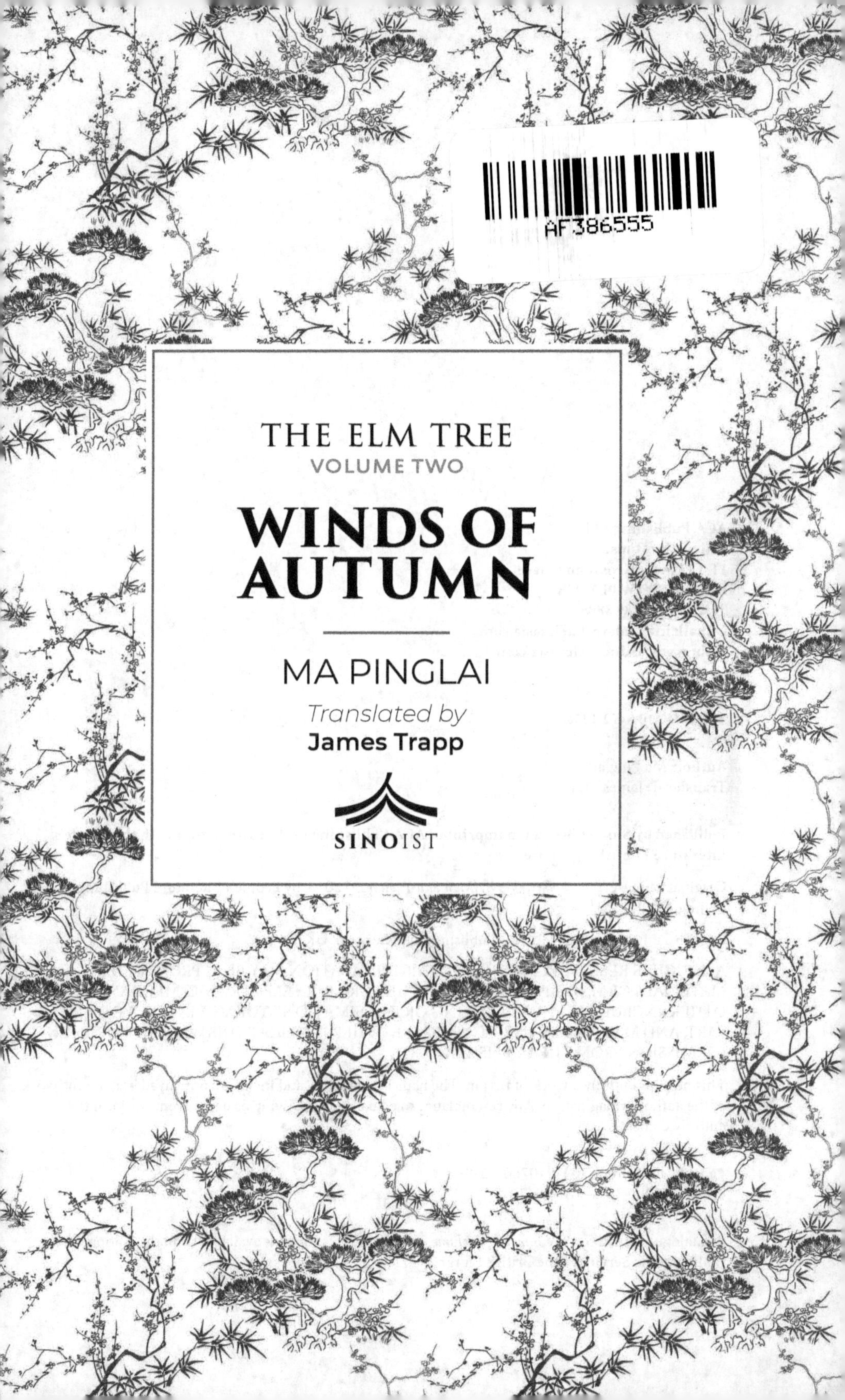

THE ELM TREE
VOLUME TWO

WINDS OF AUTUMN

MA PINGLAI

Translated by
James Trapp

SINOIST

ACA Publishing Ltd
University House
11-13 Lower Grosvenor Place
London SW1W 0EX, UK
Tel: +44 20 3289 3885
E-mail: info@alaincharlesasia.com
Web: www.alaincharlesasia.com

Beijing Office
Tel: +86(0)10 8472 1250

Author: Ma Pinglai
Translator: James Trapp

Published by Sinoist Books (an imprint of ACA Publishing Ltd) in association with the People's Literature Publishing House

Original Chinese Text © 满树榆钱儿 (*Man Shu Yuqian Er*) 2018, by People's Literature Publishing House, Beijing, China

English Translation © 2021, ACA Publishing Ltd, London, UK

This novel is entirely a work of fiction. The names, characters and incidents portrayed in it are the work of the author's imagination. Any resemblance to actual persons, living or dead, events or localities is entirely coincidental.

Paperback ISBN: 978-1-910760-75-8
eBook ISBN: 978-1-910760-76-5

A catalogue record for *The Elm Tree (Volume Two): Winds of Autumn* is available from the National Bibliographic Service of the British Library.

THE ELM TREE

VOLUME TWO: WINDS OF AUTUMN

MA PINGLAI

Translated by
JAMES TRAPP

SINOIST BOOKS

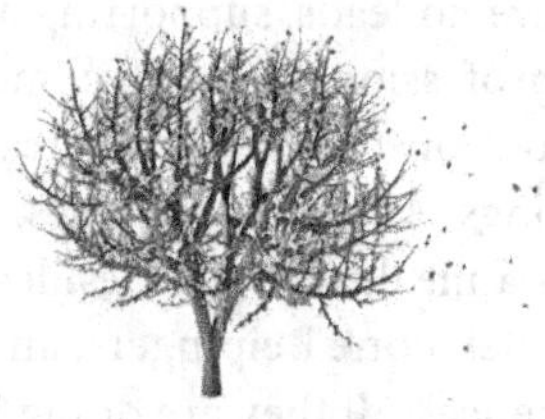

Chapter 1

The Japanese-sponsored 'New People's Assembly for Japanese-Chinese Goodwill' is about to be established. Although this assembly carries the label of a humanitarian organisation, its constitution is entirely for the benefit of the puppet governments of Beiping and the rest of North China. According to the people themselves, it is just a basinful of dogshit put out to attract flies, a random congregation of scabies-ridden curs. Nonetheless, the Japanese are planning to mark the occasion by holding a great party in the square in front of the main hall of the Thai Temple, with seven days of theatrical performances in the inner courtyard. At the appointed time, all the Japanese military and civil commanders, representatives from the puppet state of Manchukuo and traitorous VIPs from Beiping, Tianjin and every county in Hebei Province are all to gather in attendance.

WHEN A MASTER SPEAKS, it's bad news for his slaves who have to do the hard work. In the past, even excluding the clapper song, local *ping* opera and shadow puppets, there were dozens of opera troupes in the capital. But either side of the occupation of Beiping, many of these companies fled the city to escape the chaos. Not everyone left as part of a troupe, and individual performers fled independently south of the Yangtze River or into the northwestern provinces of Shanxi and Shaanxi, either to re-form as companies or to seek shelter with family. Even those who didn't take such drastic action still sought refuge in the rural areas around Beiping, abandoning their former profession. If the supporting pillars are taken away from a stage, leaving only the empty space below, can it still be called a stage? Liu Chenglong was an executive administrator for the new assembly, and his men were in charge of maintaining public order on the streets through all the local area offices. However, although they raised financial contributions to fund two days of performances, they were still unable to rustle up a single decent star artist.

It is Zhou Si's suggestion, although it is indeed a counsel of desperation, that it doesn't matter if there are no leads, supporting actors, juniors, gong-beaters or warm-up artists. If the professionals won't come, then amateurs will have to suffice, and if they can't put on full-blown operas, they'll have to make do with sideshow acts and folk songs. As the saying goes, if you can't find any meat, eat beancurd instead; it's still a meal, after all. Besides, the event is being laid on by the Japanese, not Chinese, let alone Beipingers, and how many of them are going to be able to tell the difference? All they are doing is planning a bit of a knees-up. It doesn't matter how good it is, as long as there are a few songs and some music.

Providing no one looks at it too closely and everything comes together one way or another, the job is done, and they've managed to put on a two-day programme. Zhou Si also appoints Li Fenggu to oversee the production, and in trying to cobble everything together, rehearsals in the courtyard of the local government office often go on well after midnight. Autumn is the season of noisy cats, and at the third watch of the night, the combination of the performers' caterwauling and the cats' mating calls increases the noise and general nuisance considerably.

One day, Li Fenggu arrives particularly early, and she hurries over to the western chamber of the main building where Zhou Si lives. She pushes open the door and goes in. Shaken awake, Zhou Si asks blearily: "Eh? Why are you so early today? Do you need money?"

"You're not far wrong," Li Fenggu replies, her lips twitching into a smile. "It is indeed money I'm on about."

"Ah! Is it really urgent? Can't you wait outside a minute? I haven't got any clothes on here."

Li Fenggu claps him on the back. "Ha! Surely we know each other well enough by now for you to stop playing the shy little virgin. Anyway, why would I want to look at what you've got down there?"

Zhou Si scrambles out of bed and throws on some clothes, as Li Fenggu continues: "If I've got good news, I tell you straight out. Not like you – if you have a little windfall, you stay mum and keep it all to yourself."

"Are you really saying I don't look out for you? What about now? You're not just supervising the show, you're acting in it, so you'll get all the glory and have a chance to show off your talents too."

"Alright, alright, so you say," she says. "But I'm putting in all the effort for no reward. These Japanese are so stingy, it's like I'm doing a charity show."

"Keep your voice down, aunty. Who ever gets any money out of the Japanese?"

"Me for one! I'm going to get my hands in their wallets."

"Dream on."

Li Fenggu smiles, slows down a bit and lowers her voice: "I know a Japanese quartermaster. His name's Ono Ichiro..."

"Stop! Stop!" Zhou Si says uneasily. "If you want to poke the tiger and stir up trouble, that's got nothing to do with me."

Li Fenggu is unconcerned and smiles broadly. "Don't be so suspicious. Someone's given me an opportunity to make some real money. Did you know the Japanese army has comfort stations?"

"What's a comfort station?"

"Well, er, basically it's a brothel specially for the troops."

"Ah! I'd heard something of the sort. But I'd also heard that all the girls are Japanese and Korean. Why? Are you thinking of getting mixed up in that business? Is there really a lot of money to be made? Aiya! You'd not just be risking your reputation, you'd be risking your life too!"

Zhou Si can't help bursting into astonished laughter, but he is pulled up short by a slap from Li Fenggu.

"Stop that nonsense! How many Japanese soldiers are there in Beiping? Too many to count. Do you think a hundred Japanese girls are going to be enough to satisfy them? My contact tells me they may be looking for some Chinese girls to work in the comfort stations too, and I want to get the monopoly on that cushy number. You'd be crazy not to come in with me."

"Ha! And what exactly would you want me to do? Do you expect me to empty the brothels of the red-light district, or scour the stews?"

"That just shows how little you know. Do you think the Japanese are idiots? Most of the brothel girls have got the clap, and if they give that to the Imperial Army, how long do you think their heads would stay on their shoulders?"

"Well then... are you expecting girls from good families to do the job?"

Li Fenggu raises an eyebrow. "That's where you come in. If there aren't enough girls, we'll just have to take them by force. Once they're with us, like it or not, it'll be out of their hands. If you can lay on a few lads as security, I'll take care of the details. That way, you'll not only get in the Japanese's good books, you'll make some money too."

Tempted, Zhou Si considers this for a while, then asks: "How much money do you think?"

"Plenty. When the Japanese soldiers go to those places, they settle their bills once a month. Food and necessities for the girls aren't going to amount to much. A couple of melons and a handful of dates will do. Even if we give them a few coppers so they don't leave and scatter to the winds, the bulk of the money will end up in our hands, won't it?"

"Well then... how will we split it between us?"

"We don't need to talk about splitting it." Li Fenggu's voice becomes girlish, but her overall tone remains that of the middle-aged woman she actually is. "You're all alone, and I'm a widow, so there's no need for us to mess around. If we're going to manage the Japanese business to their satisfaction, then we should shack up together. I've already arranged the accommodation, not too big, and very quiet and discreet. There's no need to lay on sedan chairs or drinks. You can save your pennies, get yourself a wife for nothing, and there'll be no need to talk about splitting the money because we'll be keeping it all in the family. So, are you in or not?"

"I'm in, I'm in!" Zhou Si says hurriedly. "One hundred per cent! And from now on, I'll do whatever you say. Alright?"

Li Fenggu is all smiles, but Zhou Si is still a bit troubled by the business. "It's going to be a bit of a bother, though, isn't it?"

When he sees Li Fenggu glaring at him, he quickly explains: "I mean the comfort stations. It's big stuff. We may be able to keep it secret from everyone else, but we won't be able to keep it from my Junior Master."

"There's no need to. He's not going to do anything to antagonise the Japanese, is he? Besides, Liu Chenglong's nobody's fool, and he isn't going to pass up the chance to make some easy money. All we have to do is cut him in for a share."

Before Zhou Si can reply, the door is hurled open, and Chenglong stands composedly in the doorway.

"Ah! It's you, Junior Master," Zhou Si says, hurriedly putting on his jacket.

Chenglong ignores him and inspects the two of them, before saying, with a cold smile: "I *am* going to pass up the chance to make some easy money. Zhou Si, if you want to get involved in this rotten business, I can't stop you. But don't drag my name into it, and don't get ideas above your station – there's no more in the pot after you've finished this bowlful. Now fuck off and open your brothel with your slutty girlfriend, so you can play the pimp like you always wanted."

Li Fenggu blushes furiously, clearly stung by Chenglong's words and is about to answer back, but Zhou Si surreptitiously restrains her. He steps forward with an obsequious smile.

"Don't be angry, Junior Master. Fenggu and I were just shooting the breeze. Even the biggest flood can't swamp a mountain, I know that. If you don't give the nod, there's nothing anyone can do about it, not even the Japanese. They could offer me a mountain of gold, and no matter how tempting, I wouldn't dare."

Although Chenglong knows Zhou Si is a champion bullshitter, he is still pleased by his words, so he snorts in amusement and his severe expression relaxes. Seeing this, Zhou Si continues: "On the other hand, Young Master, the matter has been decided by the Japanese, and we're already in there, so we don't have much option."

This only serves to rekindle Chenglong's anger, and he glares at Zhou Si. "Every railway policeman has his own section of track to look after, and that section has got nothing to do with me. You'd better stop trying to use the Japanese to pressure me. Do you expect me to believe they would punish me over something like this?"

"No, no, of course it wouldn't go that far." Zhou Si laughs nervously, and he changes tack. "But just think about it, Junior Master. This business could become a free-for-all if no one takes control of it. If we don't get involved, everyone else will be fighting over it, and they won't just be fighting over the rich pickings, they'll also be fighting to get in the Japanese's good books, won't they? Look, the

Japanese respect you and they know you're not one of those arse-lickers. They value you for your talents and abilities, so you can do your brothers in the society a good turn and foster international relations at the same time. But just remember, there's no point in doing something quietly, because there are always blowhards who'll claim the glory. Think of all those bigwigs in the New Assembly – which of them wouldn't do just that? You wouldn't even get a look-in as a committee member. Do you think our folk will put up with that kind of humiliation?"

These words really irritate Chenglong, but he just snorts and gives a long sigh.

Zhou Si takes up again where he had left off: "So then, if we get on board with the Japanese and really put our all into it, then we can grab the opportunity and put all those loud-mouths and pen-pushers in their place. None of the new government officials are properly sworn in yet, and if we don't act now, it will be too late. Fenggu and I are only thinking of what's good for you, and what's good for you must be good for us too. Isn't that right, Fenggu?"

Li Fenggu catches Zhou Si's meaningful look as he says this and bites back her annoyance. She forces a smile and nods in agreement. Chenglong looks up at them, mutters to himself, but doesn't reply.

Zhou Si leans in closer to him: "I'm being straight with you, Junior Master. You've got to take the lead in this. Can you... can you give me the go-ahead?"

There is a long pause before Chenglong finally sighs again and says: "Ai! If you're going to do it, go ahead and do it."

Wreathed in smiles, Zhou Si replies happily: "Great! Don't worry, Fenggu and I will make a fine job of it. We'll make sure the Japanese..."

"Enough!" Chenglong interrupts him angrily, then pauses for a moment, before adding: "Just remember, it's never a good idea to shit on your own doorstep. Make sure you find somewhere as far away as possible, not around here, or we'll have too much explaining to do."

Zhou Si and Li Fenggu acknowledge this enthusiastically, nodding their heads like hens pecking at corn.

IT'S APPROACHING MIDDAY, and the workers at the Liuji night soil depot are still busy laying out the dung to dry. They've been at it without a break being called since early morning. Although it's already autumn and the hottest days of summer are over, meaning that the mornings and evenings are a bit cooler, the sun is still fierce during the day. The workmen all have rivers of sweat running down their backs, and their long trousers are wringing wet. On top of this, they are so hungry their stomachs are growling; it's too much for even the strongest to endure. Two of them have already fainted from exhaustion, and several others are struggling, their heads swimming and their sight blurred. It's not uncommon to see men dealt with harshly, but it's something else to see them treated this way, as if they were no longer human beings. Things are even worse than when Chenglong was in control. Why is this? It's because 'Sergeant Lian' is in command, and he is the ultimate in work-shy bullying bosses. He is very much the new broom trying to impose his authority. It's not easy to move from worker to manager, and in the transition he has done more than just ruffle a few feathers.

One of the workers straightens up, leaning on his pitchfork, but before he has even had time to draw breath, he is hit on the back by a clod of earth. This is immediately followed by a shout from Sergeant Lian: "This is a night soil yard. If you want to stand there like a telegraph pole, then you can do that out on the street. You're a waste of space!"

"We've been working all morning," the worker shoots back. "Can't a man catch his breath occasionally?"

Sergeant Lian grins back at him. "Who's stopping you? Go ahead and breathe, but breathing doesn't stop your arms and legs working, does it? How many times do I have to tell you, we need to take advantage of these sunny days. If we get a run of wet, cloudy days, with the shit sticking to your body, how's it going to bake dry? Ha! Do you all stop work at the sound of someone's voice now? Get on with it! If you want to rest, then go home and lie on your *kangs*."

The worker doesn't dare answer back, and he just goes back to shovelling dung. But Clown, who is standing next to him, straightens up and says, making a great show of earnestness as he points at the man: "You're new here but you actually dare bandy words with the great Manager Lian? You've got a nerve! Don't you know who he is? If this yard was a country, then he'd be the father of the nation. Do you know what that is? It's the emperor's father-in-law. Like the character Pan Renmei in the opera – big white face and hiding the truth from the people..."

Before he can even finish, all the other workers have begun to snigger. They all know that, earlier in the year, if it hadn't been for Clown riding to the rescue, Sergeant Lian would have sold off his daughter Lian Yuxiang. Recently, she has gone with Chenglong, and although it is an entirely unofficial arrangement, it is certainly better than being sold into a brothel.

Sergeant Lian looks very put out, but before his anger can flare up, Clown smiles obsequiously at him and says: "I was just making a comparison, Manager Lian. I didn't mean anything by it."

"Ha! I know you're not the sort to hold a good fart in! But I've seen a thing or two in my time. I'm no novice. If you get on my tits..."

Clown doesn't wait for him to finish but picks up a pitchfork handle and begins to beat out a rhythm:

Ai! Ai! Our Sergeant Lian, he's the man.
Talk of the army across the northeast,
Ladle in his left hand,

Cooking pot in his right.
He drove the Japs into three provinces,
Liaoning, Jilin and Heilongjiang,
Into Rehe
And into Beiping!

All the workers on the drying field roll about laughing. Furious, Sergeant Lian drops his pipe and comes charging over. Still giggling, Clown dodges this way and that behind his pitchfork handle, so Sergeant Lian can't lay a hand on him. On the move, Clown keeps up his teasing:

Ai! Ai! Manager Lian, he knows a thing or two,
Keeps having daughters to earn his keep.
If you've got money or if you've got clout,
He'll sell you one straight, no questions asked.

Still unable to catch him, and lost for a suitable reply, Sergeant Lian stops and points at Clown.

"You… you just wait!" he pants. "You just wait till tomorrow, and I'll fuck you over good and proper."

But Clown takes no notice, striking up his rhythm again: "Ai! Ai!…"

But before he can get going, a voice shouts from behind him: "Enough! What's all this racket? You should be ashamed of yourselves."

Everyone turns to look, and they see Wangtian glaring at them.

Wangtian has turned his back on the depot, and he no longer has anything to do with its running, but he still brings the night soil he collects there. In fact, over the last few days, he has been bottling up his anger at Chenglong, and today, on arriving at the depot with his cart and seeing these carryings-on, that anger explodes out of him. The fury in his voice and in the expression on his face is truly terrifying.

Sergeant Lian is the first to react and hurry forward: "Boss, you can be the judge here. This little…"

Before he can finish, he sees Wangtian looking daggers at him, and he swallows what he is about to say.

"Don't call me 'boss' any more, I won't answer to it. And don't talk to me about depot business. It's nothing to do with me. If you see me here, it's only because I'm making a delivery for you. I sell, you buy, and that's it."

Wangtian keeps pushing his cart as he speaks, and after he's gone a couple more steps, he adds: "There's no need to bust a gut, you fellows. You're not likely to get a storm out of a clear sky!"

After some thought, Sergeant Lian just maintains a stolid silence, but Clown scurries forward to help Wangtian push his cart over to the dung pond. He lowers the shute to unload and then says: "Brother Wangtian, I really wasn't…"

Wangtian interrupts him with a wry smile. "Ai, little brother! I'm not getting on your case."

"Then you..."

"I'm not getting on anyone's case, only my own."

"I... I don't understand."

"No, nor do I. Aiya..."

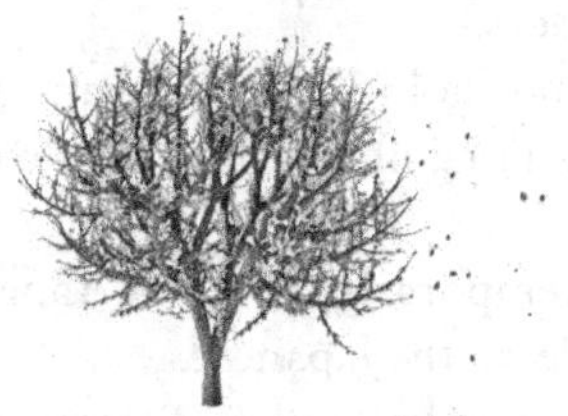

Chapter 2

Just as Lao Zhang had predicted, the ruse of 'jumping out of the bowl' proves entirely effective, and Qi Yuexuan leaves the city on the pretext of offering sacrifices to his ancestors. What is unexpected, however, is that Matsuzaki Harayama doesn't cause any difficulties; he is not the least put out, obstructive or annoyed. In fact, he agrees to the idea with the greatest alacrity. Even more unexpectedly, early on the following day, before Qi Yuexuan has even got going, Yamaguchi of the Kempeitai arrives at the head of a squad of Japanese military police carrying incense sticks, sacrificial goods and a scroll. This is not the fearsome Yamaguchi of the last time they met, and although there is still something of a swagger about him, he does at least observe the proper etiquette.

When he sees Qi Yuexuan, he stands to attention and bows. "Chairman Qi, as a mark of his respect, Mr Matsuzaki has personally written a memorial scroll and specially prepared these offerings. We are here representing both the Beiping Special Action Assembly and Mr Matsuzaki personally to accompany you in observing your ancestral rites. There are carriages at the gates, so shall we get on our way?"

"You Japanese are always a little hasty," says a laughing Qi Yuexuan. "Don't you know these things have to be done by mutual consent. Why didn't you ask me first if I could accept all this stuff – the official recognition, the gifts and the guard of honour? Ah, I get it! You're worried, aren't you? Are you going to guard me on the way there and make sure I come back safe? Ha! That's it, isn't it! Come on then – are you going to handcuff me or tie me up?"

Yamaguchi is more than a little put out by this remark, and he splutters: "Please don't misunderstand, sir. This is only for your own safety. There's a lot of anti-Japanese activity in the area. The situation in the mountains is uncertain, and it's very dangerous."

"Huh! And won't having you with me just make it more dangerous?" Qi Yuexuan snorts. "I'd be safer if you tied me behind the carriage with a sign saying 'Anti-Japanese Faction' round my neck."

"I haven't got time for your jokes. Let's get a move on."

"Are you insisting on coming with me?"

"Yes, those are my orders."

"Very well then, I'm not going," Qi Yuexuan says huffily, and he heads back into the inner chambers. "I'm going to have a little nap, to sleep on it, and then I'll decide what to do."

While Yamaguchi is temporarily at a loss, Yang Zhixing enters the room and turns an obsequious smile on the Japanese.

"I'm sure it's all a misunderstanding. Please ignore the Young Master's bad temper. I'll go and talk to him."

So saying, he follows Qi Yuexuan inside, speaking in a deliberately loud voice: "Don't be like that, Young Master. Today is the designated day, and we must go. We can't miss the appointed hour." Then he adds, in a lower voice: "We're not likely to get another chance like this, so don't be so stubborn."

"Even so, I prefer not to go."

"Let's get out of the city first, and then we can see what to do. Now's not the time to get in their faces."

"When *is* the right time then?"

"We must play it by ear. There'll be more opportunity once we're out of the city and up in the mountains. Just for the moment, do as I say."

Without wasting another word, Yang Zhixing pushes Qi Yuexuan out of the house. Not wanting to rouse suspicion by bringing along the clothes and provisions they had so carefully prepared, they take only the necessary sacrificial items. Once outside, Qi Yuexuan stops and stares in amazement. Parked outside the main gates are a limousine, a truck and three motorcycles and sidecars. The truck is already decorated with a banner, on which is written a couplet: 'Joint Ancestral Commemoration of the East Asian Republic, The Joint Promotion of Japanese-Chinese Goodwill'.

Qi Yuexuan stares at the message, lost for words, his anger swelling inside. Yang Zhixing pinches him hard, twice, only just forcing him to control his impulses. The journey is real torture, as the truck purposely drives as slowly as an old ox-cart, and the gaze of the people on the street stabs his eyes like a sharp knife and gouges into his heart. If anything can be called a living death, for him, this is it. If it weren't for Yang Zhixing keeping a tight hold of him, pacifying him, he would certainly have caused a scene.

The road ends when the convoy finally reaches the foot of the mountains. Yang Zhixing sticks by Qi Yuexuan's side as they get out of the limousine, and he whispers to him: "Now's the moment."

Qi Yuexuan nods his head in silent acknowledgement. He waits until the Japanese soldiers have finished unloading, then says to Yamaguchi: "A good journey. You can leave us here. There's no need for you to scramble up and down the mountain. Uncle Yang, give all the men some money for a drink."

But Yamaguchi shows no sign of relenting, and he shakes his head firmly. "No, no. We must escort you to the spot and bring you back safe."

Qi Yuexuan raises an eyebrow and replies: "Very well, I'm not going to stop you doing your duty, as long as you don't mind tiring yourselves out. However, once we start making our offerings, we must follow our Chinese rules. Is that alright?"

"Of course. What are these rules?"

"These Western Hills are dragon's territory. To the west they lead to the Western Tombs of the Qing dynasty, and to the east they connect with the cenotaph of Dr Sun and the thirteen Ming Tombs..."

"I don't need a history lesson, just tell me what these rules are," Yamaguchi says, interrupting Qi Yuexuan's leisurely exposition.

"Alright, just the rules then," Qi Yuexuan says with a laugh. Still taking his time, he continues: "The peace of the sacred territory of the dragon must not be disturbed. There must be no talking, no fire, no digging, no blood-letting or violence..."

"Yes, yes, that's all fine."

"Hold on, there is one more thing," says Qi Yuexuan, pointing to the pistol at Yamaguchi's waist. "No firearms. All weapons are forbidden."

"No! That, I cannot accept." Yamaguchi shakes his head decisively.

Yang Zhixing joins in from beside him, stirring the pot: "This rule cannot be violated. If the gods are angered, there will be retribution. Didn't you Japanese learn your laws and customs from the Chinese? Surely you must accept this."

Yamaguchi hums and haws for a moment, then says: "Hmm... no, no, you're right, the same is true in Japan when we worship the gods. I truly believe in the gods, but I have a duty towards my men too. It is difficult terrain here, and it is too dangerous for them to be unarmed."

"Ha, this is your fear speaking," says Qi Yuexuan. "You are not respecting the dead and putting your faith in men rather than the gods."

Yamaguchi's face flushes in indignation, and he bows deeply, saying: "I am very sorry, but in time of war, my soldiers cannot be disarmed."

"In that case," says Yang Zhixing, "suppose you don't come up the mountain. You can either wait here or go back to the city and return here later to meet us. That would work for both of us, wouldn't it?"

Yamaguchi grunts in acknowledgement of the suggestion, but then he stiffens his neck and says: "No, that won't do."

Yang Zhixing is about to reply, but Qi Yuexuan restrains him: "That's enough. There's nothing more to say. He's afraid I'm going to run away. It's quite understandable that he's on edge. Come on, let's go! We might as well return home. I won't offer any sacrifices this year. It's better to be unfilial this once than to commit a blasphemous act."

So saying, Qi Yuexuan begins to walk away, with Yang Zhixing holding onto him and trying to dissuade him. Yamaguchi finds himself at a loss as to what to do, and he stands, muttering to himself irresolutely.

At this moment, Lao Zhang, of whom there has been neither sight nor sound until now, suddenly pops up next to Yamaguchi.

"Heehee, great lord," he says, with a giggle. "I think there may be a way. You're Japanese, aren't you? So why should you worry about Chinese gods. There's no need to be scared." He turns to Qi Yuexuan. "Young Master, you've had enough trouble getting here, so don't turn back now. Hurry up and get up the mountain. We haven't brought any guns or swords, so we've got nothing to fear."

"Shut up!" cries Qi Yuexuan, glaring furiously at Lao Zhang. He restrains himself but is still cursing inwardly. "What do you think you're doing, interfering in such an important matter? Who do you think you are helping?"

Yang Zhixing also grabs hold of him. "Yes, we don't need you sticking your oar in."

But Yamaguchi laughs and slaps Lao Zhang on the back. "You're right!" he says and turns to one of his subordinates. "Nishimura, you stay behind with some of the men. The rest of you, follow me."

Looking very put out, and avoiding Qi Yuexuan and Yang Zhixing's eyes, Lao Zhang sets off up the mountain, saying: "I'll lead the way."

Yamaguchi hurries after him but stops when he reaches the beginning of the path up the mountain. He turns and says: "Don't be so stubborn, Chairman Qi. Come along now."

When he sees Qi Yuexuan still not moving, he throws a meaningful look at his men, two of whom hurry forward and take Qi Yuexuan firmly by both arms. What can he do? He can't move even if his life depends on it. Yang Zhixing reaches out to help him, but he finds himself held on both sides too. Just at this moment, Yamaguchi suddenly begins to shout and dance about, waving his hands. Startled, the Japanese soldiers all reach for the guns at their waists. Closer inspection reveals a swarm of wild mountain bees buzzing like a black cloud around Yamaguchi's head and body.

Still yelling and slapping himself, Yamaguchi hurriedly retreats. Two of his men try to go to his assistance, but they are driven back, shouting, by the stings of the wild bees. Yang Zhixing pulls Qi Yuexuan away to a safe distance, where they nervously take cover. The remarkable thing is, however, that the bees seem to have recognised Yamaguchi and are concentrating solely on him, leaving everyone else alone. By now, he is rolling around on the ground, trying to protect his head from their stings.

Lao Zhang stamps his feet and cries out in delight.

"Shit! Would you credit it! It seems that our Chinese gods *do* have power over you Japanese. Look, there's no doubt about it – they're ignoring everyone else and just stinging him. Talk about karma! This is no deferred retribution, it's instant justice!"

Yamaguchi's discomfiture is complete.

"Hurry up and do something! Help me! Ai!... Hurry!"

"Aiya! You must kowtow to the gods in apology. Quickly! Kneel down and kowtow... That's it. Don't stop."

Lao Zhang hurries over to the side of the road where he picks several handfuls of mugwort, which he sets fire to, then puts out with his feet. He hands half of it to Yamaguchi, saying: "Here now, do as I do, and offer it like incense. Kowtow each time you offer it, and we'll see for sure whether the old god of the mountain forgives you or not."

What else can Yamaguchi do but follow Lao Zhang's instructions and kowtow twenty or thirty times? Amazingly, the wild bees stop attacking him, circle around a few times and fly off.

"Ah! The mountain god has forgiven me!" Yamaguchi cries out in relief.

His face is swollen and covered in dozens of reddish-purple blotches, his eyes are closed and his lips are twisted, though it is impossible to say whether in a smile of relief or a grimace of pain. The sight is so comical it brings a smile to Qi Yuexuan's face, and even the Japanese soldiers can't help grinning surreptitiously. Lao Zhang goes over to inspect him.

"Aiya! Amazing! The poison of those bees is really powerful. It could be fatal. You'd better hurry back and get to hospital as quick as you can."

When he hears this, Yamaguchi's head begins to swim, his eyes blur and his body begins to sway. His men rush to hold him up.

Only then does Qi Yuexuan go over to him and ask: "Do you, er, still want to go up the mountain?"

Yamaguchi doesn't reply and just shakes his head.

"In that case…"

"Ah! You do what you like. We're all going back."

As soon as they hear this, the Japanese soldiers eagerly carry Yamaguchi over to the car, load him into it, and the convoy disappears in a cloud of dust.

As he watches them fading into the distance, Qi Yuexuan gives Lao Zhang a smack on the head, not too hard but enough to be heard.

"What did you think you were doing playing up to the Japanese? If those bees hadn't come along, we'd never have got away from them."

Lao Zhang doesn't reply, but Yang Zhixing speaks out instead.

"You mustn't be unfair to Lao Zhang, Young Master."

"What?"

"Ha ha, Young Master!" Lao Zhang says, delighted with himself. "You may have all the book learning and military strategy, but when it comes to playing dirty, you have a lot to learn. I've got to tell you, I brought those bees here myself today."

"Nonsense! How could you have brought them?"

"I already knew there was a big bees' nest around here, and I pissed on it to winkle the queen out. Do you think the other bees weren't going to come looking for it?"

"But why didn't they sting you, or anyone else, and only went for that devil Yamaguchi?"

"Ha! You saw me trying to make up to him, didn't you? Well, that's when I slipped the queen in his pocket, wasn't it?"

Qi Yuexuan can't help laughing and nodding his head in admiration: "You're really something! But..."

"I'll tell you all about it later," Lao Zhang interrupts him, "but now, we'd better get a move on."

They've only gone a few paces when Qi Yuexuan comes to a sudden halt and points at the sacrificial goods Lao Zhang is carrying. "Take the stuff the Japanese gave us, and throw it all in the ditch for me."

"No," Lao Zhang says. "The Japanese may have given it to us, but it's all Chinese-made, and it would be a shame to waste it. If the thought of it is too much for you, give it to me, and at least I'll get a full belly out of it. Even those banners will come in useful – what the Japanese have written on them may be shit, but it's good quality paper. I can tear it up and make paper tubes out of it for the cricket-hunting season. I'm all on my own, with no sons or daughters to worry about, so what have I got to be afraid of? And we'll be getting our own back on the Japanese ancestors too."

THERE IS AN ANCIENT BUILDING in the old bannermen barracks belonging to the Qi family. Long ago it was given over as a residence for the family tombkeeper, and it looks like an ordinary county farm. The farmyard is of no great size, with three rooms in the northern range and three in the western; to the south is a shed for the animals. Houses built in the mountains have to follow the terrain, so there is no east gate. Although Lao Zhang has swept the place inside and out, it has been unoccupied for many years, and, on entering it, the stale, mouldy smell is very strong. In particular, the faded bedding on the *kang* is dank and sodden. Because they knew they were to be accompanied by Japanese troops, they hadn't dared bring any fresh bedding or even a change of clothes. Qi Yuexuan has never in his life had to stay in a place like this.

Yang Zhixing knows what he is thinking and says hurriedly: "We'll take the bedding out to air in the sun straight away, Young Master. You'll just have to put up with it for one night, and tomorrow I'll go back and get some fresh."

Rather embarrassed, Qi Yuexuan says quickly: "No, no, let's wait a few days and see whether the Japanese come back. Then we'll see. In any case, we're a hundred times better off here than those refugees who have to sleep in alleyways or out on the street."

Lao Zhang hastily joins in: "You'll have to put up with the accommodation, Young Master, but you don't need to worry about food. I'll make you something really tasty."

"Oh yes? Or are you just bullshitting?"

"You'll see tonight whether I'm bullshitting or not."

At dinner-time that evening, Lao Zhang is like a conjurer as he lifts the fly-covers off the dishes on the table and Lo! Cold dishes, hot dishes, meat dishes, vegetarian dishes, they're all there. The quantity is not huge, but the variety is impressive. Qi Yuexuan only recognises the delicate, finger-size cucumbers, but there are many other fragrant dishes unknown to him. Lao Zhang points them out: "These are cold-dressed fern fronds, these are quick-fried sour-pickled cucumbers, this is plain-stewed wild pigeon, red-cooked mountain frog, plain-fried vine tubers... the cucumbers I grow myself, but the rest comes wild from the mountain. You can get all of them in the city, but no one has dared cook them for you. Try them! Are they crisp and crunchy enough for you? Tasty? Ha ha, those are deep-fried field crickets. So, was I bullshitting or not, Young Master?"

Qi Yuexuan's mouth is full, and he just nods his head. Then he realises that gesture might be misinterpreted, so he shakes his head instead. This confuses the expectant Lao Zhang: "Are they... are they not to your taste?"

Qi Yuexuan swallows his mouthful and laughs. "It's amazing!" he says. "So many restaurants in the city, and none of them come close to your cooking. So now, we're fine for the time being, but I guess the Japanese will starve us out eventually. But let's not worry about that now. What are you two staring at? Sit down and eat! We're not going to stand on ceremony here. Is there any wine?"

"Yes, but it's not very good."

"I don't care whether it's good or not, as long as there is some."

Lao Zhang produces a small keg of *gaoliang* and sets some to warm. Qi Yuexuan isn't used to such strong spirit, and the first mouthful sets him spluttering. He sips slowly at his cup, and soon he begins to feel he is getting used to it.

The day has been wet and unusually close, and by the time the wine has been passed round three times, the trio are sweating freely. In normal circumstances, Lao Zhang would have stripped to the waist, but today, with the Young Master at the table, he doesn't dare.

Qi Yuexuan understands and says with a smile: "Strip off if you're too hot, there's nothing stopping you."

"Well... I don't want anyone to say I'm taking liberties."

"Ha! Given the circumstances, who's going to notice? From now on, we don't stand on ceremony."

"If we're not standing on ceremony," Yang Zhixing asks with a smile, "why aren't you stripping off too? The two of us are in our undershirts, and you're still wearing your long gown."

"Ha! I'm not being stand-offish, I'm just not in the habit... Alright, alright, I'll strip off. In fact, I'll go first."

So saying, Qi Yuexuan takes off his gown, and then his shirt and undershirt, revealing his rather puny physique. When he sees the other two staring at him, he self-consciously wraps his arms around himself. The three of them give a great guffaw of laughter.

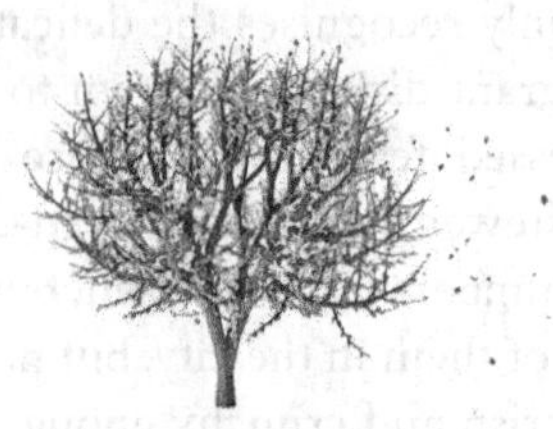

Chapter 3

The autumn weather is cold and wet, and after a few rainy days we are into the period of the White Dew; the Indian summer is well and truly over. It's almost the Mid-Autumn Festival, but the streets of Beiping are desolate and deserted. No more than half the shops are open for business, and apart from the grain stores and grocers, those that are have got no customers. There are more people trying to sell things than buy them. This is not surprising since no produce from Hebei, Chahar, Henan, Shanxi, Shaanxi and the provinces south of the Yangtze has been able to reach Beiping since it has been occupied by the Japanese. So even those shops that do open have little to sell. If it weren't for the Japanese troops and the police bullying them into it, no one at all would be willing to undertake this thankless task on their shrivelled and empty bellies. The Japanese have, in fact, brought in some supplies from Rehe and the three eastern provinces, but it's really only a token gesture, as these supplies comprise mainly wet-weather clothing, rubber shoes, backless sandals and suchlike. Things of practical use are far outnumbered by the useless.

So, after several months of the occupation, prices have soared, especially for food, which gets more expensive by the day. And even if you have money, that's not enough; if you don't have the specially issued purchase permit, you can't buy whole grain from the grain store, just a kind of blended flour instead. Nor is this what used to be called two-grain flour, or mixed grain flour; those, at least, are made out of grain. This blended flour, apart from a bit of maize flour and powdered maize stalks, is mostly made up of ground acorns, maize cores, millet straw and sweet potato shoots. With the addition, also, of a little sand and earth, it is dry, sour and gritty in texture. Swallowing it is easy enough, but it is more difficult getting rid of it at the other end. Many children and older people get bad stomach aches and become severely constipated after eating it. It is hardly surprising that, despite the Japanese mantra of 'Japanese-Chinese goodwill and mutual prosperity', few locals have any faith in this. Giving people animal feed to eat surely shows that the Japanese don't even consider the Chinese to be human.

. . .

OF COURSE, Chenglong doesn't have to eat this blended flour. Although he and the other society members are not in military uniform, they are better off than the soldiers of the Puppet Army. After the establishment of the New People's Assembly, Matsuzaki Harayama took up the post of chairman of the Beiping Special Action Committee and co-opted the society members as his direct subordinates so that they could enjoy the same provisions as the Japanese Army. When you also include the graft they collect at will on the street, even a small fry like Zhou Si is much more comfortably off than before, and the same is even more true of a shark like Chenglong. In order to avoid the hostilities, many of the households in Beiping have upped sticks and left, so there are a lot of empty houses. Under the pretext of setting up public offices, Chenglong has taken personal possession of several courtyards. Although none of them are as grand as the Minister's Residence, they are all the former homes of prosperous families. He doesn't, however, take up residence in any of them, for fear that the Japanese might start investigating. In any case, the houses aren't going anywhere, and he can bide his time and enjoy them at ease sometime later.

So, when he takes in Lian Yuxiang, he evicts two neighbouring families and gets some of his men to touch up the whitewash and bring in some furniture and bedding. He divides his time between his home and this new establishment. He doesn't hold a party or send a sedan chair, nor does he confer any official status on Yuxiang, but the society members, and other people on the street, all know this is his 'second home' and that Lian Yuxiang is his mistress.

On this particular afternoon, Lian Yuxiang knows that Chenglong is coming that evening, so she goes to the late market outside the Desheng Gate to buy some meat and other delicacies. Having done the shopping, she doesn't want to hang around on the streets, so she hurries home. Although she no longer has to service customers, or worry about food and clothing, she still does not feel entirely comfortable. Her previous life was one of poverty and suffering, but at least her feet were planted firmly on the ground; now, however, she feels herself floating in mid-air, unable to catch hold of anything, or find a firm foothold. She has money in her pocket, but it feels like she has just borrowed it from a loan shark. She is wearing brand new clothes, but to her eyes she looks like a boutique mannequin.

Although Chenglong has made all sorts of vows and promises, and has set her up in a big house as his 'second wife', she still doesn't dare believe it is all really happening. She doesn't regard any of this as actually hers; it feels more as though she has stolen it. When she is in the Minister's Residence, she is afraid of catching the eye of her sister-in-law Yue E, but when she goes home, she can't bear the looks she gets from her neighbours either. Her father now tells anyone who'll listen what a good daughter she is, but she herself regards herself as a commodity that has been sold. She has been over this time and time again, and she is quite clear that this is not the life she wants, nor is Chenglong the husband she would choose. But like a butterfly caught in a net, however much she wants to fly far away, there is no point. However you look at it, a woman's virgin body will always be defiled, so what use are idle day dreams? She might as well be a silly girl eating silly porridge until her head and belly are full of silliness.

"Aiyo! Is that you, Yuxiang?" someone calls out from right in front of her.

When she looks up, she sees it's Chun'er, the eldest daughter of the Sun family next door. Before Chun'er went off to get married to a mechanic on the Fengtai Railway, the two of them were good friends. However, since the wedding she has seldom returned to her family home.

"Sister Chun!" cries Yuxiang, also delighted. "Have you just arrived?"

"I've been back two days." Chun'er looks her up and down. "Hey, I like the clothes you're wearing. So restrained and tasteful. Clothes and shoes really do make a person. All that white makes you look so healthy and full of life. You quite put your sister to shame!"

"Oh, get away with you," Yuxiang says, smiling sweetly.

"Are you still working at the Minister's Residence?"

"No, er... no I'm not working. I'm staying at home at the moment."

"It's good not to be working," says Chun'er, lowering her voice. "Isn't the master at the Minister's Residence a bit of a prick. He's always been shifty, and now, I hear, he's gone over to the Japanese. His name stinks now. I've even caught a whiff of it in Fengtai. Our innocent connections with the Minister's Residence will always be suspect to others, so how can we possibly ever serve them again? Isn't that right?"

"Er, yes, yes it is," Yuxiang replies vaguely, feeling her cheeks redden.

Chun'er doesn't notice anything and goes on: "Ai! It always seems that the more brazen you are about things, the better you get on, and modesty and inner virtue only hold you back. Just look what happens if you're a little late going to buy a few *jin* of that blended flour – it's all gone, and you go home empty-handed." She glances casually at the contents of Yuxiang's basket, and her eyes widen. "Shit! How much does meat cost these days? Your family certainly likes its food! Have you been collecting gold ingots or something?"

Yuxiang's normally pale face blushes furiously and she stammers: "It... it isn't my shopping... I'm doing it for someone else."

Chun'er is about to continue her interrogation, but she is interrupted by the rumble of an engine behind them as a motorcycle and sidecar hurtles up. The Japanese officer sitting in the sidecar is shaven-headed and bare-chested, clutching a wine bottle and bawling at the top of his voice. It is none other than Yamaguchi of the Kempeitai. He had been very seriously stung by the wild bees at the foot of the Western Hills and was unconscious by the time he got back to Beiping, needing urgent treatment to save his life. The swelling reduced after several days in hospital, but he was left with a number of dark purple scars. He has just been discharged from hospital today and has been enjoying a welcome-back party thrown by his friends. Yamaguchi has never been one to let sleeping dogs lie, so when he hears that Qi Yuexuan has still not returned home, he immediately wants to take out a squad of men to arrest him. But Matsuzaki Harayama has forbidden him to go and torn him off a strip, saying that he is just a soldier and pig-ignorant about politics. Moreover, this affair has become a standing joke among Yamaguchi's colleagues, which has just made him even more angry and resentful. Fuelled by wine, he is now running amok on the streets.

Seeing the commotion, Yuxiang and Chun'er hurriedly duck to the side of the road. As the vehicle goes past, a squeal of brakes makes them turn to look and it stops in front of them.

"Pretty ladies!" Yamaguchi calls out, and he leaps out of the sidecar without waiting for it to come to a halt. He grabs hold of Chun'er and pulls her towards the sidecar. She cries out for help, but, of course, no one dares come to her aid. She struggles as though her life depends on it, but she can't break free. Yuxiang is shaking with fear, but her courage asserts itself, and with a swing of her arm, she smacks Yamaguchi with her basket. Taking advantage of this distraction, Chun'er escapes and runs off into one of the hutongs. Yuxiang tries to follow her, but Yamaguchi chases her down after only a few steps, catches her round the waist and swings her into the sidecar. The rumble of the motorcycle's engine fades into the distance.

Li Fenggu's 'North Beiping Institute for Young Women' is situated in a small, two-storey building beside the Houhai. It has been open for a fortnight or so, and business hasn't really taken off yet, especially during the daytime, and the more so because of the cold weather. Over time, Zhou Si has brought her a dozen or more girls, the youngest fifteen or sixteen and the oldest over forty. The majority of them are refugees he has found sleeping rough on the streets and alleyways. Of course, when they discover what they are expected to do there, none of them are willing participants, but once the doorman has beaten one of them half to death, they are scared into staying.

Li Fenggu and the doorman are sitting in the hallway, chatting and joking, when Yamaguchi drags Lian Yuxiang in through the door. Yuxiang is still struggling, but she is weakening, and her voice is now hoarse.

Yamaguchi sticks a finger in Li Fenggu's face and says: "Get me a room."

Li Fenggu doesn't know Yamaguchi but can see at a glance that he is a Kempeitai officer, so she instantly replies: "Of course, of course. But... we have our own girls here, and they've all gone through quarantine. If you bring your own, I've still got to see a certificate."

"What certificate? I haven't got one."

"Well, that puts me in a difficult position, because..."

"Bugger that!" says an enraged Yamaguchi. "Hurry up, or you're a dead woman."

Li Fenggu goes white with fear. She hurriedly nods and bows, smiling obsequiously. "*Hai, hai.* Please go upstairs. I'll show you the way."

After a while, Li Fenggu comes down the stairs, still chattering away: "Ha! We haven't opened a single tab all afternoon, and it's just our luck that, when a customer does come along, he brings his own rations."

"That piece the lord brought along is a bit of alright though," the doorman replies. "If he doesn't take her away when he's finished, you might want to keep her. Wouldn't cost us anything."

"Not a bad idea," Li Fenggu laughs, adding rather haughtily: "I'm not familiar with this particular Japanese devil, or I'd lodge a complaint with the Kempeitai and get him punished. This isn't some backstreet stew. We only cater to the top flight, and status is a major consideration. I'm doing quite nicely here, and it's always easier to take an official salary rather than have to earn a living by yourself."

"Absolutely, absolutely." The doorman nods in agreement, but inwardly he is cursing the woman.

GOING BACK to the other side of the story, when Chun'er sees Yuxiang being taken away, she rushes out through the Desheng Gate to the Liuji night soil depot to find Yuxiang's father. She tells him it looked as though they were heading for the Houhai. All fired up on hearing the news, Sergeant Lian tells one of the workers to go and find Chenglong, while he himself hails a rickshaw. He heads over towards the Houhai, looking and asking as he goes. Fortunately, there are quite a few eye-witnesses along the way, so it's not long before he finds himself in front of the small, two-storey building. He is daunted by the size of the plaque hanging over the front door, so he doesn't dare rush straight in. Instead, he decides to peer through the glass. Before he can see anything, the door is thrust open, hitting him hard on the head.

"What are you doing poking your nose in around here, you old bastard?" the doorman yells.

"I'm… I'm looking for someone," Sergeant Lian says, rubbing his head.

Before the doorman can say anything more, Li Fenggu arrives: "Looking for someone, eh? Who are you looking for?"

"I'm looking for my daughter. Some Japanese soldier… no, I mean some Japanese lord brought her here."

"How do you know it was here?"

"Lots of people saw it."

Li Fenggu realises this really must be the girl's father at her door and that it's going to be difficult to deny everything. After a moment's thought, she says: "Something of the sort did happen, but if I let you in, are you happy to get on the wrong side of the Puppet Army? Aren't you afraid? If you don't get shot, at the very least you'll get a good kicking. Do you think you can take it?"

"Can you tell me what to do? Please, I'm begging you!" Sergeant Zhang cups his hands in entreaty.

Li Fenggu smiles: "Alright, alright, I'll see what I can do. Give me fifty yuan and your daughter will soon be home."

"Fifty yuan? That's too much!"

"Aiya! Clearly you care about money more than you care about your daughter."

Sergeant Lian knows she is taking advantage of him, but for the moment, there's nothing he can do about it. Then, he suddenly thinks of something and straightens up from his bow.

"I think we have something in common, elder sister."

Li Fenggu glares at him. "You've got a nerve! Who do you think has something in common with who?"

"It's, er... it's just that you work for the Japanese, don't you?"

"That's right."

"My son-in-law also works for them. He's got some status with them."

"Who's that then?"

"Liu Chenglong."

Li Fenggu is initially taken aback by this, but then begins to chuckle. "You're having a laugh! There was a big wind last night – was that you bullshitting? Master Liu is married to the daughter of the Yang family of the Minister's Residence, and Master Liu has a stake in this house of mine. So who do you think you're kidding?"

Sergeant Lian is stumped for words and stammers evasively: "Well, er, that is..."

"Huh! I don't have time to waste on you. If you've got the money, give it to me. If not, fuck off!" Li Fenggu stares at him, then turns to go back inside.

At this moment, a motorcycle and sidecar comes hurtling up, and Chenglong leaps out and bounds up the front steps. Sergeant Lian hurries forward to greet his saviour, but Chenglong ignores him and goes straight inside.

Li Fenggu starts in astonishment. "Aiyo! Master Liu..."

Without waiting for her to continue, Chenglong asks abruptly: "Did a Japanese bring a girl here?"

"Ah... yes."

"Where are they?"

"Up... upstairs, second room on the left. Master Liu, please don't..." Li Fenggu cries out in alarm, but there's nothing she can do to stop him.

Sizing up the situation, Zhou Si hurries after him.

Chenglong reaches the door of the room on the second floor and is about to pull aside the curtain and storm in, when Yamaguchi comes out, swinging his arms. He is grinning lewdly and reeking of alcohol as he buckles his trouser belt. Chenglong explodes with fury, grabs the Japanese by his collar, and, stepping in with a twist of the hip, he straightens up, lifting him upside-down off the floor.

He is about to hurl him to the ground, but Zhou Si, who has come up behind, stops him. As Yamaguchi's feet touch the floor again, before he can flare up in anger, Zhou Si breaks in with a smile and says: "You really mustn't be angry, Lord Yamaguchi. He's just having a joke, ha ha. That's it, just a joke."

Still flushed with pleasure, Yamaguchi surprisingly doesn't take offence. He glances at Chenglong and says: "A joke, eh? I don't... don't need any jokes. But your *gongfu*... that's good. Come and find me later... and I'll try you out."

So saying, he staggers off but turns back when he reaches the top of the stairs. "Ah, your *gongfu*... ha ha." He points towards the room. "It's not... not as good as hers."

Chenglong explodes with fury and is about to rush Yamaguchi, but Zhou Si hangs onto him for grim death. After watching Yamaguchi stagger down the stairs, Chenglong finally turns and pulls aside the door curtain. The room is in semi-darkness, clothes are strewn over the floor, and Lian Yuxiang is curled up in a corner of the bed, wrapped in a bed sheet. Her face is grey as river silt, there is blood at the corners of her mouth, and her hair is dishevelled. She is trembling uncontrollably and her eyes are fixed in fear.

Li Fenggu has caught up now and says: "Oh, Master Liu! Is this your..."

Zhou Si blenches and stops her finishing her question.

"The cowardly bully!" Chenglong curses and punches the wall, dislodging a big lump of plaster.

Yuxiang gives a heart-rending howl of anguish.

"Hurry up and get her home," Zhou Si shouts, and he finally allows Sergeant Lian into the room, who has just come out of his daze. Li Fenggu follows him.

Zhou Si pulls Chenglong to one side: "Junior Master, the way you manhandled Yamaguchi just now was really dangerous. Almost dumping him upside down and ramming his head into his chest like a concertina. Wasn't that a bit reckless?"

"I'm going to..." Chenglong spits out through gritted teeth.

"Aiya, you've really got to forget thinking this way," Zhou Si sighs. "We're on this boat now, and there's no turning back. Don't sacrifice the big stuff for something trivial, or you'll find yourself neither on the boat nor on the bank, but floundering in the river. Your brothers are relying on you totally, and if you... Ai! Nothing good will come of it."

"So we just let people bully us, shame us and mock us, and do nothing about it?"

Chenglong glares at him, and Zhou Si softens a little. "Just think about it. Which is more important? Our future or the girl? Your life or your face?"

Chenglong doesn't utter a word.

At this moment, Sergeant Lian emerges from the room carrying Yuxiang on his back. Yuxiang is still sobbing softly, but Sergeant Lian is wailing more loudly, high and shrill like a steam whistle.

"Enough!" Chenglong shouts. "Do you want the whole city to know?"

The wailing stops immediately.

Chenglong falls silent himself for a moment, then says in a more composed tone: "I've got some official business to see to, but you two get a carriage to take you home as quietly as possible, and don't come out unless there's an emergency. Get on with it!"

Sergeant Lian doesn't dare say anything, and he heads off with Yuxiang still on his back. When they reach the bottom of the stairs, Yuxiang starts to wail again.

Zhou Si steals a glance at Chenglong, then says tentatively: "Don't get all worked up again, but are you going to be able to put this little affair behind you? After all, were you two actually engaged? Did you get married? No, none of these. It's not worth falling out with the Japanese over this chit of a girl. Just think about it. Even if there are some people we don't dare offend, there are a lot more who don't dare offend us. Let's go. I'll take you somewhere that'll open your eyes and cheer you up."

"No, I'm not in the mood."

"Ha! I'm going to take you anyway, and you'll find you are in the mood once you're there. Let's go."

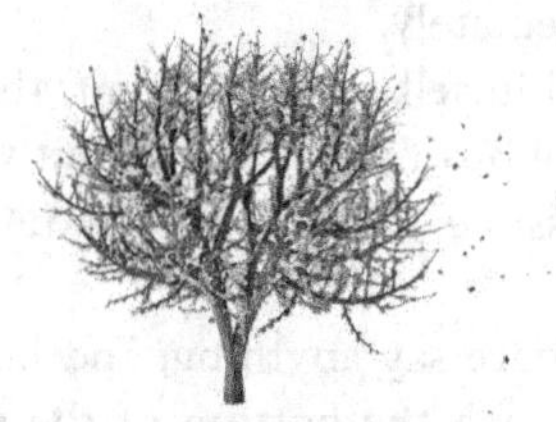

Chapter 4

In fact, Zhou Si doesn't have anywhere new in mind to take Chenglong but heads straight for the Tianjiang tea garden. As the pair enter, the manager immediately notices them and personally escorts them to a square table right in front of the stage.

"Bring us a pot of good tea, nice and strong," Zhou Si orders before his bottom has even touched the chair.

"Aiyo, I'm very sorry but we've run out of all my best tea. Longjing, Houkui, Wulong, Biluochun, even Xiangpian, all gone to the last speck of dust. It's all because... well, you two gentlemen know better than I... Anyway, will you make do with a pot of 'big leaf'?"

"Alright, we won't have tea. Bring some wine and some dried fruit and cold dishes."

"Of course. Please sit down."

The manager hurries off, and the wine and dishes soon appear on the table. Zhou Si hurriedly pours Chenglong a cup.

"Come now, Junior Master, drink up," he says.

But Chenglong doesn't touch his cup. He looks up sharply and replies: "You bring me to this broken-down old place and still promise me something special to look at. What's that going to be then?"

"The surroundings don't matter, it's the people we're interested in."

"Who's that then? That old bloke on stage? Is he your father or something?"

Zhou Si knows Chenglong is in a bad mood, and he does his utmost to placate him. "It isn't time for their performance yet. Drink up while we wait."

"Who is it then?"

"Wait and see."

"Ha! You're just messing me around. Either tell me, or I'm off."

"No, no, don't do that!" Zhou Si is getting agitated and finally he says: "You know Fenggu has got a girl under her, called Noble Red – voice like an angel and a real looker too. You'll see for yourself in a bit. I guarantee you won't think your time's been wasted. Now drink up."

Chenglong finally finishes his cup. After a while, the male performer who's on stage takes his bow and departs, to be replaced by a pair of crosstalk artists. Zhou Si can see that Chenglong is getting restive, so he stands up, waving his hands.

"Get off, the pair of you! Let's have Noble Red."

As it happens, Dong Caiping is just mounting the steps to the stage, and when she hears someone shouting her name, she twitches aside the curtain to take a look. One glance leaves her rooted to the spot in astonishment. There he is, the man who beat up the Japanese at the folk music tea house last year, risking his life; the man who looks a lot like her cousin Chenglong.

"Up on stage with you, Noble Red, quick now!" The accompanist gives her a shove, and, distractedly, she mounts the stage.

As she comes to a halt, her eyes lock with Chenglong's down in the audience. Her heart starts pounding and her mind goes blank. Luckily for her, the accompanist sees that something is wrong, and he plays her entrance music rather louder than usual, which brings her back to her senses. It helps also that the number she is singing is one she knows inside out and backwards, so although she is still distracted, it doesn't show on stage.

Chenglong is also temporarily stunned, as he too remembers the scene at the folk music tea house. And the more he looks, the more he feels that this singer Noble Red closely resembles his cousin Caiping. Zhou Si can tell there's something odd going on, and he cautiously asks: "What's up? Do you know her?"

Staring at Caiping, Chenglong mutters to himself: "She is like her... very like her."

"Like who?"

Chenglong doesn't reply, but his eyes are fixed on Caiping's face. As for Caiping, she doesn't dare catch his eye again, so scared is she of its burning intensity. She just about manages to finish the song she is singing, *Visiting the Multi-Coloured Clouds*, but she forgets even to take a bow, picks up her drum stand and hurries off stage. Her heart is still pounding when she arrives backstage.

"What craziness has got into you today?" The accompanist can see that she's still not with it, and he continues sternly: "It's really dangerous out there. If you'd mucked up the performance just now, it surely wouldn't have ended well for you. Didn't you see they're all carrying Mausers? Nowadays, if they're not Japanese, then they're gangsters. Didn't you recognise Zhou Si?"

"But... who was that sitting beside Zhou Si?"

"That was the leader of that pack of wild dogs."

"What's his name?"

"Liu Chenglong."

Caiping's heart lurches when she hears this. She had never thought she would be reunited with her long-lost cousin in such a fashion. Even more unexpected is that his appearance, which she dimly remembers, should have turned out so ugly and dirty. In an instant, her heart is plunged from fire into ice. She doesn't feel the pain or the cold, she just feels numb.

The accompanist grabs hold of her. "Don't stand there like an idiot," he says. "They're getting a bit excitable out there. Put your stuff together and get out of here."

She has gathered together her drum and stand and is about to leave, when someone shouts from behind her: "Hey, don't go!"

Chenglong and Zhou Si have appeared backstage, and as soon as the other artists see them, they huddle together to one side. Smiling ingratiatingly, the accompanist says: "We have to get to our next job, Master Liu."

Chenglong gives him a look. "Surely you have a moment to answer a few questions?"

"Of course, of course. Ask away, ask away." The accompanist nods and bows simultaneously and continuously.

Chenglong goes over to stand in front of Caiping, looks her straight in the face and asks with a nervous smile: "Are you... are you from Beiping?"

Caiping lowers her head. "No... no, I'm from Yangliuqing."

"And your name is?"

"Noble Red."

"I didn't ask for your stage name."

"My family name is Wei, and my given name is the single character Ying."

"Is that your original name?"

"No."

"So what is it?"

"My family name was Zhu. It was changed in the time of my grandfather."

"Is there anyone else in your family?"

Caiping doesn't reply.

Chenglong is about to continue his interrogation, when Zhou Si interrupts: "It's not good to open old wounds, Young Master. I know all about this. She's been an orphan since she was little and grew up with her grandfather, but she's not an outsider. Her grandfather was Fenggu's music teacher, and she calls Fenggu 'aunty'. Anyway, after her grandfather died, she threw her lot in with Fenggu. There's no doubt about any of this."

Chenglong listens with a wry smile. "She really does have something of the look of my cousin... Hah! It's a shame that when Moxiangzhai burned down when it did, not a single body survived the flames..." He falls silent, his eyes misting over.

Zhou Si signals unobtrusively to the accompanist, who takes his meaning and makes to slip away with Caiping in tow. Before they can move, however, Chenglong calls them back: "Wait! Wait! The eighteenth of this month, the day after tomorrow, is my birthday. I'd like Noble Red to come over to my place and sing some songs. How about it?"

Without waiting for Caiping or the accompanist to reply, Zhou Si breaks in: "Huh! There's no need to ask them. Fenggu and I will make sure they're there."

After she gets out of the door, Caiping's eyes fill with tears the size of soya beans, which roll freely down her cheeks.

It is raining again on the eighteenth, from early morning until the afternoon. Wangtian has already been back in his old place for several days. He has just re-plastered the roof, which hasn't dried fully yet, and the rain is leaking in. So that afternoon, after he has finished work, he is back up there with the mud, hoping to fix it. He has just climbed the ladder with a basket of mud, when Yue E comes into the courtyard.

"What are you doing here, Yue E?" he asks, clambering back down.

Yue E doesn't reply immediately but pulls open the door to look inside, before saying: "Good! You really don't want to spring a leak. But you need to see what happens when the sky clears. If it's still coming through in the evening, then all your plastering will have been in vain."

"Ha, if it's still coming though in the evening, I'll just slap on some more mud. I can't let a little rain get the better of me, or I won't get any sleep. That's all it comes down to – more leaks, more mud."

"Or you could... you could come back to our place to stay in the meantime and wait for the weather to clear, fix it properly and then see."

"No."

Yue E can hear how determined he is, so she doesn't pursue the matter and decides to change the subject: "Brother Wangtian, are you going to keep your word or not?"

"What do you mean?"

"Didn't you say you'd come and have a proper talk with Chenglong?"

Wangtian laughs bitterly. "I was thinking about it, but if he comes home at all, it's in the middle of the night. It's impossible to get to see him. He just says he's too busy at the moment with public affairs, but he'll come and find me in a couple days. So I wait a couple of days, and of course there's still no sign of him."

"He's coming home this evening for sure."

"And pigs might fly!"

"Ha! Today's his birthday, isn't it!"

"Oh! Alright then. I'll just finish off this load of mud, and then I'll go along."

"Take my advice, and don't bother with the mud," Yue E says, going inside and rolling up Wangtian's bedding.

Wangtian follows her in. "Alright, alright, I'll come with you."

"Fine, but don't bring all that muck with you."

Wangtian looks at his mud-plastered hands and laughs. Scooping some water out of the basin to wash, he says: "I'll do my best, but if he won't listen, it'll all be a waste of time."

Yue E gives a wry smile and sighs softly. "Ai! Let's just see what happens. I really didn't expect he'd be as selfless as the Young Master, just that he might show a little integrity. Even less did I hope he might emulate his master and his brother-in-arms Zhicheng, and stake his all against the Japanese. Alas! However high the sweet potato plant grows, its fruits stay on the ground. He's signed up with the Japanese, and once you're on the pirate ship, it's very hard to get off. As long as he doesn't tie himself too closely to them, holds back wherever he can, doesn't commit any atrocities and doesn't lose all moral decency, that's all I ask for."

"Huh! Even that won't be easy. He's their golden boy and riding high, so self-restraint won't come easy."

"I'm not so sure. Last night he came home drunk around midnight, and he was raving against the Japanese into the small hours."

"Is that so? Why?"

"Who knows? Perhaps the Japanese are being a bit tight-fisted at the moment. Or..." Yue E stops abruptly, hesitates a moment, then asks: "Have you heard what happened to Yuxiang?"

Wangtian is already aware of the affair, but he hasn't mentioned it out of respect for Yue E. Now she has brought it up herself, he just grunts and nods. Yue E goes on: "They say the Japanese are very like us Chinese, but are we that lacking in human decency? Chenglong is grinding his teeth with fury over this. I was thinking we might be able to use this as leverage with him."

Wangtian nods.

"That poor girl Yuxiang has had a hard life. I've given it a lot of thought, and with things as they stand, the best thing to do is get Chenglong to marry her properly. It's got to be better to give her some status, rather than leaving her neither here nor there."

Wangtian nods again.

Yue E doesn't say any more but picks up Wangtian's bedding and heads for the door.

"I'll take that." Wangtian dries his hands on his body and reaches out a hand.

Yue E avoids him. "I can manage. But what we've just been discussing... you've got to talk to him about it."

EVENING IS DRAWING IN when Chenglong does indeed arrive home. As soon as he goes in, he realises just how much he has drunk at lunchtime. His face is flushed, and he reeks of alcohol. Instead of being in a black mood as Yue E described, he appears very pleased with himself.

"Hah! You've come, Brother," Chenglong says. "It's great you've remembered my birthday. We haven't spent any time together for ages. Sit down, sit down."

The birthday feast is already laid out on the table, and Chenglong sits Wangtian down next to him. Yue E brings in the children to kowtow to their father and congratulate him, and they both sit down too. She sees him pull out his pocket watch and asks: "Who else have you invited?"

"I've invited a singer to add to the fun. Zhou Si has arranged it with Li Fenggu." Seeing Yue E's anxious look, he hurriedly picks up his cup. "We won't wait, we won't wait. I didn't give a specific time, and they won't necessarily want to eat anyway. Come on, let's get on with the meal."

The two children are ravenous, and they quickly set to work with their chopsticks. Wangtian and Chenglong both drink a cup of wine. For quite a while, apart from the occasional "Drink up" from Chenglong, no one says anything.

It's Chenglong who can't contain himself any longer: "You've been wanting to talk with me for some time, haven't you, Brother? Why not spit it out now? I'll listen to whatever you've got to say."

"In a few days, it'll be the anniversary of our father's death."

"Is that all it is? Ha! I've worked all that out. This time we'll make a proper job of repairing his tomb, really do it in style. You don't have to worry about the money, I've got it covered."

"That won't do," Wangtian blurts out, before feeling he's been too cold and abrupt, so he hurriedly backtracks. "Don't they always say, 'the living don't show filial piety, and the dead don't need to'? We can fix up the tomb and make grand sacrifices, but the memory we hold in our hearts is more important. We two should live like our father, be just as steadfast and big-hearted. The old man will know this, even in his grave, and be content."

"You mean I'm not steadfast? Not big-hearted?" Chenglong raises his eyebrows, his expression darkening. When Wangtian doesn't reply, he goes on: "I get it, we're back to that are we? You despise me for working for the Japanese, don't you? I've already told you, I've got a family and a business to look after. I'm not going to gamble with my family, and I'm certainly not going to play the martyr."

"And the rest of Beiping doesn't have the same obligations? Only you?"

"Ha! What other people think is their affair, I can't control it. Take you, for example. You went to war and got wounded, and where did that get you? You're discharged after three months with two silver dollars. And what about Qizi? Killed in battle and his body never found. Has anyone made him a grave or raised a memorial tablet to him? Then there's my master – yes, they found his body, but he lost his life and destroyed his family, and what was left behind? Condemned as a bandit! Life is cheap and it's not even yours to sell."

Wangtian lets him stew over his grievances without speaking. Then, finally, he says sorrowfully: "And if you're left with a clear conscience, does that count?"

"Oh, listen to you, Brother! Are you a commander or a city mayor? Have you profited by money or by land? People come and people go, but you're still carrying barrels of shit on your back and pulling a heavy cart, aren't you! Do you still want to talk about clear consciences? You've made some big mistakes yourself, haven't you?"

Wangtian doesn't reply but stares silently at his brother's face, as though searching for something. Yue E starts clattering the dishes around on the table and says: "What kind of talk is that?"

"The truth," Chenglong snaps back.

Wangtian is unruffled. "Chenglong, the Gao family has never produced high officials, or earned big money, and our trade has always been one that ordinary folk hold their nose at. Who else has shown you any respect? No one, ever. But just consider – we of the Gao family are so far beneath you, but when God turned his back on you, and you were starving and freezing on the street, how was it that there was no general, no mayor, no moneybags to take you in, but it was us, a family of night soil collectors, who gave you a home? How was it that we took you in like a phoenix in a chicken coop, and I put up with all the deprivations and rebuffs? Didn't I even apologise to you on behalf of our father?"

Finally, Chenglong looks a little embarrassed and flustered. He smiles placatingly. "Stop now, Brother, no need to go on. Let's not get ahead of ourselves. Don't..."

"What you've said is quite right, but you've only said half of it. When people are poor with no authority or support, and find it hard to stand on their own two feet, then they have to stiffen their resolve. I may not have read as many books as you, but I have never forgotten the very first lesson I learned at school – I am Chinese."

Chenglong begins to lose patience. "Yes, yes, yes – Chinese, Chinese, all I hear is Chinese. But how can anyone be Chinese when warlords are all setting up their own private fiefdoms? Where is your China now, eh? So, let's not talk about affairs of state at my party, alright?"

Wangtian doesn't reply, but he just looks up fiercely and drinks a cup of wine.

Hearing the grown-ups bickering like this, the two children quietly slip away.

Chenglong pours Wangtian some more wine. "Let's get things straight, Brother. The Japanese are not my father, and I am acting under compulsion, but I have my limits. They can use me, yes, but I'll never be their lapdog."

Wangtian remains quiet, but Yue E can't stand by without saying something: "What kind of talk is that? If that's really what you think, then perhaps you'll be too busy to come home. And if you're acting under compulsion, why are you so enthusiastic about it?"

"You're just a woman. What do you understand? Do you think the Japanese are so easy to deal with?"

"You're right, I don't understand. You say this hasn't worked out, or that hasn't worked out, so I don't understand what good are the Japanese getting out of all your blood, sweat and tears."

"You think things haven't worked out? Forget about how I've safeguarded the family property, and my family. How many other houses have I added? How much money have I brought in? But forget about that too. The most important thing is that I've taken the night soil business to the top of the tree, and I'm king of the streets of north Beiping. Nowadays I've got both the straight world and the underworld covered under one roof, and the Japanese respect and value me..."

"Ha! Trying to keep up with you is like trying to keep up with a whirlwind! Yesterday you were like a frost-bitten aubergine or a deflated frog, so what's so different today?"

Chenglong takes Yue E's interrogation with equanimity, and he actually starts laughing uproariously.

"Ha ha! Good question! That was one situation, this is another. At lunchtime today, I was a guest of Mr Matsuzaki for lunch, and we ate Japanese food and drank sake. Then, right in front of me, he chewed out Yamaguchi and boxed his ears, just to give me face. If that's not enough, the most important thing is that they're setting up a CID Division in Beiping, and today, I was appointed its chief. Don't underestimate how important this post is. It reports directly to the Special Operations Committee and is answerable only to Mr Matsuzaki himself. It's better than being a brigade chief in the Puppet Army. That's what I call rising on one's own merit!"

Unable to respond, Wangtian is about to make his excuses, when Zhou Si and Li Fenggu enter the courtyard with Caiping and the accompanist in tow.

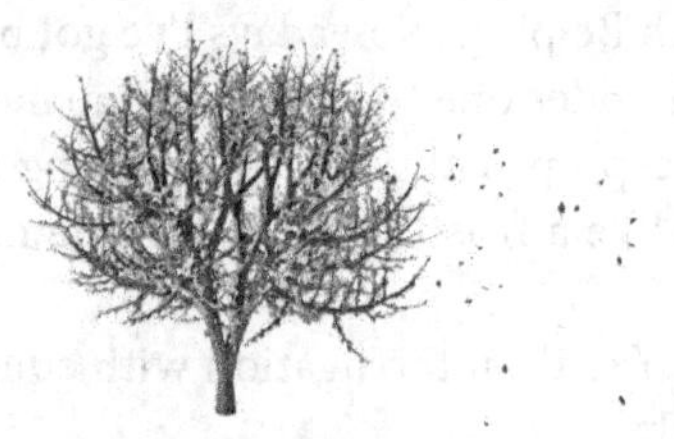

Chapter 5

"Congratulations and many happy returns, Commander Liu!" Zhou Si and the others call out before entering the room.

"Aiyo! What fantastic news, Commander!"

"Hai, your promotion is in the bag. There's no one else qualified for the job. I'm happy to wait, if it gives me a chance to ride on your dragon's tail."

Chenglong is delighted by all this. "Sit down, sit down everyone," he says.

But before they can take their seats, Wangtian stands up, encourages them to go ahead and sit down, before he heads for the door. On meeting Caiping, he just looks at her briefly and moves on. Cold-shouldered by him, Zhou Si looks at Chenglong and says: "Ai! Master, what's the..."

"Take no notice. He's a shameless fellow who shouldn't be seen out in public. Sit down."

Zhou Si and Li Fenggu duck their heads and bow again, then sit down making polite conversation. Yue E is extremely uncomfortable when they both address her as 'aunty', and to cover her embarrassment, when she sees Caiping still standing with lowered head together with the accompanist, she hurriedly calls out: "Hey, you two must come over and sit down too."

Caiping has had her head down since entering the room, and when she hears Yue E call her, she bows and flashes a quick look at her. That glance is enough to revive memories of her childhood: why does this wife of Chenglong standing in front of her seem so familiar? Who is she? Just for the moment, she can't pin her down.

"Where do you want them to sit, aunty?" Li Fenggu asks, before she turns with a wave of her hand. "Sit in the top spot to the side."

But Chenglong stands up and says with a laugh: "No, today, Noble Red is the guest of honour, and you two are the second rank. Come on now, folks, sit down, sit down."

As the second-rank guests are sitting down opposite, Yue E has a chance to look at Caiping more closely, and she too feels there is something familiar there, but she can't pin it down either. Suddenly, her eyes light up and she nudges

Chenglong excitedly, whispering: "Hey, don't you think that girl looks rather like your cousin, Caiping?"

"Ha, so you see the resemblance too? That's the reason I invited her. Ah well, she may look like her, it's just a shame it isn't actually her."

"Did you ask her?"

"There's no need. None of the adults survived the big fire that year, let alone any of the children. Besides, I haven't changed my own name, so if it was her, she'd have to know me."

At this point, Caiping suddenly realises who Yue E is.

"Come on everybody, eat, drink!" Chenglong raises his cup, but the only person he is looking at is Caiping.

Li Fenggu puts on her best smile. "Haven't you heard the saying, Master Liu? Play on a full stomach, sing on an empty one. If you get her all muddled with food and drink, she'll be no good for singing. When she opens her mouth, all you'll get is a belch."

Chenglong nods in agreement. "Right then," he says, "shall we have the singing first?"

Caiping stands up and arranges her drum stand. Drumstick in hand, she bows and says: "This humble girl would like to congratulate Master Liu on his birthday, and to wish Mistress Liu every good fortune. I am going to sing *Baoyu Explores the Multi-Coloured Clouds* from *Dream of the Red Chamber*. Please make allowance for my meagre talent."

In a moment, the *sanxian* and the drum strike up, and when the introduction is over, Caiping flexes her bright and sonorous voice and sings a coloratura number.

Although Yue E doesn't cheer as loudly as Chenglong, in her heart she is shouting 'Bravo'. As she calms down inside and listens more carefully, she becomes more and more hooked by the performance. She hums along inside, and taps her hand to the rhythm. The singing stirs deep emotions in Caiping and draws her into the drama. For her part, Yue E finds herself floating on the waves, her face to the wind, as the song weaves its magic on her.

In the meantime, Zhou Si and Li Fenggu are not idle with their hands or mouths, as they keep the wine flowing. Chenglong is in his element, and, of course, no one is turned away. The many years he has spent in the underworld have left him with quite a head for booze, but even he can't take this constant drinking from lunchtime into the evening, mixing Japanese sake with Chinese *baijiu*. Before the song has finished, the wine has rushed to his head, his face has become flushed, his eyes are bloodshot and his tongue is thick, as he becomes more and more annoying, and his voice gets louder and louder. Just as the song reaches its most moving part, he shouts: "Enough... enough of this depressing rubbish. Sing something... sing something cheerful."

Yue E, who has been enthralled by the song, turns on him furiously: "What are you yelling about? She's singing beautifully. You're an educated man, but do you know what's really depressing? You, shouting and yelling and drinking yourself to death. That's what I find depressing."

Yue E's abuse is too much for Chenglong, and he is about really lose his temper, but Li Fenggu manages to keep him quiet.

"I'm on Aunty Yue E's side, Master Liu. What woman doesn't like a sentimental ballad? Even if you don't appreciate it, can't we have a little bit more?"

Chenglong decides to let it go: "Alright, alright. Go on, go on and sing."

The *sanxian* strikes up again, but before Caiping can open her mouth, a maid comes rushing in and whispers in Yue E's ear: "Mistress, Master Wangtian is about to walk out."

Yue E stands up and heads out of the room, with the maid hot on her heels.

"Hey, where are you going? I let her go on... and you're not listening?" Chenglong gestures with his hand. "Stop... stop singing. Don't sing anything... Noble Red, come on... come on over here... come and sit down. Have a few drinks with me."

Li Fenggu hurries to drag her over, and Caiping sits down beside Chenglong. Zhou Si prompts her: "Go on, drink a toast to Captain Liu."

Caiping looks at Chenglong, and a secret stab of pain pierces her heart. Her past flashes before her eyes, but she can't make any connection with this man. When she raises her cup, no words come, but her eyes fill with tears.

"Get a move on!" Li Fenggu prompts her.

Caiping forces a smile: "Master Liu, from now on I am your servant, and I drain my cup in your honour."

Chenglong stares hard at her: "My servant... that's fine, but I really... I really don't want... don't want you to sing any more. I want to say this now... no one... no one from now on, from the inner city to Tianqiao... will dare... dare let you sing for them."

Certain members of the party are stunned.

"Aiyo, Master Liu! What kind of talk is that?" Li Fenggu is distinctly agitated. "Please don't be angry. Noble Red only knows these standard songs. I could sing you something a bit different if you want." She claps Chenglong on the shoulder.

Chenglong pushes her hand away and says with a laugh: "Give it a... give it a rest... and don't... don't try to soft-soap me. I'm not angry... why... why should I be... angry. I'm just being honest... I really don't... don't want her to sing."

"You do like a good joke..."

"Who's joking?"

Li Fenggu is going to persist, but Zhou Si stops her: "It's the drink talking."

Chenglong hears this, and his face darkens. "I could drink another three bottles and... and it wouldn't be too much... too much for me."

"Of course not, of course not. Let's raise a glass together."

"No, we'll... we'll get this matter settled... then drink." Chenglong points at Caiping. "She's... she's in hock to you?"

"Yes."

"How much?"

"Several hundred yuan."

Chenglong laughs. "Alright, sign her... sign her over to me."

"Aiyo, no! No, I can't do that," says Li Fenggu, beginning to panic. "I've got everything riding on that girl."

Chenglong stares at her. "How's that? Doesn't that stew you're running for the Japanese bring you in... some extra? Isn't my suggestion... helpful?"

Zhou Si pulls Li Fenggu back to stop her answering. "Fenggu wouldn't dare sell her to you. Perhaps she is afraid of what Aunty Yue would say..."

"Hah! Do you think... I'd let a woman... tell me what to do?"

"Of course not," Zhou Si says tactfully. "But Fenggu has spent a lot of money and taken a lot of trouble over that girl, so..."

"It's really just the money... isn't it." Chenglong shoots a look at Li Fenggu. "Can you... give me a figure?"

Li Fenggu really doesn't want to do this, and she prevaricates for a while. Zhou Si gives her a hard look and kicks her under the table. She realises she can't put it off any longer and says coldly: "I can't take less than four hundred silver yuan."

"Ha! Do you think I'm rolling in money?" Chenglong snorts with laughter. "It would take two years... to bring that in on the streets. I'll give you... two hundred and... not a cent more. I'm telling you straight now... but if she's not pure as the driven snow... you can give me the money right back!"

Li Fenggu is about to make a counter-offer, but Chenglong's bloodshot eyes and terrifying sneer make her think again.

Zhou Si hurriedly takes over: "Alright, you're the boss. Anyway, we're all singing from the same songbook, aren't we? Of course, we will treasure any money you care to give us. Even if you don't give us a cent, you just have to say the word, and you must know that we'll give you the girl."

"How very... tactful you are."

At this point, Caiping leaps wildly to her feet and cries: "Impossible!"

Li Fenggu catches hold of her and tries to persuade her: "Ying'er, Master Liu values you very highly, and I..."

"Aunty, our contract is quite clear," Caiping says, shaking off her hand. "My voice is yours, but my body is my own. You may agree to this deal, but I don't. I, Noble Red, am not a beast of burden for you to buy and sell as you please." So saying, she turns on her heel and storms out of the room.

Chenglong slams the table with his fist in fury and follows her out. When Zhou Si and Li Fenggu recover from their shock, they hurry off in pursuit.

As Caiping runs out of the eastern side courtyard and into the main gateway, she bumps into Yue E, who is seeing Wangtian out of the residence. Chenglong's words at the banquet have made him determined to leave, and since Yue E has been unable to dissuade him, all she can do is see him off. Who could have expected this new turn of events to occur before he is even out of the gate? Unable to get out of each other's way, Caiping and Wangtian collide head on. Wangtian drops the bedding he is carrying, and Caiping stumbles and falls to the ground. Wangtian is about to help her up, when Chenglong emerges into the front courtyard.

"Trying to escape?" says Chenglong, wagging his finger at Caiping. "Don't you understand... how long my reach is. There's nowhere for you to... run."

Li Fenggu hurries forward: "Ai! Don't be so pig-headed, Ying'er. Don't you know what I'm planning for you? I'll tell you what – good food, good clothes and a good life!" She reaches out to help Caiping to her feet. "Now, Master Liu..."

Caiping pushes her away and stands up by herself.

"I'm nothing special. I admit to being poor, but I'll never admit to being base and lowly. If you want to sell anything, sell yourself."

Li Fenggu chokes with fury and can't utter a word.

Chenglong seems to have sobered up a little, and he smiles coldly. "What's this?" he says. "Am I... Liu Chenglong... not worthy... not worthy of a little song from you? I'll tell you what... what it's all about. My aunt and uncle made a childhood be... betrothal between me and... my cousin Caiping. You're her... spitting image. She's... she's dead, but you're... you're the very picture of her. If you'll agree... today, tomorrow... I'll send a grand sedan chair and... bring you home with... all the bells and... whistles. Once you're... through the gates... you and Yue E will... be equals... both my proper wives... not... concubines. How about it?"

Caiping meets his gaze: "And... if I don't agree?"

"Then... don't be surprised if... if I take you... by force."

"In that case, I will kill myself right here!"

She takes a couple of steps back and gives every indication of being about to hurl herself at a corner of the wall. Luckily, Wangtian is still close-by and catches hold of her with one hand.

"What do you think you are doing, Chenglong?" Wangtian thunders. "You've drunk too much of that horse's piss. Fuck off home and sleep it off! Don't make a spectacle of yourself in front of everyone here."

Chenglong has had Wangtian as a brother for a very long time, but he has never seen him this angry before, and he stiffens in apprehension.

"I haven't... haven't drunk that much. This is none of your business... Big Brother. Don't... get involved."

Yue E seizes the opportunity to push Chenglong back towards the house, saying: "Really, Chenglong, the drunker you are, the more you overstep the bounds. Hurry up and get back inside."

Chenglong shakes her off furiously. "Just what... bounds...do... I overstep? I'm a... a man of substance... three bedrooms and four concubines... what do you say to that? I've made up... my mind so... don't try any of your... women's tricks... with me. Hah! Anyway, as for you... there's no need... to be jealous."

"You..." Yue E is shaking with anger.

"Chenglong," Wangtian interjects, "if you're willing to take the consequences, no one's going to stop you having as many concubines as you like. But what you can't do is shelter behind the Japanese and act like a tyrant."

Chenglong looks surprised. "How... how am I acting like a tyrant? I bought this girl... she's... my property."

"Yes, master, yes, that's quite right," Zhou Si chips in.

Chenglong laughs: "No one got... anything to... say? Noble Red... are you still refusing... to come back with... me?"

"How much did you pay for her?" Wangtian asks.

Chenglong bursts out laughing at this: "Ha ha... you...want to... know the... price? Alright... I'll tell... I'll tell you. Two hundred silver... dollars."

"And you've got that much?"

"What... do you mean?" Chenglong is taken aback, then his laughter redoubles. "Ha ha... I forgot... you're still... a... bachelor. Have you got... your eye... on this girl... too? I got there first... but if you... can produce... two hundred silver... dollars ... she's yours . If not... then go... find somewhere to... cool off."

"You can't tell me what to do."

"What I... can tell you... to do... is show me... the hard cash. If you... can't, then stop... trying to... show off!"

At this point, Mother Yan can't resist joining in: "How can you talk like that, Chenglong? He's your elder brother."

"Of course... he's... my elder... brother," Chenglong sneers back. "And I'm... doing... my best for him. How about it... Big Brother?"

"I have your word on it?"

"Of course. Everyone here... heard ... me."

"Right!" Wangtian nods, turns round and opens up his bedroll. From it, he extracts a stoppered gourd bottle, which he holds up and then drops to the ground. The gourd shatters with a crash, scattering banknotes and silver dollars all around. Wangtian points at them: "There's one hundred and thirty-seven yuan and fifty cents there. You can count it."

"Then you're... still ... short."

"My night soil route is worth another eighty. That covers the full amount."

Chenglong has recovered his composure: "I've got enough routes, Brother. I don't need any more. It's cash on the... nail... today."

Wangtian appears to have run out of luck and can't go on. He steals a glance at Caiping and stamps on the broken pieces of bottle in frustration. Then Yue E, who has remained silent through all this, steps forward and says: "You really do have a terrible memory, Brother Wangtian. Have you forgotten the eighty yuan you left with me? I'll go and get it for you."

This takes Wangtian by surprise. What money had he left with Yue E? But without waiting for him to reply, Yue E runs off into the eastern courtyard.

"Alright! So that's... the way of it! You're going... to insult me like... this? You really are my fucking... elder brother!"

Wangtian meets his gaze and says in a level tone: "Chenglong, all I'm doing is expiating some of your sins, so your punishment will be reduced. Neither your birth father nor the father who brought you up ever had people pointing their finger at them behind their backs. You're a father now, you have a son and a daughter. Aren't you concerned what they will think of you when they grow up? Have you forgotten the significance that your son is called Liangxin and your daughter Xinliang? That is something you mustn't traduce."

This infuriates Chenglong. "What the fuck... do you know about it? I haven't got... time for people's... mealy-mouthed morality. Liangxin? ... Xinliang? Tomorrow... I'm... going to... change their... names to... Ren'e ...and E'ren!"[1]

"How can you say such a thing!"

"I'll... say anything... I like. You lot... can all stop... pretending you're... saints. Do you... think... Liangxin... will grow up like me?"

"What nonsense are you talking now?"

Chenglong's face contorts, and he says fiercely: "I was never... going to bring any... of this... up, but you forced me to."

This is too much for Wangtian. He swings a mighty slap at Chenglong, which makes Chenglong stagger back a couple of paces. To everyone's surprise, Chenglong bursts out laughing.

"Ha ha... a good hit... very good! No one else dare lifts a finger... against me... so good for you! I'll take that... slap from you...but it ends... any fucking... friendship between us... from now... on. You go on and... play the... goody-two-shoes and... I'll be... the bogeyman... and we'll leave... each other... to it."

Wangtian stands up without a word, and it is as though the slap he has just delivered to Chenglong's face has landed on his own, too.

At this moment, Yue E returns and thrusts a stack of banknotes into Chenglong's hand: "There's sixty-three yuan there. You owe me fifty cents."

This just serves to enrage Chenglong even more. He hurls the money to the ground and leaves, without looking back.

THE RAIN HAS SLACKENED, but the wind is getting up and making the elm tree in front of the Minister's Residence rustle and sway. Wangtian is dragging his feet as he comes out of the main gate, carrying his bedroll. At his side, Caiping nudges him a few times until he finally reacts: "You go home, girl." When she doesn't move, he thrusts at her some of the silver dollars Yue E has given him. "Take these and be on your way."

Caiping is taken aback. "You want me... to go?"

Wangtian nods.

"I... But you spent all that money."

"Ai! Just go home."

"I... I don't have a home."

"In that case... just go somewhere far away, and find a nice family to marry into."

"Don't... don't you want me?"

"Me?" Wangtian says with a wry smile. "What have I got to offer? Nothing, and I've wronged you enough already. Ai! This affair isn't just about you. I've put up with Chenglong for so long, it's for my own pride too. You have nothing to apologise for, and if, later on, things can be sorted out and you still want to know me, then come back and we'll see."

So saying, he puts the silver dollars he is carrying into Caiping's hand, then he turns and walks off.

Caiping hurries after him and throws herself to her knees in the mud and rain.

"Elder brother, although I am just a paid singer, I still have my self-respect."

"Aiyo! That's not what I meant. Get up, get up." Wangtian is rather flustered.

Caiping stubbornly remains on her knees. "Now you've bought me, you can't just abandon me."

"I'm a poor man, little sister..."

"I know."

"I'm just a night soil collector."

"I know."

Wangtian is temporarily lost for words. After a pause, he finally says: "If you really have nowhere else to go, come with me, and we'll muddle through somehow."

When Caiping hears this, she stands up without his help.

"Please don't misunderstand me," Wangtian continues. "I may not have much of an education, but I understand proper conduct and would never take advantage of someone who is down. If I was like Chenglong and thought I could just buy you, and do whatever I liked, then I would deserve any curses and blows people cared to throw at me."

"Then..." Caiping looks at him in surprise.

"Since you call me 'elder brother'," Wangtian says solemnly, "I count you as my younger sister. You will never go hungry while you are with me. If you ever find somewhere better, and want to leave, just say the word and you're free to go."

The two of them move off, one in front of the other, heading for the mouth of a nearby small hutong, their figures casting long shadows in the light of the streetlamps.

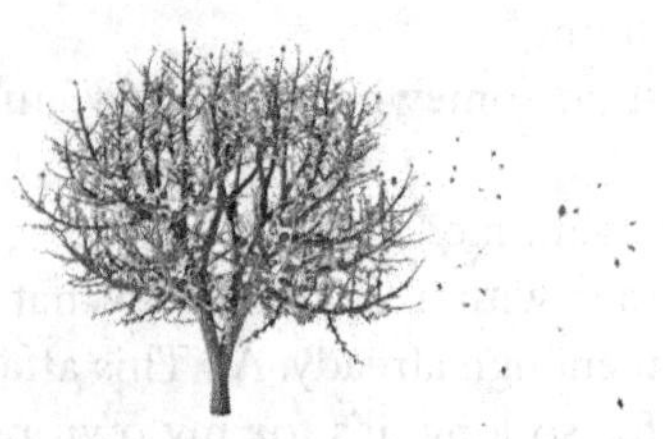

Chapter 6

Next day, the weather finally clears. The sun, which has been absent for several days, finally shows its face, suffusing the dripping wet streets and rooftops with golden light. Meizha Hutong off Dongsinan Avenue is reckoned a large hutong by Beiping standards, wide enough for three carriages to pass, in fact wider than many thoroughfares that call themselves streets or roads. The spot prepared for the New People's Assembly and the New Government established by the Japanese is a large courtyard residence on the north side of this hutong. There are sentries inside the courtyard, and two police posts are located at the gates; a detachment of military police is also stationed diagonally opposite, so it can certainly be considered heavily-guarded. Nor is this close security very surprising, given that this nest of Japanese collaborators is situated in the midst of more than a million loyal Beipingers. In fact, even this level of protection has proved inadequate, and quite a few people have already been assassinated, either side of the establishment of the New People's Assembly. It is being reported that they have been executed in their homes, in playhouses, in restaurants and on the streets, by shooting, by stabbing, by strangling, by bludgeoning with a rock: the whole works. It is also said that a sheet of paper is pinned to every corpse that reads: 'So die all traitors to China'. It is signed 'The Traitor Elimination Squad'. Where has this mysterious group come from? Nobody knows. One thing is certain, however – no matter from what party or faction, they are Chinese. It is because of them that the Japanese have redoubled their security measures and increased the number of personnel.

At 8.20am, a limousine appears from the north, slows down at the crossroads with Grain Market Avenue and turns into Meizha Hutong. Anyone who lives here knows that this limousine will arrive every day at the same hour and the same minute, give or take a few seconds. The owner of the car is called Wang Youde. He has spent time in Japan and was once a bureau chief in the Beiyang Government's Ministry of Finance, but he lost the post because of corruption charges. His nickname is 'Small-Eyes Wang', not because he has small eyes, but because he is like a fine-meshed sieve in his quest for financial gain. With the establishment of the National Government, he made a considerable outlay of money mobilising connections in the hope of securing a part-time government position; but his name was still so tainted, no one dared employ him. It was only when the Japanese came that he re-entered public life. He is only a council member in the New People's Assembly, but it would appear he is a candidate for head of the Ministry of Finance in the new government. The Japanese have assigned him an official car and two personal bodyguards.

Wang Youde's car is halfway round the corner, when a rickshaw suddenly pulls out from the kerb directly across its path. The driver hurriedly stops the car, and before it has even come to a halt, the rickshaw man has produced a gun. Almost at the same moment, a man hawking cigarettes at the side of the road also draws a gun and rushes over. Shots sound, and the car's windscreen and left-side window shatter. The street erupts into chaos. Before the military police and CID men on the street can arrive, the assassins have disappeared. The two bodyguards in the car are dead. Wang Youde has been hit twice and dies a few days later in hospital. Only the driver survives, with a few scratches on his head.

It turns out that this isn't the only incident of the day; two other key members of the New People's Assembly have also been attacked. One was stabbed and seriously wounded just as he stepped out of his front gate, while the other was killed before he had even left home, drowned in his own fish pond. But neither of these is as startling, as animating or as exciting as the daring attack in Meizha Hutong. Across the city, everyone is whispering about it and laughing up their sleeves; and cronies sitting around in groups in courtyards and houses are all boasting about it and laughing uproariously. Everybody has heard about it, and the details are discussed in vivid detail. This outpouring of emotion is hardly surprising since there has been a sullen mood hanging over the ordinary citizens of Beiping for several months, and they have been looking for an opportunity to vent it.

Of course, Matsuzaki Harayama is enraged by the news. Just when he thought things were settling down, this comes along and shatters his illusions. They've made a great fuss about appointing these pro-Japan Chinese to office, and they're all being assassinated and making the Japanese lose face. The same day, the Japanese impose martial law across the whole city, and they institute house-to-house searches. Several arrests are made, but in the end, not a single person actually involved in the assassination is apprehended.

SINCE THE ARRIVAL OF THE JAPANESE, business in the better class of restaurant on Houmen Avenue, including Xiao Yuerong's Yuerong's Place, has been ticking over quite nicely. Matsuzaki Harayama, who was a regular customer there when he re-opened Moxiangzhai when he was still calling himself Liu Yu, is particularly partial to its Huaiyang cuisine.[1] Now he is head of the Japanese spy network in Beiping, naturally he is an even more frequent visitor. This is the place where he arranges welcome and farewell parties, and other celebrations too. Because of the food shortages, he has specially arranged for Yuerong's Place to have a 'military certificate' that allows Xiao Yuerong to buy rice and other ingredients not generally available in the markets. Along with Xiao Yuerong's talent for making the best of what is available, personal recommendations and favourable comparison with other establishments mean that Yuerong's Place is doing pretty well.

It's still early, and there are no customers yet in Yuerong's Place. Xiao Yuerong, himself, is supervising the staff as they wipe the tables and mop the floor. Suddenly, two men pull aside the door curtain and come in. One is twenty-something and the other is in his early fifties; both are wearing long gowns with Western-style hats.

"We're not open yet, gentlemen," says one of the waiters, ducking his head courteously.

The two men ignore him and seek out the table furthest inside the restaurant and next to a window. Sitting down, the older one says: "Are you not going to bring me some food, even though I'm hungry? Is that because we're too early, or because you don't like the fact we are Chinese?"

The waiter's voice sticks in his throat, and Xiao Yuerong, realising the newcomers are bad news, puts on an ingratiating smile: "You are joking, gentlemen. A restaurant doesn't care how early its guests arrive, or what nationality they are. If you've got money, of course I'm not going to show you the door. Just order whatever you want. The staff are here, the provisions are here, we just have to light the stove."

"Fair enough," the older man says, turning to look him over.

Xiao Yuerong can see him clearly now. The man's face is covered in a criss-cross of deep wrinkles, and a dark purple scar, about six inches long, runs from the right of his forehead to his left cheekbone. The scar has caused a big tuft of hair to sprout above his left eyelid, and it gives a crooked slant to both eyes. His devil-take-you stare is startling and a little scary. He pulls out a handful of silver dollars and throws them down on the table, saying: "Alright then. Bring a catty of wine and whatever food you've have to go with it."

"Ah... of course... of course, thank you." Xiao Yuerong picks up the money and orders the waiter: "Quick now, bring some tea."

Xiao Yuerong's eye happens to fall on the two men's trouser legs and shoes under their gowns, and he gives an involuntary start of surprise. The scar-faced man notices and automatically pulls the edges of his robe together and puts his feet under the table.

"Have you sung *Finding a Jade Bracelet* recently, Master Wang?" he asks.

"What... Ah! You recognise me?"

The scar-faced man smiles wolfishly: "How could I not recognise you? You were a big star back then. So, you're a restaurant owner now? Very good. They say a big mouth is useful for eating, but it should also know when to keep quiet. I'm sure that if any brothers were to run into a little trouble, they could rely on Master Wang. Isn't that so?"

"Eh? What's that?"

"I'm sure that you still enjoy some opera here. It would be a shame if the song was *Wu Song Smashes up the Inn*."

"I... I don't know what you mean."

Xiao Yuerong goes back to the serving counter, thinking about the meaning of what the man had just said. His heart starts pounding harder. He gives himself a moment to settle down, then hurriedly finishes writing out the menu. He hands it to another waiter, saying: "Hurry up and take this back to the kitchen. Tell them to get on with the cold dishes first."

"Yessir! Marinated beef, salted pig's tripe, chicken and mushrooms, sweet and sour pork..." The waiter calls out the list of dishes as he heads towards the kitchen.

At this moment, a police siren is heard outside, along with a confusion of running footsteps.

"Police search!" someone shouts. "No one leave! Arrest anyone you don't recognise, or anyone who looks suspicious, and we'll question them later."

The twenty-something-year-old Officer Song enters the restaurant with two of his men. Xiao Yuerong hurries over to greet him.

"Are you sheltering anyone here, Master Wang?"

"No, I can vouch for all my staff."

"Have you seen anyone suspicious?"

"Ah, what do you mean by suspicious?"

Officer Song doesn't return his smile, as he looks over the waiters in the dining room. Then his gaze settles on the two men, and he asks: "Those two early birds – what are they doing?"

"I... I, er, didn't ask." He leans closer and whispers confidentially in Officer Song's ear: "I can't afford to offend any of my regular customers, least of all those early birds. Can you, er, trust me to handle them?"

Officer Song takes his meaning. "Hmm, I just thought they looked familiar... Alright then, I'll take my leave." So saying, he leaves the restaurant.

Xiao Yuerong escorts him out, asking: "All this rumpus, Captain Song. Has something important happened?"

Officer Song knows the street well, so he is familiar with Xiao Yuerong's history and knows that in recent days there have been Japanese looking out for him. He is also keen to curry favour with him, so he discreetly tells Xiao Yuerong about the events in Meizha Hutong, as if imparting a confidence. Seeing Xiao Yuerong's frightened expression, he adds: "Now the rooster has been shot, anyone else eating the Japanese corn shouldn't stick their necks out too far."

Xiao Yuerong can guess about ninety per cent of who his two customers are and what they're about, and he takes their food over in person. As he serves them, he says casually: "Have a drink, gentlemen. The hot dishes will be with you shortly."

The scar-faced man stands up to offer Xiao Yuerong a cup of wine. "Master Wang, when one meets a man of understanding, words are unnecessary. It's all in the wine." He finishes his cup.

"What has happened in Meizha Hutong is... I must raise a cup to you two."

The younger man looks admiringly at Xiao Yuerong, and he can't help asking: "How did you know, Master Wang?"

"I can tell you that. You forgot something when you were getting the disguises ready."

"Ha! Yes, there was a saying in my theatre troupe – better to wear rags than wear the wrong clothes. The Western-style hats and long gowns are fine, but those trousers and those shoes..."

The three men laugh knowingly, and Xiao Yuerong says: "I'll go and get you two some other clothes, and once you've changed, you'll be safe to go out."

"Excellent. And don't worry, once the flap has died down, we'll..."

"That's not what I meant," Xiao Yuerong says. "I just wanted to ask you... will you answer me truthfully?"

"That depends on what you ask."

"Tell me, do you think someone like me is a traitor to China? If you do... I'll shut up shop tomorrow."

The two men laugh. The scar-faced man claps him on the shoulder. "Ai! How will you eat if you do that? What will all these waiters eat? Two nations are at war, but it's nothing to do with us ordinary folk. Just remember you are Chinese, and you'll be fine."

Xiao Yuerong's relief is immediately apparent. "Gentlemen," he says, "when I performed in *Resisting the Jin Army*, I used to play Liang Hongyu. I cherish that memory."

Qi Yuexuan has been hiding out in Laoqiying in the Western Hills for more than a fortnight now, and the provisions Lao Zhang had stowed away are fast running out, given that they have had to feed three people. They can't think of any way of getting more supplies, so they are reduced to three meals of thin congee a day, and even that will only last another two or three days. Yang Zhixing has several times thought of returning to the city, but Qi Yuexuan has always stopped him. Today, however, he has no option but to let him go. He doesn't have any presents to take back with him, except for two fine-voiced grasshoppers for Liangxin and Xinliang, along with two woven grass cages.

Yang Zhixing leaves the mountain early, and since he has no vehicle, he walks the whole way, more than thirty *li*. Although he has some basic skills in *gongfu* and is still pretty robust, he is over seventy years of age. This year, in particular, has taken a mental and physical toll, and he is not as strong as he used to be. Still, he is spurred on by emotion and by the task in hand, so there is no way he is going to dawdle, let alone give up. All he can do is endure what is ahead and put suffering behind him. It is approaching midday when he reaches the outskirts of the city.

There is a spiked barrier blocking the city gate, leaving passage for just a single vehicle, and a dozen or so soldiers and CID men are standing on either side. People leaving the city are free from any formalities, but anyone entering undergoes a body search. Seeing Yang Zhixing travelling all alone, one of the Japanese soldiers gestures to him, saying: "Raise hands. I search."

Yang Zhixing knows there is no way out, but he doesn't raise his hands, just unbuttons his jacket.

"Don't do anything hasty," he says. "I'm really itchy, and I'm just taking it off. Watch."

The next instant, he has taken off his jacket and his undershirt. Wrapping them round his arm, he displays his still sturdy chest. The Japanese soldier looks on blankly.

Yang Zhixing says with a smile: "Can you see everything? Hurry up! You're not a girl, staring at me like that! I'm not going to marry you!"

The bystanders all laugh up their sleeves. The two grasshoppers that have been wilting in the heat seem to come back to life and begin singing loudly. The Japanese stiffens in surprise and asks abruptly: "What is this?"

"Grasshoppers."

"Ah! I have them in my home too." The Japanese grins and reaches out to take them.

Yang Zhixing snatches his hand back quickly, so the Japanese just grasps thin air.

"You go on, leave this behind."

"No!" Yang Zhixing says bluntly.

"No?" The Japanese glares at him.

Yang Zhixing just laughs. "There's no point in glaring at me. Beiping men aren't that easy to frighten. I can't give you these two grasshoppers since I've caught them specially for my two grandchildren. If I hand them over, it will bring you bad luck."

He doesn't finish, but a laugh escapes him, and the Japanese soldier gets really angry. He continues to glare at Yang Zhixing, clenching his back teeth. Then, suddenly, he raises his rifle and gestures with the tip of his bayonet, shouting sternly: "Underclothes take off! Take all off!"

Yang Zhixing stares at him, unconcerned. "Eh? Do you Japanese not have a home of your own, or have you just forgotten how you got here? I'm too old to be coy. If you want me to strip, I'll strip. But let me tell you, what I've got down there could never produce a thing like you."

So saying, he begins to unbuckle his belt.

At this point, one of the plain-clothes CID men comes over and stops him.

"Aiyo! Please don't! Aren't you Manager Yang? I must be blind not to have noticed you. Quickly, put your clothes back on. He's one of the good guys, my lord, one of us."

"One of us? In what way?"

"He's the father-in-law of our CID Chief Liu – his wife's father."

Yang Zhixing breaks in stubbornly: "I really don't want to benefit from that distinction, or even mention it. It's better to lose my clothes than forget who I am."

"Aiya! Don't be so perverse, sir!" the plain-clothes man says, dragging Yang Zhixing away. "Let's say you let me rescue you now, and you keep quiet about all the ins and outs of it. Next time you see me, you can get in my face and say whatever you like, alright?"

SINCE MOTHER YAN HAS BEEN REMARRIED to Yang Zhixing, the two of them have never been apart. Now her husband has been away in the Western Hills with Qi Yuexuan for more than a fortnight, and she has not even received a letter from him. The experience of old age stops her from saying anything, but the doubts and fears that are kept locked in her heart keep bubbling out, and she worries over them constantly. What is more, it has been one thing after another over the last few days, each one divisive and frustrating in the extreme. It really is a case of 'when the cat's away, the mice will play'. Several times, she has packed to go out to the Laoqiying herself, but each time she has held back. She knows Yue E is bitterly unhappy, and she cannot bring herself to leave her or the two grandchildren. She is reduced to spending her sleepless nights tearing up rags to use to re-sole shoes during the day. She has mended countless shoes and has hardly stopped talking, but her anger and indignation are undiminished. Now she has just finished her dinner, and she is sitting on the edge the *kang*, mending shoes, each thrust of the needle fiercer than the one before, as she pulls the thread tighter than if she was hogtying a pig. All the time she is swearing under her breath: "God-cursed little Japanese, I hope you go mad... Chenglong, you little bastard, you stuck-up thankless wretch... how unfair, Heavenly Father, for you to turn a blind eye on good people who worship you till their knees are raw. You treat men and women differently, so why don't you do the same for good and evil..."

"Are you re-soling shoes or doing *gongfu*?" Yang Zhixing asks with a laugh, as he comes through the door.

"Aiyo! So you've come back have you, you wretch!" Mother Yan stops what she is doing and slips down from the *kang*.

He hurries towards her, and she notices he is limping. "What's up with your feet?"

"It's nothing. I'm just not used to walking very far."

"Are you trying to tell me you walked all the way back? Your stinginess will be the death of you!"

"Do you actually think there's any kind of vehicle to hire out there?"

Mother Yan quickly brings him some hot water in which to soak his feet, and she pours him some tea. She looks at him lounging on the *kang* and says with a smile: "Right, let's get you some food. You rest there, and I'll go and make you something."

"There's no rush for that. Go over to the eastern courtyard first and fetch Wangtian."

"What for?"

"I want him to find a cart and load up some supplies. He can come back with me this afternoon."

"Eh! You've only just got home, and you're already thinking about leaving?"

"If I don't hurry, the Young Master will run out of food."

Irritated, Mother Yan's voice rises: "And how old are you! Look at you – your toes are about to fall off! An old crock like you can't stand this kind of treatment. You've been your own man for a long time now, not a household servant. You don't need to risk your life like this. What are you planning? An early burial in the Qi family tombs?"

"Bullshit!" He knows that Mother Yan is really worried about him, so he tries to shut down the argument. "I, Yang Zhixing, am nobody's servant. If I die, this bag of bones can be dumped any old where, I don't mind." He points fiercely at the pit of his stomach. "What I am planning is to be at peace with myself here."

Mother Yan realises that, at this time, any further objections will just be ignored, so she says no more.

Seeing that she is giving way, Yang Zhixing says: "Enough! There's no need to tear at the heart strings, I have full command of the situation. These old bones are not about to fall apart. They'll serve me for a few years yet. Now, be off with you."

"But... Wangtian is ill."

"What's wrong with him?"

"He's been in bed for a few days. The doctor says his body is overheated and it's affecting his heart, and now he's caught a fever."

"Then I will go over to the eastern courtyard to see him."

"He... he's gone back to stay in his old place... but don't worry, there's someone there to look after him, and he seems to be getting better."

"And whose stupid idea was that?"

"Ah! It was that son-in-law of yours..." Mother Yan breaks off before she can say any more.

"What exactly is going on here?" Yang Zhixing asks furiously.

Yue E has beseeched her not to tell her father about what has happened, for fear of his angry reaction. But now Mother Yan has blurted it all out to him. All she can do is try to back-pedal: "It's nothing serious, I'll tell you all about it later.

Now I'll go and get you a cart and some men. When you've eaten, you can take a nap and then be on your way as fast as you like." So saying, she leaves the room.

Yang Zhixing is thinking about all this when he hears the two voices that have been filling his dreams: "Grandpa! Grandpa!" Liangxin and Xinliang come running into the room, jostling each other to be first into Yang Zhixing's embrace. He hurriedly reaches for the two grasshopper cages on the *kang* and puts them in the outstretched hands.

"There you are," he says, "one for each of you."

The two children run off happily, as Yue E, out in the courtyard, tells them to slow down and then she comes into the room herself.

In her eyes, her father appears to have aged in the several weeks they have been apart, and for his part, Yang Zhixing thinks his daughter looks much thinner and paler. Both born into troubled times, their lives have not been easy, and as they take each other's measure, neither knows quite where to start.

It is the father who first finds his voice. "What has been going on in the family, Yue E?"

"Nothing... nothing at all. Everything's fine." She lowers her head, avoiding Yang Zhixing's gaze.

"Don't try to fool me. Are you ill?"

Yue E shakes her head, her eyes already glistening with tears.

"Is Chenglong mistreating you?"

Yue E keeps shaking her head, but the tears begin to flow.

Yang Zhixing begins to get agitated. "Whatever it is, you can tell me. As long as I have a breath in my body, I'll..."

"It's nothing, father. Really it isn't." Yue E remains tight-lipped.

Yang Zhixing stoops down and lifts Yue E's face to him. She can hold out no longer, and burying her face in her father's embrace, she wails.

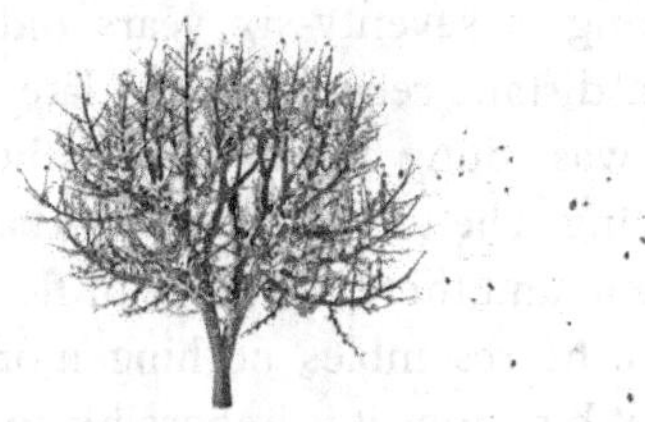

Chapter 7

After her death, Flower Branch was buried in the Qi family tombs, which, at the time, were derelict and overgrown. All that marks her grave is a wooden plaque. During his time at Laoqiying, Qi Yuexuan has begun to feel more and more ashamed of this, so he has rewritten the epitaph and ordered Lao Zhang to find a stonemason to carve an appropriate stone stele. When the stele is finished, a group of men bring it over, just after Yang Zhixing departs for the city.

Erecting a stele is the same as burying the dead; it must be done before noon. Once the stele is up, the men lay a surrounding wall of mountain stones and set out the offering table. When everything is ready, Qi Yuexuan dismisses Lao Zhang and the stonemason's men. Stroking the stele, he says with a deep sigh: "Xiulan, I have been neglecting you all this time, but now I hope I have given you a fitting memorial. I didn't dare express myself too clearly in the inscription, in case it attracts attention and has to be taken down."

A life of lonely sorrow,
An unbending character,
A hero among women,
The most loyal of humans lies here.
Two worlds yearn for each other,
Too late to reunite.
One life cannot contain them both.
Two hearts in one eternal sacrifice.

"Do you understand? From now on, I will come here every day to tell you what is in my heart. I know you want to listen, and that you trust me, so know what kind of man I, Qi Yuexuan, am. I am no hero, so treat me as a stranger, separate your heart from me..."

"Young Master Qi!" Someone behind him is calling him. He wipes away his tears and turns to look. It is the mayor of Laoqiying, Grandpa Dong.

This Grandpa Dong is seventy-six years old. His proper name is Dong Fuzhong, and he is a distant relative of the late Dong Fuxing. He is short in stature, and when he was young he was slender, but as he has grown old, he has inflated with good living. The top of his head is balding to the extent that he no longer needs to shave it, and there is a ridge of flesh across the back of his shiny pate. When he walks, he resembles nothing more than a large, slow-moving rubber ball. Looking at him now, it is impossible to believe he was a *baturu*[1] of his banner, could draw the stiffest bow, wrestle a bull and catch a leopard bare-handed.

His clan was formerly part of the servant class of the Plain Yellow Banner. Their original name is forgotten, and they use the name their overlord changed it to, which is Dong. After the foundation of the Republic, all the members of the Tunggiya clan of the Plain Yellow Banner took the Chinese name Tong. Because 'Tong' and 'Dong' sound very similar, there are many servant families who had their name changed to 'Dong'. This is the reason people are wont to say 'Tong and Dong are two sides of the same coin'. In the time of Emperor Qianlong, the servant class of the top three banners were transferred into the Imperial Household Department, so the Dong clan were considered to be under the direct command of the emperor. They were falconers, dog trainers and keepers of the imperial hunting grounds, charged with supplying offerings of game to the palace. At that time, commoners were strictly forbidden to live in the Western Hills, or to hunt there, so the place teemed with wild animals. In addition to hares, roe deer, all kinds of birds, badgers, jackals, foxes and wolves, there were even occasional leopards and bears. Laoqiying was then the site of the Left Barracks of the Imperial Army whose area of command extended in the south to Badachu, in the north to the Fragrant Hills, and in the west to the Twelve Villages in Jiufeng. With the Central Barracks at Zhaitangchuan on Shijingshan, and the Right Barracks at Shijiaying on Fangshan, these formed the Three Barracks under the control of the head of the Imperial Household Department. During the Qianlong period, Qi Yuexuan's forefathers held the post of deputy to the head of the Imperial Household Department, and had command of the Three Banner Barracks.

Grandpa Dong's father finally shed his servant status in the twenty-fifth year of Emperor Guangxu, and he became an aide at the Left Barracks. By the time of the Republic, he had also been mayor for several years, and after his death, his son took over. With more than a hundred years of this relationship behind them, the Dong family continued to hold their old master's family in the highest respect, and right up until Grandpa Dong's generation had never gone against the established customs. Every time Qi Yuexuan came to sweep the family graves, Grandpa Dong never once failed to convey his most respectful greetings. But this time, when Qi Yuexuan came to hide out in Laoqiying, Grandpa Dong only came to say a brief hello on that first afternoon, and he has not visited again. Nor is it just him and the other members of the Dong clan, but all the hundred and more families in the village, close to a thousand people, have kept themselves at a respectful distance. Qi Yuexuan is puzzled by this, and neither Yang Zhixing nor Lao Zhang can offer any explanation.

"Ah, Mr Mayor!" says Qi Yuexuan, brushing the earth off his clothes. "Is something the matter?"

Grandpa Dong bows. "Young Master Qi, I haven't paid my respects for many days, nor have I done anything to look after your needs. Please..."

"Ai, there's no need," says Qi Yuexuan with an easy laugh. "This isn't the Qing dynasty any more. There's no need for such ceremony."

With Grandpa Dong looking embarrassed, Qi Yuexuan continues: "Is there anything else? If there is, please tell me. If not, please go home."

Grandpa Dong hesitates for a moment, then says: "There is one thing I'm not clear about."

"What's that?"

Grandpa Dong points at the newly-erected stele in front of Flower Branch's tomb. "Is it really the Young Master's wife buried in this tomb?"

"It is."

"Were you formally married?"

"What... what do you mean?" Qi Yuexuan is greatly put out by this line of questioning.

Grandpa Dong is unperturbed. "It's just that I feel it is not proper to bury her here, let alone to erect this stele."

"Not proper?" Qi Yuexuan gives a harsh laugh. "Ha! Whether it is proper or not is a matter for my family. Don't you think you are exceeding your authority in questioning who is buried in the Qi family graves?"

Now Grandpa Dong defines the problem more clearly: "Ai! If it was just me and my family in Laoqiying, you could do as you please. But if the whole village objects, I can't ignore it. I wouldn't dare try to tell you what to do, but I do want to alert you to the situation."

Qi Yuexuan is baffled by this conversation, but he manages to keep a lid on his rising anger. "Right, well, you had better explain what you mean. What exactly is 'not proper'?"

"Aiya, isn't that obvious? Here in front of you is buried your principal wife from the Niohuru clan. Then, a few years ago, you remarried a girl from the Zhou family. I even went to the wedding. Her whereabouts are unknown, and her death was never announced. In these circumstances, can it really be fitting to bury Miss Xiulan here?"

Qi Yuexuan can no longer restrain his anger: "There is nothing improper about it! Xiulan and I were separated by fate when she was alive, and I cannot deny her her status in death. Xiulan died a brave death, a hero's death, and she is worthy of sacrifices. No matter what you say, even if my parents were still alive, even if the whole of Beiping objected, I would ignore them all."

While Qi Yuexuan becomes agitated, Grandpa Dong remains calm and says with a smile: "You may not care, and we cannot know whether the dead care or not, but the villagers can see what is going on. How did Miss Xiulan die? The Japanese announcement was quite clear about that. Since she was a hero and a patriot, is it fitting for someone in your position to honour her with burial, with sacrifices and with a stele?"

"How is it not fitting with my position?" Qi Yuexuan stares at him in astonishment.

"From a private point of view, it doesn't matter." Grandpa Dong takes out a newspaper and points to it, saying: "But from the public point of view, it can't be ignored. Are you not the honorary chairman of the New People's Assembly for Japanese-Chinese Goodwill? Would it be appropriate to mention that on her stele, or would it be completely wrong? Would it be an adornment or a blot?"

Qi Yuexuan is flummoxed by this approach.

"I am afraid these two things are completely at odds, are they not?" Grandpa Dong continues. "If you let the Japanese see this stele, you must be prepared for it seriously to affect your standing with them. If the anti-Japanese faction see it, they are likely to tear it down because of your position..."

Qi Yuexuan doesn't let him go on, but snatches the newspaper from him and tears it into pieces.

"This is a put-up job. They're trying to frame me. I won't dignify it with a reply. Although I, Qi Yuexuan, am not in a position to take up arms against the Japanese pirates, I will never bend my back to them. If I really cherished my crappy status with them, would I be keeping watch over this grave? Would I have even come up this mountain? Master Mayor, according to our ages, I must honour you as my uncle, but do you not know how my father died? Are you unaware of my behaviour towards others? Yes, the world is a dangerous place, and people act from the most mysterious of motives, but there is an explanation for everything, which is not necessarily evil or sinister. Do you still have the nerve to talk to me about status? If you really want to go back over my record, I will make you eat your own words."

Grandpa Dong can see how furious he is, but he just smiles meekly and nods.

Even angrier than before, Qi Yuexuan yells: "You can wipe that treacherous smile off your face! What will make you believe me? Right! These are the Qi family tombs – in front of the spirits of all my ancestors I swear..." As he speaks, he points to the heavens and then is about to fall to his knees, but he is stopped by Lao Zhang, who has appeared at some point during these proceedings.

"Aiyo, Young Master! Don't do it. Oaths should not just be sworn on a whim." He turns to the other man. "Master Dong, you may not believe me, but surely you have to believe him now."

When Grandpa Dong still doesn't say anything, Qi Yuexuan takes one look at Lao Zhang, and anger floods through him. "I don't need you trying to smooth things over for me. You've just made matters worse with your 'jumping out of the bowl'. I may have 'jumped out of the bowl' but in jumping out of the city, I certainly haven't jumped out of the arena, have I? There's no need to keep tugging at me, I haven't sworn anything yet. Huh! How stupid I am! If they're determined to judge me by their own standards, what use is swearing an oath? I'm going back to the city today. It's a hundred times better to go down in a blaze of glory, than to stay cowering here..."

"Quite right, Young Master, quite right!" says Grandpa Dong doubling up with laughter. "Now I believe you. Now I'm convinced."

Seeing Qi Yuexuan at a total loss, Grandpa Dong goes on: "Please forgive my ill manners, Young Master. Lao Zhang and Zhixing had already explained things to me, but when great matters are at stake, one can't baulk at causing offence in testing them."

"Great matters? What great matters?"

It turns out that, since the Japanese occupation of Beiping, Grandpa Dong and the men of the neighbouring villages have been discussing how to organise a resistance movement. None of them, however, want to drag their own countryside into the path of destruction. Everyone believes that, although the Japanese haven't reached their area yet, it is only a matter of time. The twelve villages have joined forces to defend their land and their families. Some of these villages were formerly military posts for the Banner Barracks, and some defences are erected to protect them against bandits, which were originally manned by militia. They just need someone to coordinate them, and with no great difficulty they could assemble a force of a few hundred men, armed with several dozen rifles. In addition, this range of mountains is high, with deep valleys, dense woods and treacherous paths. Such terrain is a great deterrent to those unfamiliar with it. An incursion out of the mountains into Beiping is out of the question, but a defensive response is certainly possible. Everyone has been urging Grandpa Dong to take up the standard of commander, but he has already refused three times. This is not because he is afraid but because he feels he is just a coarse fellow, with no prestige, and also too advanced in years to take on such a great responsibility. When Qi Yuexuan returned to Laoqiying, his eyes lit up. But he knew he could not lightly entrust him with such an important task, and that is why he has devised this test at the family tombs. Such a possibility had simply not occurred to Qi Yuexuan, and he looks at this comfortable, portly old man with new respect. In comparison, he feels like an innocent.

Grandpa Dong can see what he is thinking, and he says with a smile: "The pretence is over now. Let us move on to important matters. Do you accept command of our defence force or not?"

To Grandpa Dong's consternation, Qi Yuexuan shakes his head.

"Does that mean you refuse?"

"Ai! I'm a scholar, not a soldier."

"Ha! Zhang Liang, Zhuge Liang, Liu Bowen... they were all scholars too, weren't they?"

"That's right," Lao Zhang chips in. "When you have warriors such as Guan Yu,

Zhang Fei, Zhao Yun, Ma Chao and Huang Zhong on the battlefield, you need a general like Zhuge Liang in command."

"Hmm, there is some reason in that." Qi Yuexuan thinks deeply for a while, then continues: "Grandpa Dong, I feel that whoever takes the lead in this should be someone born and bred in these mountains. He must have prestige, be familiar with the geography and understand the mind of the people. You may be advanced in years, but you are the man in control. As for me, I may have some knowledge of Sunzi's *Art of War* and the other classics of military strategy, along with some experience of current political and military policies, but that's all theoretical. I was also once an adviser to the Beiping military government, so I can come up with ideas and act as a messenger, but I am not the man to hold the reins. What is more, the Japanese have set me up, and I'm afraid it will be hard to clear myself of the suspicion I am a collaborator. I know I am innocent, but how do I convince others of that? I'm not just making excuses, I'm looking at the big picture."

Grandpa Dong can see that Qi Yuexuan also has a point, and he is temporarily stumped for a solution. So he laughs and says: "Clearly we need to talk about this some more."

But Qi Yuexuan won't let it go: "We can't mess around here. If we are going to act, we have to act big. This can't just involve a few villages in these mountains. We have to link the mountain ranges to the west, to the south and to the north of the Western Hills. The bigger the area under our command, the better we can organise our resistance. I think we can unfurl the government flag in order to rally more men. Not only can we unite the surrounding villages, we can link to the north with Changping, to the west with Huailai, and to the south with Wanping, Liangxiang and Fangshan in a chain of immediate mutual support. We can also incorporate any stranded soldiers, mercenaries and local bandits into our strength. It doesn't matter whether they are officials, commoners, soldiers or outlaws – as long as they reject being citizens of a vanquished nation, and want to resist the Japanese, that's all we ask. As for maintaining secrecy and security, and establishing confidential lines of communication, we'll deal with those as they arise. It seems too petty to call ourselves a local self-defence force. We should look to the whole northeast, and call ourselves the North China Anti-Japanese Volunteers and Western Pacification Army, dividing ourselves into detachments and platoons as appropriate. The more organised we are, the more men we will attract, and we must also give due thought to establishing a proper military hierarchy..."

"I'm afraid that won't work," says Grandpa Dong. "The government's flag may be big, but where is that government? If you want to rally people to a flag, they must first believe in it."

Qi Yuexuan raises his eyebrows. "I am special adviser to the Beiping Municipal Government and its defensive garrison, personally appointed by

Mayor Qin himself. Doesn't the saying go, 'If there is no great general in the Kingdom of Shu, let Liao Hua take the lead'?"

"So... do you have access to official government seals?" Grandpa Dong asks.

"Nothing could be easier."

"Really? Do you have them here?"

Qi Yuexuan laughs, and Lao Zhang takes over: "Aiyo! Don't you get it? Ha! What do you think the Residence's Moxiangzhai does? If we want to go for broke, forget about the municipal government, we can even get hold of the presidential seal if we want."

Qi Yuexuan glares at him and gives a dry cough. Making a great show of standing on his dignity, he says: "Stop talking such nonsense! Do you really think a private company can cut government seals for personal use? Anyway, Moxiangzhai is currently in the hands of the Japanese. Even if it wasn't, we couldn't do such a thing."

Lao Zhang and Grandpa Dong hear Qi Yuexuan out, not knowing where he is going with this. Unable to keep a straight face any longer, Qi Yuexuan chortles: "Who needs Moxiangzhai for this anyway? I can do it myself – a potato, a sweet potato, a radish, any of them will do."

Since his birthday, Chenglong has not returned home. Yue E is indifferent to him, and he resents the way she has turned against him by siding with Wangtian rather than her own lord and master, and causing him to lose face in front of everyone. If he happens to bump into Wangtian and Noble Red, that just increases his embarrassment. He even hates going into Minister's Residence Hutong because, as soon as he sees the old elm tree, he feels an inexplicable, illogical, irresistible, inescapable sense of regret. Every evening, he makes his way to Yuxiang's small room in the Lian house, and lets strong drink and a woman's company further dull his already weakened mental state. Even so, he often wakes from his dreams shaking, as he stares up at the blackness of the ceiling.

On this particular evening, he has just drifted off into a restless sleep when he is woken by a shout from Sergeant Lian.

"Do you think you can call me your son-in-law?" Chenglong explodes. "Don't you fucking dare presume on your relationship with me! You've stuffed yourself silly at my expense, so what are you yelling about now, in the middle of the night?"

Outside his window, Sergeant Lian is panting with fear, and it is Zhou Si who answers: "It's me, Master Liu."

"What's up?"

"Lord Matsuzaki wants you immediately."

"What for?"

"How should I know?"

Chenglong lights a lamp and says: "Get the car and take me to him."

"Lord Matsuzaki has sent a limousine. It's at the gates. I'll wait for you outside."

Yuxiang hands Chenglong his trousers and drapes a lined jacket over his shoulders, saying: "It's cold outside. Put on some extra layers."

Chenglong shrugs off the jacket with a laugh: "Don't worry, the cold doesn't matter. Didn't you hear? He's sent a limousine."

Yuxiang doesn't insist and just helps him do up his buttons.

"Master Liu…" she says softly, but she doesn't continue.

"What is it?"

"Couldn't you… let me go back to the Residence? I… I don't want to stay here."

"Hmm, go back, eh?" he grunts. "As my concubine, or as a maid again?"

Yuxiang is prepared for this. "Either. Whatever you wish. Just don't make me stay here any longer."

"You don't want to live at home, and I don't want to go home," Chenglong says with a wry smile. "If you go back to the Residence, where do I go?"

"Where does that leave me, then?" Yuxiang takes him by the arm and kneels on the *kang*. "Since all this happened, I haven't even dared leave the house. If you…"

Chenglong shakes off her hand as he says: "Alright, we'll talk about this later."

Yuxiang wants to say more, but, before she can, Chenglong fishes out some banknotes and hands them to her. Yuxiang looks at the money dumbly and doesn't take it. Chenglong throws it onto the *kang* and leaves the room.

Sergeant Lian's voice is heard from outside: "Son-in… I mean, Master Liu, you go on, I'll look after things here for you."

Hearing this, Yuxiang can't restrain a sigh. She picks up the money and is about to get off the *kang* to go and lock the door, when Sergeant Lian enters the room. Yuxiang is only wearing her undergarments, and she scurries back to the *kang* and pulls the cover over her.

Sergeant Lian looks away and babbles: "Alright, alright, but I don't know why you think you can still keep on playing the shy fucking virgin!"

"What do you want?"

Sergeant Lian doesn't reply, but, keeping his face averted, he holds out his hand and rubs his fingers together.

"Have you no face left at all, father?" Yuxiang asks angrily.

Sergeant Lian is unabashed: "Ha ha! How can I have face without money. Money is face."

"Take it!" Yuxiang says, throwing some of the banknotes at him.

"Is that all?" he says, picking them up. "I saw what a thick bundle it was from outside."

This is too much for Yuxiang: "Father, I used to hate mother for leaving home, and leaving her children… but now I understand, I understand everything. It's all your doing. But you're... you're not going to do anything more to me, you're not going to do anything more to me!" Then she begins to wail.

"Alright, alright, alright. Stop bawling, it's the middle of the night," Sergeant Lian says as he slips out of the room.

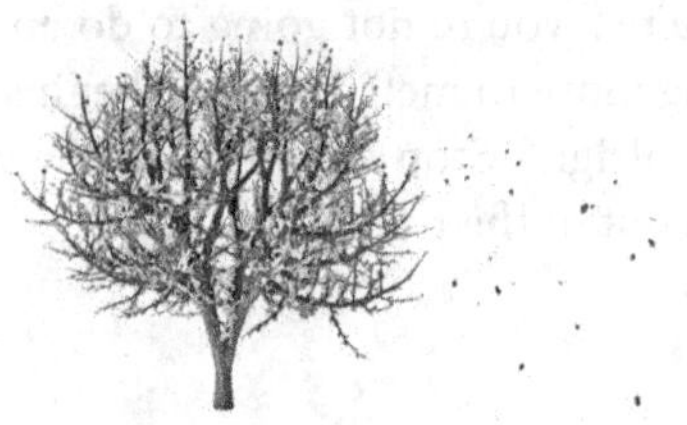

Chapter 8

Matsuzaki Harayama is living in the rear courtyard of the compound housing the Beiping Special Operations Committee to the west of the Houhai and next door to the Kempeitai command centre. This Special Operations Committee comprises no more than twenty or so men, but it has overall control of all the intelligence work in Beiping, Tianjin and the rest of the North China area. From the age of sixteen, Matsuzaki was hand-picked by the founding father of the Japanese intelligence services to undergo special training in military intelligence at the Ministry of Military Affairs, and he has been there now for more than twenty years. Before the war, he spent a long time intelligence-gathering in Beiping, and his substantial contributions mean he is now considered a veteran warlord of the intelligence services. Given all this, it should only be natural that he occupies his current position as director, but this is not the case.

At this time, the Japanese civil and military authorities are seriously divided over whether or not to expand the theatre of operations in the war against China; one faction wants to push on for a rapid victory, while the other wants to consolidate and take things step by step. Superficially, it is a battle over tactics, but in fact, it is a power struggle of self-interest between the new and old guards. In addition, the current Japanese North China Army is made up of the troops originally stationed in North China, the Guandong Army that came through the Shanhai Pass and troops newly transferred from Japan. Each faction is vying for control of its own territory, and they all have something to protect, so the key job of chairman of the Beiping Special Operations Committee is also something they are all fighting over. Matsuzaki Harayama's long period spent undercover in Beiping and Tianjin before the war is neither one thing nor the other to any of the factions. Their open warfare and covert manoeuvres resulting only in stalemate, the Japanese Ministry of Military Affairs finally gives Matsuzaki the direct appointment as chairman of the committee. He is secretly delighted, and his private opinion is that it is his unique understanding and knowledge of the close ties between Japan and China that got him the job. He is also very aware that the rewards in front of him now are like a hot meat pie, fresh out of the oven

– a lot of hungry pairs of eyes are staring at them and just waiting for him to slip up. Over the last few days, the succession of assassinations in Beiping is already causing him sleepless nights. This evening, the commanding officer of the North China garrison, General Tada, has personally telephoned to inquire about the circumstances of the assassinations, sounding extremely dissatisfied, and this has only served to increase his feelings of trepidation. This is the reason he has summoned Chenglong tonight. Compared with his own agents and the military police, he would rather put his faith in his Chinese underlings because he is confident he understands the Chinese, and because he believes in the principle that even a mighty dragon cannot match a snake on its own ground.

Chenglong is summoned into Matsuzaki Harayama's inner sanctum, which is a newly-altered Japanese-style room. This is the first time he has sat on tatami, and he doesn't know what to do with his legs, so he just kneels in front of the desk. He looks very ill at ease.

Seeing his awkwardness, Matsuzaki laughs: "Ha, Liu-san. In Japan, you have to pay particular attention to how you sit. When people of different status sit down together, the way they sit is also different. But here, that doesn't matter, just sit as you would on a *kang*, whatever way makes you most comfortable. There is no special reason I asked you here today, I was just feeling a little depressed and wanted a drinking companion. So, come now, have a drink."

Chenglong relaxes a little. He hastily drinks a cup with Matsuzaki and scrambles to pour refills. Feeling the mood lighten, Matsuzaki changes the subject: "Liu-san, I am not very satisfied with the work of your CID squad."

Chenglong hasn't yet swallowed the wine, and these words make him choke on it.

"I am not very satisfied, but equally, I am not dissatisfied. As for you, you absolutely have the capability to do even better than you are, but you are held back by your limited vision."

"I would welcome your instruction, sir." Chenglong puts down his cup and then stands up and bows.

"There's no need for such ceremony, this is just a friendly chat. Drink up, drink up!"

Matsuzaki waits until Chenglong picks up his cup, then asks: "So, let's look at this. Are you quite happy being just a gang boss, or do you want to be a major player in the political arena?"

"Well…" Chenglong doesn't immediately know how to reply.

"I think, in your heart of hearts, you don't really want to be limited to the former," Matsuzaki says, half encouraging, half teasing.

"Yes… yes, that's right."

"Then you need to weaken the power of the gangs until they are gradually squeezed out of existence. You need to reel in anything or anybody that can be of use, regardless of whether they are in the gangs or not, or which gang they belong to. You need to understand that the only thing that matters in selecting men is not their gang ethos, but their profitability. I think you understand this principle."

Chenglong profoundly agrees with these sentiments. "You are very wise. I will certainly do as you say."

Matsuzaki looks at him, smiling faintly. "The reasons I value you so highly are your instinct for profit and your ability to weigh up the pros and cons of an opportunity."

Chenglong's expression shows that he has been fully convinced, so Matsuzaki now throws out the real bait. "The New Government of North China is about to be established. Would you like a post in it?"

Not knowing exactly what he means, Chenglong just smiles and doesn't reply.

"Ha ha... that's given you something to think about, hasn't it! Well, I've offered you the stage and set the standard of performance, now you have to decide for yourself whether you can play the part."

"Yes, yes, yes."

Matsuzaki suddenly changes the subject and asks: "What's your view on all the recent assassinations in Beiping?"

Chenglong realises this is the real reason for his summons. "I think they are all the work of one gang... but the methods suggest they are not professional agents, nor do they feel like the work of the Communist underground resistance. I think it's a breakaway cell."

"Eh?" Matsuzaki is taken by surprise. "Are you saying there's no larger organisation behind these assassination squads?"

"No, no, an organisation clearly exists, but I can't yet say for certain where its allegiances lie. What I can say for sure is that the assassins themselves all have experience in the criminal underworld."

"Why?"

"Because when specialist agents undertake an assassination, they are primarily concerned with efficiency, directness and neatness. A breakaway cell is different – they don't just want to kill someone, they want to terrorise and to establish a reputation. That's why they make a big show of it, and go for effect. Subtlety is superfluous with such amateurs. It doesn't matter where their allegiances lie, they'll always do things the way they're used to. Given time, we can work out their patterns of behaviour and catch them. What is more, this doesn't feel like the work of a Manchu gang, because they're much more rough and ready. This feels more like the work of a gang from Laiyuan or Laishui, west of the capital."

Matsuzaki knows he's got the right man. "So, where do you think their lair is most likely to be?"

Chenglong doesn't even pretend to have to think about this. He replies immediately: "It's highly unlikely to be in the city. We've been through it with a fine-tooth comb over the last few days and haven't found anything. After the incident in Meizha Hutong, my men found a rope on the outer city walls north of the Xizhi Gate. It was tied to the battlements and hanging down outside the walls. I reckon that's how the assassins got out of the city and, judging by this, their hideout is probably somewhere to the northwest. It can't be too far from the city, either. It's most likely to be in the district between the ruins of the Yuanmingyuan to the east, and Xiyuan to the west. There are scattered villages in that area, and shantytowns – quite a few universities too, so the population is pretty diverse. Lots of people are living in broken-down old temples and abandoned courtyards, so it's a good place to hide. Several of the universities, schools and courtyards belong to English and Americans, and the Puppet Army doesn't have any control over them. You need to maintain closer surveillance over this area."

"Hmm, that's a very acute analysis." Matsuzaki's expression suddenly becomes stern. "But why didn't you report all this to me immediately?"

"I've already told Section Chief Imai. He said there's no use the detective squad investigating this kind of serious case, it's the responsibility of the secret service and the Kempeitai."

Matsuzaki mutters "Idiot!" under his breath, then seeing Chenglong's worried look, says placatingly: "I don't mean you. A lot of Japanese look down on you Chinese, Liu-san, and don't value cooperation with our Chinese friends. They are very stupid and don't understand the essential principle of 'using the Chinese to control the Chinese'. I disagree with them. I believe in valuing people with your kind of ambition, and any other Chinese with true ability. From now on, you can report directly to me. We must not let those dolts squander any more opportunities to advance the struggle."

"Yessir!" Chenglong is more than a little overwhelmed by this mark of favour from Matsuzaki.

Matsuzaki seizes the opportunity to bring Chenglong even further under his control: "You have a free hand to act as you see fit. Just tell me if you need anything, and I'll do whatever I can to facilitate things. Right now, drink up!"

Chenglong appears suddenly to think of something, and he asks: "Mr Matsuzaki, when the Puppet Army occupied Beiping, did it seize the records and archives of the Nationalist Government's civil and military intelligence services?"

"Yes. Why do you..."

"I would like to examine them to see if there were any circumstances where they incorporated any independent activist cells. If there are, and you follow my earlier train of thought, then there is a distinct possibility we might be on the track of this current bunch. But these are top secret documents, so I..."

"That's not a problem, I'll give you special clearance. Do you have any other requests?"

"This traitor-assassination squad is undoubtedly attached either to the Nationalists or the Communists, and it's more than likely to be in radio contact with one or the other. Please get the army eavesdropping departments to train their equipment on the area I just mentioned. If they can find them out, break their code, or even pinpoint their location, that will make things a lot quicker. Also, is it possible to order the foreign-controlled universities to re-open enrolment? That way I can infiltrate some more men to carry out surveillance and inspections. It's a bit of a blunt implement, but effective."

Matsuzaki hears Chenglong out, nodding continuously. He has a whole new level of respect for this confident and ambitious young man. He congratulates himself on his sound judgment. He remembers the old saying: introduce a dog into a wolf pack, and it becomes the other dogs' worst enemy.

Ever since Caiping came to Wangtian's little courtyard, that man, who has endured many years of solitary sweat and toil, has begun to enjoy the happiness of family life. But he has failed to live up to his own expectations recently, and for three days he has been lying in bed as the slight chill he took on the evening of Chenglong's birthday has turned into a raging fever. This morning, he is feeling somewhat restored, so he stealthily picks up the handle of his cart and tries to slip quietly out of the gate.

"Big brother!" The cry comes from the northern room of the courtyard, and Caiping follows him into the yard, draping her robe over her shoulders. "You haven't got your strength back yet, big brother. Don't be stubborn. It would be a real pain if you relapse."

"It's not a problem, I'll be alright."

"I know you're just putting on an act. Are you going to burst into song next? Listen to reason and come back in." Caiping grabs hold of the cart handle.

"Nice try," Wangtian laughs, "but collecting the night soil isn't a part I can just abandon. I've been lying here for three days, and if I stay off work any longer, people's toilets will be overflowing. Then I'll really get it in the neck."

"In that case, you should at least go out on a full stomach."

"There's some cornbread in the room. I had a couple of those."

"That's no good, they're all dried up. You might as well be eating air. Are you determined to stay sick?"

"It's fine, I'm used to it. It's always been like this before."

"Well, I wasn't in charge before. Things are going to be different from now on. A man grows weak if he doesn't eat properly, even more so given the kind of hard labour you're doing. Now hurry up and put that cart down. Relax and have something hot to eat, then you can go out to work."

The two of them go into the northern room together. Caiping ladles out some water, lights the fire and sets about things. Wangtian stops dead in amazement when he enters the room. The room, which had been filthy and in complete disorder only a few days ago, is transformed, with everything clean, neat and tidy, back in its proper place. When he was living there by himself, it was a mess, but now it's a proper home.

"I didn't expect you to do all the housework. I thought…" Wangtian stops mid-sentence.

Still working away, Caiping laughs. "You thought all I could do was sing and look pretty? Well, you underestimate me. When my grandfather was alive, even though we were broken down and destitute, we didn't drop our standards. If you've got a bowl of savoury noodles, do you really need nine or ten other dishes? If you have some pickles, you just have to cut them up as fine as possible. I looked after him alright, so you'll be no problem at all. Now, while you're waiting for your food, change into some clean clothes. What you've got on now isn't just filthy, it's as full of holes as a rivetted old cooking pot. Put on what's on the *kang* – it's freshly washed and I've mended all the tears."

"With the job I do, what's the point in having my clothes spick and span?"

"People sneer at rags but not at patches. It doesn't matter what your job is, you can't look like a beggar. All the neighbours have seen me coming in and out of here, so if you want to keep living your bachelor life like before, then they'll all be laughing at me for being so useless and stupid."

Wangtian looks at the pile of clothes on the *kang*, at how spotless they are, how well mended and neatly folded, and a warm feeling floods his heart. Like drought-stricken fields welcoming the longed-for rain, his whole being relaxes and blossoms.

Wangtian grins foolishly and doesn't say anything more. He turns his back and changes his clothes.

"Ai, big brother!" Caiping calls out, having also turned her back.

"What?"

"I wrote a little song while I was staying up looking after you. Shall I sing it to you?"

"Yes, yes do. I've only ever listened to professional singers on the phonograph. This would be a first."

Caiping hums the introduction, leads in softly, then sings with deep emotion:

A year of famine or a year of plenty:
The earth never knows which.
We never know what the next dream will be,
All we can do is muddle through.
We plant melons and harvest beans,
Long for rain and only get wind.
What is suffering? What is pain?
What is love? What is hate?
Elm tree seeds are a childhood dream.
Why does there have to be a winter after the spring?
Evil men full of malice are more to be feared than demons.
Why are good men always dealt the weakest hand?
Ai! Aiyaya! Aiya!

When she has finished her song, she turns and hands Wangtian the noodles she has been cooking. She sees that his eyes are full of tears and says, reproaching herself: "Enough! I wouldn't have sung it if I thought it was going to make you sad."

"No, no, not at all. You sang it beautifully, much better than the phonograph."

Caiping smiles. "Then I'll sing some more for you later. I'll sing something happy. Now eat up while it's hot."

Wangtian takes the bowl and stirs the noodles with his chopsticks. "These are 'two-face strip noodles'! Where did they come from?"

"Sister Yue E sent them over."

"Oh!" Wangtian replies. "Next time she sends over anything, you're not to accept it. We owe her too much already. That eighty yuan she pushed on me that evening wasn't anything I'd given her to look after. It must have been her own personal money."

Caiping nods in reply, but inside, she can't help feeling that bit closer to Yue E. Suddenly, she remembers something, and tapping herself on the head, says: "Ai! I almost forgot. A few days ago, someone else came looking for you. You were burning up and completely out of it, so I didn't wake you."

"What did he look like?"

"He was an old man, in his fifties or more, wearing a long gown and a Western-style hat... yes, and he had a scar on his face, long and slanting. He looked really scary, but once he smiled and opened his mouth to speak, he seemed quite nice. It sounded as though he knew you quite well."

Wangtian sucks his teeth and shakes his head: "No, I don't know anyone like that... who can it be?"

"I asked him why he'd come, but he didn't say. But he did start asking me stuff."

"What did he ask?"

"He asked right out if I was your..." She stops with a little laugh.

Wangtian is slow on the uptake. "My what?" he asks.

"Work it out for yourself."

The light dawns on Wangtian, and he can feel his ears reddening as he stutters: "What er, what did..."

Caiping grunts, not sounding particularly happy: "It's alright, I didn't embarrass you. I just said that you'd bought me, and I'd only been here a day or so."

"Aiya! Why did you say that?" Wangtian asks, getting agitated.

Caiping's voice also rises: "What was I supposed to say?"

Wangtian chokes to a halt, and Caiping laughs and goes on: "He asked a whole lot of other stuff too. If he asked about me, I told him the truth. If he asked about you, I just said I didn't know."

"Did he... did he leave any word for me?"

"He, er... he left his excuses and hoped you got better soon. He said he'd be sure to come back later. He also left you a little bundle. He said you'd understand when you opened it."

She feels around on the *kang* and pulls out a bundle wrapped in blue cloth from under the bedroll.

"This is it."

The bundle contains a fairly new pair of trousers and an unlined jacket, along with a pair of new cloth shoes. There is something heavy stuffed into the shoes, and when it's tipped out onto the *kang*, it turns out to be two one-*liang* gold bars and a red sword-tassel. Wangtian picks up the tassel and inspects it closely. He can't stop his heart from pounding.

"This is from my father's sword! I tied this tassel myself! My father took it with him when he went off on that armed escort job. I'm certain of it."

"Then was that man... was it your father?" Caiping stares at him wide-eyed and open-mouthed.

Wangtian sounds suddenly cast down: "My father died more than ten years ago."

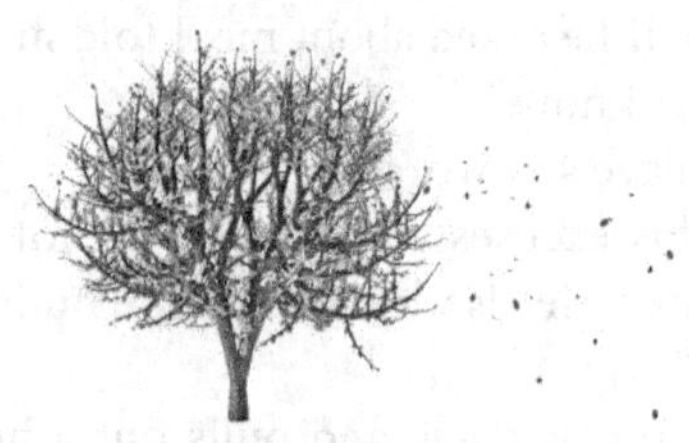

Chapter 9

I t's already been almost a year since Yanjing University suspended its classes. Before the Marco Polo Bridge Incident, the majority of the teachers and students had already moved to Wuhan and then, later, further west along the Yangtze River to Chongqing and Chengdu. The final stage of the migration has taken them to Dali in Yunnan Province. The only people left behind to look after the college grounds are Director Charlie and a dozen foreign teachers, along with a handful of Chinese teaching and administrative staff. The majority of the students still there are refugees who have been moved on from the Three Provinces, Rehe and eastern Hebei, numbering, in all, only a thousand or so. Compared with when the place was in full swing earlier in the year, it feels cheerless and deserted.

At first, the college authorities and the student union still organise a few activities and make every effort to increase the number of academic courses, but after the occupation of Beiping, it pretty much grinds to a halt. Most of the students, however, have no homes to go back to and are living in the university for the time being. They are not attending any classes, so private political organisations flourish. These include the openly-run Nationalist Party and the Three Principles of the People Youth League, but there is also the Communist Party that has secretly been gathering support among the students for some time, not to mention the Anti-Japanese Vanguard, the Iron Blood Group, the Students Against the Japanese Alliance and other groups organised by the students themselves. The college authorities are turning a blind eye to these organisations, neither supporting nor participating in any of them, and not opposing or attempting to close them down. All they have done is organise a university security squad, which is on duty and on patrol twenty-four hours a day, protecting college property and keeping order on campus.

CAUTIOUS AND CONSCIENTIOUS AS EVER, Director Charlie continues to go to work each day. A fortnight or so previously, a young man came looking for him. He said he had been entrusted with something by a friend, and he had an important issue to report. Full of suspicion, Charlie watched him take a strip of paper from inside his shoe, produce a small medicine bottle and brush some of the liquid it contained onto the paper, before handing it over. On the strip of paper now is a line of English in blue ink. It reads: 'I am safe and will be back within the next few days. My colleague, Zhang, has sent Brother Gui and twelve others as an advance guard, and I hope you can help them find somewhere to hide out. Hao Bingchen.'

Charlie has known for a long time about Hao Bingchen's position in military intelligence; and Hao Bingchen, in turn, is relying on his knowledge that Charlie is secretly working for the American Department of State. Quite apart from considerations of mutual interest and shared intelligence, thirty years of personal friendship mean there is no way Charlie can ignore this.

In fact, the leader of the twelve agents Hao Bingchen has sent is the scar-faced man who so vividly demonstrated his skills in Meizha Hutong. He is currently known as Brother Gui, but his real name is Gao Guigeng. He is, indeed, Wangtian and Chenglong's father.

Charlie finds a place for the twelve men in a long-disused building in the northeast corner of the university grounds. It is surrounded on three sides by thickets, and to the north there is some wasteland that is well off the beaten track. After their arrival, Beiping has seen the continuous stream of assassinations of traitorous Chinese, carried out by the 'Traitor Elimination Squad'. With his nose for intelligence, developed over many years, Charlie is already quite certain of the identity of the men he is sheltering.

Hao Bingchen is currently a special agent of military intelligence and also the co-ordinator of the Traitor Elimination Squad. He hasn't been to see Charlie since his arrival in Beiping, but has first arranged for Mr Zhang to take him to see Captain Gui.

Greetings exchanged, Hao Bingchen says: "Recently we have been hard-pressed at the front, and neither the northern nor southern arenas are any use to me. After Beiping and Shanghai fell in such quick succession, the government has secretly moved to Chongqing to ensure a safe command centre. At the same time, they have assembled the elite troops from both northern and southern fronts, and decided that Shanxi must be defended in the north and Nanjing in the south, to the last man. I've just..."

"Ha!" Captain Gui laughs coldly. "All the top brass have fled, so what's this talk of defending to the last man? It's bullshit!"

Mr Zhang gives him a meaningful look, but Hao Bingchen doesn't take offence and continues: "I've just come from Chongqing, and I'm in Beiping to coordinate the assassination of traitors. Since the radio transmitter I established is already being monitored by the enemy, there is a possibility our codes have been broken. So I have been ordered to bring the list of assassination targets personally identified by the bureau chief to you in person. I met with a few difficulties on the road, so I'm a few days late."

"But these assassinations are like harvesting garlic chives, aren't they?" Captain Gui says with a wry smile. "Cut down one traitor, and another just springs up in his place. Our energies would be better used on the battlefield."

"This *is* a battlefield," Hao Bingchen says. "The nation's woes are paramount, Brother Gui, and we must each play our part to the full. Hasn't what you have done here already borne fruit? At the very least you have served warning on all traitors and would-be traitors, and harassed the enemy from the rear. You have also shown the nation that there are still Chinese who dare to fight."

Captain Gui nods as he listens and then says: "Right then... now show us your list, so we can see which of the bastards are on there."

"To tell the truth, I haven't seen it myself." So saying, Hao Bingchen takes off his hat and goes on: "Lend me your knife a minute."

Captain Gui takes the knife from his belt, and Hao Bingchen carefully slits the rim of his hat. He extracts a strip of white cloth and lays it out on the table. He also takes a little bottle of 'revealing' fluid from inside his jacket, and, rows of characters soon begin to appear on the cloth. The characters 'Qi Yuexuan' make Hao Bingchen's heart lurch in shock, as he has never expected to see his old friend's name on a list of traitors to China. Even less has he expected that the sight of the same name would cause Captain Gui such distress.

WITH WANGTIAN OFF WORK for several days, all the toilets in the hutong are full to overflowing. The resulting work keeps him busy from early morning until the stars are out and his cart is full. He pulls it to the Zhangji night soil depot, which has already shut up shop for the night. On hearing Wangtian's shout, the depot's Manager Qu opens the main gate.

"Aiyo! What time do you call this? Any later, and I would have been asleep."

"I've been out of action for a few days. The work has really piled up."

Manager Qu goes over to have a look. "Ah right, yes, a few days and you're looking all hollow-eyed. I hear you've bought yourself a good-looking girl. There's no point denying it, everybody's been talking about it. Good for you, you deserve it, but you'll need to take it a bit easy."

Wangtian doesn't feel like explaining the real story, so he just smiles, picks up the handle of his cart and asks: "Which pool do you want it in?"

Manager Qu doesn't reply directly but says: "There's no rush. Put the cart down, I need to talk to you."

"Alright, go on then."

Manager Qu hesitates for a moment, then says: "I've got to tell you, Wangtian, I can't take your night soil here. From now on, I'm not allowed to."

"Why not?" Wangtian is flabbergasted. "I've been bringing it here for years. It's always good stuff, I never dilute it."

"I know all that, but... well, with the war going on and everything all over the place, I don't need as much as before."

"It doesn't matter what's going on, people have still got to live, still got to eat. You're taking everybody else's and refusing mine. I don't believe your excuses."

Manager Qu sighs: "No, I wouldn't either... alright, I'll tell you how we stand. We've done business together for a long time, and if I have to turn anyone away, I'm not going to do it to you. But... but if anyone comes to inspect what's going on, we can't get on the wrong side of them, can we? I reckon..."

"Hah! You don't need to go on, I understand."

"You really chewed Chenglong out this time. Couldn't you... go and apologise?"

"Not while my name is still Gao," says Wangtian, picking up his cart. "Let's get on with it. Where do you want it? I haven't had dinner yet."

"At least you've got something to eat today. But what about tomorrow? And the day after?" Manager Qu asks with concern.

"I can go somewhere else tomorrow, can't I?"

"Don't play dumb! They'll be checking everywhere. Who's going to want to stir up a hornet's nest just for you? I'll tell you what I really think – you two have got to find some way of getting along together. You are brothers after all's said and done. He's the one standing on his dignity, but if you go and give him back his face, he's bound to forgive you, isn't he?"

"And if I don't?" Wangtian asks, putting down his cart.

"If you don't, what are you going to do for work?"

"Heavy loading, pulling a rickshaw, portering, messenger boy. I've done it before, haven't I?"

"What about your night soil route? If you don't do it, won't people notice when the shit backs up? Once the streets start stinking up, you can be sure they'll be round your place cursing you."

"Well, I can sell the route, can't I?"

"But that was a really good area your father left you... can you really bear to give it up?"

"Like it or not, I've got to."

"So what are you planning to do?"

"I'm planning to strike a hard bargain," Wangtian says resolutely.

Manager Qu can see that he's serious, so he rolls his eyes and asks: "Have you got a buyer, then?"

"No."

"Well then, how about I take it off your hands?"

"That would be good."

"But... given the current market, the price can't be too high."

"What are you offering?"

"Sixty," Manager Qu says. Then, seeing the look on Wangtian's face, hurriedly adds: "Alright, since we've been friends for so long, I'll add another five. Sixty-five."

Wangtian is silent for a moment, then says, with a bitter laugh: "Alright, it's a deal."

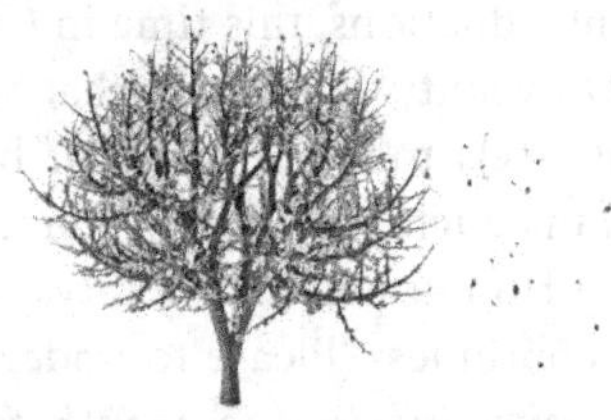

Chapter 10

The next morning, just after nine, three Kempeitai motorcycles and sidecars arrive at the main gates of Yanjing University and drive in without stopping. A number of security patrol on duty at the gates flag them down. In the sidecar of the lead bike, Yamaguchi yells at them to get out of the way.

One of the students replies firmly: "Yanjing University is an American college. According to international convention, you can't enter the property of a neutral country without permission."

Yamaguchi shakes his head. "Mine is general staff of Kempeitai. My want see university authority. Official business. Now get out of way."

"The university is a big place," another student laughs. "If you go in by yourself, you might still be trying to find your way in the dark."

"Then... you show way."

"Alright, but I have to make a telephone call first. If the director wants to see you, I'll show you the way. If not, I'm sorry but you'll have to turn round and go home."

Yamaguchi nods grudgingly. "Hah! Quick, quick, then."

Charlie is in his office, chatting with Hao Bingchen. After he takes the call from the porter's lodge, he hangs up hurriedly and says in a low voice: "The Kempeitai are here."

"What do they want?"

"I don't know, but if I refuse to see them, that'll be it. They won't dare force their way in."

Hao Bingchen gestures excitedly and leans in close to Charlie. "You'd better see them, and find out what they're up to."

A little while later, Yamaguchi is escorted in by the security patrolman, while Hao Bingchen hides in the inner chamber. Charlie smiles faintly and launches a stream of English at Yamaguchi, who stares at him blankly, not understanding a word. Charlie laughs and shrugs his shoulders, before switching into Chinese: "I'm sorry, I don't speak any Japanese, and you don't understand English, so is it alright if we converse in Chinese?"

"Alright."

Charlie repeats his introductions, this time in Chinese: "I am Heunis Charlie, the director of Yanjing University. May I ask what brings you here?"

Yamaguchi snaps his heels together and half bows, his face expressionless: "Lieutenant Colonel Yamaguchi, Military Police Office of Great Japanese Empire. Bring notices to Honourable University. Here is text." Without waiting for Charlie to reply, he continues: "Please to understand our notices are orders. Honourable University must inside one month take new students, next year January must restart classes. This is first notice, last warning. If no do in time, we close university. Goodbye."

When Charlie sees him turn and make to leave, he says: "The United States of America is not at war. By what right would you close down the university of a neutral country? Have you no regard for international law?"

"Huh! We Japanese Empire long ago withdraw from international agreements. You Westerners' international convention to us are not binding."

"I see, so your troops are now free to occupy, arrest and massacre as you please!" Charlie slams his fist down on the desk, and says, slowly and clearly: "But please now hear what I have to say. This is an assault on the United States of America, it is a declaration of war. Does a mere lieutenant-colonel like you really have that kind of authority?"

Yamaguchi understands the import of Charlie's words, and he immediately changes his attitude. "It's not so serious. International convention not binding on Japan, but we surely not want to make war with United States. Otherwise we not be so polite. But your neutralness must be correct. University without classes is not university, so we have reason to suspect this place maybe is hiding anti-Japanese factions. So, this place belongs to you Americans, but outside walls does not. If you not start classes again on time, I send men here to protect gates for you, stand guard, close all roads in area to keep you Americans safe."

It is highly unusual for a simple soldier to be able to speak so confidently and comprehensively. In fact, Charlie isn't to know it, but before he despatches Yamaguchi, Matsuzaki Harayama has given Yamaguchi a lot of special instruction. These 'dress rehearsals' are Chenglong's idea, with Matsuzaki as dramatist and director, and Yamaguchi proves himself to be a more than competent improvisational performer.

Charlie can see the dangers the man presents, and he also knows that meeting force with force is not the way, so he moderates his language a little: "We fully intend to start registering students again, but where are the young people in China today who have the desire to study? And those that do have the desire, don't have the money. Even if I do open the register, I doubt I will get enough to restart classes."

"No, no, no!" says Yamaguchi, shaking his head and smiling. "Just open register and I guarantee you get students."

"But they have to sit an examination to register, and it takes time to prepare the examination questions and the papers themselves. One month..."

"One month, no delay. I have told you consequences, please consider. Goodbye."

When Hao Bingchen hears that the Japanese has left, he emerges from the inner room and says to Charlie: "It seems not opening the register is not an option. Well, if we have to do it, we have to do it."

Hearing him so relaxed agitates Charlie. "Register students? You heard him guarantee there would be enough, and you can bet they will all be their men, can't you?"

Hao Bingchen smiles faintly: "Didn't you say yourself, they have to take an exam? So let them register, but if they foul up the exam, they can't force their way in, can they?"

"Ha! Yes, good... very good! You'll have to help me set the questions."

"That will be no problem with the mathematics. I guarantee they'll be so confused they won't know which way is north. But as for the humanities, especially the Chinese language essay..."

Charlie sees that he is looking a little embarrassed, and he jumps in: "I know just the man."

"Who?"

"Qi Yuexuan."

When Hao Bingchen hears this, he shakes his head vigorously: "No! Not him, not him!"

Charlie understands his misgivings and says with a smile: "He's your best friend, and you still don't understand what kind of a man he is? I don't believe the Japanese propaganda. If he really is going to take up a post with the Japanese, why is he hiding out in the Western Hills?"

Hao Bingchen is about to say something, but he changes his mind.

"As his friend, I really hope he isn't like that. But at the moment, I can't confront him with that friendship... Mr Charlie, there are some things I can't explain to you."

"How will I ever understand if you don't tell me?" Charlie's voice rises a little. "I think I understand everything. I understand your position. I understand what you have come back to do. I have lived in China for so many years, I think I understand the Chinese. Out there you can put up a façade, but here, it's just the two of us. I believe in Qi Yuexuan, he is the kind of sincere man rarely seen among you Chinese. I didn't expect an American-educated man like you to be so hypocritical."

Unexpectedly, Hao Bingchen gives a wry laugh. "Huh! You're right, but not completely. Apart from being a hypocrite, I am also cruel and heartless. I have to be at the moment. These are extraordinary times. We are at war. You are more straightforward than me because you are an American. You are an observer, an outsider."

"No, no, not at all!" Charlie's face goes red with indignation. "When good and evil come face to face, no one can be an outsider. Yes, I am an American, but I am also a Christian. In the Lord's name, I curse Judas. But..."

Hao Bingchen doesn't let him finish, but pats him on the shoulder. "Alright then, I'll send some of my men with you. But whatever you do, don't mention anything about the understanding the two of us have."

THAT AFTERNOON, the house belonging to Grandpa Dong, the mayor of the village of Laoqiying, is a hive of activity. In the courtyard, a feast is laid out on three large square tables. Grandpa Dong himself is seated in a wide armchair right in the middle. Around him are the mayors of all the other villages. The mayors and village elders are seated in rows along the two sides, each with their own entourage who stand in random formation behind them. The other villagers are standing around in twos and threes, exchanging greetings, chatting and laughing, shouting and whispering, creating a background buzz of noise.

Grandpa Dong bangs the table leg with his stick a few times, and the courtyard gradually quietens down. He stands up and cups his hands in respect to his audience. "Honoured guests," he announces, "everybody who should be here, is here. Anyone who is not here must be avoiding us, so we won't wait on them. All of you are leaders of your communities, and we are gathered here today to finalise plans for the mustering of our forces. If you have something to say, speak freely and don't keep anything bottled up. If any of you are here against your better judgment, there is still time for you to leave."

"There is no need to talk about mustering our forces, Mayor Dong, we are all already agreed on that." This is the mayor of the neighbouring village of Fucha speaking. His name is Fu Zhanxiang, but everyone calls him Grandpa Fu. He is the elder of the Fu clan, ten years younger than Grandpa Dong, but already in his sixties.

He hesitates for a moment, then continues: "There are several families today who are advocating retreat, with good reason, in my opinion. What we all originally discussed was establishing a self-defence force to protect our own homes and our ancestral lands. But over the last two days, you have been wanting to change the ground rules and set up an 'Anti-Japanese Resistance Army'. To be honest, I myself am in two minds. We are very close to Beiping here, right next to the dog's jaws and the wolf's claws. Dare we act so openly? Isn't it just asking for trouble, making ourselves a nail in the eye and a thorn in the flesh of the Japanese like that?"

A middle-aged man sitting opposite bangs the table in front of him and says: "Ha! You're absolutely right, that's just what we want to be – a nail in the eye and a thorn in the flesh. You're from one of the old hunting families of Laoqiying, aren't you? How come you don't have the same gumption as Grandpa Dong, who is your senior by many years? Beiping has fallen in the past to the Anglo-French forces, and to the Eight-Alliance Army, but no one has ever fought their way in here. Why not? Because of the mountains."

Grandpa Fu gives a little laugh. "Yes, you're right, we're in the mountains here, and it is treacherous terrain, but what about the great mountain ranges of the northeast, of Rehe, of western Hebei and northern Shanxi? How do we compare with them? Yet none of them have been able to resist the Japanese."

This reply irritates the middle-aged man. "In that case, is there even any point in establishing a self-defence force? Is it all nonsense to talk about protecting our homes and lands?"

"That is timid, defeatist talk and meaningless breast-beating," the old man replies disdainfully. "What you're saying is that there's no point in worrying about anyone else, and every man for himself is the best policy. If you're facing a murderous enemy, and you know you can't defeat him, are you still going to risk everything against him? Putting on exaggerated airs and shooting your mouth off is just courting disaster."

His words draw out quite a few murmurs of agreement in the courtyard.

"There's a lot in what Grandpa Fu says."

"That's right. If the Army of the Centre, the Northeast Army and the Northwest Army, with all their troops, couldn't do anything, what chance do we have?"

"It's true. We aren't going protect our wives and children with just this handful of rifles, and we have no control of anything outside the mountains. If the Japanese are showing no sign of coming up into the mountains, we don't want to do anything to provoke them."

Amid this hubbub of debate, the middle-aged man gets abruptly to his feet. "Pah! In the past, if anyone tried calling you country hicks and wild mountain men, there'd be an outcry! You'd puff out your chests and say: 'We are bannermen, our roots are in the imperial city.' So how is it now you start finding a difference between inside the mountains and outside? We men of the Left Barracks fight wolves and eat eagles for supper, we don't skulk in the mud like turtles at the first sign of danger."

"Who are you calling a skulking turtle?"

"Anyone who deserves it!"

The courtyard suddenly degenerates into a free-for-all, as each side rolls up their sleeves, and the battle of words becomes a battle proper.

"Enough!" shouts Grandpa Dong, and the two sides quieten down. "The war hasn't even started yet, and you're already fighting each other? This meeting is a place for debate. Those of you who can do this in a civilised manner sit down, and those of you who think brawling is the answer, please leave."

Grandpa Dong succeeds in calming things down. No one leaves, and, one by one, they all sit down.

Grandpa Fu hurriedly tries to explain: "Grandpa Dong, I really..."

Grandpa Dong gestures to him to be quiet. "Brother Fu, I understood your intentions quite well."

"Then you mean..."

"As for intentions, the only thing that matters to me at the moment is to explain to you all the intentions of the Japanese and of the National Government. You can go over the ins and outs of it all again, and I will follow your wishes." So saying, he slaps a piece of paper down on the table and continues: "This is a document sent by the Japanese, ordering us to establish a 'preservation committee'."

"What is a preservation committee?" somebody asks.

Grandpa Dong grunts and then explains: "It's a committee charged with preserving the so-called new social order of Japanese-Chinese Goodwill, supervising local security and also collecting grain taxes and other levies, and informing on any anti-Japanese factions. The choice of chairman of the committee must be ratified by the Japanese. Ha! I just have one thing to say to you – if you are going to work for the Japanese for free, you're worse than their dogs."

Before he has even finished speaking, the courtyard erupts.

"We'll just shun anyone who takes on the job."

"The ancestors will turn their backs on us if we hold this place for the Japanese."

"I'll look after my own business. I'm not joining this group."

Grandpa Dong begins to laugh, and everyone stops talking to stare at him. Unruffled, he says: "Everybody feels we shouldn't obey this order, and I agree. But throughout history, the path of self-government and self-defence has never been a successful one to travel. It doesn't matter who here is Han Chinese or Manchu, at heart we are all Chinese, and we all have to be loyal to our nation and to our government. When two countries are at war, standing in the middle to watch the fun is not an option. If we are not going to accept Japanese control, then we have to listen to our own government. China has already lost a number of provinces, but the country is not yet lost..."

"The country may not be lost, but where is the government?" says Grandpa Fu. "Where are the officials and the soldiers? They abandoned us common people long ago. Why be filial to a heartless mother and father? Why be loyal to a country that doesn't love its people?"

Grandpa Dong leaves the question unanswered, and it has clearly hit a sensitive spot with the crowd, who heave a collective sigh of sorrow and pain.

At this very moment, the door curtain of the main building is pulled aside and Qi Yuexuan comes hurrying out, saying in a loud voice: "What he says is correct, but not completely."

Many of the crowd recognise him and look at him with suspicion.

"Our country is not one man, one clan or one party," Qi Yuexuan says with a smile, "nor is what we call loyalty devoted to one man, one clan or one party. But we are loyal to this land, and we are loyal to this amalgam of the lifeblood of Han, Manchu, Mongol, Hui and Tibetan. We are loyal to this civilisation of shared knowledge that has lasted several thousand years. These are things that can't be destroyed, and nor can the nation. As long as it remains, it has our loyalty. A man may fly away like a bird when he is startled, draw in his head like a tortoise when in danger, be submissive as a dog when overawed, but if he sets no store by wealth and prestige, and never submits to force, then he may still truly call himself a man. In perilous times it is inevitable that there will be people who bow and scrape, and do things that harm the nation, but there will also be great heroes who give their lives in the cause of righteousness. Which do you all want to be? Which do you want to stand comparison with?"

You could hear a pin drop in the courtyard. Grandpa Fu nudges Grandpa Dong and whispers to him: "And who is this?"

Grandpa Dong and Qi Yuexuan had discussed in advance how to handle things, from Dong's initial appearance, fanning of the flames, to Qi showing up in the role of the official, when the flames had died down a bit. But they hadn't anticipated that the turn the meeting was taking might force him to appear earlier than planned. This change to what they have rehearsed means they have to ad lib, and it has caught Grandpa Dong a little off-guard. At Grandpa Fu's question, he immediately smiles and turns to the crowd to make the introduction.

"Everybody, this is Qi Yuexuan from the Minister's Residence in Beiping. His ancestor was the first Imperial Supplies Administrator for our section. You probably already know that we of the Left Barracks were all servants of the Third Banner of the Imperial Household Department, from households with powerful connections and upstanding masters. Young Master Qi is still an outstanding senior official in the Beiping National Government and the Army Garrison Command Centre, and he is also the official left behind as caretaker by that same government. Who says the government has gone? Commissioner Qi here represents the Beiping National Government. Please listen to Commissioner Qi's admonitions."

Even before he has finished speaking, the courtyard breaks into celebration. Qi Yuexuan waves both his hands and says in clear tones: "Elders, fellow countrymen, everybody. I, Yuexuan, am of no outstanding talent, but I have been entrusted by the government with the guardianship of Beiping. In this time of national peril, how could I refuse this task? I shall do my utmost to carry it out. Although in the current state of play in the war, I have retreated and the enemy has advanced, and we have suffered the heavy loss of Beiping and Tianjin, even so, in the overall picture, at the outset of this great war, it is by no means certain who will emerge victorious. The tiger may be ferocious, but after three pounces he is exhausted. The flood may be violent, but once it drains away, its power is gone. Japan cannot compete with China in terms of size or population. It's like a small river trying to flood a desert – the intention is there, but its waters are insufficient. If we, in our tens of thousands, are all of one heart, and army and people combine forces, we can certainly drive the Japanese bandits out of North China, and out of the whole of China itself."

He produces a scroll of paper from inside his gown and raises his voice several pitches: "For this reason, the Beiping National Government has specially appointed Dong Fuzhong as commander of the Wanping County Division of the Heroic Popular North China Anti-Japanese Resistance Army, and he may himself make all other subsidiary appointments and dispositions on his own authority. Here in my hand is the letter of appointment."

Grandpa Dong takes the letter, and when he sees on it the great red seal of Republic of China Beiping City Government, he can't restrain a smile. Seeing Qi Yuexuan glaring at him, he hurriedly hands the letter to the man standing next to him and says, somewhat nervously: "Look everyone, the army we recruit has official status. Anyone who wishes to join is welcome, but we will not force anyone who is unwilling."

"Our village will join!" the middle-aged man calls out. "We have more than twenty men, and not counting old muskets, we have three long-barrelled and two short-barrelled machineguns. That surely makes up a detachment, doesn't it, Commander Dong?"

His speech prompts another shout: "Our village will join too. We have two cast-iron cannon."

"Us too. We'll join! We'll join now it's an official army."

"Count our village in also!"

Grandpa Fu remains seated and doesn't speak. Several men standing beside him take one look at his expression and stay silent too.

Grandpa Dong taps Grandpa Fu on the shoulder and whispers: "Let's act together, Brother Fu. How about I make you Commander Fu?"

Grandpa Fu gives a wry smile and points to the document sent by the Japanese. "And how shall I reply to this?"

Grandpa Dong doesn't respond, but the middle-aged man has overheard the question and grabs the document. "This is no good to us. Let's tear it up and be done with it," he says, making to do just that.

"No! Stop, don't do that," Qi Yuexuan says, hurriedly holding him back and retrieving the document. "We can't tear this up. Tearing it up would be like spitting in the face of the Japanese. I think we should comply with the setting up of this so-called 'preservation committee'."

The crowd falls silent in amazement when they hear this, and even Grandpa Dong wonders what exactly is going on. This isn't part of the scenario they created. Seeing that everyone is baffled, Qi Yuexuan laughs and waves the document he is holding. "What I mean is, we should run our own business under their shop-sign. On the surface it will be a 'preservation committee', but underneath it will be the Heroic Anti-Japanese Army. As long as we walk softly and hide our tracks, we can look good to the Japanese while flying our own flag."

Grandpa Dong slaps his thigh. "A cuckoo in the nest! Excellent!"

The crowd all join in with their assent, and even Grandpa Fu nods and smiles.

"We mustn't just concentrate on these dozen or so villages of the Left Barracks, we can spread all along this range of mountains," a smiling Qi Yuexuan says. "Anyone who genuinely wants to fight against the Japanese is welcome. If we gather enough strength and influence, the government may also reinforce us. Beyond Wanping, to the south, there is Liangxiang, Fangshan, Laiyuan and Laishui. To the west, Huailai and Yu County, while to the north there is Yanqing and Changping. We'll make the chain as large as we can. The larger it is, the more territory we'll have at our disposal. The larger it is, the more difficult it will be for the Japanese to shut us down."

At this point, he stops smiling. "Listen everybody – heaven has laid a great responsibility on us. How many times in a life, in a generation, does one get an opportunity like this to restore the fortunes of the nation? If we can come together to work for the common good, when we recover our lost territory, each and every one of us will be considered a true hero."

As the crowd in the courtyard overflows with emotion, a young lad comes panting through the gates and goes over to speak to Grandpa Dong. The courtyard is so noisy, Grandpa Dong can't make out what he is saying, so he bangs his stick on the table and calls out: "Stop shouting, all of you!"

Finally, he picks up what the young lad is saying: "They'll... soon be at... the entrance to the village."

"Who?"

"A foreigner."

"Is he... Japanese?"

"No, a Westerner. Big nose, deep-set eyes, you know the sort. He says... he's an American."

"How many altogether?"

"Four. They came by car. The Westerner and two others have come up the mountain. The back side of the mountain slowed them down, and I came ahead to report."

"Did you ask him what he's doing here?"

"Yes, he says he's looking for Professor Qi, Young Master Qi, that is."

When Qi Yuexuan hears this, he says: "It's the director of my university, Mr Charlie. Don't worry, he's a friend. I'll go and see him. Keep talking, all of you, but try to keep the volume down."

From behind him, he hears Grandpa Dong's voice: "Did you hear? An American has come to cheer us on. That's what I call a seal of approval."

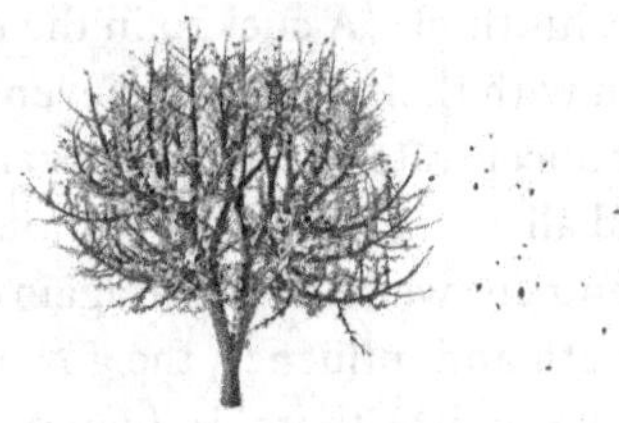

Chapter 11

As Qi Yuexuan reaches the entrance to the village, he sees Charlie following a narrow path up the mountain. He calls out his name and hurries over to greet him. The two men embrace for a long time. Although they've only been apart for a few months, it feels more like ten years to them, even almost a lifetime. To Charlie's eyes, Qi Yuexuan seems to have aged greatly, having become so pale and haggard. His cheeks are sunken in what was already a thin face, as are his eyes, and his hair is snowy white. His straggly, half-length beard makes the wrinkles on his face look even deeper. Only his eyes themselves haven't changed, and they are still penetrating, agile and full of life.

"Yuexuan, how are you..." Charlie stops short, because this seems such an inadequate greeting in the circumstances. However, he doesn't know what else to say.

Qi Yuexuan instinctively understands his emotions. "Ha ha! Yes, I'm still alive. Events haven't yet battered me to death. Did I feel a little extra warmth in your embrace just now?"

"Alright, yes, it's good to see you. It is good to see you. But the reason I've come today is that I need to beg a favour..."

"Of course, I knew it was something important. But you have no need to beg – you can just order me."

Charlie acknowledges this, and the two of them enter the village, side by side. The mountain villagers have no experience of the outside world, and they surround Charlie as he walks along as though he is some kind of rare beast.

As soon as he sits down, Charlie explains everything about the Japanese demand that the university re-opens and starts enrolling students, and his strategy to get out of these difficulties. Qi Yuexuan listens, then laughs and slaps his thigh.

"Ha ha! Brilliant! That's what I call beating them at their own game. If you get it right, the Japanese will just have to suffer in silence." He stops suddenly and narrows his eyes. "I think maybe... this wasn't your idea. Who is the bright spark behind it?"

"No, no, not at all," Charlie says defensively. "I thought of it all myself. Do you think me incapable of having a good idea of my own?"

"Of course you can," says Qi Yuexuan, probing a little further. "Nevertheless, could your American way of thinking really come up with such a sneaky trick? You're not a very good liar, you know. Look! You're blushing."

Charlie continues to give nothing away and just laughs self-deprecatingly.

"Alright, alright, I won't push you," Qi Yuexuan says. "Go on, what do you want me to do?"

Charlie becomes more animated: "I need you to write a Chinese culture exam paper, the harder the better. Ideally, I want the examinees to get zero per cent."

"Aiyo! That's not so easy. Languages and culture aren't like mathematics. Unless they hand in a blank sheet, they're bound to get at least one per cent."

"They can have a few per cent, but they mustn't reach the pass mark. They've got to do really, really badly, so the Japanese can't find any excuse for them."

"Well, if you want them to do really badly, the general knowledge paper and the classical translation and commentary are both too easy. The difficult part is the essay. The essay is compulsory, but what topic will ensure they do sufficiently badly? Of course, the marking pen is in our hands, but we have to do everything fairly and by the book, so no one can find any fault with us. Not easy!"

"If it was easy, would I have come looking for you?"

"Hah, don't get agitated. Just let me have a proper think about it."

"Alright, I'm quite calm. Think away, think away."

YANG ZHIXING IS HEATING WATER in the kitchen, but he is no more relaxed than the other two. As soon as they come in through the door, he feels there is something not right with the two companions Charlie has brought with him. On the face of it, they are perfectly polite and respectful, but there is the ominous glint of the thug lurking behind their eyes. As they chat inconsequentially about this and that, there is something halting and false about their answers, and all the time they are chatting, one of them is squatting by the door of the main room, looking much more as though he is eavesdropping than simply taking a rest. The other one is wandering around the courtyard, and he gives every impression of being on a reconnaissance mission. From time to time, the two of them also exchange meaningful glances. When the one who is squatting in the doorway bends forwards, he reveals a bulge at his waist that clearly shows he is carrying a gun. Yang Zhixing is quite certain now that these two are up to no good, and he hides a small meat-paring knife at the small of his back. He also gives careful consideration as to how to warn Qi Yuexuan.

When the water boils, he makes the tea and hurries over to the main room with the tea tray. When he gets there, he says to the man squatting by the door: "The tea's made. Take some if you're thirsty. You'll only miss a few words of whatever crap it is they're spouting in there."

He turns to the other man and says loudly: "You'd better stay in the courtyard and not go outside if you're carrying a gun. The villagers here are all hunters by tradition, and they gang up when they're annoyed. Just one shout will bring half the village out, so don't cause an incident."

Qi Yuexuan takes no notice of what Yang Zhixing is saying outside the room, and even when he comes in with the tea, he doesn't let him catch his eye. Getting agitated, Yang Zhixing goes over to Qi Yuexuan, hoping to warn him, but to his surprise, just as he is about to whisper in his ear, Qi Yuexuan says irritably: "Don't disturb me now. Tell me later."

"It's important."

"I'm not listening."

"It's just one thing!" Yang Zhixing puts heavy emphasis on the word "one", stretching it out.

"Hah! Even one..." Qi Yuexuan is sounding even more impatient, but he suddenly stops, mid-sentence, and his eyes light up. "One... one? One! Aha! Yes, that's it! One! Ha ha, I've got it! That's the subject for the essay."

"What is?" Charlie asks.

"One!"

"One? What do you mean, one?"

"One, two, one, of course! Uncle Yang has just given me the idea."

Yang Zhixing laughs bitterly to himself, thinking: But I didn't even get to say one word!

Charlie is shaking his head vigorously. "No, no, that won't do. It's too simple."

"The simplest things are the most complex, the most profound," says a delighted Qi Yuexuan.

"Eh? You'd better explain."

Qi Yuexuan dips his finger in some tea, and writes the character for 'one' on the table: "Look at this character '一'. It only has one stroke. It's the simplest of all the characters, but there is a whole world of meaning in that one stroke – so much that you could be explaining it for three days and still not cover it all. As a number, you have to have 'one' before you can have 'two', 'ten', 'a hundred', 'a thousand' or 'ten thousand'. It's the beginning of a man's life, the first step of a journey, the start of everything. It can represent eternal unity, loyalty, love, belief, perfection. It stands for agreement and completeness. Coherence, integration, harmony, stability, nation, clan, society, humanity, the root of religions and philosophies, the unity of heaven and earth... 'one' represents everything that mankind seeks."

He stops for a moment. "Of course, it can have negative connotations as well as positive. We have sayings such as 'one grain of rice in the wide ocean', meaning something insignificant, or 'one body all alone', meaning orphaned or abandoned. Then there is 'one leaf covers the eyes' to mean narrow-minded, and 'a one-person viewpoint' to mean biased or self-interested. When a single person or a single family wields all the power, we call it 'one nation, one party, one leader': a dictatorship, in other words. Ha, everything in the world starts with this character '一'. The simplest of strokes, so small and negligible, yet so big and powerful. It is no exaggeration to say it is infinite in both scope and meaning."

Charlie seems to get the general point, but then he expresses some doubts: "But doesn't that mean they could write anything and still be on topic?"

"Quite the opposite," Qi Yuexuan argues. "Whatever they write, they can't cover the topic. The thing about infinite scope and meaning is that you can't set limits or criteria as though you're setting up targets for gun practice, because where's the bullseye? They can lay it out neatly, one, two, three, with every phrase beautifully crafted, and I can still slap them with a fail. If they ask why, I'll just tell them that if they can't even define 'one', how can they expect to go to university?"

"Very good! But doesn't this seem a little..."

"I understand," says a laughing Qi Yuexuan. "You feel this might be a little unethical, a bit dishonest, is that it? But in these circumstances, you shouldn't think that way. When the dog pack is circling you and about to attack, do you still try to play the gentleman? If you can't run, and you can't hide, you don't argue, you attack! Ai! You and your Western hypocrisy!"

"Hypocrisy!"

"Yes, just like you thanking God for your food before you tuck into a steak – if He doesn't give permission, do you not eat it?"

Charlie realises he is being teased, and he shrugs his shoulders with a rueful smile.

Yang Zhixing sees his opportunity and whispers in Qi Yuexuan's ear: "Be careful, these newcomers are up to no good."

Qi Yuexuan shows no surprise but smiles calmly and turns to Charlie: "Talking of hypocrisy, I realise that allowance must be made in exceptional times. As your friend, I believe that in your heart you are both honest and trustworthy. Otherwise, you would surely not bring men of such bad reputation with you when you come looking for me. But I am also afraid that there may be an ulterior motive in your coming here today. So, did anyone else give you a message for me?"

"No, no, not at all."

"Well, in any case, I would like you to take a message back to them. Tell them that I, Qi Yuexuan, can bear humiliation and am not afraid to die. If their organisation is as sharp as it likes to think it is, how is it that it can't tell the difference between the good and the rotten?"

At this point he turns to the door and says in a loud voice: "Did you two hear that? This foreigner's Chinese isn't that good, so I want you to report exactly what I said."

The two men outside don't dare reply, but without saying so, they are amused by Qi Yuexuan's wit and impressed with how far the Young Master has progressed. Charlie, however, is deeply embarrassed and heaves a long sigh: "Yuexuan, truly, I was speaking for myself..."

"Enough, enough," says Qi Yuexuan, "have some tea. Tea and people are the same, they must be taken slowly. It's only after several infusions that the tea reveals its true flavour. While you taste it, I will draft the general knowledge and classical Chinese papers."

Now Wangtian has sold his night soil round, he has no way of earning a living. Although his previous work was dirty and exhausting, it was the business his father had left him, and he was good at it. Losing it suddenly like this is genuinely heart-wrenching. Many times, he gets up in the morning and pushes his cart out of the gate, only to realise, once he is on the street, that he has sold his route to someone else. When things reach this point, and nothing he thinks of is any use, a man must look to the future, but what skills does he have to offer? Although he has a little money in hand, with two mouths to feed, it's not going to last very long. Within a few days, Wangtian finds himself working as a heavy porter at the goods yard outside the Xizhi Gate. When he's finished there, he makes his way over to the labour market in the hope of picking up any odd job that's going. Every day he leaves before dawn and only gets back after dark.

Caiping is deeply distressed to see him suffering like this. She wants to find a job at a folk music tea house, but Wangtian is afraid that, with things the way they are, Chenglong will seize the opportunity to stick his oar in again, and he won't countenance it at any price. With nowhere to turn, she suddenly remembers her grandfather's New Year woodblock prints. She had done every stage of the process with her grandfather: he taught her how to trace the design, cut and polish the blocks, use a stone to rub the paper over the block, and trim and finish off the final work. Hiding them from Wangtian, she buys some ink and brushes and a woodblock knife, scrounges some peach wood planks, and secretly starts work at home. She hasn't done anything like it for a long time, and hand and eye are out of practice. But with great difficulty, she carves a pair of bodhisattvas seated on lotus thrones, although she has had to discard a few planks, and her hands are covered in blisters.

One afternoon, Caiping is rubbing down a plank with fine sandpaper, when someone knocks on the door. She knows immediately it is Yue E come to visit, and she calls out: "Coming! Coming!" She puts down the plank and opens the door.

"Is Wangtian back?"

"It's still early. He's never back before eight."

"Hasn't he sold the night soil route?"

"Yes, he's working as a porter now and picking up odd jobs."

"Ai!" Yue E sighs. "As long as you've got food to eat. I don't have anything special, I just thought I'd look in and give you some grain. Eating that blended flour all the time is not good for you. This maize flour will at least make a change. Come on, take it."

"Thank you, big sister, please..." As she is talking, she sees that the edge of the *kang* is covered in dust and wood shavings, and she hurriedly brushes them away with her hand, before finishing: "... sit down."

"What's this? Are you a carpenter as well as a singer?"

"No, no, it's not carpentry. It's woodblock carving to print New Year pictures."

"Show me, show me!" Yue E takes one of the woodblocks and laughs delightedly. "You're really talented. Is this one Guanyin? Can you make money selling these blocks?"

"I don't sell the blocks, I sell prints."

"You know how to print too?"

"If you've got the blocks, the printing is easy."

Smiling, Yue E scrutinises Caiping's face and then sighs: "Wangtian is a good man, and it seems he's being rewarded for it, having found such a fine little sister as you... oh, look at me still calling you 'little sister'! However you look at it, I'm going to have to call you sister-in-law now."

Caiping blushes, lowers her head and falls silent.

"Ha! What is there to be embarrassed about? Wedding party or not, you're part of the Gao family now. Do you want me to set up the ceremony some time?"

"Why are you trying to stir things up like this?" Caiping snaps back. "There's nothing like that between the two of us. All the time I've been here, he's been sleeping in the western side room. So you can wipe that stupid grin off your face."

Yue E looks at her in astonishment, then retorts animatedly: "What? You mean he's spent all that money for nothing? You've got a man like Wangtian, and he still not good enough for you? Are you some kind of con merchant, setting him up like this?"

"If that was my intention, I'd be gone already. Do you think I'd be hanging around for you to poke fun at me like this?"

"Then... why aren't you getting married?"

"You'll have to ask him."

"Is it that he doesn't want to?"

"Hmm..."

"What has he said?"

"He says he doesn't want to take advantage of my situation and will treat me only as a sister."

"Nonsense! Is he just messing you around, or is there something wrong with him? If he's got the money to buy a sister, he's got the money to buy a wife." Yue E can't help smiling at her own words. "Ai! I can't believe he's changed that much, but if he's really not ready yet, perhaps it's because he's been on his own too long. But feelings develop through proximity, don't they? Now you're together all the time, perhaps family feelings can turn to love, and a little sister can become a sister-in-law. So just be the little sister for now and..."

"Huh! Not necessarily, in my opinion."

"What do you mean?"

"I think he's already given his heart to someone else, so there's no room for me."

Yue E is taken aback by this, and she hesitates before saying: "You... you should put that thought out of your head and stop making wild guesses."

Caiping just lowers her head without replying.

Yue E steals a glance at her, and asks hesitantly: "Has he... has he said anything to you?"

"Not a word, but I've kept my eyes, and my heart, open." She looks at Yue E. "I've seen it, and I've worked it out, big sister. You and I are the same, both hostages to fortune." Tears gather in her eyes as she speaks.

Yue E's eyes also begin to glisten. Silently, she takes Caiping's hand and draws her down to sit next to her.

"Little sister," she says gently, "it's too late for me, and there's no point my looking back, but it's not too late for you. I'm just going to ask you one thing – you must put your hand on your heart and answer honestly."

Caiping nods.

"Do you love him? Do you want to marry him?"

Caiping says nothing, just nods emphatically as she blushes to the tips of her ears.

Yue E smiles. "And you have done nothing about it because you're afraid you are fire and he is ice? Have you heard the saying? When a man goes after a woman there is a mountain between them, but when a woman goes after a man, it is only a sheet of paper. I don't think he will be able to put up much resistance."

"Aiya! Stop, please! I can't listen to this."

Caiping is so embarrassed, she tries to get away from Yue E. But Yue E gently pulls her back down and says firmly: "If you love him, there is nothing to be ashamed about and nothing to be afraid of. There are millions of people in the world, and when two people are fated to meet, the only regret should be if something goes wrong."

"But he still loves..."

"Hah! There is no one with him now, and all he has in his heart is a memory. It's a ghost. A dream. You're a living, breathing woman, a beautiful woman. Surely you can get the better of a ghost."

Seeing the tears falling from Caiping's eyes, Yue E wipes away her own and stands up. "It's alright, there's no need to say anything. I understand. If you don't marry Wangtian, then I won't come back again. Alright? The sixteenth of this month is Wangtian's birthday, so why not take advantage of that to get all this out in the open? If he is still intent on chasing a ghost, then you tell him: 'You have already disappointed one heart. If you regret that, then don't disappoint another. Otherwise, you have no right to call yourself a man.'"

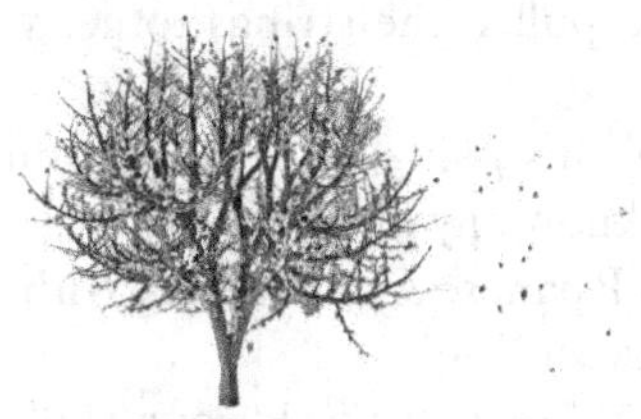

Chapter 12

A notice appears at the main gates of Yanjing University reading 'New student enrolment and resumption of classes', and there is an announcement the same day too. Its general import is: unlimited enrolment of new students, both Chinese and international. Specialist classes in physics, mathematics, English, history, Chinese language and literature etc. The entrance examination to be held in seven days' time on the twenty-fourth of this month (sixteenth in the old calendar). All who meet the minimum required standard will be admitted.

Chenglong is delighted when the announcement appears. Matsuzaki orders him to work with Yamaguchi of the Kempeitai to select a cohort of students, with the aim of ensuring that as many as possible of their own people, or people useful to them, enter Yanjing University to act as their eyes and ears. Chenglong gathers together all his subordinates and goes through them, filtering out quite a few. After eliminating more than thirty who are barely literate enough to read the announcement, they still have twenty or thirty left. Working on the principle that money talks, he announces that whether they pass or not, he will pay five silver yuan for each person brought in to sit the exam. Those who pass will have their fees paid and receive a salary. Spurred on by this, all of Chenglong's subordinates bring their relatives, friends and even passing acquaintances to have a go. Some of them even decide they can take the money from both ends and put themselves forward, regardless of their ability. After a few days, the tally rises to several hundred. On the day of the exam, ten Kempeitai trucks are loaded up with candidates, packed like sardines. They stop about a kilometre short of the south gate of Yanjing University so that the examinees can enter on foot. These 'young' men and women span a wide range of ages, from children to bearded, wrinkle-faced men and heavy-breasted, pot-bellied women. Their clothes are even more varied: long, short, new, old, foreign, local, heavy enough to make you sweat, skimpy enough to make you shiver, they're all on show. Do they look like student hopefuls about to sit an entrance exam? Or a motley crew on their way to an early morning market?

A man taps the woman in front of him on the shoulder. "It's little Pear

Blossom, isn't it? Who pulled the strings to get you here? I'm taking the exam too."

"Huh, do you think it's going to be like reading a menu? Apart from 'with sesame sauce', do you know any other characters?"

"With the Imperial Japanese Army to fuck with, do you think the university is going to dare turn us down?"

The woman laughs. "So you think your skills as a pot-boy in a mah-jong house are going to be just what they're looking for here, do you? I'm not so sure."

Everyone around them laughs.

They all go into the morning mathematics exam in high spirits, but they emerge listless and discouraged. They sit for the afternoon Chinese culture paper nervous and uncertain, but they come out considerably cheered. With a topic as simple and straightforward as the character '一', everyone could at least write something. If the examinees outside the hall are laughing up their sleeves, the examiners inside are even more delighted. This is hardly surprising, since what they see written on the essay papers is stuff like: 'One: I am one person, I have one home with one mother, one father and one dog. I have one head, one mouth, one nose, one eye (the other being recently scratched out by my cat). I have both ears, one on one side...'

Three days later, the examination results are published. The highest overall score for the four papers is forty per cent. The lowest-scoring paper is the Chinese culture paper, where the highest mark is ten per cent, and of that, the worst part is the essay, where most candidates don't answer the question and score zero. So out of the glorious throng of several hundred candidates, not a single one is admitted as a student.

Of course, Matsuzaki, doesn't believe a word of this. He immediately orders Yamaguchi to collect all the exam scripts so he can audit them personally. Yamaguchi supervises the collection in person to prevent any funny business; he also gets hold of Liu Chenglong, and they go to see Matsuzaki together.

After half an hour looking at the scripts, Matsuzaki's expression has been getting blacker and blacker. "Who wrote these?" he asks, hurling the scripts on the desk to the floor. "They're all morons, and so are you two! You're all morons!" Then he picks up several of the scripts, tears them into small pieces and throws them in the faces of Yamaguchi and Chenglong. "Alright, which of you is going to explain?"

Yamaguchi snaps to attention, keeping his head lowered. He stays silent and snatches a glance at Chenglong, who bows and says: "I found all these people, Mr Matsuzaki, sir. They have nothing to do with Commander Yamaguchi. They come from all walks of life and were put together at short notice. We just had to make the best out of what was available. If they failed in their task, then I'm the one who should be punished. But..." He stops abruptly.

"But what?" asks Matsuzaki, glaring at him.

Chenglong continues: "Mr Matsuzaki, sir, the main reason we failed today was not because we are morons, but because our opponents were too clever for us. I have looked at all the questions, and although they're all within the scope of the high school curriculum, they are all very tricky and complicated. The culture paper essay subject, in particular, is chosen so that almost anybody could fail. Whatever you write, the examiner can still say you haven't addressed the topic. The worst of it is that, although they are clearly part of the anti-Japanese resistance, they have planned everything so cunningly that we can't catch them out in their treachery. I'm sure that the American is just fronting for someone higher up."

Matsuzaki thinks there is probably something in what Chenglong says. "You have been very straight with me. Hah! Well, that's the Chinese for you! Nonetheless, I think I see the hand of just one man behind this culture paper."

"Who?"

"Qi Yuexuan."

"Shall I take some men and go and arrest him?" Yamaguchi butts in eagerly.

"No. It's just a feeling at the moment." Matsuzaki laughs coldly. "And even if it is him, it would be no good. Do you think I'd have waited until now if I wanted to arrest him? He's the honorary chairman of the New Peoples' Assembly, and everyone knows it. Who do you think would put this kind of trust in him? The Nationalists? The Communists? Neither of them, I'm afraid. Even the Americans wouldn't think it worth the candle. If they really trusted him, they would have let him hide out in the university. I can't afford to mess this business up, but why would the Traitor Elimination Squad ever let him out of their hands? Let's see if we can't get them to force him to come back for us. Assuming he's still alive, that is."

He sees Yamaguchi nodding in agreement and goes on: "Good, then let's leave it like this. You notify the university authorities that... that this office agrees their request temporarily not to resume classes, and that, as another matter, they should re-start enrolment when a suitable opportunity presents itself."

"Mr Matsuzaki, sir, I think there may be a way of remedying this situation," says Yamaguchi.

"What way?"

"We could find some scholars to redo these papers, burn the originals and then claim the marking has been unfair. They won't have any evidence..."

"How do you know they won't have any evidence?" Matsuzaki says irritably. "They might have made copies, mightn't they? Or taken photographs. They handed over the originals happily enough, so of course they took precautions. If this affair becomes public knowledge, and the Ministry of Foreign Affairs gets involved, it will be the worse for us."

"Well then... now what?" Yamaguchi mutters.

Chenglong takes hold of him. "Don't you understand, Lord Yamaguchi? Mr Matsuzaki's strategy is to retreat in order to advance. Very clever!"

Even Matsuzaki is surprised by this. Chenglong continues: "On the surface, it looks as though we have taken a step back, to make them think they have succeeded, whereas, in fact, we have got just what we wanted. At the very least, we know where the American stands, and we know there is a very good chance Yanjing University is sheltering anti-Japanese factions. Making a show of retreating allows us secretly to advance. Have I understood you correctly, Mr Matsuzaki, sir?"

Matsuzaki takes advantage of the hint Chenglong has dropped him, and he nods, smiling. Chenglong continues, very solicitously: "Mr Matsuzaki, sir, I have another idea to advance your strategy."

"Go on."

"I was thinking that, if we were to take away all the Kempeitai checkpoints on the roads around Yanjing University..."

Matsuzaki encourages him to go on with a look.

"I was thinking, obvious roadblocks aren't a lot of use. With armed Kempeitai men standing around there, the anti-Japanese factions aren't blind. Are they going just to walk straight into them? Much better to conceal the checkpoints and get the men to keep watch disguised as fruit and vegetable pedlars, shoe-repairers, mechanics and so on. You could also post some plain-clothes men to keep a closer eye on the side-roads and alleyways – a lot of them aren't even marked on the maps, and some can't even be called roads, but if I were an anti-Japanese faction, I would find these places both convenient and secretive. We do, however, need to find men who are very familiar with the locality. If they come across anyone suspicious, they must arrest them in the utmost secrecy, as that will save us a lot of bother."

"There is something in this plan." Matsuzaki nods his head, and when he sees Chenglong looking as though he has more to say, hurriedly asks: "Is there something more?"

"Yes, sir. That just looks after things outside the university. There is also the inside to consider." Chenglong laughs. "Actually, it's not going to be too difficult to act inside the university."

Matsuzaki can hardly conceal his surprise and delight: "You mean you already have someone on the inside?"

"Not at the moment. But aren't we just about to introduce Certificates of Good Citizenship? That will give us the chance to investigate people really closely. Just think how many people there are at the university. Can they all really present a united front? Even if they do, we'll find some way of prising them apart and boring our way in. If we secretly snatch a few of them, and mix a bit of torture with some bribery, we're bound to get one or two. Then, of course, they need water and electricity, don't they? Well, we can stop both of them and send in our own men to check the wiring and inspect the pipes. They can't hang around in there too long, and they won't have time to search the whole site, but they will have enough time to check the most important areas. And of course, that's not all. If we infiltrate every line of communication between the university and the outside world, we're bound to strike lucky at some point, aren't we?"

"Yes, very good. I can see you've really thought it all through." Matsuzaki laughs, but then he stops abruptly and fixes Chenglong with a stare. "Why didn't you say any of this sooner? Didn't I tell you, you could report back to me at any time?"

Chenglong answers hastily: "You're right, Mr Matsuzaki, you did indeed say that, but our CID squad doesn't have any authority outside the city walls, and I thought that if you took up the idea when I suggested it to you, you would have to hand it over to the Kempeitai or even the Senior Investigation Department to implement. Even though my own plan is based on my expert knowledge of how we Chinese go about things, I still didn't want to be seen to be snatching the job away from less experienced Japanese officers... I didn't want it to look as though I was deliberately exceeding my authority. Not all you Japanese lordships are as easy to get along with as yourself and Lord Yamaguchi, and I know that it's not always easy for you."

Matsuzaki mutters to himself for a few moments, then says: "Let's handle it like this – as soon as possible, give me a written plan, and I will give it back to you to implement. We'll create an independent special action group, with you as leader, answering directly to me. You recruit your own personnel, and you can get your authorisation documents from the Beiping Special Action Committee, with permission to act without restriction in any administrative district. If the plan works out, after the new government is established, you will form the foundation of its Intelligence Bureau." He stops and asks Chenglong with a laugh: "How's that? Are you satisfied?"

"Yes, yes, absolutely..."

"But you have to make sure I'm satisfied too."

"Of course! Of course!" Chenglong nods eagerly and bows, feeling extraordinarily pleased with himself.

THE MOON IS HIGH IN THE SKY when Wangtian finally gets home. After work at the goods yard, he found another job at the doors of the grain retailer and delivered four or five large sacks of grain outside the Qian Gate. It has meant a return journey of almost twenty *li* pulling his cart, so it is, of course, much later than usual when he reaches his gates. Once in the courtyard, he smells the long unfamiliar scent of cooking meat, which immediately makes his stomach growl. On the road home, he had considered the moon to be particularly round, like a large white pancake, and now here he is smelling the scent of meat to go with it. Laughing at himself, he thinks it must just be his imagination, born out of hunger. But much to his surprise, it turns out to be the real thing. There is Caiping in the act of taking from the steamer a bowl of pork with stewed cabbage, which shimmers with oil and gives off billows of fragrant steam.

"Don't stand there like an idiot, big brother, you're late enough already. Aren't you hungry? I've already heated it eight times. Aiya..." She hurriedly puts the bowl down on the *kang* table, shakes her scalded hands and laughs.

"Hurry up and wash your grubby paws, and eat it while it's hot."

Wangtian nods in agreement, splashes some water on his hands and sits down on the edge of the *kang*. He picks up his chopsticks and seizes a piece of pork. "So," he says with his mouth full, "you can afford to buy meat... this year... eh?"

"Can't even poor people be liberal once in a while?" Caiping laughs. "I've saved a bit of my allowance over the last two years so we could celebrate when we hit a good day."

"It's not New Year, or any other festival – what's so good about today?"

"Isn't it your birthday?"

"Ha! What birthday?" Wangtian chuckles. "I've never celebrated a birthday in my life! When I was little, I really envied Yue E her birthdays... Ah! Yue E told you, didn't she?"

When Caiping hears him mention Yue E yet again, she can't help feeling a little jealous, and she just grunts in reply, stony-faced. She turns and brings out a dish of fried potato shreds, a plate of stir-fried mustard greens, a bowl of pickles and a basket of cornbread nests.

Wangtian is so hungry, he doesn't notice her expression. He stuffs a couple of cornbread into his mouth and then picks up another one. Caiping is delighted by his appetite. "Slow down a bit! I've got another treat for you. Can you guess what it is?"

"Wine! Is it wine?" But he shakes his head, even as he speaks. "Even the wineries have all shut this year. Where could you dredge up some wine from?"

Caiping grins in delight, hums the tune from a grand introduction, and, with a flourish, places a bottle of wine on the table.

Wangtian's eyes widen. "Ha! There really is some wine! How did you manage it?"

"Ah! Manager Sun from the Shanxi Winery was a regular customer at the tea house. He came to listen to me sing. He recognised me out on the street. His shop ran out of wine for sale some time ago, but he let me go there and empty out the dregs from all the big jars. I tipped up ten or more of them, and this is all I could get. Is there about half a catty?"

"A bit less, about seven *liang*. Hey, don't give it all to me. Keep some for yourself."

"Alright. I don't normally drink, but I'll take a cup to sip with you."

Perversely, however, the wine doesn't serve to draw out any conversation, and the atmosphere just gets more awkward. The two of them are sitting face to face, but they don't look directly at each other, and when their eyes do meet by chance, they swiftly look away again.

It is Caiping who first breaks the mood: "That heavy lifting at the goods yard is exhausting you, big brother, and the pay isn't nearly enough. You've either got to get a raise out of the gang master or find some other kind of work."

Wangtian shakes his head. "Now I've lost the night soil route, what else can I do? At least I can make a daily living at it. And if I do some extra odd jobs for people, and add it all together, you don't have to worry. I'm not going to let you go hungry."

"I'm not work-shy, big brother. I can earn some money too."

"I know you're talented, but you'll have to wait till things settle down out there before you can go singing again. You don't want to jump out of the wolf's jaws into the tiger's mouth."

"I'm not talking about singing. Grandfather taught me some other skills too," Caiping says, taking out her woodblocks from under the bed roll and showing them to him.

"What's this?"

"It's a woodblock for printing."

"Did you carve it?"

"You don't believe me?" Caiping laughs as she also takes out a paper scroll and unrolls it. "See, this is what a print looks like. It's just the first impression, so there's only the black outlines. Once I've carved another couple of blocks, I can add in the colours. If I finish it off by adding some more coloured detail with a brush, do you think we could sell it?"

"It looks good to me, really good."

"Do you think you could do it too?"

"No, no, that won't work. I can't carve, and I can't draw."

"Couldn't you learn? Drawing the outlines is a bit tricky, but the rest is just a matter of practice. You already know a bit of carpentry, don't you? It would only take a couple of days to get the hang of woodblock carving. If you give it a try and it doesn't work out, you could still take the prints to sell at the temple markets. You could see how things go and maybe set up a little business. Anything's got to be better than the hard labour you're doing at the moment."

"It might work," Wangtian says, clearly tempted. "But how much start-up capital would we need?"

"Ha! Don't be silly. We don't need capital. This is craftsmanship. We don't have to worry about that sort of thing."

Wangtian slaps his thigh. "Right! Let's do it! I'll be your apprentice."

"Alright then, but you shouldn't put me in such an honoured position."

Caiping pours Wangtian some more wine and fills her own cup too. She thinks of something, but bites back the words. She doesn't drink and just blushes deeply. Then she picks up her cup and says: "Come on then, big brother. Bottoms up!"

"If you're not used to it, just sip it. You don't have to down it in one."

"It's alright, the wine will help. I want to ask you something."

She finishes her cup and chokes so that the tears come to her eyes, and her face goes even redder.

Wangtian swallows his own wine in one gulp and shows her the empty cup. Then he sees the ardent look in her eyes, and he stops dead in surprise. He feels the heat rising in himself too, making his head swim. His eyes slip away from hers in confusion and panic.

"What is it? Can't you look me in the eye?" Caiping stares fixedly at him. "Am I so ugly?"

Wangtian blushes to the tips of his ears, and he doesn't know where to look.

"No... no, not ugly... just too... too intense."

Caiping takes his hand. "I... want to be intense with you."

Wangtian snatches his hand back as though it has been thrust into a fire. He is about to speak but stops himself, and he gets up to go. Caiping scrambles over to him and stops him, saying resolutely: "Wait, big brother, wait. You have to let me finish asking you what has to be asked, now."

"Alright, go ahead and ask."

"Do you not like me because I'm a singer?"

"No, absolutely not."

"Are you afraid I'm not a virgin, and I'll bring shame on you?"

"No."

"Then what is it about me that means you can't take me to your heart?"

Wangtian doesn't answer but just glances at her and sighs.

Caiping laughs, but there are tears in her eyes. "Ai! I understand. There's someone else in your heart, and the two of us are fighting in there. That's it, isn't it?"

Wangtian doesn't say a word.

"I won't hide anything from you, big brother. There used to be someone in my heart too, the man of my dreams. But dreams are just dreams, whether they're full of beauty or nightmares, and we always have to wake up from our dreams. Miss Yue E gave me something to say to you."

"What is it?"

"She said that, if she knew you were happy, then she would be happy too. She told me to tell you that you have already broken one heart, don't betray another."

Wangtian's heart pounds when he hears this, and he says, haltingly: "I... I just think... I just think I'm..."

"Why are you always doing yourself down?" Caiping interrupts him angrily. "Do you think because I'm a woman, all I'm interested in is money? There are women like that, but they're fools. I don't want to be part of the Minister's Residence, I want to be part of your home, part of your heart, part of you. Your name is Wangtian, and what shame is there in that? In my eyes, you are a better man than anyone."

Wangtian remains silent.

Caiping sighs deeply. "Big brother, I am indeed a virgin, but today I have put shame aside in saying everything that needs to be said. You have no reason to leave. If anyone must go, it is me, and in case it makes me look like a gold-digger, I will pay you back every cent, with interest. As long as I am alive, I won't renege on this debt..."

Finally, Wangtian chokes out some words: "Yingzi, don't go! I..."

"I don't want your pity! It's no use to me!" Caiping struggles free and goes to collect her belongings.

Wangtian's tears flow freely down his cheeks as he rushes over to her and folds her in his embrace.

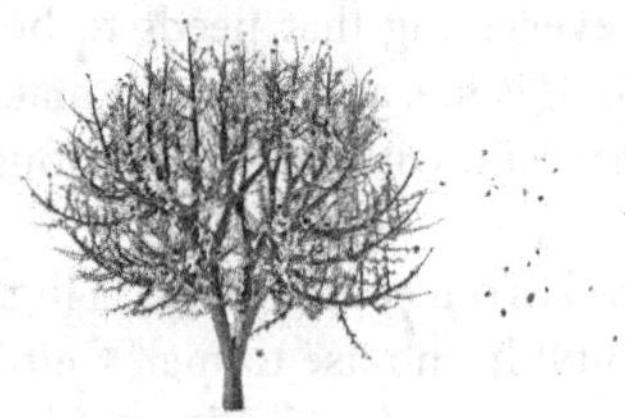

Chapter 13

Following the meeting of the twenty villages of the Left Barracks, the Wanping County Division of the North China Heroic Anti-Japanese Army is considered to be established. A sparrow may be small, but it has all the vital organs, and this army is the same. Fu Zhanxiang, the man generally known as Grandpa Fu, is appointed its commander. Various men are also given the posts of chief of staff, general secretary, combat coordinator, head of logistics, head of training, chief security officer and so on. Most of these sections consist of only two or three men, and some of them only of the section head himself. The seven eastern villages and the five western ones are combined into Divisions One and Two, mustering, according to the local registers, more than three hundred and twenty men. However, in total, counting both long- and short-barrelled varieties, they only have eighty or so machineguns. Of them, some are missing parts, and others have rusty mechanisms and can't be fired; but they are good enough to be carried for show. There is a shortage of ammunition, with not even five rounds per weapon. There are more than a hundred crude hand-made rifles, and because they are the normal weapons of the local hunters, most of them are in working order. They also have reserves of gunpowder, and many of the villages have facilities for the manufacture of saltpetre, which are at the disposal of the army's logistics section. There are also five crude cannons and twenty or more ancient blunderbusses, which have survived since Qing times, the oldest of which were used in the rebellion led by Li Zicheng.[1] Although their range isn't great, they can do considerable damage when loaded with shrapnel and pellets, and they were used to great effect in the past against robbers and bandits. Together these form an artillery company under the direct command of army headquarters.

Because of Qi Yuexuan's appointment within the government, he is not directly involved in these arrangements, but the establishment of the different departments and the allocation of personnel are mostly his ideas. Following his suggestion, the army is divided into five administrative detachments, with the twelve villages of the West Barracks forming two of them. The remaining three detachments, as yet unassigned, he intends to use to forge links to the south and west in anticipation of further recruitment. He has already sent a dozen or more men into Zhaitangchuan, up Miaofengshan, across the Juma River and into Huailai City to expand their communications network. He himself has spent a whole week travelling on horseback, accompanied by Lao Zhang on a donkey. He has covered many *li* of the surrounding territory, picking up a lot of useful information, and, on his return, has compiled a strategic map of the Beiping-Western Hills area. A number of small local resistance cells have expressed their intention to join in. Moreover, the areas between Zhaitangchuan and Xiayunling have already raised a considerable number of troops to form what they have called the Save the Nation Army, the Self-Defence Army and the Xianfeng Army. Whether they are genuinely anti-Japanese, or just putting on a show, is not clear, but they have all raised the flag of resistance. In the area around Changping, there is also the People's Anti-Japanese Army, which is said to have already fought several skirmishes with the enemy. Then there is the Communist Party's Eighth Route Army whose main force has crossed the Taihang Mountains, and, although it has not been sighted yet, it is reported that its vanguard has already reached Yu County in Zhangjiakou.

This news is a great boost to morale, and it encourages them all the more to want to show off their abilities. But Qi Yuexuan understands that the current troops are stronger on paper than they would be in battle, and that they are still far from being a proper army. All these plans and preparations must be carried out in secret. Having revived the Old Banner Barracks Division, they ensure all the villages of the mountains and passes establish lookout posts to keep communications open by bugle call, with whistle-arrows to relay news and signal fires to warn of attack.

In order to put up a smokescreen to keep the Japanese quiet, the twelve villages of the Left Barracks have set up the Wanping County Northern District Preservation Committee. The problem is that no one will agree, at any price, to serve as chairman of the committee. In the end, Qi Yuexuan is forced to say: "I know you all want to play the hero in this, but someone always has to play the villain. I suppose it comes down to me again. After all, I'm already wearing one big 'traitor's hat', so what does it matter if I put on a small additional one! Go on then, don't hold back, put me forward."

And so, Qi Yuexuan, who already holds the nominal post of honorary chairman of the New People's Government, is now also a bogus local countryside official.

Yang Zhixing has mixed feelings about Qi Yuexuan's sanguine attitude. It's obvious why he is pleased, but why is he also concerned? He is concerned for Qi Yuexuan's safety, of course, but he is also afraid that he is endangering the Minister's Residence. Fortunately he had himself taken steps to sell off all the family businesses before the outbreak of war, converting them into gold bars, and had even buried all the household's valuables in Lao Litou's tomb. He has kept all this from Qi Yuexuan, and other than himself, only Lao Zhang and Gao Wangtian are in on the secret. If Qi Yuexuan had known about this before the fall of Beiping, this family fortune would certainly have been squandered. In the beginning, Qi Yuexuan had often badgered Yang Zhixing, but the latter's phlegmatic temperament never gave way even in the face of curses and taunts. Later on, as other events unfurled, all this has finally been forgotten about. But now, with Qi Yuexuan wanting to raise an army, these concerns have naturally resurfaced. So Yang Zhixing has exhorted Lao Zhang in every way he can think of and made him swear to heaven not to breathe a word. He hopes that is the end of the matter, but being an honest and conscientious man, he has also considered how he might make some concessions. If everybody else is contributing funds, the Young Master can't be allowed to lose face for not following suit. He has even thought about what would be an appropriate sum, complete with upper and lower limits. However, getting the money is not the problem; letting the secret out, is. Nor is he willing to risk the capital he has so carefully amassed to restore the family fortunes. But to his astonishment, Qi Yuexuan seems to have completely forgotten about the whole affair, and he doesn't say a word. Nonetheless the whole thing leaves him ill at ease and very much on edge.

ONE EVENING, after dinner, Yang Zhixing pours Qi Yuexuan a cup of tea as he tries to probe the Young Master's intentions.

"Young Master, I've heard that the villages are all complaining that there are more men than guns, and that there aren't enough to go around."

"That's right."

"And there's even less ammunition?"

"That's right."

"And they're making a fuss about the distribution of rations?"

"That's right."

At every question Yang Zhixing asks, Qi Yuexuan just sips his tea and gives the same short reply.

"So what are you planning..."

"Wait and see."

"Wait and see? Surely we must strike while the iron is hot."

"There's no rush," Qi Yuexuan replies, still quite unruffled.

"Then why were you in such a rush at the start, throwing your weight around like that? You've drawn the bow, but not loosed the arrow..."

"We appear to have switched roles today, Uncle Yang. I'm quite calm, and you're all worked up."

"Well, yes... I seem to have been doing the worrying for you."

"Ha! I could see for some time you've been worrying about the Residence's family property."

Qi Yuexuan's uncanny reading of his thoughts leaves Yang Zhixing speechless.

"Ha ha, you are in a state!" Qi Yuexuan continues. "What's up? Are you wondering whether this inveterate beggar has really learned to change his ways? You needn't worry, I'm not asking where you've hidden the family jewels. I'd never expect an old miser like you to tell me, anyway."

Yang Zhixing sighs gently. "Well, if I wasn't so miserly, those family jewels would have gone long ago. To tell you the truth, I'm not concerned about spending the money as such, I'm just worried that it will be spent in vain. At the moment..."

"At the moment we are short of guns, ammunition and food, but even if you give me the money, where can I buy them? What is more, this army we've raised is under a government flag, it's not the Qi family's private army, nor is it the villages' local defence force. If we need funds, we should start off by looking to whoever we're fighting for." Qi Yuexuan has the look of a man with an ace up his sleeve.

"So, are you yourself still going to take up the gold seal of office?"

"Gold seals are always nice, but a base metal one would do just fine – even no seal at all, as long as we have right on our side. Do you really think I have any respect for this government? They are just a bunch of self-interested ingrates, stripping the flesh from the people on a daily basis to make themselves rich. Once they were confronted by real soldiers, none of them looked twice, but they all ran away with their tails between their legs. If they want us to act as their rearguard, they'll have to give us the money first."

"Do you think they will?"

"Whether they give it or not is up to them, but I've still got to ask."

"It sounds hopeless to me."

"Oh, there's hope all right. We just have to wait for the right opportunity."

"But where are you going to find them?"

"If you can't find a magistrate, there's always the bailiffs. Anyway, it doesn't matter if I can't find anyone else. I *am* the government."

"I don't understand."

"Ha, don't worry about it. You'll understand when it's done." Qi Yuexuan turns away and starts singing some opera to himself: "I sit quietly in the tent, sipping fragrant tea and fanning myself. / I'm waiting for the scouts to return and tell me how much."

A SHORT WHILE LATER, Grandpa Dong arrives with several others in tow. Once inside, he says with a laugh: "You were right, Young Master Qi, these mountains do contain a lot of resources..."

"Eh? Sit down and tell me exactly what you mean." Qi Yuexuan can't conceal his pleasurable surprise.

Grandpa Dong sits down and calls out to a young lad who is with him: "Make your report to the commander, Er Hun'er."

"Here it is," the young lad replies. "Thirty or so of us split into two groups to make a special survey of the mountains, taking only trails and bypaths. We went south as far as Baihuashan and crossed Miaofengshan in the west. There are quite a few stragglers and disbanded soldiers in that stretch of mountains, some from the Twenty-Ninth Army and some from the Central Army, along with several from county self-defence groups. From some of them, we collected..."

"What do you mean by 'collected'?" Qi Yuexuan asks.

"We followed your instructions and just took their guns. We didn't kill anyone. We didn't fire a single shot on the whole trip, but we did collect fifteen long-barrelled machineguns and one short-barrelled. I haven't got an accurate total for ammunition, but it's got to be more than a thousand rounds. On the way back, we came across a large group of men who are heading here to join us."

"How many?"

"More than fifty."

"Where are they?"

"At the moment they're in Lijiapu, south of the Yongding River, about twelve *li* away. They weren't up for a night march, so they took shelter halfway up the mountain in a temple to the Mountain God."

"Do you know what division they're from?"

"According to the locals, they said they are from the One Hundred and Eighty-Seventh Division of the Twenty-Ninth Army. Their leader is the regimental commander. He says they were going to head west across Fangshan, but the roads were jammed with Japanese, and they couldn't get through, so they had to retrace their steps."

Grandpa Dong interjects: "By the sound of it, they must have been intending to go through Big Stone Valley and Ten Li Gorge, then over Little Mount Wutai. They would have had to go through our Left Barrack village of Fucha."

Qi Yuexuan listens to all this without a word, until Grandpa Dong snaps impatiently: "I'm not sure about this at all. Do you think... can't we just seize their weapons and equipment?"

"Ha! They're not God Almighty, so why shouldn't we?" Qi Yuexuan grunts.

Without waiting for anyone else to reply, an agitated Yang Zhixing breaks his silence: "Don't make difficulties for yourself, Young Master. These men are anti-Japanese, and what is more, they are battle-hardened topflight soldiers, not a ragbag of stragglers you can mould into what you want, like a mound of clay. If real fighting breaks out, you'll find yourself fighting your own side before you even get to grips with the Japanese. Get it wrong, and they could end up turning on you and even killing you."

Qi Yuexuan looks at Yang Zhixing, whose face is mottled with anger and frustration, and he just keeps on smiling. Further provoked, Yang Zhixing explodes: "Why are you smiling? You think matters of life and death are a joke? You..."

"I'm not that stupid," Qi Yuexuan says, still smiling. "Why are you getting yourself into such a state, Uncle Yang? Did I say anything about fighting? Anyway, if the guns they use to fight the Japanese get into our hands, are we only going to use them for making a noise at New Year? We are all against the Japanese together, like brothers. There's no 'them and us'. If we take some of their guns, is that going to turn them against us? Do you think everyone is as petty as you? If we get this right, we might even keep the family fortune intact." Qi Yuexuan giggles mischievously as he says these words.

"That's just a pipe-dream..." Yang Zhixing knows all too well what Qi Yuexuan is like when he is playing the Young Master, and, full of doubt and suspicion, he retires into the inner room.

THE NEXT MORNING, around ten o'clock, a troop of men does indeed appear in the distance, in the valley below the village of Fucha. The men's clothes are all ragged and dirty, but the grey of army uniforms can still be made out. Although they aren't carrying any wounded, many of them are bandaged on their heads and bodies, and are leaning on makeshift crutches and sticks, as they pick their way over bumps and dips, and across the stony beds of streams. Although they total only fifty or so, they are stretched out irregularly over half a *li* or more. One of them, who looks like an officer, is being helped along by two of his men.

Suddenly, a bugle call is heard halfway up the mountain slope and both sides of the valley, and the mountain slopes immediately begin to ring with answering calls. Deep and resounding, bleak and powerful, the sound echoes mightily in the valley, making the soldiers' ears ring and terrifying them into taking cover or throwing themselves flat on the ground. They crane their necks to try to find out where the noise is coming from. At this moment, Qi Yuexuan appears on top of a large rock, and he waves the hat he is holding in his hand. The bugles stop abruptly. He shouts down to the bottom of the mountain: "Hey there! Are you, down there, our brothers from the One Hundred and Eighty-Seventh?"

Down below, someone shouts back: "Yes. Who are you?"

"You're the commander of the Fifth Brigade, aren't you? I'm Qi Yuexuan. Do you remember? Last year, in Walnut Tree Valley..."

Commander Xiao doesn't wait for him to finish, but calls back: "Is that you, Counsellor Qi? How could I forget that silver tongue of yours?"

As it turns out, before the war, Qi Yuexuan had led a group out to his command post to give a benefit performance for the soldiers. They encountered a Japanese foraging party that had crossed the lines, and the Japanese had opened up with their rifles to provoke a firefight. Because he had no orders to engage with the enemy, Commander Xiao did not return fire; it was only at Qi Yuexuan's urgent persuasion that he found the courage to fight back. Twenty or thirty Japanese were killed or wounded, but by following Qi Yuexuan's advice, he was able to report that he had suffered no casualties. Officially, the government apologised to the Japanese for the incident and offered reparations, but privately, even General Qin praised the initiative.

"Why are you here, Counsellor Qi?" Commander Xiao asks.

"I have been appointed by the government. I am under orders from General Qin as the commissioner left in charge of Beiping. When I heard you would be passing through here today, I brought the local villagers to welcome you, and to prepare a banquet for our heroic troops."

"Are there any other soldiers on the mountain?"

"Soldiers? Of course not, only locals." Qi Yuexuan waves his hand. "Show yourselves, good villagers!"

At the sound of his voice, a great press of people appears from among the rocks and trees on either side of the gorge, waving their arms, carrying flags, and banging gongs and drums as they shout out in welcome. Qi Yuexuan waves his hat and calls out: "Come on, friends, let's welcome the troops into the village."

The throng of men, women and children, two or three hundred in all, come down from the mountain sides. As they meet the soldiers, they spontaneously take them by the arm, lend their shoulders for support, pull them along from in front, push them on from behind, and some even pick them up and carry them. As they walk along, the soldiers find themselves helpfully relieved of the packs and ammunition boxes on their backs, and the rifles and machineguns they are carrying. The warmth of their reception makes the soldiers feel as though they have just moved straight out of the icehouse into the bath house, and the change is almost dizzying.

FOLLOWING THE MARCO POLO BRIDGE INCIDENT, the central Nationalist Party government retreated to the interior, and, under international pressure, it was obliged to put on a show of total opposition to the Japanese. However, internally, it dragged its feet over peace talks, pinning its hopes on intervention by Britain, America, Russia and the other major powers, and on mediation by the League of Nations. So its military operations were purely defensive, with no aggressive moves of any kind. Even after taking a pounding over several years, it still did not officially declare war on the Japanese. Only after the US declared war on Japan in 1942 did the Nationalist Government finally issue its declaration. Entering the battlefield with such a lukewarm and hesitant attitude, how can it be expected to show the strength and determination for a bloody fight to the death?

With the Japanese opening a second front at the end of July, and advancing on Shanghai, the Nationalist Government has further concentrated its defences on the southern front. Their forces on the northern front are now holed up in Shanxi Province, and the majority of the north of China has been handed over to the Japanese. Commander Xiao and his men have already been up in the mountains for more than two months. He was originally the rear guard of an operation moving a battalion to Baoding in Hebei Province, but the Japanese caught up with them at Yancun in Liangxiang County. Only a hundred or so of the original battalion were left, and as the main roads were impassable, they had taken to the mountains. Sticking to the mountains and valleys, and with great difficulty, they finally reached the southwest of Hebei, where once again they encountered the Japanese and were forced to retreat. Although this time they did not encounter the enemy, they were continually harassed by irregular troops of unknown allegiance. In several surprise attacks, they lost more than half their number. In the end, they no longer dared enter any villages, and they suffered great hardships sleeping in ruined temples or out in the open.

Once they are all in the village, Qi Yuexuan takes Commander Xiao and several of his officers straight to the Fucha clan memorial hall. Already laid out inside are two rows of tables and benches. The food has not yet been brought out, but on each table there are bowls, chopsticks and a big jar of wine. When Commander Xiao realises that only a few of his men have come in with him, he is somewhat alarmed and a little suspicious.

Qi Yuexuan notices this and says good-humouredly: "I've arranged everything. Your lads can have a hot bath first and then join the feast. The village doesn't have a communal bath house, so we've had to divide them up between households. We also have a doctor who can treat your wounded. We don't have any Western medicines, but we do have the herbal medicines to treat battlefield wounds. Why don't you few come in here, and when you've washed and changed clothes, we can sit down and chat over some tea. How does that sound?"

"You are very thoughtful," Commander Xiao replies, smiling. "Ai! I don't know how long it's been since I bathed – these clothes must really stink. Alas, even I only have the clothes I stand up in."

"Don't worry, it's all arranged – a set of clothes for each man, undergarments included. The women and girls of the village will wash and mend what you're wearing now."

Once he and his men are in the big wooden tubs, the hairs on the back of Commander Xiao's neck stand on end, as each man is surrounded and scrubbed back and front, so they don't even have time to exchange looks. They are not sure what exactly is going on. It is only once they are washed and dressed in long gowns and button-up jackets, and get back their army belts, that they relax a little as they see they still have their weapons.

When Qi Yuexuan sees them all come back into the hall, he hands them tea and asks: "So, Commander Xiao, what are you going to do now."

"Ha! I'm a soldier, so what choice do I have? I hear the army has withdrawn to Lingqiu in Shanxi, so we'll try to find them there."

"What route will you take?"

"Follow the valley to Dashiyu, then through Ten Li Gorge. We should be able to get to Little Mount Wutai, and then, if we follow the mountains west, we should make it to Lingqiu."

Qi Yuexuan shakes his head with a laugh.

"What? Is that not right? That's what the map shows."

Sitting next to them, Grandpa Dong chips in: "Tell me, Commander Xiao – if your maps were reliable, would you have ended up wandering the mountains until you found us here? Ten Li Gorge was blocked by a landslide some time ago." So saying, he unrolls his own hand-drawn cloth map on the table and points to it. "There's a three or four *li*-long weir here. Do you think you can fly over it? Even if you can get past it, you won't get out of the pass. There are big concentrations of Japanese troops, here... here... and here too."

Seeing Commander Dong's doubtful expression, Qi Yuexuan says: "That's exactly how it is. I've seen all this for myself, recently. He's quite right. You're not going to be able to get out that way."

Commander Xiao sighs mournfully.

Seizing the opportunity, Grandpa Dong says: "If there's no point in you going, why not join us here, and we can work together."

Commander Xiao shoots him a look and then asks Qi Yuexuan: "Who's this?"

Qi Yuexuan hurriedly makes the introductions: "This is Dong Fuzhong, commander of the Wanping Division of the North China Heroic Anti-Japanese Army."

Commander Xiao's eyes bore into Qi Yuexuan: "Didn't you say there were no soldiers in the village?"

"We're still recruiting the soldiers. We just have the organisational framework in place."

"Huh! So, there we have it – the beggar laying out his stall. You want to use us as your foundation, don't you! Well let's be clear about this now, I never trust a mob."

Angered, Grandpa Dong is about to flare up at him, but he is stopped by Qi Yuexuan.

"I need to get us straight on this, Commander Xiao," Qi Yuexuan says with an encouraging smile. "If we're both fighting the Japanese, surely there's no need for 'yours' or 'mine'. Even if you and your men don't stay here, you can always leave us some guns and ammunition to help our action behind enemy lines, can't you?"

Commander Xiao looks him up and down and says through clenched teeth: "So, you've gathered us here to gobble us up, have you? You were very convincing. Last time when I let myself be persuaded by your silver tongue, I didn't know what a wolf in sheep's clothing you are! Let me tell you now, Mr Bullshit-Commissioner Qi – if I ever seem hesitant, it's not because I'm afraid. I'm not a stingy person, but nor am I going to pluck out my own hair. I'm not going to fall for your soft soap, but if you want to play hard ball, I'm up for it."

With these words, he signals to his men: "Assemble the troops!"

Before the men can even reply, there is a bark of laughter. Forcing himself to restrain his mirth, Qi Yuexuan says: "Calm down a little if you can, Commander Xiao. Your troops are scattered round the village, bathing. Now they've got all the dirt off their bodies, is that all you're going to leave behind for us?"

Commander Xiao's face flushes with anger, and his voice rises to a shout: "Are you... do you want me just to lay down our weapons and surrender?"

"No, not surrender. I'm just afraid one of them might go off accidentally and start something," Qi Yuexuan says, quite shamelessly.

Commander Xiao is so angry his hand flies to his pistol on the table, and several of his subordinates' hands also go to their belts. But Qi Yuexuan just sits there, waiting without turning a hair, and still smiling all the while. He looks as if he is in a tea house, watching an opera. Suddenly, Commander Xiao's anger disperses like air from a pig's bladder. He doesn't unbutton his holster, but puts it down and says to his men: "Ai! Alright, no point fighting. They've already got us where they want us."

He collects several pistols from his men, puts them on the table too and says furiously: "I admit defeat, but I'm not going to surrender to riff-raff like you. I'm a proper soldier of the national army, and I've risked my life against the foreign devils..."

"Cut the crap!" Qi Yuexuan bangs the table. "How do you have the nerve to talk like that? The three eastern provinces, Rehe, Beiping, Tianjin, Shanghai... you and your proper soldiers of the national army have lost them all. Turning your arse to the enemy, is that what you call risking your life? A hundred thousand troops, and how many days did you fight? One battle and you turned tail, so why should the common people look after you? With you lot as an example, why wouldn't the people take up arms themselves? It doesn't matter whether it ends in defeat or victory, but what kind of soldiers don't want to go down fighting, without shame or disgrace?"

After a lot of sharp and angry questioning, Commander Xiao and his men, their faces alternately flushed and pale, finally let their heads droop, as though the tendons had been pulled out of them. Seeing this, Qi Yuexuan swiftly changes tack: "Of course, no one... no one is blaming you for this. If anyone must be cursed, it should be your tyrannical and incompetent leaders, the descendants of Qin Hui."[2]

"Then... how are you going to punish us?" Commander Xiao asks.

"It's not a question of punishing. I just want to arrange things for you. I've thought it all through – if you want to stay, you will be welcome, and if you don't, no one's going to force you. I'll be happy to arrange for some men to lead you to a safe location. In any case, why don't you listen to everything I've got to say?"

"Go on then, let's hear you out."

"As I see it," Qi Yuexuan says, pointing at the map, "the only possible route is across Miaofengshan, along the Kong Stream and through Guanting Township."

"Isn't that occupied territory?"

"There are no devils along the rivers and streams, only a squad of river police from the newly arrived security force, and they only have a couple of boats." Qi Yuexuan appears to have everything already covered. "In ten days' time, there will be a fair at the Fertility Goddess Temple on Miaofengshan. Each year, everyone from the surrounding area goes to see the fun. Here, we've got all the banners, stilts, martial artists, shaman drums and upwards of a hundred men. If you all put on festive clothes and carry some martial arts weapons of some kind, as long as you've learned enough not to make too many stupid mistakes, why shouldn't you mingle in with everyone else? If you're stopped at any roadblocks, just say you've just left the Daoist temple at Miaofengshan, and you're on your way to the Buddhist temple at Little Mount Wutai – it's a credible cover story. Don't worry, I'll find the right men to show you the way and look after everything."

Commander Xiao nods slowly.

"But you can't carry any rifles or machineguns. You'll even have to leave your uniforms behind. And you must remember, this isn't asking you to lay down your weapons, it's just that it's not possible for you to carry them, and you are volunteering them for use by the anti-Japanese resistance. I'll give you a receipt for them. You can give it to General Qin when you get back, and explain everything. I'll leave you some short-barrelled guns for self-defence and even add a few more if they're not enough. But you've got to keep them well hidden, and only use them if you absolutely have to. Your badly wounded men can stay here until they're mended, and we'll send them on after you. What do you say?"

"You seem to have it all wrapped up. So you have the final word, and I don't get a look in?" Commander Xiao gives an ironic 'thumbs-up', and says with a wry smile: "You're quite something! What it is to have an education! If all local bandits were this erudite, the only weapon they'd need would be emotional blackmail! Well played. Well played."

As he says this, the room erupts into laughter.

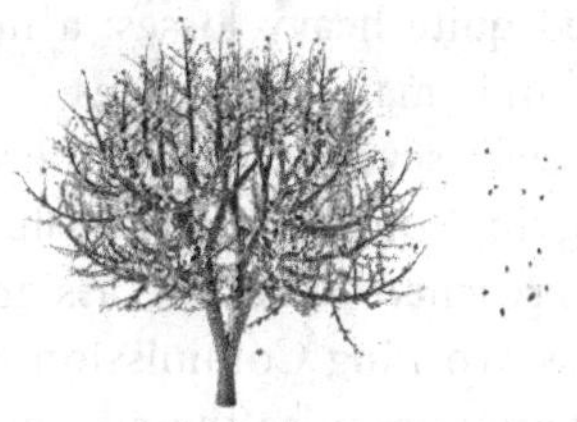

Chapter 14

Zhou Zhengying has already spent a good few months travelling with Zuo Xichuan from the south of Shanxi to Rehe. To make it easier to move through enemy-occupied territory, Zuo Xichuan had adopted the disguise of a Japanese merchant, and she has been posing as his wife. With the additional burden of having to carry her son, now several months old, she has taken lifts in carts, ridden horses and travelled on sledges; she has also, on occasion, had to cross rivers and mountains on foot. They seem to have covered most of Rehe Province, through Xinglong, Fengning, Luanping, Hushiha, Yingshouyingzi, Guojiatun and so on, until they reach Erdaohezi in the south of the province. They have come across a few independently established bands of resistance fighters, like the one led by Zhang Zhicheng, but they haven't yet been able to find the main force of the resistance army. At the beginning of October, they take a diversion to make contact with the Rehe Provincial Party Committee at Honghuagou, and it is only then that they learn that circumstances have changed – the military situation outside the Pass is now just as grim as the early winter conditions that have struck.

Around the time of the Marco Polo Bridge Incident, the Japanese armies in the northeast of China united to mount a full-scale advance on the north. Their first move was to assemble their troops to encircle and annihilate resistance in the three northeastern provinces of Liaoning, Jilin and Heilongjiang, along with Rehe. In order to break the enemy encirclement, the combined resistance of Heilongjiang and Jilin mounted many counter-attacks to the west, hoping to unite with fellow-resistance forces in Rehe. Their most strenuous efforts all being met with defeat, and casualties accounting for more than half their number, the remainder crossed the western reaches of the Jiaolai River and broke out to the north.

In order to meet up with these forces breaking out to the west, the main resistance force in Rehe came east out of Liaoning, but they also suffered heavy casualties. With their retreat to Rehe now blocked, they had no option but to link up with the remainder of the northeastern resistance and move to the border north of Dadingzishan, in order to regroup. The Communist Party's regional organisation also suffered quite heavy losses: a number of its communication posts were destroyed, and many comrades were arrested. The regional committee's vacillation over several months because of all this causes Zuo Xichuan and Zhou Zhengying considerable hardship.

Now these two have reached Rehe, the assignment given to them by the Northern Bureau Military Working Commission is this: make contact with the united Rehe resistance army; organise the advance of the main force into the mountain areas north and east of Beiping; and assist the Eighth Route Army in sending a detachment to set up operational bases behind enemy lines in those areas. Although the pair are conversant with the overall state of play between the fighting in the northeast and the country-wide war of resistance, the sudden change in circumstances makes this assignment ten times more difficult. But if it is possible to open up fighting in the environs of Beiping at this time, it will be like plunging a knife into the back of the Japanese devils. So, however difficult it may prove, it is essential not to leave the Eighth Route Army launching its attack with one hand tied behind its back. The comrades of the Rehe Provincial Party Committee decide to knit together the scattered pockets of resistance fighters and send troops north of Beiping to support the Eighth Route Army.

Of course, Zhang Zhicheng's troop is part of this operation. When he is informed he is to make his way back to Beiping, and that his troops will stop being known as part of the unified resistance and become part of the official Eighth Route Army, he naturally claps his hands and stamps in delight, and is itching to set out immediately. But the plan, which first involves drawing several small bands and units to the high mountains where the borders of Beiping and Rehe meet, requires mobilising, then organising and finally training the troops. Five hundred-plus men are temporarily united into one squadron, then subdivided into three battalions. Zhang Zhicheng is appointed battalion commander, and the military political commissar and battalion political officer are chosen by the Rehe Provincial Party Committee. Zuo Xichuan first shows up as they start up the mountains, but as he doesn't know where they are heading, he leaves Zhou Zhengying behind as a temporary political instructor. In the blink of an eye, more than a fortnight has passed, and the order to advance on Beiping has still not been issued. Zhang Zhicheng is getting anxious, but as battalion commander, he has to keep up outward appearances, and he is reaching boiling point.

At noon on this particular day, Zuo Xichuan finally reappears. Once in the barracks, he orders that more men be sent to carry supplies down the mountain, while he himself heads over to Zhou Zhengying's cellar room. She is sitting on a mattress on the floor, feeding Nan'er some maize porridge.

"Can the child eat that alright?"

"Ai! I'm not producing enough milk for him." She is pleasantly surprised to see it is Zuo Xichuan.

"I've got some Japanese milk powder here. Mix it up with some warm water and give it to him." He takes off his overcoat and fishes several tins out of the inside pockets.

"I'll make it up later. This will fill him up for now." Itching to get down to business, she asks: "What have you been doing these last few days, coming and going like a ghost?"

Zuo Xichuan laughs: "I went to find the Kwantung Army[1] to do some business."

"Fine, if you don't want me to know, I won't ask. Just stop talking nonsense."

"What do you mean 'nonsense'? I've brought the goods back. I'm really not trying to keep any secrets from you, it's just that I didn't know if I would be successful or not. I was afraid it wouldn't be safe for you to go, so I didn't tell you."

"Did you really do business with the Kwantung Army?"

"Of course I did. Why don't you believe me?"

"What exactly went on?"

"Let me have some water first." Zuo Xichuan picks up a pottery jar from the floor, but the water has frozen. He knocks out the lump of ice, and, with considerable difficulty, gnaws off a chunk. Sucking on it, he says: "My father had a nephew from his clan called Shoi Toyoki, who was one of his students at the Japanese Military College. He often used to come to our house then, and I was good friends with him. He's now the commander of the Fourteenth Brigade of the Kwantung Army, stationed at Chengde."

"Is he a comrade?"

"Fellow townsman, fellow clansman, but not a comrade. It was only when I heard our comrades on the Party provincial committee mention him, that I learned about his circumstances. When I went to do business with him this time, it was by way of a test. I was quite open with him about my being with the Chinese Army of the Northwest and the Shanxi Army. It was just as well that I was, because he'd already heard all about it. He even knew about me going to the Soviet Union."

"So he knew about you being in the Communist Party too?"

"Do you think I'd have made it back if he'd known that? I just said I'd left the army long ago because I didn't want to get involved in a war between China and Japan, and now I'm trading in furs and other mountain goods. I sold all the furs and other stuff we'd collected on the road, and took two cart-loads of maize in return. After all, our troops won't be able to go north without grain."

"What did he do that for?"

"The Japanese soldiers are all doing dodgy private black market deals. And they have some way of spiriting the stuff back home by sea. But getting hold of the grain this time was a useful extra – the main purpose was to buy access to the route." He fishes out a piece of paper. "This is an official pass. If you've got one of these, you don't have to worry about having any other documentation to travel and trade in and out of the Pass."

"That's fantastic!" Zhou Zhengying is genuinely excited.

Zuo Xichuan hurriedly gestures with his lips, and she realises Nan'er has fallen asleep. Zuo Xichuan waits for her to settle the child on the mattress, and then he says quietly: "He also mentioned some other students of my father, not only in the Kwantung Army, but also in the North China Garrison Army. If we can make use of them, it will be an enormous help to our work. He said that he was thinking of going into business with me. He doesn't have any working capital, but he can supply the goods and open doors. He's also considering using my trade network to gather secret intelligence for the Kwantung Army."

"Aiya!" Zhou Zhengying exclaims. "That's terrific! We'll never get another opportunity like it." Still excited, but now lowering her voice a little, she continues: "If you really pull this off, you'll have two-fold cover, and not only can you help our intelligence work, you can also get hold of desperately needed supplies for the Party organisation. Such a great..."

"But... Ai!" Zuo Xichuan seems a little less excited, and he clearly has something more he wants to say.

"But what? Does he have some... conditions?"

"Mmm..." Zuo Xichuan nods and says hesitantly: "He says that running all over the place doing business will be too exhausting, and he wants me to move and settle in Chengde. He says it will be better for my wife and child. If he's still suspicious of me, he'll have you two as..."

Zhou Zhengying understands all that the word 'hostages' means before the word is even out of his mouth. There's a long moment's silence before she asks: "So, did you ask for instructions from above?"

"They've already wired back their agreement. They've ordered me to Beiping as soon as possible to meet the head of the army working committee, to gather information on the deployment of troops inside the Pass and to make a detailed feasibility study of this business. But they also ordered me to ask your opinion." Zuo Xichuan speaks lightly, but he doesn't raise his head to look at her.

"And if I don't agree?" Zhou Zhengying asks with a wry smile.

Head still down, Zuo Xichuan replies: "I don't think... you could go against the Party's decision."

"If the committee has already decided, then why ask me?" Zhou Zhengying snaps back angrily. She looks at the sleeping Nan'er and then says loudly: "I agree. But our child is not a member of the Party, so why should he go? If you travel to Beiping, I'm going with you, but I'll send him to Yuexuan. He hasn't seen him yet..."

"No, that won't do!" Zuo Xichuan interrupts forcefully.

Zhou Zhengying doesn't argue, but her eyes have clearly filled with tears.

"You have to have the child with you," Zuo Xichuan says with a sigh. "He's the most valuable one in Shoi Toyoki's eyes. But... if you can come around to the idea of going to Beiping, we can think of a way for you to take him to see his father. You'd both have to come back, though."

Zhou Zhengying stays silent for a long time before lifting her drooping head. Tears flow as she says: "In that case... I'd rather not go. I'm not going to Beiping."

Zuo Xichuan doesn't reply, but behind him someone laughs: "Ha ha! Is going back to Beiping something to cry about? If you told me I could go, I'd be delighted!"

Unaware of exactly what is going on, Zhang Zhicheng comes into the room, laughing.

Zuo Xichuan hurriedly welcomes him in, saying: "There's no need for you to go, Lao Zhang. You're a battalion commander, and a commander has to remain in the garrison to maintain morale among the troops. You can't just go wandering off."

"In this case, I have to go. I know you don't need me for what you're doing, but I've got my own business to attend. If you don't take me with you, I'll go by myself anyway."

"But haven't you just been made a provisional Party member?"

"That's still provisional, like you say, not confirmed, so it wouldn't be breaking Party discipline, would it?"

"What's so important you have to go to Beiping?"

"I'm going to get myself a wife."

"Get yourself a wife?"

When Zhang Zhicheng sees the amazement on Zuo Xichuan's face, he gives a great shout of laughter: "You're quite something if you don't understand that!" He taps the Mauser at his waist. "This is what old bachelor soldiers call their 'wife.'"

SINCE RECEIVING his military warrant from Matsuzaki, Chenglong has certainly not sat on his hands, and he has spared no effort in establishing his Special Operations Squad. He has selected a dozen or so experienced and capable men from his CID squad and seven or eight case-hardened officers from the police department. With the help of Yamaguchi, he has also dug out a handful of convicts from the cells of the Kempeitai prison. They have all worked for the Chinese civil or military intelligence services, or come from the Twenty-Ninth Army, and every one of them is willing to co-operate to avoid further physical punishment. They may not be major players, but on the principle of setting a thief to catch a thief, they are going to be more effective than any novice to this world would be. Chenglong's view is that strength is not in numbers but in ability, and each of the twenty and more chosen men have particular skills. Moreover, they are all single, with no home or family ties in Beiping. Once they get Chenglong's nod on interview, they are assembled for a brief period of training, during which they are kept almost as if in prison and not allowed out under any circumstances.

After a fortnight's training, his Special Operations Squad is officially up and running. With three men to a team, six to a watch and three watches every twenty-four hours, they patrol and keep watch over all the key areas. Their first move is to cut off the electricity supply to Yanjing University and then send in men disguised as electricity company workers to patrol the campus under cover of inspecting the supply cables. Following this, the men keeping night-watch over the low-lying ground to the west of the university grounds observe three men coming back through the fields after midnight and pushing through the shrubs and reeds from the direction of the city. On reaching the northern wall of the campus, they disappear without trace. The next morning it is reported that Officer Guo, the Kempeitai interpreter who lives outside the Desheng Gate, and his wife, have both been assassinated. Once the connection is made between these two incidents, an important lead in the case is exposed, and Chenglong feels that the establishment of his Special Operations Squad is already bearing fruit.

There is another thing that greatly pleases Chenglong: in a batch of documents recently seized in Baoding and sent up to the capital, he has discovered the documentation and list of names of prisoners bailed from Baoding Jail. The bailed prisoners total seventeen in number; the bail station is the Beiping office of military intelligence, and the bail licence is dated the end of July in the twenty-sixth year of the Republic. Before he received this, Chenglong had already found, in the records seized from military intelligence offices, a plan to establish a commando team behind enemy lines. This mentions commandeering a number of bandits bailed from prison, and it is dated just a few weeks before the Baoding document. The two things are clearly connected. What is more, the Baoding prison files contain the case notes of these seventeen men, complete with photographs, and they all prove to be co-defendees in a case against a troop of bandits from Dawangshan in Laiyuan County. This is further proof that his own previous analysis of the Traitor Elimination Squad was right on the money. But when he pulls out the prison registration form of the bandit known as Two-Ox Gui, his heart turns a somersault. However he looks at the scarred, lined face of the man in the photo, he bears a remarkable resemblance to his adoptive father, Gao Guigeng. On the one hand he berates himself for thinking he is seeing a ghost, and he tells himself that his adoptive father has been dead for years and couldn't possibly have risen from the grave. On the other hand, he can't rid himself of the thought that the man in the photo corresponds so closely with his memory of his adoptive father. In the end, he tucks the photo carefully into his pocket. He doesn't go home but heads for the army stores, where he cuts himself a few catties of meat, weighs out a sack of rice and drives over to the old Gao home. He stops the motorcycle and sidecar at the mouth of the little hutong, unloads his stuff and goes into the courtyard.

Wangtian has just got home from the Longfu Temple fair, where, in one morning, he has sold a dozen or more New Year prints. With Caiping, he is happily counting up the handful of coins he has just thrown down on the *kang*, when he hears someone calling at the door. "We're here," he replies in an off-handed manner. "Come on in."

Caiping tries to stop him, but she isn't in time. As soon as Wangtian sees it's Chenglong coming through the door, he gets to his feet and asks: "What... what are you doing here?"

Chenglong hesitates: "I've just come to visit, Brother, and bring you some meat and rice."

With this, he is about to put the food down on the table, when Wangtian stops him abruptly. "No, don't put it down. Didn't you say you came to see me? Well, you've seen me, haven't you? I'm not going to let you keep hounding me. Enough! Go home, and take that stuff with you. I wouldn't be able to swallow your special supplies crap."

Chenglong scratches his head. "Aah! I know I've really offended you this time. I'd drunk too much. Ai! Brothers should be able to get past something like this, shouldn't they? Brothers are like hands and feet, but wives are just clothes. For the sake of a woman, are you..."

Caiping throws the knife she is holding down onto the table with a clang. Chenglong puts on a smile and says: "No, no, that's not right, what I said is not right. Everything I did then was not right either. I was drunk, and it made me crazy. Now, I just want to give my brother, and my... ah, should I call you sister-in-law? Ha ha! I've just come to try and make up for things. We're on a new page now, and we can still be brothers, can't we?... Ai! If you won't answer to 'Brother', at least let's not act like enemies."

Wangtian's reply is still icy cold: "Say what you've got to say, and be done with it. There's no point in grinning like an idiot and going round the houses."

"Alright, alright!" Chenglong finally takes out the photograph and hands it to Wangtian. "I've brought a photo to show you. Who do you think it is?"

At first, Wangtian is not going to take it, but one glance locks his eyes on it and he blurts out: "That's... that's Dad, isn't it?"

"Is it really him?"

"... but it also isn't him."

"So is it him or not?"

"Dad never had that big scar on his face. The eyes are a bit too slanting, and he looks older than Dad... no, that's not right, it's really like him."

Chenglong thinks for a moment, then says: "Have another good look. If Dad... if Dad is still alive, he'd be that age. If he's really not dead, he must have got that scar later."

"Bullshit! Dad's been dead for more than ten years, so where did you get that photo? You can't go around saying anyone who looks a bit like Dad actually is him." He takes another look at the photo. "This name isn't right and nor is the occupation. Dad would never be a bandit. Take this piece of trash with you and leave!"

Caiping moves closer and just a passing glance at the photo is enough to make her cry out: "Isn't that..." She breaks off and comes to a dead stop. Casting a sidelong look at Wangtian and Chenglong, she goes on, haltingly: "Isn't that... isn't that a prison mugshot?"

Very put out, Chenglong takes back the photo and replaces it inside his jacket.

"Is this man... in a Japanese prison?" Wangtian asks.

"No. He was in the National Government prison at Baoding for several years, then someone bailed him out."

"Then... what are you up to?"

"Well, I came across it in the archives, and when I saw how much it looked like Dad, I had to come over and show you. I remembered that whatever happened to Dad, happened in Shanxi, and that's not far from Laiyuan County. If, by any chance, he's still alive..."

"Didn't you see his ashes? Weren't you there when we buried them?"

"We only had Lao Litou's word for it then. We never saw a body."

Wangtian doesn't immediately know how to respond.

Chenglong continues: "Where's Lao Litou now?"

"He's dead. Killed by the Japanese."

"Is he... really dead?"

"How could it be faked? I brought his body back myself and buried it. It's in the Qi family plot."

Chenglong can see he's quite definite about it, and there's no point enquiring further. It's at this point that an indefinable feeling begins to bubble up inside Wangtian. Just the word 'Dad' resurrects in him all the responsibilities of being the older brother. In a less harsh tone, he says: "Alright, let's not get carried away with wild conjecture. If Dad really is still alive, wouldn't he be concerned for us at home? Wouldn't he come back to see us? Even if he could let go of me, do you think he could let go of you?"

Wangtian sighs. "Ai! I suppose if you're still concerned about Dad, it means you still have a few shreds of decency left. How much enmity can there really be between two brothers? However you worry at me, and go against what our dad stood for, you'll never really hurt us. But there's more to it than just you and me, you and your older brother. At the heart of it all, I am still a Chinese, and I still try to be an honourable man. If you are truly still concerned about our dad, then you must distance yourself from the Japanese. Hah! Even if you turn your back on Dad completely, as long as you aren't bereft of the greater virtues, as long as you don't make yourself an object of universal contempt, as long as you don't disgrace the name of Gao, then Dad's life will not have been in vain, and he can rest in peace..."

"Enough of that for now, Big Brother," says Chenglong who has become a little restive listening to all this. "We'll talk about it again sometime. I've got to go now. I've got other things to do." He turns away and is about to leave.

"Wait! Wait!" Caiping cries out.

Chenglong whirls round and looks at Caiping in amazement: "Have you... thought of something else?"

"You've left your things behind. If you don't take them away with you, I think he'll probably throw them out in the street."

Chenglong looks at Wangtian and grunts angrily. He picks up the meat in one hand, the rice in the other, kicks open the door and swaggers out. Caiping hurries over to close the door, then tugs at Wangtian's sleeve and whispers: "I've seen that man in the photograph."

"Where?"

"Here."

"What? When?"

"That time when you were ill. It was him that left that cloth bundle here."

"It... it was really him?"

"I didn't trust Chenglong just now, so I didn't dare say anything. Who is it really? Could it be your father?"

Wangtian doesn't reply. Inside he thinks he has the answer, but he can't suppress an indefinable worry that overlays his surprised delight.

Chenglong has just put the meat and rice in his sidecar, when he discovers that two of the three wheels are flat. On closer examination, there are triangular-shaped punctures in the outer walls of the tyres, exposing the inner tubes. It's obvious someone has slashed them. He's never experienced anything like this before. He doesn't usually go out by himself, but he didn't want anyone else to know about today's business, so he hadn't called for a driver or bodyguard to go with him. He stamps his foot in anger and yells: "Who slashed my tyres? Fuck it! Have the guts to show yourself!"

Of course, no one is going to own up. He keeps up this pointless shouting for quite a while with no response, but all the passers-by on the street stop to watch the fun from a distance, and householders open their doors a crack to peer out. All he can do is push the vehicle the ten yards or so to the gates of the Minister's Residence. The old porter is no longer there, and for the sake of security, Chenglong has assigned four men from his CID squad to guard the gates and courtyards in teams of two. But just at this moment, there is no one in sight, so he shouts even more angrily and leans on the motorcycle's horn. One of his men finally emerges from the porter's lodge.

"Fuck you!" Chenglong yells at him. "If you have a watch-dog, you chain it up outside, so what do you think you're doing skulking around indoors?"

The man hurriedly greets him and smiles obsequiously. "Aiya! Commander Liu, I... it's not my fault. Your wife ordered us not to stand outside. She said..."

"What did she say?"

"She said... Ai! It's what your wife said, it's nothing to do with me."

"Stop making excuses! Are you going to tell me or not?" Chenglong glares at him fiercely.

"Your wife said... she said if we want to stand around looking fierce, then we need to move further away, so as not to frighten the children and block the street. And not to think that we can make ourselves look good by prancing around outside and pretending to be watch-dogs, not scuttling little crabs. She said the Minister's Residence has its status to consider, and just because you've dishonoured yourself, that's no reason to bring dishonour on the Residence too."

"Enough!" Chenglong interrupts him sternly, his expression clouding over ominously. "This household doesn't need her to run it. The days when a bunch of old women with bound feet run things are over. Haven't you noticed the trouble we've got throughout the city?" He points at the punctured tyres. "Someone slashed my tyres right outside these gates today, and more than likely tomorrow it will be someone's belly that's slashed. You've got to guard me much better. Understand?"

"Yessir! Yessir!" The man nods like a chef pounding garlic.

"Hurry up and get some men to repair the motorbike, and take that stuff in it back inside." Then something occurs to Chenglong, and he asks: "Are you the only one here?"

"Lao Bangzi is inside sweeping the courtyard, San Qingzi..."

Before he can finish, another man comes running out of the courtyard: "Commander Liu, I... I was just delivering something to your family. Someone gave you a box of pastries."

"Who was it?"

"He said he was a friend, and that you'd ordered it for your family."

Chenglong stares at him. "Was it just a box of pastries?"

The man laughs uneasily. "There was certainly something in it. I could tell by the weight."

Chenglong grunts pensively, then suddenly thinks of something and breaks into a run towards the western side courtyard. As he gets there, he hears his two children squabbling over the pastries. Yue E calls out to them: "It won't hurt to wait a minute, will it? Just be good and hold on. I'll be right there."

Chenglong is shaking all over as he reaches the threshold in a couple of strides and hurls open the door, yelling: "Don't move!"

Yue E has already undone the ribbon on the box, and she jumps in surprise. The two children are even more startled. They burst into tears and hide behind their mother.

"What are you crying for?" Chenglong says harshly, striding over to the table and grabbing hold of Yue E.

"Haven't I told you not to open anything strangers send me?"

Yue E also flares up. "What's the matter with you? It's just a box of pastries."

"There might be something else in it."

Yue E looks at his fraught expression, laughs and opens the box, saying:

"They're cakes, not bombs. Look at the state of you! Haven't you had enough? If you're feeling so bad, stop doing wicked things. Otherwise, if you don't get blown up, you'll die of fright anyway." With that, she takes one pastry and gives it to Xinliang, and takes another for Liangxin.

Chenglong is so taken aback by this, he can't speak, while Yue E leads the two children into the inner room. He is still uneasy though, and he picks up the box of pastries, weighing it in his hand. He examines it closely for a while, takes out the top layer of pastries, and tears open the paper lining. It's only half open, when it reveals a round, black object. Chenglong gives a cry of alarm, hurls himself backwards and crouches on the floor. He stays there not moving for an age, before lifting his head and seeing Yue E bending over him.

"Don't move!" he yells.

Yue E reaches out and takes the object out of the box. It's a jumbo-size doughnut. Yue E gives a bark of laughter.

"How evil can they get, giving you something like this?"

Chenglong takes the pastry and inspects it. Apart from being a bit larger and firmer than usual, there's nothing odd about it. He breaks it open, and finds a ball of paper stuffed inside. He opens it out, and shudders as though he's just stepped on a live wire. On the crumpled paper are written four large characters – 'Your life's in danger' – and three small characters – 'Traitor Elimination Squad'.

Seeing his expression, Yue E gives a bitter laugh: "Ha! Go on then! Throw your lot in with the Japanese, and next time, when someone comes to assassinate you as a traitor, see how much good it does you! Ai! They've given you a warning today. Think it over carefully – do you think you'll ever feel safe again?"

Without another word, she turns and goes back into the inner room. After a long silence, Chenglong can be heard shouting hysterically: "You think you can kill me? Think on! Let's see who fucking kills who!"

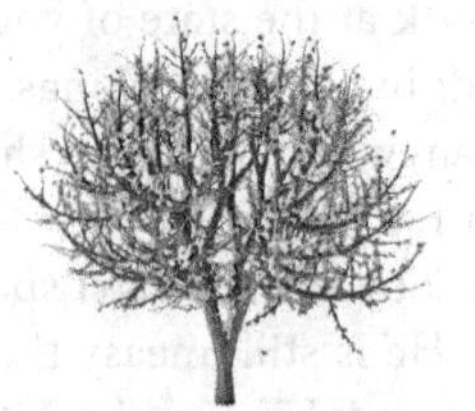

Chapter 15

The sky is just getting light as the group from Number Twelve Village of the Left Barracks set out for the temple fairs. A large apricot-yellow banner carried on either side of the road leads the way and is followed by a continuous stream of percussionists, stilt-walkers, flag-wavers and martial artists. They walk down the small mountain path for no more than two or three *li*, then take the main road from Beiping to Miaofengshan. In past years, this was the route pilgrims took to go and burn incense at the temples, so it's commonly known as 'Incense Road'. Once they are on Incense Road, Grandpa Fu, at the head of the column, sounds a bugle, and the troops immediately fall into formation. A signal flag is raised, the drums and gongs begin to play, and everyone starts to dance as they make their way along the road. Commander Xiao and his men are all in make-up and their faces are every colour imaginable: red, white, black, blue, yellow, they're all there, and they are designated Number Seventy-Two Demon Troupe. They are, however, all novices at this kind of thing, and with only a few days' practice, can't be expected to be too convincing. Fortunately, the part of a demon isn't demanding; it just requires a lot of baring of fangs and claws, and jumping about wildly. Out of the whole group, only Qi Yuexuan and Grandpa Dong seem unconcerned, strolling along in the middle of them all. Bringing up the rear are three great vats of wine, which each take four men to carry.

THE FAIR AT THE HARMONY TEMPLE on Miaofengshan has a long history with a story attached to it. The mountain is not considered particularly high among those in the area west of Beiping, but 'it is not height that makes a mountain, but the immortals that live there'. There is a cave at the top of the mountain, known as the Cave of Favour and Relief, where legend has it that five female deities practised Daoist asceticism. They are called the Queen of Progeny, the Queen of Posterity, the Queen of Disease, the Queen of Vision and the Queen of the Earth Treasures. They look after all aspects of human affairs, including happiness and long life, children and illnesses. Of the five, the Queen of Progeny, the Primordial Lady Immortal of the Purple Clouds, is the most revered and has the greatest mystical powers, so she is considered the most important. In the Liao dynasty, a Daoist temple called the Palace of Insight was built next to the Cave of Favour and Relief, and it is also called the Temple of the Lady of the Purple Clouds. Ever since it was built, the mountain became famous among Daoists and a place of pilgrimage, known as the Gold Peak of Miaofengshan.

After the Ming dynasty, five more similar Queen Goddess temples were erected in the area around Beiping, known as the Five Peaks. The Eastern Peak is in a small pass beyond the Dongzhi Gate; the Western Peak is by the indigo factory outside the Dongzhi Gate; the Southern Peak is divided into two, the Greater and the Lesser. The Greater Southern Peak is at Maju Bridge, and the Lesser Southern Peak is at the Dahong Gate. The Northern Peak is at Tucheng, beyond the Desheng Gate, and the Central Peak is at Cao Bridge outside the Youan Gate. Of the five peaks, the Western Peak is the closest to Miaofengshan, and it also neighbours Yiheyuan Imperial Park, Jade Spring Hills and the Fragrant Hills. So from Ming times onwards, pilgrims going to burn incense all first travel to Miaofengshan, and then come back to hold a temple fair at the Western Peak. On the days of the temple fair, the road through the mountains is thronged with people. Troupes of all kinds, jugglers and acrobats, martial artists and dancers file along the road, in a procession more than ten *li* long, singing, dancing and performing as they go. When the temple fair was held during the time when the Dowager Empress Cixi was living in the Summer Palace, she would sit on a garlanded dais erected beside the road, watching these troupes pass by on their way to the fair. Beiping has many temple fairs of all kinds, but for more than a hundred years, this forty *li* round-trip pilgrimage between the fairs at Miaofengshan and the West Peak was by far the most popular. After the establishment of the Republic, however, the Western Peak Temple has gradually fallen into disrepair, and both pilgrimage fairs have been combined into one event at the Palace of Insight on Miaofengshan.

Despite, or perhaps because of, the uncertain and disruptive times, the people are more determined than ever to ignore all obstacles and worship the goddess and pray for blessings. Moreover, the Japanese, in trying to maintain the pretence that all is just as before, have been encouraging attendance at these fairs. So this year's fair, although far removed from its former glories, is still very lively. Troupes of worshippers have come, not just from Beiping, but also from Wanping, Changping, Yanqing, Huailai, Yu County and all the counties along the Xiang River. In the old days, all the temple fairs ran for three days, and the troupes that had come from any distance away spent the nights outside the temples where the 'Matting Shed Guild' put up shelters and the 'Congee and Tea Guild' laid on free food and drink. But none of that is allowed this year, and the Japanese have restricted the fair to only one day. No matter how far people have come, they have to return the same day. Moreover, performances are not allowed inside the temple gates, and incense is prohibited from being taken into the main hall. This is because a small detachment of troops stationed on the mountain are billeted in the main hall. Although this is a hardship for the people, the added confusion is a blessing for Commander Xiao and his men. They can mingle with the parties from Huailai and Yanqing, as they make their jumbled way down Incense Road from the west side of the mountain.

Qi Yuexuan summons over some of the men detailed as escorts, gives them a few extra words of instruction, then goes over to make his farewells with Commander Xiao. Seeing him approach, Commander Xiao is about to say something, but he stops, pulls him to one side and only then says: "I still have some reservations about all this, Mr Qi. Are we really going to get through, looking like this? If, by any chance, we give ourselves away, and we don't have our weapons…"

"Ha! Well, if you don't have weapons, what's going to give you away?" Qi Yuexuan reassures him. "Even if you had your names and army numbers tattooed on your foreheads, no one could see them under this make-up. What you are now is a Group Number Seventy-Two of devils and demons, and you don't have to talk to anyone. Just listen to what the leader of the troupe says, follow when he says follow, stop when he says stop, and leap about like madmen when he says dance. If you remember that, you'll be fine."

"But," Commander Xiao says, "I just heard someone from Huailai County say there is another group of demons at Miaofengshan from the mountain pass on the west side – quite a big group, several dozen of them."

Qi Yuexuan shakes his head. "More than that. For this fair, the Japanese have ordered in a Chinese troupe and a hundred traitors from the security police. Even that group from the west must number more than a hundred too."

Commander Xiao is even more worried by this. "Then… there really is cause for worry. I have heard there are going to be individual searches at the start of the way up the mountain and that they will arrest anyone who has gunshot wounds or the mark of a rifle strap on their shoulder. And it's going to be even stricter coming down from the summit…"

"Ha! Don't worry about it. You're already going down the mountain, and it will be dark by the time you reach the pass, so it will be much more difficult for them to search properly than in daylight. Besides, there are bound to be incidents up on the mountain this evening. If those disturbances are big enough, the Japanese aren't going to be able to pay any attention to you, are they?"

Commander Xiao still hasn't got the point. "What do you mean? Are you…"

"Don't ask," a smiling Qi Yuexuan reassures him. "Just stop worrying and go. If I wasn't at least ninety per cent sure, I wouldn't let you all take the risk."

Commander Xiao finally realises that he has some plan or other up his sleeve, and he relaxes somewhat. None the less, in his experience, anything is possible before an affair is actually brought to a conclusion, and there are all sorts of ways this trip could still end in disaster. But having got so far, all he can do is steel his nerve and proceed.

Just at this moment, he hears a shout from the leader of the expedition: "Seventy-Two Group ready! On your way!"

Commander Xiao takes Qi Yuexuan's outstretched hand, grips it with all his might and only lets it go when he sees Qi Yuexuan wince with pain. Laughing with satisfaction at the other's discomfort, he hurries off to join his men. Grandpa Dong watches them disappear into the distance and goes over to Qi Yuexuan.

"Do we move on to the next song now, Young Master Qi?" he asks.

"Not the next song, the next act!" Qi Yuexuan says, teasing him. Then he signals to the young men standing beside the vats of wine, and he calls out: "Alright, lads, take them into the temple and offer up the wine!"

The twelve young lads shout their assent, and, at the orders of the team leader, four to a vat, they crouch down to shoulder the poles and straighten up. With small, neat steps they follow Qi Yuexuan, Grandpa Dong, Grandpa Fu and several others in through the gates of the Palace of Insight. They make their way straight over to the main image hall of the Lady Goddess of the Purple Clouds. They have just reached the doors, but not crossed the threshold, when a Japanese soldier bars their way with his rifle and bellows something at them in a stream of Japanese. Grandpa Dong signals to the men to put the vats down, and Qi Yuexuan steps forward. He looks straight at the guard and says: "What are you saying?"

The soldier looses another string of Japanese. Qi Yuexuan stares at him and shakes his head. "I still don't understand."

Hearing the noise, a Japanese officer comes out of the hall and also addresses Qi Yuexuan in his native tongue.

"Enough!" Qi Yuexuan laughs. "We sound like a crosstalk act. I don't understand what you're saying, and you don't understand what I'm saying – ribbit-ribbit ribbit-ribbit, like two frogs."

The others burst out laughing.

Hearing this, the officer beckons to someone in the group of people standing behind him, and Qi Yuexuan sees a Daoist monk stepping forward. He is a man in his forties, dressed in black, thin and spare with a long beard that makes him look very scholarly. He advances swiftly, flicking a horsehair fly-whisk, clasps his hands and bows.

"My friend, this is Major Hamada," says the monk, "and he says that this hall is already requisitioned by the army, and there is no admittance for worship allowed."

Qi Yuexuan returns the bow. "Very well, I will stay outside the hall to make my offerings of incense and wine, and leave when I have finished. May I ask Master Abbot's name?"

"My name in religion is Qinglu."

"Ah, and are you the abbot of the Palace of Insight?"

"That is my humble role."

Although Qi Yuexuan has never met Abbot Qinglu before, he has often heard Zhou Zhengjie mention him. In fact, they were classmates at Peking University; the abbot formerly worked as a journalist, and he once had radical views. In the fifteenth year of the Republic, he was implicated in the court case against Shao Piaoping[1] and sentenced to imprisonment in the military jail. People from all levels of society called for him to be pardoned, and Qi Yuexuan himself signed the petition. Later, after the Shao clan had been put to death, he was bailed and released. Disheartened and disenchanted, he withdrew from the world and became a Daoist. For twenty years he has not gone out into the world, and he has gained the reputation of being a semi-immortal. Meeting him here and now, like this, Qi Yuexuan can't help but be deeply moved. He looks up at the huge plaque over the entrance to the hall, sweeps his gaze over the Japanese major, smiles icily and says: "Dark purple clouds beside the sun, I fear, in the end, there is no True Way. Could it be there is no true justice and righteousness, only people who propound them?"

The quick-witted Abbot Qinglu immediately picks up the pointed allusion in the first line of this couplet, and he blushes to the tips of his ears, as though he has just swallowed a whole chilli pepper.

The Japanese major comes down from the threshold and points to the vats of wine. In rough and ready Chinese, he asks Abbot Qinglu: "This! What is?"

Grandpa Dong takes it on himself to answer: "Wine. For offering to the Lady Goddess."

The major peers into the mouth of one of the vats, looking and smelling, before laughing. "Wine! *Yoshi! Yoshi!*" He waves his hand and utters another stream of Japanese.

"The Lord says you are not to leave the wine in the courtyard, but take it into the hall," Abbot Qinglu translates.

"The Lord has spoken!" Qi Yuexuan says. "Don't stand there gawping – the Great Lord is more powerful than the Primordial Lady. Hurry up and take them inside."

Laughing, the men carry the three great vats into the hall and place them in front of the image of the Primordial Lady of the Red Clouds. Either side, the floor of the hall is covered in futons, and several Japanese soldiers are sitting or lying around idly. A dozen or so ammunition boxes are stacked up behind the image, rifle racks line the walls of the passage leading to the rear hall, and there are two machineguns laid out on the floor. Once they have carried in the vats, and kowtowed nine times, the men file out of the hall.

"Please wait a moment, my friends," the abbot calls after them.

Qi Yuexuan shoots a look at Grandpa Dong, who takes his meaning and leads the men out of the monastery gates. Qi Yuexuan then stops and asks: "What enlightenment can you offer us, Master Abbot?"

Abbot Qinglu bows and says, in a low voice: "My friends, enlightenment is to be found in quiet and solitude, and in the place of non-action. If there is bright gore, then the gods will be angry. If ruin is wrought on sacred places, the sin is even greater, but if you rein in the horse before the cliff-edge, it is still possible to find peace."

Qi Yuexuan pretends not to understand and asks: "What does My Lord Abbot mean?"

Abbot Qinglu shakes his head with a gentle sigh. "If you are meant to understand, what need is there to explain?"

"Your humble servant is very slow and truly does not understand what My Lord Abbot is indicating." Qi Yuexuan stares at him fixedly.

Abbot Qinglu quietly spits out a single word: "Wine!"

Qi Yuexuan's stomach tightens at the abbot's perspicacity. The vats that they have just carried into the main hall contain the best and purest wine produced by the little still in Laoqiying. But the vats have two layers: the top half is indeed full of wine, but underneath is packed with gunpowder. The fuse is an improvised, slow-burning spiral, which can be set to burn for more than an hour. A ventilation hole has been drilled in the bottom of the barrel to stop the fuse going out. Grandpa Dong and his men have carried out a good many experiments before perfecting its use, and they certainly didn't expect to be seen through so easily by this Daoist abbot.

Seeing Qi Yuexuan lost for words, Abbot Qinglu says: "My friend is an educated man, so why kick against fate?"

Qi Yuexuan calms down when he hears this. With things having gone this far already, there is nothing for it but to go for broke. He laughs wryly. "Ha! Do you think all an educated man can do is play the knight errant in fairy tales, or the great hero in dreams? Does My Lord Abbot not know that a man may lay down his pen and take up the sword? So now you have seen through our ploy, are you going to go and claim your reward from the Japanese?"

"My friend should not misunderstand me," Abbot Qinglu says hurriedly. "I have no evil intentions. A Daoist does not carelessly betray others. But have you not thought that, if heaven is overturned, how can it be supported by the trees and grasses? All things under heaven stem from nature whose power can be harnessed but never overturned. If something is useless, why seek it out? If something is practicable, it leaves traces, and if it leaves traces, it may be discovered. Once you engage in shady nefarious deeds, thenceforward you will never find peace. If you are bent on death, I fear you will drag everyone down with you. I long ago ceased enquiring about human affairs, but even so, I cannot stand by and watch innocent people being led into bloody slaughter. Just listen to my words and stay your hand."

Qi Yuexuan looks at him, then changes the subject. "My lord, I know you call yourself Abbot. You live in the temple and spend every day debating the nature of the Dao. But what I don't know is whether you truly believe in it yourself."

Abbot Qinglu stares blankly at him for a long time, then stutters: "Of... course! I have spent twenty years contemplating the true nature of the Dao..."

"Ha ha! Twenty years? Twenty years and you still come up with those banalities? And you still dare boast to me with your 'of... course'?"

Abbot Qinglu finds this rebuke hard to take. "My friend, if you have a principle to expound, there's no need to mock me in doing so! Bravo! Bravo!"

"Well then, let me take you through the twists and turns of the Dao." Qi Yuexuan stops laughing and goes on in a serious tone: "The law of the Dao is the law of nature. Heaven naturally has ordained the four seasons. The warmth of spring and the heat of summer are part of nature. The austerity of the winds of autumn and the snows of winter must necessarily be ordained by nature too. Man by nature is divided between good and evil – evil men naturally do evil deeds, and it is also natural to punish and eliminate this evil. The Japanese have occupied my country and it is natural for them to murder and plunder. It is equally natural for the Chinese to oppose them. How can you talk of quiet and solitude? A tree may wish to be still, but what if the wind still blows? The Japanese have brought their racks of rifles into the temple, so where are you going to find quiet and solitude? What is this talk of non-action? If it rains, do you not put up an umbrella? If it is cold, do you not put on an overcoat? If a wolf attacks, do you not kill it? If a dog bites, do you not drive it away? Non-action is not apathy, evasion or weakness – it exists between doing nothing and doing something. To put it crudely, it is like stifling farts and suppressing thunder."

"Mountains soar effortlessly, and water floods with ease," says Abbot Qinglu with a bitter laugh. "Great deeds in this world require great power."

"Hah! What is 'great power'? The Chinese people have survived five thousand years without destruction, but only great power can ensure their survival now. Using this great power to inform our actions is what is called 'following the Dao on behalf of heaven'. Our nation does not belong to one man or one party, but however lowly their status or negligible their words, one cannot abrogate responsibility for the common people. Why do we concern ourselves with a single moment's failure or success? Why do we worry about a single person's safety or peril? Daoism has always condemned evil and upheld virtue. It talks of capturing monsters and subduing demons, but today the sacred hall of the Queen of the Crimson Clouds has become the lair of these Japanese dogs. In the face of this extraordinary shame and humiliation, where are your demon-slaying swords and devil-deflecting talismans now? Where are your magic powers acquired through ascetic practice? Alright then, let's suppose your arts are not truly efficacious, and good only for hoodwinking the common people – if your arts are not efficacious, then surely your intentions must be false too. You may believe in the Dao, but are you willing to defend it? If you are not willing to risk everything and put your body on the line for the Dao, what use is your belief? Mystics like you transcend the order of the Three Realms,[2] so why fear life or death? How many Daoist immortals are there in *Fengshen Bang*[3] who are not also generous-hearted martyrs in the world of men? If you have no arts, if you have no sincere belief in the Dao, if you don't have the courage to die for a just cause, if all your quiet and solitude, and your non-action are just fig leaves to hide your shame, if you hide behind your holy altars like a tortoise in its shell, then just what kind of Dao do you believe in? Does Chinese Daoism not distinguish between right and wrong? Between good and evil? Does it have no integrity and no courage?"

Even though Abbot Qinglu was once a journalist, he doesn't have the eloquence or scholarship to match Qi Yuexuan, and this rapid-fire interrogation leaves him unable to reply.

Qi Yuexuan knows in his heart that the man before him is not one of those who cannot distinguish between right and wrong, but someone who has been worn down by the ways of the world and forced to seek seclusion from them. So he says, more compassionately: "But I have been speaking foolishly and letting my words run away with me. Please forgive me, Lord Abbot, but please also consider three things. Every individual has his own will but cannot impose it on others. If he recognises a danger, he should remove himself from it. And he should be prudent in what he says. These are the only things I ask. It is entirely for My Lord Abbot to choose whether he leaves behind the sweet smell of a fine reputation, or the stench of disgrace. Farewell!" With these words, he leaves the temple.

Two hours later, as evening closes in, the peak of Miaofengshan is a magnificent site, blood red in the glow of the setting sun. But nightfall comes quickly, and soon the forests and temples on the mountain disappear into the boundless twilight. At this time, the area around the village at the bottom of the mountain reverberates with an outburst of gunfire, as a group of men mount a surprise attack on the Japanese sentry post at the entrance to the village. Three of the four sentries are killed, and the other is seriously wounded. The strange thing is that the attackers do not go on to fight their way into the village, but wait for the Japanese to come out to them, then retreat back into the mountains. They make another attack using the advantage of the higher ground, killing or wounding another seven or eight Japanese, then disappear into the darkness of the trees. The Japanese don't dare follow them. Instead, they use their walkie-talkies to report to the troops at the top of the mountain that they have suffered a surprise attack by the enemy, and that, judging by their uniforms and equipment, they are troops from the regular Chinese army. In fact, what they have encountered are soldiers of the Heroic Anti-Japanese Resistance Army from Number Twelve Village of the Left Barracks. There were more than thirty of them, and they were all wearing the uniforms left behind by Commander Xiao and his men.

Just as the Japanese have recovered from their surprise, an explosion rocks the summit of the mountain, followed by a shock of flame. A moment later, the noise of the explosion rolls down the mountainside, flames shoot into the air, growing larger and larger, until half the pitch-black night sky turns fiery red. When the commander of the Japanese forces at Wanping County receives the report of this event, he immediately orders emergency reinforcements to be sent to Miaofengshan. The sentry posts west of the mountain suddenly appear deserted, and Commander Xiao and his men seize the opportunity to make a forced march through the night. By daybreak, they are already over the borders of Wanping County, and into Huailai County. Qi Yuexuan's ploy to lure the tiger out of its mountain lair to provide cover for a break-out has gone precisely to plan, and surprise has won the day.

But there is something Qi Yuexuan hasn't anticipated, and which takes him completely by surprise. Before the Japanese reinforcements have reached the top of the mountain, the main hall of the Palace of Insight is completely in ruins. Extraordinarily, the small garrison of Japanese on the mountain have been killed to a man, and even the men in the lookout post at the Cave of Favour and Relief, at the very top of the mountain, have not escaped. When a clean-up operation is mounted, not one single complete body is found, and the remains are all black and charred. Some of them have lost their human form and are just piles of broken body parts. One such pile shows the tattered remnants of Daoist robes, and the Japanese maintain that these are, indeed, the remains of Abbot Qinglu. No one can be certain of what exactly has happened here. The locals have many different opinions: some say that the government army has a huge cannon that it used to bombard the temple; others that the Japanese drank too much wine and self-combusted. Even more are of the opinion that the Queen of the Crimson Clouds manifested herself, and brought the thunder and lightning of the heavens crashing down. In the end, people propound whatever theory gives them the most satisfaction.

Although Qi Yuexuan himself cannot explain all the oddities of the event, the death of Abbot Qinglu does shock and grieve him, to the extent that he feels himself responsible, that it was he who set the abbot on the road to destruction. From this time on, he does not talk about the incident, and even in his declining years, if someone brings it up, he still feels the pain and replies only with silence.

After this, right up until the war is over, the Japanese never dare to occupy a Daoist temple again. The biannual temple fairs are banned, and they do not resume for eight years.

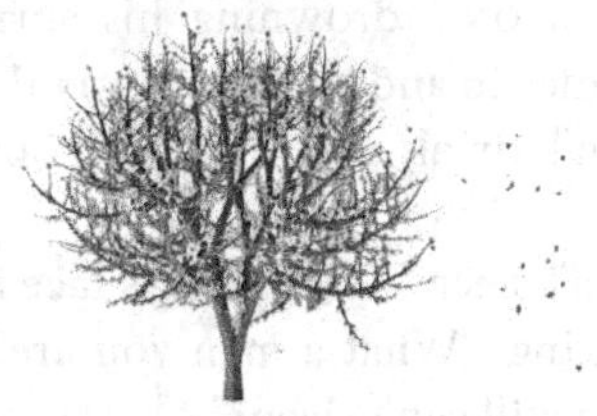

Chapter 16

Outwardly, Chenglong remains as fierce as ever. However, since receiving the warning from the Traitor Elimination Squad, he feels inside like a man alone on a road at night, who is startled and frightened by everything around him. He hasn't told anyone about the warning, but the same day, he increased his bodyguard squad by seven or eight men. During the day, a guard post is installed at the main gates and a sentry at the inner gates; at night, there is a man on patrol in the outer courtyard and a watchman in the inner courtyard. He has also brought in a Japanese wolfdog, which is chained on the veranda of the main building during the day and loosed to roam the Residence at night.

Over these last days, Yue E's heart has been broken by the things Chenglong has done. Before, she would complain that he was never at home, but now she longs for him to stay away, and as soon as she sees his face, her heart lurches and every tendon in her body tautens. That time when Yang Zhixing came back, he told his daughter that, if her husband got really bad, she and the children should flee to the Western Hills. But although Yue E is angry and exasperated with him, hates him even, she has been his wife for so many years and he is the father of her children, tied by flesh and sinew. So, for the moment, she cannot harden her heart enough actually to leave him. But now, with the arrival of this warning from the Traitor Elimination Squad, she sees a glimmer of light and a sliver of hope. She knows exactly what he is like, acting on the spur of the moment, then finding it hard to retreat. Of course, she also knows what he is thinking: once the skin of a drum is broken, no matter how hard you strike it, you'll get no sound. Looking at things through Chenglong's eyes, she can see a lack of confidence and fear that is most unusual for him, and this only serves to increase her satisfaction. Is there not a saying that he who does no wrong to others has no reason to fear the knock in the middle of the night? But then again, someone who goes crying for help because he's afraid of ghosts is clearly lacking in heart and open to fear. All this tells her that he is not completely lost yet, and may still be saved.

· · ·

Chenglong is sitting alone, drowning his sorrows, pouring one cup after another, when Yue E comes in and snatches away the bottle.

"That's enough. Don't drink any more. Or are you planning to drink all night?"

"Give it back! I... I can't sleep." Chenglong's face is flushed and sweaty.

Yue E's tone is mocking: "What a man you are! Guards patrolling outside, a dog on the loose and you still can't sleep?"

"Ai! I've... I've got things on my mind."

"Well, you've got a lot to think about. So you need to think, not drink any more. Take advantage of it while you're still sober, and do some serious thinking. If you wait until you've drunk yourself under the table, you're thinking won't be worth a fart."

Chenglong doesn't reply, just stares at her expressionlessly, puts his elbows on the table and cups his head in his hands. Seeing him like this, Yue E softly puts down the bottle, sits down herself and watches him silently. Of the two of them, one doesn't want to talk, and the other doesn't know where to start. Wanting to talk and not wanting to talk are the same – you turn the words over and over inside you, but nothing fresh comes out.

It is Yue E who breaks the silence, asking softly: "What are you going to do, Chenglong?"

"What am I going to do?"

"They told you, next time they'll be playing for keeps."

"Ha! I'm not scared."

"Still the hard arse? Have you got the nerve to say you're not quaking in your boots? They are outside in the dark, and you are here in the light..."

"Ha! But I have my own men out in the dark too. When you beat a wolf with a stick, there's fear on both sides. It just depends on who can bite the hardest or grip the strongest. Don't you get it? I'm a special agent now. I'm not some cop on street patrol, I'm on special duties."

"It doesn't matter what you are, you've only got one life. Is this cursed job worth dying for?"

"I think so, and what's new in that? How many times have I said that I'm like a tightrope walker between two mountains – if I don't keep going, how can I get down? If I fall and perish, it just means my death has come quicker."

"They didn't come after you with a gun or a knife, did they? They gave you a way out. Have you heard of that happening anywhere else in everything that's been going on? It's clear they don't see you as the same as those Japanese devils they've killed. If you ignore this opportunity, then you're just asking for it."

These words stop Chenglong in his tracks, and he considers them for a while, before saying in a low voice: "There is something in what you have just said. But you don't need to worry, I'm not stupid. If I've got two legs to run with, I'm not going to hop, am I? The Japanese aren't my father, so what's in it for me to wave the banner for them on my own? Still, I'm not yet sure exactly what their game is, so I need to give it some more thought."

Yue E finally relaxes a little and stands up, with a smile on her face: "Well I'm just happy we've got a couple of things straight this evening. Let's leave it at that. We've begun to see a little daylight today, and tomorrow we can look at things more closely. Now, get some sleep."

She goes over to the bed, pulls back the cover and begins to undo her buttons.

For most couples, such a domestic scene is commonplace, but it is something Chenglong hasn't experienced for a long time. He can't remember the last time the two of them shared a bed. Over the days, when he has not slept at his office, he has slept in Lian Yuxiang's place. If he has happened to come home at night, Yue E has disappeared like a ghost, leaving him a cold and lonely bed. Perhaps because of today's scare, or perhaps because he is flown with wine, but after one quick look, Chenglong finds himself rooted to the spot, a warmth spreading through his body, his eyes reddening and his heart in turmoil...

Yue E has just got under the covers, and as she has undressed to her underclothes, the cold of the quilt makes her shiver. She says with a reproachful laugh: "Well, are you coming to bed or not? You're not getting in here once I'm all warm and asleep."

Grinning foolishly, Chenglong hurries over to the bed, stripping his top half down to his undershirt. Then, just at this moment, as Chenglong's trousers are halfway off, the telephone in the outer room rings. Chenglong swears, and, not bothering with his belt, he clutches the trousers round his waist and leaves the bedroom. He picks up the receiver and snaps angrily, in a strangled tone: "Who is it?"

He hears Matsuzaki's voice: "You don't sound yourself, Mr Liu! Has the Traitor Elimination Squad's box of pastries put the wind up you?"

Chenglong is taken aback, as he has told no one apart from a few trusted confidants about this. Without giving him time to think, Matsuzaki goes on: "Of, course, since Mr Liu is still riding high, even they didn't dare go through with a real bomb."

Chenglong finds it hard to keep his cool. "Mr Matsuzaki, you... you mustn't..."

"Ha ha, I was only joking. I am just concerned for Mr Liu's safety and wanted to ask after you."

"Thank you. Thank you for your concern."

"There is something else I want to call to your attention."

"Please go on."

"When two armies face off against each other, the safest tactic is to attack and annihilate the opposition."

Matsuzaki speaks slowly, pausing between each word, hammering them home into Chenglong's trembling heart. Greatly flustered, he replies: "Yes, yes, I understand."

"Aren't you already on the track of the Traitor Elimination Squad? So when are you going to act?"

"Yes, yes I am on their trail. I can already say for certain that they are military intelligence men, and there are only a dozen or so of them. But the majority of them are hardened bandits. I've also ferreted out their base, which is in the grounds of Yanjing University. The thing is, they are on American territory, and I can't act against them there. All I can do is spread my nets outside the university and wait."

Matsuzaki grunts and says: "It's not that you can't do anything on American territory, you just can't leave any trace. Do you understand what I'm saying?"

Chenglong considers this for a moment, then says: "Ah, yes, I understand, I understand."

"Very well, go and get some sleep. Or maybe today's been too unnerving for that. Ha ha. Just put your mind on your work, and, if you need him, I'll send Yamaguchi to keep you company. Once you've got this matter all tied up, then you'll be able to sleep soundly."

It's only when he hangs up the telephone that Chenglong realises he is cold. He puts the phone down and hurries back into the bedroom and under the covers. No matter what Yue E asks him, he doesn't reply. He just curls up in Yue E's arms, shivering uncontrollably.

Yue E didn't hear any of what Matsuzaki said on the telephone, but she can guess its general import. From nowhere, a strange thought pops into her head: at this moment, Chenglong is like a pitiful child still dependent on his mother's breast. She doesn't ask any questions, she doesn't shrink away, she just holds him tight to her, sharing her warmth. Gradually, Chenglong's breathing begins to thicken, until, suddenly, he turns over, bringing his wine-laden breath close to her face, and he begins to paw frantically at her underclothes... but, on this evening, his usually impressive virility has deserted him. The two of them thrash round until they are covered in sweat, but to no avail. Yue E doesn't say anything, but Chenglong begins to berate himself, hissing through clenched teeth: "Fuck it! Does everyone think I'm a soft touch now?" He sits up abruptly and begins to get dressed.

"Are you crazy?" Yue E demands, not at all pleased.

Chenglong just ignores her and goes on talking to himself: "I'm no toothless pushover. If anyone tries to fuck with me, they'll find out just how sharp my teeth are. Hah!"

"And who is 'anybody'?"

"Anybody, everybody! Who cares?" Chenglong yells, eyes blazing.

He puts on his shoes, throws on his jacket and leaves the room. A moment later he can be heard making a telephone call: "Is that 071? This is Liu Chenglong. Get Number Two Team on duty immediately. That's right, I want my guard duty doubled for the next two days. Tell them that if they see anyone suspicious, they're not to wait for instructions, just arrest them on the spot. And if they resist, shoot them. If we don't use force when it's called for, we'll just look like weaklings. And another thing, send some men over to my house early tomorrow to install an electrical circuit, then move the whole unit over here...”

HAO BINGCHEN HAS BEEN WORKING in technology and communications for a long time now, and he is no great field operative. But he has spent many years in the military intelligence system, and he has developed quite a nose for danger. Over the last few days, a number of suspicious things have happened in the environs of the university that have put him on the alert. He knows their hidey-hole is already under observation, and exposure is only a matter of time. In fact, on the first day of his return to Beiping, he terminated all contact drop-offs and radio communications with the Traitor Elimination Squad. He did this because the first time he set eyes on Gao Guigeng and his men, he could see they were too amateurish. It didn’t matter that they were brave and had a few tricks up their sleeves; their bandit’s instincts were too strong, and it made them undisciplined, slack, reckless and headstrong, all major shortcomings in secret agents. Any one of these faults could bring about their undoing, and perhaps even annihilate the whole squad. Even though he is a special commissioner, these gangsters are not good at taking orders, to the extent that he has had to hold back quite a lot of information from them, and take more precautions. Not only does he not fully trust his subordinates, he has even less faith in his superiors.

The focus of the government’s defences is on the Yangtze Basin, and the elite sections of military intelligence have been transferred to the southern front, even though the war on the northern front is much more significant. The stations in Beiping and Taiyuan are both short of funds, and although a number of personnel are being transferred to maintain surveillance on the operations of the Communist Party, responsibility for the actions of the behind-the-lines Traitor Elimination Squad has been left in the hands of an academic and a bunch of bandits. Given the National Government’s disregard for Beiping and the whole of the rest of North China, it’s not hard to believe that, in time, they are going to abandon the whole area. Or perhaps their defence of the northern front is all just for show, and they have no intention of any serious engagement with the Japanese but instead are going to use it as a bargaining chip. It could even be that the united war of resistance is an unintended necessity, and keeping watch over and limiting the operations of the Communist Party is more important than resistance against the Japanese.

Hao Bingchen is no fledgling agent on his first mission, and he has experience of relations between Japan and China both at peace and at war, and of the constant swings between friendship and enmity of the Kuomintang and the Communist Party. He is very well aware of how the policymakers weigh up advantages and disadvantages. He also knows that, in the great scheme of the war between China and Japan, he and the Traitor Elimination Squad are very small fry indeed. What it comes down to is that the Traitor Elimination Squad is not going to have a huge influence on whether the war of resistance ends in victory or in another humiliating peace treaty. All he can do is promote the activities of the squad as far as possible, kill as many traitors as possible and in general be as big a threat as possible to the enemy. For all these reasons, he suggests that the squad withdraw from Yanjing University immediately and scatter into different hiding places in order to maintain their efficacy.

Gao Guigeng immediately flares up at this idea: "Do you really think it's good management to split us up? Let me remind you that, when I first joined this group of yours, there was just one condition – we live together, and we die together. So how is it that, as soon as you come along, you want to change the rules?"

Hao Bingchen controls his temper and says: "I'm only saying we should split up to go into hiding. We'll still have the same leadership, still be the same group. A bunch of a dozen or so of us all together is too big a target. Moreover, there are clear signs that you are being watched. Over the last few days, the campus water and electricity have been cut off, and there have been more and more suspicious characters hanging around outside. Who do you think they are after? If anything goes wrong, it could end up annihilating the whole army. Splitting up and going into hiding is all for your own safety."

"Safety? I think we're safest here. Even if the bastards are onto us, they can't do anything to us while we're on American territory."

"Do you really think the Japanese are going to be bound by international conventions? What they can't do openly, they can certainly do covertly. Whatever they do or don't do, they won't admit to anything."

"Who's supposed to be afraid of who, here? If we want to stop them coming against us, all the more reason to stick together."

"What is your mission? It's to root out Chinese traitors, not to risk your life with the Japanese."

"If we scatter and we're found out, they can pick us up piecemeal. Can you guarantee we won't be found out?"

"I'm a secret agent, not an insurance company. But I have chosen a few places that are all well hidden and secure, and they have proper cover stories. I've also got some back-up places you can relocate to if you're discovered. If the worst comes to the worst, we will be in a position to sacrifice a finger to save the arm."

"Alright, alright, I know you were born with a brush in your mouth and were suckled on ink, and I can't match your eloquence. But there is one quote I do know: 'A general in the field is not bound by orders from his ruler.' Have I got that right? In normal circumstances, I would have to show you respect because you've been sent here by the big bosses. But if we apply that quote to what we are doing, then we should be allowed to act as we wish, shouldn't we?"

Hao Bingchen's expression darkens, and he glares at Gao Guigeng. "I'm sure you are familiar with military intelligence rules, Captain Gui."

"Ha ha! Are you trying to browbeat me with rules? Isn't death the worst thing you can threaten us with? Well, get the lads in here and ask them one by one, and you'll discover there isn't one of them who hasn't already died several times. If you really think we have no regard for the rules, then ask the bosses to send some men here, and they can either kill us all or send us back to jail!"

Now Hao Bingchen finds himself at an impasse, as he runs into the brick wall of Gao Guigeng, who drives home his argument: "And do you lot obey the rules in what you do? When you arrived, you agreed there would be a bounty for every traitor we killed, on top of our salary. So you just count up how many of the devils we have killed, and tell me when you're going to settle the bill. This sort of blood money is not something you can hold on account."

This is all too much for Hao Bingchen. He slams his fist down on the table and sticks his finger in the other's face. "You lot are just a bunch of mercenaries. You don't care about anything except money."

Undaunted, Gao Guigeng yells back, even more fiercely: "And you think you bunch of misers are worth me giving my life for?"

"Then what are you doing it for? And don't try telling me it's for Party and country..."

"Ha! Don't give me any of that Party and country bullshit. I wouldn't fight for them if you gave me a mountain of gold!"

"Then..."

"Then what? Don't you get it?" Gao Guigeng gives a cold laugh. "Ha! I can tell by the way you're looking at me that you still think you're a real soldier, and we're just a bunch of bandits. Well, let me tell you, I haven't always been a bandit. Under the Great Qing dynasty I was an officer. I've lost count of how many people I have killed in my life, enough to give me nightmares, but all of them when I was a soldier. Great Qing, Republic, whatever party or country, they're all one in my eyes. They all treat their soldiers like wild dogs, and they even turn the common people against them. Is it really worth killing for them and risking one's life for them?"

"So you're not going to do it any more?"

"I'll still do it, but not for them. I don't give a fuck for country or whatever, I just don't want to see this place being taken by the Japanese."

It had never occurred to Hao Bingchen that Gao Guigeng could think like this, and it is as though he is seeing him for the first time.

"Of course, if you don't pay, I'm not going to go on," Gao continues. "Not for the money itself, but because I've earned it. I'm not like those officials who take the money and run away. Once I'm sure of the reward, I'll attack. An honest reward is honest money, and honest money can't be held back, it must be paid on the spot. If it isn't, then don't be surprised when I quit."

Hao Bingchen nods his head. "You're right. Don't worry, I'll ask for instructions immediately..."

"Pah! Ask for instructions, and we'll be waiting till the cows come home. I don't know about the others, but I need the money now."

"What... what do you need it for?"

"So my son can get married."

"So your son can get married? So, you have..."

"What are you gaping at? Aren't I allowed to have a son? And does my son have to be a lonely old bachelor like me?"

Hao Bingchen laughs. "Not at all, not at all. It's just the first I've heard of it. This is really important. So, er... how about this? Even though I'm really low on funds here, I'll squeeze out your share for you now."

"I'm very grateful for that," Gao Guigeng says, before heaving a sigh. "The boy has been without a mother since he was little, and I'm his father and have been away from home for more than ten years. Those years have been hard for him. But things are good now. This money is honestly earned and I don't have to be ashamed of using it."

Seeing the emotion in the man's face makes Hao Bingchen remember his own home, which he hasn't seen for so long, and the daughter he left there. At this moment, the two of them are just two homesick fathers.

"How old is your son?"

"He was born in the Year of the Ox."

"So just over thirty?"

"That's right."

"And you've never met your future daughter-in-law?"

"Last time I was out on a job, I caught a glimpse of her on my way back. She's beautiful. A son marrying late is a lucky thing, and she really is as pretty as a picture."

"Ha ha, excellent! And is your son out in the countryside?"

"No, in the city, in Minister's Residence Hutong."

"Minister's Residence Hutong?" Hao Bingchen looks at him in amazement, and the smile disappears from his face. Frowning slightly, he asks: "Doesn't Liu Chenglong live there too?"

"Yes."

"Are you... neighbours?"

"You could say that," Gao Guigeng says, avoiding Hao's eye.

Hao Bingchen looks at him more acutely: "So you... wouldn't want to take action against him?"

"Nonsense. Nothing like that."

"So why have you kept putting it off, time and time again?"

"I just want to push him into the background."

"That might do with someone else, but not him. He's the Japanese's blue-eyed boy. He's got to be a prime target."

"I thought he... he doesn't seem to be fully committed."

"What makes you say that?"

"Because," Gao Guigeng says evasively, "because he is Chinese not Japanese."

Hao Bingchen laughs incredulously. "You think that's a good reason? All the traitors are Chinese. If he was Japanese, he'd be a devil not a traitor."

"Then... why aren't we killing the devils and only killing traitors?" Gao Guigeng asks stubbornly.

"Who says we aren't killing devils? But our most important task is to kill traitors. The traitors who serve the Japanese are no better than dogs, and dogs should be killed, shouldn't they?"

"I didn't say they shouldn't be, but if you only kill the dogs, not their masters, isn't that just picking off the low-hanging fruit? And can we really exterminate the dogs? You kill the yellow ones, and you've still got the white ones. When the white ones are all gone, you can be sure some black ones will come along."

"Even if we can't kill them all, we can make them cower."

"Hah! You're just talking about frightening them. Are we supposed to be scaring them or killing them? A frightened dog just sticks closer to its master, doesn't it? If it's standing by its lair, wondering whether to go in or not, frightening it will just send it scuttling for shelter. If we really want to scare both master and dog, then we should go after the master first. If the master starts throwing his weight around, the dog will be scared, and if it can't trust its master, who will it follow then? If we kill the Japanese first, the traitors will immediately start pissing themselves with fear, and we won't need to kill them too. How about we keep the same arrangement, a bounty on every killing, but we concentrate on the Japanese, officers only, not ordinary soldiers. If you don't believe me, wait and see. It will surely be more effective than what we're doing now."

Hao Bingchen thinks there might be some merit in all this, but he doesn't dare be heard to agree: "Obeying orders is a soldier's duty, and military intelligence rules are to be observed, not questioned. We can't change the orders sent down to us, we can only follow them. Forget everything you have said today, and from now own, for heaven's sake keep your mouth shut. I too have my orders to follow, so don't embarrass me again."

Gao Guigeng doesn't reply.

"How about this? We'll compromise on the special operations. We'll stay at the university for the time being, but we'll have to spread ourselves round the campus. We can't stay together here, all in the same place. Tomorrow morning, we'll find ourselves hideouts. We can't compromise on the traitors, and everyone on the list has to stay there."

Gao Guigeng glares at him. "So why don't you make a move on Qi Yuexuan? He outranks Liu Chenglong."

Hao Bingchen is silent for a moment, then says: "Ah, him... he may not really be a traitor..."

"Hah! Didn't you just say everyone on the list has to stay there? Who is it we're supposed to take action against? The people you say, or the people the high-ups say?"

Hearing his own words turned back on him, Hao Bingchen has no reply.

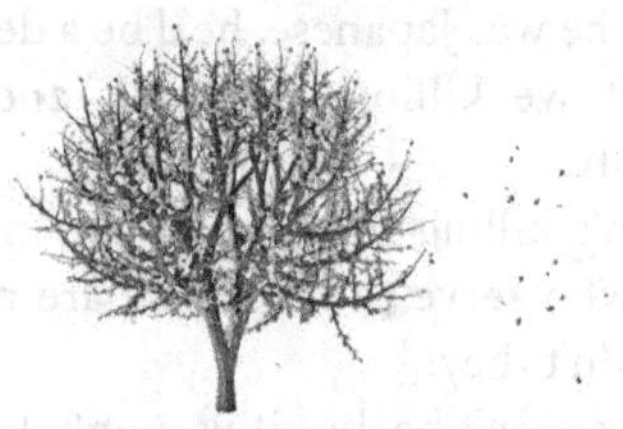

Chapter 17

Lao Zhang has spent half a lifetime raising crickets for a living, so it's not something he can give up easily. He has continued, no matter what the circumstances, to raise the crickets that live through the winter: long-horned grasshoppers, bell crickets and field crickets. These winter insects are bred in his own home and looked after very tenderly, but they are not as easy to care for as the autumn ones that are born and grow up in the wild. Their environment can't be too cold or too hot, too dry or too moist. They have to be kept out of draughts, but need a free flow of air; they can't go hungry, but should never be more than half full. They need particular care when they are changing from nymph to adult cricket: they have to be wrapped in a cotton quilt and kept in covered wicker baskets lined with hot common frogbit;[1] the soil has to be well-matured, and the water used to keep it moist must be warmed in the sun; then you have to monitor the temperature and moistness of the soil by touch. It's easy enough during the day, but the monitoring must be maintained through the night as well. If you nod off and don't keep your eye on them, then all your previous hard work is wasted. According to Lao Zhang, when he did this work as a boy, he used to go to sleep holding a lit incense stick, which would wake him up by burning his hand. Now he's been doing the job for so many years, he has long ago developed the ability to wake up as needed, and he no longer has to use an incense stick. In fact, this ability is more reliable than any alarm clock.

Previously, he has always kept his insects in the north building of the courtyard, but now the Young Master has returned to Laoqiying, he has to put them in the west building. Yang Zhixing still maintains the old customs by which the master sleeps in the main building and the servants sleep in the side rooms. But this small courtyard only has buildings on two sides, so he can't sleep in the main building, and he has to join Lao Zhang in the west building. The *kang* in there already has a dozen or more cricket baskets on it, leaving less than half the space free for the two men. So, old customs or not, the next day he takes his bed roll back to the north building.

"You're just money-mad, Lao Zhang. People haven't even got food to eat, so who's going to buy crickets?"

Unperturbed, Lao Zhang replies: "If anyone wants to buy them, I'll sell them, but otherwise I'll give them away. I'm not after money, I just want the crickets to have a few more days of life, however many or few. You mustn't be annoyed with the noise they make, because if you can hear them chirruping, at least you know you're still alive. One day, when you're lying in your grave, the crickets will gather round and sing to you, and you won't be able to hear them."

Yang Zhixing finds himself laughing in spite of himself, and Qi Yuexuan slaps his thigh and exclaims: "He's right, you know!"

They hear that there is another temple fair in the city. Lao Zhang checks his dates and sees that the next day is the fifteenth, so it must be at the Longfu Temple. After dinner, he asks the Young Master's permission to set off down the mountain in the small hours. The lining of his long jacket is already sewn with several rows of small pockets, all of which are stuffed with cricket cages, so the coat bulges out and makes him look as round as a ball. He makes good time and has already reached the city gates before it is light. At the gates he encounters the main ID card check, where his unusual attire raises the suspicion of the Japanese soldiers on guard. Fortunately, his quick tongue and the gift of a cricket help him avoid a thorough search.

When he arrives at the Longfu Temple market, the sky is just lightening, but all the good pitches have already been taken, and all he can do is squeeze in next to someone selling New Year prints. He has just got himself set up, when the print seller suddenly calls out: "Uncle Zhang!"

Lao Zhang turns to look, and, to his delight, sees it is Wangtian.

"Oh! It's you! Since when have you been messing around with temple markets? What's happened to your night soil route?"

"I sold it. I'm not doing that any more. Now I do odd jobs and sell these New Year prints at temple markets."

"Not a bad idea. It pays to be adaptable. Being a businessman, however small, beats lugging night soil around." He bends down to look at the prints laid out on the ground. "You've bought in good stock. These prints are really pretty."

"They're not bought in, I printed them myself."

"Ha! Is there no end to your talents? Did you carve the woodblocks yourself too?"

"I'm just the dogsbody, I don't know how to carve the blocks. They're..."

An old man selling birds next to them sees Wangtian's embarrassment and interrupts with a laugh: "His old woman carves the blocks. His household is all topsy-turvy. She's the one who wears the trousers."

Lao Zhang laughs. "Well just look at you, Wangtian! Where did you get such a talented wife?"

Wangtian is really embarrassed now. "It was nothing to do with me," he mumbles.

"You can't afford to hang around getting married at your age. You've been lucky to find a partner. If you hum and haw over it too long, you'll end up losing her."

"You're right. We have it all worked out. My wife's family all died a long time ago, leaving her an orphan with no one to fuss over doing things properly. We don't want anything big, just some food and wine, and everybody having a good time. I don't have any parents either, so I'm going to have to ask Uncle Yang to fix the day. The fair's still running tomorrow, so the day after that I'll go and find him."

"Good, that's the proper way to go about it."

"Then... will you go with me?"

"Yes, of course."

The market is all hustle and bustle, and when a CID street patrol arrives, wandering around looking for suspects, the busy market quietens down considerably. They continue to do this until breakfast is laid out on the hawkers' stalls, at which point their leader stops in front of a table where two middle-aged customers are seated, and he looks them up and down. These men are wearing sheepskin coats and hats, so they appear to come from beyond the Pass.

"Where are you two from?"

"Outside the Pass."

"Where outside the Pass?"

"Rehe."

"What are you doing here?"

"Business."

"Where are you staying in Beiping?"

"At the top of the street, in the Japanese Club."

"I didn't think Chinese could stay there."

At this point, the other man spits out a few sentences in Japanese, at which the CID captain's expression immediately changes to an ingratiating smile.

"I'm sorry, I'm sorry! Enjoy your meal, my lord."

Lao Zhang sees that Wangtian is still staring fixedly at the scene, and he asks: "What are you looking at? Nothing's going on."

Wangtian ignores him, and he keeps on looking. Sucking his teeth, he mutters to himself: "It's like him... very like him."

"Like who?"

"A friend."

"A Japanese? A friend?"

At this moment, the two men stand up, and the one who was speaking Chinese turns so that Wangtian can see him full-face. Wangtian's eyes light up and he blurts out: "It's him! It's Brother Zhicheng!"

His gaze follows the two men as they hurriedly disappear among the crowds, and only then does he stop staring and say to himself: "Ai! How is it that everyone has changed since the Japanese came?"

Standing beside him, Lao Zhang looks on uncomprehendingly.

. . .

WANGTIAN IS NOT MISTAKEN; it is indeed Zhang Zhicheng, and the man with him
is Zuo Xichuan.

Zuo Xichuan really had not wanted Zhang Zhicheng to accompany him to
Beiping. Secret service work is completely different from army work in that it
emphasises individual lines of communication and a vertical chain of command.
Only in exceptional circumstances is it permitted to establish horizontal lines of
communication. Zhang Zhicheng is a military cadre, with no experience of
undercover work, nor has he been part of the revolutionary army for very long,
so it would be inappropriate to use him as an accomplice. On the other hand,
Zhang Zhicheng's reason for wanting to go to Beiping is quite compelling, and it
would be difficult for anyone to refuse him.

Several months ago, when Zhang Zhicheng was leading a group of stragglers
and displaced soldiers north, away from Beiping, they came across an overturned
truck on the roadside at Weizikeng, beyond the Desheng Gate. It was piled high
with guns and ammunition, all in unopened packing cases. This can only be a
special munitions transport truck, whose driver got careless in the dark and put
it in the ditch. In a panic, he had left it unattended. Zhang Zhicheng couldn't
possibly leave it for the Japanese, but he only had a few dozen men, and couldn't
take it all away even though he wanted to. So apart from exchanging a few
weapons, and filling up their ammunition pouches, the best he could do was
unload most of the gear from the truck, stash it in a nearby depression and blow
up the sides of the depression, so it was completely hidden from view. He
carefully marked the spot, set fire to the truck, and hurried on to Rehe to join the
allied resistance. He can't give an exact inventory of the weapons and
ammunition, but he knows there were five or six cases of German-made light
machineguns, two to a case, so at least ten guns in all; ten or more cases of rifles,
eight to each large case and four to the small ones, so about seventy or eighty in
total. There were also thirty or forty cases of ammunition containing both bullets
and hand grenades. When the army had formed up and set off to the northwest
of Beiping, they were short of both weapons and ammunition. So it's hardly
surprising that, when Zhang Zhicheng said he was going back to Beiping to find
a wife, he wasn't looking for any betrothal gift when the bride came with a
dowry like this.

It was only after long consideration that Zuo Xichuan agreed to let Zhang
Zhicheng come with him. Even then, in order not to compromise his main
mission, he imposed three conditions: first, he has to wait for Zuo to complete
the most important business before he can move on his; second, if he's not sure
of success, he's not to act rashly, but wait for another opportunity; third, he has
to obey orders, and not act independently or make contact with any old friends
and acquaintances. Naturally, Zhang Zhicheng immediately agreed to these
conditions.

The two men have already been in Beiping for two days, and the evening before, made contact with their comrades from the northern office. They arrange a noon meeting at the Dongxinglou restaurant. With no business to conduct before that, and having risen very early and eaten breakfast at the temple market, they hail two rickshaws and head off for Weizikeng. They get out of the rickshaws quite some distance away. Zhang Zhicheng pays off the rickshaw men and leads Zuo Xichuan to a spot out of sight of any human habitation. In the distance is a large pool of water, from the recently frozen surface of which a few dried-up reeds still protrude. Closer to them, there is a large mound of earth. The wreck of the truck has already disappeared from the ditch beside the road, and there is no longer any sign of fresh earth. The collapse of one side of the slope, however, is still evident, and the mark cut with a knife into the bark of a young tree is also clearly visible.

Zhang Zhicheng breaks a branch off the tree and shoves it into the earth a few times. He squats down to prise out a flat slab of stone, digs down no more than a foot and reveals the planks of a packing case. Not daring to excavate any further in daylight, they hurriedly replace the earth. Nonetheless, they are relieved to find the goods are still there and haven't been discovered. What they have to think about now, is how best to excavate the stuff and transport it away.

On the return journey, Zuo Xichuan says: "Lao Zhang, this place is too close to the city, and it's going to be difficult to move such a large quantity of goods without being seen. From now on, this affair is your only priority, so forget about anything else. Come up with a plan as soon as possible, then we'll discuss things again. Given all the problems and risks, it's vital that we don't act precipitately."

"Ha! I can't afford to waste valuable time and let this opportunity slip. I've been thinking about this for so long, do you think I haven't got it all worked out?" Zhang Zhicheng begins to speak with great animation, and as soon as you hear him talking at such a pace, without even pausing for breath, you know it is a real obsession with him.

Zuo Xichuan nods. "I think that will be alright. But you mustn't pin all your hopes on the one plan – there must be a back-up. I didn't know your military affairs could be so complicated. No wonder you've been so quiet over the last few days, if you've been trying to work out how to make money out of this."

Zhang Zhixing laughs. "You and I can each do our own thinking for the moment, then come together to eat at the same table. You need to bear in mind that, whenever the high-ups call you to the table, that's when you've got to act. What I have to bear in mind is that, no matter when and no matter where, I've got to have the bowls and chopsticks ready, because we can't eat with our hands."

Zuo Xichuan giggles and is about to say something when their rickshaws arrive.

. . .

Clown has filled his first cartload of night soil and is pushing it back to the Liuji depot. Just as he is about to reach the main gates, he sees a woman walking up ahead. He can't see her face, but from behind, she is neatly dressed in bright-coloured clothes and her petite frame is shapely and well-proportioned. Clown can't resist the urge to exercise his wit:

> *Ai! Ai! Turn your face away and stand to one side,*
> *You don't want to dirty your nice clean clothes.*
> *How fierce we bachelor shit-shovellers are,*
> *We can't see a beautiful young girl.*

Hearing his clapper song, the girl steps aside to make room for him to pass, but she doesn't turn her face away. She even flashes him a smile. Clown sees that it is Lian Yuxiang, and he is momentarily flummoxed. It's been a long time since he has seen her. In the past, every few days he had found an excuse to go to her home, and even if they didn't exchange any words, at least he could catch a glimpse of her. Since she has been with Chenglong, other than in his dreams, he hasn't even had that treat. Bumping into her today, it seems to him that she is even more piercingly beautiful than before; more even than in his dreams.

"Brother Clown! Still as sharp-tongued as ever then?"

Clown blushes furiously, and lowers his head smiling foolishly.

Lian Yuxiang sees his embarrassment and says gently: "Ai! If only I could be like you, all would be well."

"Eh?" Clown is stumped.

Lian Yuxiang smiles faintly. "When times are hard, you're happy. When you're poor, you're also happy. How good it is to be so simple-minded."

So saying, she turns away and walks the few steps that take her through the main gate of the depot.

Clown mulls over her words, and the more he considers them, the less he likes what he thinks she is saying. He picks up his cart and hurries in after her. On catching up with her, he wants to strike up another conversation, but he doesn't know what to say. Every time he is face to face with Yuxiang, his normally glib tongue deserts him, and he becomes mute as a fish.

Yuxiang slows down and asks: "Is there something you want?"

"I... er, I just wanted to ask... how you are," Clown finally manages to stammer out.

Yuxiang's face doesn't show any emotion. "I've got food to eat, clothes to wear, money to spend. I also have a rope to drag me by, a cage to shut me in and fingers to point at me. I don't know whether that means I'm well or not."

When she sees that Clown is lost for words, she goes on: "Well or not, it's my fate, and no one can fight against fate."

What she says makes Clown's heart ache, but no words come out.

At this moment, they hear Sergeant Lian yelling: "Hey there, you! Just because you've seen a girl doesn't mean you have to stop. There's no time for chatter, just hurry up and get your load of shit inside."

With Yuxiang there, Clown doesn't dare answer him back. He just glares at him and pushes his cart over to the cess pond. Sergeant Lian goes over to stand in front of Yuxiang, and says, with cloying solicitude: "Aiyo, my little lady, did you just go to see the doctor? What are you doing here when you should be going home to lie down?"

Yuxiang pulls him to one side and whispers something. Sergeant Lian laughs when he hears it: "Such good news! Now you've really got it made, Yuxiang..."

"Shh, not so loud!"

"Is it a secret? If you wait... Aiyo!" He yelps as Yuxiang pinches him.

Having deposited his load, Clown is still stealing glances at her, and when he sees her whispering, and looking worried, his curiosity is roused. He also sees Sergeant Lian shaking his head, reducing Yuxiang to tears, as her voice gradually rises: "Are you my father or not? If you don't do it, who will?"

"Huh! Can't you wait till he comes home?"

"How long has he been away already? We can't wait for that. I can't go brazenly into the Minister's Residence myself. Are you trying to shame me to death?"

"Alright, alright, alright, I'll go. I haven't got time this morning, but I'll go in the afternoon, alright? But I don't mind telling you, it's making me fucking nervous."

BY THIS TIME, the Minister's Residence has pretty much become a *yamen*,[2] as Chenglong has moved his entire 'Special Action Group' over there. The south range and the two side buildings of the eastern side courtyard have proved insufficient, so they have also taken over the whole entrance courtyard. Although they haven't put up any kind of sign, what with the electric wires running over the walls, the motorcycles in the courtyard and the sentries at the gate, there's no need to ask: everyone knows exactly what is going on here. All of this gives Chenglong a little more peace of mind, but it's too much for Yue E. She is bitterly disappointed, but she's not inclined to argue any more, telling him just to do what he wants. In a fit of pique, she decides to go with the children to the Western Hills, but Mother Yan dissuades her.

"If you don't want to be watched, there are still bits of the Residence he doesn't have control over."

Yue E sees her point, and she and the children move into the western side courtyard. With Mother Yan there, it's really like moving back into her family home.

Sergeant Lian arrives in front of the Minister's Residence carrying a box of pastries and a basket of fruit. Luckily for him, he says he wants to see the mistress of the house, so the guard at the gates doesn't bother to search him and his belongings, but just tells the porter to take him to the western side courtyard. If he had said he was looking for the Young Master, he would have had a lot more bother.

Yue E is taken by surprise when she sees Sergeant Lian appear, and she says hurriedly: "I don't have anything to do with affairs at the depot. If there's a problem, go over to the east courtyard and find Boss Liu there."

"I'm not looking for Master Liu," says Sergeant Lian, smiling ingratiatingly. "I've come specially to see you today, mistress." He puts the gifts down on the table.

"Why do you want to see me?"

"Ha ha, ah well, it's nothing much, I just want your permission for something."

"Then you'd better sit down."

Smiling even more, Sergeant Lian says: "The thing is... it's Yuxiang. She's pregnant."

Yue E is stunned into silence by this announcement, but Mother Yan immediately flares up: "Hah! You're a fine piece of work! What's it got to do with my daughter whether the girl's pregnant or not? Have you come here on purpose, just to annoy people? Take your sorry tale over to the other courtyard and tell it to Liu Chenglong!"

"Don't be angry, old mistress. It was Yuxiang who told me to come and find Mistress Yang."

"I don't care who told you to come, take your things and go. If you..."

Before Mother Yan can finish, she is interrupted by Yue E: "Let's hear what he has to say first."

Sergeant Lian starts his tale again: "Mistress, Yuxiang said that even a river in flood can't swamp a mountain. However you look at it, you have the place of honour and respect here. Of course, any fault lies absolutely with her. She just begs you to consider the status of the child she is carrying, and show some magnanimity by allowing her to become part of the Liu family."

Yue E gives a wry laugh. "Ha! You really overestimate my importance. There's no point in coming to me with something like this. Let me make it clear – if he wants to set up an imperial harem and take seventy-two concubines, there's nothing I can do to stop him. He can do what he likes. Alright?"

"But Master Liu... he won't discuss it."

"If he won't discuss it, why on earth should I?"

"But you are the mistress of the household..."

"I'm his wife, not his mother."

"Maybe so, but you're still in a better position than us!"

Mother Yan's anger flares again, and she tries to stop any further discussion. "So we have to do your pleading for you, do we? Why should we? Go and find whoever's responsible. We weren't the ones who sent her to work in someone else house. It's got nothing to do with us. You're Yuxiang's father, aren't you? It's your job to talk to Master Liu. If your daughter's being mistreated, why are you acting like some kind of servant? Grow some balls! I don't have a gun here, but I've got a vegetable knife. Take that with you and go and find him. If he agrees to what you want, all well and good. If he doesn't, then you should fight him for it."

Sergeant Lian lets her shout herself out until she is only moaning and mumbling to herself. Seeing his distress, Yue E softens her tone a little. "Lao Lian, I have watched Yuxiang grow up. Her life hasn't been easy. I know she is not to blame for this."

Sergeant Lian perks up again when he hears this, and he immediately follows it up: "That's right, you're right. Yuxiang has always remembered your kindness, otherwise she wouldn't have asked me to come here now. You have to help her with this."

"Does the Liu family really inspire such affection in people?" Yue E asks. "Who? Where? Why? Yuxiang is still young, and as her father, don't you have to stop and think? What do you want for her? Money? Influence? Even if you have them, how reliable are they? If they are dishonestly come by, they will be blown away by the wind and washed away by the water. You need to be very sure not to ruin your child's life just for some temporary advantage."

Sergeant Lian understands what's behind these words, but he has always been a man who only thinks of today, and lets tomorrow look after itself. This is especially true in the current circumstances, as he is confident Chenglong's future is particularly bright.

"With things as they are, what's the use of being sure of anything? Anyway, anything is better than worrying so much you can't eat and starving to death! Do you..."

"It doesn't matter whether we're talking about the current circumstances or not, it's not up to me," says Yue E. "You've got to talk to Chenglong about this. I can back you up, but even if he listens to me, his brother Wangtian won't get involved, the Minister's Residence won't want any part of such shenanigans, and I'm certainly not going running to my father. The Japanese are in charge now, and my husband calls himself their Number Two, so he's not going to listen to anyone. Anyway, he hasn't definitely said he won't take Yuxiang as his concubine. Now she's carrying his child, he's bound to take her into the family."

"Right, yes, yes!" Sergeant Lian nods eagerly.

Yue E thinks for a moment, then says: "How about this? You don't go over there either. This is a matter where his honour is at stake, and we don't want to turn it into something where he feels he's the outsider, losing face. I'll call him over here, so it's more like neutral territory. Will that do?"

"Very well, seeing how things are."

Yue E sends her daughter, Liangxin, over to fetch her father, and to tell him there's something really urgent and exciting to discuss. It's not long before she returns, with her father in tow. He is all smiles when he comes into the courtyard, but, as soon as he enters the room and sees Sergeant Lian, the smiles disappear.

"Is it you who's looking for me?"

Sergeant Lian just smiles ingratiatingly and looks to Yue E.

"No, it's me who called you over," says Yue E, laughing. "Lao Lian has come to give you some good news."

"Yes, it's Yuxiang..."

As soon as Chenglong hears the name 'Yuxiang', Chenglong cuts him short and spits out: "We'll talk about it outside."

Before Sergeant Lian can gather his thoughts, he finds himself grabbed by Chenglong and bundled out of the door, speechless. Yue E is worried by this and makes to follow them, but Mother Yan holds her back. After a moment, she says: "What do you think you're up to? I've seen some stupid people in my time, but you take the biscuit."

Once Chenglong has dragged Sergeant Lian out of the western side courtyard, he lets go and glares at him.

"What's so fucking important you had to come to my home?"

"Aiyo! It's... it's Yuxiang... she's expecting."

A fleeting expression of delight crosses Chenglong's face when he hears this, and Sergeant Lian is quick to pounce on it. "We only found out this morning, and I came straight over to tell you the good news."

To his surprise, the smile disappears from Chenglong's face, and he's looking very serious. He sees Chenglong take a banknote from his jacket and hand it to him. He has still been a bit apprehensive up to this point, but as soon as he sees the money, his face lights up and he reaches his hand out for it quicker than Chenglong can give it. Then he hears Chenglong say: "I can't be doing with this now. Take this money, and hurry up and take her to get rid of the baby."

Sergeant Lian can't believe his ears. "What? Get rid of it? Your own flesh and blood!"

Chenglong smiles coldly: "My own flesh and blood? How do I know that Japanese isn't the father?"

"Ah... Oh... well, we counted the days and they work out... the doctor says..."

"Crap! Is everyone in Beiping a doctor now? Who lent you their fingers to count the days?"

"It's true..."

"How do you know it's true or false? Listen to the gossips and backbiters, and they'll tell you that false is true and true is false. I'm not going to have my reputation trashed like this. Do you understand? Right, now go and buy her something to build her strength."

With this, Chenglong turns away and is about to leave, but Sergeant Lian pulls him back.

"What do you think you're doing?" Chenglong asks impatiently.

Sergeant Lian picks his words carefully: "When... er... when do you think you can take Yuxiang into the family?"

"We'll talk about it afterwards," Chenglong replies carelessly.

Steeling himself, Sergeant Lian asks: "Master Liu, you say we should get rid of this baby, and I agree. But you must still give Yuxiang some proper status. The mistress there agreed, so why are you being so cagey? I know you cherish my daughter, and she is devoted to you..."

"I said we'll talk about it afterwards. What's wrong with that?" Chenglong glares at him.

Although Sergeant Lian doesn't dare meet his gaze, he keeps his own eyes steady, and says resolutely: "You talk about your face and reputation, Master Liu, but surely you have to leave us some too. So how about this instead? If this is all too bothersome for you, then release Yuxiang, and I'll pay whatever compensation you want. I'll marry Yuxiang off to someone else..."

Chenglong smiles frostily and says through gritted teeth: "As if you'd dare!"

"Master Liu," Sergeant Lian almost sobs, "if you won't marry her, and won't let her go, then... then where does that leave us?"

"Where does it leave you? Ha! Do you want me to spell it out for you? If you're tired of the easy life you've been living, then just keep trying to force me to take Yuxiang in, and don't be surprised if I show no mercy. You want to live off the fat of the land? Well, let me make it quite clear, I can be really mean, and I'll have my eye on you. You can try to marry her off, but no one will dare marry her. So get your position clear in your head, and fuck off. You just do as I tell you, if you don't want me to really lose my temper."

These words seem to stun Sergeant Lian, and all he can do is stare foolishly.

At this point, Zhou Si appears. "There's been someone in the office asking for you, Junior Master," he says.

"Who is it?"

Zhou Si is uncomfortable talking in front of Sergeant Lian, so he whispers in Chenglong's ear. Chenglong gives a start: "What's he doing back here?"

"I'm told he's a trader now. He's staying at the Japanese Club in Dongsi."

"And?"

"When he saw you weren't there, he said he had something to do this afternoon, and he left. He told me to tell you to meet him this evening at the Tiancheng restaurant, and that I should come too."

Chenglong considers this in silence, a deep frown on his forehead. He looks up and sees that Sergeant Lian is still there, and he glares at him angrily.

"Why haven't you gone home yet? Do you think you live here?"

Sergeant Lian finally comes out of his daze, and he hurriedly slips away.

Chenglong turns back to Zhou Si. "Did he really say he was staying at the Japanese Club? Go and sound things out quietly, so I'll have some idea of what's going on when we meet."

"Got you. I'm on my way."

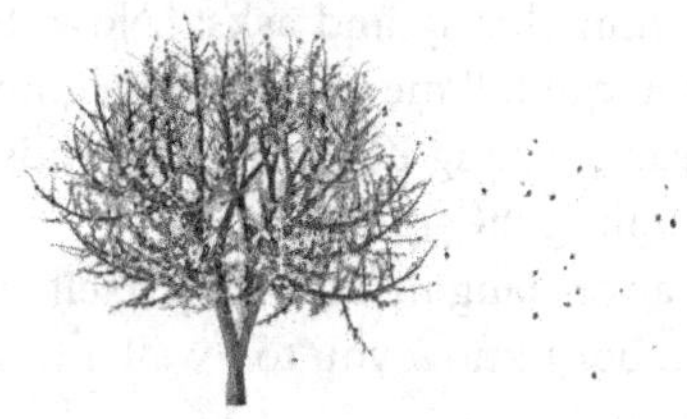

Chapter 18

When Chenglong and Zhou Si arrive at the Tiancheng restaurant, a waiter immediately leads them up to a private room on the second floor, where Zhang Zhicheng and Zuo Xichuan are sitting at a table waiting for them. Chenglong and Zhang Zhicheng grew up together from when they were very little, but they haven't seen each other for some years, so there is much exchange of greetings and enquiries. Without waiting to be asked, Zhang Zhicheng launches straight into how he got separated from the main army; how he knew the Japanese merchant Shoi Keisen; how he has been trading beyond the Pass; and how they have come to Beiping together to replenish their stock. Chenglong can't spot any hole in Zhang Zhicheng's story, and it corresponds with what Zhou Si has found out. But, while he can't put his finger on why, he finds himself only half believing it.

When the wine has been round a few times, Zuo Xichuan smiles at Chenglong and says: "I'm not familiar with business in Beiping, Captain Liu. I asked Zhang-san to lead the way this time, but next time I couldn't do better than ask for your help."

"Although this is the first time we have met, Mr Shoi, I feel like we're old friends already," Chenglong replies immediately. "Brother Zhicheng and I were childhood friends in the same village, and we're members of the same society, friends for life. All you have to do is ask, and I'll do whatever is within my power. If business is good, you can give me a small commission. Let's have another drink."

After a few more rounds of wine, Zuo Xichuan stands up and says: "I must make my excuses, Captain Liu. I have a social engagement this evening at the North China Army Division HQ, and I must make a move now. I'll let Zhang-san sort out the business details with you, and we'll meet up again next time."

"That's fine, please do leave if you have to." Chenglong also gets to his feet, and he orders Zhou Si: "Get the car, and take Mr Shoi wherever he needs to go."

Zhou Si, who knows what's behind this order, acknowledges it immediately and leaves the room with Zuo Xichuan. Chenglong pours Zhang Zhicheng some more wine, looks at him closely and asks: "Now it's just the two of us, Brother Zhicheng, perhaps you can tell me what's really going on."

"What do you mean?" Zhang Zhicheng responds, sipping some wine. "Do you think I haven't been telling the truth?"

Chenglong gives a wry laugh. "The story itself is good enough, and I'd believe it from someone else, but I know you too well. I think your story's a front. I can't see you being so devious."

Zhang Zhicheng sighs. "Ai! I'm not surprised you're suspicious. A year and a half ago, I would have been surprised at myself too. But once the army's got its hands on you, what's the use of looking back? What is more, I'm scared as well..."

"Pah! How can you be scared? You've always been braver than anyone I know."

"Ha! Well, times change. What about you? Are you fighting fit? Other than Third Brother Shen, have you killed any Japanese? Now you're head of the CID, and living the good life, aren't I allowed to help someone run a few scams for a little hard-earned cash?"

Chenglong lets him stew for a while without speaking, then he takes a big gulp of wine and says: "You said you wanted to join the Allied Resistance in Rehe, so could it be..."

"I said a lot of things. I've been looking for a wife since I was eighteen, but I'm not married yet. And when I think about resistance, it's not resistance against the Japanese, it's resistance against the high-ups."

Chenglong gives a shout of laughter: "I didn't mean anything by what I said, I just felt you were shutting me out a bit. Our friendship goes back to our fathers, so why can't we be straight with each other?"

"Straight about what?" Zhang Zhicheng asks, but when Chenglong doesn't reply and just sits there staring at him with a half-smile on his face, he drinks an entire cup of wine and takes a certificate and several other pieces of paper out of his inside pocket. He puts them down on the table and points at them.

"This is my certificate of good citizenship, and that is the official seal of Manchukuo. There's also a pass for the checkpoints. Take a good look at them. Mr Shoi is persona grata in Rehe, and I'm not exactly without my own reputation either."

"Pick them up, I'm not going to look at them. What use are those tatty bits of paper to me?"

"Tatty bits of paper? Those are the seals of Manchukuo and the Kwantung Army!"

"So what? Anyone could forge them with half a radish."

Zhang Zhicheng stares at him in amazement and leaps to his feet. Startled, but always alert, Chenglong's hand unconsciously reaches for the holster on his belt. Zhang Zhicheng just laughs.

"You're very jumpy. It's seems your courage hasn't kept pace with your cunning. If I wanted to attack you, do you think I'd let you draw your weapon?"

Embarrassed, Chenglong withdraws his hand.

"Ha! Well, from what you say, we brothers..."

"Forget the 'brother' stuff," Zhang Zhicheng interrupts him. "Just what's your game, Captain Liu? It's up to you to convince me. Aren't you tired of all this going round the houses? So tell me straight, what exactly do you want with me? Tell me and I'll accept it. Alright? Let's forget this stinking wine. Go! Go to the authorities, but will you go to that *yamen* of yours, or to the Kempeitai?"

Seeing that he's serious, Chenglong smiles placatingly. "Calm down, calm down! You're not really angry are you? Can't you take a joke?" He pulls Zhang Zhicheng back down into his seat. "I just didn't think that trade was one of your strong points, Brother Zhicheng. It's a real pity that your martial talents are being wasted. I need people like you here at the moment, so how about you stay and help me?"

"No, I won't do it," Zhang Zhicheng replies bluntly. "It's no use glaring at me. If I stop now and pull back from the fighting, I'll lose all my contacts. I'm not worried about losing out on the money or the business opportunities, but it's more important than anything else that I make a few more trips. As for you, you need to listen to me. This filthy job you're doing is no way to earn a living. If you sell your soul, there's no going back. One way or another, you need a trick or two up your sleeve, you need to leave yourself a way out."

Chenglong grunts and nods, then asks: "What are you hoping to take back with you, this trip?"

"Ha! There's no sure business to be done this year, so anything I can lay my hands on."

"For example?"

"Well, cloth, for example, coarse or fine, it doesn't matter. Dark colours, but no patterns... best of all, plain, undyed cloth. Cotton's good too, lint and gauze..."

"Plain cloth and cotton are both prohibited goods."

"I know that." Zheng Zhicheng laughs without humour. "At the moment, everything profitable is prohibited. I could take a cartload of cabbages back, but I wouldn't earn enough to pay the porter. Anyway, these prohibitions are graded – plain cloth and cotton are done by quantity, and it's only going over the limit that's prohibited. But if you can't trade in iron, or copper and weapons, how much can you actually earn? Then again, if you've got connections to get round the regulations, and can spread a little money, who isn't going to turn a blind eye? Suppose you're on a route where you don't have any connections, and you chance upon sticklers for observing those kinds of prohibitions. The worst that's going to happen is that you won't get all your goods through, and you'll pay a few fines. You may be detained for a few days before they let you go on, but your life's never going to be in danger. I won't touch the most prohibited goods, because no money is worth losing my head for. But if they're trifling prohibitions that can be overcome by bending the rules a little, that's some kind of business isn't it? And at least I'll get home to hold my child again."

"Yes, you're right," Chenglong nods. "So are you going to let me help you?"

"That's the idea. But if you help smooth my way, I'll help you earn some money for nothing. I don't need you to source the merchandise, I just need you to arrange for me to get the stuff safely through the checkpoints."

Chenglong is tempted, but he remains suspicious, and he silently weighs up the options. Seeing his hesitation, Zhang Zhicheng says: "You don't need to worry. We're not trying to put you in an impossible position. Do you think Mr Shoi doesn't have a few tricks up his sleeve himself? It's just that he's too important to bother with trifles like this. Anyway, it's not that important. Even the Japanese are in on this, as is anyone with a bit of capital who's not too fussy about the rules, so there's no danger of a shortage of willing volunteers."

"I haven't said I wouldn't do it. But... I have to see the goods first, just to set my mind at rest."

"That's not a problem."

"So how much am I going to make?"

"Depending on the cost of the stock, twelve per cent."

"That's too little. I've got to bribe the Kempeitai, so it has to be twenty per cent."

"I can't do twenty per cent. You can have some of my share, and I'll go to fifteen per cent."

"It's not worth my while for less than twenty."

Zhang Zhicheng begins to get frustrated: "These goods are Mr Shoi's, I'm just picking up a little extra cash by helping. I'm getting twenty per cent in total – if I give it all to you, I'll starve. So be it. If you won't do it, I'll find someone else."

"Enough, Brother Zhicheng! Listen to you quibbling with me over such a small amount. Maybe you are a proper businessman after all. Alright, just for a bit of peace and quiet, fifteen per cent it is."

Zhang Zhicheng picks up on the undertone of what Chenglong says, and he bursts into genuine laughter.

CLOWN HAS UNLOADED his last collection and is pulling his cart homewards, although home is perhaps the wrong word as it is in fact just a place to sleep in. He and two other single young men rent a small room in a large courtyard to the west of the Drum Tower. On his way there now, he is feeling rather apprehensive. That afternoon, when Sergeant Lian came back to the depot, he had a face like a frostbitten aubergine. Normally he is a high-handed manager, dismissive of other people, but today he resembles a sulky young girl. Remembering that Yuxiang had come looking for her father in the morning, Clown knows something serious must be up with her. He doesn't know the details, but he's quite sure that it has something to do with Chenglong. Normally, he and Sergeant Lian avoid talking to each other, and now he wants to ask but the words won't come out.

But, he tells himself, even if you can steel yourself to ask, is he going to talk to you? Who are you anyway? If she really is in trouble, what can a wretched thing like you do to help?

He sees himself quite clearly for what he is, but he still can't stop worrying about her. So after he has gone in through the Desheng Gate, he doesn't head east towards home, but keeps going south. He has decided to go to the Lian house and eavesdrop at the doorway. If there's no commotion, he can stop worrying.

As he turns into the narrow hutong, he sees someone else hurrying out of it. It's dark and at first he can't make out who it is, but as he gets closer, he sees it is Sergeant Lian.

"Clown? Ai! Did you... did you see Yuxiang coming out here?"

"No. Why? What's up?"

"She threw a tantrum and ran out on us. I only stopped to put on my shoes, and now there's no sign of her."

"We'd better check both ends of the hutong."

"Yes! Yes!" Sergeant Lian turns to scurry off.

"What's happened?" Clown asks.

"It's... Aiya! I can't bring myself to talk about it. Let's find her first, and hope that we're not too late and only find her corpse."

Clown's heart lurches as he puts down his cart and follows Sergeant Lian, saying: "You go to the east end, and I'll go to the south, then look for her along the Houhai. Don't search blindly, ask anyone you see."

Twisting and turning through the narrow hutongs, all he sees are trees and telegraph poles. There's not a single person in sight. As he reaches the shores of the Houhai, he finally spots a rickshaw man and his rickshaw.

"Hey there, brother," Clown calls out to the man.

Thinking he's got a fare, the man pulls his carriage over and asks: "Where to?"

"Ah, sorry to bother you, but have you seen a young girl go past?"

"Aiya! I've seen a lot of girls."

"This one's eighteen or nineteen, well-dressed and very pretty."

"I haven't been paying that much attention."

Disappointed, Clown is about to go, when someone startles him by appearing suddenly from a passageway. Recovering from his surprise, he sees it is a young beggar boy.

"Hey, are you talking about the Lian girl?"

"Yes... do you know her?"

"Of course I know her, she's been bringing me a dish of her leftovers for the last two years. I just saw her, but she didn't see me. I kept calling out to her, but she didn't answer."

"Where was she heading?"

"That way, along the shore of the lake." The little beggar points with his finger in the direction he means, then suddenly freezes. "Ai! Look! There's someone on the ice!"

Clown follows his finger, and sure enough, a shadowy figure can be seen shuffling along, far away on the ice. His stomach turns over for a moment, then he breaks into a run towards the banks of the lake. The beggar boy pulls him back: "You're too big. The ice won't support you."

Clown looks more closely and sees that the ice is indeed not yet fully formed, and the middle of the lake is still moving water. All he can do is stop and shout as loud as he can: "Yuxiang! Yuxiang! Stand still!"

The beggar boy joins in too.

But the figure on the lake doesn't reply, and just keeps on shuffling forward. Clown looks around in panic, then grabs hold of a branch of one of the willow trees that line the lake, and pulls with all his might. There is a sharp crack, and the big branch snaps off. Carrying it, Clown climbs down onto the ice, but after only a few steps, there is an ominous creaking sound from the ice.

"Stop! It won't hold!" the little beggar shouts from the bank.

Clown ignores him, and slips and slides as fast as he can towards the middle of the lake, shouting all the time. Yuxiang hears his shouts and sees him following her, but she shows no sign of stopping.

"Yuxiang! Don't be crazy!" Clown shouts himself hoarse.

Yuxiang slowly turns around, and seeing Clown's reckless look, shouts back: "Don't go any further."

The two of them are quite close now, and the howling of the wind and the terrifying creaking of the ice are enough to freeze the blood.

Clown steadies his feet, collects his wits and says carefully: "Whatever you do, don't move, Yuxiang. I'm coming over..."

"Don't!" Yuxiang cries, her voice full of tears. "Whether I die or not has got nothing to do with you. My life isn't worth living any more. Forget me."

"Yuxiang, there's no trouble in life we can't overcome."

"No, it's too much. I'm tired of life."

"You're only eighteen, don't be so foolish."

"I'm a fool. How else could I have shamed myself like this?"

"But if you want to get rid of that shame, you have to keep living."

"Keep living? To let people hate me? To let people curse me? To let people laugh at me behind my back?"

"Old women's talk! I'll take on anyone who doesn't treat you fairly. You've been deceived, taken advantage of, made to suffer, but heaven has eyes, and people can judge for themselves, and know that you are a good person. Come back and start your life again."

Clown's words are all the more forceful because he has suppressed them for so long, and Yuxiang listens in silence, shivering in the icy wind. Suddenly her voice rises in a heart-rending wail.

Clown heaves a sigh of relief and says hurriedly: "Don't cry. Quickly now, lie down and grab hold of this branch."

Yuxiang has just got hold of the branch, when there is a rending sound from the ice between them, and it splits open. Yuxiang's body tips forward, but Clown is quick enough to reach out a hand and catch hold of her clothes. Nonetheless, the bottom half of her body has already slipped into the water.

"Hold onto my hand. Don't let go!" Clown says, lying down on the ice. Using all his strength, he hauls her out of the water, and up onto the ice. But just at this moment, the ice all around them begins to groan and slowly split open.

"Stay as still as you can and don't move!" he shouts.

The two of them lie side by side on the ice, motionless and holding their breath. Gradually the groaning of the ice subsides, then stops completely. Only then does Clown slowly attempts to stand up. Yuxiang tries to say something, but she is shivering too much to get the words out. She just points, soundlessly, towards the banks of the lake. Clown understands, but instead of standing up, he wraps her in a tight embrace, and starts to roll, slipping and sliding, across the ice.

The spectators standing on the bank scramble the two of them out of the water. Yuxiang has fainted from fright and from the cold, and when Clown sees her in this state, his relief at getting out turns to alarm. He scrambles to his feet and reaches out a hand to feel for her breathing. Then he shouts to the bystanders: "Quick, give me a hand." And he tries to pick her up and put her over his shoulder.

"Stop! Stop!" Sergeant Lian yelps, anxiously. "You can't carry her like that!"

"Why not?"

"She's pregnant."

Clown's mind suddenly goes blank, and he freezes, as a shard of ice pierces his heart.

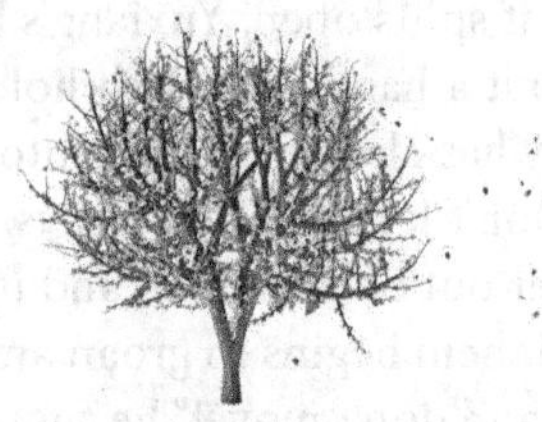

Chapter 19

Wangtian sets out even earlier than usual for the last day of the Longfu Temple fair. He has just left the narrow hutong, carrying his roll of prints, when a rickshaw comes up behind him.

"Is your name Gao, sir?" the rickshaw man asks when he is close enough.

"It is."

"Do you sell New Year prints?"

"Yes."

"Then you're the man I'm looking for. Please get in."

"No thanks. It's no distance. I..."

"There's no charge, the fare's already been paid. Don't worry. Someone who wants to buy your prints has sent me to get you. Where else are you going to find someone who wants to buy your entire stock? Why hesitate?"

Without any further explanation forthcoming, Wangtian gets into the rickshaw, but he can't help asking: "Where are we going?"

"You'll know when we get there. Just sit back and enjoy the ride." The rickshaw man picks up his poles and sets off at a steady trot.

Wangtian is still uneasy as he sits in the rickshaw, and as he watches the rain and hail, he reflects that, as far as he knows, there's no such thing as a free lunch. Still, he reckons kidnappers and blackmailers usually target those with money, so who'd pick a penniless fellow like him? And human traffickers only want pretty young girls, so what would they be doing with a hulking great bearded fellow like him? Quite soon, the rickshaw stops outside the doors of the Tianjiang tea house, and the rickshaw man leads him up to a private room on the second floor. Zhang Zhicheng stands up, smiling, as he sees Wangtian enter the room.

"Why are you looking so surprised, Wangtian? It's really me."

Wangtian had never expected to see this man, this brother, who had inspired such admiration in him, and he is about to step forward to greet him warmly. But then he remembers how he had seen him yesterday, at the temple market, deep in conversation with a Japanese, and his heart lurches.

Seeing his hesitation, Zhang Zhicheng says with a smile: "What's this? Are you cross with me for not saying hello to you yesterday?"

"You saw me yesterday?"

"Well, if you saw me, aren't I allowed to see you too? I walked past your stall, then went on to have breakfast. You were busy talking to a couple of old chaps about finding a wife. Didn't you notice me?"

"But you didn't..."

"Ah, well, I had a lot on yesterday, and I didn't have the time."

"You mean you didn't have the time to greet a poor Chinese friend in front of a rich Japanese businessman?"

Zhang Zhicheng just smiles at Wangtian's mockery, and he says: "I'm afraid you're doing me an injustice, if that's what you think." He lowers his voice. "That man with me was indeed Japanese, but he's a Japanese who's on the side of China."

"Are there Japanese like that?"

"Of course there are! Are all ten fingers on your hand the same? Aren't there good men and evil men, heroes and villains, among us Chinese too?"

Wangtian considers this and sees the truth in it.

"But... aren't you in the National Army?" he asks.

Zhang Zhicheng confirms that he is, and after a moment's pause, he goes on: "An army like that, that turns tail and runs at the first whiff of battle, is not worth joining. The National Army of Tianjin and Beiping has more than a hundred thousand men, and the Japanese devils only have several tens of thousands. If they had fought tooth and nail as they should, could they really have lost the whole of Tianjin, Beiping and Hebei Province within a month? In the past, they cursed my Army of the Northeast for losing our territory in three months, but hasn't the Army of the Northwest proved to be just the same? Ai! It's not that the Chinese soldiers lack courage, it's the top brass who are weak and treacherous. When Qin Hui is in charge of the country, all the Yue Fei's in the world can't out-manoeuvre him. Ai!"

This speech reminds Wangtian of the time he had spent in Chahar, in the Allied Anti-Japanese Resistance Army, to such an extent that the scar across his stomach began to ache dully.

Zhang Zhicheng's face is wreathed in smiles, as he goes on in a low voice: "This time things will be different. I've found an army that really wants to fight the Japanese devils. I'm ready to give my life for them, truly."

The beginnings of hope and pleasure can be heard in Wangtian's suspicious expression: "What... which army is this?"

"Outside the Pass, they're called the Allied Resistance, but inside the Pass they're the Eighth Route Army, and they report direct to the Communist Party leaders."

"The Communist Party? I've heard they don't offer any amnesty to renegade soldiers from other armies."

"It's not a question of amnesty, but of uniting against the Japanese. The Eighth Route Army see themselves as the successors to the National Army."

"Then they're finished. As soon as you use 'National' in your name, you're at everyone's beck and call. I'm afraid the time will come when they find themselves just the housekeepers, not the owners."

"It's not the same at all. As the saying goes, 'a general in the field is not bound by the orders from his sovereign'. If everyone makes resisting the Japanese their focus, and there is advantage to be had in attacking those devils, then they'll listen, but if there's no advantage, then any pleas will be as useless as the clicking of crayfish."

"So... will your plan work?"

"Why shouldn't it work? We haven't taken a single rifle from the central government, nor a cent of pay, so everyone's a winner. From the Mukden Incident up till now, the Allied Resistance has waged six years of warfare against the Japanese, and now, as the Eighth Route Army, they want to move into Hebei from the east and establish a base of resistance behind enemy lines at Pingxi. If they order me to fight, I'll fight, and if they don't, I'll still want to fight. If they retreat, why shouldn't I advance? If they lose territory, why shouldn't I take it back? The common people see the big picture. They can tell truth from lies, and know the difference between traitors and patriots."

Although Zhang Zhicheng has kept his voice low, each sentence falls like a hammer blow, making Wangtian's blood surge. He takes Zhang Zhicheng by the hand, gripping it tight. Zhang Zhicheng returns the grip equally sincerely and says: "Wangtian, I sought you out today..."

"To get me to join your army? No need to ask. I..."

"Ha ha! Not now, I'm afraid. There's plenty of time. Wait until we have a foothold around Beiping, and then, any time you come, you'll be welcomed. For the moment, you concentrate on marrying that girl of yours, and planting a seed as soon as possible, so that next time you go into battle, you'll do so with some peace of mind. I came to see you this time with an important request."

Wangtian is blushing, but when he hears this last sentence, he says immediately: "There's no need to ask, just tell me what you want."

Zhang Zhicheng's voice sinks even lower: "I need to get a load of weapons out of Beiping."

"Weapons? How many?"

"A whole truckload."

"That... that won't be easy."

"I know. Yesterday evening I went to see Chenglong..."

"What? Don't you know what Chenglong is now? Aren't you afraid to put your head in the lion's mouth like that?"

"Ha! I'm not that stupid. I haven't given him the real story. I'm stringing him along." Zhang Zhicheng pauses, looking at Wangtian with a grin. "But you have to help me keep that string taut."

Wangtian isn't clear exactly what he can do. "And my part is to..."

"You're vital to the whole affair."

He moves closer to Wangtian and whispers to him.

IT GOES WITHOUT SAYING THAT, since Li Fenggu took on the business of the comfort stations, she has had frequent contact with the Japanese. She has made her living as a singer since she was a little girl, and for twenty years was the mistress of Third Master Shen, the Master of the Beiyu Lodge of the Green Society, so she may be considered a fully fledged member of the underworld. According to her, the high-ups in the Green Society were the most demanding clients she ever had, so if she could keep them happy, and pull the wool over their eyes, sweeping the doltish Japanese off their feet should be simple.

Within a few months, she has become the most famous social butterfly in Beiping. When a Japanese holds any kind of event, it is not complete without her. Although she is already in her forties, she has never had children, and she has looked after herself very well. Her overall appearance is fundamentally still pretty fine, and with the judicious use of powder and rouge, and some fashionable clothes, she can pass as an attractive woman half her age. On top of this, she has retained all the skills and tricks of the trade from the many years of her singing career, and she often performs at all sorts of parties and gatherings. Sometimes she even dons a kimono and wooden pattens, and has practised enough small talk to string together a few sentences of Japanese, which is quite an achievement. There is only one fly in the ointment, which is that the Japanese are especially fond of Peking opera and she doesn't know how to sing that. In fact, she does know a few verses of opera, but, whenever she sings them, they still have a flavour of drum singing. The voice production, breathing and underlying spirit of the two genres are completely different. It is in her posture that the difference is most marked. She hasn't ever practised the fundamentals of hand, eye and body movements, not to mention wearing the specialised costumes. So, even when singing 'in mufti', as soon as she makes her first gesture, it is so wooden that people laugh and jeer, calling her a 'marionette'. Fortunately, she knows how to preserve her dignity, and although the Japanese often call on her to sing opera, she always politely declines, not daring to go beyond her limits. But as she watches the successes of other performers, she resents them and seethes inwardly. She decides to go for broke, and learn opera. She intends to find a famous teacher, not for reasons of study, but for the reflected glory of his name plate. But who to seek out? When people are barely able to earn enough to keep body and soul together, who is going to have time to teach her? Then Zhou Si thinks of someone. Who? Xiao Yuerong, of course.

Around noon one day, waiting until after the lunchtime rush, Zhou Si accompanies Li Fenggu to Yuerong's Place. They ask a waiter to find them a private room, where they sit down and order some food and wine. When they are settled, they tell one of the staff to ask the owner if he could come up to see them. Xiao Yuerong is exchanging pleasantries with a group in another room, and when he hears it is Zhou Si and Li Fenggu, his heart sinks. But he has spent more than enough years in underworld circles to understand the principle that, if you're going to offend anyone, make sure it's a gentleman, not a thug. So he hurries over to make them welcome. To his surprise, they turn the tables and treat him as a guest rather than the owner of the restaurant. They are all smiles, polite enquiries and invitations to sit down.

Xiao Yuerong gives a small exclamation of surprise, then asks with a smile: "You've come to eat at my restaurant, but you two are the one's doing all the work? What can that be about?"

Zhou Si hastily replies: "You don't know me, Proprietor Wang,[1] nor is there anything very much to know. The truth is, I have come with Fenggu today to ask if you will take her on as your apprentice."

Li Fenggu smiles modestly with lowered brows, all the bashfulness of a sixteen-year old on her forty-year old face. The overall effect of mutton dressed as lamb is actually a little toe-curling. Xiao Yuerong can't stop his amusement showing briefly, but he suppresses it quickly to avoid any embarrassment.

"Yes, yes, good, very good," he burbles, completing the cover-up.

"I know it is an odd request, Proprietor Wang." Reading people is one of Li Fenggu's particular skills, but she doesn't take any offence. There is a Tianjin lilt to her Beiping speech, as she says: "Why is someone my age going back to school, eh? But what else can I do? All because someone let Mei Lanfang[2] take Peking opera to Japan, that's what the Japanese all love now. Someone like me, who has a lot to do with our Japanese friends, has to be able to sing a few excerpts of Peking opera if I want to be taken seriously. Our country mustn't lose face. If you take me as your apprentice, at the very least my singing will enhance your reputation, even though you yourself no longer perform. At best, it will not just be good for Sino-Japanese relations, it will spread our reputation through all East Asia."

"I understand, I understand," Xiao Yuerong says with a smile, though inside he is cursing. "However, taking you on as an apprentice would certainly not be within the rules of the Pear Garden Company."

"Aiyo! If I want to learn, and you are willing to teach me, who cares whose rules it's under?" Li Fenggu says, with a curl of her lip.

Unperturbed, Xiao Yuerong smiles faintly. "The rules are not generally known outside the profession. Unlike the way you sing your songs, the Pear Garden Company has many rules. The most important one from our point of view is that a female impersonator like me can't take a female apprentice, as it is an offence to public morals. Under the Qing, it was an offence punishable by imprisonment, and quite apart from the law of the land, the weight of gossip and public opinion was enough to crush you. Zhou Si and you are people of quite some standing now, so you have to decide if this is worth doing."

Zhou Si can't restrain a snort when he hears this, but Li Fenggu stops him from saying anything. She addresses Xiao Yuerong: "You don't need to worry about that. I'm not concerned with that kind of thing."

"Well, *you* may not worry, but I'm more sensitive. I'm not sure I can go through with it. What is more, I lodged a complaint with the grand-master of my profession and retired from the Pear Garden Company. If I do chance to sing anything now, it's as an amateur, and how can an amateur take on an apprentice? It would be even worse for your reputation to have people saying your teacher is a rank amateur with no qualification to teach!"

Li Fenggu knows that Xiao Yuerong is really just making excuses, but she can't think of any way of talking him round, so she gives Zhou Si a meaningful look and he hurriedly responds: "Proprietor Wang, it would be just as good if you don't officially take her as a pupil. If you could just find the time to teach Fenggu a few popular excerpts, that would surely be alright, wouldn't it?"

"So, not learning opera proper? Not a problem, given what you know already," Xiao Yuerong replies briskly.

The smile returns to Li Fenggu's face on hearing this. "The way I see it, I can't deprive you of this little bit of prestige, Proprietor Wang. So from now on I'll change how I address you, and even if you don't accept me as your official apprentice, if you teach me just one line, you will still be my master. I offer you my most respectful thanks..."

"Let's not stand on empty ceremony," Xiao Yuerong says hurriedly. "Just sing a few lines for me."

Adopting an operatic pose, Li Fenggu replies: "Very well. Please excuse my poor performance. I will sing *Leaving the Cave-Dwelling.*"

Xiao Yuerong hums the percussion introduction and the entrance music, tapping out the rhythm on the table. Following the tune, Li Fenggu begins to sing. But before she has finished more than a few lines, Xiao Yuerong tells her to stop.

"Enough, don't sing any more. I've got your measure. You'll never be able to sing the female lead."

"Why not?"

"The female lead requires particular attention to gestures and mannerisms. It must be dignified and composed, staid but natural. When she sits, she must look as though she is sitting. When she stands up, she must appear to be standing. There is nothing feminine about it – every expression must transmit rectitude. No matter whether the character is rich or poor, is an empress, a prostitute or a heroic warrior, her heart must be honourable and dignified, indifferent to danger and stoical. No matter whether it is Wang Baochuan, Du Shiniang, Yu Tangchun or any of that sort of woman, storm-tossed on the seas of fate, they all must follow this model. If they don't, they are no longer the brightest and best among all the flowers, but become no better than whores, standing on the street touting for custom. Just consider carefully whether your expression just now, your gestures and posture were those of a female lead."

Li Fenggu's face goes red with the effort of restraining herself. Zhou Si gnaws his lip and says: "How about... how about studying for the juvenile lead?"

"That won't do, it won't do at all," Xiao Yuerong says, shaking his head vigorously.

"Won't do?" Zhou Si explodes. "The juvenile lead won't do? Aren't *Shen Hong* and *Picking up the Jade Bracelet* ideal for her?"

"The juvenile lead must have some charm, some coyness, some vivacity and some wit," Xiao Yuerong replies unhurriedly. "Most important of all, she must be truthful, genuine and natural, and if those qualities aren't apparent, then she is false, and vulgar and mannered. If it's not on the inside, how can it show on the outside? This role is that of a girl or young woman. If I didn't have the nerve to tell you all this, you would soon discover for yourself that all the make-up in the world won't cover the wrinkles when you smile. A young girl can simper coquettishly, but if I try to do that at my age, won't I just look like an old floozy? In this job, acting comes first, then learning your lines, and last of all, singing. If you want to study this part, that's fine, but first you must learn how to be lithe and graceful. Go home and practise tightrope-walking for at least two hours every day. Tie a bundle of incense sticks under each foot, and practise your movements, lithe and graceful as a swallow, for half an hour each day. If none of the sticks are broken by the end of it, then you've succeeded."

Li Fenggu is losing her patience with all this, and she snaps: "Alright then, you've had your say. Now tell me, just what part should I study for?"

"Let me think about that for a moment," Xiao Yuerong says, making a great show of pondering the matter deeply, clicking his tongue continuously. "A mounted soldier? No, you couldn't wear the tights. At your age, I can't see you kicking your legs, bending over backwards and doing handstands. The old woman? No, that won't do either. Granted it's an old woman, but it's a starring role, just like the lead female part..." Suddenly he slaps his thigh. "I have it! I'll teach you *Picking up the Jade Bracelet*."

"Ha! You spend all that time thinking, and all you come up with is the coquette part?"

"I'm not going to teach you Sun Yujiao's part," Xiao Yuerong says, keeping a straight face. "I'm going to teach you the old matchmaker role."

"The old matchmaker? You want me to play the... the ugly old woman?" Li Fenggu's voice rises about eight pitches.

"The ugly old woman part is still a woman's part," Xiao Yuerong replies, completely deadpan. "Do you think there were no old woman specialists among the thirteen great actors of the Qing Palace?[3] There aren't many movements, they're easy to learn, they're saucy and they get laughs. Your background in your kind of singing should make this a walk in the park. Besides, aren't you going to be performing specifically for the Japanese? How many of them are going to understand the words of your songs or your speeches? Why not just go for it, and play the clown? Whether they understand or not, you'll still get the belly laughs."

This time, Li Fenggu is really furious, and with staring eyes she asks through gritted teeth: "Now you're just taking the piss!"

"What do you mean?" Xiao Yuerong asks, smiling calmly. "Didn't you just say that, at best, it will not just be good for Sino-Japanese relations, it will spread our reputation through all East Asia? For such a grand undertaking, what does it matter whether you play a beautiful woman or an ugly one? As long as the Japanese like it, why shouldn't you be happy to play an ugly old woman? By sacrificing your appearance to please the Japanese, wouldn't it demonstrate even more clearly that you are a person of loyalty and filial piety? Tell me I'm not right."

Li Fenggu has flushed bright red with anger. She stamps her foot and points at Xiao Yuerong. She is about to unleash a steam of curses, but all she manages to get out is: "You... you... you..." before Zhou Si slams a fist down on the table and leaps to his feet. But he knows Xiao Yuerong has stayed just within the bounds of decorum, and he doesn't know how to vent the fury in his belly. He is like a dog trying to eat a hedgehog – he really wants to take a bite out of him, but he doesn't know where to start.

Just at this moment, one of Zhou Si's henchmen comes running into the room, and Xiao Yuerong manages to make it over to the doorway. With a laugh and a wave of his hand, he says: "Right, well, you have a chat about it, and if there's anything you two need, just say." The words are scarcely out of his mouth before he has slipped out of the room.

Li Fenggu's anger finally spills out, and she begins to curse furiously: "You stinking skunk! Pissing me around like that! I don't give a stuff about your reputation! You're just an actor turned restaurateur, but you think you're God's anointed! He likes me much more than you! You just wait and see what Aunty Gu is going to do to you."

As she's huffing and puffing like this, Zhou Si pays her no attention, but whatever his henchman is whispering in his ear is clearly causing him considerable unexpected pleasure.

"Good! Keep a close watch on him. I want you to find out what the goods are, how many there are, where they came from and where they're being kept."

"Yessir! But," the henchman replies, rather hesitantly, "this is Commander Liu's business, and if he knows that..."

"Use your brains! I said keep watch, not make a spectacle of yourself. So what if he knows, anyway? Let me tell you that Mr Matsuzaki is uneasy about him, and has told me to keep an eye on him. Get the picture? I've got orders from above, so what have I got to be afraid of? All I've got to do is get something against Chenglong, and his goose is cooked with Mr Matsuzaki. With him out of the way, who else is going to take control of the CID squad? And when that time comes, do you think I'm not going to look after you lot too?"

"Yes, yes, I understand. I'll be off then," the man says, and he hurries away.

Zhou Si waits until he has left the room, then pounds the table, chortling happily, until Li Fenggu turns her anger on him: "What's the matter with you? Xiao Yuerong insults you, and you just roll over and take it..."

"He's just an actor, who cares about him? He's not even enough for a snack. If you really want to sink your teeth into something, it must be something big."

"Get on with you! Something big? Who do you mean?"

"Liu Chenglong!"

"What?" Li Fenggu positively quivers with amazement, and her eyes are as round as saucers.

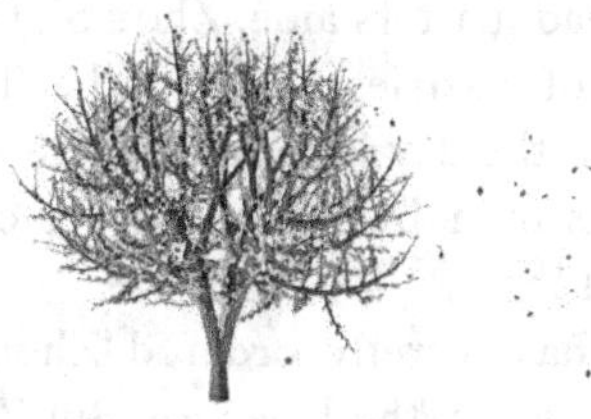

Chapter 20

For the next few days, Zhang Zhicheng and Zuo Xichuan are busy moving the merchandise. At this time, there are restrictions on the transportation of goods in Beiping, and high-demand items are not easy to acquire. The Japanese merchants' trading companies and warehouses have free movement everywhere, but the big-name Chinese companies are denied this opportunity, and in the end, even the temple fairs have all moved on, some eastwards and some westwards, until there's hardly a cartload of goods to be bought. There are many imported goods, and all the daily necessities are there, but plain cloth and cotton are still the most important. In accordance with their agreement, the goods are gathered centrally at an empty house belonging to Chenglong, and stored just as they arrive. Chenglong has appointed two men to check and inspect the merchandise, and he himself finds time to go over several times to have a look. When he sees that there is nothing untoward, he finally relaxes.

However, not every checkpoint on the way out of Beiping is under the control of his CID squad, and they all have Kempeitai guard posts, which are a constant nuisance to Chenglong. Commander Yamaguchi of the Kempeitai is rude, unreasonable, hot-headed and above all, unpredictable. After Matsuzaki has bad-mouthed him a few times, he and Chenglong have finally worked out a modus vivendi. Now, they often go out drinking together and swap notes on martial arts, and gradually a sense of brotherhood develops between them, or at least an amicable truce. As soon as Chenglong raises the question of the movement of goods, he slaps his chest and declares that he can count him in. Of course, he is bound to take his share of the extralegal tolls that are extorted.

Chenglong has anticipated every eventuality, except for one blind spot that is right in front of him. What he has failed to take into account is that the ever-respectful and deferential, sweet-talking and honey-tongued Zhou Si might be plotting against him. From the first time Chenglong fell in with Third Master Shen, when he served the Beiyu Lodge, and now after joining the Japanese and establishing the CID squad, Zhou Si has been his trusted confidante. Over the last few days, all his energies have been directed to the organisation of his new enterprise, and he has handed over responsibility for the day-to-day running of the CID squad to his headquarters aide, Zhou Si. He had sent someone to report the affair of the box of pastries sent by the Traitor Elimination Squad to Matsuzaki Harayama on the day it happened. He was also well aware that there were traitors among his men, but he had never considered the possibility that Zhou Si might be one of them.

In fact, Matsuzaki has secretly ordered Zhou Si to spy on Chenglong, a control strategy often used by the Japanese. But Zhou Si gets the wrong end of the stick, in that he believes the Japanese want him to turn against Chenglong completely. In fact he has long been disappointed with Chenglong; he feels that Chenglong is flavour of the month: he lives in a big house, earns a lot of money, whereas he, Zhou Si, is just left lapping up the dregs, applauding Chenglong's every move and laughing at his lame jokes. And now, with Li Fenggu sharing his pillow, his anger and bitterness have increased, and he's itching to engineer Chenglong's fall from grace. With his boss wanting to help Zhang Zhicheng transport his merchandise, Zhou Si sees a heaven-sent opportunity. Although Chenglong has ordered him to spy out exactly what Zhang Zhicheng is up to, he hasn't found any holes in his story; the Japanese merchant is clearly genuine, and although the goods they have been acquiring are all rationed, there's no evidence of any great transgressions. Nevertheless, he still thinks there's something fishy going on, but if he can't make a searching examination, how can he ever get to the truth of the matter? Even with a free hand to act, he is still not satisfied, but he has no clear evidence to present to his superiors. He knows all about what Chenglong has done to others in the past, and the consequences he faces if he is exposed and doesn't turn up anything. So he wracks his brains and eventually comes up with a plan. First, he orders one of his men to secretly switch one of the bales of cotton for a package of assorted army supplies, bandages and iodine. Then he sends an anonymous letter to Matsuzaki Harayama, saying that Chenglong is conspiring with people unknown to smuggle contraband goods. The Japanese will be bound to investigate, and if they are successful, he will reveal himself as the source and take credit for the operation. If that's not enough to bring down Chenglong, then he won't go so far as to expose him himself, and will continue to work for him. With his plan in place, Zhou Si sits back to watch the fun.

MATSUZAKI RECEIVES the letter in the morning, but it's already four in the afternoon before he summons Yamaguchi by telephone.

Yamaguchi comes through the door, stands to attention and salutes. When Matsuzaki doesn't say anything, but just looks at him through narrowed eyes, he begins to feel rather nervous.

"What are your orders, sir?" he asks carefully.

Matsuzaki grins. "Nothing urgent. I hear you've had a bit of a windfall, and I've been wondering where my invitation to the celebration is."

Yamaguchi hesitates a moment, then stammers: "You... er... you're talking about the... the job I helped Liu-san with?"

Matsuzaki doesn't reply, but motions Yamaguchi to continue.

"It's like this," Yamaguchi explains, his gaze dropping rather. "Liu-san's friend came to Beiping to trade. He asked me to keep an eye on things for him, and I agreed. Yes, there's money in it for me – he said he'd see me right when the business was done, but I haven't had a cent of it yet."

"What is he trading in?"

"I'm not sure exactly, but I heard Liu-san say they're restricted goods."

"Where is he taking them?"

"Again, I'm not sure of the details, but I heard him mention Rehe."

"Whose goods are they?"

"I'm not sure of the details, but I heard..."

"What exactly are you sure of?" Matsuzaki interrupts him coldly.

Yamaguchi's head droops even further, and he stammers: "Sir, I... I know it was wrong... I guarantee I won't take any further part."

Seeing his distress, Matsuzaki laughs. "That er... that's not necessary. I'm not worried about trifles like that, even less where there are Chinese concerned. You can't keep a dog chained up all the time. If it happens to find a bone and bring it back to its mother, that's fine. A hungry dog can be a good dog. It might even be useful to me. The key thing is not to let it out of your control, and not tolerate it being unsure of the details."

"Yessir!" Yamaguchi replies. "I'll go and find out immediately, and report back to you."

"No need," says Matsuzaki, waving his hand. Then, seeing Yamaguchi looking doubtful, he continues: "These goods belong to the overseas Japanese merchant, Shoi Keisen, and he has influence in high places. His father, Shoi Takashi, served in both the Chinese Army of the Northwest and the Shanxi Army, and last year he left the military and went into business in Rehe. Major General Shoi of the Fourteenth Division of the Kwantung Army is his nephew, and he has connections in the North China garrison. Staff General Akira Yamano and Colonel Kinoshita of the Thirty-First Division are both his father's students. His second-in-command is called Zhang Zhicheng, a former soldier and member of the Green Society, who's very thick with Liu Chenglong."

Matsuzaki smiles tolerantly and continues: "I've already got a man on him, and I've even investigated things on the Kwantung Army side. If he sticks his neck out, or gets up to anything, I need to know the details."

"Yessir, yessir!" Yamaguchi replies immediately.

Matsuzaki stops smiling and goes on: "I've just received an anonymous letter that says there is a large quantity of military necessities hidden in among that merchandise. These are extraordinary times, and if this information turns out to be true, it cannot be allowed, no matter who is responsible."

Yamaguchi has recovered his composure now: "I think the possibility is remote, sir. Liu-san wouldn't take that kind of risk, and anyway, if the writer of the letter was sure of his facts, he wouldn't have sent it anonymously. If this isn't just someone's guesswork, then it's a stitch-up."

"There's an old Chinese saying: 'It's better to hope for the best, and believe the worst.'"

"So... should I go and carry out a search immediately?"

"No, no, no, you shouldn't be seen searching. Nor should I. If we didn't find anything, it would destroy our carefully nurtured relationship with Shoi Keisen, and it might also affect our relations with the military. I think the best thing would be for the army to be seen doing the search, so we should pass on the information to them. Once you know the goods are on their way out of the city, tell the army to conduct a search at the Qing River checkpoint. If they find anything, then you won't be seen to have any responsibility, and if they don't, you will still earn Shoi Keisen's gratitude. We win either way, don't we?"

"That's right, sir! You've thought of everything, sir!"

For the last two days, Caiping has been feeling uneasy. Their business is going very well, and once the two days of the Longfu Temple fair are over, Wangtian makes the journey to Laoqiying to ask Uncle Yang to fix the day for their wedding. But for some reason, this life-changing event is pushed to the back of his mind, and he doesn't even raise the question of setting the date. Of course, it is not proper for the girl's side to press the matter, so Caiping approaches it in a roundabout manner.

"It doesn't matter," she says with forced gaiety. "Look how busy you've been for the last couple of days."

Of course he hasn't really been busy with work, it's just that he hasn't been seen at mealtimes during the day, and at night he still hasn't come back by the third watch. One day, when he finally comes home with the dawn, Caiping has been awake all night, anxiously waiting in the doorway. If he is busy, she doesn't know what at, and every day when he comes home, he doesn't bring any money, just a body covered in dirt and sawdust. Nor is he being busy by himself, as he has also summoned Clown and some others who cluster together muttering about who knows what. He goes off with the long-unused night soil cart to who knows where, and the various bits of broken wooden plank and slabs of wood that pile up in the courtyard are treated as though they are a precious treasure. Even the bed boards in the little western chamber are not ignored, and everything is carried off by a procession of carts until there is nothing left. Caiping is not concerned that he might be up to something illegal, but she is angry that he is keeping it secret from her, not giving anything away. Although nothing is formally settled and she is not sharing his bed, she is living in the Gao family courtyard, and she and Wangtian have made their feelings for each other clear. Even so, she is still not his real wife, so how can they be considered a real family? And now Wangtian is keeping these secrets from her, it's clear he doesn't trust her, so how can she be expected not to feel hurt? And since she is unhappy, she can't resist hurling a few taunts and curses at him behind his back. However, like pounding a hammer into cotton padding, they provoke no response at all.

ONE AFTERNOON, Caiping is about to start making dinner, when Uncle Yang calls round with Yue E. This is an unexpected visit since Wangtian has still not been back to the Western Hills. Caiping has not seen Yang Zhixing since she was little, but she still remembers quite clearly what he looked like. Although he is much older now, that good-natured, benevolent, smiling face is instantly recognisable. Without waiting for Yue E to make the introductions, she calls out "Uncle Yang".

"Eh?" says a surprised Yang Zhixing. "So, young lady, you still recognise me?"

Suddenly feeling she has been impolite, she smiles hastily and replies: "You've come with Miss Yue E. Who else could you be? Brother Wangtian is always talking about you. He says you will be a father to both of us. He has not yet paid his respects to you, and you have come here first. Sit down, Uncle Yang. I'm afraid we don't have any tea in the house, but please take a cup of hot water."

"Don't trouble yourself. I'm not staying long. I had to attend a meeting in Wanping on behalf of the Young Master, and I just thought I'd look in on you on my way back. I have to go home shortly."

Yang Zhixing sits down on the *kang* and scrutinises Caiping.

"You do indeed look a bit like Fuxing. Ai! If she had lived, she would have been the same age now."

"What do you think you are doing, Father?" Yue E reproaches him. "What's the point in talking about this with Ying'er?"

"You're right, you're right," Yang Zhixing nods with a smile. "Young Wangtian is like a sweet potato – the later you pick it, the sweeter it is. And as for this young lady... she's called Ying'er, you say? Ha ha, so charming! Well-spoken, diligent and industrious. A fine companion to pass one's days with. These are the fruits of the previous generations of the Gao family." Seeing Caiping's blushes, he continues with a smile: "If you want to marry, Ying'er, you will do so in style. You have no family, so you can treat my home as your family home. You will stay with me there to get married from. The wedding sedan will collect you from there and make a circuit of the streets to bring you here. It will be as though my own daughter is getting married. How does that sound?"

These words warm Caiping's heart and bring tears to her eyes. "Of course, of course! Uncle Yang... no, from now on I must call you 'Father'!"

"Ai!" Yang Zhixing replies, laughing. He takes two silver dollars from inside his coat. "These can serve as your dowry, and as a gift to my daughter-in-law, since I am now father to both of you. A double gift. Please accept it."

"No, no. We aren't short..."

"Ha! If you're not short of money, that doesn't mean you should ignore the correct etiquette and my good intentions. Take it now."

Caiping takes the silver dollars as tears run unheeded down her cheeks. She bends down and is about to kneel, but Yang Zhixing stops her.

"There's no need for that now, Ying'er. Wait for the day you join the family, and then you can kowtow."

Caiping smiles through her tears.

"What about Wangtian?" Yue E asks.

"Ah, these last two days, he's been..." Caiping chokes on her worries and grievances, and just manages to utter the word "busy".

Yue E clearly wants to say something, but Yang Zhixing shushes her: "Busy is how he should be. With life as it is at the moment, busy is the right thing to be. Saying that, though, my old lady has all the bedding you need already packed up. It's not that she doesn't trust you young people's needlework skills, it's just..."

Before he can finish, Yue E signals to him unobtrusively. He has no idea what he has said wrong, and he gives her a puzzled look.

"What about setting the day?" Yue E says softly.

Yang Zhixing slaps his chest and says: "Ha! I've completely forgotten the most important thing. I consulted Lao Zhang and have chosen the day for you. How does the twenty-sixth day of the eighth month suit you, Ying'er?"

"The twenty-sixth... Today's... today's already the twenty-second!"

"I know it's a bit rushed, but it's a very auspicious date," Yang Zhixing says, taking out his almanac. "Look, it says here that that day is suitable for weddings and reunions, and that everything will go smoothly. The year also promises happiness in marriage, and is propitious for a son and for wealth. You would have to wait six months for another such day. Given that neither of you are youngsters, I thought you wouldn't want to delay. What is more... ah, to be blunt, the fact you are living together, and all your comings and goings are bound to set tongues wagging. The sooner you get officially married, the better, and the fact your parents are no longer with us is another good reason to get on with it. Don't you agree?"

He sees Caiping nodding in agreement and continues: "Time isn't on your side. With the year as it is, you don't want to put on any great show because you need to leave some money for day-to-day living. It won't take long to give this place a lick of paint, tidy up, put up some lucky characters and window decorations. We just need to give it some festive spirit, and it will do fine. My old lady can look after the bedding, I can guarantee you of that. There aren't many other preparations to be made, except to book the wedding sedan. Neither of your wedding clothes have to be new, and when the Young Master hears about this, I know he'll give you the suit and wedding dress from his own marriage. They've only been worn once, they've never been laundered, and they're good quality material and well made. They'll be perfect. The wedding party is more pressing, but since neither of you have any family, it will just be friends and neighbours, so four tables will be enough. Yue E can look after all that..."

"No need, I'll do it myself," says Caiping. "As it's only a few tables, I can manage."

"If you do it," Yue E laughs, "won't the bride find herself busy in the kitchen? And if she doesn't go into the wedding chamber, how can anyone lift her veil?"

"Ha! Paupers have to make do with paupers' arrangements, don't they?" says Caiping. "Do you think I need someone else to plan a party and organise the ceremony? If you ask me, we should save money on the wedding sedan too. That's how I want it, and since I've got no family to look askance at all this, who else is going to?"

Yang Zhixing slaps his thigh. "Right! Yes, you're right. With you in charge, I know your future is going to be smooth."

"But…" Caiping starts to speak, but stops herself.

"But what?"

"There's no problem with the food, but the wine… there's none to be bought anywhere."

"Ha! What vital task am I good for, if it's not seeing to the wine?" Yang Zhixing says with a laugh. "There's a pot still at Laoqiying, so you can leave it to me. You won't go short. Besides, the quantity isn't really a problem. This is first-run stuff, and it's pretty lethal, so when we water it down a bit, we'll be all set, won't we?"

Everyone laughs so heartily that it makes the paper in the windows rustle.

It's only after supper has been reheated several times that Wangtian comes home. As soon as he gets in, he pulls the lid off the steamer basket, ravenous as a hungry ghost, and snatches out a piping hot cornbread. Even though it scalds his hand so he has to blow on it, he still manages to wolf half the bread down. Caiping chuckles at the way he is eating and uses a bowl to scoop out some more cornbread.

As she turns to pour him some vegetable and dough-drop soup, she says: "Drink a little soup first to settle your stomach. Don't choke yourself."

Wangtian laughs, swallows a couple more mouthfuls of bread and just manages to splutter out: "Ha! I only… had… a bowl of congee… for lunch."

"Really?" Caiping stares at him. "What's keeping you so busy that you can't even come home to eat?"

Wangtian grunts a couple of times and avoids the question. "It's been a good day today. I got the job finished."

"And what about the pay?" Caiping puts the bowl of soup down on the table and abruptly holds out her hand, palm up.

Wangtian evades the question again: "I… er… I'm not quite done yet. I need to get the cart fixed, and then, in a couple of days' time, I've got to transport some stuff for them, and then they'll pay me."

Caiping knows he's not telling her the full story, but she can't be bothered to argue. She just changes the subject quietly: "Uncle Yang came here this afternoon and he... he fixed the day for our wedding."

"Eh? What? When?"

"Uncle Yang says that the twenty-sixth is a particularly auspicious day."

"The twenty-sixth!" Any delight disappears from Wangtian's face when he hears this, leaving only shock. He shakes his head furiously. "That's no good, no good at all!"

Caiping assumes that he just thinks the timing's too tight. "Don't worry," she says, "Uncle Yang has thought of everything. We're sure we can manage."

"Ah... that's not the problem."

"Then what is?"

"It's... er... I'll tell you afterwards." Wangtian turns away and makes to leave.

"What do you think you are doing?"

"I'm going to find Uncle Yang."

"You just stay where you are!" Caiping grabs hold of him and stands in his way.

Seeing that she is really angry, Wangtian says coaxingly: "The twenty-sixth won't do, Ying'er. I've got to transport those goods for someone. I'll go and talk to Uncle Yang, and push it back a couple of days. What does a day or so matter?"

"Alright, alright, off you go." Caiping lets go of him and waits until he has turned to leave, before continuing: "But you're wasting your time. Uncle Yang went back to the Western Hills this afternoon."

"Then..." Agitation and annoyance vie with each other in Wangtian, and he doesn't know what to do for the best. He looks around, and his eye falls on the cornbread. He grabs one of them and takes a couple of furious bites out of it.

Seeing him like this, Caiping can't help laughing. She pushes the bowl of soup towards him: "Don't take it out on the bread. You're so fierce you're in danger of taking a bite out of the bowl once you've finished the soup."

Wangtian just puffs out his cheeks and shoots her a look, without replying.

In response, Caiping plonks herself down opposite him. She looks at him, smiling, and asks: "You've got me puzzled. What exactly are you transporting in your old night soil cart? What's so important that you can't delay things by a couple of days, but you can push back our wedding day? How much are they paying you that makes you so set on doing it?"

"Don't be so greedy. If you want the truth, I'm doing it for nothing."

"What's all this about?"

"It's..." Wangtian hesitates a long moment. "It's about fighting the Japanese devils."

Hearing these words, Caiping freezes, but then, after a moment's thought, she begins to rock with laughter: "Aiyo! Don't mess me around! Are you going to use your night soil cart as a gas bomb? Or..."

"Don't make so much noise! Do you think I'd joke about something like this?"

Pulled up by how solemn he looks, she chokes back her laughter. "Are you really serious?"

Wangtian nods solemnly. Then, seeing how alarmed she still is, he takes her hand and pulls her over to sit beside him. He holds her tenderly in both hands and says: "I wasn't deliberately keeping this from you, Ying'er, I just wasn't allowed to talk about it. I would have told you everything afterwards. I'm really not angry at you, I'm just sorry these two such important events have clashed. I know you want to get married openly and above board as soon as possible, so we can be a proper couple and live peacefully together. I want that even more than you. But this business is too big, too important and it can't be delayed. If I can see it through, it will really be good for my reputation. And if I do pull it off, I'll show I'm a proper Chinese, and a proper husband to you."

"Is it dangerous?"

"Anything this important always involves risk. But it's been well planned and well organised, and I've been around a bit myself, and I know how to handle myself. Moving some goods can't be more dangerous than fighting. I've been to war. You see this scar? I got it when a traitorous dog shot me. But I got him with my sword, and I've ended up fine and he's fucked. Don't worry, I've always been lucky. Actually, you've always been lucky too, so together we can take on Yama himself, no problem."

Seeing him so confident, her own heart begins to beat a little faster: "So... do we change the date? Then you can have that really auspicious day for your important business."

"How can we have time to change it? Wouldn't I have to talk to Uncle Shu, anyway? I can't tell him the real reason, but if I don't come up with some excuse, won't he take offence?"

"Then..." Caiping is stumped for an idea too. Suddenly she asks: "What time are you due to move the goods?"

"It's fixed for eight in the evening. The return journey will take all night."

"Then there's still time. We get married during the day, and you can get on with your business at night."

"That's it! Why didn't we think of it before?" Wangtian's face is wreathed in smiles, but he quickly stows them. "But that means our wedding night..."

Caiping gives a shy smile, nestles her head on his chest and says softly: "I'll wait for you."

"But... but I can't... wait for you." Wangtian's breathing has grown a little rough.

"Get on with you! Didn't you just want to change the day?"

"Can we only push the day back, not bring it forward?"

"To when?"

"Well... today!"

The moonlight outside creeps through the window papers to sneak a look.

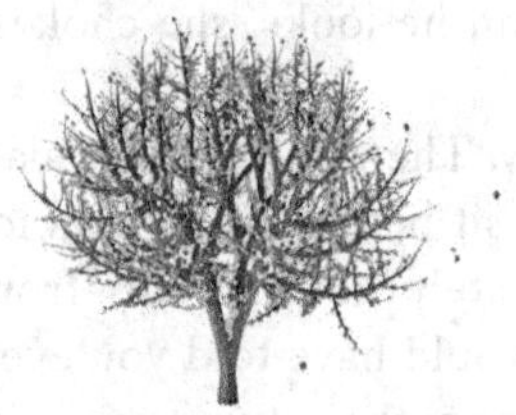

Chapter 21

With Miaofengshan so manifestly at war, it naturally attracts close attention from the Japanese. What comes as a shock to them is the fact that the troops that killed several dozen of their men in one night are a newly formed peasant militia. According to the battle report sent to his superiors by the commanding officer of the Wanping garrison, it was the work of the regular Kuomintang Army, and the size of the attacking force was at least a battalion.

In addition, a large number of resistance armies have recently sprung up in the area between Changping and Huailai, giving the commanders of the Army of North China grave concern, and causing them to immediately transfer two brigades of Japanese troops to reinforce Changping and Wanping counties. They also withdrew a brigade from beyond the Pass to reinforce the encirclement campaign in the mountain area to the north of Pingxi. They ordered every county to enact measures to 'clear the countryside',[1] starting with using the 'preservation committees' to conduct population counts in every village and township, enacting the *baojia* system,[2] issuing good citizenship certificates, and levying public security taxes and military provisions contributions. Then they started searches of the mountainous regions, pulling the net tight around any insurgents, as part of their plan to purge the whole region of any resistance forces within three months, and consolidate the whole area behind their front lines.

Of course, this is only an aspiration. The mountain district of Pingxi encompasses the three counties of Wan, Fang and Liang, but to the south, there is also Laiyuan and Laishui; to the north it adjoins Yanqing and Changping, and to the west, Wei County and Huailai. It is crisscrossed by the great mountain ranges of Lüliang and Yanshan, while the Yongding, Juma and Laishui rivers run through it. Given the scale of this region of mountains and rivers, valleys and ravines, how can the Japanese possibly cover the whole area with their limited number of troops? Mustering them together was like making a piece of patchwork cloth, only just enough to cover one's modesty, but scattered, they were even less effective, since how can you make a large pot of congee with just a handful of grain?

The twelve villages of the Left Barracks are part of Wanping District, and relatively close to Beiping; if the Japanese fart, the people here are the first to smell it. A squad of a dozen or so Japanese soldiers commandeer the county preservation committee to act as guides and interpreters, and make their first stop at Laoqiying. Over the next two days, they summon the chairman of every district preservation committee to ascertain their loyalty from the start. Qi Yuexuan finds an excuse not to attend, and sends Yang Zhixing in his place. By keeping out of sight in the lead-up to the meeting, this little deception plays out without a hitch. By the following night, Qi Yuexuan knows exactly what is going on in each village, and over the next two days of frantic activity at every level, he ensures that everything that needs to be hidden or concealed is well and truly buried. Rifles, ammunition, uniforms, even the ancient blunderbusses and cannons with their makeshift charges, any swords and spears, everything has been gathered together and safely cached. Household valuables, grain and other produce are tightly wrapped and stowed, and horses and cattle, domestic animals and poultry are all hidden in caves and valleys.

OF COURSE, they have to make a show of complying, so the registers of households and family names are all presented neatly and correctly; but at the same time, the people charged with running the *baojia* system are all members of the Heroic Anti-Japanese Army. Slogans and catchphrases are colourfully displayed along the streets, but Qi Yuexuan has written them in archaic seal script, so needless to say, neither the Japanese, nor even the local Chinese, have any idea what they say. When the noisy troupe of drums and gongs arrives at the village gates of Laoqiying, what really makes the ground shake is a great shout of "Hai". The Japanese think they are saying the Japanese word for 'yes', but in fact, the countryfolk are just playing along with Qi Yuexuan's plan and enjoying the show. Of course, when the Japanese arrive they want food, and Qi Yuexuan's house is well stocked. Watered down, one vat of wine becomes two, which is more than enough for ten people. There is a huge pot of pork and vegetable stew boiling away, to which Lao Zhang adds a ladleful of cold water, making it particularly fragrant and toothsome – even if, halfway home, most of the Japanese are struck down with diarrhoea. But we are getting ahead of ourselves; at the time, the Japanese were just delighted to see the good food and fine wine laid out to greet them.

When it comes to the levying of money and grain, paring flesh from the bones and bleeding people dry, they are all business. As soon as the Japanese start talking, Qi Yuexuan is extremely attentive, and he immediately agrees to everything. They have made all their calculations and estimates in advance, so the whole process is watertight and comprehensive.

"Very well," Qi Yuexuan says. "None of our twelve *bao* and thirty-two *jia*[3] have any objections to the figures you have given us. However, the farming families all beg you to relent, as they are all so poor. The best way to think about it is that, the further you go into the mountains, the poorer the inhabitants. The villagers don't have enough money to live off, they can't afford even to set up workshops or run any kind of small business. Pestilence and disease have decimated the human population, along with the pigs, sheep, chickens and ducks too, so they have even less chance of producing any money. Of course, even though they have no money, they must still pay the public security tax, but don't worry, I'll take care of that. Since they have no money, I told them to pay in grain and goods, using the current market price, not a cent less, and to combine the surety and the army grain tax into one."

When the Japanese captain hears these words translated, he nods with a curt exclamation of "*Yoshi*".

Qi Yuexuan goes on: "What is more, I have everything arranged. Once the amounts came down from above, all the villages collected them together the very next day."

So saying, he pushes open the door of the western room to show that it is full of hemp sacks, piled up to the ceiling. "It's all here. The money has been converted to grain, correct to the last *jin* – one thousand five hundred and fifty-six and a half *jin*. When you've checked it and verified the accounts, please give me a receipt, and I will consider my duty discharged."

The interpreter quickly translates this to the Japanese captain, who, to Qi Yuexuan's considerable surprise, shakes his head firmly.

The translator says: "The great lord says that the exchange for grain is no good, as he has no way of taking it back. You'll have to send it to the county town in Wanping."

Yang Zhixing, who is standing to one side, can no longer restrain himself: "Actually, there's no trouble him getting it back. Even if he doesn't have any horses or oxen, he can hire a cart. But you can't get a cart along the small roads in front of the mountains. He'll have to use Incense Road behind the mountain. That's not a very safe road – in the past it was full of bandits, and now it's even worse, and is crawling with anti-Japanese troops from the regular army. I've heard this resistance force has a good few hundred men, and they're ferocious fighters. They might kill dozens of Japanese in one go. Do you think the sight of grain being transported isn't going to get their blood up? It's not worth the risk, it's really not worth it."

Qi Yuexuan backs him up: "That's right, there's absolutely no doubt about it. It would be best if you don't go now, but wait here on the mountain for a few days until we can hire a cart, and you can take it back under escort. To tell the truth, even keeping that grain here isn't safe. If they get wind of it, they're sure to attack the village. But with you and your men's guns on guard, although I don't know how you'd cope if things get really serious, at least you'll put some heart into the villagers."

The interpreter tells Qi Yuexuan: "The great lord says that, without clear intelligence on the enemy's dispositions, he doesn't dare risk spending the night on the mountain, and he is determined to leave by dusk. Your hard work sets an example to the whole county, so he trusts you to arrange the transport yourself." Seeing the difficult position Qi Yuexuan finds himself in, the interpreter goes on, in a low voice: "You made the situation sound so dangerous, Mr Qi, the Japanese don't dare wait here."

Qi Yuexuan seizes the opportunity and says: "In that case, may I make a request? Could you leave us a few rifles? We have the men here, but no weapons, and we can't be seen to be escorting the shipment empty-handed, can we?"

The Japanese captain doesn't commit himself immediately, and considers the matter for a long time, before finally nodding his head.

"The great lord agrees," the interpreter says. "He'll give you three rifles and a hundred rounds of ammunition, but the guns have to be signed for and you will have to account for any ammunition used. Moreover, you will be responsible for any damage or loss."

Qi Yuexuan laughs heartily and agrees.

Replete with food and wine, the Japanese captain hardly even bothers to wipe his mouth before belching out: "I'm off!"

Making a great show of solicitude, Qi Yuexuan pulls him back. "Don't go now, nightfall's still a long time off. What's the rush? Let me take you round some of the villages higher up the mountain..."

Immediately after seeing these Japanese soldiers out of the east gate of the village, a dozen or so strapping young men from Laoqiying set off on the narrow path down the mountain from the west gate. Following Qi Yuexuan's instructions, they take a shortcut to get ahead of the Japanese, though, for the moment, it's just a matter of herding the ducks, not turning them into dumplings. A little later, there is a random burst of rifle fire; the Japanese don't even catch sight of a shadow, but two of them lie dead, and four or five are wounded. It's every man for himself now as they flee headlong, much more like rabbits than ducks, and the bodies of their comrades are left behind without a second thought.

The next afternoon, Grandpa Dong takes a handful of men and a cart to retrieve the bodies of the two Japanese and take them to the county town of Wanping. There, he cunningly makes a false report to the effect that they had heard the gunfire the day before, and had detailed some men to go and provide reinforcements. They had caught up with the attackers and killed one of them; then they had gone on to collect the bodies of the two noble Japanese. Two of the villagers were also killed, and several wounded. They also handed over an army uniform, saying it came from the body of the man they killed, and a rifle, broken into two pieces, which they said they had also seized. Grandpa Dong also enquires whether they should still send the military grain. With the road in such a dangerous state, its safety couldn't be guaranteed. The Japanese have no option but to reply that the shipment should be temporarily postponed, feeling that they are lucky to be in an area that serves as a model of co-operation with the Japanese. The same day they order a draft plan to be produced, which appears in the newspapers the next day. It says that the district preservation committees will faithfully enact the policies of the imperial Japanese army, strictly enforce the *baojia* system, vigorously pursue the levying of taxes and grain, and particularly, cooperate with the imperial army in the elimination of anti-Japanese factions. And that this announcement will serve as formal notification of all these measures.

When Grandpa Dong returns to the village and reports all this, everyone laughs till their bellies ache. They reckon that, for the cost of half a pig, a vat of wine, an army uniform and a broken rifle, they have gained two dead Japanese devils and five wounded, along with seven or eight rifles. They have also managed to get the collection of taxes and grain postponed, and have been honourably mentioned in dispatches. They feel they have done a pretty good piece of business. Only Qi Yuexuan doesn't seem particularly happy with the affair.

He is still depressed when he gets home. In the time it takes to smoke a pipe of tobacco, he loads a brush with thick, black ink, exhales deeply and writes a verse. When he has finished writing, he feels that he hasn't quite given his feelings full expression, so he reads it out in a bright, clear voice:

> *When a hero plays the square-cloth clown,*
> *Clever plots just drag him down.*
> *The red flag he carries remains unflown*
> *Behind white powder, his true self unknown.*
> *Jointed bamboo won't bend to a frame,*
> *Stifled courage has nothing to gain,*
> *A slash, a yell, the master's here,*
> *I wake from a dream, the night's long, I fear.*

At his side, Yang Zhixing fully understands his Young Master's discomfort. A man like him finds heavy responsibilities easy to bear, but disgrace hard to endure, the more so because of his upbringing in the Residence, hemmed in by books and poetry. Considering what he has had to do recently, his conscience must have been working overtime. Yang Zhixing wants to find some words to comfort him, but they stick in his throat. When the poem is finished, he goes over to him. But to his surprise, just as he starts to move, he hears a voice expressing its approval from outside the room. It's Lao Zhang, who pulls aside the door curtain and comes in, carrying a bundle of firewood.

"Eh?" says Qi Yuexuan, looking at him in surprise. "I... I didn't know you understood poetry. Good, you say? Which bit do you like?"

Lao Zhang puts the firewood on the stove counter, and says with a smile: "I lived in the Residence for so many years, I picked up a taste for it. 'The Master's here'? That's really good. That's all about putting on airs and having a chip on one's shoulder, isn't it? And the whole second half is all about putting on a grand and imposing manner when you go into battle against the enemy. That's what you mean, isn't it?"

Qi Yuexuan remains expressionless. "Is there anything else?" he asks.

Lao Zhang scratches his bald head. "I only remember that phrase, but it is the most expressive, isn't it?"

Qi Yuexuan can no longer keep a straight face, and he breaks into a grin.

"Alright then, I'm amazed you could read so much into the rest of the poem, when you only remember one line. Off with you now, and light the *kang*."

Yang Zhixing chortles, then carries a dish of peanuts and a pot of wine over towards Qi Yuexuan, asking with assumed deference: "Young Master, how would it be if I were to have a cup or two of wine with you?"

Qi Yuexuan groans slightly, then nods and sits down. He watches Yang Zhixing pour the wine, then asks with a blank stare: "Is that all we're doing with the Japanese? Just a bit of play-acting?"

"Not at all! Not at all!" Yang Zhixing says with a laugh. "At least Lao Zhang came out well from it in the end."

"Don't talk about me getting any benefit, Manager Yang," Lao Zhang interjects. "I was just afraid of messing things up. What I didn't expect was that, after a few cups of wine, my stomach would start hurting. I'm still not comfortable even now. You added too much water to the wine, and the Japanese were bound to get the runs. If I were them, I'd be coming back to arrest you."

"So you're allowed to add cold water to the cooked stew, but I can't water down the wine? If the Japanese do come back for the people who poisoned their stomachs, it'll be you they're after first!"

"That's enough!" says Qi Yuexuan ill-temperedly.

Yang Zhixing has just been trying to cheer up the Young Master, and he isn't sure what he has said that has annoyed him. He doesn't dare say anything more, and just fills Qi Yuexuan's wine cup.

Seldom the most tactful person, and not knowing when to shut up, Lao Zhang carries the firewood over to the stove, feeds the fire to warm up the *kang* and asks: "Who are you sulking at, Young Master? I may not have got much benefit out of the business with the wine, but you certainly came out on the right side with the way you dealt with the Japanese. You didn't lead any troops, you didn't fight, but you delivered some telling blows..."

"I don't need anyone to blow my trumpet!" says Qi Yuexuan, slamming his wine cup down on the table. "From now on, I'm done with these petty little plots and minor victories. They're not how we're going to drive the Japanese out. Ai! I'm not blaming you, I'm no better myself. I don't have the skills or ability to challenge the Japanese head-on. All I can do is plot and plan. Here I am, itching to take the stage as a heroic warrior, and all the time, all I've got is my clown's make-up. When am I ever going to be able to play that part? As for me shouting

'The Master's here' or whatever, that's just a dream, and when I wake up, I'll still have to stitch a smile on my face, play the conman, praising them to their face and kicking their shins under the table. It's an insult to my education, it's unfair and it stinks to high heaven."

Angry as these words are, they delight Yang Zhixing and Lao Zhang.

"Hearing you talk like this," Lao Zhang dares to say, "makes me think of a good comparison."

"What's that?"

"It's like being hungry for three days, then getting a bowl of leftovers – you swallow it in one gulp, then complain it's too oily. What you..."

"What I'm doing is buying cheap and selling dear? Is that it?" Qi Yuexuan scowls. "Bullshit! Where there are gains, there must be losses too. These small gains I've made are because I'm selling myself. If you were in my shoes, you wouldn't take the same risks. The Japanese have published my name in the papers, singling me out for praise, so my traitor's hat seems to be fitting me pretty well at the moment. You two realise that I'm out on my own on this. The few people in this little district may know I'm no traitor, but how many people are there in the city and the surrounding countryside ready to stab me in the back? Do you think Liu Chenglong and the prestige of the Minister's Residence are going to stop people cursing me as a traitor? If I return now, I'll need eyes in the back of my head to avoid being beaten up. Who's going to write the story of these times? It's you two, isn't it? I'm really afraid that, if I don't make everything as clear as possible, I'll be made the scapegoat when I'm gone."

"Ha, Young Master!" says Lao Zhang. "It just like fighting crickets..."

"You and your crickets!" Qi Yuexuan exclaims angrily. "Men aren't crickets. Men know what shame is, they have a sense of honour."

"So do crickets. How would they know not to admit defeat if they didn't have fighting spirit? You've seen it for yourself, haven't you? How they'll hang on for grim death even with broken teeth and one eye put out!"

"You're right. Surpassed even by an insect!" Qi Yuexuan says, with a bitter smile.

"No, no, that's not right," says Lao Zhang. "Men are more formidable than crickets, otherwise it would be crickets rearing men, not the other way around. When a cricket tastes defeat, it runs away or jumps right out of the arena. Does it still bare its teeth in defiance then? And here you are, unscathed, having bitten several lumps out of them, and still proclaiming continuously 'I'm on your side, I'm on your side!' They've lost several of their legs, but they don't even know who's bitten them! There's no cricket as cunning as you."

"That's typical of you, Lao Zhang. Finding some way to use crickets to deride me!"

Qi Yuexuan throws away the peanut he's been fiddling with.

Caught on the hop, Lao Zhang exclaims: "I wouldn't dare do anything like that. I was praising you! How else are men better than insects if it's not in their ability to plan, to have vision and to exercise self-restraint. The Japanese do not act like gentlemen, and there's no trick they won't stoop to. Do you remember when you matched crickets with the Old Prince? Our cricket, Tu Xingsun, wasn't even six centimetres long, and was up against General Copperhead, which was at least eight centimetres, but we ended up winning the five hundred yuan. And why was that? General Copperhead was a large insect but reared in captivity, its strength not reflected in its size, despite its large abdomen, supple legs and substantial frame. Although our Tu Xingsun was smaller, it had the strength that comes from being born and raised in the wild. It was a good match because it could use its small size to attack General Copperhead's legs from underneath. Fighting crickets and going to war are the same, it comes down to a battle of wills."

Qi Yuexuan sighs, but then remembers something and asks: "Hey, Lao Zhang, Tu Xingsun was a loser, wasn't it? It had been discarded by its previous owner, so how did it become, in your hands, such a fierce creature? I asked you over and over again, but you never told me. Can you reveal your secret now?"

"But that's one of my trade secrets! However, since you're not fighting crickets any more, I'll tell you a little. Some of that cricket's qualities were given by heaven, but more came from the way it was reared. Apart from food, soil, water and warmth, there's one additional thing they can't do without..." He pauses for effect, keeping Qi Yuexuan in suspense.

"Well? What is it? Come on, tell me!" Qi Yuexuan says excitedly.

"You have to put a female cricket in its gourd, and raise them together."

"Is that it?" says Qi Yuexuan with a disappointed look on his face.

"Aiyo! It's only the most important thing! If it has a mate, then it has a family, and when it fights, it's not just fighting for status, for food, for itself alone. It's the same with people, who call it fighting for home and country. Of course they're willing to fight to the death to defend them."

Qi Yuexuan gets the point immediately, and nods: "You're right."

"There's another secret, but... I can't reveal it."

"Hey! You can't string me along like that! Can't reveal it? Alright, you just wait. I'll throw out all those insects of yours."

Lao Zhang knows the Young Master is so agitated he wouldn't think twice about doing it, so he goes on: "Alright, alright, alright, I'll tell you. Do you remember, Young Master, at the Old Prince's residence that time, before I put Tu Xingsun into the basin, I shook it a few times and blew on it?"

Qi Yuexuan grunts and nods.

"The shaking was to rouse its spirit, but the blowing was the key. I had a little bit of a secret formula in my mouth, and when the cricket smelled it, it drove it wild."

"What secret formula?"

"That's all I can tell you, Young Master. The details wouldn't interest you. Besides, they wouldn't be any use to you either."

Qi Yuexuan knows just how far he can go, and he doesn't ask any further, but simply asks: "So just how long have you been keeping these dishonest practices of yours from me?"

"I didn't want to spoil things, Young Master. All bets are crooked, one way or another, and the trick is to win them. It's the same with war, isn't it? It's hard to tell what's real and what's sham. Look at you – you can't stop being a gentleman, an intellectual. For a lowly insect to be raised well, or a lowly person to live well, can be a hard burden to bear, and a tiring appearance to maintain. When you are involved in great affairs, if you are so frustrated it becomes intolerable, do you continue? Men have an interior self, and an external appearance, and it is the interior self that is more important. At the moment, you have lost face – that's your external appearance. But your interior self is unchanged. As the days pass, your interior self remains, but for some reason you seem to be afraid you'll never regain your face! What you mustn't do is let your heart fight against itself, but keep that spirit to turn on the Japanese. Isn't that so? If you can't do that, then don't do anything. Who cares if the country is lost or not? You and I can just keep playing with our crickets."

Qi Yuexuan knows that what Lao Zhang is saying is quite reasonable, but what he actually says is: "Well, now you've taken such a roundabout route, it's good of you to wait for me to catch up. Of course I understand the principle. How could I not? It's just that I can feel a sullenness in my heart."

Then he changes the subject and points at Lao Zhang, reprimanding him: "Do you think a Young Master like me is the same as you? Thin-lipped and thick-skinned? I'm doing alright here. I'm not used to playing the clown, but I haven't fallen over on stage yet, have I? So what's wrong with me grumbling a bit when I come off stage? And here you are deliberately driving me crazy with your own grumbling. And if you're not doing that, you're trying to force me to shout my war cry from the top of the Qian Gate!"

"Aiyo! Listen to you! Talk about wanting to have your cake and eat it!" Lao Zhang knows that Qi Yuexuan has vented his frustrations now, and he continues, with a broad smile: "Alright, alright! You grumble away. When you can't take it any more, and you go down into the river, you can be Qu Yuan, and I'll be the villain who drove you there."

With this, the three of them break into laughter.

At this moment, there is a thud from outside the room, as though someone has bumped into something. Qi Yuexuan and Lao Zhang are laughing too hard to notice it, but Yang Zhixing hurries over to the window and looks out. There's no one to be seen. Heart thumping, he rushes out of the room to investigate.

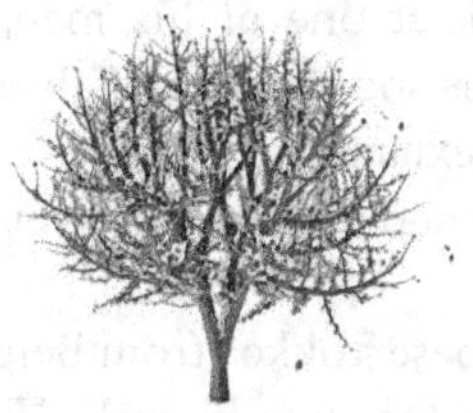

Chapter 22

There is nothing unusual to be seen in the courtyard. The noise had come from a galvanised iron piss bucket under a tree by the south wall, which had fallen over. Yang Zhixing discounts it, assuming a cat must have knocked it over, and he stoops down to set it upright. Glancing around, he sees a leather shoe poking out from under the tree. A shiver runs through him, but he doesn't betray any emotion; he just rights the bucket and ambles slowly back to the room.

The man behind the tree is in plain clothes, with a strip of black cloth hiding half his face. He waits until Yang Zhixing is safely in the room, then slips over to the main entrance, where he quietly lifts the locking bar and opens the gates. Several masked figures file in, carrying handguns. Once in the courtyard, they follow the base of the wall, feeling their way round to the lamp-lit windows of the northern room. The leader signals with his hand, and the men crouch below the windows on either side of the door.

What they hear is the voice of Qi Yuexuan: "Ha ha! Living here, deep in the mountains, I really didn't expect so many people to be concerned for poor little me. Even in the middle of the night, there are still people coming to pay their respects. Now you're here, come right in. Don't skulk around like dogs. The wind is bitter up in these mountains, and you don't have fur to keep out the cold. Uncle Yang, pull back the curtain and welcome them in."

On hearing this, the leader signals again to his men. Two of them, either side of the door, come into the room, guns levelled at Yang Zhixing and Qi Yuexuan. Only then does the leader himself enter the room. The remaining men stay outside, standing up now, with guns raised, watching every move inside the room.

"Well, gentlemen, which road have you taken to get here?" Yang Zhixing asks, cupping his hands respectfully in welcome.

The leader doesn't reply immediately, but looks carefully around the room, before asking coldly: "There is someone else, isn't there?"

Yang Zhixing smiles and replies: "Yes, yes, he's the family tombkeeper. He's gone to make his night-rounds of the tomb enclosure."

The leader shoots a look at one of his men, who takes his meaning and hurries out of the room. He is soon back and gives his leader a nod. Seeing this, Yang Zhixing winks at Qi Yuexuan.

The leader coughs quietly and asks: "So, are you Qi Yuexuan?"

"I am. And you are?"

"We are the imperial Japanese Tokko[1] from Beiping."

Yang Zhixing hurriedly interposes himself: "I don't know exactly what the Tokko is, brother, but does that mean you answer to the Japanese? Our Young Master also..."

"Stay out of it," rasps the leader, glaring at Yang Zhixing. "It's none of your business."

"Don't say anything more, Uncle Yang," Qi Yuexuan says hastily. "It's me they've come for." So saying, he meets the leader's gaze, and asks with a faint smile: "So, tell me, what is it that has brought you here in such secrecy?"

The leader doesn't reply, but directs an intimidating stare at Qi Yuexuan, looking him over carefully from head to foot. Yang Zhixing has also been examining the leader, and even though half his face is covered in a black cloth mask, a slanting scar is clearly visible. Although one eye is half-closed due to the scar, the glint in it strikes Yang Zhixing as somehow familiar; he just can't remember where he has seen it before.

Of course, it is Gao Guigeng, and when he sees Yang Zhixing looking at him, he is afraid he will be recognised, so he turns away towards Qi Yuexuan and says: "Qi Yuexuan, we believe you are only paying lip service to the cause of Sino-Japanese goodwill, and are secretly working against it. The explosion on Miaofengshan, which killed those Japanese soldiers, and the recent ambush in these mountains, are both connected with your twelve villages of the Left Barracks. So our superiors have sent us here to execute you." With this, he points his gun at Qi Yuexuan's head. "Do you have anything to say, before you die?"

Qi Yuexuan just laughs.

"What are you laughing at?" The muzzle of Gao Guigeng's gun presses a little closer.

Qi Yuexuan grunts softly: "That's enough, brother. You are not that good an actor. As soon as you mounted the stage, your words and your character were all wrong."

"What do you mean?"

"You're nothing to do with the Tokko. You're not even working for the Japanese in any capacity."

"How... how do you know?"

"Ha! Well, if you were in the pay of the Japanese, why would you be wearing masks and sneaking up on me like that? If it had been me doing those things, I'm quite sure you'd have questioned them, and wanted to know who I was working for, how many of us there were, who we were, whether we'd actually used our guns. Isn't that so? I'm really not that important a figure, but if Matsuzaki

182

Harayama were to come in person, without conclusive proof, there's no way he'd treat me like this. So put your gun away, just in case it goes off accidentally."

Gao Guigeng looks rather embarrassed, and he lets the gun barrel drop a little.

"Sit down, sit down all of you. Take your time and say what you have to say," Qi Yuexuan says with a laugh. "Tell your comrades outside to come in and get warm too, and have a cup of hot tea. If you're going to stand guard over me in such cold weather, there's no need to be formal about it – we're not in the Qing dynasty any more."

Gao Guigeng glares at him. "You can keep your smarmy smiles. Do you know what it is that we do?"

"I don't need to eat pork to know how a pig runs. You've got more muscle than sense, and you can't tell who the good guys are."

This speech is too much for one of Gao Guigeng's men, who flares up angrily: "Hey! Who do you think you are insulting!"

Gao Guigeng can see he is about to lash out with his fist, and he hurriedly puts out a hand to stop him, saying with an icy smile: "Well, *Mister* Qi, since you already know why we're here, let me explain a little more to you. Today, the Traitor Elimination Squad have come for you."

As he speaks, he has already thrust a dagger into the table, pinning a piece of paper to it, which reads: 'So dies another traitor. The Traitor Elimination Squad.'

Yang Zhixing jumps up and down in agitation: "The Young Master is no traitor! You can't..."

"Stop that, Uncle Yang." Qi Yuexuan waves his hand, and he sits up straight. "It's not for you to say whether I am a traitor or not."

"The list of traitors for punishment has been compiled by the government."

"Which government?"

"The National Government."

"The National Government? Huh! And where is that now?" Qi Yuexuan raises his voice. "Just at this moment, where is the Government of the Northeast? Where is the government of Rehe? Where is the Tianjin-Beiping Government of North China? Where indeed is the central government of Nanjing now? I am just a mere scholar, but I haven't run away. I've stayed here in the Beiping district. Where are all the great officials of those governments? Republican? Nationalist? Whatever flag a government is waving, its job is to protect the country and the people, not lose the country and desert the people, let alone damage the country and bring suffering to the people. They've levied excessive taxes and pared the people to the bone, but what did they use that money for? To fight a civil war! Now they're fighting an invader, why have they turned from fierce tigers into frightened rabbits? They raise their fists but neither attack nor defend. They just let themselves get beaten around the belly and buttocks. They've got the power, they've got the soldiers, they've got the guns and cannons, and they've all disappeared without trace, leaving it to the common people, totally unarmed, to resist the Japanese. What's that all about? And now they run away a hundred *li*, a thousand *li*, but find the time to look back and throw around random accusations of treachery. Isn't that the biggest joke under heaven? Traitor? Who's the traitor?"

Gao Guigeng secretly admires this Young Master from the Minister's Residence, and his expression begins to soften. Just at this moment, there is a dry cough from outside the door, which breaks the mood, and he says sternly: "Let's not talk about things beyond our control. Let's talk about you. It's very hard to believe that the honorary chairman of the New People's Assembly is not a traitor!"

Yang Zhixing scrambles to rescue the topic: "That is doing him the greatest injustice. The Young Master never accepted the position. He's never received a cent of salary and has never undertaken any duties. The Japanese... the Japanese insisted, but the Young Master made the excuse that he had to offer sacrifices to his ancestors and come back here to Laoqiying, precisely so no one would suspect him of collaborating. You don't just have to believe me, you can see with your own eyes and work it out for yourself. What kind of traitor gives up his fine mansion and easy life, and suffers the hardships of the mountains and valleys instead?"

"Even supposing he never took up his post as chairman of that committee, wasn't the act of being appointed an act of betrayal?"

"Hah! Didn't you just mention the explosion on Miaofengshan, and the ambush? How can you just forget about them?"

"Were they... were they really your work?"

"Don't say another word, Uncle Yang!" says Qi Yuexuan.

"Well, why don't you tell me if you won't let him talk?"

Qi Yuexuan replies coolly: "Why don't I tell you? Because of that tatty piece of paper, and because of your guns and knives."

"Hah! I gave you the chance to speak, but you wouldn't. That's the sign of a guilty conscience, or are you really not afraid that I will punish you as befits a traitor?" Gao Guigeng simply can't work out Qi Yuexuan.

Qi Yuexuan fiddles with an oil lamp so the light flickers on his face, illuminating his indignant expression. He says in a low-pitched voice: "Slander comes from the stupid and lands on the wise. I know my own heart, so what use are further words? I make my own judgment on loyalty and treachery, good and evil. All regard for whether the nation is destroyed and our homes lost, for life or death is long gone from me. All I can do is implore you to wait and see, just as when... just as when, at the end of the Ming dynasty, Yuan Chonghuan[2] suffered the plottings of the eunuchs, and was unjustly executed at Caishikou for collaborating with the enemy. Then all the bystanders fought for a piece of his flesh so they could eat it. Fortunately, this grievous injustice was later wiped clean and all subsequent generations have revered him as a hero. I don't know whether you are willing to wait to see whether the future will turn out as when the treacherous eunuchs were reviled for all time, or as when those ignorant people in the market spat on his memory."

The room has gone silent, as though everyone has stopped breathing. Gao Guigeng just turns and walks over to the doorway, where he shouts: "Alright, you can come out now, so I don't have to do your dirty work any more."

A voice answers from outside, and a man comes in. He is also in tight-fitting clothes with a mask covering half his face, but as soon as he stops, he cups his hands in greeting to Qi Yuexuan and says with a smile: "Brother Yuexuan, it's been a long time."

As soon as he hears the voice, Qi Yuexuan's eyes widen in surprise, and he leaps excitedly to his feet. Then he has a change of heart, and slams his fist down on the table, saying furiously: "Hao Bingchen, you little bastard! You think wearing a piddling little mask means I won't recognise that fat arse of yours? Do you think you can still deceive me? Ha! Even if you were burnt to ashes, I'd still know you!"

Hao Bingchen accepts the insults without demur. He takes off his mask and gives a bark of laughter: "Ha ha! I deserved that, Brother Yuexuan. Well cursed! If you still haven't got it out of your system, hit me a couple of times, I don't mind. We've been friends for so many years, how could I not believe in you? Even so, with the world in turmoil as it is, and fish and dragons sharing the same river, I really had no choice but to arrange today's little test."

When he hears this, most of Qi Yuexuan's anger vanishes, and he asks with a smile: "Are there any more tests?"

"No more tests."

"Are you letting me off easy because we're friends?"

"No, no, it's based on facts and a desire for the common good."

"And are you still working for that National Government of yours?"

"A general in the field doesn't always heed his ruler's orders. Captain Gui and I report things as we see them to our superiors, and act as each other's guarantor."

"Captain Gui?"

"That's him there." Hao Bingchen points to Gao Guigeng.

Gao Guigeng removes his mask too, and cups his hands with a smile on his face: "Please forgive me, Young Master Qi. We can consider ourselves old acquaintances too."

Qi Yuexuan certainly feels his face is familiar, but it is Yang Zhixing who slaps his thigh and exclaims: "Young Master, it's Lao Gao the night soil collector, Gao Guigeng! Wangtian and Chenglong's father!"

"Ah yes..." Qi Yuexuan remembers now, but then stands stock still in amazement. "But aren't you..."

"It's me alright, Young Master Qi. You are not seeing ghosts, Yama hasn't taken me yet," Gao Guigeng says, bowing deeply to Qi Yuexuan and Yang Zhixing. "Young Master, Manager Yang, I know I was in the wrong just now. I,

Gao Guigeng, am not the kind of man who forgets a favour or ignores justice, but I really..."

"Everything's clear now. It's fine," says Yang Zhixing, his face wreathed in smiles. "The only people to blame are the Japanese devils."

The warm expressions of friendship, old and new, are interrupted by loud shouts from the courtyard and the roof of the building.

"Stand where you are!"

"Don't move!"

"Nobody move or you'll be killed!"

A myriad of torches lights up the area outside the room.

Gao Guigeng, Hao Bingchen and the other men all draw the guns they have just put away. Seeing this, Qi Yuexuan exclaims urgently: "Don't do anything rash, gentlemen! They're my men."

With this, he and Yang Zhixing go out of the room, with Gao Guigeng and Hao Bingchen close on their heels. There are already a dozen or so men rushing into the courtyard through the main gates, and heads are peering over the roof and walls. In the torchlight, there is the glint of numerous machineguns, flintlocks and blunderbusses. A number of the masked men are forced under the eaves of the northern room, and although they're still armed, they can see they are surrounded and heavily outnumbered, and they lose the will to fight.

This is the rescue force brought by Lao Zhang after he slipped out of the back window.

"For heaven's sake don't fire!" Qi Yuexuan shouts at the top of his voice.

Grandpa Dong pops up from behind a large tree: "Don't fire! You'll wound the Young Master!"

Then, pointing behind Qi Yuexuan, at Gao Guigeng and Hao Bingchen, he yells: "Hand over your weapons now, and let him go, or I'll let you go... to your deaths. If you're not careful, none of you will leave Laoqiying on your feet."

Qi Yuexuan hurries forward a few steps, but before he can start to explain, one of the villagers draws him to one side to protect him.

"Hand over your weapons!" Grandpa Dong yells again, and in an instant, the cry is taken up on all sides.

A moment later, three guns are thrown onto the ground, and they are collected by Grandpa Dong's men. Then, Qi Yuexuan shakes himself free of the villager, rushes through the throng of men in the courtyard and raises both his arms. Shouting himself hoarse, he yells: "Listen to me, all of you! They're anti-Japanese resistance. They're with me. It's all a mistake. Everyone put down your weapons, come down and go home."

Grandpa Dong still has his suspicions: "What group do they belong to?"

Qi Yuexuan pulls him over to Gao Guigeng and Hao Bingchen. He introduces each of them and provides a lengthy explanation before Grandpa Dong finally believes him, and he leaves with all the others.

At this point, Gao Guigeng furiously seizes hold of one of his men who has handed over his gun, and he raises his hand, about to slap him. Qi Yuexuan hurriedly stops him: "Don't! Don't! You can't blame them. They could see everyone was Chinese, ordinary folk. What else were they going to do but hand over their weapons?"

"Those guns... I still can't..."

"Ha ha, it was all a bit chaotic," says Grandpa Dong. "I really don't know who took them. I'll ask around, of course, but it's a bit like trying to find which dog stole a bun – if you don't see one with the food in its mouth, it's hard to tell which is the culprit."

"That won't do!" Gao Guigeng says angrily.

"Enough!" Qi Yuexuan laughs. "It's only a few guns. They don't really matter very much to you, after all. Show a little largesse. If you leave them behind, they're still going to be used against the Japanese, aren't they? Besides, you spent all that time scaring me out of my wits, and I think something more than just words is needed as an apology. Don't you agree?"

Gao Guigeng looks around him and smiles ruefully. "Alright, so be it. I'll report the loss, and that'll be that."

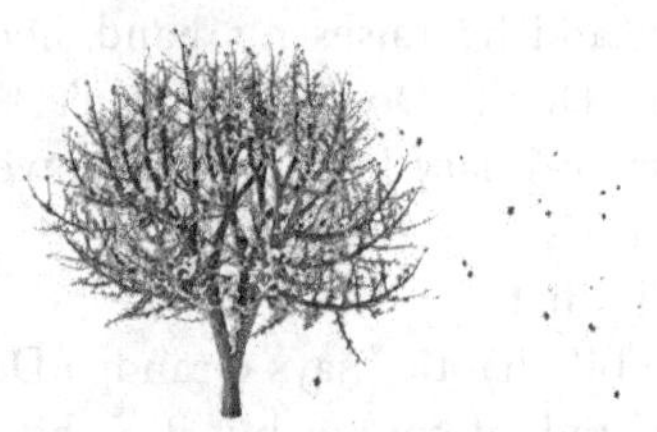

Chapter 23

Wangtian's wedding is settled as Yang Zhixing has suggested, with the celebrations taking place on the twenty-sixth. The evening before, Yang Zhixing hurries home. Mother Yan and Yue E have already prepared the marriage bedding and daily necessities, and they make up two full loads. He takes his wife and daughter over to receive Caiping. Thus, the western side courtyard of the Minister's Residence becomes the family home she will get married from, and early the next morning she will set out from there in the wedding sedan, to be carried on a roundabout route to the Gao family home. This isn't just a case of wandering around just for appearances; it is, in fact, an old city custom, and essential for the wedding to be seen to be done properly.

Although there is no wedding marquee in the small Gao family courtyard, the gates are adorned with lucky characters, lanterns have been strung up, and the hired tables, chairs and benches are stacked up inside. The little northern room has been tidied and cleaned, there's a lucky character on the door, cut paper decorations in the windows and a celebratory hanging scroll over the *kang*. In fact, it's only the happy couple-to-be who aren't quite up to scratch – one is covered in dirt, and the other is slippery with cooking oil.

"Just look at the two of you!" Yue E says, grinning at them. "A right pair of earth gods!"

Wangtian laughs sheepishly and makes to brush himself down, but Caiping stops him.

"Go outside if you're going to do that, all the food for tomorrow is in here!" She turns to Yue E with a smile. "Everything for the feast that needs steaming has been steamed, and everything that needs frying has been fried. All I have to do tomorrow is reheat them, and we're all set."

Mother Yan shakes her head. "And what would a new bride be doing in the kitchen? That's my job tomorrow. It's what I'm good at."

"But you're the bride's mother! I can't let you work," Caiping says, rolling down her sleeves and taking off her apron. "Don't worry, the feast is being held outside tomorrow, and no one will go inside. I'll just slip in and do it all secretly. If we don't make a fuss about it, no one will ever know."

At this point, Yang Zhixing interrupts, trying to hurry things along: "That's all settled then. Now be off with you. The three of you go home, have a good wash and go to sleep. You have to be up early tomorrow. There's lots to get ready – clothes, make-up, all that kind of thing. You'll be busy all day."

Yue E agrees, and she leads Caiping out of the room. Mother Yan is about to follow, when she sees that Yang Zhixing hasn't moved. She pulls up a wooden bench, sits down and asks: "What's this? Aren't you coming with us?"

"I need to talk to Wangtian."

"What's so urgent? You've had a long journey back today, and tomorrow you're going to be the master of ceremonies."

"I know. I only need a couple of words. You go on ahead. Off you go."

Only when Mother Yan is out of the room does he beckon Wangtian over and indicate that he should sit down. Still covered in dirt, Wangtian squats beside him. Yang Zhixing remains silent for a long time.

"What is it, Uncle Yang? Spit it out."

Yang Zhixing grunts, and says conversationally: "I've put your clothes for tomorrow on the *kang*. You can go and have a wash in a moment, and when you're clean, you can try them on. They're the ones the Young Master wore for his wedding..."

"You've told me that already. That's... that's not all you wanted to say to me, is it? I can see there's something more important. Whatever it is, you can tell me. You'll know I'll take notice."

Yang Zhixing sighs and forces a smile. "Ai! Lao Litou and I lied to you, and now Lao Litou is dead, it's up to me to..."

"What can be so important that it's made you like this?"

"Your father..."

"What about my father?"

"Your father's not dead."

Wangtian isn't particularly surprised that Yang Zhixing should be thinking of his father on a day like this, and he says with a wry laugh: "What are you on about, Uncle Yang? We buried my father's ashes more than ten years ago..."

"Ai! The fact is, Lao Litou never even saw the body back then, so how could there be any ashes?"

"But I buried the urn with those ashes myself."

"Those were just the ashes from some twigs and grasses. When your Uncle Li and your father went off together as armed escorts that year, they met with some bandits. Your father ordered Lao Litou to protect their employer and his family, and he himself drew off the attackers. When Lao Litou went back to look for him, he found no sign of either your father or his body, only a heavily bloodstained patch of ground. He searched everywhere on his way back too, but there was still no sign. He was afraid of returning with nothing at all, so he burned some vegetation to create the ashes. I worked out what was going on the day of the burial. Although I was pretty sure your father must be dead, I was afraid you and your brother wouldn't let it rest, and would worry about it needlessly. That's why I've kept the story quiet all these years."

"So... how do you know my father's not dead?"

"I've seen him. Yesterday evening."

There is a buzzing in Wangtian's head, and he stares blankly at Yang Zhixing for a long while. Then, half questioningly, half to himself, he mutters: "Does he look like a bandit? With a scar half across his face? And he's calling himself Gui, not Gao?"

It's Yang Zhixing's turn to stare, speechless. All he can do is nod his head and grunt an affirmative.

Wangtian leaps to his feet, eyes blazing. "He's still my father, isn't he? Why has he stayed away so long, without even a letter? Did he like playing 'king of the mountains'? Was he enjoying all the killing and the plundering too much? Is his family lost to him? Doesn't he still have any sons?"

As he's speaking, he takes a New Year picture down from the wall and pulls out a brick. He removes a cloth bundle from the hole in the wall and throws it furiously down onto the *kang*. Yang Zhixing hurries to open it. Inside, there is a sword tassel and two gold bars.

"He gave me these."

"You've seen him?"

"He gave them to Ying'er, that day when I had the fever. I had my suspicions when I saw the sword tassel, but I didn't really believe it was him. Ha! I'd like to think it was clean money, but if it's come from a bandit, it's bound to have blood on it. You're going to see him again, aren't you? Give it back to him. I can't spend this money."

"You young idiot!" Yang Zhixing shouts at him. He picks up a broom and aims it at Wangtian, raising it high above his head.

Wangtian makes no move to get out of the way, but just looks at Yang Zhixing, tears running down his cheeks. "Hit me, Uncle Yang! Go on, hit me! You've seen how these last few years have treated us. Do you think it's been easy for me? How many crimes have been committed against me? How many times have I been wronged? But I always remembered what he told me: don't cheat anyone, don't do anyone harm. I have always played straight. So how can he have changed so much? Why hasn't he come home? Am I supposed to believe that our whole relationship, father and son, is only worth two gold bars? I haven't spent that money, and I'm not going to. I'd rather have my poor, old father back." Unable to go on, he begins to wail and sob.

Yang Zhixing's own eyes are moist now, as he says gently: "I know you're a dutiful son, Wangtian, and these years have not been easy for you. I also know that, in your heart of hearts, you have never let go of your father. But it hasn't been easy for your father to survive these years either. When he became a bandit, it was only because he had absolutely no alternative. You know how stubborn and determined he is. Do you think anything short of death would allow him to come home bearing such shame? As for those gold bars, never doubt that they have been hard-earned. They are his reward for killing Chinese traitors. Have you heard of the Traitor Elimination Squad that has been operating in Beiping recently? Your father is its captain."

"Is that... is that really true?"

"Absolutely and completely."

Wangtian stands there dumbstruck. When he hears Yang Zhixing detailing his father's past experiences and current circumstances, a smile breaks out across his tear-stained face.

"Can he come tomorrow?"

"How could he? Those Chinese traitors and the Japanese all want to arrest him and the rest of the squad, so how could he dare show his face at your wedding feast? He says, wait till this state of affairs is over, then he'll find a way to come home."

Suddenly, Wangtian remembers something, and he gives an involuntary shudder. "Fuck it!" he exclaims.

"What's the matter?"

"Out of the blue, a few days ago, Chenglong brought a file from some prison records round to show me, and he asked me whether it was Dad. At the time, I didn't dare believe it was, but he must have had his suspicions."

"It doesn't matter if he did recognise him," Yang Zhixing says with a laugh. "Maybe he'll stop that little bastard's wild ways. Your father said that, if his soft heart hadn't held him back, he would have killed him a long time ago. He's planning to find an opportunity to see Chenglong face to face, and lay his cards on the table. He wants to give him a way out, and see whether he's willing to change his ways. Ai! I really hope your father can rein him in."

Wangtian nods and says quietly: "Uncle Yang, are the Traitor Elimination Squad and the Communist Party one and the same thing?"

"No, no, they were formed by the old government." Yang Zhixing decides this isn't quite right, and he corrects himself: "Actually, you could say that they are pretty much the same thing. Not so long ago, the people running the Communist Party were also called bandits, and weren't they granted an amnesty? At the moment, if you're both killing traitors and Japanese devils, then you're on the same side."

"In that case, Dad and me are on the same side."

Yang Zhixing feels there's something odd in his tone, and he asks: "What's going on, eh? What have you got yourself involved with, you young fool?"

"Nothing."

"Really?"

Wangtian realises he's been a bit loose-tongued, so he bites his lip, not wanting to give any more away, and he burbles on: "Nothing... really."

Yang Zhixing doesn't pursue the matter, but just urges Wangtian: "If it's nothing, that's fine. You need to be a little more open with me, young lad, and settle down. If you want to pass your days happily when you're married, then, for heaven's sake, don't keep rocking the boat. When the country is in trouble, the most important thing is to remain true, and country and family are the same. If you're thinking of risking your life over something, you must also always remember your place and preserve your heritage. In due course, there's something I want to discuss with you, something much more important than killing a couple of traitors or Japanese devils."

"What is it?" Wangtian asks excitedly.

"You'll find out when the time comes."

THE NEXT DAY, the marriage ceremony follows its prescribed order, and, when the appointed time arrives, the wedding sedan party is already assembled in front of the gates of the Minister's Residence. Of course, appearances are everything in these circumstances, and Wangtian is wearing the outfit Qi Yuexuan gave him: a long robe and a buttoned Mandarin jacket, draped in red and with gold decorations. He is riding a black mule and looks like a different person altogether. Even the neighbours in the hutong do a double-take, wondering which residence's young master it is, and needless to say, they all come rushing over. There hasn't been such a commotion on the street since the Japanese occupied Beiping; of course, there have been other weddings, but none as grand as this. The neighbours throng around this rare and precious sight, clustering three deep, inside and outside the gates of the Residence. The young kids of the hutong run in and out of the wedding sedan troupe, clamouring for wedding sweets and picking up unexploded firecrackers.

The matron of honour goes in to collect the new bride, while the sedan troupe stays outside blowing their instruments and beating their drums. When Mother Yan and Yue E lead Caiping out, it is as though some star performer has just taken the stage, and, although her head is covered, her tastefully selected outfit draws shouts of acclaim.

Caiping has just climbed into the wedding sedan, but the head bearer has not yet given the command to lift the poles, when Chenglong comes out of the doorway where he has been hiding, with an angry expression on his face. He glares at Wangtian and asks: "What kind of behaviour is this, when my big brother gets married and tries to keep it from me?"

Before Wangtian can reply, Yue E interrupts fiercely: "Your brother has been completely open and above board about getting married, so what's this nonsense about hiding it from you? We haven't seen hide nor hair of you for days. Did you go to visit him? No!"

Chenglong has been preoccupied with arresting the Traitor Elimination Squad, and has been out at all hours, sometimes not even coming back at night. Even so, he continues to twist things: "Hah! I know you still didn't want me to find out."

"It was me, Chenglong. I didn't tell you on purpose," Wangtian says unapologetically.

"Why? Do you want me to lose face completely?"

"It's not that I want to make you lose face. I was trying to avoid it."

"What do you mean?"

"What is your job now? A gun at your waist, smoke coming out of your arse, the whole city shakes when you stamp your foot. How can that broken-down old home of ours be a fitting place for you? Besides, even if you don't despise your pauper of an elder brother, I was afraid you'd frighten everyone away. But if, deep down, you still want me as your brother, then stop putting on airs, and afterwards, we'll have a drink together."

"You?" Chenglong replies, looking Wangtian up and down. "Poor? How can a poor person put on such a show? What you've got on today is a hundred times better than anything I ever had to wear."

"So that's it!" Wangtian shouts back at him. "The Young Master gave me this. It's the very best quality workmanship and material. It would have been worth five hundred silver yuan back then. Don't worry about *him* being poor today, because it's likely that tomorrow he's going to be richer than you."

Not wanting to say anything rash, Chenglong huffs and puffs: "So... if he's sending the wedding sedan, why is it going from my house, then?"

"Your house?" Yang Zhixing laughs. "Aren't you exaggerating a little? The west courtyard is the bride's family home. Don't stare at me like that. As for your brother from the Gao family, who's to say, in the future, he's not going to be bigger than the Minister's Residence!"

This speech confounds Chenglong, and even Mother Yan and Yue E are completely at a loss.

"Right, up with the sedan. We don't want to be late."

On Yang Zhixing's command, the head bearer gives a loud cry of "Lift", and the matron of honour begins to recite the wedding verse: "The new bride mounts the sedan, her whole road is one of joy. She leaves behind her lucky home, on her way to new riches."

Just as when Chenglong married Yue E, the sedan chair troupe leave Minister's Residence Hutong at the east end, and turn south. When they reach Di'anmen Street, they turn west and follow Shichahai Hutong back round to the west entrance to Minister's Residence Hutong, making a large circuit. After the sedan has been put down at the entrance to the small courtyard, the matron of honour helps the new bride step over the brazier, and the bridegroom shoots three arrows to frighten off evil spirits. Only then does the bride stand in front of the doorway. Yang Zhixing and Mother Yan are already sitting on two chairs that have been placed in the doorway. Amid a chorus of good wishes, Wangtian and Caiping bow to the gods of heaven and earth, bow to the bride's parents, bow to each other, and finally the happy couple enter the bridal chamber. Clown has taken on the role of door guardian, blocking the doorway to keep out strangers and stopping anyone from creeping up under the window to peek inside. This isn't just because they are following tradition, but also because, for the time being, the bridal chamber has become the kitchen. As soon as she enters, Caiping removes her veil and turns into the head chef. Wangtian works the bellows as sous-chef, while Mother Yan and Yue E take on the role of kitchen assistants.

Yang Zhixing takes charge of arranging the tables and benches, occasionally whispering instructions through the window: "Make sure you look after the wedding clothes. Don't get them dirty or scorched. If oil gets on them, you'll never get it out yourselves, and it will be even worse trying to repair them if they get burnt. Just one small hole in that kind of finery would cost two silver yuan to repair..."

"Keep your nose out of things, you old busybody," Mother Yan replies from inside the room. "Do you think these two poor kids need your instructions? Are the tables ready yet? Can we bring the food out?"

As soon as the tables and benches are properly arranged, the wine and cold dishes are laid out. Just as Yang Zhixing tells the guests to sit down, the large bowls with the hot dishes are also brought out. The four tables fill the entire small courtyard, and with twenty or so people all gossiping away, shouting and laughing, the place is as noisy as a battle scene on an opera stage.

Of course, the festivities are not complete without the groom, and as soon as Wangtian comes out, he goes over to toast his guests. Before he is halfway round the four tables, clinking cups, his face is already flushed and sweating.

"Hey Brother Wangtian," Clown says, smiling mischievously, "it's terrible for you to be doing all the chit-chat by yourself. Why don't you call the bride out here, to show her face and drink some toasts. That would be much more fun."

Yang Zhixing gives him a slap. "Don't mess with things that aren't your business, you young fool. You're not out in the sticks now, sleeping three generations on one *kang*. This is the capital, and the bride doesn't come out and carouse with the guests here. That's not our custom."

"Aiyo, grandad!" Clown laughs. "These customs of yours are so lame. Why not change them for the better? After all, since the bride has done all the cooking, why shouldn't she join us to eat? Don't worry, this country hick has been knocking around the city for some years now. I won't go too far. It's traditional for us all to have some fun with the bride and groom. If you don't bring her out to let off some steam, she's going to be so noisy in the bridal chamber tonight, she'll make the walls rattle!"

The courtyard echoes with everyone's laughter.

"He's right. Bring out the bride."

"Maybe her face is covered in pockmarks, and she won't let anyone see."

"Could be she doesn't have a nose."

"Bullshit! I heard she used to be a singer, pretty as an angel. They think that, once you see her, they won't be able to drag her away from you."

Wangtian feels like his head is going to explode with all the noisy heckling, and Yang Zhixing and Mother Yan are even more agitated, caught between anger and embarrassed laughter.

Then a crisp, clear voice makes itself heard: "What are you all squabbling over? Are you picking on these old folk?" Caiping is standing four-square in the doorway. "Take a good look. Do I have a face full of pockmarks and no nose?"

Caiping has just finished doing her face. She has painted on her eyebrows and rouged her cheeks, and when you add on the effect of the red wedding outfit and phoenix headdress, her natural beauty is now enough to render anyone speechless. Quite apart from those who've never seen her before, even Wangtian stares at her in awe.

Caiping walks over with small, quick steps, and when she sees Wangtian coming up to greet her, she whispers: "You've got an important job to do tonight. Don't drink so much, I'll cover for you."

"Can you handle it?"

"Don't worry, I can hold my drink."

As she speaks, she makes her way over to the main table, pours herself some wine and quietly clinks cups with Wangtian, expecting him to say a few words. Wangtian coughs a few times, but can't get his words out, so Caiping raises her cup and says: "Today is a joyful day for my husband, Gao Wangtian, and myself, Wei Ying, and we are sincerely moved that you have all honoured us by coming to share in our happiness. My husband is the kind of good man it is hard to find, and it is my good fortune to be marrying someone like him. Neither of us have our parents, so Uncle Yang and Mother Yan are our mother and father, and all of you sitting here are our uncles, elder bothers and elder sisters. There are no strangers here, so please enjoy yourselves as much as you please. The food and wine may be poor, but there is enough for you to eat and drink your fill. The two of us would like first to drink a cup in your honour."

Stroking his snowy white goatee, Yang Zhixing turns to Mother Yan with a smile: "She's a steady girl, this Ying'er. Wangtian could do worse than copy her. She speaks sense and with propriety, and she is adaptable in how she acts – neither listless and timid, nor rash and angry, and very self-possessed in public. She's not the least petty-minded. In fact, she's just the person to be the mistress of a household."

Mother Yan can't help smiling at this. "Steady is steady but as for being mistress of the household, mistress of what? Mistress of the earth and dust?"

Yang Zhixing smiles and looks at her askance. He doesn't say anything, but there seems to be something lurking in his expression. Mother Yan is sure there is more to what he has said than meets the eye, and she curses him inwardly: You old devil. What are you up to now?

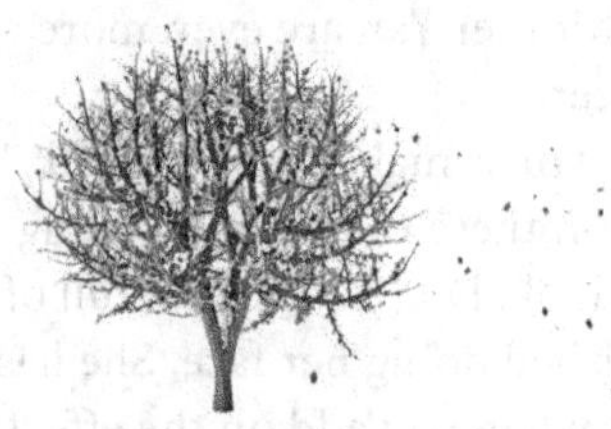

Chapter 24

That evening, a little after nine o'clock, Zhang Zhicheng, Zuo Xichuan, Chenglong and Zhou Si leave the Tianhe restaurant and go to the warehouse where the goods are being stored. A large truck has already drawn up outside the gates, with five or six men standing around beside it, waiting for the owners to inspect the merchandise and supervise the loading. Zhou Si barks an order, and the men spring to life. Zuo Xichuan and Chenglong stand to one side, smoking, but Zhang Zhixing doesn't dare take his eye off things, and he stands by the truck, holding an inventory and watching every package as it is loaded.

"I've got it covered, Brother Zhang. Don't you trust me?" Zhou Si says.

"It's not a question of trust. But when you're in a Buddhist temple, you recite Buddhist scriptures, and since I'm being a merchant, I want to do it properly."

"Yes, yes, you're right," Zhou Si replies, but his eyes are everywhere, sweeping over the merchandise and occasionally stealing a glance at Zhang Zhicheng.

At this moment, one of the men comes out carrying a large package, and Zhou Si hurries forward so that he is blocking Zhang Zhicheng's line of sight as he helps load it onto the truck. But Zhang Zhicheng claps him on the shoulder and calls out: "Wait, wait", and he steps forward to take a careful look and to feel the package all over.

Zhou Si is rather flustered. "What's the matter, Brother Zhang?"

Zhang Zhicheng points at the package. "This isn't one of ours."

"That's not possible! No one else's stuff was stored here. We had a man on guard specially. What could have gone wrong? I came here myself several times." Zhou Si then takes the opportunity to slip out into the yard.

"What's up?" says Zuo Xichuan, who has made his way over too.

"This package isn't one of ours," Zhang Zhicheng repeats with a smile.

"If it's not one of ours, whose is it?" says a puzzled Chenglong. "You don't think..."

Zhou Si comes hurrying back out of the courtyard. "I've checked," he says. "There are twenty-three packages in here, and twenty-seven have already been loaded onto the truck. That's fifty in all. The count is correct."

"The count may be correct," Zhang Zhicheng says, "but there's definitely something wrong with this package." So saying, he pulls out another package and points to an indecipherable seal on it. "This is what our packages look like. I put a secret sign on them – on the bottom corner for cotton, top corner for cloth and in the middle for daily necessities. This package doesn't have any sign."

Zhou Si silently curses his own carelessness. In the past, when grain taxes were shipped by boat, every landing stage had its own unique secret sign, and, although he has never seen one, he has heard fellow society members talk about them. He'd had no suspicion that Zhang Zhicheng might have used this ploy. Nonetheless, he puts a brave face on it and says with a dismissive laugh: "When you play mah-jong, there's always a tile you forget to declare... perhaps that's what's happened with this package?"

"That's right," Chenglong chips in.

Zhang Zhicheng doesn't say anything, but takes the unmarked package down off the truck, pulls out a small knife and slashes it open. He thrusts a hand in, feels around and pulls out a bundle of bandages and a bottle of iodine.

"This package is full to bursting," he says. "There's an awful lot more in there. Chenglong, everything of ours is on the inventory, and there are no bandages or iodine. These are military necessities, and it's not that they wouldn't be good business, rather that I don't have the nerve to do it, and I'm afraid it might cause problems for you. What I can't work out is whether this stuff is a well-intentioned gift or maliciously planted contraband."

Standing beside him, Zuo Xichuan says: "Trading in military necessities is completely off-limits. So what's going on here?"

Chenglong points at Zhou Si and the other men, and yells at them: "You useless fuckwits! Tell me? What's going on? If I find out someone's up to mischief, I'll have his guts!"

"Leave it," says Zhang Zhicheng. "It's best not to make a fuss about it now. Tell your men to start loading the truck. We've still got to get on our way. It's not one of my packages, which is why I pulled it out for checking, but even if it was one of mine, I'd be happy for you to open it up and search it. There shouldn't be any misgivings or complaints among partners."

Chenglong orders his men: "Get a move on and bring out the rest of the goods."

Several of them hurry out into the yard, followed by Zhou Si. Zhang Zhicheng moves a bit closer to Chenglong, and says in a low voice: "You've got a traitor in your midst, Chenglong. This was almost certainly aimed at you."

"Yes, I know. The Japanese know I've farted almost before I do. I'm just not sure who it is yet."

"Ha, yes, hiding in plain sight, I expect."

A man of Chenglong's intelligence is not going to mistake Zhang Zhicheng's meaning. He nods and says: "We've got some other business on later tonight, and I can't get out of it. Originally, I'd arranged for Zhou Si to escort, but... I can change him for someone else if you want."

Zhang Zhicheng shakes his head. "As long as we're only carrying my goods, as they are packed and loaded, then I don't care who it is. Just make sure you take care, that's all."

They check and double-check the merchandise until they are finally satisfied, and then it is all loaded onto the truck.

"Chenglong," says Zhang Zhicheng, calling him over. "Forty-nine of the fifty are ours, and I haven't opened them. Do you want to take a look?"

"No need. The only thing is, you're short one package, and it's a little…"

"Don't worry, I'll accept liability. I'll leave that extra package with you, as I'd really rather it didn't mess up the whole business."

"That's fine, let's just say I owe you for now, and we'll discuss it later."

Quite soon, the lorry is covered in tarpaulin and tied down firmly with rope. Zuo Xichuan and Chenglong take their leave of each other, and the former climbs up into the driver's cab. Zhou Si waves his hand, and a motorcycle and sidecar drives over to him. Chenglong reminds him: "I've seen to all the exit permits from the city. The two of you escort them as far as Changping, and then come back."

"Yes, I know, don't worry," Zhou Si replies, then calls out quickly to Zhang Zhicheng: "You sit in the sidecar – it's warmer."

"No, it's fine, I'll leave that to you. It's too cramped for me and my long legs. I'll sit here." So saying, he takes his place on the pillion seat of the motorbike.

NIGHT HAS FALLEN, and the countryside outside Beiping's city walls is plunged into darkness. Fortunately, the weather has been quite clement recently, so a few stars are visible, shedding a little light on the scene. Through the gloom, a file of dark silhouettes can be seen heading straight along the road leading north. There are two men to a cart, one pushing, one pulling, six carts in all. In charge of the lead cart are none other than Clown and the newly-wed Wangtian. The men behind them are all brother workers from the night soil depot, and their carts are all night soil tankers.

Today's wedding party had gone on until after three in the afternoon, and it was almost evening by the time they left the city. By now, they have already covered twenty *li* and will soon be at the Qing River. To look at, their night soil carts don't seem any different from the usual, except the tanks are a little bigger, and their wheels are not the traditional wooden ones with rubber rims, but are almost exactly like imported pneumatic tyres. In fact, these vehicles are considered the last word in night soil equipment. By the look of them, the carts are making heavy weather of it – their tyres are bulging under the pressure of the load, and the two men to each cart are having their work cut out.

Quite soon, a light appears up ahead. In the distance, they can see sandbags piled up either side of the road, and a spiked barricade across the middle. There are two gas lamps, one hanging from the guard post and the other from a tree, and seven or eight Japanese soldiers loafing around on either side of the road. They have reached the Qing River checkpoint.

"Take it easy, brothers," Wangtian calls softly. "We'll have to play it by ear. We don't want to raise their suspicions."

"Yessir!" the men at the rear reply.

As the carts approach, a sergeant of the guards shouts: "Stop! Stop right there!"

The carts all come to a halt and form a line in front of the checkpoint. As the sergeant steps in front of the lead cart, the smell hits him, and, with his hand over his nose, he asks: "What do you do? What do you carry?"

Wangtian bows, smiling: "All we have is night soil, great lord. We're taking it to Zhangwang Village up ahead. They use it for growing vegetables."

The sergeant looks him up and down, then glances at the carts and asks: "Why you not send them in daytime? Why has to be night-time?"

"We collect the stuff during the day, and they wanted it urgently. They said it's for their hothouse vegetables and... they said they're growing them for the Imperial Army. So we've been busting our guts, working round the clock, in order to get it there, even if it means travelling through the night."

The sergeant only understands half of what Wangtian is saying. He grunts and signals to the soldiers behind him. He barks a couple of words of command, and two of the soldiers acknowledge them and go at the double to the last two carts. Of course, they are intending to search them.

Without waiting for a sign from Wangtian, Clown lifts the covers of one of the front carts. A ferocious stench gushes forth, making the sergeant, who has come up close to look, grimace and cover his nose with his hand. He shines an electric torch inside and sweeps his eyes over the contents, then, immediately steps back a good few paces, and turns away to gulp in several lungfuls of fresh air.

What is in the carts is not fresh night soil, but some of the dregs from the depot reservoir that have been festering there for a good few days. Old wine is particularly fragrant, old shit is particularly rank, and there is no faking either. If you're not used to it, the first breath chokes you, and the next two take your breath away completely.

In no time at all, the two soldiers come running back from the rear carts, and from the sight of their hands clapped over their noses, it's clear they've been on the receiving end of the stench too. The sergeant hastily waves his hand and shouts: "On your way!"

Wangtian shouts back to the rear carts, waits until the last one has passed the checkpoint, and only then moves on with his own cart. He has just passed the checkpoint, when, to his shock, the sergeant calls out from behind him: "Stop!"

The sergeant is staring at the bottom of the night soil vats, and he taps them all over with a wooden baton. He seems suspicious of the sound it produces, and, with a poke of his stick, he unhooks the filler hose from where it hangs. Not a good move. The end of the pipe jerks forward, and the shit soup inside the vat spurts out like a fountain. The sergeant tries to dodge it, but he's not quick enough, and some of the liquid splatters across his legs and shoes.

Hearing his squeals, Clown rushes forward nimbly to roll up the hose, and he hangs it back up on its iron hook. His tongue is as nimble as his hands, as he says: "Aiya, great lord! What a prankster you are! You've been dying to mess around with a shit cart, haven't you! Well, don't worry, it's all the real stuff, not a square of stinky bean curd mixed in."

It's not clear how much of this the sergeant understands, but he waves his baton in exasperation and yells: "On your way! On your way! Quick, quick!"

HALF AN HOUR OR SO LATER, the sound of motor engines is heard on the road from the direction of Beiping, and the light from several headlamps pierces the dark. The Japanese sergeant immediately orders the spiked barrier to be lowered, and he leads several of his men to stand across the carriageway. A few moments later, a motorcycle and sidecar and a lorry pull up in front of the checkpoint. The Beiping city gate pass is the joint responsibility of the Kempeitai and the CID, and because Chenglong has had a word with Captain Yamaguchi, their passes are stamped and they are let on their way there without any inspection. The checkpoints on the two roads at the Qing River and Changping, however, do not come under the Kempeitai, but are the responsibility of the Twenty-Third Division of the Japanese Army of North China. In normal circumstances, their inspections are more rigorous going in than coming out. Vehicles on their way out of Beiping just have to show their seal of inspection from the Kempeitai in the city, and they have their passes stamped and are let on their way, with only a token inspection. More recently, however, conditions have tightened, and the Japanese army has begun to take a serious interest.

"What your business?" the sergeant demands, stepping forward.

Zhou Si stands up in the sidecar, nods and bows. "We are from the Beiping CID, escorting some goods out of the city, great lord."

"What goods?"

Zhang Zhixing dismounts from the motorbike, and hands over his pass and the certified inventory. "Just daily necessities."

"Transporting to where?"

"Rehe."

"You goods?"

"They belong to Mr Shoi Keisen."

"Where him?"

Zuo Xichuan sticks the upper half of his body out the driver's cab and says, in Japanese: "I'm here. I'm Shoi Keisen."

The sergeant hurries to the front of the truck, stands to attention and salutes: "My apologies, sir, but please show me your identification documents."

Zuo Xichuan hands over his passport, which the sergeant inspects in the light of his electric torch.

"My apologies, sir, but I need to inspect your merchandise."

Zuo Xichuan nods. The sergeant turns to Zhang Zhicheng, and says in rough and ready Chinese: "You! Untie rope! Unload good! Us want look inside."

Zuo Xichuan is infuriated, and cursing as he climbs down from the cab, waves his finger under the sergeant's nose. In Japanese, he demands: "What unit are you from? What's your name?"

The sergeant half bows, and he replies, also in Japanese: "I am Sergeant Mikimoto of the Hameda Brigade of the Yamamoto wing of the Twenty-Third Division of the North China Expeditionary Army."

"The goods were inspected when they left the city. Why do you need the packages opened up again?"

"Apologies, sir, those are the commanding officer's orders. He says someone is trying to smuggle out a large quantity of prohibited goods by truck, and that all loads must be inspected."

"Who is the commanding officer who gave those orders? Telephone through to the general headquarters of the Army of North China, and check with General Yamano."

"Apologies, sir, but I can't by-pass my chain of command. I only take orders from my central control."

"So how long is this inspection of yours going to delay me?"

"Please be patient. I'll be as quick as I can."

"Let him look, Lord Shoi," Zhang Zhicheng interjects. "If we end up in a stalemate with him, it will waste even more time." With this, he turns and asks the sergeant: "Is the checkpoint up ahead at Changping also under the same central control, great lord?"

"Yes, yes, the same."

"Does that mean after you've done your exhaustive search here, we have to undergo another one at Changping?"

"No. We open search everything and check it thoroughly here, with my signature, you can pass through ahead without search."

"Good, we'll take your word on that," says Zhang Zhicheng, before he calls out to Zhou Si and the driver: "Come over here and give them a hand. Unload the truck and let them search everything."

In fact, the Japanese don't break open the packages and scatter the contents. They just make an opening where the packages are sealed, thrust in a hand and rummage around a bit. After about half an hour of this, they haven't found any prohibited goods. The sergeant is rather embarrassed as he stands to attention in front of Zuo Xichuan, and his bow is considerably deeper than before.

"My apologies, sir, for having caused you such inconvenience. Please excuse me. There are no contraband goods in your merchandise. Once you reload the truck, you can be on your way." When he sees Zuo Xichuan is still looking at him sternly, he hurriedly calls out to his men: "Come over here, and help them load the truck."

Their combined efforts mean the truck is reloaded quicker than it took to unload. Before Zhang Zhicheng has had time to retie the ropes over the tarpaulin, the sergeant has already signed and sealed the inventory, written a line of Japanese and is handing it back to Zuo Xichuan with the utmost respect.

"I have signed off on the inventory, Lord Shoi, and have clearly written that the whole load has already been opened and inspected. There are no contraband goods, and you should be allowed unhindered passage. I was just following orders. Please forgive me."

Zuo Xichuan still doesn't say anything, but he smiles faintly and nods.

With the CID motorcycle and sidecar in the lead, the truck passes through the Qing River checkpoint and speeds along without a hitch. After they've been travelling for ten minutes or so, a number of towering, ancient pine trees appear on the right-hand side of the road. Although there are trees along both sides of the road, they are mostly poplars, and in the winter they are just tall, thin poles, all branches and no leaves. But these few pine trees have strong, sturdy trunks, intertwined branches and luxuriant foliage, and are very eye-catching. Not far behind the trees is the entrance to a small country track that leads to Old Pine Village, about one *li* away.

Since they left the checkpoint, Zhang Zhicheng's gaze hasn't left the right-hand side of the road ahead, looking far into the distance, his eyes alight. He leans forward and says to the driver: "Pull up by those pine trees ahead, brother. I need to piss."

The driver doesn't reply, but Zhou Si, who is sitting beside him in the sidecar, says: "What would we be doing stopping in the pitch black there? Just hold it in for a while, until we get to Changping, then we'll see."

He sounds very impatient – which is not unreasonable for a man who has sweated blood devising a plan only to see it come to nothing and end up spending the night freezing his balls off.

Zhang Zhicheng keeps his temper and says with a laugh: "Alright, don't stop then. I wonder if a man can die from crossing his legs. Now, if I just lean over this way a bit, I can let loose a torrent worthy of the Dragon King." So saying, he does indeed lean over and thrusts a hand under his coat. "Lean forward a bit, Zhou Si, I don't want you to get a faceful."

This alarms Zhou Si, and he begins shouting: "Don't! Don't go! Stop! Stop! Stop the bike!"

Once the bike has stopped, Zhang Zhicheng hurriedly dismounts. But he doesn't head to the side of the road, but instead he steps behind Zhou Si. In the twinkling of an eye, he puts his right arm around Zhou Si's neck, pulling him tight into his chest, so he can't move an inch. At the same time, he draws his revolver with his left hand and sticks it into the small of the driver's back. In a low growl, he says: "Neither of you move. The first one who does is a dead man!"

With his head on one side, Zhou Si says in a strangled voice: "Stop... Brother Zhang... stop kidding around."

"Shut up! Another sound and I'll wring your neck," Zhang Zhicheng says, tightening his grip.

Zhou Si gestures in pain, but he doesn't say any more.

Zuo Xichuan and the driver of the truck come hurrying over and strip the two men of their weapons. Zhang Zhicheng fishes out a length of rope and begins to tie the two men up, back to back.

"Leave that to me," Zuo Xichuan says. "You two hurry up and load the goods."

A FEW DAYS BEFORE, Zhang Zhicheng had led Wangtian and his men to the reed-covered pit to the north of the city. They started excavating the weapons and ammunition, and wrapping them in oil paper. Following Zhang Zhicheng's diagrams, Wangtian and his men carefully built a hidden compartment into several night soil carts.

Wangtian leads Zhang Zhicheng into the undergrowth, where the carts have pulled up. He points to a pile of goods beside them: "We've unloaded all the goods, Brother Zhang. You can count them."

"No need for that," Zhang Zhicheng says, feeling the bundles. Are you sure none of the shit got into them?"

"Don't worry. You won't find a drop on them. We converted these carts according to your designs and used mortice and tenon joints on the secret compartments, and sealed all the cracks with putty. You've got a lot of space in that lorry of yours – the stuff on my six carts will only fill half of it."

Zhang Zhicheng laughs. "If we hadn't rewrapped it, and left it in its original packing cases, you wouldn't have got it all in ten carts. It may not take up as much space as before, but it doesn't weigh much less. You must be tired out after dragging it all this way."

As they're talking, the truck has driven up, and, at Zhang Zhicheng's command, everyone rushes to open the packages already on it. After they have half-emptied each package, they put the guns and ammunition into them, and then cover them up with the cotton and cloth they've just taken out, so they are completely concealed.

"Put the tarpaulin back on, Xiao Li," Zhang Zhicheng orders the driver. "Pull it down tight over the top packages."

Clown steps forward to point something out: "There's something over there, Brother Zhang. Don't leave it behind."

"Ah, no, that's for you. It's some cotton and cloth. Share it out among yourselves," Zhang Zhicheng says with a smile.

Clown is about to thank him, but Wangtian interrupts urgently: "We can't accept this, Brother Zhang. We can't let the troops fighting the Japanese freeze..."

"Alright, no need to go on," says Zhang Zhicheng, realising that he is going to keep on refusing. "This is your fair share. If you're willing to risk your lives against the Japanese, that makes you part of our Eighth Route Army, and this can be reckoned your army pay."

Wangtian can't see any way of continuing to refuse. "Alright, I'll pass on the cotton and cloth. But you must write to me when you've established your base camp, and settled in. Then, if I want to come and join your army, you've got to accept me. Alright?"

"Alright, that's how we'll leave things." Zhang Zhicheng claps him on the shoulder.

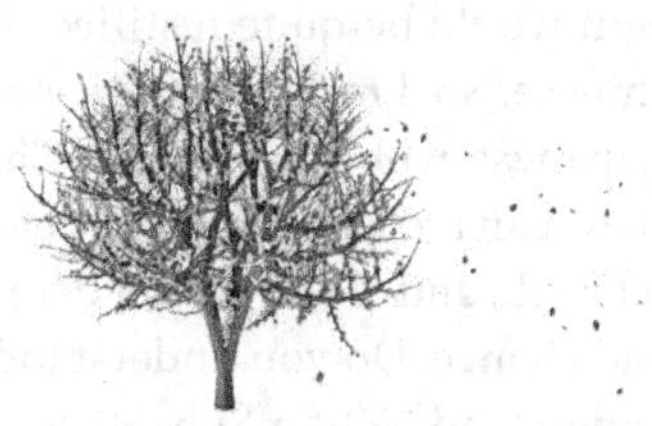

Chapter 25

When Zhou Si sees Zhang Zhicheng coming back, he raises his drooping head and says piteously: "Have you forgotten who I am, Brother Zhang? I've always been your errand boy, your cheerleader, your whipping boy. It's not fair. We are members of the same society, after all, so please show me some mercy and let me go."

"Ha! Let you go? You're a coward, but you're cunning and you have a loose mouth, so what would I be doing letting you go back to destroy someone else by informing on them? Here seems as good a place as any to..."

"Don't, Brother Zhang! Stop!" Zhou Si cries out in distress. "I wouldn't dare, I really wouldn't dare do anything so stupid. I haven't seen anything today. I don't know who you are. I haven't listened to anything you've said. I'm begging you! Just let me off this once."

At this, the driver joins in with his own piteous entreaties.

"Enough!" Zhang Zhicheng interrupts them sternly. He exchanges a look with Zuo Xichuan, and continues: "Maybe we can let you two go back, but you have to see us through to Changping first, and make sure you don't give anything away."

"No problem. Don't worry. We're not going to try to match wits with you, we surely won't give anything away," Zhou Si promises desperately.

Zhang Zhicheng finally unties the two men, and says, pointing his gun at them: "You've got this one chance, but a single word out of place, and you know what I'll do."

They are only about twenty *li* from the sentry post at Changping, and by quickening their speed, they find themselves in front of it in a quarter of an hour. Things turn out just as the Japanese sergeant had said, and when the guards at Changping see the message and the signature on the inventory, and realise that Zuo Xichuan is Japanese and that the truck has a Beiping CID escort, they let them on their way without an inspection.

Once past Changping, they continue north for several *li* until they come to a fork in the road. Zhang Zhicheng orders the truck to stop. Zhou Si and the driver are terrified, wondering whether this is a good sign or a bad omen. Zhang Zhicheng gets down from the truck and says to them: "You're both Japanese lapdogs, and killing you would be quite justified. But I am bearing in mind that you are both also Chinese, so I'm letting you go on your way. Don't for one moment believe the Japanese will ever destroy China, and I don't just mean the whole of China – they can't even keep the peace in Beiping. So think very carefully when you get back, and if you're still determined to play the traitor, you won't be given a second chance. Do you understand?"

"I understand, I understand," Zhou Si babbles. Then he stammers cautiously: "Brother Zhang... can... can you..."

Knowing what Zhou Si is going to say, he picks up the gun he had confiscated: "What? The gun? You want it back?"

"If I don't have a gun, Brother Zhang... the truth is... Ai! I don't want to say it."

Zhang Zhicheng hands him back the gun. "Since I seem to be doing good deeds today, I'll help you one more time. Alright, take it, but I'm keeping the magazine."

"Aiyo! I'm eternally grateful." Zhou Si clasps his hands and bows continuously. "Don't worry, when we get back we won't breathe a..."

"Enough!" Zhang Zhicheng gives him a chilly smile. "You can be sure that, if you do say anything, and if I don't kill you, then the Japanese certainly will. Enough of this bullshit now. Just fuck off and be quick about it."

"Yessir, yessir, yessir!" Zhou Si replies, then nudges the driver. "Turn this thing round, turn it round."

Zhang Zhicheng watches the motorcycle and sidecar turn around and disappear into the distance. He is just about to get back into the truck when he sees, to his surprise, that it too is turning round.

"Hey, Lao Zuo! What are you up to?" he asks in agitation. "We've got to go east to get to Rehe. Are you lost?"

Once the truck is pointing west, Zuo Xichuan opens the truck door and says: "Get up here, quick, and squeeze in with me."

Zhang Zhicheng has no choice but to scramble up into the driver's cab. The cab is designed for two people not three, and with all of them wearing thick winter clothes, they can scarcely even close the door. The truck does indeed set off westwards, and Zhang Zhicheng asks again, with some urgency: "So... what's going on here?"

"We're not going to Rehe... Ai! Ai! You're too big! Don't sit full on my leg like that, I can't take it!"

"Serves you right," Zhang Zhicheng says ill-temperedly. "Now spit it out. Where are we actually going?"

"We're going to Phoenix Ridge, northwest of Beiping."

"What for?"

"To rejoin the army, of course," Zuo Xichuan says. Then, seeing Zhang Zhicheng's blank look, he goes on: "This is how it is – there's an anti-Japanese resistance army mustered to the west of Phoenix Ridge, and a lot of my Party comrades are with it. They've just established communications with the Party leadership. Only yesterday I received orders from the leadership of the army working committee to link up with this army. The leadership has already sent a radio message to Rehe, ordering all troops currently in the mountains to move west of Beiping within a week, to join up with the army there. The two of us are to go on ahead and establish a forward position."

"That's... well, to tell the truth, I'm loth to let you use this equipment. I don't want it wasted." Zhang Zhicheng narrows his eyes and keeps a lid on his temper. "I came looking for a wife for myself, not to make a wedding dress for someone else."

Zuo Xichuan laughs. "Once we've joined forces, we'll all be one army, so what difference does 'yours' and 'mine' make?"

"Ha! You're so full of it!" Zhang Zhicheng mutters. "And full of yourself, keeping all this secret from me."

THE ARMY ON PHOENIX RIDGE is called the National Anti-Japanese Army. It's not very big, numbering only four or five hundred men, but it seems that a third of them are Communist Party members. Quite apart from the fact it is a recently levied army of resistance, this is a larger proportion of Party members than even in the regular Eighth Route Army. In fact there is something remarkable about its origins, something almost theatrical.

The Kuomintang's Number Two Prison was situated at Gongdelin outside the Desheng Gate, and at the time of the Marco Polo Bridge Incident there were several hundred prisoners locked up there. Most of them were political prisoners arrested by the civilian secret service, either Communist Party members or student activists. As hostilities increased, the agents of the secret service quickly slipped away, but they did nothing to evacuate their prisoners. The Japanese Army occupied Beiping at the end of July, but by the beginning of August they had still not established control over the whole of the city, and were even less inclined than their predecessors to take responsibility for the prison. Most of the guards had fled, but a few conscientious ones remained, who, unsure what the future would bring, simply locked the prison gates and stood guard over the prisoners. A small resistance force took advantage of the hiatus in authority and mounted a successful rescue operation. This small force had only been established a few days before and numbered no more than twenty or thirty men, mostly refugee students from the northeast. A good number of them were Party members, all founder members of the Northeast National Salvation Assembly. But due to the exigencies of war, they had kept their status secret.

In the course of the prison rescue, however, they were intercepted by the Japanese Army, and, as they fled southwest to the foot of the Western Hills, the majority of them were either killed by the Japanese, or scattered. Only a hundred-plus men were left. Although a few more found their way back, they still mustered no more than two hundred, armed with around thirty weapons.

Over the following days, they frequently encountered small bands of Japanese troops, and, fighting as they retreated, they finally reached Heishan County, northwest of the Fragrant Hills. Here they found a few groups of armed students, with whom they combined forces, and they unfurled a new banner as the 'National Army of Japanese Resistance'.

Quite soon, two detachments of Japanese troops launched a campaign of encirclement and annihilation against Heishan County, and the fighting lasted from midday until nightfall. Taking advantage of the terrain, the newly formed army gave a good account of themselves; they lost twenty or thirty men, but the Japanese left thirty or forty bodies behind. As evening approached, a formation of Japanese aircraft arrived to provide support, but they only managed to drop a handful of bombs before a burst of machinegun fire from the mountain top strafed into the sky and forced them to dip their wings and turn for home, heading due north of Beiping to the west of the Qing River.

Under cover of night, the National Army of Japanese Resistance broke out of the encirclement and headed to the north of Miaofengshan. Because the Japanese had committed most of their troops to the encirclement, the army was able to withdraw to the region of Changping and Phoenix Ridge. At the end of autumn, the Party members in the army finally managed to make contact with the underground command centre in Beiping, who thoroughly grasped the strategic implications of the situation and made an urgent report to their superiors.

The commanding officer of this new force was a young man called Zhao Ran, who was neither a member of the Communist Party nor the Kuomintang, but of the fascist Chinese National Socialist Party. He was born in Xiuyan in Liaoning Province, and after the Mukden Incident, while still a child, he went with his mother, Hong Wenguo,[1] to join the Heroic Northeast Army of Japanese Resistance, and he even established his own Iron-Willed Youth Brigade. Not only did he have enormous innate tactical ability, he was also a heroic fighter, and was given the nickname 'Little Hero' in the northeast. He and his mother went to Beiping to raise funds for equipment, but they were unable to return to Rehe after its occupation. After the Marco Polo Bridge Incident, he gathered a force of thirty or forty men, and once again raised the flag of resistance against the Japanese. His mother left the army in August that year to go to Wuhan to seek military aid from the government there. After the prison break from Number Two Prison, the power of the Party within the new army increased enormously, and it became the backbone of the force. Differences in political beliefs were unimportant as long as everyone was united to resist the Japanese in this time of national emergency. Consequently, the deputy commander-in-chief of the Eighth Route Army, Peng Dehuai, personally sent a man with a letter to Zhao Ran, inviting him to join forces with the Eighth Route Army. Zhao Ran agreed. When Zuo Xichuan changed the route to go to Phoenix Ridge, it was with orders from the military working committee to implement this union, and to organise certain tasks. Because this was all top secret, he could not reveal any of it to Zhang Zhicheng, who was still only a probationary Party member.

Now, putting aside one matter, let us turn to another. That evening, after Chenglong leaves the warehouse, he hurries back to the Minister's Residence. The dozen or so members of the Special Operations Squad who had not been out on the job were already gathered there, according to his orders. The thirty-plus men transferred from the lower divisions of the CID are also stationed at various locations awaiting orders. Of course they are all aware that there is important business to be done, but no one knows exactly what it might involve. Not only has Chenglong failed to inform his subordinates, the Kempeitai don't know anything either, and even Matsuzaki Harayama is unaware that there is a CID operation taking place that night.

In fact, there is a member of the CID squad, a man called Li Shitong, who had once been a staff captain in the headquarters of the Twenty-Ninth Division of the National Revolutionary Army. Secretly he was also an agent of Beiping military intelligence, acting as their eyes and ears on army security. When the Twenty-Ninth Division was transferred out of Beiping, he accompanied the Beiping Army representatives in negotiations with the Japanese. After the negotiations broke down, he was unable to escape with the chief negotiator, Zhang Zizhong, but was detained by the Japanese and transferred to the Kempeitai prison. When Chenglong discovered who he was from military intelligence files, he used a carrot and stick approach to reel him into his employ. Later on, he arranged for him to be brought into the Special Operations Squad, with responsibility for four teams, and also made him team leader of the motorised section.

When Li Shitong first puts himself in the hands of his new master, he is very keen to please and to provide meritorious service, but when he takes some people to mop up several of the meeting places of the military intelligence agents he knows about, everywhere they go is deserted, with no one to arrest. He knows that the favourite tactic of military intelligence is to lie low in busy places, and hide out in dives, so he turns his attention to the low-grade brothels of the Eight Great Hutongs, especially the second-tier brothels with long-term residents in short-let rooms. With no little effort, using the gossip and other information wormed out of brothel regulars, stool pigeons, madams, pimps and bouncers, he finally succeeds in discovering suspicious activity at a brothel called The Boat of One Hundred Flowers.

A prostitute known as Pink Apricot has been working as an independent operator at the brothel for no more than three months. Aged twenty-five or twenty-six, she hasn't had a single client, but the day comes when she agrees to become someone's kept woman. The man's name is Zheng, and he calls himself a merchant middleman. However, he has seldom come out of his room over the last few days, even sending out to a neighbouring restaurant for his meals. There is no evidence of him running any merchandise, or doing any kind of business at all, but he has been very open-handed and paid the girl a month's allowance in advance. Li Shitong has been watching the place for three days, and he is surprised to discover the man is a military intelligence agent he knows. This man was a fellow student of his on the special training course at Baoding. His real name is Sun, he was a class above Li, and he is now a station sergeant at the South Beiping Police Bureau. Working from what he knows about the man, he discovers his immediate subordinate is a furnace worker at the Rongyuan bath house called Lao Tian, and the man below him is a rickshaw puller called Zhu Gui. The way Li Shitong sees it, the best thing is to proceed cautiously, laying a long line to catch his fish. But Chenglong does not want to wait, first because he is worried other distractions might arise, second because he is under pressure from above to speed things up and third because he doesn't want someone else to get the glory. He decides to act this very night.

At ten o'clock, he allocates his men their duties, dividing the specially assigned group into three sub-groups, which have responsibility for making the arrest; the CID squad are responsible for containing the area and raising the alarm if necessary. All groups are to go into action simultaneously at eleven o'clock. They are to leave their vehicles some distance away and approach on foot, to be sure of taking their targets alive. After the arrest, the men are not to be handed over to the Kempeitai, but instead taken straight to the Minister's Residence. Their lodgings are to be carefully searched, and all documents, books, clothes and other personal effects are to be removed. Success will be amply rewarded, but if anyone escapes, the penalty will be severe. As his men set out according to their orders, Chenglong doesn't dare relax, but sits watching the telephone, waiting for news.

Within ten minutes, the three groups all report in. Apart from Zhu Gui, who put up some resistance before shooting himself, the other three are all taken alive, along with six short-barrelled machineguns and a radio transmitter that is discovered at the Boat of One Hundred Flowers.

Chenglong orders his men to interrogate the prisoners through the night, and although they have no interrogation room or torture equipment, they have plenty of ways to grind a man down. They play good cop bad cop, use carrot and stick, are alternately fierce and emollient, and within two hours, all three prisoners have confessed.

These people are, without doubt, agents of military intelligence, part of a special detachment operating behind enemy lines, the one known as the Traitor Elimination Squad. There are, in fact, more than twenty members of the Traitor Elimination Squad established by the Beiping branch of military intelligence, divided into two sections, one for intelligence and one for operations. Police Captain Sun is an old-stager left behind in charge of the Beiping branch as head of the intelligence section of the Traitor Elimination Squad. Zhu Gui, the rickshaw man, and Lao Tian, the bath house attendant, are his subordinates; there are another twenty or so intelligence officers. Their principal responsibility is to ascertain chosen targets' addresses and their layout, any defences, routines and activities, and so on; and they report back to Captain Sun at the Boat of One Hundred Flowers. That brothel is the communications centre of the squad, Pink Apricot is its communications officer, the businessman Zheng is its radio operator, and the radio transmitter is in Pink Apricot's room. These latter two are not familiar with the rest of the intelligence section, but report directly to the man appointed by their superiors, Special Agent Hao. However, they have not been told where Special Agent Hao lives, or when he will next appear. They know very little about the operations squad, except that it is located outside the city, consists of a dozen or so men, and most of them are new recruits.

Based on the three prisoners' confessions, Chenglong sends some men to mount a second manhunt that same night. Although some of the squad get wind of what is going on, and make a get-away, the majority of the intelligence sections are unable to escape. By early morning the next day, nine people are under arrest. Chenglong is delighted, and his recent fears and worries are swept away. He opens a bottle of good wine, and drinks a hefty cup with Li Shitong and the others. Flushed with pleasure, he picks up the telephone and makes his report to Matsuzaki Harayama.

Matsuzaki is naturally delighted, and, although he hasn't cleaned up the whole Traitor Elimination Squad, at the very least he has broken one of their wings and put out their eyes and ears. He has undoubtedly ensured the safety of the soon-to-be established provisional government, and provided a successful case study for his policy of using Chinese to control Chinese. This seems to give him a chance to counter the criticisms levelled at him by his colleagues, and to stand back and draw breath.

Matsuzaki is effusive in his praise and goes on to say: "Don't worry, I will surely recommend you for a suitable position in the provisional government. Transfer all the prisoners to the care of the Kempeitai immediately. Your place isn't secure enough. I won't let anyone else muscle in on this. You are still in full command."

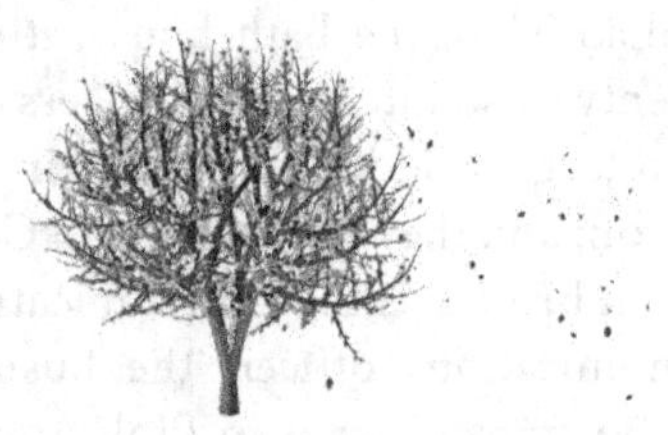

Chapter 26

On the evening of the wedding, the little north room of the Gao home has a lamp burning all night, and Caiping sits up until dawn. Although Wangtian hasn't given her the whole story of the movement of the goods, she has figured out for herself how dangerous it must be. What is more, Minister's Residence Hutong has been much busier and noisier than usual, with motorcycles and cars to-ing and fro-ing, and it seems as though several people have been arrested. All of this means that her nerves are drawn as tight as bow strings.

When daylight finally comes, there is still no sign of Wangtian. Although the house lacks a clock, just by looking at the sky she knows it's already past seven. She is really worried: the city gates opened at six, and he should be home by now. Could it be that... she doesn't let herself continue down that line of thought, and she hurries out of the room and heads towards the street. She has already opened the gate when she suddenly comes to her senses: what would a new bride be doing out so early looking for her new husband? Quite apart from making her look foolish, more important, it would raise suspicions. She has only just gone back into the room and started reheating some rice and vegetables, when Wangtian and Clown come into the courtyard. Seeing them is more than she can take, and she throws herself at Wangtian, tears streaming down her face. Wangtian has a cloth bundle under one arm, so he uses the other to hold her close and stroke her gently. To his surprise, just as he embraces her, she suddenly begins to wail.

Clown doesn't dare say anything, and he just stands to one side savouring the scene with a mischievous smile. Distressed and embarrassed, Wangtian just exclaims "Ai!" a couple of times. Caiping also blushes through her tears. At first, she only has eyes for Wangtian, so she gives a start when she realises there is someone else there too.

"Ai! I'll... I'll be off now, Brother Wangtian," Clown says tactfully.

"Don't go. Wait till you've eaten. You must be hungry after last night."

"Being hungry's bad, but playing the gooseberry is worse."

"You little so-and-so..." Wangtian says, raising his hand as if to slap him.

Clown laughs and pulls a face, then follows him into the room. But just as Wangtian steps over the threshold, he is pushed back out through the door by Caiping.

"Look at you! You're filthier than the Earth God!"

So saying, she starts scrubbing at Wangtian's body with the small brush from the *kang*. Then, when she sees Clown absent-mindedly dusting himself down, she goes over to him too.

"Stop acting like a cat burying its shit! If you don't clean yourself properly, you're not coming in. Stand still and raise your arms."

Clown does as he's told, but he can't resist a cheeky comment: "Hey, sis, I didn't get back in time to prank the bridal chamber last night. Shall I make up for it tonight?"

"Alright then," Caiping replies briskly, but she turns the brush she is holding round in her hand and gives him a couple of sharp raps with the handle. When she hears him exclaim in surprise, she hands him the brush, saying: "Do it yourself!" and she turns to go inside.

Clown makes a face at Wangtian. "That one's pretty feisty," he says. "I hope she's not too much for you."

Caiping sees that all Wangtian can do is grin foolishly and keep quiet, so she pulls aside the door curtain and says: "Still full of it, then? Well, I'm going to find you a matchmaker, and we'll see where your nonsense gets you with that! Enough now."

"Don't do it," Clown exclaims, following Wangtian into the room.

Wangtian takes up the suggestion and asks in a serious tone: "Hey, Ying'er, do you really have someone in mind?"

"Of course."

"Then you have to make allowance for Clown's age. He's knocking on a bit."

"How about a country girl?" Caiping asks, as she serves the food.

Clown doesn't say anything, so Wangtian replies for him: "Yes, a country girl would be just the thing."

"And a little on the plump side?"

"Yes, fat even!"

"Not too pretty?"

"Definitely not. Ugly is good."

"Of course, ugly doesn't actually have to be ugly if you get it right – a nice bristly coat, a little curly pigtail, two big ears like fans, four neat little leather shoes..."

"Alright, alright," Clown says. "You two jokers can cut the comedy act. What you're suggesting is a pig, not a wife, and that's even better – if I don't get enough profit out of her, I can slaughter her and eat the meat!"

The room fills with laughter.

As she watches the two men piling into the food like ravenous tigers, Caiping continues the conversation: "Seriously, Clown, do you want me to give some proper thought to this?"

"I'll tell you straight, sis – you don't need to worry."

"You've got someone?"

"Ah! A memory in my heart, the reflection of the moon in the water. What's the use?"

"So, whose daughter is she?" Wangtian asks.

Clown is about to say something, but he stops himself. He takes a large bite of cornbread and chews morosely. Wangtian clearly wants to pursue the matter, but they are interrupted by a knock at the door. Caiping hurriedly gets up and pulls aside the door curtain. To their surprise, Yang Zhixing is standing there, looking very serious.

"Uncle Yang? You..." Caiping stares at him in amazement. Forget about the old customs, even in these modern times, it's unheard of for the bride's relatives to come calling the day after the wedding. Yang Zhixing is about to go in, but stops when he catches sight of Clown.

Wangtian hurriedly goes over to greet him: "Uncle Yang! Come in, come in!"

"No, Wangtian, you come outside."

Realising it must be something both important and confidential, Wangtian hurries out, closing the door behind him.

"What were you up to last night, you young fool?" Yang Zhixing asks, his face taut.

"I... nothing, nothing..."

Yang Zhixing doesn't wait for him to finish, but interrupts with a grunt: "Ha! Don't bother trying to come up with a story. I saw you coming back with my own eyes. I told you last night to show some restraint and not rush blindly into things, but did you listen?"

Wangtian laughs awkwardly. "I... I was taking some carts of night soil to the Qing River. They'd ordered it ages ago."

"Night soil? You gave up your wedding night for a couple of loads of shit? Who are you kidding?" When Yang Zhixing sees he has no answer, he sighs and changes the subject. "Alright, I'll ask you again later. Anyway, I've got something important to tell you." He lowers his voice: "Chenglong has got several plainclothes cops in the front and eastern courtyards. There was a big rumpus all last night and a lot of arrests. I hear they're from the Traitor Elimination Squad."

"The Traitor Elimination Squad? But my dad..."

"I wanted to make sure he wasn't here. I saw Chenglong looking very pleased with himself. If he'd caught your father, I don't think he'd have been so happy."

"Then..."

"He's still in danger. It just takes a loose word from someone, and he'll be done for."

"We'd better send my dad a letter."

"That's what I thought."

"So, do you know where they are now?"

"I've heard they're at Yanjing University, but where exactly, I don't know. It's a big place, and there's no way of asking. Have you got any ideas?"

Wangtian furrows his brow and sucks his teeth, but he can't think of anything for the moment.

"How about this?" Yang Zhixing asks. "The university director, Charlie, is an American, and he's good friends with the Young Master and Mr Hao. Mr Hao and your father are in this business together, and I reckon Director Charlie knows what's going on. You'd better go and find him."

"Do you think a VIP like him will see me? I'm afraid I won't even get through the gates."

"You just say Young Master Qi has sent you with a message."

"But the Traitor Elimination Squad is top-secret stuff. Do you think he'll trust a stranger like me? Do you think he'll take me to see..."

"Ah! It doesn't matter whether you actually get to see your father and Mr Hao, as long as word gets to them, and they understand the situation. That will be enough. You need to be quick, so take a rickshaw."

"Right, I'll go and find one now."

It's already past eight in the morning when Hao Bingchen appears in the hutong where the Boat of One Hundred Flowers is situated. He and Gao Guigeng only got back to Yanjing University from the Western Hills the evening before, and Hao has hurried out this morning to send a radio message to his superiors to protect Qi Yuexuan, and to ask for instructions to counteract Chenglong's plans. He notices that something is amiss before he reaches the door of the brothel. Normally this is the quietest time of day in this hutong, but today there is someone leaning on the telegraph pole at the entrance to the hutong, and there are two or three others strolling around further down. None of them look as though they belong there. There's a rickshaw driver sitting on his contraption outside the main entrance, and there's no way he can be expecting any business there at this time of day. So Hao Bingchen doesn't stop at the door, but passes on by and out the other end of the hutong. After he's gone quite some distance, he finds a breakfast stall and sits down. He orders a bowl of fried liver and strikes up a conversation with the stallholder as he eats.

"So, is this the famous Eight Great Hutongs then?"

"You're not from the city, then?"

"No."

"Good deeds go unnoticed, but a bad reputation travels a thousand *li*! But this isn't the Eight Great Hutongs proper. If you want to find them, go east then south. The hutongs around there are what you're looking for."

"I'm not going there, just asking. I heard an old countryman of mine talking about it. He said he had several old flames somewhere around here. I think he said... yes, that's it, The Boat of One Hundred Flowers."

The stallholder starts at the sound of the name, looks all round him and says in a low voice: "Whatever you do, don't go there."

"Why not?"

"It was raided last night, and they arrested a whole load of people. I saw them being taken away past this very door."

"Why were they arrested?"

"Who knows? But by the look of it, it was something big, not just to do with the brothel business. Most likely they were anti-Japanese factions."

Hao Bingchen's heart lurches, but his expression doesn't change. He carries on chatting for a while, bolts a few mouthfuls of fried liver, then stands up and leaves. Back on the street, he hails a rickshaw and hurries off to the Xizhi Gate. Urging the driver to ever greater speed, they enter the grounds of Yanjing University. Not daring to risk any delay, he goes off immediately in search of Gao Guigeng, but finds no sign of him. It's only when he sees Mr Charlie that he discovers someone has beaten him to it with a letter, and Gao Guigeng has already passed the news on to his men. Those of them who were still in the original hideout have now emerged from it, and are scattered among the student dormitories. Those who had already moved on have also changed their locations. Hao Bingchen finally feels he can relax a little.

He takes stock of the current situation: his force has already suffered heavy casualties, and his lines of communication and intelligence have been cut. The whereabouts of his action squad have been discovered, and although the grounds of Yanjing University are protected by international convention, he is afraid the enemy may ignore convention and play hard ball. Not only are his own men in danger, that danger may extend to the innocent as well. The radio transmitter is lost so he has no way of asking his superiors for instructions; he will just have to make the decisions for himself. He orders Gao Guigeng to take his men to Laoqiying in the Western Hills that very evening, to cease all activities and wait for further orders. He himself intends to make a dash for Taiyuan to see his superiors.

IN NO TIME AT ALL it is early January 1938, and the 'Temporary National Government of the Republic of China', put together by the Japanese, has been formally established in Beiping. Although it labels itself 'National', this sham government, from its establishment to its downfall, never extends its sphere of influence beyond Beiping and northern China. So, in order to distinguish it from the later Reorganised National Government of China, not just the people, but even the history books refer to it as 'the Sham Government of North China'. When we say 'put together', we mean just that: even though it uses the grand title 'National Chinese', it is a mere façade, supported only by a handful of men. The

Japanese themselves are not greatly involved with it, as its establishment just means they have one more puppet, one more pretence of self-government, which in fact only serves to tighten their grip on military power. All they are doing with it is to help their invasion masquerade as cooperation, and to provide a fig leaf for their military operations. It is a shame for them that it produces the opposite effect, and only serves to reveal the truth behind the invasion, to interrupt the retreat of Chiang Kai-shek's Nationalist Party Government, and force him to return to his roots in persevering with resistance to the Japanese.

Matsuzaki Harayama is as good as his word, and he makes Chenglong head of the intelligence service of the new government. But because time is so pressing, he does not succeed in getting the appointment ratified by the relevant government committee, so it is necessary to put a 'provisional' in front of the title. It is, in fact, a very large hat on a head that doesn't entirely fill it. The Japanese keep their own firm grip on military intelligence, so Chenglong's provisional headship doesn't really extend beyond his current responsibilities, and is limited to activities in Beiping and the surrounding countryside. But even if the hat is large and the head small, leaving plenty of vacant space, in the end it does increase Chenglong's prestige, and he is deeply moved by the generosity of his superior and enormously grateful.

When it rains above, what's below gets wet too. Following the establishment of this ad hoc central government, every provincial town and every county occupied by the Japanese army follow suit in establishing their own sham local authorities. Wanping, Liangxiang and Fangshan County to the west of Beiping are no exception. The division of the area still follows the existing traditional pattern, except that there are no district commissioners, as they are replaced by the so-called 'preservation committees'. County commissioners are no longer called county commissioners, but the old Japanese term is used, and they are known as *kentiji*. The Japanese also take the captured Kuomintang troops and other ragtag soldiers and turn them into the Imperial Army of Cooperation; every county establishes its own home guard battalion, and every district has its own company. The twelve villages of the Northern barracks receive orders to form a home guard company, and are issued with several dozen short-barrelled machineguns. This suits Qi Yuexuan very well. In fact, the company is already well established, but it can now emerge from its clandestine existence largely unchanged.

From this time on, the Japanese Army intensifies its efforts to clear the mountains and countryside, but this has little effect in the succession of mountains and valleys in Pingxi. If a large force enters the area, the locals just hide, and if smaller groups of soldiers venture in, if they don't disappear altogether, they certainly suffer heavy casualties. At this time, the front line in Shanxi is under great pressure but the Japanese have no troops to transfer as reinforcements, so they have no option but to hole up in the county towns and their other principal military bases, and guard the major transport hubs of road and railway. They are seldom able to make any kind of sortie, so the vast area around Pingxi remains home to all kinds of anti-Japanese forces.

After Zuo Xichuan and Zhang Zhicheng make contact with the National Anti-Japanese Resistance Army assembled at Phoenix Ridge, and combine forces with the troops coming west out of Rehe, they officially become Number Five Troop of the Shanxi, Charhar and Hebei Brigade of the Eighth Route Army, with command remaining in the hands of Zhao Ran. This brigade is, in fact, the main force of the 115th Division of the Eighth Route Army, and they have already established bases behind enemy lines in Guangling, Yixian, Kaishui, Laiyuan, Fuping and other places. They open a broad offensive against the enemy from behind. In order to establish reliable supply chains, the main body of Number Five Troop makes its way through Miaofengshan and across Yu County; then they cross to the south of the Lai River and set up a base in Fuping County. Zuo Xichuan does not accompany this advance, but after fulfilling his orders, returns to Charhar and Rehe. Zhang Zhixing becomes a platoon captain but does not go to Fuping. Instead, he receives orders to lead a force of three hundred men as a traitor elimination squad into the region between Wanping County and Baihuashan, to link up with the local Party organisation. His brief is to mobilise the masses, increase the number of troops and open up an anti-Japanese resistance base. The establishment of this Number Five Troop opens a new chapter in the war of resistance in the Beiping area, and from now on, the Communist Party and its Eighth Route Army become the backbone of the struggle against the Japanese. Beiping is no longer a bulwark of defence for the Japanese devils, but gradually becomes an isolated island in the vast sea of the people's war.

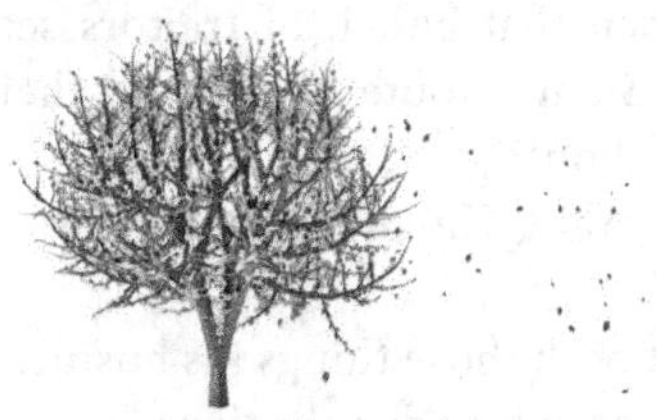

Chapter 27

Qi Yuexuan is suffering from insomnia. Although this is not unusual for him, it is particularly bad today. For three days now, his eyes have stayed wide open and he hasn't had any sleep. By day, if he isn't criss-crossing the mountains, climbing the peaks to view the surrounding countryside, then he is sitting in silent contemplation in the family tomb enclosure. In the evenings, he sits at the table until midnight, then tosses and turns on the *kang* until daybreak. He gives every appearance of thinking, but no one knows what about. His face serene, he goes the whole day without uttering a word. He doesn't waste time over food, and his capacity for wine, as if he is drinking to drown his sorrows, has been turned upside down.

After watching the Young Master go without sleep for two nights, on the third night Yang Zhixing encourages him to drink more than usual, hoping that he will sleep if he gets drunk. But to his surprise, the Young Master just gets more animated as he drinks, whereas he, Yang Zhixing, finds his body swaying, his words slurring and his eyes growing heavy. Qi Yuexuan, who has quietly stayed awake all night again, is still writing at the table in the inner room when Yang Zhixing resurfaces. Actually, there's no paper on the table any more, but there is a great pile of it on the floor.

In the western room, when Lao Zhang gets up to check on his precious winter crickets, he sees the light on in the north room. He is just thinking of creeping over to the window to have a look, when Yang Zhixing pulls aside the door curtain. He hurriedly gestures at Lao Zhang, afraid he will speak too loudly.

Lao Zhang acknowledges this and says in a low voice: "Is the Young Master still not sleeping, Manager Yang?"

"Not a wink."

"That makes three nights! Has he turned into an immortal?"

Yang Zhixing just sighs, so Lao Zhang goes on: "So, tell me, what's the matter?"

"I'm not sure."

"There's been a lot going on over the last few days – first Nanjing is lost, then there's a big fuss when that bunch of traitors set up shop inside Beiping, and outside the city, the Eighth Route Army raise their flag. Is that what the Young Master is all riled up about?"

These words jerk Yang Zhixing awake. "Eh? No, I'm not sure that's what's bothering him."

"But… well, aren't both those things his business?"

"Ai! Even if they weren't, he'd make them."

"What do you mean?"

Yang Zhixing doesn't answer, and Qi Yuexuan's voice is heard calling from inside the room: "Bring me some tea! You get up and all you do is chat away! Don't you know how to make tea? Do you want me to die of thirst?"

Yang Zhixing and Lao Zhang are delighted to hear Qi Yuexuan grumbling like this, and they hurry into the room. It doesn't matter to them what kind of mood he is in, they're just happy he's talking and hasn't come to any harm from not sleeping for three days.

"Let Lao Zhang get the tea, Uncle Yang," Qi Yuexuan says. "You run over and fetch Grandpa Dong. Quick as you can."

Yang Zhixing grunts in acknowledgement, but he also raises an objection: "It's the middle of the night, Young Master. Do you really want me to get Grandpa Dong out of bed? Is it urgent?"

Qi Yuexuan looks out of the window and grins. "Alright, go when it's light. It is important, but waiting an hour or so won't hurt." He stands up and stretches.

Yang Zhixing can't help asking: "You've been on edge for three days, so what's happened today?"

"Ai! I've been puzzled for three days, which has, of course, put me on edge. And now I've worked it out, why wouldn't I be happy?"

"So what is it that's kept you so puzzled?"

"Family affairs, state affairs, world affairs – affairs of huge importance."

"Ai, Young Master! I'm afraid you've let your imagination run away with you."

Qi Yuexuan chokes off a laugh: "Ha, Uncle Yang! You really do have an answer for everything! Sit down, and I'll tell you all about this great affair."

The water has just boiled, and Lao Zhang brings it in to make some tea.

In fact, Yang Zhixing has guessed right, and what has been preoccupying Qi Yuexuan are the major consequences of the loss of Nanjing, the establishment of the sham government and the consolidation of the five units of the Eighth Route Army. One moment he is full of righteous indignation, and the next his heart is surging with optimism. He feels the time has come when he has no option but to stand up and be counted; that he must raise the banner of the Heroic Army of Anti-Japanese Resistance and carry the fight to the enemy. But it is easy to be carried away by a fit of hot temper; actually to carry through this determination is more difficult. For himself, he gives little thought to life or death, but he does have to consider the danger to the great host of his fellow countrymen. The twelve villages of the Left Barracks are situated in Wanping County, which is right next to Beiping, and if he unfurls the banner of anti-Japanese resistance, they will bear the brunt of any retaliation. Although it is mountain territory, its single range can't compare to the mountainous hinterland of Hundred Flowers Mountain and Red Cloud Ridge. If the Japanese are willing to risk the casualties of an all-out assault, the depth in defence is not great enough, and they will be very hard to withstand. The Japanese have been employing the *baojia* system for keeping track of the population, and if they attack, it is inevitable that a good number of innocent people will be implicated in supporting the resistance. He has been turning all this over in his mind, looking for a strategy that will accommodate both sides. For three days and nights he has been considering possibilities from every angle, and he has thought of all viable responses. Now, finally, he has come up with an idea. But as for what that idea is, he quietly sips his tea and keeps the others guessing.

Yang Zhixing's interest is aroused: "So, what are you actually going to do?"

"I'll explain as simply as I can," Qi Yuexuan replies calmly. "Our base is the Left Barracks, and we have raised our standard in the mountains. We shelter in them and attack outside them. We rely on the mountains to provide for our needs, and take water where we find it. When there's thunder in the sky, there's fire under foot. Someone else can repair the road, and I'll advance along it. I don't care how far I have to travel to eat, as long as it's cheap. I won't bother rolling out noodles, I'll just stuff dumplings. While there's food, I'll keep eating, and then I'll wipe my mouth and leave."

"Aiyo! And what exactly does all that mean?" Yang Zhixing asks with an exasperated laugh.

"I deliberately put it as plainly as I could. Do you really not understand?"

"Not... er... not entirely."

"Ha! Well, what I mean is that, if our army is going to raise its standard, then we must be open and above board about it. But the Left Barracks are our home, and we can't just invite the Japanese in. If our flag is raised in the mountains, we need to conduct our operations away from there, the further the better, so we don't end up showing them the way in."

Yang Zhixing looks at him in astonishment: "But... doesn't that just make us bandits?"

"Bullshit!" Qi Yuexuan glares at him. "Weren't the leaders of the Communist Party bandits in the past, and haven't they made good now? As long as we're fighting the Japanese, why should I worry if people call me a bandit?"

"So these mountain villages are..."

"HQ!"

"That's right, HQ! Our HQ!"

Qi Yuexuan finally lays bare his plan: "Ten *li* or so away from here is the Baolong Convent. It's strategically located and easy to defend. It contains buildings that are ready for use, and in the surrounding mountains there are lots of caves, big and small and some of them are even interconnecting. We can attack from them, and retreat into them. We can handle any domestic matters that may arise there too."

"Ah! So that explains 'we can rely on the mountains for all our needs'. What about the 'water'? And the 'thunder' and 'fire'? Are they…"

"That's all about taking advantage of the terrain, relying on the ruggedness of the mountain and harnessing the power of the river."

"Hold on a moment. I'm with you about the mountain, but the water in this ravine is in the hands of the gods. If there's heavy rain, it's a river, but after a dry spell, it's just a stream. How can we exploit that?"

"Have you never heard of damming a river to cut off the water? Could we not cause a landslide in the gorges of the upper reaches that would dam a stretch of more than two *li*? It should only be done *in extremis*, but once in effect it would be like the drowning of the seven armies."[1]

"Yes, that makes sense. And the 'thunder' and the 'fire'?"

"That's much more straightforward. At the entrance to every mountain pass, we prepare rocks, boulders and logs, and drill holes in the cliffs on either side at strategic points. We fill the holes with gunpowder, and when the time comes, we set them off. However many Japanese devils there are, they'll all be buried."

Lao Zhang can't help interrupting: "Can I stop you there a moment, Young Master? Both sides of our valley here are rocky cliffs, and really hard. How much gunpowder are you going to need to get the effect you want?"

"You just go and look after your crickets," Qi Yuexuan grins. "This isn't your field of expertise. We've got the TNT that Captain Xiao and his men left behind. It's much more powerful than the local gunpowder. We just need to make sure we choose the best of it, and it'll be fine. In any case, if that doesn't work, we can use the local method, and heat up the rock. Then, when you pour water on it, it splits like an explosion, and breaks up. So that would work too."

Yang Zhixing realises that Qi Yuexuan has thought everything through, and he tries to get him to lay out the whole plan: "Alright, so that's the thunder in the heavens sorted. Let me have a guess at the 'fire underfoot'. You mean to use a fire attack, don't you? And then there's the… what did you say? Something to do with roads, wasn't it?"

"Ha ha, you mean 'someone else can repair the road, and I'll advance along it'. We're fifty *li* from the Beiping-Suiyuan Railway here, thirty from the Beiping-Baoding line, and only twenty from the road to Huailai. These are all vital supply routes to the frontlines for the Japanese devils, and all within range if we want to attack. I'm not going to neglect them, am I? If we're going to exterminate these Japanese devils, we have to do our homework and get to know the enemy's circumstances inside out."

Qi Yuexuan is warming to his subject as he continues: "That's why I said 'I don't care how far I have to travel to eat, as long as it's cheap'. If we do attack, then we have to go all out to exterminate them, and not let any word leak out, and that's what I mean by 'I won't bother rolling out noodles, I'll just stuff dumplings'. We have to be sure of the enemy dispositions before we attack, and if we're not certain of the outcome, it's better to hold back. If we mount a lightning attack, we've got to be able to withdraw at equal speed. Isn't that the same as my saying 'while there's food I'll keep eating, then I'll wipe my mouth and leave'? Well, that's given you the general idea. If you want to hear it in more detail, that would take at least two hours. Raising the standard is easy, but if you haven't thought through the subsequent moves, it will all be over in three days."

"There's nothing new in all this," Qi Yuexuan continues as he gets to his feet. "Fighting a war is not just a matter of risking one's life. More than that, it's a battle of wits. Needless to say, Sunzi's *Art of War*, *The Six Strategic Teachings*, even *The Romance of the Three Kingdoms* and *The Water Margin* don't cover the whole subject. Even so, you must read what the books have to say, whether it's useful or not. I've really had to squeeze out my courage and sharpen my wits."

Despite what he says, Qi Yuexuan can't quite hide his self-satisfaction, not to say conceit. He has his hands clasped behind his back, his head slightly raised and his chest puffed out. His eyes are bright and full of spirit as he gazes ahead, just like a general considering his battle plans. Suddenly, he seems to remember something, and his expression changes and becomes very solemn: "Once we raise the standard, Uncle Yang, there is only one way for us to go, and that is to fight the Japanese to the death. I long ago stopped worrying about life and death. Provided it's in a good cause, I don't mind whether death comes in a hundred years or today. But there is one thing I can't let go of..."

He stops at this point.

"Sit down and tell me about it," Yang Zhixing says, trying hard not to laugh. "Just don't make it sound like your dying words. You're still alive, and while you're alive you can keep killing Japanese devils, can't you?"

"Ha! For every ten thousand devils we kill, we lose three thousand of our own. Of course I want to live to see victory, but I can't help feeling it is my time to die. If I do, I can leave my country, happy in the knowledge that there are still four hundred million more Chinese, but I can't leave my family. I can't leave Yue E. I think..."

"Ah, is that what this is all about? Didn't I tell you long ago you should let her know her true ancestry. But you've kept insisting otherwise. I'm going into the city tomorrow, and I'll bring her and the children back."

"It's not just that. I also think..." Qi Yuexuan sees that Yang Zhixing is waiting impatiently to hear what he is going to say, and he goes on resolutely: "I still want you to hand over half the family treasure to help the army. And I want to give the remaining half to Yue E, while I'm still alive."

"It can't be done. Most certainly it can't be done." Yang Zhixing shakes his head vigorously.

"Why not?" Qi Yuexuan's temper is rising, and he glares at him. "Raising the standard of resistance against the Japanese is an unstoppable process once started, Uncle Yang, like an arrow mounted on the bowstring. I've only asked you for half the treasure, not all of it, and you still refuse? Isn't it the Qi family's money? How about giving me half of it as my coffin money?"

Seeing how angry he is, Yang Zhixing smiles placatingly and says: "Don't agitate yourself, Young Master. I've already got the money you want, ready for you. But fighting the Japanese is not something that is going to be over in a couple of weeks. Nor is it the business of just one family. If all we ever do is take money out and not put any in, then there won't be much left for any other major family business. You have to raise chickens to collect eggs. You can't kill the chickens and then extract the eggs."

"So how are you going to raise the chickens then?"

"I want to start up in business again."

"What kind of business?"

"Whatever makes money. And once I've made some money, I'll provide you with whatever you need here. Collecting the eggs is fine, but not killing the chickens. Taking the profits is no problem, but using up the family treasure is."

"So... what can I say to keep you happy?"

"You can say what you like, and call it what you like. In the end, as long as I'm alive, I'm not going to see the Minister's Residence suffer." Yang Zhixing is quite calm, and despite Qi Yuexuan's protestations, he insists that the capital shouldn't be touched for this business, only the interest.

Qi Yuexuan has run out of ideas: "Ai! Alright, alright, alright, I won't go on. But your words have made me realise something. War is no joking matter, and if you get in the way of great events... Ah well, Zhuge Liang wept when he had Ma Su executed, but perhaps you won't even bat an eyelid when I die."

"Enough, enough!" Yang Zhixing says, laughing.

"And what about Yue E?" Qi Yuexuan asks.

"I'm even less willing to give her anything."

"Even though I have acknowledged her as my own, isn't she still the girl you brought up? If the family property is passed on to her, won't you still be supervising it? You..."

"Don't get me wrong, Young Master," Yang Zhixing interrupts him again. "Yue E will get her due share. But just think about it. Yue E is a married woman, and what kind of a person is your good-for-nothing son-in-law? If you give Yue E the family property now, is she going to be able to hang on to it? Wouldn't that just be throwing food into the lion's mouth? A lion called Liu!"

"Then... what if you go back? If you're there to hold on to it, won't that do?"

"If you hand over the property, even if it's you who goes back, not me, there's no guarantee you'll have any control over things."

"Then..."

Seeing Qi Yuexuan at a loss, Yang Zhixing smiles and says: "I've given this matter a great deal of careful thought, Young Master, and I have come up with an idea. I just don't know whether you will agree to it."

"Tell me and see."

"I think..." Yang Zhixing suddenly stops when he sees Lao Zhang.

Lao Zhang takes the hint: "I'll leave. You go on with what you're saying."

As he heads for the door, Qi Yuexuan stops him. "I haven't even kept important military affairs secret from him, so why should I worry if he hears about family matters. Lao Zhang may look like a rogue on the outside, but there's an honest man on the inside."

"Ha! How wise you are, Young Master," Lao Zhang replies.

Yang Zhixing sighs and says: "I didn't say he wasn't honest. I'm just afraid he's a little loose-lipped."

Lao Zhang flares up at this: "Hah! If you don't want me to know, Manager Yang, I won't listen, but don't accuse me of being loose-lipped. When we buried Lao Litou..."

Yang Zhixing doesn't let him finish, but gives a sudden dry cough and glares at him. Lao Zhang realises he was just about to break his promise of secrecy, and he stops short. Qi Yuexuan doesn't notice, and he urges Yang Zhixing: "Go on, Uncle Yang. Are you going to tell me or not?"

"Yes, yes!" Yang Zhixing replies, and he begins to explain, calmly and unhurriedly. What he says leaves Qi Yuexuan and Lao Zhang wide-eyed and open-mouthed. However, once Qi Yuexuan has mulled over every detail, he gives his approval.

THE ARRANGEMENT of family matters is secondary to great military affairs.

As the cock crows for a second time, Qi Yuexuan can't wait any longer, and he tells Yang Zhixing to fetch Second Master Dong. When he hears Qi Yuexuan's plans for formally raising the banner of resistance against the Japanese, Second Master Dong gives his enthusiastic approval, saying that he had had the same idea himself ages ago, and great minds think alike. He immediately sends men to summon the key personnel from each village to come and discuss the matter over the course of a morning. When the meeting is over, a dozen or so men go over to the memorial hall to burn incense and swear a sacred oath in front of the ancestral tablets.

As he is seeing these men off, Qi Yuexuan at last begins to feel tired, and he actually falls asleep where he sits. He doesn't even wake up when he is carried over to the *kang*. After being awake for three days, he sleeps long and sound, from noon of that day until noon of the next. That afternoon he is summoned to attend a meeting of dedication in front of the troops. After considerable pinching and prodding, he finally wakes up and gets out of bed; and after a pot of strong tea and a wash in cold water, he finally emerges from his stupor.

At the dedicatory meeting, Second Master Dong announces the rules and discipline the army will observe: military orders are immutable as a mountain and must be obeyed at all times; independent action is forbidden; no one is to shirk battle; the ordinary people are not to be harassed nor their property stolen; there is to be no plundering or looting for personal gain; and the wounded are never to be abandoned. These six prohibitions come from Qi Yuexuan. He also adds one more, which is simply "accept death rather than be captured". Moreover, following the rules of the former banner armies of the Qing, anyone breaking these rules is subject to a punishment of thirty to a hundred lashes, and desertion, surrender or treachery of any kind are all subject to execution without the chance of pardon. Of course, there are rewards as well as punishments: killing one Japanese soldier is to be worth five yuan, and killing a Chinese turncoat is worth one yuan; the surrender of one enemy soldier is worth two yuan; other meritorious service will be rewarded with a commendation. In addition, all wounded will receive treatment, the dead will be buried properly and their families cared for. As well as all soldiers receiving an allowance, rations will be issued to their families. Of course, anti-Japanese fervour is on a high at the outset, so the addition of a salary and extra rewards and the fact that his whole family will benefit if a man joins up, further whips up enthusiasm. Initially, more than three hundred men sign up, and a further hundred or more come forward after the meeting. When this is witnessed by Gao Guigeng and his men, who were temporarily hiding out at Laoqiying, they are also moved to action. There are other spontaneous volunteers too, anxious to follow the army into battle.

THE NEXT DAY, Qi Yuexuan, Grandpa Fu and several others lead the bulk of the army into the mountains, taking four divisions out of the existing five, leaving Grandpa Dong with one division of new recruits to stay behind on guard.

The Baolong Convent is an ancient temple on top of a ridge that was built back in the Liao dynasty. Although the mountain itself is not that high, it is very steep, and there is only one stony track that winds its way to the summit. In fact, the convent is an imperial shrine, and from the Ming dynasty on, the majority of the nuns there have been retired palace maids with no other home to return to. After the end of the Qing, fewer and fewer pilgrims came out there, and years of dilapidation without repairs have left it in ruins. Almost all the nuns have gone their separate ways, leaving only a venerable old nun in her seventies and a novice of thirty-four. When these two women see such a large force of armed men approaching, they assume it must be bandits again, and they take refuge at the top of the bell tower and don't dare come down. They are only discovered after some men climb the tower to raise the army's flag, and when they finally realise these are anti-Japanese resistance fighters, not bandits, they descend from their refuge and help organise accommodation.

Gao Guigeng has many years' experience as a mountain bandit, and it is easy for him to organise the setting up of a camp, the arrangement of defences and the posting of sentries. Qi Yuexuan is quite happy to accept his criticisms and follow his advice, and within four hours, the defence of the mountain, front and rear, is properly organised, and three sentry beats are arranged, both open and covert, to cover the ground all the way to the base of the mountain.

That afternoon, Qi Yuexuan and Grandpa Fu assemble the officers from each division for a tactical meeting, with the only subject for discussion being when to mount the first attack.

"Gentlemen," says Grandpa Fu, opening the meeting, "today, we of the Wanping wing of the Northeast Heroic Army of Anti-Japanese Resistance officially raise our standard. Now we need to agree on our slogan, so how about 'Death to the devils'? But we cannot rely on empty words. We must mount our attacks to show we mean business. We must fight like heroes. We must fight honourably and show ourselves worthy of that slogan. Then the men will be willing to follow our orders as officers."

Qi Yuexuan stands up to speak: "I am not here to issue orders today, but to confer with all of you over the plans for our first move. I will speak first and then we will all discuss it." So saying, he unrolls a map. "Look at this everyone – here is Beiping, here is Laoqiying, and this is our current location at the Baolong Convent. The red circles are Japanese defensive positions, and the red triangles are the puppet army and public security squads. The red arrows indicate the directions of the enemy's countryside clearance operations. Over the last few days, we have sent men out to clarify our intelligence on all the enemy's dispositions, and if we want to plan for the first engagement not to be on our own doorstep, but to take advantage of the Japanese sending their troops on an abortive attack to the rear of the mountain, we must make a pre-emptive sally. So, one of our divisions, along with Commander Gao's Traitor Elimination Squad, will make the first attack on Sanjiadian on the banks of the Yongding River."

He has hardly finished speaking, when the captain of one of the divisions calls out: "A couple of dozen men against Sanjiadian? That's no good. Look, there's a chain of public security squads here, and sentry towers to the east, the south and the north of the township. The Japanese have a sentry post at the entrance to the bridge, and there is a squad of Japanese troops at the railway station. There is another small troop of Japanese in the outlying village on the west bank of the river, which could quickly be summoned as reinforcements. I'm afraid our attack can't succeed."

"Actually," Qi Yuexuan smiles, "we don't want you to mount a real attack, just to create a diversion, the noisier the better. The main aim is to draw the Japanese away from the bridge and ambush the reinforcements here, at Wulituo."

"And what if the devils don't come?"

"Then we'll find out whether you can play for real or not, and whether you can actually hurt the enemy."

At this, Gao Guigeng slaps his thigh and says: "So far so good, but what kind of attack are you ordering us to make?"

"We need a great show of martial fervour to cover some more sneaky manoeuvres," Qi Yuexuan says, taking out an old hand-drawn map of the area around Donglaodian and Xilaodian, and spreading it out on the table.

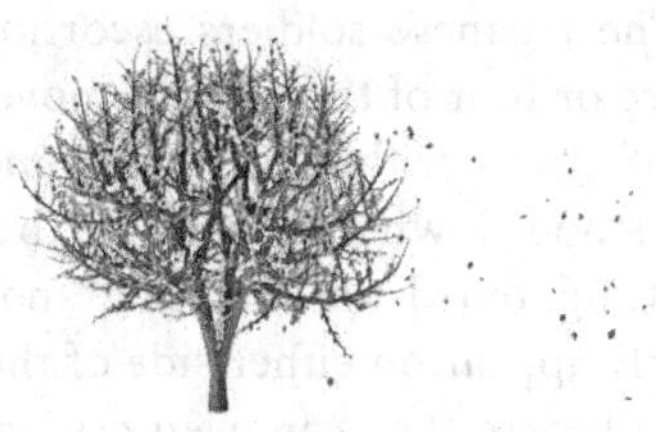

Chapter 28

anjiadian is situated at an inlet on the Yongding, where the river flows towards Beiping, and on the public highway between Mentougou and Beiping. Its history can be traced back to the Liao dynasty. It is said that the original inhabitants came from three families: the Gao, the Wang and the Yin. Each family opened a shop, and that is the origin of the name Sanjiadian, which means 'three family shops'. After the third Ming emperor, Yongle, moved the capital to Yanjing, it became the centre of coal mining for tribute coal west of the capital, and it also controlled the vital coal transport route. At that time there was no bridge over the river, and transport relied on ferries. To facilitate the transport of coal, the emperor ordered a wooden bridge to be built. However, the bridge could only be used when the river was low, and had to be disassembled when it was in spate. It was only at the end of the Qing dynasty that a concrete bridge was considered, and it would become the first modern bridge in Beijing municipality. Once it was built, both horse-drawn carts and motor vehicles could use it, and the village of Sanjiadian began to thrive. Businesses of all kinds sprang up along its main street and it became a flourishing township in the western suburbs of the capital, which people called 'Little Beijing'. A railway, built at the end of the Qing dynasty, passed through the middle of it. At the time, the Fengtai-Shacheng line had not yet reached Shacheng in Hebei Province, and trains that set out from Fengtai joined the Beijing-Suiyuan line at Shahezhen, north of Beijing. After the Japanese occupied Beiping, they stopped all passenger trains and used the line solely for the transport of troops and supplies to the frontlines in Hebei and Suiyuan. Thus the little township became a vital part of the Japanese defences in the western suburbs of Beiping. This is why Qi Yuexuan has chosen it as the target of their first offensive.

BEFORE DAWN ON THE NEXT DAY, a freight train passes by, travelling south to north. When it is still five or six kilometres from Sanjiadian, it comes screeching to a halt. The train driver has seen an obstacle on the tracks up ahead, and he immediately applies the pneumatic brakes. A large boulder lies across the tracks. The Japanese soldiers escorting the convoy pile out of the guard's van, and three or four of them try to move the boulder; but it is too big, and they can't shift it. Another three or four come to help, and they eventually manage to roll the stone down the slope of the embankment. The Japanese soldiers have just straightened up, moaning and cursing, when a number of black figures suddenly appear on either side of the tracks. A flurry of 'pop-pop' noises rings out, and before they can even cry out, the Japanese tumble to the ground. Immediately afterwards, several men leap up into the guard's van. This time, there is rather more of a commotion, but in no time at all, someone is waving a signal lamp up and down to show that the job is done. The train driver and his assistant are trembling with fear, and they stutter out: "We... we are both Chinese."

"Don't worry, we're not on your case. Get back up and drive the train while you can."

The man speaking is Gao Guigeng, and the reason they have attacked the Japanese on this freight train is to gain access to Donglaodian. To enter by road you have to pass through a checkpoint, so the train is much more convenient.

Gao Guigeng signals with his hand as he speaks, and his men load the bodies of the Japanese soldiers onto the train. After a few blasts of the whistle, the train moves on. It's not long before it reaches Donglaodian, and, a moment later it has already passed the township's southern blockhouse.

Gao Guigeng claps the driver on the shoulder and says: "Stop the train for me. Stop it at the top of the bridge."

As the train comes to a gentle halt, Gao Guigeng jumps down from the driver's cab. He shouts an order to the rear, and seven or eight of his men, who have changed into Japanese uniforms, along with a dozen or so regular soldiers, descend from the guard's van and form up.

Gao Guigeng issues his orders: "Number One Group take a detachment and look after the Japanese sentries at the head of the bridge. Wait for my signal before you make a move, and whatever you do, don't open fire. If the Japanese in Xilaodian send reinforcements, stop them, and don't let a single one get away. Number Two Group come with me to take care of the public security squad's headquarters. You are now soldiers of the Imperial Japanese Army, so act naturally and take your lead from me."

"Yessir!" His men acknowledge their orders and go their separate ways. Most of them head for the lights of the guard post at the head of the bridge, while the remaining few follow Gao Guigeng at the double towards the public security squad's barracks some three or four hundred metres away.

These barracks were originally the guild hall of the Shanxi Merchants' Association, but the two front courtyards are now accommodating the squad offices and a single platoon. Gao Guigeng and his men are soon at the main gates.

"Ai!" Gao Guigeng says in a low voice. "Shoulder your rifles and move carefully. You're the sergeant, Chengzi. Go and say something in Japanese at the gates."

"Japanese? Since when did I speak Japanese?"

"Ha! Just jabber a few words of nonsense, and as long as they sound a bit Japanese, they'll do. And if that doesn't work, try 'baka' and 'surasura'."[1]

The puppet army sentry at the gates of the barracks springs to attention when he sees a group of soldiers of the Imperial Army approaching. All he hears from the stream of babble is the word 'baka'.

"This soldier of the Imperial Army is asking where your commanding officer is." Gao Guigeng wags his finger under the man's nose.

The sentry smiles ingratiatingly and asks in a low voice: "You are... whose command are you under?"

"We're from the Railway Guard, and we want your commanding officer."

"Then... can I go and make a report?"

"Stop babbling, and hurry up and take us to him. Are you tired of life or something, holding up the execution of high military affairs?"

The sentry doesn't dare drag his feet any longer after hearing this. He hurriedly leads Gao Guigeng into the inner courtyard. Gao Guigeng secretly signals to his men, and two of them take up position inside the main gates, watching the rooms in the southern range. Two others stop inside the inner gates to keep an eye on the eastern and western side ranges. Only Gao himself and Chengzi, the man designated as sergeant, follow the sentry to the front of the northern range.

"Captain! Captain!" the sentry calls out.

A light goes on in the room, and a voice curses back: "Do you know what fucking time it is? Is someone dying?"

"The Railway Guard have some urgent business with you. They're from the Imperial Army."

As soon as he hears there are Japanese at the door, the man inside goes quiet. There is the sound of rush and confusion from inside, then the door opens and a tall man, thin as a stalk of flax and dressed in military uniform, invites them in, nodding and bowing.

"Great lord, you..."

Before he can finish, Gao Guigeng takes a stride across the threshold and the barrel of his gun is thrust into the man's chest. The sentry too finds a gun being ground into the small of his back by Chengzi. He puts down his own weapon and is shoved into the room. Like lightning, Chengzi snatches up the dropped rifle and ducks into the room.

The flax stalk captain keeps pleading with Gao Guigeng: "Brother, tell the great lord that if it's a girl he's after, I'll find him one. There's only my old lady in here."

"What's this? Have you still not worked out who we are?" Gao Guigeng gives a chilling laugh. "Haven't you heard of the Traitor Elimination Squad?"

The flax stalk captain finally realises what is going on. He is paralysed with fear and his face goes ashen. He just manages to whimper: "Brother... no, I mean master... I... I had no choice... I used to be part of the Wanping garrison, but our commander went over to the Japanese, and we... Ai! I haven't done anything wrong. I... my body is in Cao's camp but my heart is with Han!"[2]

Standing beside him, the sentry echoes these sentiments: "That's right. That's how it is."

"The Traitor Elimination Squad only deals with big fish, not small fry like you," Gao Guigeng laughs. "Today, the main force of our North China Heroic Army of Anti-Japanese Resistance is outside the township, but Chinese do not kill Chinese, we only kill Japanese devils. Stop just mouthing the words 'my heart is with Han'. Today you have the chance to really stand up and be counted, so how about it?"

"Of course, of course! Just tell us what to do," the flax stalk captain replies immediately.

"Wait a while until the shooting starts at the station, then order the blockhouses to the north, south and east to open fire for me with all they've got. Then telephone the Japanese devils at the bridge and tell them to send reinforcements as quickly as possible."

"I don't dare, I don't dare! I really don't dare..."

"What do you mean, you don't dare? I just want you to help our little charade, and the noisier you are the better. If you can draw out the devils from the bridge, then you'll be making a real contribution."

This seems to take a great weight off the flax stalk captain's mind, but Gao Guigeng adds a proviso: "But, if I do this for you, you surely can't let me go away empty-handed."

"Of course, I won't. Of course, I won't. I've got more than a hundred rifles, four machineguns and two small cannon. Just tell me..."

Gao Guigeng casts a glance at the old Hanyang rifle on the floor, and he interrupts him with a laugh: "Ha! Enough! I'm not interested in crappy old weapons like that, and, anyway, if I take any more of them you'd really be in trouble. I don't want to cause you any harm, and if I deprive you of your rifles so you can't defend yourselves against the Japanese, I might as well be killing you myself. But what I need from you at any cost is a horse-drawn cart, so I can take away the machineguns and the cannon, and some more ammunition to go with them. I also want hand grenades and explosives. I'll leave you all the rifles, alright?"

"Fine, fine, fine," the flax stalk captain keeps repeating, bending double like a dried shrimp as he bows. He goes on obsequiously: "Aiyo, master! You really know how to do things properly. Don't worry, if you need me any time in the future, just send a message, and I'll bring my comrades to help you."

"That's enough. Let's not talk about the future. For the moment, get all your men assembled in the courtyard, then bring them in here when they've handed over their weapons, and don't give us any grief about it. Don't worry, you can trust my word on all this."

"Yessir, yessir, I'll do it now."

A hubbub breaks out inside the buildings and out in the courtyard, and it's not long before forty or so public security officers are gathered in the inner courtyard. Although they may not be smartly dressed, none of them have forgotten to carry their rifles. When they see a number of armed soldiers of the Imperial Army in the courtyard, they have no idea what is going on, and they look round in bewilderment, their hearts thumping.

"I have an urgent commission for you, so listen to my orders. Attention!" When the flax stalk captain sees that none of them have moved, he grows angry, stiffens and yells at them: "Didn't you hear me?"

His men finally thump their rifle butts into the ground and stand to attention. The captain bawls out another order: "Everyone present and correct! Now, by shift, in order, proceed to the northern room and sit on the floor."

Sensing that the time is right, Gao Guigeng raises his rifle and fires three shots into the air. Just as he lowers his rifle, the sound of gunfire and grenades is heard from the direction of the railway station. Of course, the public security men in the northern room all react, and the room buzzes like an angry wasps' nest. Some of the men are startled to their feet, looking to run out of the room.

At this moment, Gao Guigeng pulls the flax stalk captain into the room and says sternly: "Don't get agitated, brothers. We are from the North China Heroic Army of Anti-Japanese Resistance, and we only kill Japanese devils. We mean you no harm today. But each of you must remember that you are Chinese, and if you persist in running around like dogs at the heels of the Japanese devils, then you will be killed. Do you hear me?"

"We hear you, we hear you!" The room echoes with a ragged chorus of agreement.

Gao Guigeng then gestures to the flax stalk captain: "Go and make the phone call. Do you need me to remind you what to say?"

"No need, no need. I understand," the captain replies, moving over to the desk and picking up the telephone.

A minute or so later, the three blockhouses have all received his orders, and he has told them that the resistance fighters kill only Japanese, and won't harm them. They are not to actively take part in the battle, but just fire into the air and make as much noise as possible. Nor are they to set foot outside the blockhouses. Before he has even put down the telephone, the sound of gunfire comes from the direction of the blockhouses, so thick and fast you can't hear the individual shots.

The captain is just about to phone the bridge, when Gao Guigeng stops him: "Slowly does it. Don't call them yet. You wouldn't announce a person's death when he's only just started running a fever, would you?" He listens carefully to the gunfire and says to Chengzi: "The fighting has started at the bridge, Chengzi. It must be the devils on the opposite bank coming over in support. I'll take care of things here. You take two men with a machinegun to back up Number One Squad."

Chengzi acknowledges the order and sets off with the two men, just as the telephone rings. Gao Guigeng slips the hemp stalk captain a look, and he answers the phone. The sound of a Japanese, speaking rough and ready Chinese issues from the receiver, so loud that Gao Guigeng, standing next to it, can hear every word.

"I am Inoue. Sanjiadian's circumstances are what? Why haven't your report?"

The hemp stalk captain follows the plan and says: "It's... it's not good, Lord Inoue. We are already surrounded here. The three blockhouses and the railway station are under attack, and the bridge is undefended. The attackers are regular army. I don't know exactly how many, but there must be several hundred of them. You must send reinforcements quickly. We can't hold out here... yessir, yessir."

A DULL-WHITE GLOW, the colour of a fish's belly, has just appeared in the east. It is the moment before daybreak, when the darkness is at its deepest. The dew is falling in a misty haze, and even if a thousand soldiers were to advance out of it, you wouldn't be able to make them out clearly.

Qi Yuexuan and Grandpa Dong, leading the two hundred and more young soldiers of the North Barracks, have spent the past three hours on the mountainsides that flank the road at Wulituo. Their position is to the southeast of Sanjiadian, only five or six *li* away, and the sound of the gunfire carries to them with complete clarity. At this moment, Qi Yuexuan is unaware that, contrary to any expectation, Gao Guigeng and his men have been able to bluff their way into position without firing a shot, undermining the enemy's defences by stealth. But when he hears the extent of the gunfire, he is satisfied that things are going well. The bridge is only about ten *li* from Sanjiadian, and with the township in such straits, the Japanese are bound to mount a rescue operation. He is not afraid that the Japanese won't come, just that there may be too many of them. He is even more afraid, however, that his untried troops won't be able to maintain their morale. If the first mouthful doesn't go down, but sticks in the gullet, that becomes hard to bear. Ha! What's the point in him worrying that his men are untried, when he himself, the commander of the army, has never fought the Japanese devils face to face. Although he has gone over and over the coming battle in his head, and has faith in his meticulous planning, in the end he has only ever fought battles on paper. Although he has previously scored two minor victories, his weapon has been his mouth not his hands, and he has never been up to the frontline. When he was four or five years old, a firecracker went off in his hand, and since then he has been afraid of letting off firecrackers, and of any unexpected explosions. As an adult, if he sees a child setting off a firecracker, he hides as far away as possible, but keeps his eye fixed on the firework so he will know when it is going to go off. If he doesn't know when it is going to explode, he waits for the noise with every nerve stretched to breaking. This time he is not waiting for a firework to go off, but for a thunderclap that will split the sky and shake the earth. If he were to tell himself he is not nervous and afraid, he would be lying. Fortunately, he is lying face down on the ground so he can't feel his legs go weak, and the sky is still dark, so no one can see how pale his face has become. But he can feel the cold sweat running down his spine, and the chill of his underclothes as they stick to his body.

Grandpa Fu comes up to him and asks: "Well, General, why haven't we seen any sign of movement from those devils yet?"

Qi Yuexuan settles his nerves, looks at his pocket watch and says with a laugh: "Don't fret, the fighting at Sanjiadian started less than twenty minutes ago. It's going to be at least another half an hour before the reinforcements from the bridge reach here. I'm afraid this fog is going to hang around a bit."

"It will brighten up when the sky clears."

"I can't wait that long. Daylight will bring its own advantages. Once it's no longer dark, the Japanese will relax. What is more, our first move is an ambush, and the better we can see, the more accurate and the fiercer we can make it. If we can knock them out with our first strike, then what do we have to fear? So pass this on down, and order everyone to hold their nerve, and make sure they don't waste their first shots. They are all born hunters and can hit a rabbit with their eyes closed, so they shouldn't miss a target this big."

"Yes, you're right," Grandpa Dong says, scrambling to his feet and making to leave.

Qi Yuexuan stops him. "Go and check the rocket tubes," he orders. "We don't want them failing to go off when the time comes."

"Stop worrying, I've checked them all. If they don't fire, you can shoot me instead."

These rocket tubes are one-offs made by the master craftsman at the North Barracks gunpowder mill, and are a refinement of the old 'fire tubes' of earlier centuries. Those fire tubes used to be loaded with loose black priming powder, and fired iron grapeshot and shrapnel. However, these modern ones have been adapted to use black gunpowder in cartridges, on the same principle as a firework tube, except that, in this case, the cartridges are made out of thin galvanised iron, and packed with TNT. They may not look very neat, but they have considerable power. There has been a test firing, which blew away one side of the Earth God Temple at the base of the mountain. The fire tubes of old fired on a horizontal plane and only carried forty to sixty metres. These modern one are mounted at an angle, so their charge describes a parabola and can carry much further. Today, they are sited on high ground, and if they get the elevation correct, should have no difficulty reaching the enemy. There are eight of them in total, and if they are all fired together, they will take out plenty of Japanese devils.

Half an hour has passed, and the sky is now light, when the rumble of engines is heard in the distance. Qi Yuexuan hurriedly picks up his binoculars to take a look, and he sees that it is indeed a motorised column of Japanese devils. Spearheading the column are four motorcycles and sidecars, with three trucks following about three hundred metres behind. Qi Yuexuan draws his pistol from his waist, straightens up and calls to either side: "Keep under cover, brothers, and prepare to join battle. No one open fire before the order is given."

Grandpa Dong comes up beside him. "Ha, General!" he says. "I've never seen you with a gun in your hand before."

"Yes, but it's really just for show. They're too far away for a hand gun to reach, aren't they? Then again, will this actually be any use if I launch myself into battle?"

The Japanese convoy is getting closer and closer, and the motorcycle and sidecar outriders are within range of the ambush. Grandpa Dong is beginning to get agitated. "Why haven't we attacked yet?" he whispers. "Go on, order the attack!"

"Calm down. We'll let the motorbikes go past, drop in a roadblock, then concentrate our fire on the trucks," Qi Yuexuan says, not shifting his gaze from the base of the hill, but raising his weapon and preparing to give the order.

The four trucks are right below them now, and Qi Yuexuan points his gun up in the air and pulls the trigger to give the order. It doesn't go off. He pulls it twice more, but there is still no sound. Grandpa Dong excitedly raises his own rifle and fires it. Within a second, gunfire erupts from the hills on either side, as rifles and machineguns open up together. Hard on their heels, the cannons begin their bombardment. Apart from one shell that lands short, and one that overshoots, the rest land square on the road. Hemmed in by these violent explosions, the Japanese soldiers begin howling and screaming, and the noise is deafening. Unable to contain himself at the sight, Qi Yuexuan shouts out: "Bravo!" He shoves the useless pistol at Grandpa Dong, muttering angrily: "Huh! Whether I know how to use it or not, you've no business giving me a gun that doesn't work."

Grandpa Dong looks at the pistol and grins: "There's nothing wrong with this gun, my General. It's just... ha ha... it's just that you didn't take the safety catch off."

Qi Yuexuan is mortified. "I did some target shooting when I was at school, but they were single-shot guns, and didn't have safety catches. Right, give it back to me."

The smoke from the shelling at the bottom of the hill has dispersed now, and the lead truck can clearly be seen, its front end rammed into the slope of the hill, and its rear end sticking up in the air, unable to move. The third truck is on fire, slanting across the road and stopping the second truck from being able to reverse. The bodies of Japanese soldiers are strewn around – inside the trucks, on the road, at the bottom of the hill. It seems that the burst of firepower has been well directed, and at least a third of the enemy have been wiped out.

The Japanese soldiers stationed at the bridge are an elite unit of seasoned troops recently transferred in from the Kwantung Army, and not raw recruits fresh from Japan. After a short period of confusion, they quickly regroup. Some of them take cover behind the trucks, while others shelter in ditches at the edge of the road and keep firing at the slopes on either side. The motorcycles and sidecars turn back too, and lend their weapons to the counterattack. Although the Japanese don't have the territorial advantage, they are well organised. Seven or eight machineguns open up, and two mortars continuously bombard the slopes on either side. The return fire from the Chinese begins to dwindle. Under cover of this superior firepower, twenty or so Japanese devils scramble up the slope opposite Qi Yuexuan, seeking to take control of the higher ground on one side.

"Keep firing those cannons," Qi Yuexuan yells at Grandpa Fu. "Take out the devils' machineguns and mortars for me."

Grandpa Fu gives a wry laugh: "We have to pack our rocket tubes with gunpowder before we can fire them. I'm afraid the tubes are so hot they'll explode. They're nowhere near as good as the devils' ones."

"Then we're in trouble if we want to mount an attack."

"Then... we're not withdrawing?"

"Withdrawing?" Qi Yuexuan glares at him wide-eyed. "We might be able to withdraw on this side, but the three divisions opposite are pinned down by those devils. How can they withdraw? If they lose the advantage of the higher ground, they'll be sitting ducks."

"Then let's go for broke and charge them."

"We can't risk everything like that, or the ambush will fail. I'm not going to spoil everything on such a manoeuvre."

"Then what are we going to do?"

Qi Yuexuan looks down the mountain and thinks for a while, before saying determinedly: "Tell the Number Four Group to detach twenty men and sneak down the slopes on either side, and attack the enemy's flanks. They're not to carry any long-barrelled weapons, but gather together all the hand grenades, and give them those. They'll have to move quickly and launch an attack as soon as they're close. They are to withdraw straight after they've got our men out. Once they're safe, we'll mount a full-frontal attack."

"Alright. But the grenades are round. It's impossible to hold more than a couple."

"Where there's a will, there's a way. They can take their trousers off, can't they"

"Take their trousers off?"

"If they take their trousers off, and tie off the legs, then they got a kind of sack, haven't they? If they sling it over their shoulders, it won't get in the way."

"Listen to you! I'm surprised a toff like you knows such tricks!"

"I used to do it when I was scrumping apples as a kid."

"Ha ha! Good for you!" says Grandpa Fu.

Qi Yuexuan straightens up and shouts to the people either side of him: "Keep under cover everybody. Stay calm when you raise your heads, and aim carefully. The devils outgun us, so we've got to be more accurate. The most important thing is to knock out their machineguns, and those of them that have climbed the opposite slope. They're just flesh and blood like us. One bullet and their game's over. Fight fiercely for me, and don't be afraid!"

Most of these lads from the Left Barracks have grown up playing with rifles, and they are experts with them. But fighting in a battle is not the same as hunting. As the bullets whizz over their heads and thud into the ground nearby, or when they see the bright red blood spurt as someone is hit, many of them are too frightened to raise their heads. How can they aim properly in these circumstances? But as they begin to calm down and overcome their nerves, the advantages of the higher ground and their concealed positions start to become apparent. They aim directly at the Japanese devils trying to climb the slope opposite, killing five or six of them, and forcing the rest to retreat. Several of the Japanese machineguns are also silenced. As the fighting settles down, the moans of the wounded on either side can be heard.

Qi Yuexuan now feels he can relax a little, and he snatches up his binoculars to inspect the situation either side of the valley. He sees that the party of men from Number Four Group have slithered down the side of the hill and are approaching the two flanks of the enemy with great determination. Unable to restrain his emotions, he stands up and waves his arms, shouting: "Give them some covering fire, brothers, fierce as you like!"

No sooner are the words out of his mouth, than Grandpa Fu pulls him back down to the ground from behind.

"Are you trying to get yourself killed? Do you think you're on stage putting on airs and striking a pose like that?"

Qi Yuexuan is about to make a riposte, when he raises his arm and sees the bullet hole in one of the sleeves of his padded jacket. He thinks better of it. He is amazed at himself. Normally he is scared of firecrackers, but today here he is in the middle of a firefight, totally unafraid, and even his initial nerves have disappeared.

In a moment, the commando unit are right up on the enemy. Grenades seem to rain down from the sky. There is a continuous storm of explosions that makes the ground underfoot and the sides of the valley shake. The road along the bottom of the valley is engulfed in fire and smoke.

"You lay down some cover with the machineguns, and I'll lead the attack," Qi Yuexuan whispers in Grandpa Fu's ear.

"It would be better if I lead it."

"Oh yes? And just how fast can you move that fat body of yours?"

As the two men squabble, someone beside them says: "Look! Troops are coming from the north!"

Startled, Qi Yuexuan looks through his binoculars, and he can see that there is, indeed, a body of soldiers moving south along the road. Although they are still some distance away, he can make out that they are wearing the uniforms both of the Imperial Army and of the sham army.

"It must be Number Nine Troop and Lao Gao and his men," he exclaims. "Right! It's time to spring our trap. No shirkers now. Attack on the bugle call!"

A few seconds later, through a lull in the sounds of battle, a bugle call rings down from the top of the hill. Actually, they don't have regulation army bugles, but are using brass trumpets from the old banner barracks. Although no one can produce a proper bugle call, several trumpets combined produce a properly martial and stirring effect.

"Kill them!" the men shout as they stream down the hills on either side of the road.

The attack proceeds perfectly, exceeding everybody's expectations as Gao Guigeng's feint to draw out the Japanese turns into an all-out battle, and the relief force is almost annihilated. There is no way of assessing the cost of the blockade of the bridgehead at Sanjiadian, but for the moment, it doesn't matter. Sixty-two Japanese devils have been killed in the ambush and the attack on the railway station combined, and one is taken prisoner. Six machineguns have been captured, along with three pieces of artillery, seventy Type 38 rifles and two Nambu pistols. Of course, the Heroic Army has also suffered casualties, with seventeen killed in battle and thirty-seven wounded, six of them seriously.

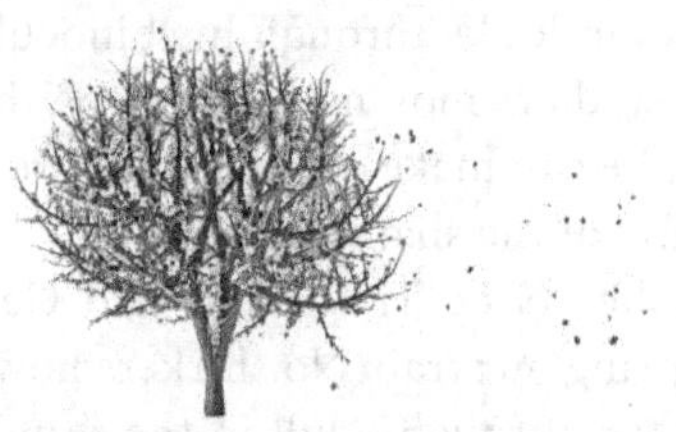

Chapter 29

Wangtian has been at the Fertility Goddess Temple outside the Xizhi Gate where the market is held in the morning, so he is home particularly early. However, that doesn't mean he has nothing to do, and he is now in their room, polishing some finished woodblocks.

In these last few days since the wedding, even though Caiping hasn't emerged from the inner door, let alone been out into the street, she hasn't been idle for a single day. She has carved several new designs of woodblock and made new sets out of the old ones, with three or four blocks to each set. She has also freshened up the colours of the New Year prints, so they are even easier to sell, but her hands are covered in cuts and calluses, dried blood crackles on the bandages she has wrapped around them, and they really hurt when she unwinds them.

Wangtian's heart aches as he lifts her hands.

"You mustn't do any more carving," he says.

"Who's going to do it if I don't?" Caiping asks with a smile.

"I will. Last time, didn't you trace out the design, and I carved it?"

"And how did that turn out? A line too many here, a block missing there. We ended up with a Guanyin with a crooked nose and slanting eyes, which we couldn't sell when it was printed."

"Well then... how about you do the face, and then mark a dotted outline of the rest for me to follow?"

Seeing how happy and excited he looks, Caiping feels a warm glow inside. "Alright, alright, have it your way. What would you have done if I hadn't agreed? Flooded the Jinshan Temple?"

Wangtian grins and sighs gently: "Ai! You're perfect, except maybe a little too ambitious sometimes. We have plenty of time ahead of us, so is it worth risking your life for a couple of yuan? You have to leave me a little face, so people don't go around saying I only got married so my wife could do all the donkey work. I'm a big strapping fellow, so I should be able to support you, one way or another."

Caiping flashes him a smile. "Is it just me you can support? Not a child, as well?"

"Of course, a child as well. I just haven't got one, have I?"

"Oh! Do you have to wait till the event is upon you before you do anything? Do you really want to be like Yue E and have two or three at one go, then have to tighten our belts to try and get by on what little food you can afford?"

When Wangtian doesn't reply, she goes on, more quietly: "Ai, if you want to know the truth, I'm late this month."

"Late? Late for what?"

Exasperated, Caiping thumps him on the back with her injured hand, which has no effect on Wangtian, but hurts her enough for her to cry out.

Wangtian stops what he is doing and lifts her hand up to inspect it. "Just look at you, still using your hand even though it's injured. If you need to let off steam, kick me instead. Do you really think I don't know what you mean? Are you really pregnant?"

"I'm about eighty per cent sure."

"Ha ha, just like you not to commit yourself. Well, from now on, I'm going to do everything for you. I'll do the cooking and the cleaning. All you have to do is eat and sleep. Eat till you're full, then go to bed. And when you've slept enough, have some more to eat. You're going to look after yourself properly."

Caiping begins to laugh along with him. Wangtian sweeps her into his embrace and holds her as tight as he can. Caiping tries to wriggle free a couple of times, then sees her husband's eyes are filled with tears.

"Don't worry, Ying'er, I'll... I'll make sure..."

Caiping doesn't let him finish: "I know. What makes a family? Having you makes a family. But when we have a child, and when your father can come home, then our family will be truly complete. I just have one thing to ask of you. You are the lynchpin of our family, so whatever you do, please don't get involved with anything like that business again. Alright?"

Wangtian hesitates for a moment, then nods.

Caiping smiles sweetly and begins to sing in a low voice:

There is no god in the broken-down old temple
When a careworn couple go inside.
We don't even feel the bitter north wind
When you hold me, and I hold you.
The real god is in the warmth of human hearts.

The melody of the final line lingers and reverberates, swooping and sweeping, and seems to last forever. Inside the room, Caiping is lost in her song, and Wangtian is entranced by it. Sadly, the mood is broken by someone calling out impatiently outside.

"Ai! Spare me the sickly sentiment!" Yue E says, laughing. "Alright, I won't come in, I'll just give you the message. My father wants the two of you to meet him at the Tianjiang tea garden at nine o'clock this evening."

"Is something up?"

"Something's definitely up, but I don't know what. I asked him, but he wouldn't say."

"In that case, I'll go now."

"Ai! He won't be there if you go now. It's no distance. You can set off in a couple of minutes. Anyway, there it is – I've delivered the message and I'll be off. You two keep on spooning."

THAT EVENING, the two of them arrive at the appointed place at the appointed time. Caiping used to sing at the Tianjiang tea garden at the height of her fame, and as soon as she goes through the door, the manager recognises her. His jaw drops but he quickly recovers himself.

"Ai! It's Noble Red! Why aren't you singing any more? Aiyo! It's such a shame, what with you being so pretty, and having such a good voice and being so graceful. People still ask for you. I heard you got married. Which Young Master did you marry? I'm sure you've done well for yourself, you're so..."

Caiping just grunts in reply, but Wangtian loses patience and interrupts him abruptly: "Has Manager Yang from the Minister's Residence arrived yet?"

"Ah! Yes, yes, he's here. He's in the second room on the right upstairs."

Even having been given the cold shoulder, the manager is still unable to keep quiet, and he chatters away to the waiter next to him: "See? She's really made it! She's got a bodyguard now. Look at the size of him! He could take the two of us with one hand..."

Outside the door of the private room, Wangtian and Caiping hear someone coughing badly inside. They go in and see Yang Zhixing, coughing incessantly. They hurry over and pound him on the back. Wangtian can't help scolding him: "You're not well, Uncle. What are you doing out and about? What is there that couldn't be said at home?"

Yang Zhixing gives a wry laugh: "Hah! The dogs are in charge at the Residence at the moment, and too many eyes are watching everyone's comings and goings. With something this important, we're better off being cautious and coming here."

"What's so important then?" asks Wangtian.

Yang Zhixing looks at him, slowly taking his measure. "Wangtian, do you remember how I said that, in order to make sure you're looked after, there was something really big I want to entrust to you in the future?"

"I remember."

"Well, now the time has come." Yang Zhixing strokes his goatee and lifts his chin a little. "I've discussed it with the Young Master, and we've decided to set up a trading company open to private investors. We already have a dozen or so investors who want to come in on it. Some of them are ex-managers of our old businesses, and some of them are old clients. The initial agreement is that the investors will all contribute to an opening capital of fifty thousand silver yuan."

Wangtian is amazed. "Fifty thousand? What kind of business is it that needs so much money?"

"Anything that makes money. Anything that comes in low and sells high."

"Well then... I... if you want someone to do the legwork, just tell me what needs doing."

Yang Zhixing shakes his head, smiling: "No, no, no, we already have people for that kind of thing. I was thinking of getting you to run the business."

"Run the business? As manager?"

"As a majority shareholder."

"Now you're pulling my leg. Where would I get that kind of money? Even if I could invest, it would be a drop in the ocean. How could I be a majority shareholder?"

Caiping pulls Wangtian towards her and looks him straight in the eye. "Just listen to your Uncle Yang."

"Ha! You need to learn to stay as composed as your wife. "You won't need to find the money to become a majority shareholder. Don't gawp at me like that. The Minister's Residence will put up twenty per cent and you will put up twenty-five per cent for a total of twenty-two thousand five hundred, but it will all come from me. Outwardly, you'll be a majority shareholder, but, in fact, I'll be paying you a manager's salary, and you'll get ten per cent of our two dividends. Do you get the idea?"

Wangtian just grunts, but Caiping replies immediately and straightforwardly: "We understand. The Residence will collect all the money, with Wangtian as front man, and there will be two sets of accounts, one set for public consumption and one set of real ones."

"That's right. But Wangtian is not there just for show. He will genuinely be in charge of the operation. What do you think, Wangtian?"

Wangtian just grunts again and doesn't say anything. Caiping nudges him, urging him to speak, but he stays mum. He shuffles to one side a little, but still doesn't reply. So Caiping takes it upon herself to speak for him: "Of course, he's delighted at such a wonderful offer. He's just stunned by such a gift from heaven."

Wangtian shoots her a look and just manages to say: "Who's stunned?" Then he turns to Yang Zhixing, and stammers out: "Ai!... I... I still don't get it."

"Alright, alright, tell me what you don't get?"

"If the Residence is funding the project, why are you insisting on putting an outsider in as the figurehead?"

"That's just a ruse. There are a few things going on that I can't tell you about at the moment. But I can tell you that the Young Master has fully embraced the anti-Japanese cause, and I have no idea how things will turn out after all the upheavals that will cause. This whole business of the Residence putting up the capital for the business, and making it a stockholding company but not being the major stakeholder, is all to guard against the Japanese getting their hands on things. So if by any chance they sequester the Residence and its property, they won't get their hands on the business."

Wangtian thinks about this, then nods and asks: "If you want your money to be safe, isn't the best place underground? Why take risks with it in these troubled times?"

"That's part of the ruse." Yang Zhixing sighs again. "Underground is certainly safe, but fighting the Japanese costs money. Burning through the capital at the expense of the family makes my heart ache, but if I don't put my heart into resisting the Japanese, not only would I be being disloyal to my country, my life wouldn't be worth living with the Young Master. So using some capital to set up a business and earning some money to use against the Japanese has got to be a good long-term plan. What is more, it's a good cover for laundering contraband, isn't it?"

A faint smile plays over Wangtian's face, as he says: "But the Japanese are all over everything at the moment. Do you really think you can bypass them with this business? Won't you have to come to some arrangement with them? And if that's so, won't you be turning anyone involved into a traitor?"

"Ha! Do you think it's that simple to turn someone into a traitor? There are two sides to every coin. If a man is sure of himself in his heart, if he is honourable in who he is and what he does, if he can look his ancestors in the face, why should he fear what other people say? Are you a real man, or a timid widow mourning her husband?"

Wangtian is too choked to say anything. He blushes and laughs uncomfortably.

At this point, Caiping, who has been quiet for a while, breaks in reproachfully: "Just look at you! You piss people off when you don't say anything, and you piss them off when you do open your mouth. What's with all the questions anyway? Just do what Uncle Yang says."

Yang Zhixing gestures to her to calm down: "Ai! These are important matters. It's best to get things clear, face to face, and not keep any worries bottled up. Is there anything you still don't understand, Wangtian?"

"The main thing is," Wangtian says, "I've never... I've never been involved with big business before. Do you think I'm up to it?"

Yang Zhixing nods emphatically. "I think so. The principle's the same whether the business is big or small. If you want it to last, you must be honest, trustworthy, have some intelligence and be light on your feet. Besides, aren't I still going to have a say in things, and keep an eye on you?"

Wangtian is still uncertain: "The open side of the business will be governed by rules and statutes, won't it? But the under-the-counter side will run on trust. Aren't you... worried?"

This annoys Yang Zhixing, and his voice rises: "If I was worried, would I be employing you?"

"But I..." Wangtian chokes on his words before finally getting them out: "I don't want to do it."

Now Yang Zhixing is really agitated. "Why not?"

Caiping tugs urgently at Wangtian's sleeve, but he shakes her off. Head lowered, not daring to look Yang Zhixing in the eye, Wangtian says: "Uncle Yang, I know you have specially chosen me for this, but the burden is too heavy. I don't dare accept it. It's too great a favour, and I can't take it. But please don't worry, it goes without saying that I won't breathe a word about this. If you have any other tasks for me, no matter how demeaning, I'll do them without a word of complaint, but as for this affair, you'll have to forgive me. I just can't do it."

Yang Zhixing is really angry now. He thumps the table and jumps to his feet. "You young bastard..."

His words are cut short by a violent paroxysm of coughing. Alarmed, Wangtian and Caiping rush over to slap him on the back as they babble with concern. Yang Zhixing pulls out his handkerchief, hawks into it and finally manages to catch his breath. Caiping sneaks a look and sees that there's blood in the phlegm in the handkerchief. She gives a cry of alarm and snatches away the handkerchief.

"We must get you to hospital immediately, Uncle Yang," Wangtian says, hurrying over to take him by the arm.

Yang Zhixing waves him away. "It's nothing to worry about. I probably just coughed too hard and damaged my windpipe. It's nothing. I simply lost my temper with you." With this, he grasps Wangtian's hand and looks him in the face, long and hard, before saying: "They say the child is father of the man, Wangtian, and I've watched you grow up. If I can't trust you, who can I trust? The business world is a dog-eat-dog place, and what it lacks is honest men, sincere men, straightforward men who are not just out for a free lunch. I have been manager of the Minister's Residence for more than thirty years. Upheavals in the world have come and gone, and I have kept it intact. I truly believe I have done so without giving way to greed or covetousness. But I am getting old now, and there's nothing I can do about it. There are so many things I have to look after for the Young Master, but it's a real struggle to find the energy. I may be able to hide it from other people, but I can't fool myself. While I still have breath in my body, I need to find someone that the Young Master can depend on, someone I can entrust things to in the future. But it is no easy burden given the way things have gone with my generation where the worthless is valued and wrongs are not acknowledged. The Residence's property and wealth may not bear the name of Yang, but I have used the money that has come in where it needed to be used. The Young Master has dedicated his life to the service of the country, but haven't I too earned my share? I have chosen you specially so I can hand that share on to you. This is not me offering you advancement, it is me putting my honour on the line, and begging you. It is not me conferring a favour, it is me handing on a heavy responsibility. I am not offering you a life of riches and ease, but a life of hard work and toil. If you really can't see your way, I..." He finds he can't go on, as the tears gather in his eyes.

"Uncle Yang!" Wangtian exclaims, his voice choking as he runs over to Yang Zhixing's side. "Don't be angry with me. Forget I said any of that nonsense. I agree. I'll do it. I'll do it."

"Not just because you feel you have to?"

"No."

At last, Yang Zhixing breaks into a laugh, and he laughs until the tears run down his cheeks.

"Alright, that's enough. Stand up. You can wait till I die, then you can kowtow. I've already agreed with your father – since I have no son of my own, you will perform the son's duties at my funeral."

"Uncle Yang, that..." Caiping says before stopping herself.

"What's this?" Yang Zhixing says, greatly amused. "Has he finished with his questions, and now it's your turn?"

"I was just thinking," Caiping says, "it's easy enough to call him a majority shareholder, but who is going to believe he has that kind of money? What is he going to say if people ask?"

"She's right," Wangtian concurs. "Apart from robbing a bank, where am I going to get a heap of money like that?"

Yang Zhixing is unconcerned. "I was coming to that, and of course, any lie has to be convincing. That's why I wanted you here too, Ying'er. I heard the Young Master say that the man who brought you up, Master Wei, wasn't really called Wei."

"That's right. Grandfather's real name was Zhu, Zhu Weixu."

"He was a descendant of the Ming dynasty imperial family, and during the Qing dynasty he inherited the title of Marquis of Extended Grace?"

"That's what Grandfather told me, but he also told me it was an empty title. All the time I was with him, he earned his living making New Year prints and playing the *sanxian*. If he had had money, would I have been unable to give him a proper funeral and been forced to mortgage myself to Li Fenggu?"

Yang Zhixing strokes his goatee as he listens to her and purses his lips in a smile. "As long as he actually had that title, then our story will be based in fact." He takes a small cloth package from inside his gown. "If you sell this, that will get you some money, won't it?"

"What is it?" asks Caiping, taking the package.

"It's one of the Young Master's album leaves." Yang Zhixing unwraps the bundle for her and points to what's inside. "The Young Master says this is in the calligraphy of Cai Jing[1] of the Song dynasty. He is the treacherous minister in *Water Margin* – not much of a man, but a fine calligrapher. I've arranged a meeting for you with the manager of the Jubao Tang Antiquaries tomorrow. You just tell him it was left to you by your grandfather as a keepsake, and you want to sell it on commission."

Wangtian's eyes widen. "Is it... is it really genuine?"

"Huh! You're not taking account of who gave it to him. This was a present from his brother-in-law, Zhou Zhengjie, Mr Zhou. Do you think someone as tight-fisted as that could bear to part with the real thing? But the Young Master says it's a high-quality fake, and looks the part."

Caiping is taken aback: "Can a fake still be worth tens of thousands?"

"It's not even worth a hundred," Yang Zhixing laughs.

"Is it going to fool the dealer?" Wangtian doesn't sound very happy.

"Tomorrow we're turning fiction into reality. You just take care of making the real sale, and getting the real money. I'll look after the fiction part."

The next morning, in the same private room, Wangtian and Caiping have arrived early, and are waiting. On Yang Zhixing's instructions, they have brought along Zhou Si and Li Fenggu. Those two weren't invited to the wedding party, so Li Fenggu is a little wary of this invitation out of the blue; an invitation from a poor relation usually means a request, either for a favour or to borrow money, and she's not inclined to either. But then again, Wangtian is Chenglong's older brother, and Caiping still calls her 'aunty'. Moreover, it was her household Caiping left to join the Gao family, so all she can do is swallow her doubts and come along. Once she's in the room, and hears Caiping say she has a treasure to sell, that she wants her to give an opinion on, her eyes light up. Her inspection is in vain: if it had been some precious object in gold, silver or pearls, she would have known what she was looking at, but she has no clue at all about antique paintings and calligraphy. Zhou Si is even more of a layman in such matters, and no matter how long he looks, he can't even read a single character.

"I can't take this on, Ying'er," Li Fenggu says.

Caiping smiles. "I'm not asking you to. I just want your opinion, and for you to give me some support. I've got someone who wants this thing."

Li Fenggu gives a crooked smile. "Someone wants it? You mean someone's willing to pay money for this crappy old thing? Do you still want my opinion? Well, I don't think it's even worth the price of two catties of meat."

"If that was the case," Caiping sighs, "I would just have sold it willy-nilly, but I didn't expect anyone to offer this much. It's got me paralysed."

"So how much are they offering?"

"Eight thousand yuan."

"Eight thousand!" Li Fenggu can't believe her ears, but when she sees Caiping nodding earnestly, she asks excitedly: "Where did you get it from?"

Caiping lowers her voice a little: "My grandfather left it to me. I didn't know it was worth anything myself. I thought he'd left it to me just as a keepsake. But I happened to show it to a southern gentleman, and he told Uncle Yang he's got to have it. He started off by offering five thousand, but when he saw I wasn't going to sell, he upped the price himself, and ended up at eight thousand."

"And... and you still didn't sell at eight thousand?" Zhou Si interjects.

Wangtian takes up the story: "If it was up to me, we would have sold it, but Uncle Yang was more cautious and wouldn't let us. He invited the manager of Jubao Tang to come and give a second opinion. Then we can discuss the price again."

"It's good to be cautious," Zhou Si says. "If you don't fix a price, it can always go up."

Li Fenggu is still suspicious: "Ai! I still think there's something fishy going on. When I was studying drum singing with the Old Master, I never saw that he had anything valuable. How..."

"Have you forgotten?" Zhou Si says in a low tone. "Master Wei's original name was on his grave tablet, and his family name was Zhu. He was a descendant of the Ming imperial family, and a marquis under the Qing. It wouldn't be so odd if he had a little something left after he lost everything else. Your trouble is you're too narrow-minded. Otherwise, you might have something from him of your own."

This irritates Li Fenggu enormously, and her bile surfaces. She glares at Zhou Si without speaking; her face falls and she looks very discontented.

At this point, Yang Zhixing comes into the room accompanied by two middle-aged men. He performs introductions all round: "Wangtian, Ying'er, this is Proprietor Mou from Jubao Tang, and this is Lu Chaofeng, who is the owner of the biggest antique dealers in the city and right at the top of the profession."

They all exchange pleasantries, and everyone sits down. Tea is served and Yang Zhixing says: "Proprietor Mou, Master Gao's wife is the granddaughter of Zhu Weixu, the Marquis of Extended Grace under the Qing dynasty. This album leaf was left to her by her grandfather. Hurry up and fetch it out, Ying'er, so these two gentlemen can take a look."

Caiping hastens to hand over the cloth package, but Proprietor Mou doesn't take it. He smiles faintly and says: "Master Yang, I won't try to deceive you. I know more about this Marquis Zhu than you do, and his family lost everything a long time ago. During the reign of Emperor Guangxu, his father betrayed his trust at the Imperial Ming tombs by selling off trees for firewood to outsiders. When all the trees were gone, he spread some bribes around and just managed to escape exile. He was sentenced to ten years in prison instead. When my father was in charge of the business, he took possession of everything of value that the Zhu family owned. When I took over, I had some dealings with him too, but he had nothing worth selling. He produced a few bird and flower paintings of his own to consign for sale, but they didn't even sell for peanuts. Later, I heard he had gone off somewhere else, apparently to work as an accompanist. Ai! If this really is something handed down by Old Marquis Zhu, then I'm not even interested in looking at it."

"That's fine if you don't want to look, Proprietor Mou, but let's be clear about things." Caiping keeps her temper and just gives a bitter little laugh. "Everything you say is quite correct. I had no personal experience of those events, but Grandfather often talked about them when he was alive. Just remember, the building may collapse, but the ground remains firm. The family may lose everything, but people don't die. So why shouldn't there be some precious object like this tucked away at the bottom of a trunk? When you're trading, you look at the merchandise for what it is, not for who's selling it. My grandfather said this is a relic from the Ming dynasty palace. If the nation had not been overthrown, and my family made destitute, you would not have the opportunity to feast your eyes on this great treasure."

Her words shock Proprietor Mou into a temporary silence, and he just gives a little dry cough. Yang Zhixing hurriedly redirects the conversation: "Proprietor Mou, if the piece isn't right, or the price doesn't suit you, nobody's going to force you to buy. But since you're here, you might as well have a look."

When Lu Chaofeng sees that Proprietor Mou has remained silent, he joins in instead: "Master Yang, we are not trying to make you lose face. What you don't know is that surviving works by this Cai Jing are exceedingly rare, but I have seen many pieces – centrepiece scrolls, wall scrolls, personal correspondence and so on. It goes without saying that even the paper and ink on them were wrong, so..."

"Ai!" Yang Zhixing interjects. "I'll be straight with you too. The Young Master has looked this piece over. He wants it for himself, but I've put a block on that. Nonetheless, he says this painting is a very honest piece of work. The ink and paper are genuine, and even the silk mount is period silk."

"Oh!" Proprietor Mou has a change of heart when he hears this. "Perhaps we might take a look then."

"Of course," Yang Zhixing says, taking the package from Caiping and handing it over.

Proprietor Mou opens the package, and before it is even fully open, he gives a grunt of recognition at the cover: "Hah! Not bad. Your Young Master has a good eye. This is a genuine Ming dynasty silk mount."

So saying, he opens it up properly, looks at it, feels it, smells it, then nods: "The paper is old, so is the ink, at first glance at least."

"Alright, Lao Lu, come over and have a look. Give it a proper inspection."

Lu Chaofeng takes the album leaf and opens it out on the table. First, he examines it closely with his naked eye, then he takes out a magnifying glass. At this moment, a middle-aged man in Western dress bursts in through the door. Once in the room, he begins to berate Yang Zhixing in Mandarin with a heavy southern accent: "This just isn't right, Manager Yang. Aren't Beiping businessmen supposed to be the most sophisticated in the country? This album leaf is promised to me, so what are you doing talking to other buyers? Are you going back on your word?"

"Aiya! Don't be angry, Mr Cai." Yang Zhixing hurriedly puts on a conciliatory smile. "Sit down and take your time."

"I won't sit down." Mr Cai points at the document on the table and says angrily: "I've got the money here, so let's settle this business right now. Alright?" He flicks a disdainful glance at Proprietor Mou and Lu Chaofeng.

When Lu Chaofeng sees this, he stops his inspection of the manuscript, and hastily picks it up and hands it back to Caiping. Mr Cai stretches out his hand to take it, but Yang Zhixing stops him: "Mr Cai, it's true you were the first to see the document, but the final price wasn't settled. If you could…"

"What?" Mr Cai protests. "Isn't eight thousand enough? Do you really think it's worth that much? The truth is, I am the thirty-eighth generation descendant of the Cai family, and if this wasn't a precious heirloom of my ancestor's, I could take it or leave it."

Yang Zhixing laughs. "Well, in that case, Mr Cai, I'm very sorry, but I am still going to show it to these other buyers, and hear their offer."

When Mr Cai sees Caiping about to hand over the album leaf, he says hurriedly: "Hold on! What do you think you're doing? This isn't an auction house! Look, how about this – I'll offer another thousand, cash on the nail, here and now."

"Mr Cai," Caiping says, pursing her lips in a smile, "this may be an heirloom of your ancestor, but it is also a treasured possession of my grandfather. You may gain face by buying it, but I lose face by selling it. You've got as far as nine thousand, but when all's said and done, the figure I see to compensate me for my loss of face is ten thousand. If you agree, you can take it away now, and I won't even consider a higher offer from anyone else. If not, we'll go back to where we were and let these two gentlemen get on with it."

"There's no room for a little discussion?"

"No."

Mr Cai frowns and considers for a long time, before he heaves a deep sigh and says: "Very well then."

He raises his hands and claps twice. Two of his men enter the room in response, one of them carrying a small leather-bound box. Mr Cai takes the box and puts it on the table. He opens it and points to the gold bars inside.

"I don't have any white gold, only yellow. There are ten half-catty bars here, which are worth, if anything, a little over the agreed amount, at current gold prices."

Yang Zhixing steps forward to check the purity of the gold, and to count the bars. He nods to Caiping, and she hands over the album leaf. Mr Cai opens it out to check it, then tucks it safely inside his jacket. With a smile, he clasps his hands in farewell, and Yang Zhixing escorts him out of the room. Proprietor Mou whispers in Lu Fengchao's ear: "Ai! Do you think it's the real thing?"

Lu Fengchao whispers back, in an even lower voice: "I think it must be. Otherwise why would that thirty-eighth generation descendant of Cai Jing be so happy?"

There is a certain bitterness underlying these words.

Li Fenggu and Zhou Si just sit there, looking baffled, not understanding what has been going on. They don't see what all the fuss today has got to do with them. In fact, quite apart from them, even Wangtian and Caiping themselves only half understand. They are not at all sure which parts of today's goings-on are real and which are fiction; nor who are the actors and who the audience.

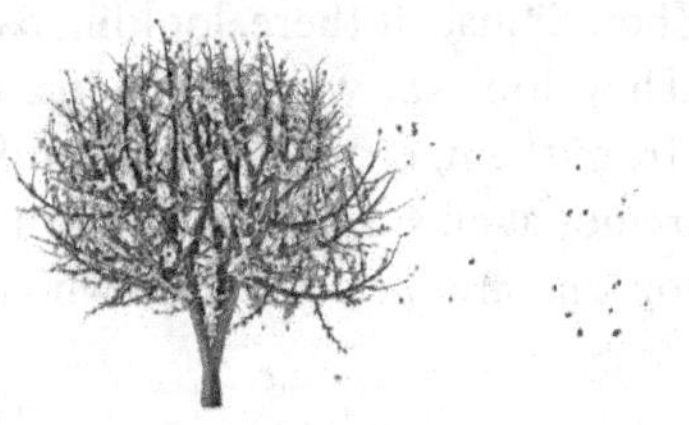

Chapter 30

Following the night attack on Sanjiadian, and the relief of Wulituo, the Heroic Anti-Japanese Resistance Army of the North Barracks takes two days to regroup. Then Qi Yuexuan leads a hundred or more men down the mountain by night. They follow the Yongding River westwards, before launching a surprise attack on the Japanese military outpost at Mayucun. The outpost is at the eastern entrance to the village and is only manned by around a dozen men. There is also an outpost of the sham army at the western end of the village, with a strength of one platoon. The attack is no great affair: they start by sending some men to cut through the wire-mesh fence and take out the sentry post. Then, with one bundle of explosives and a dozen Molotov cocktails, they turn the blockhouse into a bargain-basement roast duck oven. Most of the men inside are panicked into flight and are easily mopped up. The blockhouse is no more than a wooden-framed building, with a mud-brick rampart reinforced with sandbags, and surrounded by a fence no sturdier than a regular peasant farmhouse. It has no chance of withstanding fire and explosion, and it soon collapses. The three or four remaining Japanese soldiers come running out naked, and they are met with a rain of machinegun fire that peppers them like sieves. Only after the battlefield is clear does a single, dazed survivor clamber out of the ruins.

The sham army soldiers in the west of the village hear the commotion and initially intend to make a rescue sortie, but as soon as they emerge, they are met with a volley of shots, which fells seven or eight of them. They rush back to the cover of their blockhouse like turtles retreating into their shells. At the given moment, Qi Yuexuan calls off the attack. Their sole target has been the Japanese blockhouse, and once that is destroyed, they withdraw. When all's said and done, the sham army soldiers are still Chinese, and all Qi Yuexuan wants to do is teach them a lesson and lay down the law; there's no point in slaughtering them all. So the soldiers stay inside, and the attackers hold off outside, while maintaining a constant hail of bullets. The sham army soldiers show they understand the situation, and they fire their rifles harmlessly into the air and keep up the racket until the Heroic Army has withdrawn a good two *li*.

The next night, a detachment of troops who have not been used the previous evening mount another surprise attack, this time on the coal mine at Muchengjian. They split their force into three groups and coordinate their movements. The first group attacks the little grey mine office building, killing the dozen Japanese soldiers, foremen and security guards inside. The second group attacks the barracks of the mine police who are working with the Japanese, where they kill seven or eight, and the rest meekly hand over their weapons. The third group take possession of the explosives store and make off with several dozen cases of explosives. When they are done, they set off several bundles of explosives to destroy the machinery and equipment, after which they retreat from the mine area. They don't take any of the captured mine police away with them, but turn them all loose after giving them a good telling off. But there are twenty or so mineworkers who insist on going with the Heroic Army, so they take them along and use them to help carry the cases of explosives.

LESS THAN A WEEK LATER, a continuous attack is mounted along both banks of the Yongding River, inflicting heavy casualties. This not only terrifies the Japanese troops at Wanping; even the command centre of the North China Expeditionary Army in Beiping is profoundly rattled. At the same time, Song Shilun and Deng Hua of the Eighth Route Army are leading a detachment of troops that has already reached Zhaitangchuan in Wanping County, where they establish the Anti-Japanese Democratic Government. Moreover, five detachments of the former Japanese Resistance Army, now the Eighth Route Army in Hebei and Chahar, have also returned to the west of Beiping and mounted several attacks and inflicted heavy casualties on the Japanese Army in Laiyuan, Yu County and Huailai. The Japanese are convinced that all the attacks launched so far are the work of troops of the Eighth Route Army, so they urgently transfer the two large detachments that are currently conducting clean-up and blockade operations in the area of Baihuashan to mount a defensive operation. They also move in their motorised division to concentrate on suppressing the insurgents in the mountain area east of the Yongding River. The newly raised peasant army of the North Barracks has thus, unintentionally, been working on behalf of the Eighth Route Army, and by diverting the main thrust of the Japanese forces, has won both time and opportunity for the Eighth Route Army's subsequent successful offensives.

Several days later, the Japanese Army blockades all the roads and valleys in the mountain region as far as Moshikou and Guangningcun to the south, Tanyu and Nanmachang to the north, and Xinshikou and Badachu in the east. They also reinforce the sentries on both banks of the Yongding in the west. What is more, they dispatch aircraft to patrol the mountain peaks and carry out airborne surveillance. Several times, Qi Yuexuan sends men down the mountain only to discover large contingents of Japanese soldiers guarding access to the mountain in every direction. One of his groups escorting out the wounded exchanges fire with the Japanese on their return trip. They don't dare engage fully, and instead wait for the cover of night to cross the ridge and return to the barracks. The Japanese encirclement has not yet been completed to its fullest scope and strength, and since they are not sure of the precise state of affairs, they don't dare mount a pursuit.

Qi Yuexuan realises that they now have a tiger by the tail, and the tiger will be looking for an opportunity to kick out with its rear claws and turn around and bite them. He hurriedly summons Grandpa Fu, Gao Guigeng and every division commander to discuss their counter-strategy. Qi Yuexuan's opinion is that they should take advantage of the enemy not yet having completed its encirclement, and break out of it by crossing the mountain and heading north via the Long'en Temple, the Jingde Temple and Nangong. From north of Sanjiadian, they could cross the Yongding River south of Junzhuang. Then, between Longquanwu and Liuliqiu, they could make for Yingtaogou, beneath Miaoshengshan and Lianhuafeng.

Grandpa Fu is the first to disagree: "That won't do, General. It wasn't easy for us to establish ourselves in this foothold in the mountains, and, as our base of operations, it would be a great shame to give it up too lightly. Nor should you give the Japanese too much credit – haven't we denied them any advantage in the skirmishes we have fought so far? The mountains around here may not be that high, nor the valleys that deep, but the Japanese are unlikely to venture within twenty or more *li* of here. Even if they do, we can defend against their attack and take advantage of our superior position to fight them off. That's why I say we shouldn't consider trying to break out, but retreat to the North Barracks where we can be much more secure than if we establish a new base of operations in foreign territory."

Grandpa Fu's words are met with approval by many of the audience. This is hardly surprising since their confidence is sky-high after their victorious encounters with the Japanese, and none of them want to go too far from home. Even Gao Guigeng, drawing on his many years as a mountain bandit chief, feels that, just as a dragon doesn't leave its pool, nor a tiger leave its mountain, it is better to stay put than move on.

Qi Yuexuan remains unruffled: "Our troops are neither local militia nor bandits. We fight under the banner of the North China Heroic Army of Anti-Japanese Resistance, so if we stay within the region west of Beiping, and within Wanping County, how can that be considered leaving our base of operations? Wherever we fight the Japanese, which is all that counts, we know we will stand firm. If we move on temporarily, it is only to avoid the enemy's vanguard, to watch for an opportunity. There's nothing to stop us fighting our way back. I too find it hard to consider leaving just after we've made this base our own, but I really don't want a stand-up fight with the enemy. You may have won a few small victories, but what makes you think the Japanese devils will always be that easy? Do you think our troops can really fight a pitched battle? Why did we win those minor victories? Because we played dirty, we plotted, we blindsided them, we sucker-punched them. Now the Japanese devils have even brought up aircraft, and they are bound to have assembled a large strike force. If we really try to hold out against them, it will be a battle of strength, and you must consider for yourselves how sure you are of the outcome. How long will our food and ammunition here last? If we wait until the enemy are fully mustered, will we still be able to break out? Suppose we can defend our position here, or can break out, how many men would we lose? To risk the lives of several hundred on one throw of the dice, that is something I dare not do. My heart would break and I would never be able to look the elders of the North Barracks in the face again. If we retreat, we will be even less able to return to the North Barracks, and if we invite the Japanese into our home, how many lives of our fellow countrymen will we be sacrificing? I ask you all to concentrate your minds, weigh up the pros and cons, and consider the tortuous path of gains and losses."

Grandpa Fu points at the map and asks: "Supposing we do break out, why would we head to the northwest? We've just attacked Sanjiadian, Wulituo and Muchengjian, so do you think the Japanese devils won't be ready for us? The Long'en and Jingde temples and Nangong are no distance from there, so wouldn't we be just throwing ourselves at the muzzles of their guns?"

"What you say is common sense," Qi Yuexuan replies with a smile, "but the Japanese won't see it that way. They've just been attacked and are still suffering the after-effects. They certainly won't be expecting us to turn round and attack again. What is more, if we use the cover of night and stick to our route, avoiding conflict at all costs, then we can be sure of getting through from Nangong. I have ascertained from that Japanese soldier we captured that there are no Japanese devils in Nangong, and it comes under the charge of the public security squad in Sanjiadian. Even if we can't get past the enemy undiscovered, those public security men have already had a dressing down from Lao Gao and his men, and they won't risk their lives by trying to get in our way. If they do, they won't be able to hold us, and a few *li* further north, we're in Changping, which is outside the area patrolled by the Japanese in Wanping. If we choose there to cross the Yongding River, we have the advantage of being in an area unregulated by the Japanese."

"He's right," Gao Guigeng says. "Those public security fellows are not dyed-in-the-wool traitors. Last time, we let them off. They won't dare stand up to us this time."

"Things will be tight if we make it to Yingtaogou," someone else chips in. "It's a small place with only a few households and there are a lot of us. Are we all going to be able to live off the land?"

"Have you heard of Zhuang Shidun?"[1] Qi Yuexuan retorts.

"No."

"What about Xu Shichang?"

"No, which village is he from?"

Everyone begins to laugh at him.

"Ha! He isn't from any village. He was the president of the Beiyang Government. Zhuang Shidun was a Scotsman. He was Emperor Xuantong's teacher. Didn't you know any of that?"

Amid the general laughter, the man asks: "What have these two gentlemen got to do with Yingtaogou?"

"Xu Shichang built Zhuang Shidun a villa there. It's currently unoccupied and is ideal for us to quarter in."

"Ha, you're quite something!" says Grandpa Fu, sucking his teeth in admiration. "I was born in these mountains, and even *I* didn't know about that. We can always rely on you city folk."

"I went there in the ninth year of the Republic and stayed for a week." Qi Yuexuan stops and looks at his audience, before continuing: "But that's all history. Let's get back to what we were discussing. Everyone must have their say – should we dig in or leave?"

"No need, we agree with you," comes the great shout of approval.

That evening, they leave the Baolong Convent, with Gao Guigeng leading the vanguard, and the main body following in a tail that stretches two *li*. They go through Shangshifu and Xiashifu, past the Long'en Temple, over Cuiweishan and come down from the mountains at the village of the Dejing Temple. They go east past Nangong and then head north. Just as Qi Yuexuan had thought, they don't encounter any obstruction from the enemy for the whole journey. As they pass through Nangong, the public security blockhouse is only a few hundred metres away, but whether it is because they go unnoticed or because a blind eye is being turned, they are unchallenged and not a shot is fired. The level of the Yongding is low at this time of year, and they can ford it with the water barely reaching their knees. But in early spring it is bone-chillingly cold, and with the night wind blowing, a thin layer of ice forms on their trouser legs, so they crackle with each step. But on this occasion, no one feels the cold, as they march through the night until they are out of breath and their whole bodies are covered in sweat. Just as the sky is lightening, they finally reach Yingtaogou in the shadow of Lianhuafeng.

IN THE AFTERNOON of the day after their evacuation, the Japanese Army command send three expeditionary forces into the mountains. Not only do they find no trace of a single soldier of the Eighth Route Army, the Heroic Army has also left behind an assortment of hanging mines loaded with grenades, steel-toothed hunting traps, snares and pitfalls, which inflict quite serious casualties, killing or wounding more than a dozen men. The Japanese fly into a humiliated rage, and the ensuing massacre stretches from the Baolong Convent to the village at Xiashifu. More than thirty of the locals who haven't managed to escape, mainly the elderly, women and children, are slaughtered, and even babies are not spared. The inhabitants of Shangshifu have already fled into the mountains and escape this horror. The two nuns in the Baolong Convent ignore Qi Yuexuan's advice to flee into the mountains, and they are rooted out of their hiding place in the convent. After raping them, the Japanese throw them into the main hall of the convent and level the whole place with explosives, so the bricks and roof tiles form the two nuns' tomb. The convent is never rebuilt after this, and all that remains of it is a desolate patch of empty ground on the mountain top, with only the Liao dynasty brick pagoda still standing, lonely and aloof. Its walls, pockmarked by bullets and blackened by the smoke of the explosions, serve as a testament to the unforgettable bloody events that took place here.

Yingtaogou is situated under Lianhuafeng in the middle reaches of the Miaofengshan range, several *li* from the central peak of Miaofengshan itself. In the Yingtao Ravine, there is a naturally sited village that is home to only twenty or thirty families. It is known as Sidixia, which means 'below the temple'. Since the autumn of the previous year, Qi Yuexuan has been taking the opportunity to go and burn incense at the Fertility Goddess Temple at the top of the main peak, and he knows that, along the line of the main peak, as well as a guard post at Longjiazhuang at the foot of the southern side of the mountain, there is a lookout posted at the Huiji Cave at the summit. But Miaofengshan is what is called 'a five-peak, eight-pavilion mountain' and is many tens of *li* in circumference, so how can a lookout possibly keep up surveillance of the whole area? Qi Yuexuan leads his troops to take up position in Yingtaogou, relying on the old principle that people fail to see things that are under their very noses. But, in truth, they are extremely close to the enemy, and they have to be careful. So, before they enter the ravine, Qi Yuexuan announces some strict rules: there are to be no warning shouts or warning shots; no loud voices or general hubbub; no fires lit in the open countryside; and no one is to go out alone. In addition, before they go into Sidixia, he sends men to seal off the entrances to the village and the entrances to the ravine at both ends, and only then do they hurry over to Zhuang Shidun's villa in the north of the village.

The villa is called the Mountain Retreat of Happiness and Quiet, and its name plaque was inscribed by Puyi himself. It stands alone in a small courtyard. The main building has only five rooms, and it is flanked by several rooms that serve either as accommodation for attendants or as storerooms, all of them south-facing. The courtyard itself is not large, no more than a dozen *zhang* in either direction, and on the nearby slopes of the mountain there are three pavilions beside a pond. The original owner, Zhuang Shidun, was a Scot who had been private secretary to the governor of Hong Kong and chief magistrate of Weihaiwei in Shandong. In the eighth year of the Republic, he was hired as an

English teacher to the already-abdicated Puyi, until the emperor was evicted from the Forbidden City following the Beijing coup of Feng Yuxiang. Altogether, he spent six years at the emperor's side. From that time on, the villa became the property of the president of the Republic, and it was later gifted to Xu Shichang, who held the post of the Crown Prince's tutor in the diminished imperial court. Although Zhuang Shidun was a foreigner, he was deeply committed to the restoration of the Qing dynasty, and he kept in secret contact with the remaining members of the Qing imperial household. At that time, Qi Yuexuan was also a supporter of the restoration of the emperor. He was a follower of Zhang Xun and his Restoration Faction, until his arrest was ordered by the government of Duan Qirui, and he went into hiding for two years in his family's ancestral property in Wucheng, in Shandong. He had some dealings with Zhuang Shidun soon after his return to Beijing, and did, indeed, spend a few days' holiday at the villa, escaping from the summer heat. Later, when Qi Yuexuan was teaching at Yanjing University and underwent his political awakening in which socialist thinking began to replace his old feudalist attitudes, the contact between them lapsed. Zhuang Shidun went to Weihaiwei to take up his British Government post as chief magistrate, before returning to England in the nineteenth year of the Republic. Thus, it has been more than ten years since the owner has lived in the villa, and only the original gardener is still there, acting as custodian.

This old gardener has witnessed his fair share of things, and although he is taken aback to see so many armed men, not knowing whether they are soldiers or bandits, he doesn't panic. He listens to Qi Yuexuan's explanation, inspects the army rules of discipline, and his worries are eased. He hastens to open up all the rooms, but how can so few of them accommodate so many men? What is more, their trousers are sopping wet and need to be dried in front of a fire, which just makes everything even more cramped. All Qi Yuexuan can do is order that the wounded be looked after first, and everyone else should wait their turn in the courtyard. At the same time, he orders Grandpa Fu to take some of the men to the village to borrow the use of their rooms and their fires. Although they are not allowed to call out when they enter the village, two or three hundred men making their way along the road can't help but make some noise, and the villagers are soon roused in alarm. The Heroic Army of the North Barracks have already fought a number of skirmishes, and quite a few of them are wearing leather boots stripped from dead Japanese soldiers. Some are even wearing Japanese Army greatcoats, and there are a few Japanese prisoners among them. Looking out of their windows and through cracks in their doors, the villagers can't see clearly in the murk, and they naturally think that the Japanese have come. None of them dare emerge from their houses. In a panic, the men of the village hide all their grain and foodstuffs, along with their valuables, while the women, young and old, smear soot on their faces. When they discover that the people knocking on their doors are speaking Chinese, claiming to be troops fighting the Japanese, at first they don't dare believe them. Only when they hear the village headman go out and strike up a conversation, do they finally open their doors.

Most of the families of Sidixia Village are called Li, and so the eldest member of the Li clan is also the village headman. This Grandpa Li is a few years older than Grandpa Fu, already close to seventy, but he still clasps his hands respectfully in greeting, and says with a placatory smile: "Aiya! I am the headman of this poor village. Please accept my apologies for not coming out to greet your great army. Very sorry. Very sorry."

Grandpa Fu hastens to return the courtesies: "So sorry to disturb you. We are the Heroic Anti-Japanese Army. We have recently fought several battles against the Japanese devils, and now we have broken out of their encirclement to come here. You can see that we all got soaked crossing the Yongding River, and we would really appreciate some space and the use of your fires to dry ourselves out."

Grandpa Li blinks at him in disbelief: "What's that?"

"We would also appreciate the use of your cooking stoves to make the brothers some hot congee to keep out the cold," Grandpa Fu goes on.

"Alright, agreed, agreed," Grandpa Li says, but then goes on rather doubtfully: "Do you have any other orders?"

"Other orders? Ah well... we'll talk about those later."

"Later? Won't your honoured army be in a hurry to move on?"

"I'm afraid we may be staying for a little while."

"Aiyo, Commander!" Grandpa Li cries out in distress. "Food we can give you, money we can give you, but... we can't let you stay here."

Grandpa Fu explodes with anger when he hears this, and he glares at the old man: "That is not at all what I want to hear. Quite apart from the fact that I have been risking my life killing Japanese, is this how you treat a traveller and a guest? Chasing him out of your village? Do you think we are just a mob of beggars?"

"Aiyo! Don't be angry. Please just listen to me. We are a generous village here in Sidixia, but how can we take in so many men? But that's not what's important here. What's important is that the Japanese are so close, word is bound to get out, and then what would we do? One firefight and the village will be laid waste. You can leave when it's over, but our homes are here, our wives and children are here. Where can we run to? Remember what happened with the 'red and blue armbands'[2] last year? The Anti-Japanese Resistance Army fought the Japanese for two days at Jiangou, Dagongcun and Bei'anhe. They retreated, and the Japanese took it out on the local people. All the villages in the region of Miaoshengfeng were forcibly occupied, every house was searched and not a few people were killed. My twenty-year-old nephew, just grown into a strapping young man, and needless to say, a member of the resistance, had his head cut off with one stroke of a sword. Shortly before he died, he even left some words to be passed on to all those fighting the Japanese: 'Our people have been killed and our houses burned. I'm begging you, please leave us some way to stay alive!'"

Tears fill Grandpa Li's eyes as he speaks, much to Grandpa Fu's annoyance and exasperation, and he wags his finger under the other man's nose.

"What do you think you're doing, trotting out the same old meaningless bullshit at your age? You're worried about your homes and how much your lives are worth? The Japanese have killed your own kith and kin, and instead of seeking revenge, you want to chase away the very people who are fighting those devils? Are you bastards Chinese or not?"

"We are no traitors, Commander," Grandpa Li says, put on his mettle. Then he goes on with a bitter laugh: "You have guns and bombs, but what do we have?"

Grandpa Fu draws his pistol and hands it over. "Here, take this, and find a Japanese to stake your life against."

When he sees Grandpa Li shaking with fear and not daring to take the weapon, he snorts with laughter and points it at him, saying: "Let me tell you, everyone in this army of ours is from round here, and if the Japanese hadn't come, we would still be ordinary people like you, content with our lot and minding our own business. But we have courage, unlike you miserable cowards. What kind of ungrateful bastards are you? You need to sort yourselves out, and do what I tell you, if you don't want us to think you are traitors to China."

These words really rile Grandpa Li, and he stiffens and says: "Do you think an old man like me is afraid to die? Go on, shoot if you've got the guts. I've never seen you kill any Japanese devils, I've only seen you pointing your gun at me. Go on, shoot, and take this old Chinese life. What will that tell people? That you are resistance fighters or just bandits?"

Grandpa Fu chokes on these words, opening and closing his mouth but unable to speak. In his heart he knows he can't shoot, but he is having trouble swallowing his fury. He lowers the gun, but raises his hand to deliver a slap.

"Put the gun away! You're forgetting your place. I'm in command here." Qi Yuexuan's voice is low, but forceful.

Grandpa Fu knows he has gone too far, but he doesn't want to lose face. Holstering his pistol, he grumbles: "Did you hear what that old bastard said? It's enough to drive a man to..."

"Such anger is the sign of a narrow mind." Qi Yuexuan smiles and turns to address Grandpa Li: "May I ask how old you are?"

Hearing Qi Yuexuan's more cultured tone, Grandpa Li replies: "Not that old. A year under seventy."

"Aiya! Ten years older than me. I must respect you as my elder!"

"Not at all, not at all! I'm just an ordinary old man."

"I can't accept that. A year older means a year wiser. How else could you endure the enemy killing your loved ones without seeking revenge? And why, indeed, should you believe someone's words alone when you haven't seen them act?"

Grandpa Li is still trying to work out exactly what this means, when Qi Yuexuan laughs again and goes on: "I can see that you hate the Japanese to the very marrow of your bones, and that you wish there were tens of thousands of loyal troops lined up to fight the devils. For you, holding back is almost more than you can bear. It's not that you don't want vengeance, it's just that the right opportunity hasn't arisen. When the time does come, you will take your full revenge. Isn't that so? It's quite natural for you not to trust us, because you haven't seen us do anything yet. When the world is in turmoil, all manner of bandits, deserters and tomb-robbing traitors take shelter under the banner of the anti-Japanese resistance. They come asking for food and money, and you have no idea whether they have actually been fighting the Japanese devils. It's enough to turn the hair of ordinary folk white with fear and uncertainty. How can I be surprised at you acting this way?"

Grandpa Li nods in agreement. "That's right, Commander. There used to be a bandit chief around here, shooting his mouth off about fighting the Japanese, and demanding food and money, but he'd never been anywhere near one of the devils. Then last year along came a whole load of 'red and blue armband' resistance fighters who really did fight the Japanese, but they also looted two of the imperial tombs, robbed many of the rich families, and even kidnapped some of the foreign priests and held them for ransom. There was no way of knowing who was who!"

"So you want to know whether these soldiers really are resistance fighters?" Qi Yuexuan replies. "Of course they are. Just look – many of them are wearing Japanese greatcoats and padded jackets, they have Japanese boots on their feet, and they're carrying Japanese rifles and machineguns. Where do you think they got them? Would the Japanese just give them away? No, they were all taken in battle. In a while, you must come and see that we have two Japanese prisoners at the Mountain Retreat of Happiness and Quiet. We've sent away our most serious casualties, but we still have more than thirty of our wounded, and it's not red dye seeping through their bandages, it's real blood."

Grandpa Li looks rather shame-faced at this and says: "I believe you, I believe you."

"Then please also believe that we have nothing against you, we just want to borrow some space and your fires to dry out our clothes. We have a few supplies of our own, but not enough, so we'll pay you for some more. The only reason we want to stay here is to give our troops a rest. We aren't going to do any fighting here, and we most certainly won't bring any disaster down on you. If you agree, we'll stay. If you don't, we'll dry our clothes, eat our fill and go."

"Go? Where will you go?"

"We'll fight our way back up Miaofengshan. Last time we only blew up the main hall of the Fertility Goddess Temple, so, once we deal with the Japanese, there will still be somewhere for us to stay."

"But... you can't do that. Once you start fighting, you'll stir up the whole Japanese army."

"Then... what do you suggest?"

"Hah! You'd best stay here," Grandpa Li says, before he begins to protest: "But this many men…"

"Don't worry, we're not going to stay in your homes. If we can't all fit in the villa, there's also the Qiyin Temple on the mountainside, isn't there?"

"That's no good. That temple is in total ruins. I can't remember there ever being a whole building. Only the surrounding wall is still intact, so how can your men live there?"

Qi Yuexuan is aware that Grandpa Li knows what he is talking about, as he himself had taken a look around up there on his previous visit. This Qiyin Temple dates back to the Jin and Liao dynasties, and it sits halfway up the mountain behind the Mountain Retreat of Happiness and Quiet. It is said that, at its height, it was the most famous of all the many temples on Miaofengshan, and was one of the eight great temples of the Jin and Liao dynasties. But for whatever reason, by the time of the Ming dynasty it was in ruins and all its halls and buildings had been razed to the ground, leaving only a few brick stupas.[3] Repairs were undertaken after the establishment of the Republic, but only to the stupas, not the halls. The bicoloured brick courtyard wall and the main gate are still intact, but inside the wall it is all crumbling and dilapidated, with broken bricks and tiles lying around and head-high weeds and grasses.

Qi Yuexuan is unconcerned: "I know all that, but we can make some kind of shelter out of the broken-down buildings, can't we? If we thatch them with dried grass, they'll be fine for people to sleep in. The wall is still there to give shelter from the wind, and the weather is warming up, so we should be alright."

"That's all very well, but I am still ashamed to reduce you to this."

"There's no need to talk like that. As long as we have somewhere to pitch our camp, we are happy. But if you do let us stay, you will have to observe army discipline. We will post sentries at the entrance to the village, at the head of the ravine and on Lianhuafeng. No one is allowed out without our permission. This is for our own safety, and for yours."

"Very well, that's how it will be," says Grandpa Li, and moving briskly, he turns to go and summon the villagers.

A little later, smoke is coming from the chimneys of all the houses, and the smell of simmering congee and stewing pork is wafting through the village. The villagers have slaughtered a young pig to show their appreciation for the heroic resistance fighters.

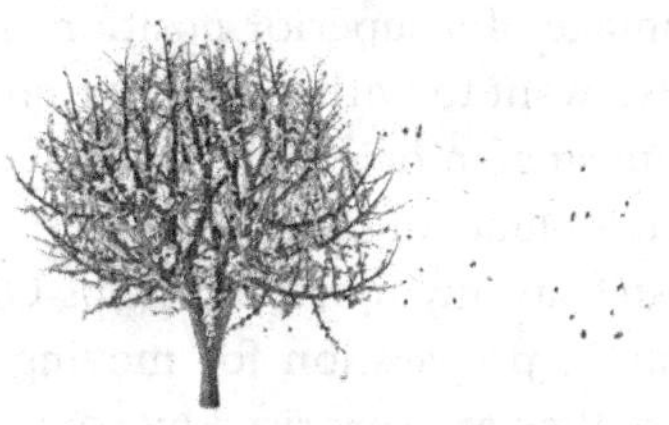

Chapter 31

On the third day after the Heroic Army of the Left Barracks entered the village of Sidixia in Yingtaogou, something unexpected happens. At the time of the morning sentry change, they discover that two of the lookouts at the eastern entrance to the mountain, one open and one covert, are missing. Each sentry shift is two hours, and the head of the sentry squad had found everything in order at the four forty-five inspection, so whatever has happened must have taken place between five and six o'clock. There is no trace of them left behind, and no one knows whether they have deserted or if someone has taken them.

When Qi Yuexuan hears the news, knowing there is no time to lose, he immediately sends someone to tell all the sentries to stay under cover, maintain surveillance and increase all precautions. He also instructs a dozen men to carry out an exhaustive search of the entrances at both ends of the ravine and report back straight away if they find anything.

Standing silently to one side, Grandpa Fu is studying a map, waiting for Qi Yuexuan to finish making his dispositions. Once everyone has left on their missions, he says, half to himself: "Could they have deserted?"

"It doesn't look like it. I think they've been kidnapped."

"By the Japanese?"

"I don't think so. If it was, they'd have attacked by now."

"Who then?"

"I don't know for the moment," Qi Yuexuan says. He turns to a sentry and orders him: "Pass the word on immediately – take the wounded and the prisoners to the Qiyin Temple. All our troops are to assemble there, prepare to mobilise and wait for orders."

The sentry acknowledges his instructions and turns to leave, but Grandpa Fu stops him. He asks Qi Yuexuan with some agitation: "In these circumstances, why are they staying where they are? Whether we decide to attack or to move out, we should do so immediately. We don't want to lose our chance."

Qi Yuexuan smiles faintly. "In this situation, all we can do is stay calm, wait till we know what's going on and then decide on the best way forward. Why didn't I order the troops to stay in the village but move to the Qiyin Temple? The temple has the advantage of a superior position, and is easy to defend. It's even more convenient if we want to withdraw. If we cross the top of Lianhuafeng, we can head north to Jiuwangfen or east to the Shuangquan Temple. Either would do. Don't worry, there's plenty of time to decide."

Grandpa Fu doesn't say any more, but helps Qi Yuexuan gather up the maps and other documents in preparation for moving up to the Qiyin Temple. But before they can leave, they are surprised by someone dashing excitedly into the room. Grandpa Fu looks up to discover it is one of the missing sentries.

Delighted and angry in equal measure, he demands: "Where have you been, you little bastard?"

Out of breath from running, the man pants out: "I... was... taken... prisoner."

"By the Japanese?"

"No, no... not the Japanese. It was the Eighth Route Army."

"The Eighth Route Army? Why the fuck are they attacking us, not the Japanese?" Grandpa Fu glares at the man. "How did you escape?"

"They... didn't stop me... it was just a... misunderstanding. Once they knew we are also fighting the Japanese... they let us go."

"Hmph, and where's your rifle?"

"They... didn't give us them... back."

Grandpa Fu's temper gets the better of him: "Fuck it! How many of them are there?"

"Twenty or thirty."

"Where are they now?"

"Halfway up the slope at the east end of the ravine."

"Go! Assemble the men. Two can play at that game. We can pretend we don't know who they are and go seize their weapons!" Grandpa Fu angrily makes to leave the room.

"Enough with your troublemaking," says Qi Yuexuan, glaring at him. "How can a man of your age act like such a child? If someone gives you a clod of earth, you make a brick out of it, don't you?"

"I was just trying to frighten him, to let them know we still have teeth."

"Haven't you thought you might accidentally start something? Would it be worth it, just to fight to a stalemate?"

"If we throw up our hands now, it will just weaken our position next time and make it even more difficult to keep our reputation."

"Do you think there's any merit in fighting just to show off? I call that petty and small-minded. Enough! I'll handle this. The Eighth Route Army are a properly regulated army. They will be open to reason," Qi Yuexuan says, himself making to leave.

"Ah, there's no point going there," the sentry breaks in.

"Why not?"

"Their leader said he wanted a meeting with you two, and he'll be waiting at the second sentry post. I came here to report and to get your agreement."

"Fine, but I'd rather spare myself the journey. Quick, go and invite him here."

As he watches the man leave the room, Grandpa Fu shouts through the door: "Come in here!"

A sentry standing outside comes running in. Grandpa Fu continues: "The whole sentry squad are to form up immediately with their rifles, and be on high alert. Also, send one group straight away to the eastern entrance to the ravine, where they are to conceal themselves and maintain the highest vigilance."

"Is that really necessary?" Qi Yuexuan asks.

"It's better to be careful," Grandpa Fu replies. "I've heard that quite a few anti-Japanese resistance forces have gone rogue. Gao Xianzhang, the man who led the Tongzhou Uprising, is one of them. He made a pretence of inviting someone to a meal, then took him prisoner and shot him. He sent some of his own men to surround his victim's troops, and several hundred men and rifles all went over to his side."

"That was nothing to do with the Eighth Route Army. That was the work of the 'red and blue armband' local resistance movement."

"It's all the same thing. I've heard that the Eighth Route Army soldiers were originally 'red and blue armband' fighters, and have only been members for a few days. Besides, their commanding officer is that man Zhao. When he's in charge, any change in allegiance is only superficial, and he remains the same underneath. And weren't the Communists all bandits once, anyway? And haven't they only just made peace with the government? If they want to fight the Japanese, I'm all in favour, but if they want me to share my wife and property and all that stuff, then I'm not ready to piss in the same pot as them."

Qi Yuexuan wants to laugh, seeing him all steamed up like this. He manages to restrain himself at first, but he can't hold out and bursts out laughing. Grandpa Fu watches him, baffled, then asks: "What have you got to laugh at?"

"Ha ha, what's not to laugh at?"

"People like me and Grandpa Dong may be leaders here in the Left and Right Barracks, but your family are real moneybags. If the Communists want to gobble up your property, they'll gnaw you to the bone first."

Qi Yuexuan's laughter abates slightly. "Listen to you! Always thinking the worst. If you were told the Communists all have red eyebrows and red beards, and gouge the hearts out of children for dinner, would you believe them?"

Grandpa Fu nods seriously. "I've heard people say that..."

"Alright, let's not dwell on the past. When there's time, I'll tell you all the details, but for the moment, we're fighting the Japanese together, and as long as we're killing those devils, we're travelling the same road. If they're at our door now, then they don't mean any harm, so are you still going to be standing there, axe in hand, waiting to slaughter them at the feast?[1] Are you just putting on an act, or are you really terrified?"

Grandpa Fu sees his point, and he turns peevishly to the newly assembled sentry squad and vents his annoyance on them: "Why are you lot standing in the doorway? Auditioning as telegraph poles? Get out! Get out, the lot of you!" He pulls back the door curtain and says with an angry grimace: "You get on with this farce of yours, and I'll sit back and watch."

Only two people turn up from the Eighth Route Army, a middle-aged man and a youth, neither of them wearing army uniform, but dressed as farmers. When they arrive at the door, the middle-aged man voluntarily hands over two handguns to the sentry, and then goes into the room. As Qi Yuexuan hurries forward to greet him, he knows he looks faintly familiar.

"Ha! So, it's Mr Qi Yuexuan!"

Still unable to place him, Qi Yuexuan says with an embarrassed laugh: "I know I recognise your face, but just for the moment..."

"I was involved in the fundraising for the Allied Army of Anti-Japanese Resistance at the Minister's Residence, and, later, I stayed in the Residence's western side courtyard with Gao Chenglong and Gao Wangtian."

"Aah! Now I remember. You're Old Man Zhang's grandson. Zhang..."

"Zhang Zhicheng."

"That's it, that's it! Weren't you with the Twenty-Ninth Army?"

"A lot has happened in a short time. I'm now commander-in-chief of the Fifth Division of the Shanxi, Chahar and Hebei Area Eighth Route Army."

"Aiya! I really didn't expect to meet you here."

"Same here! What's a pen pusher like you doing on the battlefield?"

"Blame the Japanese! Come now, sit down, sit down."

Although Zhang Zhicheng is indeed the commander-in-chief, he has not gone for training and exercises with the Fifth Division to Fuping, in the west of Hebei, but is leading three crack troops who have stayed behind in Wanping to wage a guerrilla campaign, and to open up a new base of operations against the Japanese. Following the advance to Pingxi of the Song and Deng divisions of the Eighth Route Army, once you cross to the south of the Yongding River, there is now an established opposition to the Japanese in Wangping, Yanchi and Zhaitang. Their field of guerrilla operations are now in Hebei, Dagongcun, Xugezhuang, Beianhe, Guanjialing and Qiwangfen. The main force of the Fifth Division has also returned from Huailai and Wei County, to Pingxi. To support the main force, Zhang Zhicheng and his men launched a surprise attack on the Japanese at Wenquan Township on the previous night and brought down two kilometres of telephone wires. On their return, they received a report from their communications officer that troops of unknown origin had appeared in Sidixia. Fearing these might be plain-clothes soldiers of the sham army, or even actual Japanese, they captured the sentries to interrogate. Over the last few days, the Japanese have been attacked at Sanjiadian, Wulituo and Muchengjian, and they have subsequently mounted an encircle-and-annihilate operation in the region around Cuiweishan. The countryfolk have been saying the attacks on them are all the work of the Eighth Route Army; obviously, the soldiers know this is not the case, but they don't know exactly what they actually are. They finally learn from the captured sentries that they are the work of this peasant militia from the Left Barracks. So, Zhang Zhicheng has come to visit: first, to apologise for seizing the sentries; second, fearing for their safety, to offer to escort them to the Eighth Route Army base of operations south of the Yongding River; and third, to suggest they work together in future operations against the enemy.

Naturally delighted to hear this, Qi Yuexuan is about to respond when Grandpa Fu pulls aside the door curtain and comes in, cupping his hands in greeting.

"Well, brother, our own troops are by no means amateurs. You say you have a base of operations, but don't we have one too? Why should we want to join you up that mountain of yours?"

Without waiting for Zhang Zhicheng to reply, Qi Yuexuan breaks in: "This is Second-in-Command Fu."

Seeing Zhang Zhicheng's confused look, Qi Yuexuan hastens to explain:[2] "His Manchu family name is Fucha, Fu in Chinese, and he is our second-in-command."

"Ha! That's all too confusing. A second-in-command is still a commander, so how about I call you Commander Fucha?"

Grandpa Fu finds this quite acceptable and grunts his agreement, looking a bit less grumpy.

Zhang Zhicheng goes on to say: "As long as we are both fighting the Japanese devils, Commander Fucha, there should be no talk of professional and amateur. We all take our status from our resistance to the Japanese, and if we are all truly willing to risk our lives in that cause, both our credentials are established. Once we see the Japanese running away like frightened rabbits, they won't look like a regular army any more, but a raggle-taggle bunch of amateurs."

"I think you're right," Grandpa Fu says, the trace of a smile on his face.

"In the same way, as long as we're fighting those devils, what does it matter whether it is from our mountain top, or yours? I just feel that here, we're too close to the enemy, and it can only ever be a temporary position. We will be much safer withdrawing south of the river."

"It still sounds to me as though you are trying to take us over," says Grandpa Fu, glaring at him.

Zhang Zhicheng is unfazed: "If you want to join the Eighth Route Army, you will be very welcome. If you don't, we can still work together and coordinate our war against the Japanese. As long as you are truly opposed to the Japanese, and we are not working against each other, it doesn't matter. We can both use our bases of operation to oppose the rule of the Japanese Democratic Government. If you want to link them, we will welcome you in and escort you out, and you will be free to come and go as you please."

"Some of our top men are from the grand old families of the Left Barracks," Grandpa Fu persists.

"Enough! Why do you keep trying to find objections?" Qi Yuexuan interrupts him ill-temperedly, and when he sees Zhang Zhicheng's bewilderment, he hurriedly explains: "He doesn't understand how things have changed. He thinks you'll attack him as a petty local tyrant and confiscate his land."

"Ha! What year does he think we are living in? Commander Fucha, the only thing the Communist Party and the Eighth Route Army are concerned with is fighting the Japanese, and the only people we attack are Japanese devils, Chinese traitors and opponents of the resistance. It doesn't matter whether you are rich or poor, which party you belong to, which clan you come from, as long as you are opposed to the Japanese, you are your own man. You are a commander of the anti-Japanese resistance, a hero who has risked his life in the cause, and anyone who attacks you is clearly on the side of the Japanese devils and I will be the first to cut him down."

At long last, Grandpa Fu breaks into a smile. But the smile doesn't develop, and he goes on: "But, you took our rifles..."

"Why are you still so distrustful?" Zhang Zhicheng retorts, pounding his fist on his thigh. "The only reason I haven't yet returned the gun is because it got dropped and the rear sight is broken. I was going to give it back as soon as I'd had it fixed. Our new recruits are short of rifles, and the government isn't supplying any, but I'd much rather take them from the Japanese and the sham army, than rob my own side. I was in such a hurry to come and see you that I didn't have time to prepare any proper gifts. But I didn't want to come empty-handed. So, these are a few things I just took from a Japanese officer, and I'd like to give them to you to mark our first meeting."

So saying, he turns and shouts through the door: "Bring that stuff in, Xiao Chen."

The younger man who has been standing outside comes in and hands over a cloth bundle. Inside it are a Japanese pistol, an officer's sword, a telescope and a leather attaché case.

"These belonged to a Japanese captain. I'd like to give them to you as an offering. The only problem is, there are two of you..."

"I have no use for them," Qi Yuexuan says immediately. "Give them all to the commander."

This time, Grandpa Fu's smile is genuine. He expresses his thanks, takes the bundle and puts it in the inner room, then slips away.

Zhang Zhicheng then explains what has happened to him since the Marco Polo Bridge Incident: how he stopped the Japanese Army at Nanyuan; how he led twenty or thirty stragglers to Rehe to seek out the Allied Resistance; how he searched in vain for them, and how he and his troops pretended to be the Allied Army of Japanese Resistance to restock his equipment; and how he mounted a night attack on Longwang Township.

He then stops suddenly, looks at Qi Yuexuan with a grin and asks: "Can you guess who I bumped into?"

"Who?"

"Your wife."

"Zhengying!"

"None other! If I hadn't bumped into her, I'd never have found the real Allied Resistance. She is our political education officer, and my sponsor into the Communist Party."

"Has she... has she come back too?"

"No, she's stayed in Rehe on undercover operations."

"Did she give you a letter for me?"

"No."

"Or send a message?"

"Ah, how could she know I was going to bump into you in Beiping? And there's Party discipline to think of too. But don't worry, she's in excellent health and so is your son."

"Son? My... son?"

"That's right. He's called Nan'er."

It has been more than a year since Zhou Zhengying ran off, and there has been no word of her all this time. Qi Yuexuan only found out by word of mouth from government intelligence that she was a Communist Party member, and it was also only then that he realised the Residence's Moxiangzhai had become an underground print shop for Communist Party documents and propaganda materials. Secretly, he is angry with Zhengying, not because he might have been implicated, but because she failed to trust him in hiding all this from him. Despite his anger, he still misses her and can't help remembering the unforgettable times they shared. He is deeply worried for her safety. The news, brought by Zhang Zhicheng, that she is alright, but that she has also mysteriously produced a son, has the same effect on him as if he has just downed a whole bottle of spirits. A fiery sensation spreads swiftly from his belly.

"Ha! So, has she got married again? Pah! As if anyone would want to marry her, when I have neither repudiated nor divorced her!"

Now it is Zhang Zhicheng's turn to look astonished, as he simply doesn't understand why Qi Yuexuan has changed like this: "I... I haven't heard anything... about Comrade Zhengying getting married again. She is working with a senior officer, pretending to be husband and wife, but... but that's just a cover. They're not really married."

"Hah! They've got a child as well, you say? That doesn't sound much like a cover!"

"Nan'er... he isn't your son?"

"Do you think I wouldn't know if I had a son!" Qi Yuexuan yells, jumping angrily to his feet. Perhaps feeling he has lost control of himself, he sits back down again and says with a wry smile: "Ai! Troubled times indeed. The normal rules of behaviour and feelings don't apply, but even so... has she just found some random man to be father to her child? Pah! Isn't she afraid that a miserable landowning bureaucrat like me will cast a stain on her offspring?"

Seeing him like this, Zhang Zhicheng doesn't know what to say. He considers for quite a while, then says carefully: "Don't be angry, Mr Qi. I really don't have the full story. How would it be if I refer all this to our central organisation and find some way of discovering exactly what is going on, through them. Then..."

"There's no need. If you can get a message through to her, just say that I understand everything, and that I wish her well in her new life." He hesitates a moment, then goes on: "That's enough of personal matters, Commander Zhang, let's get down to real business, serious business."

Zhang Zhicheng realises there is no point in pursuing the matter, and he says: "Mr Qi, the reason I just said I want to move you and your men south of the Yongding is because of the overall situation of the anti-Japanese resistance, and for your own safety. If you consider..."

"I know that fingers formed into a fist are more effective than the edge of the hand. How could I not be willing to fall into line to confront the Japanese devils? But we come from different backgrounds. If we are to become like brothers, then we must proceed slowly and carefully. Besides, these troops aren't my personal bodyguard, and I can't take such a big responsibility on myself alone. I think we should work on the principle that we don't believe anything until we've seen it for ourselves. I'll go across the river with you to take a look, so when I come back to discuss matters with the men, I'll have a clear idea of how things stand. Will that do?"

"Yes, let's do it that way," Zhang Zhicheng says with some relief. "The return trip is only twenty or so *li*. If we leave in the morning, we can be back the same afternoon."

WHILE THIS IS GOING ON, Zhou Zhengying is several hundred kilometres away, in Chengde. It is four months and more since she came here with Zuo Xichuan. Zuo Xichuan's nephew, Shoi Toyoki, has arranged a courtyard house for them to live in, just the other side of the wall from the headquarters of the Rehe garrison. It is in the north of Chengde not far from the Guandi Temple and Bishu Shanzhuang, the Qing imperial summer villa, and it was originally the residence of the general manager of summer apartments in the Department of the Imperial Household. The garrison command next door was formerly the official residence of the Department of Military Affairs and there is a connecting door between the two buildings. After Shoi Toyoki's Fourteenth Division of the Kwantung Army arrived in Rehe, he has brought his wife and children from Shenyang, and they are living in the same building as Zuo Xichuan and Zhou Zhengying. The aide-de-camp and the guards live in the front courtyard, the eastern side courtyard houses the officers' children's kindergarten, and the western side courtyard was originally empty and used only for storing junk, so could be made available for Zuo Xichuan and his family. Shoi Toyoki and Zuo Xichuan's joint trading company has opened its doors on Chengde Street, under the name 'The Shoi Trading Guild'.

On the surface, Shoi Toyoki is very respectful towards his uncle, but he is actually not at all happy, and he is particularly suspicious of this Chinese aunt, Zhou Zhengying. Fortunately Zuo Xichuan has always been very careful, and, other than joining the Communist Party, he has no secrets of his own from his many years in China, and he is even completely open about Zhou Zhengying once having been married into the Qi family of the Minister's Residence and about her having joined the office of the Beiping underground Communist Party. It all fits with what Shoi Toyoki has learned from the intelligence bureau of the Kwantung Army, so his suspicions are at least half allayed. He puts them up in his own residence, partly to help alleviate his own loneliness as an expatriate, but more to keep them under observation. This not only has the advantage of economy, it also feeds his hope that he might gain useful information on China, and more particularly on the Chinese Communist Party, from this China-loving uncle and Party member aunt. Zuo Xichuan is well aware of all this, and he welcomes the possibilities it presents. But the situation has to be allowed to develop at its own pace, and cannot be rushed, or he will overreach himself. So after their arrival in Chengde, he concentrates only on the business and doesn't try to probe other matters. Zhou Zhengying maintains an even deeper cover, playing the perfect Japanese-style housewife.

She follows the Japanese custom by taking her husband's surname, changing her name to Shoi Zhengying. Of course, Nan'er also takes Zuo Xichuan's Japanese surname to avoid suspicion, and the character of his given name, Nan, is changed from 难, meaning 'difficulty', to 男, meaning 'male', which has the same pronunciation. Here, unlike when they were with the Shanxi New Army, she has no choice but to sleep in the same bedroom with Zuo Xichuan in order to avoid suspicion. It is a Chinese-style room, except for the tatami mats on the floor. Every time she puts on her kimono and wooden clogs, and is addressed as Mrs Shoi; every time she sees the eye-catching little silver badge pinned to her son's breast, with the character 男 in his name; every time she kneels on the tatami, and uses her inadequate Japanese, forcing a smile, to wait on guests; every time she has to make herself swallow another slice of raw fish, before sneaking off to the bathroom to spit it out; all of these actions add an extra layer to her determination to resist the Japanese occupation at all costs. She has no idea whether Qi Yuexuan is aware of all this, but all she has to do is think of him, of her home, of Beiping, and the blood rushes to her ears and they begin to burn. It is then she seems to see the hatred in his eyes and to hear the coldness in his bitter laughter. She wants to ask Zuo Xichuan if she can be transferred, but every time she stops herself, because she knows it is not possible. She wants to weep, but the Japanese maid Shoi Toyoki has found for her is always in the house, never leaving her side from dawn to dusk. However much she wants to, she can't find a time or place where it is safe for her to let her tears flow.

On one occasion, she just can't restrain herself any longer, and when the maid and Nan'er are asleep, she buries her head under the cover, gnaws on the pillow and begins to weep. Although there is almost no noise, she cannot hide it from Zuo Xichuan who is sleeping next to her. At first, he doesn't make a sound, thinking she will soon cry herself out, but she doesn't stop. He throws on some clothes and gets up to light a lamp. Crouching down next to her, he whispers: "If you want to cry, cry out loud, cry your heart out and then you will feel better."

Zhou Zhengying shoots a glance at the door, then looks at him doubtfully. Zuo Xichuan takes off his belt and rolls his quilt up into a cylinder, saying: "Wait until I start whipping this with my belt, then weep and wail as much as you like. People will just ignore it when they hear a husband beating his wife."

Even as he speaks, his belt is landing furiously on the rolled-up quilt, and he begins to curse loudly in Japanese. Zhou Zhengying unclenches her teeth, and begins to weep and wail as though a sluice gate has just been opened. Her wailing becomes louder and louder with each thud of the belt on the quilt. This goes on for quite a while, until all her pent-up anguish has been vented.

Zuo Xichuan hands her a towel and says quietly: "Do you feel better? If you don't, have a rest and then cry some more."

Zhou Zhengying takes the towel with lowered head and an expression like a naughty child, caught in the act.

Zuo Xichuan smiles gently and says: "Go to sleep if you're not going to cry any more, don't just sit there." With these words, he puts out the lamp and turns away.

He hears Zhou Zhengying's voice behind him, asking cautiously: "Aren't you going to say anything?"

Through the darkness, she hears him reply: "You understand what's going on. What is there to say?" He pauses a moment, then says with a laugh: "I think that worked rather well. We can use it again. But next time we'll have to do it for real. It won't look authentic if aren't any marks on you after all that cursing!"

This makes Zhou Zhengying burst out laughing, and she hurriedly puts her head under the quilt, in case anyone hears her.

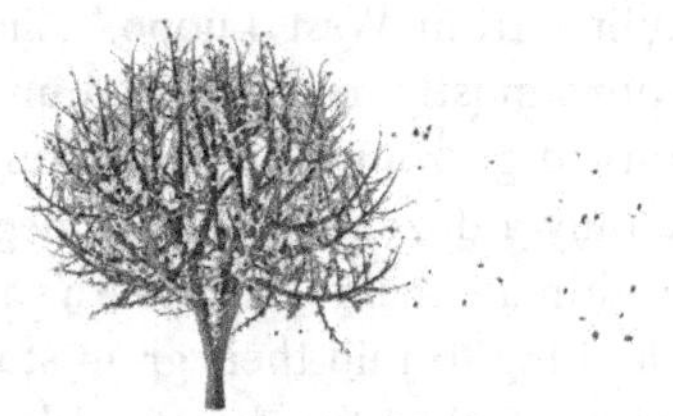

Chapter 32

On the appointed morning, Qi Yuexuan is about to go with Zhang Zhicheng to inspect the anti-Japanese resistance base. Grandpa Fu is uneasy and wants to go as well, but Qi Yuexuan forbids it, saying the camp can't be left without a commander for a whole day. Grandpa Fu also wants to send some extra men as an escort, but Qi Yuexuan vetoes this too. He says that, if they really mean them harm, it wouldn't matter how many men they took to the Eighth Route Army's headquarters, they'd still get rolled up and stuffed like a dumpling. His safest tactic is not to bare his teeth or spread his wings, not to take anyone with him, and let the Eighth Route Army welcome him and send him away as they see fit. In the end, it is Gao Guigeng who finds a compromise.

"An actor doesn't go on stage without an understudy," he says, "so how much less should a general go without back-up? To take too many men would be arrogant and ostentatious, but not to take any would be shaming. So, in case there is a repetition of the feast at Hongmen, I shall go myself, and take the part of Fan Kuai.[1] How will that do?"

Qi Yuexuan has no alternative but to agree, but he re-emphasises the necessity of Gao Guigeng keeping his status with military intelligence a secret in order to avoid any unnecessary complications. Naturally, Gao Guigeng agrees. He saddles two horses, and they set off with Zhang Zhicheng.

They leave Yingtaogou at the eastern end, where they rendezvous with the guerrilla fighters stationed there before heading northwest for several *li*. They cross the Yongding River to the south, then follow the mountain road west for a dozen or so *li*, until they come to the district of Wangping. Zhang Zhicheng tells them this is the outer edge of their base of operations, and new territory that they only took over last month. Before they have gone another two *li*, someone challenges them from the top of the mountain. Whoever it is remains unseen and under cover, and they only hear his voice. Zhang Zhicheng replies to the challenge, and only then do several youths come running down the mountainside to greet him like a long-lost relative.

Qi Yuexuan notices that they are all carrying mattocks, local muskets and broadswords, and he can't help asking: "Are these all Eighth Route Army men?"

"They're local militia from West Luopo," Zhang Zhicheng replies. "Every village has a militia now, mostly made up of young men. There are too many of them for our weapons to go round, and unfortunately, because West Luopo is new to us, there are only a dozen or so machineguns to arm seventy or eighty men. But don't underestimate them – last time a small squad of Japanese came up into the mountains looking to raid their grain stores, they didn't just send in a report to me, they also attacked the devils. We're only four *li* from the village here, but they held off the Japanese for more than two hours. When I arrived with reinforcements, the devils hadn't even reached the edge of the village. Then, when we mounted a pincer attack, the Japanese had no chance. They turned tail and ran without seizing even a single grain, but leaving several bodies behind. The Japanese have learnt their lesson now and no longer waste their time and resources sending small groups."

Qi Yuexuan nods enthusiastically, expressing his approval.

They pass through several checkpoints manned by the militia before finally arriving at Jiuyuancun. This is a large village on the road to Wangping, built in the imposing lee of the mountain close to Luopo Ridge. The eastern side of Luopo Ridge is known as East Luopo, and the western side is called West Luopo, and, not far to the north, the two mountain villages of Qiaoerjian and Jiuyuan have amalgamated to become Jiuyuancun. Qi Yuexuan has never been in this region before, but he has long known about it. Historical records show that this was the home of Ma Zhiyuan, one of the four famous Yuan dynasty Chinese opera dramatists. When he left the palace to retire, he grew old here, and many of his *zaju* and *sanqu* were written in this little mountain village. The thought stirs deep feelings in Qi Yuexuan, and, in a low voice, he begins to recite one of Ma's most famous verses as he rides along:

Withered vines, ancient trees and muddle-headed crows,
The river flows into my home under the little bridge.
On the old road, the west wind scours the horses,
The evening sun shines on the heartbroken all over the world.

But once they reach the entrance to West Luopo, Qi Yuexuan's melancholic thoughts are swept aside by the village's overpowering atmosphere of determined resistance to the Japanese. The first thing that greets his eye is a three-storey blockhouse on a high platform beside the road. The building is three or four *zhang* high, built entirely with stone blocks from the mountain. On one of its walls is written 'Give back my rivers and mountains'.[2] A couple of militia men are standing on its roof, where a red flag is fluttering in the wind. According to Zhang Zhicheng, the blockhouse is a military fortification from the Jin dynasty. As they enter the village, they see anti-Japanese slogans written in whitewash on all the walls along the street. A squad of militiamen, wearing red armbands, are drilling on the threshing floor, and shouts of "One, two, three" resound around the place. Even the little children who are playing in open-crotch trousers are chanting shrilly: "If a dog tries to bite you, take a stick and beat it. If the devils are making a fuss, take a cannon" and other such childish rhymes. Seeing what appears to be a squad of Eighth Route Army soldiers entering the village in formation, the villagers are not remotely alarmed or ill at ease, nor are they unduly enthusiastic. Mostly they just give a wave, exchange greetings, smile and pass on by, just as if they were any other young men from the village. No one treats them as outsiders.

They finally come to a halt when they reach the gates of a large courtyard house, which gives every appearance of being an ancient building. The paint is peeling from the gates, which are rotten and rickety in the extreme, and grass is growing several feet high from the stones of the walls and gatehouse. There are a five or six plaques either side of the gates. On the two biggest are written 'West Luopo Office of the United Fourth District of the Democratic Government of Wanping County' and 'West Luopo Branch of the Anti-Japanese Aid Association'. The other plaques read: 'Youth Aid Association', 'Women's Aid Association', 'People's Anti-Japanese Self-Defence Force' and other such organisations. Two cadres, one old and one young, come out to greet them and lead them into the courtyard.

As they go in, Zhang Zhicheng orders the squad leader: "Let the comrades take a short rest in the courtyard here. Then, in half an hour, go on to Datai for lunch."

The squad leader acknowledges the order and passes it on to his men. But hearing this, the older cadre, a man of about sixty, is clearly displeased: "Commander Zhang, whenever you're here, you seem to be just passing through. Is there some reason you can't stop for a meal? I know that Datai is in your base of operations, but aren't we too? What's going on? Now you've got us to join the anti-Japanese resistance, are you giving us the cold shoulder?"

Zhang Zhicheng smiles as he replies: "That's not it at all, Mr Mayor. It's just that we have our own food laid on at Datai. The Democratic Government has given us army rations, and if we eat anywhere else, we'll just be doubling up. I don't want to break the rules."

"In that case... let us say we are celebrating your victory with a feast."

"If we were to do that every time we fought, wouldn't we be depriving the villagers? A minor victory like the one we secured doesn't merit a feast. Let's wait until we've won a great victory, and then we'll see."

Zhang Zhicheng indicates Qi Yuexuan, saying: "I forgot to make the introductions. This is the commander of our ally, the Heroic Army of Anti-Japanese Resistance, and he has come to look around our base of operations. He is an honoured guest, so make some tea, if you have it, and we'll go inside for a rest."

"Yes, yes, good, we have tea. Please come in, please come in."

As soon as Qi Yuexuan enters the room, he feels there is something extraordinary about it. As he looks around, he sees it resembles neither a domestic home, nor an ancestral shrine or family temple. The roof is extremely high, but not only is there no rear window, at the front there is only a small window, about four and a half feet by one foot, positioned high up under the eaves. Fortunately, the main door is open; otherwise it would be very dark and gloomy inside.

The mayor brings the tea and teacups over, and noticing that Qi Yuexuan is frowning slightly, he asks as he pours the tea: "Do you think there is something not quite right about this room, Commander?"

Qi Yuexuan grunts and nods his head.

"It's called a *dazhai*. I'm told they had them in the Song and Jin dynasties."

"Is it a barracks?"

"No, I'm told it was originally a prison."

"Hmm, yes, it does have that sort of feel. Who did they need to lock up, to build such a big prison up here in the mountains?"

"Ai!" the mayor sighs. "The story goes that the prisoners back then were the two emperors of the Song dynasty, Huizong and Qinzong. Our village used to be called Luonanpo [Misfortune Hill], and that's how it got that name. Quite a few of the families that live here first came when the two emperors were taken prisoner. My family name is Liu, and it's said that we are from the clan of the Emperor Qin's empress, Empress Liu. But I don't know whether all that's true. It's just what has been passed down over the years."

Qi Yuexuan is familiar with the story of the Jin's capture of the two emperors, which is a humiliating page in China's past. According to the history books, after the Jin sacked Bianjing (modern-day Kaifeng), they captured the two emperors, Hui and Qin, along with more than ten thousand others, including princes, concubines and palace ladies, then moved on north from Datong in Shanxi. The prisoners were taken under guard to Zhongdu (the Jin name for Beijing), and temporarily held first in the Fayuan Temple and then in the Minzhong Temple in the south of the city. After two months, the prisoners were moved towards the northeast, and ended up in Wuguocheng, which later became Yilanxian in Heilongjiang Province. The men were sold as slaves and the women as prostitutes, which brought about total ruination. Although the historical documents do not record the two emperors were ever imprisoned at Luopo, it is situated very close to the ancient road, so it is quite possible that, if the convoy passed through here, the prison was used. As Qi Yuexuan sits in this ancient prison, the thought that today the country is once again in dire straits, under the heel of foreign invasion, prompts him to recite some lines of poetry:

Luonanpo was once called Luonan.
Inside the prison stockade, the warden sighs.
What hot-blooded man can only stand by and shed useless tears?
Who can allow a new shame to last another thousand years?

The mayor, who had been privately educated, listens attentively to this simple extemporised quatrain and nods in approval, saying: "A fine poem, sensitive and truthful. People have spoken of the tragedy of Jingkang[3] for eight hundred years, and its shame has lasted just as long. Our generation must not add to that shame. We cannot sit back and watch our country being destroyed once again. Why else would I want to follow the Eighth Route Army against the Japanese?"

"How true," Qi Yuexuan laughs. "Your words are more incisive than my poem, Mr Mayor."

"Not at all, not at all, Commander Qi. But let's talk of other things. Drink some tea."

Qi Yuexuan relaxes, picks up his tea bowl and takes a big gulp, scalding his mouth.

"Drink it more slowly and sip it carefully," the mayor says. "This is a high-quality tea. Manager Chen of the Zhangyiyuan tea company in Sanjiadian sent it to me specially last year. Nowadays, you couldn't buy it for any money."

Qi Yuexuan looks at the tea in his bowl, smells it carefully, then takes a tiny sip and holds it in his mouth for a while before swallowing.

"Very good," he grunts. "This is Fujian Wulong, probably Dahongpao from Mount Wuyi. It may not be genuine Wuyi rock tea, and it's a little stale, so it's not the very top grade, but it's certainly above average. In Beiping before the war, a catty of this would have cost ten pouches of silver yuan."

Gao Guigeng has just finished tethering the horses, and has come into the room and picked up his tea. When he hears these words, he is rendered almost speechless: "Don't frighten me like that, Young Master. Think how many white flour buns just this one bowlful would buy."

"The Young Master, no, I mean the Commander, is quite right," the mayor laughs. "But you are all heroes of the war against the Japanese, and if I can't offer you fine wine, I can at least serve you a pot of fine tea. Please drink, drink as much as you like."

When he sees Gao Guigeng gulping the tea down like a thirsty ox, he laughs and says to Qi Yuexuan: "You are a real connoisseur of tea. I hardly expected to find such a refined scholar among the troops."

"Ah, our Mr Qi is a very learned and cultured man," Zhang Zhicheng says. "He is a professor at Yanjing University, and the Young Master of the Minister's Residence in the city. The Heroic Army he now commands all used to be bannermen of the Left Barracks."

"Aiya! I'm honoured to meet you, honoured to meet you," the mayor says with an embarrassed laugh. "You can laugh at me if you want, but as mayor of this village, my heart has been pounding for the last few days at the prospect of having to deal with the Eighth Route Army. I was afraid you would want to plunder all our supplies. But now I have seen that we are forming an alliance with a man of such status, my worries have all gone away. Was my little bit of family property worth getting all het up about in the first place, anyway? Ha ha, please don't mock me for my stupidity!"

Gao Guigeng drinks the tea in his bowl, and he joins in the laughter: "Ha ha, we might not gobble up all your property, but how about we drink all your tea? Come on, pour me another bowlful."

SOON AFTERWARDS, the troops are all reassembled, and they set out again. At noon, they reach Dataicun, where the headquarters of the guerrilla force is situated. This was the first base of operations to be established, and the support of the villagers is much more solid than at Jiuyuancun. At first sight, it doesn't seem as noisy and bustling as the more recently established base, but Qi Yuexuan can see that all the works that have been undertaken are much more regular and methodical, and the initial period of frantic activity is well over.

By the time they enter the headquarters courtyard, the cooks have already finished preparing lunch and are just about to take the lids off the pots. The menu is congee and cornbread, the big slices of pickled radish known as 'coffin planks', and stewed pork and potatoes. At least, pork is what the cooks call it, but all they've actually done is sprinkle a few bits of broken meat and offal into the boiling water. Even so, the soldiers are all squatting in the courtyard tucking in with great relish, as happy as if it were New Year. Qi Yuexuan and Zhang Zhicheng are shown to the *kang* inside, but the food on the little *kang* table is just the same as that being served outside. Gao Guigeng's mouth twitches, and his lips draw back in a grimace. Qi Yuexuan tries to stop him, but he is too late.

"Aiyo, Commander Zhang! We are your invited guests, and this is what you give us to eat? Is the Eighth Route Army really that stingy?"

"Ai!" Zhang Zhicheng sighs. "It's not that we're stingy, we're just poor. The Nationalist Government only gives the whole Eighth Route Army the rations for three divisions. However, since we entered Shanxi and Hebei, our strength is already more than a hundred thousand men, so, with this change in circumstances and with the monks so numerous, how can the congee not be thin, as the saying goes. And then there are the three hundred men of the guerrilla brigade, and the two thousand men in my five brigades, who haven't received a cent in pay from the government. This base of operations was built from scratch, and the local people were already suffering, so how could we bring ourselves to add to their burden? Recently, our victories have improved the situation, but when we don't have an ongoing assignment, we eat thick congee and pickled vegetables."

"So your troops don't get any pay?"

"No pay, no, but they do get a living allowance. The amount has been set by the Eighth Route Army general headquarters – one and a half yuan per ordinary soldier per month, two yuan for non-commissioned officers, three yuan for junior officers, four for senior officers and five for general staff."

"Aiyo! That little?" Gao Guigeng shakes his head. "So there's not much difference between being an ordinary soldier and an officer?"

"The Eighth Route Army still follows the model of the old Red Army, and one of the principles is not to differentiate between officers and men. You think this allowance isn't enough, but let me tell you, I've only heard about it. My men haven't ever received it, not even once. If it had actually been issued, I would have bought you a chicken out of my own money. Anyway, enough of that. You two will just have to make the best of what there is."

Even with a mouthful of cornbread, Gao Guigeng doesn't know when to stop, and he pursues his questioning: "So if that's how the Eighth Route Army treats its men, how do you get people to join up?"

Zhang Zhicheng's smile disappears. "We rely on the fact that we are truly fighting the Japanese devils. None of our soldiers are press-ganged or conscripted. Nor do we place any value on men who are looking for wealth and promotion. That type doesn't last long with us."

Gao Guigeng falls silent, and he just munches on his cornbread.

"Well said, well said indeed," says Qi Yuexuan. "All the Nationalist Party troops have to do is ask for money and weapons, and they get them, but they still run away faster than they fight. Determination to resist the Japanese, spirit and strength of will… these are not things that money can buy. Commander Zhang, I genuinely admire your honoured army, and I value your friendship. I have made my mind up, from now on…"

"Mr Qi," Zhang Zhicheng interrupts him with a laugh, "no one is rushing you into a decision. Didn't you once say you have to spend time getting to know someone before you can conclude whether their character merits taking them as a friend? There's no hurry. Think about it some more, have a proper look around and weigh up the situation. If it was just down to you, since we have been friends for many years, I would respect your certainty and moral character. But at the moment, you are representing several hundred people and their households, so there is no harm in being cautious. In fact, even if it was just you wanting to join us, I might still have some reservations. I stand by what I said – as long as you are genuine in your resistance to the Japanese, as long as we don't act as enemies, however we deal with each other is fine, and even if we don't unite as one, we can still be friends. Go back and discuss it thoroughly, and then whatever decision you come to will not be made in haste."

"Hmm, yes, you're right." Qi Yuexuan nods solemnly, appreciating even more the honesty and sincerity of Zhang Zhicheng.

At this moment, a soldier hurries into the room to make a report: "Commander, a man from Division HQ has arrived."

Zhang Zhicheng hurriedly gets down from the *kang*, but before he can leave the room, a soldier in a brand-new grey uniform comes in, holding a riding crop. He salutes and says: "Reporting to the commander, sir. I am the communications officer from Five Division HQ. The division commander orders you to come to the front at Baihujian by four o'clock this afternoon to attend a strategy meeting. Here are your written orders."

Zhang Zhicheng takes the orders and reads them.

"Are all our divisions attending?"

"Yessir. We have fought our way through from Yu County, and our main force is now assembled northwest of Changping."

"Excellent. There is certain to be a major offensive." Zhang Zhicheng smiles as he picks up the orders, but then he looks anxious. "If they want me by four o'clock, it's thirty *li* away, and I won't make it even if I run all the way."

"In a big company like this, you don't have a single horse?"

"We don't even have a donkey, let alone a horse."

"You can take my horse, Commander Zhang," Qi Yuexuan breaks in hurriedly.

"How can I let you walk, just because you're doing someone a good turn?" Gao Guigeng says urgently. "I should do the same. It's settled – take my horse, Commander Zhang."

So saying, he hands Zhang Zhicheng his riding crop.

"Then... will you wait here for me to come back?"

"No. Once we've finished eating, we'll take a look around the village, then go home." Qi Yuexuan laughs, and then he goes on: "I have seen what I need to see, and heard what I need to hear. You only need to see one spot to recognise a leopard."

"Very well. I'll have the horse sent back to you when I return."

"There's no need. How can an important officer like you go without a horse? But if you do mount a major offensive, I expect you to tell us and let us play our part."

"Fine, that's agreed."

Gao Guigeng waits for the others to hurry excitedly out of the room, then he takes a big slurp of congee and says, in a low voice: "You're as rash as the Old Master. Don't you think the price is a bit high for a couple of cornbread and a bowl of congee?"

Qi Yuexuan looks at him with annoyed amusement. "Expensive? I'm quite happy. I think it's good value. He's a man of respect, a man of honour, and, if nothing else, he's more straight-talking than you and your men, and he hasn't accused me of being a traitor, or shoved a rifle in my chest."

Gao Guigeng can't help smiling wryly at this, but then he goes on: "Straight-talking? You're the one who isn't straight-talking, setting past events at such little value."

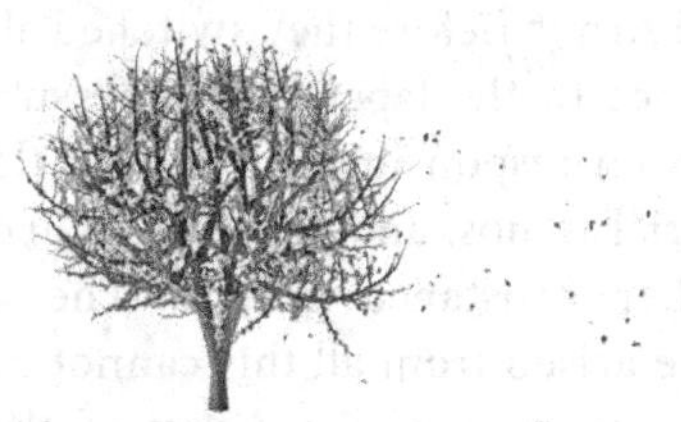

Chapter 33

This trip of Qi Yuexuan's has certainly not been fruitless, and he has gained a new understanding of both the Communist Party and the Eighth Route Army. Even though he is put out by what is going on with his wife, Zhengying, he is still able to keep things in perspective and separate his personal affairs from his public duties. He understands that, if this army from the Left Barracks wants to come through a fight with the Japanese, and if it wants to make a serious contribution to this great affair, bravery alone is not enough. It cannot act by itself, and it needs a firm base. Right from the beginning of the war between China and Japan, the Japanese have wiped the floor with the Kuomintang Army, which has fled at the mere sight of the enemy, and Qi Yuexuan no longer has any great expectations of them. But the Eighth Route Army, which has met the Japanese head on and triumphed, and which has grown so rapidly in strength behind enemy lines, has pleasantly surprised him and given him fresh hope. The Eighth Route Army has the solid foundation of the organisation of the Communist Party embedded within it, and it has experience of waging war over an extended period. It has strength in numbers and is far superior in fighting potential to Qi Yuexuan's own home-grown country militia. Looking at the overall picture of the battleground of anti-Japanese resistance in the area around Beiping, the Heroic Army certainly has a part to play, but without the help of others, it's not going to be a major one. So his mind is already made up, and he is getting ready to work with the Eighth Route Army.

ON RETURNING TO THE VILLA, Qi Yuexuan assembles the commanders of all the divisions. He explains to them, in detail, the standpoint of the Eighth Route Army, and what he himself has seen and heard. He also analyses the current state of play with the war and outlines his own understanding of it. However, everyone else's knowledge of the Communist Party and the Eighth Route Army is very limited, and the Nationalist Government has been disseminating derogatory propaganda over many years. Moreover, many of this division of the Eighth Route Army were previously 'red and blue armbands' of the

National Resistance Army. Before they switched allegiance, they had been at the forefront of resistance to the Japanese in the suburban areas around Beiping, but they had also been responsible for looting the homes of rich landowners, stealing from imperial tombs, and involved in armed robbery, kidnapping and swallowing up other resistance groups. The accumulated suspicions and misgivings that have arisen from all this cannot be swept away by a few words from Qi Yuexuan. The men of the Army of the Left Barracks are all local farmers, and they have all the courage needed to fight the Japanese on their own doorsteps to protect their families and property, but none of them want to turn their backs and leave their home turf. What is more, most of the higher ranks of the army are the major landowners in each village, and they are suspicious of the Eighth Route Army, which is made up of the poor and unsophisticated. They are afraid they will gobble up the rich families and seize their homes and lands. On top of all this, their recent small victories have meant the men's tails are up, and they have rather too high an opinion of themselves.

Grandpa Fu sums up the men's feelings in one short speech: "We raised this army to make our mark and to establish a name for ourselves, not because we were looking for some kind of father figure. They are fighting the Japanese, but we haven't been idle ourselves. They have men and weapons, but there's nothing stopping us recruiting men and buying horses. They call themselves a national army, but aren't we also fighting under a national flag? They can form a government, but why shouldn't we be able to do so? The way I see it, the best thing is for us to sit side by side the Eighth Route Army, each looking after our own affairs. Of course we can go into business with them, as long as there is profit in it."

The meeting goes on from dinner time to well into the night, but without resolution. In the end, both sides have to take a step back. The fundamental principle agreed upon is that an alliance can be formed without swallowing the whole deal; they can fight together, but the Army of the Left Barracks won't leave the environs of Beiping. There has to be discussion of tactics, the Army of the Left Barracks will not take orders of any kind, not even about movements, and all loot must be shared. The Eighth Route Army's base of operations can be used as a temporary shelter, but not over the long term, and when the wind changes, the Army of the Left Barracks will return to its base.

THE NEXT DAY, Zhang Zhicheng doesn't forget his appointment, arriving in Yingtaogou early in the morning. He hasn't ridden there alone, but has brought fifteen or sixteen men with him, all wearing new, grey army uniforms and carrying two rifles, one short-barrelled and one long. They are all riding tall Western horses apart from Zhang Zhicheng, whose horse is much shorter than the others, more the size of a mule. A tall, broad-faced young man of around twenty-six is positioned in the middle of this column of men. This is Commander Zhao Ran of the Eighth Route Army.

Qi Yuexuan is taken by surprise, as the messenger doesn't wait to be met by him at the entrance to the village, but instead gallops right on in. Luckily for him, the meeting held the previous day means that everyone knows the Eighth Route Army are a friendly force; otherwise a minor incident might have occurred with major repercussions. Qi Yuexuan is not happy, but he keeps his temper, puts on a smile and goes out to meet the man. But Grandpa Fu, who accompanies him, is not so temperate in his response, and he is suspicious of the other side's intentions, thinking they may be mounting some kind of coup. So he doesn't step forward in greeting, but turns and goes back into the courtyard where he orders the sentries to secrete themselves at various points. He also tells Gao Guigeng to take two men into the inner room and lie in wait there. Finally, he sends a man to the Qiyin Temple to move the troops to a higher position and blockade both the entrance to the village and the entrance to the ravine. These dispositions have just been made when a column of men enter the courtyard. Grandpa Fu hurries forward and invites them into the inner room with a merry laugh. In the event, only Zhao Ran, Zhang Zhicheng and another young man come in, while the others split up and take up positions at the main gate and outside the room.

Zhao Ran has invited himself along, not only taking his hosts by surprise, but even leaving Zhang Zhicheng uncertain of his reasons for coming. In fact, this is the first time in several months that Zhang Zhicheng has met with everyone together like this. Having been through the basic training at Fuping, and, more important, having fought alongside the men of the 120th Division, it is unquestionably the case that his men have changed in their military and political awareness, in their morale and in their ability to handle a variety of weapons. They now have much more the look of the regular army.

At the meeting, the orders from the general headquarters of the Eighth Route Army and the district command of the Army of Shanxi, Chahar and Hebei are passed on. They command Song Shilun and Deng Hua to combine their forces with the Fourth Brigade of the Eighth Route Army, and leave Pingxi, moving north of Beiping, to enter Hebei from the east and organise an armed uprising in the east of the province. A base for anti-Japanese resistance is to be established in eastern Hebei and northern Rehe. They are then to relieve the Fifth Division at the Pingxi base of operations and mount a series of attacks on the Japanese positions to the north and east of Beiping in order to restrict the Japanese devils' movements. After this, they are to accompany the Fourth Brigade into eastern Hebei. Finally, the commanders of the Fifth Division have laid detailed battle plans that involve splitting the new force into two. The first, second and third platoons will initially attack Yangfang Township, Xinlitun and Louzizhuang, then lay siege to the county town of Changping and take the fighting from the Sha River into the mountainous area to the west. The brigade of guerrilla fighters is to work with a detachment consisting of the First and Second

Brigades at the Yongding River in Pingxi to launch attacks as the circumstances permit, with their principal target being the area around Shijingshan and Mentougou. The base of operations at Wanping is to be protected by the Ninth Brigade of the Third Division.

The return of the guerrilla brigade into the main fighting force both pleases and concerns Zhang Zhicheng. He is pleased because it means he will no longer be operating on such a small scale; he can now get stuck into some proper fighting. He is concerned because he has to hand over the base that he has developed over the last few months to the Ninth Brigade. He is genuinely worried about this. The problem, as he sees it, is that, although the Communist Party hadn't set up shop in the brigade before it was absorbed into the Eighth Route Army, it did already have a foothold there, and most of the middle- and lower-ranking officers are Party members, or at least supporters of it. In October the year before, Zhao Ran's uncle, Ren Fuxin, commander of the First Brigade, had planned to assassinate Vice-General Zhang Zhicheng and some other cadres, then to use the army to force Zhao Ran and the Communist Party to go their separate ways. He had not reckoned with being found out by Zhang Zhicheng, who seized Ren Fuxin and his fellow mutineers, along with his son and other family members, and sent them in chains for trial before Zhao Ran.

An affair like this in any army would demand the death penalty, and although Zhao Ran is related to these men, it is not possible for him to exonerate them. He has no option but to agree to the execution by firing squad of his two maternal uncles as the principal conspirators, but, in the end, he does spare their lives after listening to the entreaties of several of his other relatives on his mother's side. The central Party organisation has no desire to see any split in the resistance to the Japanese, and it also wants to encourage Zhao Ran to cooperate with them, and to see through all the military and political initiatives currently underway. Not only do they spare Zhao Ran's other relatives, they even pardon his two uncles. They do, however, remove them from office and expel them from the army. The units that had been under Ren Fuxin's command are split between two divisions, with the majority going to the Ninth Brigade of the Third Division. When these troops were moved west to Fuping, without permission, the second-in-command, Zheng Zifeng, and the chief-of staff, Bao Xutang, took the Third Brigade eastwards, hoping to lead a mass defection, relying mainly on those still loyal to Ren Fuxin in the Ninth Brigade. Fortunately, the Party has a solid foothold in the Seventh and Eighth Brigades of the Third Division, and, although the commander, Liu Fengwu, isn't currently a Party member, he is close to the Communist Party and is able to force the Ninth Brigade to go west as originally ordered.

All this has delayed the move westwards, and they suffer considerable losses from encounters with the Japanese en route, but they have succeeded in preventing the two renegade commanders, Zheng and Bao, from luring away any of the army, and those two have to be content with packing up the treasures they have looted from the imperial tombs, and fleeing. After the troops become the Fifth Division of the Eighth Route Army, in order to keep Zhao Ran on board, few changes have been made to the personnel, and its organisation remains largely unchanged. Zhao Ran even appoints his own trusted aide, Wu Xinmin, as its commander. These are the reasons for Zhang Zhicheng's distrust of the Ninth Brigade and his uneasiness about handing over his base of operations. In fact, this distrust extends beyond just the Ninth Brigade, and includes all the measures being taken by the commander-in-chief, Zhao Ran.

Zhang Zhicheng doesn't follow the army to Fuping. Instead, he seeks clarification from the Party organisation within the division of the current situation regarding the army and Zhao Ran. After its assimilation into the Eighth Route Army, the status of the Party organisation and individual Party members within the division has become quite open, and they have already received requests to join the Party from the commander of the First Division, Xie Tingxie, the commander of the Third Division, Liu Fengwu, and several other officers. Zhao Ran himself has raised the question of joining the Party with Nie Rongzhen, the regional commander of the Army of Shanxi, Chahar and Hebei, but Zhao Ran is a member of the fascist National Socialist Party, which is the most anti-communist of all the political parties in China. Although cooperation in resistance against the Japanese cannot be viewed through a political lens, anyone being considered for membership of the Communist Party must at least have a firm belief in the Party's political ideology. Moreover, Zhao Ran was personally deeply involved with the old-time warlords and the rebel peasant outlaw bands, and quite a few of the most shameful incidences of plundering rich families, swallowing up other friendly armies, embezzlement and looting the imperial tombs were carried out under his orders. Rumour also has it that he was connected with several instances of mutiny and factionalisation within the army, and he also did his best to destabilise the process of assimilation into the Eighth Route Army. For all these reasons, the Party organisation has not immediately accepted his request to join, and instead has ordered him to raise his thinking and political awareness, work hard and allow himself to be tested by the Party.

Not long after, at the military and political meeting before the regularisation of the army, Zhao Ran resigns his position as commander to go and study in Yan'an. In fact, this isn't his real intention; rather, it is to put pressure on the Party and sound out the army cadres' attitude towards him. Much to his surprise, he is passed over by unanimous vote of the several dozen cadres participating in the meeting. Ashen-faced with embarrassment, he wishes the ground would open up and swallow him. Luckily for him, Commander Nie Rongzhen puts in an appearance and instructs the comrades to leave the anti-Japanese resistance headquarters, and he also orders Zhao Ran to continue as commander-in-chief. After this, Zhao Ran weeps and wails, trying to persuade the army district commanders that he is "the Party's man in life, and the Party's ghost in death". As the fighting moves over a period of several months, through Fuping, Laiyuan and Huailai, he makes a very good showing, directing the troops in a number of victorious battles, killing several hundred Japanese and even shooting down an enemy aircraft during the fighting at Erdaogou. He ends up receiving field and general headquarters citations.

But after his return to the Pingxi area, his actions become rather suspicious. First he proposes appointing his close aide, Wu Xinmin, to the post of head of army security, but none of the other military leadership agree, and in the end, they appoint in his place the Party member, Shi Jinqian. But Zhao Ran himself transfers a dozen or so men into the lower ranks of the unit, creating a personal bodyguard squad, and wherever he goes he is surrounded by a mounted entourage, who stick to him like glue. The Eighth Route Army has a strict principle of treating officers and men alike, and even the most senior officer never has more than one or two bodyguards. But Zhao Ran ignores all advice and even fabricates a Japanese assassination plot against him to muddy the waters. Tension is further raised in the army because, while the second-in-command, the chief of staff and the head of the political division all eat in the common mess hall, Zhao Ran and his bodyguards eat white bread, meat and chicken in the officers' mess. If anyone asks, he says he bought the extra rations with his own money, but no one knows where so much money could have come from. On the matter of the transfer of the base of operations to the Ninth Brigade, the other senior officers also differ from him in their viewpoint, but Zhao Ran argues until he is red in the face, and once he gets his teeth into the matter, he hangs on like a bulldog. In order to concentrate on the major offensive ahead of them, and to promote a unified front, the Party organisation have no option but temporarily to give way on minor matters.

The previous day, Zhang Zhicheng had made a report on the situation with the Anti-Japanese People's Army in Yingtaogou, and Zhao Ran ordered him to hand the matter over to the jurisdiction of the Ninth Brigade. It was agreed that Wu Xinmin would go and supervise the handover of the base of operations, and then proceed to Yingtaogou to oversee both sides and lay down some ground rules. As they set out, no one expects the sudden appearance of Zhao Ran, surrounded by his bodyguard, saying that he wants to go to Zhaitang to hold a meeting, and, in passing, accompany the other two in an inspection of the People's Army. Of course, Zhang Zhicheng has no way of refusing him. Just as they reach the entrance to the village, Zhao Ran orders the party to break through the guard post – an action that makes Zhang Zhicheng come out in a cold sweat, wondering what this move presages. Although this action doesn't cause open confrontation, the feeling of tension is greatly heightened, and Zhang Zhicheng tries to paper things over as soon as he enters the room.

"Mr Qi, Commander Fucha, please don't take offence at what just happened. Commander Zhao's horse took fright."

Missing the point, Zhao Ran doesn't play along: "Whose horse took fright? This is my old fiefdom. No one would dare interfere with my horse."

Grandpa Fu's temper is already smouldering away inside, and when he hears this, he says: "Commander Zhao is very sure of himself, but really, there's nothing to it. It's a horse, isn't it? A dumb beast doesn't recognise fiefdoms."

Grandpa Fu's insolent tone doesn't go unnoticed by Zhao Ran, and he glares at him. He has no choice but to change the subject, but even so, he sounds distracted as he asks: "Are you... fighting the Japanese too?"

"Ai! We've raised the troops, but we haven't fought any big battles yet. It's just that the Japanese don't look where they're going, and they keep bumping into the muzzles of our rifles, so we've killed a hundred or so of them."

"Oh! I hadn't heard about that. Which... battle was that in?" says Zhao Ran, drawing the question out.

Grandpa Fu replies with something like a recitation: "Last autumn we blew up the Fertility Goddess Temple on Miaofengshan and knocked out the guard post at the bottom of the mountain. At the beginning of winter, we beat the soldiers who came to collect the grain tax from Laoqiying. At the beginning of spring, we fought a series of battles at Sanjiadian, Wulicha, Muchengjian and Mayucun."

"You fought all those battles?"

"Yes, we fought all those battles, but the credit seems to have gone to your Eighth Route Army."

"So what's your evidence that you fought them?"

"These rifles we seized from the Japanese can't speak, but the two prisoners we took can."

Zhao Ran stares at him, momentarily taken aback, then says: "Alright then. Even if they were only skirmishes, at least they show you can fight the Japanese. From now on, under my command, you'll be part of the regular army..."

Grandpa Fu interrupts him with a grunt, then goes on: "Commander Zhao, we already have our own reputation and our own standing. Regular army or not, we hold a government commission."

"As what? The Heroic Army of Wanping?"

"It's the Wanping Division of the North China Heroic Army of Anti-Japanese Resistance, actually."

"Ha!" says Zhao Ran as he sweeps him with an icy look. "The North China Heroic Army, is it? Do you know how big North China is?"

When Grandpa Fu doesn't reply, he laughs coldly and goes on: "A person who fights under a great banner just gets on and fights. A person who has bought a big ox just stands around and boasts about it. Do you still say you have a government commission? Do you know what the Heroic Army is? It is the banner I raised when I fought the Japanese in the northeast. How many days have you been fighting the Japanese? I have been fighting them ever since 1933."

Zhang Zhicheng can't go on listening to this. He's not sure what Zhao Ran is up to, but he doesn't dare refute this version to his face, and all he can do is tug fiercely at his sleeve.

Zhao Ran glares at him and asks, with the iciest of smiles: "What is it? Have I said something incorrect?"

It is an unruffled Qi Yuexuan who answers him: "What Commander Zhao says is quite right, even though, in the past, I have heard that there were several tens of thousands of resistance fighters in the northeast and hundreds and thousands of senior officers, such as Ma Zhanshan, Feng Zhanhai, Li Du, Yang Jingyu, Zhao Shangzhi, Zhang Haitian, Deng Tiemei... more than I can name. But now I learn that they are all fictitious, and that in what was once northeast China and is now Japanese North China, there was only Commander Zhao, single-handed in his bloody resistance to the Japanese, just like Zhao Zilong[1] in ancient times."

Zhao Ran is quite taken aback, and, in some embarrassment, he tries to backtrack: "I... that's not what I said."

"Maybe not explicitly, but that's what you meant."

"Hey! I didn't..."

"If you know it's not true, next time you talk about the war of resistance, try saying 'we', not 'I'. Alright?"

Grandpa Fu steals a glance at Qi Yuexuan, wondering how he is able to keep a straight face. He purses his lips, desperately trying to contain the laughter that bubbles up inside him. Even so, a few strange little noises do manage to escape.

Seeing this, Zhang Zhicheng hurriedly gets to his feet. "Enough joking around," he says. "It's time we started discussing the matter of our mutual cooperation."

To everyone's surprise, Zhao Ran seizes control of the conversation: "There's nothing to discuss. I want you to work with me, I mean us, and there's only one way – you join our ranks."

"And... if we don't want to work with you?" Grandpa Fu asks icily.

Zhao Ran's reply is swift and decisive: "In that case, I have only one word for you: surrender!"

"Fuck you!" Grandpa Fu yells, standing up. But before he is properly on his feet, Zhao Ran's bodyguards are already rushing into the room and holding Grandpa Fu and Qi Yuexuan at gunpoint, forcing Grandpa Fu to lower his own weapon.

"What do you think you're doing?" Zhang Zhicheng cries out angrily. "Put your guns away and get out!"

"The commander is here. It's not your place to give orders," Captain Wu shouts from beside him.

Without waiting for Zhang Zhicheng to say anything else, Zhao Ran takes the pistol handed to him by one of his men and says to Grandpa Fu, with a grin: "Forget about the rifles, you're not skilled enough to use good guns like those. Give the order and tell your men to surrender. Those who want to stay will be welcome, those who don't are free to go home and look after their fields."

"They are a resistance army too. You will have to answer for breaking the policy of presenting a united front, Commander Zhao." Zhang Zhicheng keeps his voice low, but this doesn't detract from the force of his words.

"I am quite bold enough to take that responsibility."

Before these words are properly out of Zhao Ran's mouth, Qi Yuexuan begins to laugh sarcastically.

"What are you laughing at?"

"I'm laughing at the way you still think you're fit to lead troops despite your total self-obsession. Between the two of us, Grandpa Fu and I are more than a hundred years old. Do you think we're going to let a callow youth get the better of us? If you've got the guts, shoot me first, but you'll be next."

It's not just Zhao Ran who is angered by this; all his men glare at Qi Yuexuan too. In fact, Qi Yuexuan has no idea whether he really does have anyone guarding him, but he has decided to throw caution to the winds in an attempt to bluff Zhao Ran. He doesn't really expect to scare him with his bluster, and even less does he anticipate actually fooling him. He hasn't even thought what to say next when Grandpa Fu takes over.

"He's right. There are guns aimed at you all, both out in the courtyard and in here. And there are machineguns waiting for you at the entrance to the village, and to the ravine. If you attack us, not one of you will get out alive. You don't believe me?" Grandpa Fu signals with his hand and shouts: "Shout out, brothers, so the Eighth Route Commander can hear you!"

"Don't move!" "Stay where you are!" The voices ring out from behind the wooden partitions of the inner room and outside the building, but there is no one to be seen. Alarmed, Zhao Ran's men point their rifles at where the sounds are coming from. Qi Yuexuan is equally startled, and he stands there wide-eyed and open-mouthed. Zhang Zhizheng, who has also been caught off guard by this, holds his hands up in a calming gesture to both sides.

"We are all working together against the Japanese," he booms. "Whatever you do, don't shoot."

Zhao Ran's face has gone an ugly colour, but his expression changes quickly, and his formerly long face is now wreathed in smiles. "Ha ha! Alright then, it seems you can fight the Japanese devils too. You have acquired some basic military skills, have the determination to fight and are not just some kind of milk-sop army. Of course, I wasn't serious just now. If I'd really wanted to attack you, I wouldn't have brought so few men. I was just testing the strength of your army."

When he sees that his men haven't moved, he gestures at them urgently: "Why are you still pointing those rifles? Get out, the lot of you! Shoulder arms and stand easy. These soldiers are our friends. There's no need for a show of force."

As he watches the men fall out, Qi Yuexuan gives Grandpa Fu a look.

Grandpa Fu smiles in a self-satisfied manner and signals to the inner room, calling out: "You can leave off now, lads." Then he walks over to the door. "Alright, you can come out now. Get some water for the men in the courtyard, and for their horses too."

The last of Zhao Ran's anger disappears when he hears this, and he hurries to offer up his gun, holding it in both hands. "Don't be angry, Commander Fucha," he says. "At the moment there are lots of local bandits and renegade soldiers sheltering under the resistance banner but never fighting the Japanese devils and just causing trouble. Good and bad, honest men and villains are all mixed up together at the moment. You must forgive me for putting you to the test just now."

Grandpa Fu accepts the gun, and, without asking permission, goes back to sit down at the table.

Noticing this, Qi Yuexuan can only smile and divert the conversation: "Ha, come now, let's not stand around here. Come and sit down so we can say what we have to say."

When everyone is seated, he returns to the previous conversation: "You are quite right in what you say, Commander Zhao, and you are also quite right to want to test our loyalty to the Resistance. The way you went about it was wrong, though. Weren't you afraid one of the guns might go off accidentally? If two hedgehogs want to lean against each other, they must retract their spines and roll into a ball. If there are riots on the streets, and someone picks up a brick, it generally means they're going to attack someone with it. Beiping people are quick to take offence and stand on their dignity. They're not afraid to kick off, either, especially the old bannermen. If the Eighth Route Army wants to set up its base here to plan further developments, you can't behave like bandits from the wild northeast. There has to be some give and take, not just in fighting the Japanese, but in friendship in general. There has to be mutual trust and respect, surely? In such a great undertaking as this, we must be generous and forgiving, act with benevolence and righteousness to win people's hearts. Just fighting fiercely and acting like petty tyrants won't do. This isn't something specific to Beiping, like smelly beancurd. Isn't this how the whole country has comported itself for thousands of years?"

At this point, he glances at Zhao Ran and sees that he is beginning to look a little impatient, so he decides it's time to pull in his horns with a graceful smile. "But I've said enough, and if I have missed the mark, Commander Zhao will have to forgive me."

"No, no, what you said was... fine. In fact, I have always had the greatest respect for your army. Otherwise I couldn't have..." Having got this far, Zhao Ran considers for a moment, before continuing: "Ha! Let's not talk about the past. How about this – formally to show my good faith, I will give you two thousand bullets and a hundred hand grenades. Whether this agreement between us comes off or not doesn't matter. I just want to show you some support in your fight against the Japanese devils. Later on, it will be for you to decide whether we merge our armies or just work together as friendly forces. I welcome either. However, Commander Zhang has other duties. This area is now the responsibility of the Ninth Brigade, so you should discuss all specific arrangements with Captain Wu. Alright? I still need to go to hold a meeting at Dazhai, so I can't stay here with him."

So saying, Zhao Ran stands up, cups his hands and says a respectful farewell. Qi Yuexuan also jumps to his feet and makes to escort him out, but Zhao Ran says: "Stay where you are, everyone. We don't stand on ceremony in the army. You all continue your conversation."

With that, he turns and heads out of the room.

"Commander Zhao," Zhang Zhicheng calls after him, "should I…"

"You can escort me some of the way, you know this base better than me. Leave Lao Wu to discuss matters here. Do you think I haven't made myself clear enough? Is there something still worrying you?"

"No, no, nothing."

Zhang Zhicheng may say this, but, in truth, he isn't comfortable with things. Zhao Ran is so changeable, it's difficult to work out where he really stands. Although he started off on the wrong foot, he seems to have since redeemed himself. He doesn't have any good reason to insist on staying behind, so all he can do is say his goodbyes to Qi Yuexuan and the others, and set off with Zhao Ran.

Once he has seen Zhao Ran on his way, Wu Xinmin, who has hardly said more than a couple of words until now, suddenly livens up, and his whole attitude changes. Smiling genially, he becomes chatty and familiar.

"Commander Fucha," he says, "I've heard that this army of yours is made up of old bannermen."

"That's right. The twelve villages of the Left Barracks were established by the Imperial Household Department of the Ministry of Finance. The villagers all come from three banners, and most of them are hunters, but there are also plant collectors, eagle hunters, honey gatherers and fishermen."

"Ah! Ha ha! Not so different from me. My forebears were all bannermen too, but it was the White Banner of the Chinese military, nothing compared to your proper Manchu background."

"Ha! What does proper or not proper matter? The Imperial Household Department was all contained in three banners. My forebears were from the Plain Yellow Banner, but the family name of Fucha here was taken from their master's. Nobility isn't anything to do with the banners, nor does it matter whether yours was a Manchu banner or a Chinese one. Mr Qi here is the Young Master of the Minister's Residence, and his family were under one of the Chinese military banners, but the Residence produced two imperial concubines, and two ministers, and in Qing times, even royal princes didn't look down on them."

"Aiya! Mr Qi is a man with powerful imperial connections. If I'd known, sir, I would have paid my respects straight away."

Qi Yuexuan is left cold by his flattery since he feels that the time of the great Qing dynasty has vanished like a wisp of smoke, and he places no great store by the glories of his forefathers. So he just smiles faintly and says: "Ah, but we're in the twenty-seventh year of the Republic now, and I have no interest in that sort of thing. I wouldn't have accepted your respects anyway. I may have done some good for the country, but imperial connections are nothing for me to boast about."

Wu Xinmin nods in understanding, but he doesn't leave the matter there: "Our Commander Zhao's family is the Plain Yellow Banner from Xiuyan, which is one of the true imperial banners, and they only took the Chinese name Zhao at a later date. I heard the old mistress of his family say that the old master of the Zhao family was the uncle of Emperor Xuantong, and she was the emperor's aunt. So Commander Zhao is closely related to the imperial family. If we were still under the Qing, he wouldn't just be a minor prince, but a prince of the first rank, wouldn't he?"

Qi Yuexuan has no taste for this conversation and can't see why Wu Xinmen is rehashing these stale tales. But the man is staring at him, wide-eyed, waiting for his reaction, so he has to say something. Not replying directly, he asks: "What was the old master of the family called?"

"His name was Zhao Yutang. The 'Yu' is a name handed down over generations."

"And Commander Zhao?"

"Zhao Ran, but his original name is Zhao Lianxiu."

Qi Yuexuan doesn't reply, but he can't help sighing. He sighs because he knows that, while the Qing emperors still sat on the throne, being a member of the imperial family carried great privilege and prestige, and no one ever dared lay false claim to membership as that was a crime punishable by death. But now the Qing have gone, and the privilege and prestige with them, more and more people are trying to ride on their coat tails. If you believe them, then clearly it raises their social standing, and if you don't, it still seems to satisfy some kind of craving in them. Qi Yuexuan's own father had been grand secretary to the Qing court, and he himself had been a study companion of the imperial princes, and as a youth, had frequently worked as a copyist in the Office of the Imperial Ancestors. At the time of the Manchu Restoration,[2] he had also held a post on the Privy Council, and he is confident that what he has heard today is just another cock and bull story.

Originally all Manchus took their names from their clans, but after Nurhaci established the Later Jin dynasty, the imperial clan-line all took the name Aisin Gioro. 'Aisin' in the Manchu language means 'gold' just as 'Jin' does in Chinese, and they took it as their surname to demonstrate the honour and respect of the imperial family. From then on, everyone who was a direct descendant of Nurhaci and his brothers was known as part of the principal line, and, according to protocol, they were entitled to wear the yellow girdle. The descendants of Nurhaci's uncles' sons took the name Gioro, and they were entitled to wear the red girdle. During the Great Qing, as soon as a child was born, it had to be recorded in the relevant ancestral rolls. However, after the Xinhai Revolution, Manchus no longer took their Manchu names, and the Aisin Gioro clan was no exception. But Manchus could not just take any Chinese name; they had to follow the rules of the clan register. In fact, from the very beginning of the Qing, there were fixed simplified Chinese versions of their Manchu names: thus, the Tunggiya clan became Tong, and the Niohuru clan became Niu. Since both 'Aisin' and 'Jin' mean 'gold', the Aisin Gioro clan became Jin.

After the Revolution, all the important families in Beiping directly descended from the imperial line took the surname Jin. There were also some who simply abandoned their Manchu clan names and took their given names as surnames, such as those who called themselves Pu, Yu, Heng and Qi. Some distant relatives of the Gioro clan took the name Zhao, but the character 肇 was different from the 赵 of Zhao Ran's name. They took this name because Nurhaci honoured Mengtemu as his sixth-generation ancestor and founding father of the imperial line. Distant members of the same clan took this surname to mark their origins in the imperial clan, but to differentiate themselves from direct descendants. Most of the clansmen who took the other character Zhao (赵) as their surname were men from the Chinese banners or from another Gioro clan in the Manchu banners, unconnected with the Aisin Gioro, such as the Irgen Gioro, the Gerun Gioro, the Sirin Gioro and the Aha Gioro. Later on, people always believed that the Plain Yellow Banner was the most respected of the Eight Banners, so they all awarded themselves membership of the imperial clan and placed themselves under the Plain Yellow Banner. In fact, this was not the case, and, from the time of Emperor Shunzhi onwards, of the eight Manchu banners, the Bordered Yellow Banner was the most important, followed by the Plain Yellow and Plain White Banners. Moreover, all three of these banners were direct descendants of the emperor, while relatives of the royal princes belonged to the lower five banners. The three emperors who came after Emperor Xianfeng – Tongzhi, Guangxu and Puyi – did not have any direct descendants, so the vast majority of the those entitled to the yellow girdle belonged to the lower five banners, and the number of direct imperial descendants in the top three banners grew smaller and smaller. A good eighty per cent of people claiming to be members of the top three banners, and flaunting their entitlement to the yellow girdle, were, in fact, charlatans. Moreover, beginning with Emperor Kangxi, close members of the imperial clan were constrained by strict rules of seniority, and they had to choose their given names from a list of fourteen permitted: Yin, Hong, Yong, Mian, Yi, Zai, Pu, Yu, Heng, Qi, Dao, Kai and another Qi. The names 'Yu' and 'Lian', which Wu Xinmin says have been used by former and current generations of Commander Zhao's family, are not on that list. There is a poem listing the twenty-four permitted names for distant and collateral relatives, which contains the line '兴国治家永忠连' (meaning 'to reinvigorate the country and rule the family needs constant devotion'). The character for 'Lian' is there, but not the one for 'Yu', so the story about the Zhao family names is almost certainly nonsense. But Qi Yuexuan doesn't want to expose this particular man, at this particular time, in this particular place, so he contents himself with his own possession of the knowledge.

"What is it, Mr Qi? Is something not right?" Wu Xinmin asks, still wanting to get to the bottom of things.

Qi Yuexuan sighs and just says in reply: "Ah well, we've been in the Republic for a long time now. What does it matter if it's true or not, unless you want to go to Manchukuo for a seal of approval."

"What you mean is, you don't believe the story, do you? Old Mistress Zhao and the commander himself have told that story in front of everyone on many occasions. How can it be wrong?"

"The mouth says what it wants to say to suit the occasion, but the heart knows what it knows."

"You must believe it. What the commander says matches the local legends in Xiuyan. Who his forebears are, where they came from, root and branch, everything is quite clear. It has to be true."

Qi Yuexuan had really not wanted to continue this conversation, but his interest has been hooked by this solemn affirmation, so he asks, with a twinkle in his eye: "So then, do you want to examine those roots and branches for me?"

"They go right back to the time of Emperor Shunzhi," says Wu Xinmin, speaking slowly as though performing a monologue from *The Eight-Fold Screen*. "Emperor Hong Taiji's fourteenth son, Dorgon, was the uncle of Emperor Shunzhi, and was given the titles of farsighted grand prince, prince regent and commander of the Imperial Infantry and Cavalry. He fought to establish the Great Qing empire. After he died, Emperor Shunzhi listened to court gossip and stripped his family of their titles and confiscated all their property. His forebears then drifted away from the capital and ended up in Shaozigou in Xiuyan County in Liaoning Province. Those were the ancestors of my commander Zhao Ran."

When Qi Yuexuan hears this, he rocks to and fro, laughing until the tears come to his eyes.

Wu Xinmin is completely at a loss. "Hey! What's so funny? Don't laugh, just spit it out!"

Qi Yuexuan finally explains: "Ai! Dorgon was a supreme hero throughout his life and was responsible for the founding of the Great Qing dynasty. That much is true. Indeed, while he was alive, he exercised authority over all levels of society, and he was distinguished and accomplished in all fields. He married six wives and took four concubines, but only his sixth wife, Borjigit, bore him a child, a daughter called Donggo. Because he had no male issue, the line descended through his younger brother Dodo's son, Dorbo. Under Emperor

Qianlong, Dorgon was rehabilitated to the royal line, and the title of farsighted prince was restored. It was the descendants of his nephew, Dorbo, who continued the royal line down ten generations. So tell me, if your branch had no descendants, how could they have escaped to Xiuyan?"

"How... how do you know all this?" Wu Xinmin asks, unconvinced.

"It is all recorded on the jade tablets of the clan records and the historical documents, so of course I know. What is more, when I was little, I went to school at the Aisin Academy, and I had a schoolmate called Zhong Quan, who was the twelfth-generation descendant of the farsighted prince. The Qing dynasty ended before he could ascend to the title." Having got this far, he exclaims suddenly: "Oh, yes, that's right. In... yes, in the twentieth year of the Republic, that schoolmate of mine, Zhong Quan, was so poor he was at his wit's end, and he took some men to dig up Dorgon's tomb at Bangzijing. He was arrested by the police and sentenced to seven years..."

"Ha ha, that's right," Grandpa Fu interjects. "The news of it was everywhere. People were talking about it all over the city. Everyone was cursing him as being degenerate and unfilial for digging up an ancestor's tomb..."

Qi Yuexuan sees that Wu Xinmin's expression is growing ugly, so he nudges Grandpa Fu to stop him telling the story.

Wu Xinmin really doesn't believe what he is hearing, and he is still trying to find some explanation: "His family have been telling the story for eight generations. Commander Zhao's ancestors moved from Lamagou to Kaiyuan, and then on to Xiuyan. It's even recorded in the county annals that the Zhao family of the Plain Yellow Banner in Shaozigou is descended from the clan of Dorgon."

"Whatever your theory about the family," Qi Yuexuan says placatingly, "Dorgon had no direct descendants, but his residence had many servants. Those servants never came off the family roll, but took their master's surname. It's more than possible that, when their master was disgraced, they were sent out to open up new farmland in some of the poorer and more remote areas. Then, over time, word of mouth passed on a false version of events, so they could well have gone from being clansmen to direct descendants."

He can see that Wu Xinren wants to argue, but he really has no desire to carry on this pointless discussion. "Still, there is the old saying that official history is not always true, and unofficial history is not always just rumour, so who can say there is not some foundation to these country tales? Maybe, later on, there will be time to check the old records in the palace and the unofficial versions too, and you may turn up some new clues. But for now, shall we just leave it there? We should get on with our real business."

"This is real business too!" Wu Xinmin says bluntly. "In fact, do you know the reason Commander Zhao has taken a particular interest in this army of yours? It's because they are all old bannermen. He is quite serious about this... At any rate, everyone in the northeast recognises him as a member of the imperial clan, but as far as we're concerned now, what does it matter which of the barracks we used to belong to? We're all fighting under one flag now, and doesn't that make us even closer, since we're all on the same side? It doesn't matter whether you're fighting for the Eighth Route Army, the National Army or under your own banner, as long as we stick together."

Qi Yuexuan knows why he is saying this, but he also feels there is more to it than that, and there is some other reason that Wu Xinmin can't articulate. He is just considering how to get to the bottom of it, when Grandpa Fu loses his patience and offers his own blunt appraisal: "Ha! If you've got something to say, stop going round the houses. We don't have time for all this to-ing and fro-ing. Let me make our position quite clear: we are not going to merge with you, but we will co-operate as long as any loot is shared and we don't have to go too far from home. Now it's your turn for some straight talking, alright?"

"Alright, then, straight talking for a straight person," Wu Xinmin responds without hesitation. "Commander Zhao is of exactly the same opinion."

Grandpa Fu looks at him askance: "Huh! If he's not set on us merging, why all the baring of fangs just now? Was he really just weighing us up?"

"Well, yes, part of it was testing you, but really he was just putting on a show. Let me put it this way: Commander Zhao may well be commander of the Eighth Route Army, but he's not going to recruit any soldiers for it. Your own army has its roots in this place, you're strong here and you have an arrangement with the Nationalist Government. Why should you want to merge with the Eighth Route Army? In any case, our own Army of Shanxi, Chahar and Hebei isn't part of the National Army, we're just its illegitimate offspring. No one is better than the Communist Party at stirring people up, and if they bemuse you into joining them, I hate to think what will happen next. Our National Army of Anti-Japanese Resistance was levied by Commander Zhao himself, but now it has taken on the name of the Eighth Route Army, any initiative has to come from the Party. Commander Zhao brought a thousand men, but now he is reduced to a mere figurehead. If you take your men into the Eighth Route Army now, I'm afraid that, within a couple of weeks, there won't even be the dregs of you left. Ai! Enough of that. You just stay alert, and do as you have suggested."

Grandpa Fu only half gets what he is driving at, but Qi Yuexuan is quick to speak out: "Captain Wu, it's not our place to enquire about the internal arrangements of your honoured army, but will our own troops still be moved to south of the Yongding River?"

"Eh? Why would you be going to a godforsaken place like that? Commander Zhao has already arranged matters. He intends to send you to Qiwangfen, seven or eight *li* from here. There are more than a hundred houses there. Will that be enough to accommodate you all?"

"Qiwangfen? But that's not far from the main peak of Miaofengshan, and Japanese devils are stationed on the north slope at Hejian."

"Ah yes! Commander Zhao's plan is that, together, we make a clean sweep of

Hejian and the devils on the main peak. There aren't more than thirty or forty of them in the two places together, and there are several hundred of us, so they haven't got a chance. Once they're in our hands, I'll station our own men on the peak and at Hejian. There is also a detachment of Japanese in Longjiazhuang at the southern foot of the mountain, but they won't even be able to defend themselves, let alone climb the north side of the mountain."

"Couldn't they move west to Wenquan to reinforce the troops in the barracks there?"

"In a few days' time, our main force is going to advance west on Changping, so do you think they're going to pay any attention to what's going on here?"

When Wu Xinmin sees Qi Yuexuan considering this without replying, he continues: "You've got a firm footing here, and you should do your utmost to expand into the dozen or so villages to the north. This area is where we started out and it is surely better to make our nest here than to rely on other people's goodwill, isn't it?"

Qi Yuexuan still has his doubts, but Grandpa Fu stands up and laughs. Qi Yuexuan glances at him and surreptitiously tugs at the back of his robe, but he can't stop him saying: "Alright, that sounds possible, so let's do it. Mr Qi, don't you think we should agree to this excellent affair?"

Qi Yuexuan can't stop him talking like this, and all he can do is nod his head.

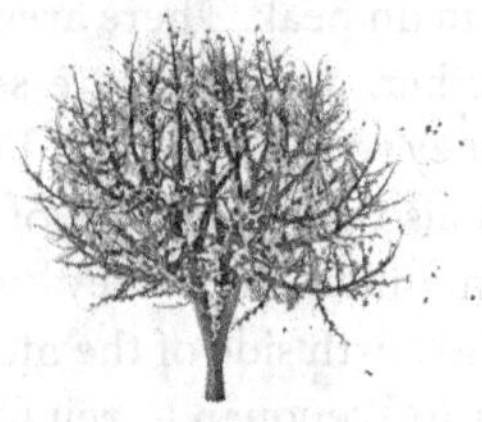

Chapter 34

Yang Zhixing's new business is officially open, with its office situated in the Minister's Residence. The full name on the company business licence reads: The Beiping Yuhua Limited Liability Shareholders' Trading Company. Wangtian is the principal shareholder, and he runs a properly constituted management board, with Manager Li of the Residence's former silk fabric business, and Manager Chen of its former general goods store, as manager and assistant manager respectively.

Chenglong has already heard that Wangtian and Caiping have come by some sort of windfall, and that his father-in-law has dragged him into a big business deal of some sort. At first he thinks it must be a kind of joke perpetrated by someone with nothing better to do, and he doesn't do anything about it. He is brought to his senses when Yang Zhixing and Wangtian solemnly pay a visit to ask him to free up his personal space in the outer courtyard, specifying that, apart from the western side courtyard, the whole of the Minister's Residence is being rented to the Yuhua Company. They show him the company's business licence and lease. When he finally realises that it's all true, he feels as though he has just fallen into a vat of old vinegar.

"Aiyo, Big Brother! You're quite something – married and rich! How come all this good fortune has suddenly been heaped on you? If only I hadn't let go when I had my teeth in you... but there's no point in going there. Fortune favours fools, it seems. But why am I the last to know about a huge windfall like this? Are you afraid I'll want your share? Your little brother wouldn't do that. I'm not blaming you, but what exactly do you think you're doing coming here to ask for something that's going to take the food out of my mouth?"

"What kind of nonsense is that?" Wangtian is not going to take any bullshit. "Young Master Qi sold you a side courtyard for Yue E's sake, but how does that mean you own the whole Residence?"

"Hah! If I wasn't here, flexing my muscles, the Imperial Army would probably have taken over the Residence long ago."

"Pah!" Yang Zhixing snorts. "Don't try that on me! Aren't you and the Japanese hand in glove? Everyone knows that. It's not as though the Residence doesn't have an owner. Bits of it may have been sold or rented, but there's no getting round the fact that it's never been commandeered. And what about you, occupying the place without so much as a by-your-leave? Which country's laws have you done that under? When we had nothing going on, we left you to it, and you've had a good few months rent-free. But now we need the space, we want you to clear out. What have you got to complain about?"

Chenglong has no real answer to this, and he just mumbles: "Since when did your elbows grow so long they need all that space at the table?"

"There's nothing wrong with my elbows," Yang Zhixing laughs. "They stay just where they should be. It's you who can't tell what belongs to who. You are my son-in-law, but the Minister's Residence isn't mine. I look after it for someone else, and I have to be loyal to them. Family property is family property, and I don't treat it as mine, because that would make me no better than a common house-breaker. Besides, you are working for the Japanese now, and even though we are father-in-law and son-in-law, looking at it from a strictly business point of view, we are representing two different countries. If I were to show you preferential treatment, from the Chinese point of view, that would make me..."

He doesn't finish his sentence, but it is quite clear what he means. The blood rushes to Chenglong's ears, and in an instant they have flushed from red to purple.

Yang Zhixing knows that he has gone far enough, and he changes the subject, softening his tone somewhat: "Ah, Chenglong! You are in a mess. You may be relying on the Japanese to fill your rice bowl, but I am your father-in-law, and he is your elder brother. Who are you closer to? Which is dearer to you? Although this business we have set up is a joint stock company, your elder brother and the Residence are the majority stockholders. No matter how well you're doing now, if the Japanese turn on you, it's game over. And if that does happen, who is going to take you in? Your nearest and dearest, of course. Surely you know what kind of man your brother is. If he makes a success of things, do you think he would forget about you? Originally we were going to ask you to join us in the business, but you're so obstinate you'd never listen to anyone's advice. Of course, you might think you can go blabbing to the Japanese and get an advantage at our expense, but you should remember that, although the Young Master isn't an active participant in all this, he does have a greater standing in the eyes of the Japanese than you do. Have no doubt about it, if he sends Matsuzaki a letter saying he wants to come back to cooperate with the Japanese, but you have taken over his house so he has no home to come back to, and he has no choice but to throw in his pot with the anti-Japanese resistance... that will cook your goose."

This speech hits the spot with the precision of a tinker's hammer repairing a broken cooking pot. Chenglong's glare softens into something much more amenable. Shamefacedly, he asks: "But... where can I find a place for my men? There's a lot of them."

"I've already thought of that for you."

"Eh? So where can we move to?"

"The rear courtyard of Moxiangzhai. It used to be the stable yard of the Minister's Residence, and there's a passage through to the western side courtyard. It was blocked off in the past, but if we open it up again, it will be just the job. The stable yard only has a gate opening onto the street, so you use that when you want to go out. That way, we each have an exit, and business and military can keep out of each other's way."

Chenglong has grown up in these hutongs, and he knows that, before the war, Matsuzaki had rented the stable yard to use as a secret intelligence station. At the request of General Qin of the Twenty-Ninth Army, his master, Flower Branch, mounted a night attack on this station, and seven or eight Japanese were killed in the yard. Matsuzaki himself wasn't there that night. After the Japanese occupied Beiping, Flower Branch was executed for that evening's work. So the sudden mention of the stable yard gives him pause for thought. He stands there looking blank for a moment, then stammers out: "But... but that yard... hasn't it been commandeered by the Japanese?"

"Whether it is commandeered or not is up to Matsuzaki. Can't you just ask him for it? If you're so popular with him, he might even give you the whole of Moxiangzhai to use. If he's being difficult and doesn't let you have even the stable yard, then your whole squad will be as much use as a paper teapot."

Yang Zhixing's words reduce Chenglong to silence, and he is sunk in thought for a long while.

"I'll... I'll give it a try," he eventually blurts out. He finds a slight smile and looks over the two men in front of him, asking: "Now, didn't you say something about bringing me along too, and making me rich. That, I'm interested in. Tell me, how much money do you want out of me? What's my share?"

"We don't need your money, and you don't get a share."

"I should have known it was all just sweet talk."

"Hah!" says Yang Zhixing. "Look how your virtue shines through! One mention of money, and your eyes go green. Your brother and I are agreed – you're not going to get any part of the business. You won't pay anything, and you won't get a share. But if you can privately source some merchandise for us, arrange official documentation, get things through checkpoints, then you can take a commission. Everything cash on the nail, no credit, because even between brothers the slate should be kept clean so no one can feel cheated. That's the best way to do things, clean and neat. Think it over carefully and see if you don't agree."

"Yes... I guess I agree." Chenglong's expression immediately brightens, and when Wangtian sees this, he exchanges a smile with Yang Zhixing, inwardly overcome with admiration for the astuteness of his Uncle Yang.

Fired with diligence and enthusiasm, Chenglong goes the same day to see Matsuzaki. Although he won't give up Moxiangzhai because he has another use for it, Matsuzaki does give him the rear courtyard. For reasons of secrecy and security, and to make Qi Yuexuan happy, he also orders him to open the other gate in the wall.

AT MIDDAY THE NEXT DAY, the official opening ceremony for the new company is held in the main courtyard of the Minister's Residence. Once the ribbon-cutting is done, the guests can stay where they are, as the food and wine are already laid out on tables. Quite a crowd has gathered: apart from clients of the Residence's former businesses, there are also several old neighbours and owners of Beiping's other major businesses, including antique and curio dealers, silk traders, general goods merchants, clothes sellers, grain and oil merchants, rickshaw men and porters, and owners of restaurants, tea houses and playhouses. Every profession you can imagine is represented here. This is all to maintain the reputation of the Minister's Residence, but also to develop supporters and contacts for the new business. The newly established interim government has sent the director of the Department of Commerce to offer congratulations, and the Beiping Chamber of Commerce, the Tax Office and the Police Department have all sent representatives too. Although Matsuzaki Harayama isn't there, he has sent Yamaguchi from the Kempeitai with a gift. Since Chenglong has also brought along several of his CID officers, the atmosphere has become a little tense. Fortunately, Yang Zhixing has anticipated this, and he invites them into the reception room, where two separate tables are laid out.

The main topic of conversation is not business but Wangtian and his wife. Although the story of how the impoverished youth made his fortune is no longer news, it is still being chewed over at the party, as a tasty morsel to wash down the food and drink. Wangtian loathes this kind of social occasion, having to meet other people's curious looks, listening to their whispered discussions, and even though he hasn't had a single drop of wine, his face is already flushed. Qi Yuexuan's long robe and buttoned jacket are, indeed, a little tight on him, but at the moment he feels as uncomfortable as if his whole body was bound with iron hoops, squeezing the breath out of him. He is by no means inarticulate, but since he was little he has been no good at idle chit-chat, and now he can't even get a full sentence out. All he can do is force himself to smile and nod at whoever catches his eye, raise his glass, and say "Cheers". If anyone asks him something, his only replies are "Cheers", "Ah" and "Yes".

Fortunately, Caiping, who is looking after the female guests, comes over to rescue him. She is wearing a flower-patterned raw silk *qipao* with silk embroidery, which shows off her slim waist to great advantage. Her long hair is coiled into a high bun, and her fringe and the tresses curling down from her temples emphasise her spirited nature. Her dignified composure increases her charm. Her outfit today was ordered by Yang Zhixing, made to measure by the master tailor at Ruifuxiang,[1] and her shoes come from Tongshenghe:[2] fine materials and fine workmanship at a fine price. Her gold hairpins, pearl necklace and jade bracelets all once belonged to the Old Mistress, and, although they may not be considered the rarest of treasures, they are ornaments to enhance anyone's status. Wangtian and Caiping both feel that everything is too expensive, too ostentatious, and they aren't worthy of them, but Yang Zhixing has a different take on things.

"In the business place, one must not be afraid of flaunting wealth, only of appearing poor," he says. "Businessmen are like insects attracted to the light, fluttering after the next bright thing they see. Just as on the stage, you have to act truthfully, but if you want to become the part, it's not your face that matters, it's your costume. There's no point comparing yourselves to me – the Minister's Residence is an old, established brand. Besides, I'm only a manager and what you're promoting today is your own business. As newcomers, if you don't go a little over the top, who are you going to attract? In the business place, women are what give men face, so it's worth them really flaunting it."

It is indeed just as he says, and without even opening her mouth, Caiping is already dominating the occasion.

"Venerable business colleagues," she says, raising both her arms. "My family is new to the market, and from now on we shall be relying on every one of you for your support and assistance. My husband's capital may not be huge, nor does he have any exceptional talent. Even in normal circumstances, he is a man of few words, but when in any sort of large gathering, he is so shy he can't even speak. But in one thing he is beyond compare, and that is his honesty. Which of you doesn't want to do business with an honest man, a man who never schemes? If you do business with him, I can't guarantee you will make a fortune, but your business will be smooth and free of any worries. There is an old saying that a simple mind is a treasure, and there is a fortune in foolishness, and it's right. If you help him with contacts, give him a leg up, then, by tapping into the hallowed ground of the Minister's Residence and my husband's profitable foolishness, you will meet with good luck and happiness beyond any of your expectations. That's all I have to say, so please take it as a toast to you all. Please drink at your own pace, but my husband and I will drain the first cup in your honour."

Wangtian hurriedly raises his cup and trots out his monosyllabic repertoire of "Yes", "Come" and "Drink". He stands up straight and finishes his cup to a round of laughter in the courtyard.

At this moment, Chenglong sidles over to Wangtian and whispers: "Hey, what are you doing wasting your time out here? All the people who matter are inside. You two get in there quick, before they start looking askance at you."

"Won't it be enough if you and Uncle Yang are in there playing host?"

"Uncle Yang is in the rear kitchen, and I'm a guest. You're top of the bill today."

Wangtian looks inside. He is feeling both irritated and nervous. He is very unsure of himself with this group of people, particularly when it comes to exchanging toasts with the Japanese, and he's not at all certain he'll even be able to force a smile.

Yamaguchi's voice can be heard shouting the odds inside, yelling and banging on the table, rhythmically: "Quick, quick! Bring wine! Flower girl, bring wine!"

His Japanese underlings and the officials from the interim government join in the racket, and they shout along with him. The noise makes the courtyard fall quiet, and everyone looks at one another and holds their breath.

Chenglong grabs Wangtian's arm: "See! You'd better get a move on."

All Wangtian can do is grit his teeth and walk towards the room, but he makes sure he looks back and orders: "I'll go in alone, Caiping. You..."

"How will that work if she doesn't go in?" Chenglong butts in. "Ha! It's nothing really. Just a question of me losing face in front of..."

"Enough! You can keep your precious face all to yourself!" Caiping says. "Ha! What do you think he's going to do to me in broad daylight in front of everyone?"

So saying, she snatches up a bottle of wine and walks off in front of Wangtian. Once in the room, she bangs the bottle down on the table with a thud. Everyone, even Yamaguchi, stares in amazement.

"Aiyo!" Caiping laughs. "It's wine, not a hand grenade! Taijun...[3] Ah, that's really not a very good title."

"Not good? Why not?" says Yamaguchi, turning to look at her.

"It's true that Taijun is a term of respect in Chinese," Caiping responds, "but it's used for old ladies."

"Old ladies?"

"That's right. In ancient times it was used for the mothers of government officials. At county level they were called Jun Taijun, and at provincial level they were Xian Taijun. If the family name was Wang, then they were Wang Taijun, and if it was Li, then Li Taijun. Have you read the *Honglou Meng*? There's a Shi Taijun in that. I'm sure you know the *Yangjia Jiang*.[4] The Old Commander's wife, mother of Yang Liulang, is called She Taijun. They're all women, aren't they. So, by calling you Taijun in China, aren't they saying you're not a man? They're calling you a woman, and not just a woman, but an old woman, seventy or eighty, and close to death."

Yamaguchi thinks Caiping is trying to hoodwink him. Throughout his time in China he has heard people calling him Taijun, and he hasn't given it a second thought. Seeing the way he is looking, none of his gangster cronies around the table dare say anything. After all, who is going to volunteer to poke a stick into a wasp nest when there's nowhere to hide? Wangtian's heart is in his mouth as he furtively tries to pull Caiping back and stand in front of her. Meanwhile Chenglong, who is also afraid of provoking Yamaguchi, pastes a smile on his face and picks up the wine bottle. He tries to divert the conversation: "Come on, come on, let's have a drink. Don't listen to her..."

"No, no, no, what she says is right," Yamaguchi says and to Chenglong's surprise. He turns to Caiping and asks earnestly: "But... they are all called like this?"

"Ha! It's just a bit of idle nonsense that's been passed on by word of mouth," Caiping explains. "You hear him say it, I hear you say it, and quite soon everybody's saying it. But nobody actually knows the truth of it."

"Hmm, I go back I search it good for sure."

Caiping looks at Yamaguchi, laughs and takes the bottle Chenglong is holding, saying: "Well, don't waste valuable drinking time on it now. Come on, drink up."

She pours him some wine. The men round the table relax, and they all chorus: "That's right, that's right. Drink up!"

A section chief from the Tax Office yawns and says to Caiping with a wicked laugh: "Hah! Stick to your own word, and drink up yourself. You started it all."

Wangtian hurriedly steps forward to take the cup, but the man says: "Stay out of it, Boss Gao! What the Tai..." He chokes off the 'jun' before continuing: "What Captain Yamaguchi meant was..."

"Who cares what he meant?" Caiping interrupts with an icy smile: "What is it with you? Always obsessing about what this Japanese means, you traitor. Aren't you afraid it will backfire on you?"

At this, the man sits down, deflated, as though he's been poked in the ribs with a fork. "Huh! Women! What a load of nonsense they talk," he mutters.

"Is it me talking nonsense, or could it be you?" says an unruffled Caiping. "Proposing a toast is an old city custom. It comes naturally to us, so how has it become something different when you do it? There's a treacherous look in your eyes and a crafty smile on your lips. Are you deliberately dragging Captain Yamaguchi down into your gutter? Don't beat about the bush, say it straight out – if you're trying to turn the Minister's Residence into something more suited to the Eight Great Hutongs, a place to hold girlie parties in safety, don't try hiding behind your Japanese friends. All the propaganda says that Sino-Japanese relations are good at the moment, so there's no place for you and your filthy mind, treating every woman you meet like a prostitute. Aren't I right, Captain Yamaguchi?"

Yamaguchi is surprisingly unperturbed and just looks a little uncomfortable as he nods, and says: "Hmm, your words have very powerful. You woman quite something worth respect!"

At this moment, Yang Zhixing appears, and suddenly the room is all laughter and respectful greetings. In fact he has already been there a while and has witnessed everything that has been going on. Caiping's bravado, persistence and eloquence alarm him at first, but then he calms down a little. He goes over to Wangtian, bows slightly and says: "Boss Gao, you have many guests outside. Will the two of you come out and see them?"

Seeing how deferential he is being, it is Caiping who reacts quickest. She understands he is putting on an act to give them an excuse to retreat, so she quickly says: "Of course, we'll go now. We'll leave you to take care of things here."

Even as she speaks, she is leading Wangtian out of the room. Then she hears someone behind her say: "Why are you behaving like this to those youngsters, Manager Yang?"

"Ah, it's not age that matters here, but status. In private, anything goes, but in public one has to observe the formalities."

"So... he and the Minister's Residence..."

"Ai! For the moment we are business partners, but in the future, who knows? Our Young Master doesn't have any children, does he?"

"Ah! I understand. That makes sense."

When Wangtian hears this, he flushes red to the tips of his ears and whispers: "Is Uncle Yang for real? He's talking nonsense. Isn't my father still alive?"

"Ha! Can't you see he's just putting on an act?" Caiping shoots back.

"Putting on an act? Well what about the way you just risked your life? Where did you get the courage?"

"That wasn't courage. I had no choice. I was in a cold sweat the whole time."

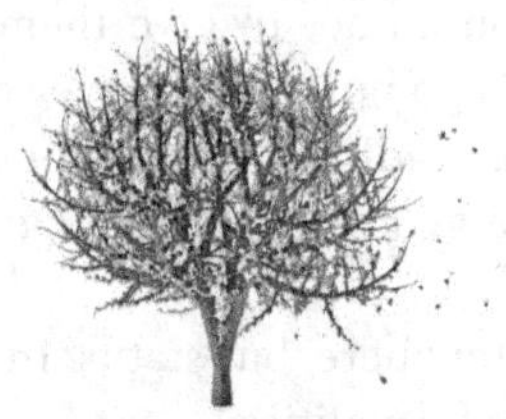

Chapter 35

Under the organisation of Captain Wu of the Eighth Route Army, the peasant militia of the Left Barracks has indeed moved to Qiwangfen. This is situated on Yangtaishan to the east of the nearby Miaofengshan. By skirting the Japanese base at Jiangou and following a small path along the ravine across the slope, the distance is just seven or eight *li*. The whole company of more than two hundred men plus horses sets out at first light, with only Gao Guigeng and his men not accompanying them. This is because, the previous evening, they received orders from above to proceed immediately to the Yunju Temple in Fangshan County. They are given an important mission, so they set out that same night.

Getting to Qiwangfen involves passing through Jiuwangfen, which sits beside the road at the bottom of the mountain. Qiwangfen means 'seventh prince tomb' and Jiuwangfen means 'ninth prince tomb'; the tombs referred to are those of princes of the Qing dynasty, both sons of Emperor Daoguang and younger brothers of Emperor Xianfeng. All Emperor Daoguang's sons had the character 奕 (Yi) meaning 'abundant' in their given names, and these were the seventh and ninth of those sons. The ninth son was honest and upright all his life, and caused no alarms or disruptions, but he did not provide particularly meritorious service, so Yihui's only honour was to be created Prince Fu.[1] The seventh prince, however, was exceptional. In the tenth year of Emperor Xianfeng, the Allied Anglo-French Army occupied Beijing and burned the Old Summer Palace. To escape the fighting, Emperor Xianfeng fled in panic to Chengde. On the road there, exhaustion and internal heat raised by anxiety debilitated his heart, and he died suddenly at the imperial summer palace in Chengde. Just before he died, he named his only son, Zaichun, as his successor. Zaichun became Emperor Tongzhi, but Xianfeng also appointed a council of ministers headed by Sushun, as regents. Shortly afterwards, a counter-coup was organised by Emperor Tongzhi's mother, the Western Empress Dowager Cixi, and the Eastern Empress Dowager Ci'an,[2] on the pretext that Sushun and the others were plotting to assassinate them both. Men were sent to arrest the Council of Regents.

Sushun, Zaiyuan and Duanhua were executed, and the other five were exiled to Xinjiang. Decades of 'rule from behind the curtain' were to follow, as the empress dowagers controlled imperial authority. In fact, it was Emperor Daoguang's sixth son, Yixin Prince Gong, and his seventh son, Yixuan Prince Chun, who led the soldiers to arrest Sushun and who helped the two empress dowagers to stabilise the political situation. After this, Cixi bestowed the title of Princess of the First Rank on her younger sister, Wanchen, and both because of his meritorious service and because of this kinship, she naturally relied heavily upon Prince Chun, even more, in fact, than on the Prince Regent, Prince Gong.

No one could have anticipated that, two years after coming of age as emperor at seventeen, Emperor Tongzhi would suddenly take ill and die. Since the emperor had died without issue, Cixi had to take her sister's second son, Zaitian, as her stepson and successor to the imperial throne, where he took the reign name Guangxu. As the father of the emperor, Yixuan Prince Chun naturally increased in rank and prestige. But under Guangxu's rule, because of his so-called 'Hundred days reform' of imperial government, he antagonised the Empress Dowager Cixi and was placed under house arrest right up until his death. Prince Chun wisely put personal safety above matters of principle, and he chose to retire into anonymity. Cixi overlooked the fact that he was the emperor's father, preferring to regard him as her sister's husband, and for this reason she endorsed his petition for retirement from public life, and under the joint authority of empress dowager and emperor, granted him fifty thousand taels of silver to buy land at Yangtaishan to build a tomb. Apart from this tomb, he also built a residence using numerological principles, which he called the Villa of Secret Retirement. He moved his household there, far from the capital, retired from worldly affairs, and after his death, was buried there. Later his wife, Wanzhen, of the Yehenala clan, and two lesser consorts, were also buried there in three satellite tombs on either side of the main mausoleum. This tomb of Prince Chun is what gave rise to the name Qiwangfen (Seventh Prince Tomb). When Emperor Guangxu died, also without leaving an heir, Zaifeng Prince Chun was adopted into the imperial line, and he ascended the throne with the reign name Xuantong. With the one house providing two emperors, and being honoured as the father of the emperor over two generations, this place, Qiwangfen, is considered to have exceptionally good feng shui.

In fact, Qiwangfen was not built out in the wilds, but, along with Jiuwangfen was constructed out of the remains of the Ming dynasty Fayun Temple. Looking further back, Yangtaishan was also the site of the Xiangshuiyuan, one of the Jin dynasty's eight imperial lodges in the Western Hills, and even today some of its ancient pines remain along with traces of buildings and steles. A stone-flagged path two *li* in length winds its way up from Jiuwangfen to Qiwangfen, which is situated halfway up the mountainside. The tomb area is divided into three levels going up the mountain. At the start, there is a flight of one hundred and eleven stone steps, more than a *zhang* wide. Once you climb to the terrace at the top of the steps, you can see a stele pavilion housing the inscription 'The late father of the emperor'. Behind it is a crescent-shaped, man-made waterway, crossed by a spirit bridge, after which you pass through the Ling'en Gate and arrive at the spirit mound with its east-west-oriented hall. Another flight of steps leads upwards, and only after you have passed through the temple gate with 'Shake off the dust and enter the world' inscribed in the space above the lintel, do you reach the prince's villa itself.

The residence gently ascends the slope of the mountain, and it comprises five levels. The first level houses the guard room and stableyard; the second level has the Hall of the Household God, beside which is a small garden in a side courtyard along with two small buildings. It is said that this is where the prince lived. On the third level is Prince Chun's Reception Hall, which is divided into five bays, with wings on either side and a cellar behind. There are several small buildings on the fourth and fifth levels, which previously served as guest rooms and servant quarters. Right at the top is an ancient pine grove in which there is a small mountain spring. This is all that is left of the Jin dynasty Xiangshuiyuan's goldfish pond.

There are twenty households of tombkeepers here, and in the past they were all servants of the Department of the Imperial Household. Apart from one family called Zhang, of which three generations numbering a dozen or more people live within the walls of the tomb compound, all the others, some seventy or eighty people, have built single-storey houses outside the compound, neatly laid out like a small village. When these families see troops climbing the mountain, they have no idea what kind of apparition this might be, so they all run off to hide in the forest at the top of the mountain, leaving behind only one old man from the Zhang family to deal with the situation. This father of Grandpa Zhang had been a five-button military official in the first squadron of guards, and had changed his name to match his position. The custodians of Jiuwangfen are from the same Zhang family. As soon as he sees they are not Japanese, Chinese traitors or bandits, but are actually familiar to him as men from the Left Barracks, he shouts to the others to come down.

Under Grandpa Fu's instructions, the troops leave the first, third, fourth and fifth levels alone. He and Qi Yuexuan settle in the garden of the side courtyard on the second level and the two small buildings there, using one as the guard house and the other as the command post. The rooms of the residence have long been without soft furnishings, and are thick with dust. However, they are structurally sound, still contain a few pieces of furniture and even retain something of their former splendour. Although the men of the Left Barracks are all former bannermen, none of them have lived in such magnificence before, and their eyes are as wide and round as steamed buns. If they had been left to their own devices, without commanding officers, there is no guarantee that some of them wouldn't have made off with some of the treasures.

As Gao Guigeng is not there, it falls to Qi Yuexuan to use his experience and initiative in setting up defences and organising sentries. He establishes a lookout post on top of the mountain, arranges a sentry patrol outside the wall, and sets up machinegun nests in the old pine forest and on either side of the terrace outside the main gates. He even puts two hidden sentry posts along the road to Jiuwangfen. The Japanese base to the west of Jiangou is extremely close, and by using binoculars at the top of the mountain, the Rising Sun flag can be seen on the blockhouse there. There really is no room for any carelessness.

Qi Yuexuan and Grandpa Zhang become more and more intimate as they talk. Although the Republic has been in existence for many years now, old bannermen still stick to the old ways. As soon as Grandpa Zhang hears that this is the Young Master of the Minister's Residence, he raises the hem of his gown and is about to make a formal salutation. Qi Yuexuan quickly stops him and doesn't even let him kneel.

The old man has difficulty accepting this and mutters: "Now we've got this Republic, no one knows who's the master and who's the servant any more. You are the master of a household that was once that of the emperor's uncle. My family have only ever been servants of the Department of the Imperial Household. How can it be right for me not to acknowledge you properly? If you won't let me perform the most formal greeting, can I not, at least, offer you a lesser one?"

So saying, he takes a pace forward, bending at the waist and leg, and stretching out his hand so that he is performing a perfect military greeting.

"Times have changed, Grandpa," Qi Yuexuan laughs. "You really mustn't stick so rigidly to the old rituals, especially not in a time of war. The sole priority now is to fight the Japanese. That's the only rule that counts. If we were still sticking to the Qing rules, would I dare bring soldiers into the prince's tomb or live in the prince's formal hall? Even if I grew eight heads, they'd still all be cut off."

This makes Grandpa Zhang laugh too, and he nods enthusiastically in agreement.

As they are talking, they have already reached the residence's stele pavilion. Qi Yuexuan looks at the inscription in Emperor Guangxu's imperial hand, and he remembers the time, long ago, when he had followed Kang Youwei and Liang Qichao in their demand for reform. He feels a twinge of melancholy, and a sigh escapes him: "Ai! If only the emperor's reforms had succeeded to begin with, I'm sure China wouldn't be as weak as it is now." So saying, he doesn't turn right to follow the stone stairs that lead to the residence, but heads for the spirit bridge at the top of the mountain.

Thinking he has mistaken the way, Grandpa Zhang says hurriedly: "The residence is off to the right, Young Master."

Qi Yuexuan doesn't stop, but says: "I'm going to pay my respects in front of Prince Chun's tomb. Even if we're not supposed to be following the old rituals any more, a man can't help having his own personal feelings, can he?"

"Yes, yes, that's right." Grandpa Zhang hurries after him up the mountain.

They pass through the Ling'en Gate, enter the inner compound, and there is the tomb itself. The compound is very large, and, apart from three reception rooms on the east side, there are the four buildings of the spirit mound, one large and three small. The overall impression is of space and emptiness. Before Qi Yuexuan has reached the bottom of Prince Chun's central ceremonial stairway, he sees that a thick slab of stone has been prised open, revealing the entrance to a cave, three or four feet in diameter. Broken bricks and earth are heaped up either side, along with some short-handled shovels and open-work baskets. There are also different size openings, dug by grave robbers, in the tomb mounds of the prince's three consorts on either side of the main tomb, and the area in front of them is jumbled and disordered. Although Qi Yuexuan has heard that the prince's tomb has been looted, he is still taken aback by the sight that confronts him.

"This must have been done months ago. Why haven't you tidied it up?" he asks.

Grandpa Zhang gives a bitter laugh: "Ha! According to the rules applied to tombkeepers, if a tomb has been robbed, nothing can be moved without authority, and a report must be made to the family involved so they can come and investigate. Prince Chun's descendants are all living outside the Pass now, aren't they? I sent a messenger to inform them long ago, but up to now, no one has come."

"Ai! But the way I see it, if you keep waiting and don't do anything, with everything open to the sky like this, won't you end up with the bodies being scattered all over the place?"

"Aiyo! Given my status, I don't dare take the initiative, so who knows what the future will bring. Now Emperor Xuantong has ascended the throne in Manchukuo, can I really wait for whenever he may come back to Beiping? Ai! If you can't bear the sight of all this, why don't you just take the role of the master of this tomb? Your men don't have to do anything. All you need to do is give permission in front of an audience."

"No, no! What good is my word?"

"Isn't your household connected to the imperial family? Even if it's not by direct lineage, a relationship by marriage is still good enough."

Qi Yuexuan shakes his head. "Ai! Even though the relationship is very distant, it could still be said to carry its obligations. Besides, I myself did spend some time as minister of the Great Qing. But that was then and this is now, and can the Great Qing and Manchukuo really be considered to be the same thing? Emperor Xuantong is now just a Japanese puppet and has sold out both his country and his ancestors. We are fighting the Japanese, risking our lives against them. We are as different from him as fire and water."

"So why come here to pay your respects?"

"This is the least formal of rites, just an expression of sympathy really. Besides, it's for the former emperor Guangxu, not Xuantong."

"So why can't you speak for the former emperor and take on the master's role? Wouldn't that be even more respectful, and show even greater sympathy?"

These words give Qi Yuexuan pause for thought, and he considers for a long while before asking: "Why is it then, that you can't break the old rules?"

"Even under the new rules, a tombkeeper can't do anything without authority. Even if he can't trace the master of the family, he still has to make an official report. So you tell me, which official should I report to? I surely can't call on the Japanese, can I?"

"Hmm, yes, you're right. I'll do as you suggest in that case."

With that, he turns and is about to leave.

"Eh? Are you not going to pay your respects?"

Qi Yuexuan doesn't stop, nor does he even turn to look back. He just says in a loud voice: "Give me a chance to speak! Aren't you going to gather everyone together? Once they're all there, we'll perform the ceremony."

It's not long before Grandpa Fu has assembled all the tombkeepers' families, and things don't end with Qi Yuexuan making a speech. He also writes out a petition detailing the time when the tombs were looted, and how many. The only things that are not specified are who commissioned the looting and exactly what was taken. He also appends a few sentences to the petition, which read:

'The prince's tomb having been robbed, and the goods taken being beyond recovery, a report has already been submitted. But despite the length of time that has passed, no reply has been received. In order to keep the bodies intact to preserve the harmony of the departed spirits, it is specially requested that Qi Yuexuan, descendant of the Minister's Residence and formerly a three-button member of the Imperial Privy Council, might take responsibility for restoring the site to order and making repairs. This testimony has been specially drafted as evidence of the above.'

The elders of the twenty households of tombkeepers add their signature or make their mark, and they request Qi Yuexuan to be the principal signatory. Qi Yuexuan initially hesitates, thinking to himself that he has already given an oral undertaking to handle this matter for them, but now, this smacks rather of them having been given an inch, but wanting a mile. But having said what he has, and with things having reached this point, he just has to put a good face on it and sign.

Qi Yuexuan has heard that the prince's tomb was looted by Zhao Ran's men, but he is not sure of the details. As for taking the lead in the clean-up and restoration, and signing the petition, the more he thinks about what he has done, the less comfortable he becomes with it. When Grandpa Fu hears him going on about it, he just laughs, saying that now he has nothing else to do, he's taking on other people's problems. Angered, that evening Qi Yuexuan goes looking for Grandpa Zhang to try to get to the bottom of the whole business. To his surprise, Grandpa Zhang himself turns up uninvited, leading his two grandsons, one of whom is carrying a jar of wine and the other a dish of red-cooked mutton, fresh from the pot.

Once inside, he gives an embarrassed laugh and says: "Young Master Qi, it is very fortunate that you have taken on this business today, otherwise goodness knows when someone would have got round to looking after it. Not only are you showing consideration to the departed, you are also freeing all of us to breathe again. This is an act of great benevolence and immeasurable virtue. Both you masters must accept my respects." So saying, he bends at the waist, sweeping back his sleeves, in preparation to performing the most formal of bows.

Before Qi Yuexuan can move to stop Grandpa Zhang, Grandpa Fu calls out: "Stop!" When he sees the old man looking at him in amazement, he laughs and goes on: "If you are going to bow to anyone, just bow to him and don't include me. I too used to be a servant of the Department of the Imperial Household, and as a tombkeeper your status is higher than mine as a hunter. I would not dare accept your bow, but I can certainly accept your food and wine. Come on, put it down on the table. Ha ha, it's a long time since I last laid eyes on mutton. I'm looking forward to this."

Grandpa Zhang orders the two young men to lay the food and wine on the table.

"Ha, it's nothing special," he says. "Every family here raises sheep, and tomorrow I'll order them to slaughter two more." He turns to Qi Yuexuan. "Young Master, you must accept my..."

"Stop it!" Qi Yuexuan says in a solemn voice. "Stop talking about imaginary things. Let's look at matters as they really are."

"As they really are? This is as they really are."

"You asked me to send a message, and I agreed. You also got me to sign the petition. But how much do I actually know about this tomb-robbing business? Now things have gone this far, I'm afraid you are not going to stop while you're ahead, but go on and make things worse. Just now, did you tell me the real reason behind it all?"

Grandpa Zhang puts on an obsequious smile and says: "I should have known you would work it out. I would refuse anyone else, but I don't dare refuse you. It's not easy to explain this affair in just one or two sentences. It would take a whole day to tell you everything in detail. First, let me pour you two masters some wine, then you can sit and eat and drink and listen to what I have to say."

In fact, the tomb robbery took place at the end of the seventh lunar month of the previous year, or the middle of September by the new calendar. The sky was clear and bright that evening, no need for lamps, as the whole place was well lit by the moon and stars.

Only Grandpa Zhang and his family live inside the tomb compound, or rather on the first level's terrace, just outside the spirit gate. Normally, once the night security round has been completed, only one dumb man stays behind to spend the night in the western reception room inside the inner compound of the spirit mound. This mute is called Shunzi. He is a bachelor of sixty or so, and one of Grandpa Zhang's brothers. He wasn't born mute, but is the last surviving of the four workmen who sealed up Prince Chun's tomb after he was interred. In accordance with the old rules, after the burial they were all given a drug that rendered them dumb, so that from then on they were unable to speak. Now, more than forty years later, three of the four mute guardians of the inner compound have died, leaving only Shunzi surviving.

In the middle of the night, at the second watch, Grandpa Zhang is frightened awake by the sound of men making a racket outside his room. He gets up and scrambles over to the window to take a look. He can see the flickering of torches in the inner compound and can hear Shunzi making the gurgling noises that are the sole sound he can produce. Grandpa Zhang knows something is amiss and hurriedly rouses his two sons. They rush outside, carrying cudgels, but before they can even cross the spirit bridge, they find themselves being held at gunpoint. Skilled as they are in martial arts, they are no match for armed men, and they have no option but to drop their own weapons, as they are forced to kneel by the men carrying the rifles.

"Whose... whose band are you from?" Grandpa Zhang asks in a low voice.

"Are you daring to suggest we are bandits?" one of the men asks, pointing at the red and blue armband he is wearing. "Can't you see? We are the National Army of Anti-Japanese Resistance, and we're fighting the Japanese devils."

"Fighting the Japanese devils? Can you see any devils around here?"

"If there aren't any devils, there are still Chinese traitors, and that's what you look like to me."

"We tombkeepers are all bannermen. We're Manchus, not Han Chinese, so how can we be Chinese traitors?"

Finding Grandpa Zhang so obstructive, the man is about really to lose his temper, when another man comes out of inner compound and takes over the conversation: "What kind of airs are these for a bannerman? We're from Xiuyan, and most of us are bannermen too. In these times of national emergency, if you don't support the anti-Japanese resistance and don't actively fight the Japanese, then you are a traitor."

The man who had just been interrupted points at the newcomer and says: "This is our Commander Zhao. He is from the Plain Yellow Banner and is an important member of the imperial clan."

"That's right," Commander Zhao interjects. "I, Zhao Ran, am an eighteenth-generation descendant of Prince Dorgon and a fellow clansman of Prince Chun who is buried here. We have come to the prince's tomb today because we have heard that the Japanese devils are intending to dig it up, and we must get in before them. I am going to take temporary loan of the goods from my forebear's tomb to raise funds for the anti-Japanese resistance. In the future, when we have driven out the Japanese, they will surely be returned in full. If you know where the entrance to the underground palace is located, hurry up and tell me, and don't be like that dumb old fool."

"What... what have you done to him?"

"That one was too tough for his own good. He tried to snatch one of the rifles, and it went off and killed him. You are old enough to know better than him, aren't you? So give me the information. Quick now."

Hearing that Shunzi is dead, Grandpa Zhang and his two sons begin to weep silently. When one of Zhao Ran's men sees this, he prods Grandpa Zhang with the muzzle of his rifle: "He said quick now. This gun of mine likes to go off."

Zhao Ran steps forward and pushes the man's rifle aside: "We don't want to have to kill anyone else, so hurry up, and when this is all over, maybe I'll pay some blood money for him."

Grandpa Zhang sighs heavily. "The men who knew the secret of the tomb weren't killed, but they were made mute. In all twenty families of tombkeepers here, he was the only mute, so you had him killed because he was the only one who possessed the secret of the tomb."

"Who do you think you're kidding?"

"You're from the emperor's clan, you should know the rules for imperial tombs."

At this moment, someone comes running out from the inner compound and whispers a few words in Zhao Ran's ear. Delight soon shows on Zhao Ran's face, and he follows the man back into the compound. After he has gone a couple of paces, he turns back and orders: "Gather everyone in the compound where I can see them. Don't let anyone get away. And tell our men outside to keep a firm watch over the road down the mountain. They are to tell all the tombkeepers outside the compound that, if they value their lives, they are to stay securely inside their homes and not come out."

More than two hours later, loud voices can be heard from the building in the inner compound. It's some distance away, so the voices can't be heard distinctly, but it's clear they are calling out descriptions of objects. There can be no doubt that the mission has been a success.

It turns out that there is a gang of experienced outlaw tomb-robbers among Zhao Ran's men. Their leader is a bandit, notorious in the area, known as Grandpa Huang the Earth God. His name isn't really 'Huang' (which means 'yellow'), but according to old Beiping superstition, foxes, snakes, hedgehogs and yellow weasels can all transform into immortals, and the honorific name for the yellow weasel is 'yellow immortal' or 'yellow grandfather'. This nickname, 'Grandpa Huang the Earth God' is no empty title, for, although no one has told them where the entrance to the tomb chamber is, by tapping here and drilling there, he quickly determines that the spirit mound of the main tomb is not a decoy. Once he has had the stone slab pried open, and dug out a few test pits, he discovers one of them no more than four feet deep in which he sees the stone slabs that form the roof of the underground palace. By enlarging the hole a little and lifting those slabs, he is able to dig down through more than a foot of concrete until he can see the empty space beneath, and he is through to the underground cavern. Once they have let out the foul air, he has a rope tied round him and is lowered into the tomb. The tomb furnishings are hauled up in a basket, piece by piece, then cleaned and meticulously recorded. It takes from the middle of the night until late morning before the tomb of Prince Chun is completely emptied. Then, following the same procedure, they also dig up the three smaller tombs of the prince's consorts, and it is dusk before they are finished. They wait until it is dark, then take everything down the mountain in different size bundles. Even the tombkeepers don't know how many precious objects there are, but they do know it takes seven or eight lorries two round trips each to transport it all. As it grows light the following morning, Zhao Ran finally leads his men away from Qiwangfen and moves on to Jiuwangfen at the bottom of the mountain. He wastes a day and a night there because the main tomb of Prince Fu and those of his several wives have already been stripped clean by tomb robbers. It's only because they hear there is a large force of Japanese close by at Bei'anhe that they move on from there, leaving the tombs of two princes in the lesser compound unexcavated.

Qi Yuexuan is confused and depressed by this account from Grandpa Zhang. He can't help saying: "However you look at it, robbing a tomb is a great betrayal and a great sin, contrary to proper human relations. No matter what flag you are under, there must be some limits."

"Yes, that's right."

"But you have nothing to apologise for. They had guns and cannons, and what did you have? There is no need for you be like the mute Shunzi and give your own life for a dead person. With things as they stand now, all we can do is think the best, and believe that if he really did loot these tombs to help the war against the Japanese, it has all been put to good use."

"Alas, all that stuff about doing it for the Resistance was just a front."

"How do you know?"

"Two months after they looted the tomb, one of the senior officers made off with all the grave goods."

"Really?"

"Do you think I'd dare make up something as important as that? I heard it from two of the sons of Lao Wang's family in Bei'anhe. Those two brothers had been in the army over there, but they didn't want to leave their home, so they deserted. They said the top brass had made the announcement. The officer concerned is called Zheng, and he has a bodyguard, so there are two of them."

"How could two people carry off all that stuff?"

"Whether they really did make off with it, or how much they took, isn't clear. But one thing is certain – it hasn't been used against the Japanese devils. We just don't know for sure who's got it now."

Qi Yuexuan falls silent after he hears what Grandpa Zhang has told him.

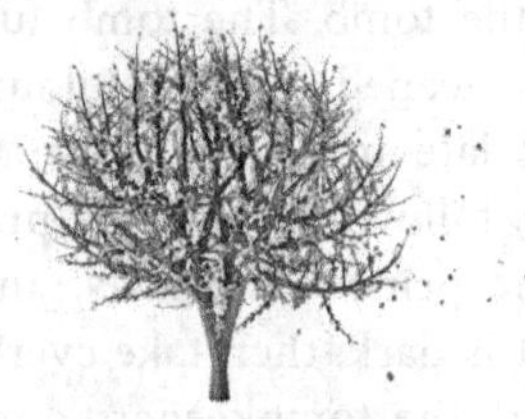

Chapter 36

Only a few days after the official opening of the Yuhua Trading Company, Wangtian sets out on a business trip. This is part of a three-pronged strategy that Yang Zhixing has been planning for some time, and the first of its three legs is to concentrate on grain.

Ever since Beiping was called Dadu during the Yuan dynasty, the city has always relied on imported grain, and there is a limit on what the surrounding provinces can supply from their own reserves. Since the Japanese occupied Beiping, the spring shortage of grain has grown more serious. The people's ration of blended flour is only available one day in three, and the farmers in the surrounding area are very worried about the spring sowing. In these circumstances, all that can be done is to import grain, and it's very difficult not be cheated on that. You may fancy a glistening piece of fatty pork, but actually getting it to your mouth is a different matter. With the country in turmoil because of the war, the harvests are poor everywhere. The Japanese at the front are in dire need, and their eyes go green at the sight of grain. In addition to them, anti-Japanese resistance groups are springing up all over the country, and far from actually fighting the devils, their empty bellies mean they don't even have the strength to raise a battle cry. So simply collecting grain is hard enough, let alone transporting it.

Luckily, Yang Zhixing already has a plan. Since the Qi family estates at Wucheng had a good harvest the year before, their granaries have plenty of grain ready to hand. Although some of it was brought up to the city last year, the majority is in store in the granaries. Moreover, there is still more than a thousand *piculs* of grain from the year before. If he gets the tenant farmers to pool their surplus grain in place of this year's post-harvest rent, that should easily bring in another few hundred *piculs*. The northern stretch of the Beiping-Hankou Railway is already complete, so you can take the train as far as Dezhou, but when you get off, there is still a another hundred *li* to go. But grain can't be shipped by train anyway; the Japanese Army has commandeered all the goods trucks, and civilian use is not allowed. All you can do is hire horses and carts on the spot. Wangtian and Qi Yuexuan take a lot of care planning the return journey; they ask many questions and sweat blood before they make their final decision. Wangtian will take the main government highway past Cangzhou, then head from Jinghai into Ba County and make his way round into Tianjin. Once he is through Gu'an, he will head across from Daxing to Liangxiang, and when he reaches Sanjiadian, he will cross the Yongding River and get back into Beiping. Although this is quite a roundabout route, the military bases and checkpoints they have to pass are easy to deal with since they are mostly manned by the puppet army. So Yang Zhixing sorts out the trade permits from the interim government and the 'tong guan' permit from the Japanese that allows travel beyond the Pass. He also gives Wangtian some extra money just in case he meets any unexpected eventualities than can be resolved by silver.

Wangtian sets out on the twenty-ninth day of the second month by the old calendar, taking only seven or eight men with him. Other than one accountant, the rest are mostly fellow workers from the night soil depot, Clown among them. A silver-tongued and quick-witted fellow like him is certainly not going to miss out on an adventure like this. The party leave the train at Dezhou, continue on through the night to Wucheng and arrive the next day at the Qi family compound.

Although Wucheng County is Japanese-held territory, the Qi family compound is well off the beaten track, a good distance from both the county town and the main highway, so there are no Japanese bases in the vicinity. The previous winter, some Japanese soldiers had escorted a squad of security police to make a grain inspection, but fortunately, the estate manager had been forewarned, and he had ordered the estate workers and tenant farmers to hide their grain. That same year, when preparing their defences against bandits, they repaired the tunnels under the village, so they could be used if the Japanese came back again. They are afraid that the Japanese won't leave without something to show for it, so they leave a little grain in the open, rather like offering alms to a beggar. Thus, the Qi family and the local families don't suffer any great losses, and what they have in store corresponds pretty much to Yang Zhixing's estimate.

Although the grain is there alright, this first time they want to test the waters and transport only a modest amount, so they settle for eight cartloads. Nonetheless, they have picked good carts, good horses and good men, so when the carts are fully laden, they are carrying at least two hundred *piculs*. For safety's sake, they only travel by day and rest up at night. Despite having scoped out the road conditions in advance, they still meet with some unexpected difficulties.

They are only ten *li* past the checkpoint at Cangzhou when they see a hundred or so Japanese up ahead turning onto the main highway from a side road. As they meet, one of the Japanese officers raises his hand, bringing the convoy to a halt. Wangtian hurries forward, holding out all his documents, and he begins to explain himself with an ingratiating smile. But having taken the papers, all the officer says is: "Grains, horses, carts, all seized."

These soldiers, newly arrived from the interior of Japan, were formerly members of the Imperial Household Guard. Despite not having seen active service, they have a very high opinion of themselves and put on airs to match. The day before, they were out in the open country on a grain inspection, and they spent all day running between villages without seeing a single person or collecting a single grain. Quite a few of them, however, were killed or injured by landmines. They are overflowing with pent-up fury, so what attention are they going to pay to any permits, no matter whose seals they bear?

Just when Wangtian is at his wits' end and can see no way out, Clown steps forward and confidently chatters out a few sentences in Japanese. To everyone's amazement, the officer behaves as though a spell has been cast on him; his attitude makes a complete about-turn, and not only does he let them go on their way, he keeps repeating the most abject apologies.

Once they've gone a little way, Wangtian finally asks: "Where did you learn to speak Japanese, Clown?"

"Ah, when I was sixteen, I was a navvy on the Manchuria Railway, and all the foremen were Japanese. I didn't need to study. I just picked up a few sentences on the job."

"So... what did you actually say?"

Clown strikes a cocky pose, a broad grin splitting his face, but when he sees Wangtian looking impatient, he says: "Ai! I've just done you a great service, and if you want the details, you're going to have to give me a reward to loosen my tongue. Don't change your ways just because you're a big boss now."

"Alright, alright! I'll give you double pay and fifty catties of grain."

Clown replies casually: "The key thing was, I mentioned someone he simply didn't dare offend."

"Who was that, then?"

"Their emperor!"

"You went on about their emperor and they listened to you? You're making it up!"

"Well, it was a lot of bullshit with a bit of truth behind it. I just told him it is soon going to be the twenty-fourth of the fourth month in the old calendar, and that is the emperor's birthday. I told him our grain is for birthday celebrations, and that if he wants to seize it, that would be an act of gross disrespect, and the punishment would certainly be very serious. Like I said, most of that was bullshit, but the twenty-fourth is genuinely the emperor's birthday, and every Japanese knows it. Why wouldn't he believe me? He didn't have any choice but to let us go."

"Alright, you lucky little bastard," Wangtian says admiringly. "Fancy you knowing about the emperor's birthday!"

It is soon the twelfth of March, and the grain convoy has crossed into Liangxiang County, and later that day they will be down the mountain, three or four *li* from Huangxinzhuang. Huangxinzhuang is a large village in the region of Pingxi, which used to be called Huangqinzhuang (Imperial Family Village) in the Ming dynasty because it was the home village of relatives of the emperor. In the time of Emperor Qianlong in the Qing dynasty, an imperial travelling lodge was built there, and it became one of the places where the emperors stayed when they went to the Western Tombs to offer sacrifices to their ancestors. It is two hundred and forty *li* from Beiping to the Western Tombs, which, back then, took the imperial party eight days, and this was the first stop. Presumably to make the emperor's journey more auspicious, at some point, no one knows when, the place became known as Huangxinzhuang (Imperial Luck Village). After the foundation of the Republic, when there were no more emperors, they simply changed the first character from 皇 (meaning 'emperor') to 黄 (meaning 'yellow').

They are forty *li* from Beiping, and if they really push themselves, they could arrive by midnight. But Wangtian decides to spend the night at Huangxinzhuang and set out early the next morning. Having passed all the checkpoints and army posts along the route and being close to their destination, now is the time for them to be at their most vigilant. They are approaching the junction where the road through the mountains from Zhoukoudian meets the main Beiping highway, and, once they are passed it, they will be only one *li* from Huangxinzhuang. Wangtian is just about to urge his men to pick up the pace, when he sees that a new blockhouse has appeared at the junction. There are sandbags either side of the road and spiked barriers across it; a good number of Japanese soldiers and soldiers from the puppet army are on guard, and every traveller is being stopped for inspection.

The fact is that, over the ten days they have been on the road, the situation in Beiping has grown more tense. In order to provide cover for its advance into eastern Hebei, the Eighth Route Army has intensified its attacks on the Japanese Army at Wanping, and the motley collection of forces fighting under the flag of anti-Japanese resistance in Liangxiang and Fangshan are providing support. Some of them are simply accompanying the Eighth Route Army in their advance, some have integrated themselves into it, and others have joined forces to form an allied anti-Japanese army nicknamed the Tenth Route Army and numbering several tens of thousands of men. So the Japanese are concentrating their attention on Pingxi and the south of Pingxi, deploying troops and strengthening their defences. The blockhouse up ahead was put up three days ago, but it does not deter Wangtian. It is, after all, only another inspection; they have been inspected all along their route through Shandong and Hebei, so what should they have to fear on their own doorstep?

The road is quite narrow at this point, and with the spiked barriers either side, it is now only wide enough for one carriage. Three or four soldiers of the puppet army accompany two Japanese devils inspecting all travellers, one by one, checking certificates of good citizenship, examining goods and carrying out body searches. There is already quite a queue, twenty or thirty at least: foot porters, packhorses and donkey carts are gradually filing through. Wangtian has no option but to halt the carts to join the line, while he goes to the front to see what's going on. Before he has taken more than a few steps, a man slips up beside him and whispers: "Are you masters heading for Beiping?"

It is a man of around sixty, wearing a long gown and a Western-style hat. He has an educated manner and is smiling broadly. Wangtian replies with a curt "Yes".

"Are you carrying grain?"

"Yes."

"There are certain formalities to be completed."

"They're all done."

"In that case, why are you waiting? Come along to the front of the queue, and I'll put in a word for you."

With that, the old gentleman pushes his way through the crowd, calling out urgently: "Excuse us, excuse us, make way, make way."

Assuming the man is connected with the checkpoint, Wangtian follows him without a second thought to the front of the queue. The old gentleman goes straight up to the sergeant of the puppet army soldiers, laughing genially and saying with every evidence of familiarity: "Hey, it's our lucky day, finding you on duty."

The sergeant doesn't seem to know who he is, but impressed by his age and air of authority, he nods and smiles uncertainly: "I'm afraid you..."

The old gentleman doesn't let him finish, and asks: "Is your company commander here?"

"No."

"Go find him, and tell him his uncle's grain convoy has returned. It's those carts at the back there. Tell him that, when he has time to go home, he'll find I've left the lucky fellow some good wine and cigarettes. Can you tell him all that?"

"Yes, of course..."

Before he can finish, he finds a pack of cigarettes thrust into his hand, and when he looks, he discovers a banknote tucked underneath it. Without waiting for him to reply, the old gentleman puts the cigarettes and money in his pocket for him, then produces several more packs of cigarettes, which he distributes among the puppet army men and the Japanese soldiers.

"What is it he doing?" one of the Japanese asks.

"Ah!" the sergeant replies. "Taijun, this... this is our company commander's uncle. He's... he's carrying grain."

The Japanese draws on his cigarette and says: "No matter who, no papers, no go."

Seeing the sergeant has no reply, the old gentleman shoots him a look and says with a laugh: "Ha, do you think we'd be moving grain without the paperwork?"

Wangtian hurriedly holds out all his permits and passes for the Japanese to inspect. The Japanese examines them closely: "Papers fine, where you grain?"

"There, queuing right at the back," says the old gentleman, pointing.

"Aiyo, Uncle!" The family relationship makes the sergeant more insistent. "The Taijun says it's fine, so what are you worrying about? Get a move on."

"No need to queue?"

"Ha! Do you think we make our own people queue?" So saying, the sergeant pushes his way through the crowd, shouting: "Make way! Move to the sides! Let the carts at the back through."

When the last cart has passed, Wangtian and the old gentleman finally leave the checkpoint. Once they've gone some distance, they take their leave of the sergeant.

"You must visit my home one of these days."

"I'm afraid the commander won't let me."

"He will. Just tell him I said so."

"Alright."

The men and carts that have gone ahead through the checkpoint are waiting for them at the roadside, when Clown discovers that a young lad he doesn't recognise has followed them through. He has managed to mingle in with them alright, but he is going very cautiously, sticking to the rear of the carts, his eyes darting all around.

Clown stops in front of him and asks: "Well, brother, you are?"

"Don't ask. The more you know, the worse for you."

"Alright, alright, I won't ask. Everyone has their own path to travel, but can you come a little further from the carts?"

"Do you think I'm standing here for fun? Traitors carrying grain for the Japanese like you stink from head to foot. Are you proud of that?"

"If we disgust you so much, why are you still standing there? Why don't you move?"

"Wait till my boss gets here, then I'll move, and you won't see me for dust."

"And who's your boss?"

The lad nods towards the old gentleman.

"It was so lucky for us you came along just now, sir. I must pay you for your trouble. Thank you. Thank you." Wangtian is babbling away as he and the old gentleman walk along.

"Ah! You are too kind, but it worked out well for both of us. If you are going to thank me, I must thank you first."

At this, Wangtian takes out some silver yuan from inside his jacket. He has heard that there are men who are in cahoots with the checkpoint guards and make a living by helping people get through. But before he can hand over the coins, the old man smiles and says: "So you really do want to thank me? Alright then. You're intending to spend the night at Huangxinzhuang, aren't you? I'm stopping there myself, so if you can give me a lift, that will do nicely. There's a little donkey meat restaurant in the village, and my thanks to you will be to invite you all to be my guests there."

At this point, all Wangtian can do is go along with things, but he does at least say: "No, it's my treat, it should be my treat. Now, please get up on one of the carts."

The old gentleman calls out to the young lad: "Changzi, hurry up and load our things onto the cart."

The young lad acknowledges the order, then turns, and like some kind of conjuring trick, produces a hemp sack from behind his back, ties it up with a straw rope and leaps up onto the cart. But Clown's quick eyes notice that there is a hook at the top of the sack, which the lad has just used to hang the thing on the back of the cart to smuggle it past the checkpoint. Wangtian has no real idea who this old gentleman is, or what goods he is carrying, but one thing he is clear about: there's something odd going on.

There is no time now for Wangtian to think about all this too carefully. In these troubled times, it is better to have one less thing to worry about than one more, particularly when you're on the road. So he remains impassive, helps the old gentleman up onto the front of the cart and sits down beside him. As the carts set off, the old man pats one of the grain sacks and asks: "Is this all wheat?"

"We've got two crops – seventy per cent wheat, thirty per cent maize."

"Where are you going to be selling them?"

"We haven't decided. We'll think about that when we get to Beiping."

"What price will you be selling at?"

"Not sure yet. We'll see what the market will bear."

"Ai, it's not easy getting through all the formalities these days."

"Certainly not."

The old man clearly knows his way around the business. "If you've got the right connections, it's better not to sell it off piecemeal, but as one big lot," he says.

Wangtian gives a wry smile and says: "You're not wrong, but there are advantages and disadvantages. Selling it as one is quicker, but you won't necessarily get the best price. Then again, in today's Beiping, there aren't that many major dealers who could handle it all. The Japanese and the interim government would surely want it, but who dares do business with them? Coming out ahead and not making a loss is what matters, and if you're going to make your own way, you can't afford to cut your own throat."

The old gentleman's eyes light up at this, and he fixes Wangtian with a look: "Well then... how about you sell the whole lot to me? You won't be disappointed. I'll give you twenty per cent over the current retail price."

"That... that's a lot of money."

"Ha ha! You're afraid I don't have it? Don't worry, it will be cash up front, a clean deal on both sides. If you've got any more to come, I'll take that too on the same terms. I'll give you an advance order for as much as you like. If you go on to Beiping, I don't think you'll find anyone to match a deal like that."

"Hmm... that may be true," Wangtian nods in agreement, but ever since he was little, he has had one abiding principle: there's no such thing as a free lunch. The money and the deal are just too good, and he simply doesn't trust the man. Buying up grain like this at above market price, even as a loss leader, is sheer madness, stupidity, burning good money. Who would dare do such a thing? But the old gentleman has such an honest face, and he doesn't look like some trick the gods are playing on him.

The old gentleman can obviously see what he's thinking: "I know the price is a little excessive, but I'm not really looking to make a profit. I'm also using money other people have earned to help them buy grain. It may be at a loss, but they've still got to have the grain. So even if I lose money, it's all in good faith."

Put like this, Wangtian thinks it sounds quite reasonable, and he even feels a little apologetic: "If you really are going to pay cash on the nail, then I can knock five per cent off the price, and reduce your losses a little."

"That would be good. Ha ha, don't worry, I've got the money available, and we can finalise the deal in Huangxinzhuang."

When they reach the village, they see the donkey meat restaurant, where the owner is coming out to greet them before the carts have even pulled up outside. The old gentleman shouts out his instructions as he gets down from the cart: "I've brought you some good business, so lay on the best stuff for us. I'm in the chair today, so make sure you've got everything we want."

"Ha! Don't worry about that."

"And find me a private room. I have some business to conduct."

"No problem. Come into the rear courtyard."

As they go in, they hear Changzi complaining angrily: "This is money for old rope. What do you need all the chit-chat for?"

"That's enough of your nonsense," says the old gentleman. "Of course there should be time to consider a deal properly, so neither side feels they've been forced into anything. Do you understand?"

Wangtian laughs, and he is just about to say something when his accountant asks: "You say you will pay fifteen per cent on top of the retail price, sir, but the retail price goes up and down. I don't know what figure you want to use."

The old gentleman laughs. "Then set it higher rather than lower, and come up with one figure for both types of grain. As long as you don't go completely off the scale, I won't quibble."

At this, the accountant hurriedly looks to Wangtian for guidance, and only when he sees him nod does he stretch out his hand towards the old gentleman, pull back his sleeve and flash his fingers to show the price: "Working in silver yuan, for each *picul* of wheat, this is yuan and this is cents, and the same for each *picul* of maize."

"Alright, I agree the price. Get out your abacus and give me a total."

"I don't need an abacus for that, I can do it in my head." Once again the accountant stretches out a hand, pulls back his sleeve and flashes his fingers. "For the total, this is thousands, this is hundreds, this is tens and this is ones."

"Alright, let's settle for that." The old man thinks for a moment, then goes on: "But I don't have that many silver yuan to hand."

"*Fabi*[1] will do too, to make up the total."

"I don't have any *fabi* either. I only have army issue notes."

The accountant doesn't dare agree to this on his own, and he looks at Wangtian for further guidance.

Wangtian doesn't even hesitate, but says immediately: "Army issue is no problem, but the ordinary people don't like that Japanese money, and it's always hard to spend. The exchange rate will have to..."

"It would have to be one to four," Clown interrupts forcefully.

"Hmm, yes, alright, that's the figure," Wangtian agrees.

These 'army issue notes' were originally only for internal use in the Japanese Army, and are officially called 'Notes for the use of the Army of the Imperial Japanese Government'. At first, only soldiers could use them, they couldn't be circulated elsewhere, and they could only be exchanged for real Japanese currency at specially designated exchange points. After the Japanese occupied Chahar and the northeast, they made this huge quantity of army issue notes an official currency and tried to force it into the marketplace. This was quite simply a ruse to plunder Chinese currency at no cost to themselves. After the Marco Polo Bridge Incident, these army issue notes became the currency of all the occupied areas. They have face values of 10 yuan, 5 yuan, 1 yuan, 50 cents and 10 cents. But the printing is very crude and there aren't any serial numbers or anti-counterfeit measures; moreover, their designs all feature famous people from Japanese history, so they are hugely unpopular with all Chinese. Although the army issue's face value is equivalent with silver yuan, at a rate of one to one, its actual value in the marketplace has fallen and fallen. At this time, the deficit between the silver yuan and the army notes on the black market is running at between 1:3 and 1:3.3, so 1:4 is definitely on the high side. To everyone's surprise, the old gentleman still raises no objection. Instead, he just smiles, nods and make a sign to Changzi.

Changzi acknowledges the signal, quickly opens his sack and pulls out a big handful of army issue notes, which he piles up into a small mountain on the table. The notes are all new and sealed in neat bundles of tens and fives.

Everyone stares in amazement, wondering how such a tatty old sack could contain so many bank notes. Changzi is pulling the notes out piecemeal, but if you took it all out at once, there had to be more than a million.

In the twinkling of an eye, the old gentleman has counted out a pile of notes, neatly divided into fives and tens, and pushes it over to Wangtian, saying:

"There's thirty or forty more than we agreed in there, but don't worry about it, just keep the lot. Now hurry up and count it, then we can eat."

"Ha! They're already neatly bundled up, what is there to check?" Wangtian signals to the accountant: "Pack it all up and put it away."

The accountant nods but doesn't immediately put the money away. Instead, he takes an army issue note from his pocket and carefully compares both sides. Reassured, he pulls out a piece of cloth and wraps the money up in it.

"Have you got any more goods coming later?" the old gentleman asks.

"Yes, at least another thousand *piculs*."

"Good, then sell it all to me at the same price." He pushes the remaining pile of notes over to Wangtian. "Take this as a down payment. I don't want it."

"Then... you're that trusting?"

"Ha! What is there not to trust? You look like an honest man, and I know your name, so why should I think you won't come through? You're from the Yuhua Trading Company, aren't you? Your name is Gao Wangtian and you live in Minister's Residence Hutong, isn't that right? I'm well-informed, you see."

Wangtian is startled and pleased in equal measure: "How do you know all that?"

The old gentleman gives a faint smile: "Didn't you give me your permits and passes to hand over at the checkpoint? I sneaked a look and memorised it all then."

Wangtian is even more convinced that there is more to this old gentleman than meets the eye. He hears him continue: "Well now, this grain I've bought. I'll need you to take it somewhere for me. Let's say I take these carts to transport the second crop, and we'll call it quits. I won't go myself, but I'll send someone who knows the way. Can you see anything wrong with that? As for you, you don't need to worry. All you have to do is give me the permits and take the down payment. Changzi, tell them out front to serve the food."

As Changzi obediently leaves the room, Wangtian tells the accountant to put the money away, then asks: "Where are you sending the grain?"

"Wanping."

"Where in Wanping?"

"I'll have to lead the way. It's a little place out in the countryside. You wouldn't know it if I told you."

"Not necessarily. Try me and see. You know where I live, so maybe I know something about your place too."

"Are you from Wanping?"

"No, but our company's majority shareholder is at the Left Barracks in Wanping."

"The Left Barracks? What's his name?"

"His family name is Qi..."

"Qi Yuexuan?"

"That's right. Have you heard of him?"

The old gentleman begins to laugh: "Ha ha! Heard of him? My best and oldest friend in Beiping is the Young Master of the Minister's Residence. But since when did he have a business brain? He has spent half a lifetime shirking his duties as head of the household, and has relied on his old manager, Yang Zhixing, to handle things for him. Isn't that so?"

Wangtian gasps when he hears this: "No, no, no, you can't say that. The way Uncle Yang puts it is that, big as this business is, it's just small potatoes, so why should the Young Master waste his brain power on it when he's got men to do it for him. He's got bigger fish to fry."

"Hmm, you could be right. Qi Yuexuan is not very bright when it comes to little things, but he's certainly no fool with really important matters." The old man smiles to himself and continues: "Didn't you just ask me where this grain is going? Well, it's going to your majority shareholder."

"What!" Wangtian stares at him in amazement. Then, after a long pause, he asks: "So he's your customer is he? How much... how much are you charging him? It's not coming out of his family money, is it?"

Seeing how agitated he is getting, the old gentleman smiles again and says: "You're right, he is my customer but I'm giving it to him for free, not selling it."

"Not... not selling it?"

"Ah but I'm not giving it just to him. Great affairs need a lot of people, and a lot of people have a lot of mouths to feed, so they can't afford to be short of grain, can they? If Manager Yang asks, you can mention me. Just say that you sold the grain to Mr Hao and I guarantee you won't get any complaints."

"Mr Hao?" Wangtian is sure he has heard the name before, but for the moment, he can't remember where. He is silent for a while, then asks: "So you know where the Young Master and the others are now?"

"Of course."

"Where, then?"

"I can't tell you that."

"It's not just me. Uncle Shu doesn't know either. They were in touch before, but for the last month or more, he's heard nothing. He doesn't even know..."

"Don't worry, he's fine, and things are going really well."

"Who did you hear that from?"

"There's no doubt about it. Several of my men have just come from there."

Wangtian's eyes light up at this news. Hadn't Uncle Yang told him that his father was with the Army of the Left Barracks? So if he knows where the Young Master is, then he can get news of his father. At this point, the memory comes flooding back: on the day after his wedding, didn't Uncle Yang give him a letter to take to Yanjing University, mentioning the name of a Mr Hao and explaining that he was working with his father? This must be the same person.

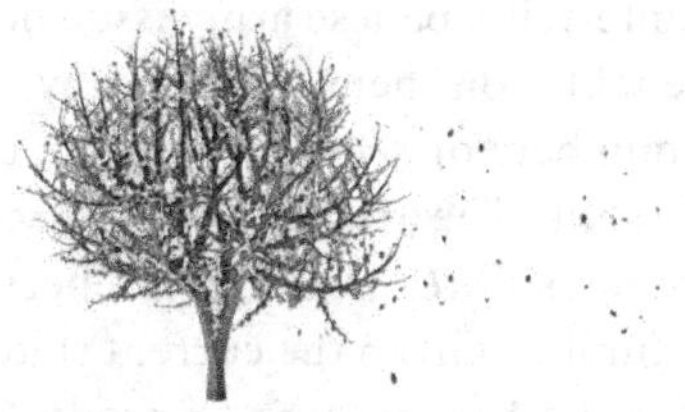

Chapter 37

The old gentleman who has shown himself so liberal with money is indeed Hao Bingchen.

After the annihilation of the Traitor Elimination Squad's intelligence section and its communications centre, he orders the untouched operations division to make a temporary move to the Left Barracks, and he himself makes a solo trip to Taiyuan. He intends to make a full report to headquarters and replenish his personnel and communications equipment so that the full Traitor Elimination Squad can be revived. But before he can even get there, Taiyuan falls to the Japanese, and the Beiping station of military intelligence has moved to an area in the south of Hebei and merged with the Tianjin station to form a joint Tianjin-Beiping section. He turns round and heads west again, and after many twists and turns, reunites with his men in the vicinity of Xingtai. There, he makes a report of all these circumstances directly to Chongqing. To his surprise, the orders come back to wind up the Traitor Elimination Squad, cease assassinations and withdraw all personnel from Beiping. Other than an individual instruction for he himself to return to Chongqing, everybody else is to transfer to the south of Hebei and join with the Tianjin station. But before they leave, they are ordered to carry out one last task, which is to dump a certain consignment on the Beiping market. They are looking for a rapid disposal, and anything they get in exchange that is too difficult to transport is to be put into temporary storage or handed over to the guerrilla outfits of the National Army operating behind enemy lines. It is only when he takes delivery of the consignment, and hears the explanation of the courier, that Hao Bingchen realises the goods are actually Japanese army issue bank notes and that they are all counterfeit.

In fact, the Japanese have not just issued the army money for use in occupied territory to plunder the Chinese economy, they have also counterfeited large quantities of the Kuomintang government's *fabi*. They have dispatched men to spread them around the whole country and disrupt the economy as far as possible behind the front lines, bringing about a devaluation of the *fabi* and causing rampant inflation in the marketplace. In response, the Kuomintang have instituted strict measures to identify counterfeit currency and have also begun test printings of counterfeit Japanese army issue notes, hoping to use the enemy's methods to turn the tables on them. As the army issue notes are crudely printed and have no serial numbers or security features, cutting the plates and printing the notes is not difficult. The tricky bit is sourcing the paper. The paper the Japanese use incorporates fibres from the mulberry tree, making it rough to the touch but also very durable. Given the current state of Chinese paper technology, it is very difficult for the Kuomintang to produce this kind of paper. But with help from American paper technicians, they reckon they have solved this problem. The batch of notes they have handed over to Hao Bingchen this time total five million yuan, and it is their test consignment that they hope to introduce into the market to see how they go. Later, they can make any necessary adjustments, then print in bulk. Hao Bingchen sends for Gao Guigeng's squad of operatives to see through this assignment, planning to divide them into three groups simultaneously to infiltrate Beiping, Tianjin and Baoding. Once their mission is accomplished, they are to withdraw immediately.

WHEN GAO GUIGENG HEARS Hao Bingchen's plan, he is in a rush to return to Beiping. Last time he devised a plan to go against Chenglong, he got Hao's approval but was unable to carry it through, even though he did get one good sharp bite in. He is not, however, willing to drop the matter and hopes to use this opportunity to meet with Chenglong in person. If he can persuade him over from the enemy, it will be a cause for rejoicing, but if Chenglong persists in his perversity, Gao Guigeng is determined to eliminate this blot on the family honour who is making such a disgraceful exhibition of himself. Whether he succeeds or not, he will at least have the satisfaction of this opportunity to vent his pent-up anger and frustration. Of course, he also wants to see Wangtian and his new daughter-in-law, since, although he has spent a good few months in Beiping, father and son have not had the chance to exchange a single word. With this forthcoming evacuation, he has no idea when he will be able to come back, and even less idea whether he will survive the hail of bullets and storm of grenades in the next battle. But when he raises these concerns with Hao Bingchen, Hao is nervous that these kinds of side issues will delay the main business at hand. So Hao Bingchen decides to send the second-in-command of the squad with several men to Baoding; he himself will go back to Beiping, while Gao Guigeng will travel to Tianjin with an old hand from the Tianjin station to help him. However, he does promise him that, once this mission is over and they meet up again in Wanping, he will personally help him achieve his wishes, and then they will move out together. Gao Guigeng has no choice but to follow orders.

Of course, Hao Bingchen hurries off to visit Qi Yuexuan, hoping to use his contacts in Beiping to spread the fake notes around the market, and maybe exchange some of them for supplies to support the people's resistance. There is no way he could have anticipated the other consequences of these actions, when, as he finally manages to buy eight cartloads of grain, it turns out that he is simply robbing Peter to pay Paul, and buyer and seller turn out to be on the same side.

ALTHOUGH HAO BINGCHEN is putting a brave face on things, like Gao Guigeng, he too is being tormented by something. Now he knows he has passed the counterfeit notes to one of their own, he feels he can't let him blindly take the loss and that he owes him some kind of explanation. He wants to do it, but at the same time, he doesn't, and he keeps weighing the options. Although the printing on this batch of notes is passable, they are still counterfeit, and although they might fool ordinary folk, once they get to a bank, the truth will be exposed. If it was just a few notes, Wangtian could get away with some excuse or other, but taking the Japanese to the cleaners like this is almost certain to result in execution. So if Wangtian is willing to cooperate, he needs to be put fully in the picture. Then he must spend as much of the money as possible without causing any major incident. Otherwise, not only will he, Hao Bingchen, be failing in his mission, he will also be involving innocent people and hurting his friends.

At this point, a waiter comes in carrying a tray, and unloads onto the table several plates of donkey meat and folded flatbread. Clown's stomach has been growling for some time, and without waiting to be asked, he reaches out to take some food, but Wangtian slaps him sharply on the back of the hand.

"Off you go and take the plates with you," says Wangtian. "Go out front and eat with Lao Xu. Hao Bingchen and I have things to talk about."

"Alright," Clown replies, and, in the twinkling of an eye, he has dextrously piled all the food back on the tray, picked it up and left the room.

Embarrassed, Wangtian says: "Ai! How annoying! Waiter, bring us some more food." He smiles apologetically. "That Clown! He's always been a bit crazy..."

"Ha! No problem," Hao Bingchen says. "This is fine. Tell me what is worrying you. We are all friends and brothers here. I can see that you are a man of principle, a man fit for great deeds."

Wangtian smiles deprecatingly, and then, when he sees the waiter has left the room, asks in a low voice: "Were you living at Yanjing University two months ago, Mr Hao?"

Hao Bingchen gives a slight start of surprise, stares at Wangtian and doesn't reply.

"Are you part of... the Traitor Elimination Squad?"

"How did you know?"

"Ah, I went to deliver a letter to you, but I never got to see you, only a foreigner."

"You've never seen me, but you still think you recognise me?"

"Well, Uncle Yang had mentioned you and said you were working with my father."

"Your father…"

"His name's Gao Guigeng."

"Ha ha, so you're Lao Gui's son! Ha! Your father told me about you. You've just got married, haven't you? I'd heard you made your living collecting night soil. When did you become a businessman?"

"That's the Young Master and Uncle Yang's doing."

"Good, very good. I just had no idea that's what you were doing."

"So where is my father now?"

"Ah, well, that's really bad timing. He and I were together a few days ago, but he's gone to Tianjin now. He's coming back to Beiping when he's finished that job, and then there'll be a chance for you two to meet up."

Changzi was one of Gao Guigeng's followers when he was a bandit chief, and as soon as he hears that Wangtian is his Uncle Gui's son, he immediately feels he has found a new relative. He comes over and claps him on the shoulder, treating him like a brother.

Hao Bingchen's light-hearted tone turns serious. "There's something I need to discuss with you, Wangtian."

"Go on."

Hao Bingchen draws closer and says in a low voice: "Those army issue notes I just gave you are all fake."

"What! Fake!"

"That's right. All the notes in this sack are counterfeit."

Wangtian stares at him, wide-eyed and open-mouthed. "You… this… what's the big idea?"

Hao Bingchen then explains the reasons behind the whole affair, leaving out any information that is secret or classified, and anything it might be inappropriate to divulge. Even so, it's enough for Wangtian to get the general idea.

"So… all this financial stuff you've been talking about… this devaluation and… what's the word… inflation, is all about making the army issue money worthless?"

"Yes, yes, that's right. So you understand?"

"What I don't get is why the government is playing such dirty tricks."

"Hah! Didn't I just say, the Japanese started it? We're just using their own methods to turn the tables on them."

"Do you really expect ordinary people to play around with these two sorts of money when it's their livelihood at stake? If they get found out, even if they're not taken to court, it's more than likely that quite a few of them will starve to death as a result. As for the currency devaluing, the people are suffering enough already, and if they've got the Japanese cheating them on one side, and their own government on the other, that's just…"

"Enough!" says Hao Bingchen, his face darkening. Then, feeling he has sounded a little too harsh, he softens his tone: "Ai! What you say is not without some reason, but there are big causes and lesser causes, and at the moment, resisting the Japanese is the biggest cause of all. Alright, forget it, let's just say the deal never happened. You give me back the money, and you keep your grain. Seeing as who your father is, how can I let you take the risk and shoulder the blame?"

To his surprise, Wangtian stiffens and says: "If you're going to talk about causes and principles, Uncle Hao, I may not have had much schooling, but I do know something about principles. As long as you stand by your reasons for doing this, then our deal can go through. If you also let me help you spend what's left of the money in that sack and cause as much trouble as possible, then I agree."

"Are you absolutely sure about this?" Hao Bingchen replies, looking at him in disbelief.

"Not in detail, but I do understand the principles. This kind of thing has to be done on the quiet, or it will be discovered. It has to be trickled out, but just like fine rain, once it starts, nothing can stop it."

"Hmm, yes, you've got the right idea, but..."

"Don't worry, I've got the men to do it. If they're not completely trustworthy, I won't use them."

"Alright, and I'll up the pay. The bigger the reward, the braver the men."

Wangtian looks a little disapproving at this. "A man's life is worth more than any money, Uncle Hao, and it won't be easy to persuade these men to risk theirs for so little profit." Seeing Hao Bingchen nod, he goes on: "I need you to give me a simple, firm explanation of exactly what is going on and why. Then, if I believe in it, I can use it to explain to the others."

Hao Bingchen finally understands where Wangtian is coming from, and he nods solemnly, saying: "When two countries go to war, Wangtian, it isn't just fought on the battlefield. What your father and I are doing with this counterfeit money is fighting the war too, but on the financial front. At the moment, the Japanese devils' guns and cannons are too many for us. They also have planes and tanks, and their battlefield strength is overwhelming. But where does all their equipment come from? A lot of it relies on the way they steal from us with this worthless army issue currency of theirs. They are using our own grain, cotton, oil, coal, copper, iron and tin against us. If we can devalue that currency, so it becomes worthless and unusable, isn't that the same as cutting off their supplies of provisions and ammunition? Isn't that a greater contribution than killing a few of the devils on the battlefield? Yes of course there are risks, and the ordinary folk may suffer some losses. Just like in battle, you may lose three thousand men to kill ten thousand of the enemy, and fighting the Japanese requires some sacrifices. Anyone who is afraid of that kind of trouble is just playing patsy to the Japanese, and there's nothing to be done about it. But not all Chinese are like that, are they?"

Wangtian nods deeply as he listens to this. "That all makes sense, Uncle Hao. Our deal stands, and I accept everything else you say too."

. . .

Qi Yuexuan and the army of the Left Barracks have been at Qiwangfen for more than a fortnight. Their army ration grain ran out some time ago, and although every household in Qiwangfen has given them some, the congee for their two meals a day is getting thinner and thinner, and it looks as if they are going to have to go down to one meal a day. They have quietly sent out several groups of men to try to raise some grain from the surrounding villages, but their success has been very limited. It is a poor region with many mountains and few people, and the mountains are all rocky and barren, with only small villages nine or ten *li* apart, each with only a limited supply of flat, cultivable land. Even the richest households have just a few tens of *mu* of sloping land that only support work for two or three farm labourers or a few tenant farmers. Last year's harvest was quite good, but once the war started, people came from all sides to plunder it, and very little is now left. The farming families are even more impoverished; in former years they had to pay rent, and they barely had enough left to eat, but now, the landlords are over-charging and demanding bigger contributions; nor are they even waiting for spring, but pushing the farmers into debt earlier and earlier. It is the same for every family: when they uncover their cooking pots, inside is simmering congee and steaming cornbread, most of which are yellow, black or green. The yellow ones have a little maize flour in them; the black ones are made from black bean flower; the green ones take their colour from elm seeds and willow shoots. The pure yellow ones are the most difficult to swallow, not because of the husks they contain, but because of the millet straw. There's no way to chew it to a mush, small bites get stuck in your throat and trying to swallow big bites would certainly end with you choking to death. Seeing the starving farming families round-eyed with hunger like little children, who could fail to be moved? They have to back up their fine words and give some of their grain to the farming families.

Captain Wu of the Ninth Battalion of the Eighth Route Army makes a trip with a dozen or so men, bringing three thousand bullets and a hundred grenades, making good the promise of their Commander Zhao. He also rams home the instructions that they are to stay where they are and not panic, and that they must make absolutely sure they remain under cover. He promises that they will soon be going into battle together. But he says nothing about when, where or how this will happen. Apart from on this occasion, they see no other sign of him, and they don't trust him one bit. In fact, the men Qi Yuexuan has sent out to collect grain come back with the news that they have heard reports that the Eighth Route Army has recently fought quite a few battles, that they have taken the county town of Changping north of Beiping, as well as Fangshan to the west; and that a large force of men is skirting the mountains, heading for the east of

332

Hebei. With his own troops soon to be out of grain completely, Qi Yuexuan is growing agitated, and when he hears that the fighting is so brisk elsewhere, he becomes as impatient as a wife waiting for her husband to come home.

If Qi Yuexuan is agitated, Grandpa Fu is even more so. It has been more than two months since they left the Left Barracks, and the men are growing homesick, particularly over the last few days, as empty bellies turn their thoughts to the warmth of the *kang* back home and the smell of real cornbread. There is a certain tension between the men and Qi Yuexuan, and for the last two days he has had a headache caused by Grandpa Fu's grumblings stemming from his anxieties for his home and fellow countrymen. As soon as Grandpa Fu hears that the Eighth Route Army is making a two-pronged attack, north and south, the thought occurs to him that this is bound to draw out the Japanese Army's main force. This will only intensify the severity of the blockade to the west of Beiping, and their best chance is to take advantage of the confusion to retreat to the Left Barracks. Qi Yuexuan can see the sense in this, but he also feels that, since they have promised to fight alongside the Eighth Route Army, which has also just replenished their supplies of ammunition, to retreat now would be a little unreasonable. After several rounds of discussion, Qi Yuexuan and Grandpa Fu come to a compromise, which is that they will wait a further two days, counting from that evening. In the meantime, they will immediately send out men to scout the route back to the Left Barracks, and they will keep waiting for news from the Eighth Route Army. If they hear nothing in the allotted time, they will mount a night retreat to the Left Barracks. But in the early hours of that very night, they suddenly hear the sound of gunfire. At the same time, someone inside the compound at Qiwangfen raises the alarm, so that everyone leaps out of bed, snatches up their rifles and hurries outside. But amid the hubbub of questions, no one actually knows what is going on.

For the last few days, Qi Yuexuan has been lying in bed, unable to sleep, and the sounds of shouting and gunfire come very clearly to him. He throws on his coat and goes out into the garden.

"Everyone stop making that pointless racket. Stay where you are and be on the alert," he shouts as he leads a group of men out of the garden. They have just reached the top of the staircase when some men come running up the steps. These are the guards stationed outside the Yinzhai Gate who report that the shots seem to have come from Jiuwangfen at the bottom of the mountain, but the precise details of what is going on are not yet clear.

Jiuwangfen is only two *li* away, and ever since the army settled into Qiwangfen, a company of men have been stationed there, manning two hidden sentry posts. The shots are almost certainly coming from those men firing at an assailant. But once Qi Yuexuan has gone out of the gate and climbed on top of the fortifications next to the staircase to look down, all he sees is a few torches flickering in the compound at Jiuwangfen.

"Has it been taken?"

"Not yet...not yet."

THE SITUATION with the tombkeepers' families is the same at Jiuwangfen and Qiwangfen, as both are under the supervision of the Zhang family. Even though Jiuwangfen is less populated, eight households still live there; but living inside the compound itself are only a young lad and his grandfather. After Zhao Ran dug up the tombs at Qiwangfen last year, he did the same to the main tomb at Jiuwangfen, but he didn't have time to get around to the lesser tombs of the prince's sons and grandsons. However, other people have targeted them, and a number of exploratory tunnels have appeared near the tombs of the lesser princes and their wives. Luckily they are discovered before any of them penetrate the actual tomb chambers, and the young lad and his grandfather block them up with branches and brambles, patrolling them by night. But the tomb robbers haven't forgotten about these tombs, and recently the guardians have discovered quite a few places where these branches and brambles have been dragged out. All they can do is stuff them back in again. This has already happened six or seven times, but still none of the attempts has been successful.

On this particular night, grandfather and grandson are out on patrol when they discover three men climbing over the western courtyard wall, into the rear courtyard, and then clambering into the smaller compound. Qi Yuexuan's two hidden sentries are both on the roofs of buildings in the front courtyard, keeping watch on the old Incense Road outside the compound, guarding against the approach of Japanese devils from either the east or the west, so the intruders have gone undetected. Seeing they are outnumbered, grandfather and grandson separate, one staying to keep watch on what's going on, the other going to call for help. Before the grandson has been able to rouse the other tombkeepers, he bumps into two men on their way to relieve the sentries, who unsling their rifles and follow him back to the lesser tomb compound. They are sure that, as soon as the tomb robbers are faced with soldiers, all it will take is the sound of a rifle bolt being drawn for them meekly to surrender. To their surprise, these three robbers turn out to be armed themselves and open fire as soon as they hear the sentries' rifles being cocked. Fortunately, it is dark, and the men dodge out of the way, so no one is injured. The robbers are as quick on their feet as they are with their guns, and the soldiers only manage to return two shots before they are off and out of the lesser compound. Perhaps because they fear the way they came in may be blocked, or because they become confused in the excitement, whatever the case, they end up in the front courtyard, where the sentries hidden on the roofs are ready and waiting for them. A rifle shot drops one of them, and the other two take cover behind an old pine tree in the corner of the courtyard wall, refusing to come out, whatever is shouted at them. By the time the soldiers work their way round the edge of the wall to flush them out, there is no sign of them. By the light of their torches the soldiers discover a drainage channel running under the wall to the outside, with one of the robbers stuck in the entrance to it. The other one must have been smaller and managed to escape, while this one's larger frame has meant he is stuck fast by his arse, unable to get through.

When he hears the story, Grandpa Fu relaxes.

"Ha ha! I thought it was the Japanese devils, but it turns out to be just a couple of petty thieves. Alright then, interrogate the one you've caught and find out where the robbers' lair..."

"No, no!" Qi Yuexuan interjects. "I'm afraid the sound of shooting will have roused the Japanese devils at Hejian. What do you want with tomb robbers anyway? We're not here as tombkeepers."

"Ha! So what if the devils have been roused? If they send a few men, we'll attack them. If they send a lot, we'll retreat. In either case, we won't just sit here." Grandpa Fu laughs. "But don't underestimate these tomb robbers – they've all made themselves very rich. We can't loot these tombs ourselves, but if we take what's in their lair, that's legitimate spoils of war, and we could reap an unexpected windfall to take home."

This idea catches Qi Yuexuan's interest and he thinks it over carefully, before saying: "Since you've caught that one alive, why aren't you interrogating him?"

"Ha!" Grandpa Fu chips in. "We've already taken him outside and got tough with him. We've dislocated the little bastard's hip so he can't even stand up."

"Then find someone who can put it back in. I need him mobile immediately."

"We haven't got anyone who can do that. We could carry him up here."

"Enough! If we waste time going there and back, it will be too late. If he can't come to us, we'll go to him. What are you standing around staring at? Let's go!"

Grandpa Fu starts heading down the mountain as he speaks. He then leaves, taking the tombkeepers and the sentry who brought the letter by surprise. They watch him go, then hurry after him.

When they reach the compound at Jiuwangfen, the tomb robber with the dislocated hip is lying on the ground in the front courtyard. Grandpa Fu seizes one of his ankles with both hands and gives it a savage tug, then puts it back where it was. Although the man doesn't dare put his full weight on the leg, he can just about hobble along with someone's arm to lean on. He is taken inside and sat down, so the interrogation can begin.

No one has expected the fellow to be such a hard arse. No matter what he is asked, he doesn't make a sound. Grandpa Fu slams his fist down on the table and wags a finger at him.

"Are you going to talk or not, you little bastard? Alright then! We just dislocated your hip didn't we? Well, now I'm going to break both your arms and both your legs, so you can't even crawl."

The man's eyes cloud over at this, but he still doesn't say anything. Grandpa Fu reaches out and grips his arms, as though he's really about to let rip. Qi Yuexuan hurries forward and pulls him off.

"Don't! Don't! Don't get carried away. Let's take a break and let me have a little talk with him."

He turns to the man, looks him over, smiles and says: "I know why you're not talking. You're afraid because you're not really an ordinary tomb robber are you?"

The man raises his eyes with a slight expression of surprise.

Qi Yuexuan thinks he's onto something, so he continues: "I'm no criminal, but I've known a few in my time. Tomb robbers are known as 'earth rats' and 'yellow weasels', and make their living digging and scouting tunnels. They know exactly how big they are just by looking at them, so how's one of them going to be as stupid as you and get stuck in a drain?"

This really hits home, and the man's face reddens. Qi Yuexuan strikes while the iron is hot: "What is more, the tomb-robbing gangs to the west of Beiping are all local men. The furthest afield they come from is Laiyuan, Laishui, Fangshan and Huailai. I've never heard of one coming from outside the Pass like you."

The man stares at him, open mouthed for a moment, then asks, haltingly: "How... how did you know... I'm from the northeast?"

"Ha!" Grandpa Fu interjects. "Just that sentence alone stinks of giant corn kernels.[1] Can you deny it?"

The man stiffens: "What's this crap about giant corn? When you lot speak as though you're being strangled, do you stink of white flour? It's no use you making fun of me, I'm not going to say another word."

Qi Yuexuan pats him on the back of the head and says: "Here, feel for yourself. The occipital ridge at the back of your skull here is flat as a coffin plank. You must be from beyond the Pass. You make your children lie on stone pillows from birth, and that's what causes this."

There is a gust of laughter in the room, and even the man himself can't help grinning as he feels the back of his skull for himself.

Qi Yuexuan stops smiling abruptly and goes on: "Look, I can see you're not a hardened criminal but come from a military background. You might as well speak and make a clean breast of it. Come on, what unit are you from?"

"I'm... I'm not from any unit... I'm a tomb robber."

"Alright then, let me ask you – how many mushrooms have you touched? Were they dry or wet? How many salt fish have you turned over? Have you seen any fire pits?"

"Eh? What does all that mean?"

"If you don't understand what I just said, you might as well stop play-acting. I was using tomb robber's slang. Any real robber would know it. Every profession has its own vocabulary. 'Mushrooms' are tombs, 'pits' are tomb chambers. If there's water inside them, they're 'wet', if there isn't, they're 'dry'. 'Fire pits' are tombs where the air is breathable, and 'salt fish' are corpses. This is just simple stuff. If I started talking about 'meat dumplings' and 'taking off the big hat', then you'd really look stupid."

Qi Yuexuan's familiarity with underworld slang leaves the man speechless as he knows he's a fraud who's come across the real thing. Even Grandpa Fu mutters that this Young Master must be related to Su Wukong, the Monkey King, the way he can change into anything he likes. In fact, there is nothing strange about this: from when he was little, Qi Yuexuan went to the Gioro clan academy in the Western Hills, and when he and his gang of friends had nothing else to do, they used to play in the tomb compounds. At that time, he had two attendants, Dong Fuxing and Third Brother Shen, who acted as bodyguard. One was like a social secretary, and the other was an old crook. Later on, the cricket expert Lao Zhang came out there from the Residence. He was practically a human insect himself, and had a whole basketful of stories, so Qi Yuexuan received an education in pretty much anything you can think of. Is any of it any use? Well, it's certainly given him a wide knowledge base.

"What? Still not going to talk?" Qi Yuexuan continues his questioning. "That's fine. To save trouble, we'll punish you as a real tomb robber. According to the ancient laws, that depends on which tomb is involved. In this case, do you know what the punishment is called? It's called 'being planted alive'."

Taking his cue, Grandpa Fu signals to his men and says, even more fiercely than Qi Yuexuan: "Right, be quick about it, but remember not to bury him completely. Leave his legs sticking out you stupid prick! Don't you understand how it works? You put traps between the legs, the legs attract the wolves and they get caught in the traps. Wolf meat is a little tough, but it's still food."

Two of Grandpa Fu's men hurry forward with some rope, but as soon as the man feels the hemp around his neck, he can't hold out any longer and begins to yell: "Don't! Don't! I'll talk! I'll talk! But... if I tell you the truth, will you let me go?"

"Bullshit! You haven't said anything yet, and you're trying to bargain? If you're a traitor, do you think I'm going to let you go?" Grandpa Fu says, putting on an air of great authority.

"No, no, I'm not a traitor. I'm a regular soldier from the Anti-Japanese Resistance Army."

"Ha! A regular soldier, are you? Show me your ID."

The man is about to speak, when one of Grandpa Fu's men comes running in.

"There's someone here, Commander," he says.

"Who is it? Who's come here at this time of night?"

"It's that Eighth Route Army man who gave us the ammunition."

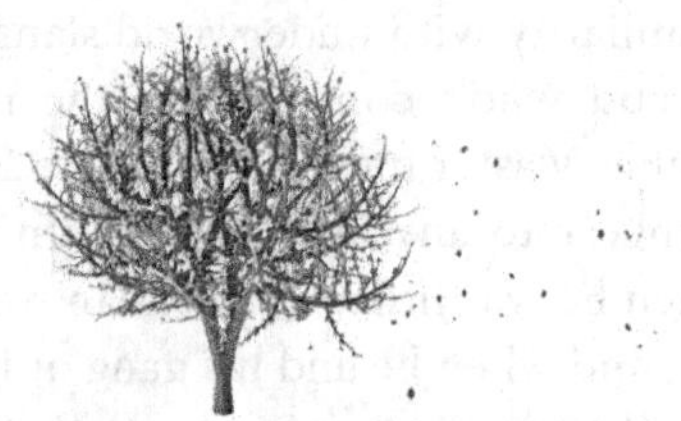

Chapter 38

The new arrival is indeed Captain Wu Xinmin of the Eighth Route Army. His arms outspread while he is still some distance away, he approaches them with a broad smile on his face.

"Aiya, Captain Wu! What are you doing coming here at this hour?" Grandpa Fu asks.

"Ah, well, if it wasn't something important, do you think I'd be playing the night owl like this?"

"Eh? What is it then?"

"I'll tell you in a bit," Wu Xinmin says pointing at the prisoner. "First, we've got to deal with this Japanese secret agent."

Everyone in the room is astonished. The man himself gasps in surprise, and he struggles to his feet, blurting out: "But Captain Wu, I... Aiya!"

Before he is properly on his feet, he gives a yelp of pain and falls back into the chair.

"Don't say any more," says Captain Wu, holding him down in his seat and glaring at him. "There's no use denying it. Your friend who escaped from here ran straight into our hands. He has confessed."

As he speaks, his hand pinches the man's shoulder in a secret signal. The man stops protesting his innocence and lowers his head.

"What? Do you know him?" Grandpa Fu lifts the man's chin to look at him, then glances at Wu Xinmin.

"No, I don't."

"If you don't, how did you know he's a captain and that his name is Wu?"

"Isn't... isn't that what you just called him?"

This stops Grandpa Fu in his tracks, and Wu Xinmin takes the opportunity to gesture towards the man: "Come here you two, and take him away."

Two Eighth Route Army soldiers, who have just appeared, step forward and support him away, one on either side.

"Wait! Wait!" Grandpa Fu glares at Wu Xinmin. "Why should we hand our prisoner over to you, Captain Wu?"

Wu Xinmin laughs. "We've caught one of them too, Commander Fucha. It will be easier to interrogate them together, won't it?"

"Then why don't you hand over your one to us?"

"We're allies, aren't we? What does 'yours' or 'mine' matter? You're not an expert in interrogating spies like me, and if I get anything out of them, I'll give you every detail. Is that alright?"

Grandpa Fu really doesn't want to agree, but he can't think what to do next, so he surreptitiously tugs at Qi Yuexuan's sleeve. To his surprise, Qi Yuexuan laughs carelessly and says: "Oh, I think we should give the man to Captain Wu."

"Eh?" says Grandpa Fu. "Why have you suddenly changed sides?"

"Who's changed sides? You should think about it." As he is speaking, he pats Grandpa Fu's arm and returns his own secret signal.

Grandpa Fu realises Qi Yuexuan has some plan in mind, so he doesn't say anything more. Then he hears Qi Yuexuan say, with a smile: "You seem to be more involved in this business than we are. Why did the one who got away run straight into your arms? Tell me about the secret script for this play. Who is the scholar and who is the soldier? Who's got to sing and who's got to fight? You've got it all worked out, haven't you? I'm right, aren't I, Captain Wu?"

Captain Wu picks up on the barb in these words, but he has to make the best of it since he can't contradict what's being said. So he responds awkwardly: "Ha ha, you give me too much credit. It was just coincidence today, that's all."

"They're all yours, Captain Wu. You can even have the dead one, but we'll keep the two guns they dropped."

"No problem," Wu Xinmin replies promptly.

Qi Yuexuan purses his lips in a knowing smile: "Alright then, you hurry up and invite your secret agent outside so you can get your story straight."

Wu Xinmin nods and heads for the door with the man, saying: "The reason I came today was to invite you to fight with us in the big battle."

"What big battle? Where? If it's too far away, we're not going," Grandpa Fu says ill-temperedly.

"Right here."

"In Jiangou?"

"Ha! There are only a dozen or so of the devils in Jiangou. Do you think they're any obstacle? We'll sweep them up in passing. The real target is Longjiazhuang at the southern foot of the mountain."

"How many men does the Eighth Route Army have?" Qi Yuexuan asks.

"Just my one brigade, three hundred men."

"That's too few. Can't you call up some reinforcements?"

Wu Xinmin shakes his head. "Song and Deng's brigades have already moved into the east of Hebei. West of Beiping, there are only our five brigades of regular soldiers, just over two thousand men. Now we're breaking out in all four directions, everyone's got their own job to do. Anyway, even though Longjiazhuang is the main

Japanese base in the area, it's only got a squadron garrisoned there. If you take the outpost at Jiangou and the lookout on the main peak at Huijidong together, there are only two hundred men. You have two hundred men, don't you? If we join together, we'll outnumber the devils three to one, and we'll have no trouble in the battle."

At this point, he smiles awkwardly and goes on: "The truth is, it's not certain that there aren't any reinforcements. On the south side of the Yongding River there are newly formed and newly recruited local militia, but unlike you, they're attached to the Eighth Route Army. There's loads of loot to be had in Longjiazhuang because this is a thriving area with all kinds of businesses. If we take it, there'll be a lot of fatty pork to throw in the pot, enough for everyone to have a few mouthfuls. So do you see now why Commander Zhao stationed you here and wants you to fight this battle with us?"

"Ha ha! Yes, I understand, I understand," Grandpa Fu says, then goes on in eager agreement: "This battle is as good as won. When we fought at Wulituo, we took on more than a hundred devils on our own and still won."

But Qi Yuexuan contradicts him: "That was an ambush. They ran straight into a brick wall and knocked themselves out. This is a frontal attack on Longjiazhuang against Japanese blockhouses and other fortifications. It's not the same thing at all. Even if there's only a squadron of the devils, they're better equipped, better trained, and their blockhouses and fortifications will only serve to increase that superiority. We don't have any heavy artillery..."

"So, according to you, we can't win this battle?" Wu Xinmin retorts angrily.

"Whether we can win it or not depends on how we fight. If you try to take them head on, there will be a lot of casualties, and even if you win, in the end, I'm afraid it will be a miserable kind of victory."

"There are always casualties in war. But I'm no novice when it comes to battles, and I've already got a plan for how we're going to fight it. See what you think – the Eighth Route Army will take out the base at Jiangou and the lookout post at Huijidong, and our main objective will be Miaofengshan Township."

"And what about us?"

"You will mount an attack from the south, and if you break through, you advance further in. If you're being held, then make a feint to draw out the enemy, and if you can keep them pinned down, you'll have done your job. Anything that's captured, we split seventy-thirty. You get thirty. How does that sound?"

Qi Yuexuan considers this in silence, so Grandpa Fu jumps in: "No, that's no good. How can you give us only thirty per cent. That's not fair."

"If you think it's unfair, we'll swap the assignments around, and you get seventy and we'll take thirty."

"Swap or not, we..."

"Don't get carried away with yourself," interjects Qi Yuexuan. "We'll follow Captain Wu's suggestions for who does what." He turns to Wu Xinmin and asks with a smile: "As for the loot, how does this sound to you? We keep it strictly fair and meritocratic. Whoever seizes something, keeps it..."

"No, no, that won't do," says Grandpa Fu, shaking his head vigorously. "If our attack is only a feint, what chance will we get to seize anything? We're guaranteed to lose out."

Qi Yuexuan glares at him coldly. "Didn't Captain Wu say that, if we break through, we are to advance into enemy territory? If we put making a feint out of our minds, we are too good not to break through."

Captain Wu laughs in approval of this sentiment.

Grandpa Fu is not entirely happy with this, but he knows how crafty Qi Yuexuan is, so he keeps quiet. Qi Yuexuan turns to Wu Xinmin and asks: "When are you going to make your move?"

"Four o'clock in the morning, the day after tomorrow. Everyone at the same time. It's not just us, either. One division, in concert with a large force of guerrilla fighters, will mount a simultaneous sneak attack on the county town of Wanping and the power plant at Shijingshan."

"Alright, but Miaofengshan Township is only ten *li* or so from the Japanese base at Junzhuangzhen, and you still need to guard against them sending reinforcements. However you look at it, we have to deploy troops to stop support coming along the road east of the township. Otherwise, if they do get through, we'll find ourselves attacked from the rear."

Wu Xinmin disagrees good humouredly: "Well, when they're being attacked from all different directions, the Japanese will be at full stretch and won't dare detach reinforcements. Now we all have our respective positions..."

"It's still better to be safe than sorry."

"Well, in that case... how about we advance the attack on Jiangou and Huijidong by half an hour? Once they've taken the outpost, they can advance across the slope under the temple and put defences in place. It won't take long to knock out the dozen or so devils in the outpost, and then it's only five or six *li* to the main highway. It would take the devils in Junzhuangzhen two hours or more to get reinforcements there, whatever route they take."

Qi Yuexuan doesn't have much confidence in this plan, but he knows the situation is urgent, so he nods reluctantly.

ONCE THEY'VE SEEN Wu Xinmin and his men off, Qi Yuexuan and Grandpa Fu take their own party back to Qiwangfen. On the way, Qi Yuexuan remains deep in silence, his brows furrowed, without any sign of his former animation. Grandpa Fu has not understood much of what Qi Yuexuan has said and done tonight, and seeing him like this disturbs him, so he explodes in fury.

"Pah! You're a piece of work, aren't you! Letting things go on a nod and a wink, and talking in riddles to me. Now it's just the two of us, are you still going to keep me in the dark? What exactly are you plotting? And why did you let them take that man away?"

"Well, he was one of them anyway."

"What? Didn't Captain Wu call him a Japanese agent?"

"He had to say that so he could get the man away."

"So what were those three men doing here in the first place?"

"They were after the goods in those tombs, weren't they!"

"If you knew that, why didn't you expose them?"

"Ai! What's the most important thing right now? It's fighting the Japanese. They are fighting the Japanese, so they are our allies. We've already killed one of them and wounded another. Not a great start! They are at sixes and sevens themselves, and already suffering, so why should we want to add to their distress and fall out with them now?"

"Ha! That may be so, but didn't you say the Eighth Route Army has strict rules of discipline? Why are they allowing this kind of despicable business to go on?"

"If it had official permission, do you think we would have had all this cloak and dagger stuff? I think that Commander Zhao's decision to station us here was all part of his devious plot. Remember, this lot were forced to join the Eighth Route Army, but their loyalty still lies elsewhere. I'm pretty sure there's a parting of the way on the cards."

"Hmm, yes, I can see that, but we're not party to their internal affairs, so what's that got to do with us?"

"A lot! I think the only reason they've wormed their way into associating with us is to secure their line of retreat. Getting us to station ourselves at Qiwangfen was all part of it. Since they joined the Eighth Route Army, they've got to observe the restrictions imposed by the Communist Party. They can't just come here any old how and open up the prince's tomb. But the various tombs in the lesser compound at the bottom of the mountain are those of the stepsons and step-grandsons of Prince Fu. They were distinguished royalty in their time, and the goods buried with them would not be inconsiderable. Where else is such easy money to be found? Once a cat has tasted fish, fish is all it can think about, isn't it? They can't go in openly, so they've decided to do it by stealth. And there we are, stationed halfway up the mountain, the perfect scapegoats. Today wasn't their main attempt at the tombs, it was almost certainly just an exploratory outing, but they didn't expect us to have posted lookouts at the bottom of the mountain. Do you see now?"

Grandpa Fu finally gets the picture, and he can't hold back an exclamation of wonder as he nods in understanding. Then he asks: "If you know all this so clearly, why are we going to cooperate with them?"

"We're not cooperating with them in tomb robbery, we're cooperating with them in fighting the Japanese. We haven't actually joined them either, so let's fight this battle and see. If we can join with them, we will. If we can't, we'll go back to the Left Barracks. After today's lesson, they may pull their horns in a little."

"Alright, but are you sure about this battle? Or are you still holding something back from me? Come on, spit it out! What's the real plan?"

"We have to outwit them, not just attack head-on."

"Outwit them how?"

"We have to infiltrate them, so we're attacking from inside and outside at the same time."

"How are we going to do that?"

Qi Yuexuan doesn't reply immediately, and Grandpa Fu begins to get impatient: "Well? Say something."

"Why are you getting agitated? Do you think I'm not going to tell you, once I've worked it out?"

"What? You mean you haven't got a plan yet? And you still want to take charge?"

"Calm down, calm down. Let me have a proper think about it. I already have the medicine. I just need the right primer." He stops there and goes back inside without looking back.

Grandpa Fu realises with a start that it is already six in the morning. Still trying to work out what Qi Yuexuan means by a primer for the medicine, he hurries after him to ask. But as soon as he enters the room, he sees Hao Bingchen, who has just brought his grain up the mountain.

Before Grandpa Fu can say anything, Qi Yuexuan bursts out laughing: "Ha ha! No need to look for the primer for the medicine any more. Mr Hao has brought it to us."

"Eh?" Grandpa Fu exclaims in astonished incomprehension.

Hao Bingchen is baffled too: "What's that? Medicine? Primer? I've brought you some grain..."

"I know it's grain. I'm not deaf. It's eight cartloads of grain." Qi Yuexuan signals to Grandpa Fu: "Why aren't you setting all the men to work taking the grain down the mountain? I don't need that much for my primer, so just leave half a cartload behind. What are you still gawping at? You can't make an omelette without breaking some eggs. If we don't dangle something decent, how are we going to get into Longjiazhuang?"

Grandpa Fu finally recovers his senses: "Ah! So that's what you've been puzzling over – what to use as bait."

"That's right."

"So, if Mr Hao hadn't brought the grain, you would have been stumped then."

"What do you mean, stumped? If Brother Hao hadn't brought the grain, then I would have trussed you up, put a halter round your neck and told them we'd captured a senior Japanese officer. But I'm afraid you wouldn't have been as attractive as the grain."

Seeing Grandpa Fu's outraged look, Qi Yuexuan can't help giving a great shout of laughter.

. . .

Longjiazhuang is situated at the southern foot of Miaofengshan and is home to more than two hundred families, which makes it a large village in terms of the area west of Beiping. It has some history to it, too. The local people say that, in ancient times, an emperor came by that way, but no one has any clear idea of when this happened, which dynasty or which emperor. The only thing they know is that this emperor's horse was spooked when he was riding along the banks of the river near Longjiazhuang. The animal galloped headlong for a good five *li*, until someone managed to haul it to a stop at the entrance to the village. From then on, that western stretch of riverbank became known as Liangjiatan, meaning 'startled horse strand', which later got changed to Dingjiatan. Moreover, the place where the horse was pulled up was called Longjiazhuang, which means 'pulling up horse village'. At some point, the first character 拢 (*lǒng*) was changed to another character 陇 pronounced the same way, which is a shorthand name for Gansu Province.

Longjiazhuang is surrounded by mountains on three sides, with a river on the fourth. Four *li* to the north is Danlicun, two *li* to the east is Xiehejian and five *li* to the west is Dingjiatan. If you go half a *li* to the south you come to Shuiyuzui next to the Yongding River, and crossing the river brings you to the ancient road connecting Beiping and Shanxi. This road has been there since Jin and Liao times, and in those days it was a major official highway. Even today it remains the most convenient route from Beiping to Wangping, Yanchi and Zhaitang, so the village is still an important boundary marker. Not long after the Japanese entered Beiping, they sent a large force of men on a mission to suppress insurgents, and made this village the centre of operations for the area around Miaofengshan in order to defend against and contain the resistance militia deep in the mountains.

A squadron of around 180 Japanese soldiers from an A-Class Division are stationed in Longjiazhuang. The Japanese have surrounded the village with a barbed wire fence, outside which is a defensive moat three metres across and three metres deep. Everywhere inside the fence are additional fortifications and machinegun posts. Soldiers are stationed at the northern and southern entrances to the village, where there are also small blockhouses. The gates are protected by triple rows of barbed wire and three sentry beats, so the whole village is very heavily guarded. There is a Christian church in the middle of the village, which the Japanese have turned into a barracks for the main squadron and another small detachment.

Since the village is on an essential trade route between Beiping and the mountainous interior, it has historically been a trading post and distribution centre for domestic and foreign trade. In the old days, markets were held on the tenth, twentieth and thirtieth days of each lunar month, such as the Miaofengshan Temple fair, and businesses from all over the place came and set up stalls here. The fair ran for several days, and they were very lucrative occasions. After the arrival of the Japanese, the markets no longer operate, but there are still a number of shops and restaurants open on the streets, as well as quite a few itinerant traders. On the afternoon in question, a large truck, fully loaded with hemp sacks, arrives at the south gate of Longjiazhuang. Sitting in the driver's cab are the driver himself, Hao Bingchen, and his underling, Changzi.

Hao Bingchen is different from Gao Guigeng in that he has been working in military intelligence since the days of the China Reconstruction Society, and he really doesn't want to get involved in this particular military operation. For one thing, the rules of military intelligence are very strict, and one is not permitted to take any action without permission, and he already has the assignment to distribute the fake Japanese army issue notes. He is afraid that this new action will delay the completion of his original task. For another thing, he has misgivings about working with the Eighth Route Army, and he is even more afraid that these suspicions may be passed on. Although the Kuomintang and Communists are currently allied in fighting the Japanese, and the Eighth Route Army is lined up with the National Army, he well knows the history of enmity between the two parties and is even more familiar with the caution with which President Chiang and his own boss, Dai Li, treat the Communist Party and the Eighth Route Army. At first, President Chiang proposed to the Communists that their two parties should unite into one, but this idea was rejected. Over time, the wariness and distrust grows with each passing day, as the Eighth Route Army penetrates behind enemy lines, rapidly increasing in strength and establishing a broad base of operations. The central apparatus of military intelligence has long grasped the importance of the Eighth Route Army as an intelligence-gathering agent behind enemy lines. Since Hao Bingchen is very clear about all this, it is hardly surprising he is caught in two minds. But in the end, he is unable to resist Qi Yuexuan's blandishments and the way he plays on his feelings of shame and self-respect. Bearing in mind that he has come alone, so word is unlikely to get back to his superiors, he finally gives his consent. Even so, he still has some conditions, and he will only take responsibility for driving the truck into Longjiazhuang, and he will not participate in the fighting. In fact, this is exactly what Qi Yuexuan has been hoping for; what he is worried about is actually getting into the village, and he really has no expectation of Hao Bingchen and Changzi charging into the enemy lines.

THE JAPANESE GUARD at the south gate is very much on the alert: "You are up to doing what?"

Hao Bingchen jumps down from the truck, takes off his hat and bows deeply: "We are from the Yanjing Christian Association, Taijun."

"What things are on truck?"

"Grain. It's a gift from Mr Charlie at Yanjing University to the church here in the village. Look, here is his hand-written letter to Reverend Sherlock."

The sentry takes the letter through the barbed wire fence, opens it and looks at it uncomprehendingly, since it is written in English, and he can't read a word of it.

"What written here?"

"It's very simple. Translated into Chinese, it reads: 'I know the church is short of grain, so I have specially commissioned some priests and brothers in Christ to come and help you through the spring shortage. If the Japanese garrison is also in need, you can use your discretion to offer them a portion of fine grain as a token of your appreciation.'"

"This is what an American say?"

"Yes, that's right."

The sentry grins broadly: "Yoshi! America is also afraid of our great Japanese Empire!"

"That's right, that's right. America is not at war with Japan. They're neutral, neutral," Hao Bingchen says fawningly.

"But you wait. I go make report."

It's not long before the sentry comes running back and says: "Captain say he get church man come take you in. Send Imperial Army grain to squadron."

After about ten minutes, a Japanese soldier arrives at the south gate leading a priest. The priest is a man of about forty, short, with a sallow, wizened appearance that makes him look very unlike a Westerner. He approaches, takes the letter and reads it, then smiles and bows slightly. He asks something in English, and Hao Bingchen replies in the same language, also smiling. The strange-sounding questions and answers go on for several rounds, and, in fact, they are only exchanging some standard courtesies.

"Hello," the priest says. "I'm Reverend Sherlock. And you are..."

"I'm a member of staff at Yanjing University. My name is Hao, Hao Bingchen. Are... are you Chinese too?"

"No, I'm Malaysian. I understand Chinese, but here it is better for us to use English."

"Yes, I agree."

"Mr Hao, I have known Mr Charlie by reputation for a long time, but I do not know him personally. What has made him think of sending my little church a gift of grain?"

"Mr Charlie is also a committee member of the Christian Association, and they are probably the ones who organised it. Of course, if you already have enough grain, and you don't want it, then I'll take it back."

"No, no, no, please don't misunderstand me. I'm just a little flabbergasted and rather embarrassed. Grain is as valuable as gold beans at the moment, of course we need it. We are all brothers in Christ, so I will stop these meaningless pleasantries and let us give thanks to God."

So saying, Reverend Sherlock makes the sign of the cross on his breast, then turns and asks the Japanese soldier in Chinese: "This is a gift of grain for us from the Christian Association. Please let them in."

"There is no problems?"

"No problems at all."

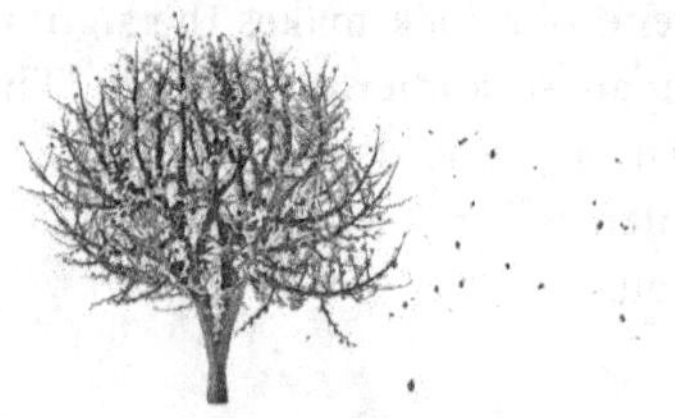

Chapter 39

The church in Longjiazhuang was built in the twentieth year of the reign of Guangxu (1894), and its first priest was the American, Halliday. Only a few years after its establishment, in the twenty-sixth year of Guangxu, it was burnt down by the Boxers on their way into Beijing from Hebei, and Halliday died under their swords. After that, when the Eight-Nation Alliance took Beijing and forced the Qing government to sign the Boxer Protocol, the church was rebuilt under the direct supervision of the *yamen* of Wanping County. Not only did they make the church building as good as new, they also built a separate barracks block behind it. The Qing court garrisoned it with several dozen troops from the artillery barracks in the Haidian District of Beijing, with a view to protecting the church against local anti-foreigner mobs, guarding the northern end of the road up Miaofengshan and patrolling Shuiyuzui to the south, on the old road that followed the banks of the Yongding River. After the fall of the Qing dynasty, these barracks were ungarrisoned, and although they were not officially church property, they ended up being used by it. At its height, the church had more than a dozen clergy and a congregation of more than a thousand. When the Japanese Army established a presence on Miaofengshan, and after they made Longjiazhuang their base in the area, the rear courtyard returned to being a barracks. The front courtyard was church property, and they didn't dare occupy it, but they did block up the passageway between the two yards and put barbed wire on top of the perimeter wall. Most of the clergy scattered, and now only Reverend Sherlock and two Chinese priests are remaining. Even including the handymen, the total staff is down to five.

After unloading a few sacks of grain and sending them to the main gate, Reverend Sherlock goes up to Hao Bingchen, looks him over, smiles wryly and asks: "Well, Mr Hao... who exactly are you?"

Hao Bingchen laughs and plays dumb: "Didn't I just say? And you've read Mr Charlie's letter. Don't you believe us?"

"Ha! I don't think I'm being over-suspicious. It's just too unbelievable."

"How so?"

"I'll tell you the whole story. For reasons of safety, the Church Assembly long ago moved all the clerical personnel from the churches around Beiping into the church in the city itself, leaving behind only a few caretakers. Here, for example, there's just five of us in total. The dozen or so others all left in turn and became refugees. The Church Assembly is very short of grain, and a few days ago they ordered me to think of ways of getting some more. Why would they be sending me grain now? I'm not a close acquaintance of Mr Charlie, but I do know he is an outstanding English calligrapher, and that letter is not in his handwriting. I'm afraid it's not just corn you've got on that truck." Reverend Sherlock keeps his voice low, but he speaks with great emphasis.

Hao Bingchen's face falls, and he eyes the priest sharply.

"So... why didn't you expose me just now?"

"How could I?" says Reverend Sherlock, smiling. "How can a servant of God side with Satan? I am Malaysian, but my forebears were Chinese from Fujian."

So saying, he quickly looks round and approaches more closely, smiling at the suspicious-looking Changzi. Hao Bingchen hurriedly shoots a meaningful glance at his subordinate, then his taut expression relaxes a little: "Your eyes see a lot, Reverend Sherlock. But please don't worry. Whatever happens, I can guarantee the personal safety of your people."

"So you are..."

"It's best you don't know."

"Then you are going to..."

"It's best you know nothing at all." Hao Bingchen falls silent, then signals to Changzi and the truck driver: "Hurry up and unload."

The two men acknowledge the order, and in no time, with one on the back of the truck and the other below, several sacks of grain are piled up on the ground by the truck. Reverend Sherlock is rooted to the spot in astonishment, as several of the sacks at the bottom and in the middle of the heap that remain in the truck suddenly sit up of their own accord. Before he can gather his wits, six men emerge from the sacks and jump down from the truck. As well as their own weapons, they also unload two machineguns and a sack of hand grenades. It is now apparent that there is an empty space in among the sacks and that the lorry is quite simply a Chinese Trojan horse.

"Listen up, everyone," Hao Bingchen orders in a low voice. "Gather all the church people in one room, leave someone to watch them and make sure no one leaves before the action starts..."

"Mr Hao," Reverend Sherlock says excitedly, "my people and I are all on your side. We're friends..."

"It's precisely because of that, that I don't want to implicate you," Hao Bingchen responds. "No matter whether our operation succeeds or not, if you are acting under duress you can't be blamed. So it's best you know nothing. Now, you go with them and help them gather your people together, and whatever you do, make sure you don't leave anyone behind."

When he hears this explanation, Reverend Sherlock finally nods in understanding.

AT THREE FORTY-FIVE IN THE MORNING, almost simultaneously, the sound of gunfire and explosions can be heard coming from the main peak of Miaofengshan and from Jiangou. The noise lasts less than ten minutes from beginning to end, then silence falls again. Soon after it becomes quiet again, pandemonium erupts from the soldiers at the village walls with shouts, curses and the sound of whistles and running feet. Mixed up in all this there also comes the clanging of bells. Other people can only hear the noises but can't see what is going on. Only Hao Bingchen and his men, who have climbed up into the rafters of the church, can watch the hubbub that is unfolding below, through the gable windows. Although the church is only one storey high, that storey is as tall as two in a normal building. Looking down from the ceiling, all the Japanese troops' activities below are within their field of vision. They pierce some holes in the roof from the inside so they can climb out onto the roof itself.

Hao Bingchen has advance instructions not to participate in the military action himself, and he intends only to see all the arrangements in place before decamping. That at least is the plan, but now the moment has come, how is he supposed just to turn and leave without climbing out on the roof to yell his encouragement and do his bit? He hesitates for a long moment, then grits his teeth and stays. After all, a general is at liberty to make his own decisions when his lord is not on the battlefield, and he is fighting the Japanese. He throws caution to the wind with a clear conscience. He orders the detachment of men from the Left Barracks to sneak up on the Japanese fortifications in the east of Longjiazhuang to support the men outside the village in their attack. He leaves two men with a machinegun on the church roof to hold that commanding position and pin down the enemy and stop them from bringing up reinforcements.

The Japanese soldiers in the barracks assemble and form ranks, preparing to go in support of their comrades on the main peak and at Jiangou, but before the squadron commander can even open his mouth, gunfire erupts from both north and south; nor is it even at any distance, as it is coming from the north and south gates of the village. Moreover, the stealthy new arrivals considerably outnumber the soldiers in the barracks, and amid the sounds of massed gunfire and explosions can be heard shouted orders and battle cries. Confusion reigns among the Japanese, and for a moment, even their officers don't know what to do.

Eventually, the squadron commander braces himself and barks out an order for his troops to reform immediately from their confusion and check that their weapons are all ready for use. He turns and is about to head for his office to telephone the other command centres to inform them of the enemy action. But before he can take a step, a gunshot rings out, his body sways and he falls to the ground. Before any of the others can collect their senses, the chatter of machinegun fire opens up, and a torrent of bullets rains in on them, followed immediately by the explosions of hand grenades, one after the other, so that the whole courtyard is enveloped in fire and smoke. As the smoke disperses, it reveals a scene of total confusion, littered with Japanese bodies. But these are crack troops: if they cannot reach the cover of the barrack room, the survivors either flatten themselves on the ground or take cover in the angles of the walls, and they begin to fight back. Those inside the main hall seal off the latticework windows and keep their heads down. All Hao Bingchen can do is lob a few more grenades into the courtyard, and under cover of the explosions, send three men up onto the roofs, where they take cover behind the curtain wall and use the advantage of height to continue the attack.

At this moment, the commander of the army from the Left Barracks leads his men in an attack on the eastern flank of the village. First, several of his men take out the sentry post, using only knives and rocks as weapons so the Japanese outer defences are taken without a shot being heard. Next, they rush another sentry post thirty metres or so away and open fire with a burst from a machinegun and a single grenade, knocking it out without any further noise. Then, twenty or thirty human figures can suddenly be seen rising out of the darkness and rushing forward carrying a duckboard formed by lashing several tree trunks together, along with bundles and sacks of rice straw. As soon as the duckboard has been laid across the defensive moat, and the bundles and sacks of straw have been leant up against the barbed wire, a voice can be heard shouting: "Up and over, brothers!"

The darkness begins to heave as, one by one, the men surge across the moat and barbed wire. The Japanese in the sentry posts on either side open fire. Some of the men fall, but their advance is not halted. The insurgents and the men giving cover from outside the village concentrate their fire and soon have the better of the enemy. In less than ten minutes, from beginning to end, all the men of the Left Barracks are inside Longjiazhuang. They divide into two parties, with one heading for the south gates of the village and the other heading straight for the Japanese squadron.

QI YUEXUAN HIMSELF is not among the main attacking force, as, at this moment, he is leading thirty or forty men in a feint at the blockhouse at the south gate. Despite being few in number, they are making a lot of noise. Although they do not press home the attack, the sound of their gunfire is more than fierce enough. In fact, apart from their rifles, they only have one machinegun, and the rest of the din comes from the strings of firecrackers they let off inside tinplate tubes. Nothing can be seen in the darkness, and the sound is sufficiently similar to machinegun fire to fool the Japanese into believing they are genuinely under attack from a large force, pouring concentrated fire into them. As Qi Yuexuan listens to the growing storm of battle in the village, he can't help smiling to himself, as he realises the coordinated plans he has laid have come together, and the feint to the east to cover the attack from the west has been successful. The Japanese defences have been principally designed to meet an attack from the outside, while inside, the place is effectively defenceless. All the attackers have to do is fight their way in, and victory is within their grasp. He orders the men to concentrate their fire to cover the approach of the explosives team. Their attack is no longer a feint, but a full-on assault. It is part of a pincer movement, and the time has come for both sides to press home with all their might. Just as Qi Yuexuan anticipates, after another forty minutes, they see the Japanese flag being hauled down on top of the blockhouse, set on fire and waved vigorously at those outside, as a voice shouts: "Don't shoot! We're on your side. The blockhouse is taken."

Once Qi Yuexuan has led the charge of his men into the village, it becomes clear that most of the Japanese devils have been annihilated, with only ten or fifteen of them escaping into the streets through a side gate. A detachment is sent after them, and they pin them down in some of the local shops.

WHILE EVERYTHING is going according to plan on this side of the village, the Eighth Route Army soldiers at the north gate are having a much tougher time. The blockhouse there is much bigger than the one at the south gate; it also has an additional storey and its surrounding defences are much more solid. To make it easier to support the lookouts on Miaofengshan and the command post at Jiangou, the devils stationed here are an augmented squad. A platoon of infantry, four machineguns, a mortar team and three small field guns are augmented by a heavy machinegun team and an artillery team. They are outfitted with two heavy machineguns and a mountain gun,[1] so their infantry strength and firepower considerably exceed the norm for that kind of squadron. The truth is that Captain Wu Xinmin's actual strength is inadequate for the task, but he overestimates it and blindly tries to force his way in. After several unsuccessful attempts, his casualties are mounting alarmingly. As he listens to the sounds of fighting inside the village getting louder and louder, he realises that the men from the Heroic Army of the Left Barracks have already fought their way in. He doesn't know how they have done it, but he can't bear the loss of face. The chips are really down now, and he is backed into a corner. Even so, how can he possibly retreat at this point? He grits his teeth and is about to launch another major assault, when Commissioner Lin stops him, saying that he can't attack like that, as the casualties would be too high and it's simply not worth it. He offers another idea: the village is in a wind tunnel with the wind blowing directly at the blockhouse, so why not use it to mount a fire attack. The truth is, Captain Wu has been relying on the fact that he is a trusted aide of Commander Zhao Ran; he has never paid much attention to the commissioner assigned by the government to accompany the military, and he has acted as a law unto himself. But now he is flush out of ideas, he has no alternative but to listen to the man.

MANY HANDS MAKE LIGHT WORK, and it is not long before there are more than a hundred bundles of tree branches and thorn twigs ready and waiting. Under covering fire, twenty or thirty men load the bundles of firewood on their backs and crawl forwards, making their way, inch by inch, up to the enemy fortifications. They light the bundles when they are still thirty or forty paces away. In case the firewood doesn't burn, and lacking any petrol, they have sprinkled the bundles with gunpowder, so they do indeed catch immediately. A gust of the mountain wind makes the smoke and flames leap up right in front of the enemy, blinding and choking them. The command to attack rings out, and the Eighth Route Army soldiers mount a ragged charge. The Japanese firepower is still fierce, but how can they see to aim properly amid the smoke and flames? All they can do is fire blindly. The front line of the attackers who have thrown themselves to the ground take out their grenades and hurl them, using the cover of their explosions to leap to their feet and advance. Before the enemy can regain their senses, they are in among them and fierce hand-to-hand combat breaks out. At the same moment, the machinegunners on top of the blockhouse stop firing as they can no longer make out who is who, and they lose their nerve and hold fire. Presumably at the order of some officer or other, the machineguns then open up again, firing indiscriminately as they sweep they battlefield. But it is already too late, as, taking advantage of the previous interruption to the machineguns, the Eighth Route Army soldiers are already thronging round the base of the blockhouse, where they throw a few grenades in through the loopholes. The sound of the explosions can be heard, and the attackers charge into the blockhouse yelling their battle cries.

THE SKY IS JUST GETTING LIGHT as Qi Yuexuan leads his men up to the Japanese barracks in the middle of the village. Once in the courtyard, they hear Grandpa Fu's voice shouting: "Close up, brothers, and be careful. We waded through blood and risked our lives to get here, so let's not let a good thing slip out of our hands now."

On seeing Qi Yuexuan, he greets him with a laugh: "Well, Great General, I think we can call this a total success. You are better than..."

"Stop that!" Qi Yuexuan gestures at him, deliberately cutting him off short. "Shelve the flattery and speak slowly. How many casualties have we taken?"

Grandpa Fu gives him a keen look, and he says in a serious tone: "I haven't... I haven't got the exact numbers, but at a rough estimate, I would say, the casualties aren't too great. No more than twenty dead, and, excluding flesh wounds, another five or six badly wounded."

"And that... that counts as not too great?" Qi Yuexuan glares at him.

"Well, it's not a real battle without casualties. Look at how many Japanese devils we killed, and tell me it wasn't worth it."

"What I'm telling you is that you need to rethink your calculations. All our casualties are your kinsmen and fellow countrymen, so are you comfortable in the knowledge that every time you look up you will see widows and orphans? Do you actually still want to go home?"

Grandpa Fu's eyes bulge, but he doesn't say anything. Hao Bingchen limps up to him and says: "What Yuexuan is saying, Commander Fucha, is that it's lucky you came when you did, when there weren't that many devils left. Otherwise, fighting the way you were, your men would certainly have been risking their lives in vain."

Grandpa Fu is aware that Hao Bingchen knows what he is talking about, and he doesn't dare answer back. To Hao's surprise, it is Qi Yuexuan who comes up with a riposte: "Ha! We may not have fought that well, but it was still better than you and your government troops."

"Eh? Why are you turning on me now?"

"I say one should treat one's soldiers like one's children, and you disagree. But you're the odd one out here. You're the only one actually working for the government."

"You really are a piece of work! Here we are fighting your battle for you and risking our lives for you, and when we meet, you can't be bothered to thank us or even ask about our casualties! Instead..."

"Stop right there! Let's just be clear about who is helping who. We are a people's army, and aren't the people the country's clenched fist, its backbone... even its buttocks, here? You? You keep your fists behind your back and leave us with our arses exposed, and you still have the nerve to say you're helping us? If you really want to talk about help, then it's us who are helping you. Helping you and your Eighth Route Army save face, helping you play the hero, helping you satisfy your craving to fight the Japanese."

As he finishes this speech, Qi Yuexuan laughs and Grandpa Fu joins in too. Hao Bingchen shakes his head resignedly: "Listen to you, still playing the pedantic scholar. You just get more and more pretentious. Aiya!" He suddenly cries out and grimaces in pain.

"What's the matter? Are you injured?" Qi Yuexuan gives him an arm to lean on.

"No," Hao Bingchen laughs. "I twisted my ankle getting down from the roof."

Qi Yuexuan immediately crouches down and takes Hao Bingchen's shoe and sock off. He can see that the ankle is badly swollen. He feels all round it, then relaxes a bit.

"No bones broken. You've just sprained the ligaments." He stands up and says to Grandpa Fu: "Hurry up and get all the wounded down here, and take Mr Hao with you. Bring any of the Japanese who want to come, but we can't do anything about the others for the moment. Bring all the guns and ammunition we've seized, but leave everything else. It will just get in the way."

Grandpa Fu laughs disapprovingly: "Ha! Alright, I'll gather up the wounded at once, but I'm not leaving any of the plunder behind. If it was useful to those devils, then it's useful to us too. Aren't the Eighth Routers bearing the brunt of the fighting? I can hear them exchanging fire with the Japanese, so we've got plenty of time."

Before Qi Yuexuan can reply, a man comes running in: "Commander, Mr Qi, there are two men from the Eighth Route Army here asking to see whoever's in command."

"We won't see them," Grandpa Fu grunts. "Tell them we're not here and don't let them into the courtyard."

"What are you up to?" Qi Yuexuan asks urgently.

"What do you think they want here? It's bound to be because they think they've been short-changed on the plunder and are looking for more."

"Listen to you, you country monyebags!" Qi Yuexuan is caught between anger and mirth, and he heads out of the room without another word.

From behind his back, Grandpa Fu's words still carry to him: "You need to keep your lip buttoned, but if you can't, at least delay them for half an hour... Zhuzi, hurry up and bring some horses and carts to get the wounded and any weapons and ammunition away from here. Load up everything you can, and the men can carry the rest. Hurry up about it, they've come to steal our supplies."

Qi Yuexuan ignores him, but before he is even out of the door, he sees two Eighth Route Army men hurrying into the courtyard. At the sight of him, one of them, who looks like a Party cadre, hurries over.

"I am the political commissar of the Ninth Division, Lin Ke."

This Commissar Lin doesn't waste time on courtesies, and he gets straight to the point.

"I have come to notify your honourable company that the Japanese reinforcements will be here soon, and they are not just coming from Junzhuang, but from Bei'anhe too. Hurry up and organise your retreat, or you'll be too late."

"Didn't you send a detachment to stop them? I thought I heard shooting coming from the east."

"Ah, the answer to that is too shaming, and I'd rather not talk about it. The fact is, we didn't send anyone."

"What? But it was all agreed..."

"Well, we originally had two small detachments ready to take Jiangou, then immediately go on to stand guard over the southern Incense Road. But Captain Wu personally changed the plan, and the detachments never went. He only sent two lookouts."

"So where did the two detachments go?"

"That I don't know, but the lookouts have just reported that the enemy forces are no more than four or five *li* from Longjiazhuang."

"What kind of treachery is this?" Qi Yuexuan explodes with anger. "Fighting a war isn't like running a household. You can't just change things as you please. Where is Captain Wu now? I..."

"I'm afraid he is already leading the withdrawal," says a red-faced Commissar Lin. "We of the Fifth Brigade are new in the Eighth Route Army, and there are some internal affairs I can't discuss. But you don't need to worry, now we are part of the Eighth Route, we're not going to go back to being one man's private army. I'll give you a full explanation later. But for now, the situation is urgent, and you have to get out as soon as possible. Take care of yourself." With that, he salutes and leads his subordinate off at a fast trot.

Given the urgency, Qi Yuexuan shelves his anger and hurries out into the courtyard to organise the retreat. He tells Grandpa Fu to marshal the troops, lead them out of the south gate of the village, across to the south side of the Yongding River, then to make their way from Dingjiatan back to the west of Miaofengshan and follow the ravines back round to Qiwangfen. He rams home the instruction that he is only to take the guns and ammunition they have looted and to leave everything else behind. Speed is of the essence, and he mustn't, at any cost, risk lives for the sake of a bit of loot. He himself leads a small group of men at the double over to the north gate, hoping to use the Japanese blockhouse to mount a delaying action on the advancing enemy, and buy the others a little time.

They have just organised their defences at the north gate when they hear the sound of the main Japanese force approaching. The mountain track is impassable to motor vehicles, but the pounding of several hundred leather boots makes the ground shudder like an earth tremor.

The small troop that Qi Yuexuan has brought is formed of the same thirty or forty men that just made the feint attack on the south gate, and although they haven't been reinforced with any more personnel, they have added two captured Japanese machineguns and a good supply of ammunition. They have clambered inside the fortifications and are all too aware that they are vastly outnumbered and outgunned by the enemy. Qi Yuexuan gives the order to hold out for one hour, but in his heart he knows they will be lucky to survive for even half that time. The only hope he has is that the troops in the village will get a move on with their withdrawal.

"Mr Qi," the troop sergeant whispers, coming over to him. "Look, there's one of the Japanese big guns on its side in the ditch by the roadside."

"Ha! I expect the Eighth Route Army couldn't take it away, so they disabled it."

"I can't see from here. I'll go and take a look."

"Even if we have a gun, we don't know how to fire it."

"I do, I really do. Chinese ones, foreign ones, I know them all."

"Then get a move on. The devils are almost on us."

The sergeant acknowledges the order and scrambles out of the fortifications.

In a leap and a bound, he is in the ditch by the road, inspecting the gun. After a while, he stands up and gives Qi Yuexuan a thumbs-up, then he throws a rope over to the fortifications. The gun is a Japanese-made Type 92 mountain gun. It is no ordinary weapon, being of a sort used only by divisions and above. The Eighth Route soldiers had tried to drag it away and got it onto the road with the help of ropes, only to discover they had no chance of getting it along the mountain track. So they tumbled it into the ditch and lobbed in a couple of grenades, hoping to disable it. But Japanese-manufactured goods are sturdy, and although there are some pits on the surface of the gun, none of the working parts are damaged.

Qi Yuexuan is overjoyed and hurriedly orders his men to lend a hand and pull the gun up out of the ditch. Just as they are dragging it back to the fortifications, a few Japanese are appearing on the road up ahead. Fortunately, the men on top of the blockhouse have spotted them, and they are felled by a burst of machinegun fire. No more Japanese appear behind them, so it's clear this was the vanguard. But like a rat pulling a wooden shovel, when the little head appears, the big head can't be far behind. Qi Yuexuan keeps shouting his encouragement, telling everyone to keep their heads and prepare for battle. A number of men surround the gun, looking at each other.

"What is it? No shells?" Qi Yuexuan asks.

The sergeant replies with some embarrassment: "We've got two cases of shells, but…"

"But what?"

"The shells don't fit the barrel, so we can't load them." He puts a shell up to the barrel to demonstrate.

Qi Yuexuan can't help laughing: "Ha! I thought you said you knew how to fire it. This isn't a front-loader, it's a rear-loader."

"Really?" The sergeant only half-believes him. "Quite apart from our local guns, the last time I took a Japanese field gun, that was a front-loader too. You just dropped the shell in and 'boom'!"

"That was a small calibre gun. The big ones are all rear-loaders."

"So how do you do it?"

"I haven't done it, but I've seen it done."

"But there's no hole at the back, so how do you load it? Do you want to have a try?"

Qi Yuexuan had seen guns being fired when he was taking gifts and contributions out to the Twenty-Ninth Route Army, but he has never actually done it himself. He mutters to himself that he is sure he saw the guns being loaded from the rear, back then, so why can't he see a hole? At least he's more willing to give it a go than the others, and he pushes here, pulls there, trusting to blind luck – which doesn't desert him: as he tugs at a metal handle, it opens a hatch with a 'clang', revealing the gun's breech. He takes a shell that he pushes into the gun and lets go. To his surprise, the shell slips back out of the breech.

Fortunately, the sergeant has a quick eye and even faster hands. He catches it, pushes it back in and locks the hatch.

The shell is in the gun, but there is no touch hole or trigger, so how do you fire it? The sergeant and Qi Yuexuan look at each other in consternation, completely at a loss. They hear the sound of gunfire, signalling that the main Japanese force has already reached the foot of the mountain and is following the mountain track, firing as they come and swarming towards the entrance to the village.

"Brothers!" Qi Yuexuan shouts. "This is the moment of truth. Fight your hardest for me!"

Before his words have died away, gunfire erupts from the fortifications and the top of the blockhouse. In an instant, ten Japanese devils or more are lying dead, but the others keep pressing forward even as they are swept by machinegun fire. A hail of grenades follows, killing or wounding at least half of them, but still the attack continues. Suddenly, Qi Yuexuan's eyes light up and he shouts: "I remember now! It's like throwing a hand grenade – you have to set a fuse. Quick! See if we have any."

"Ah! Got them!" the sergeant replies almost immediately.

"Then take aim and fire a round to see if they work."

The sergeant acknowledges the order, and several men set to work shifting the gun into position and setting the fuse. The gun goes off with an explosion that makes the men's ears ring. The shell whooshes out of the barrel and describes an arc through the air. After a short while, an explosion can be heard far off in the distance, but it is not clear exactly where the shell has landed.

"Too far! That's gone several *li*! Aim closer," Qi Yuexuan yells.

"But... I can't shift the thing."

"Well if you can't shift it, then level it out and fire. If the barrel is horizontal that should be good enough."

These Japanese mountain guns are a type of howitzer, and they are usually fired with an arced trajectory for maximum distance, being able to send a shell up to ten *li*. But they can also be fired with a flat trajectory over shorter distances, which is how the Japanese use them in close combat and street fighting. So how does Qi Yuexuan know so much about all this? He is relying on his own experience. As a naughty little boy, he sometimes used to block up one end of a piece of pipe and shoot fireworks at passers-by. He is simply applying the same principles he learned then.

A few of the men haul up some sandbags that they use to raise the rear end of the gun. They open the case of shells, load one into the breech and fire it at the point where the attackers are most concentrated and their firing the heaviest. This time, the shell's trajectory is almost flat, with no arc, and it flies straight as an arrow at its target. There is an explosion, one of the trees opposite the gun breaks in two, and the noise of the enemy machineguns reduces dramatically. A cheer comes from the men, as this shot rouses their fighting spirit. Following the same routine, they fire off several more shells, one after the other, until the whole of the base of the mountain opposite is wreathed in the smoke of their explosions.

But the Japanese are only stopped for a short time before they regroup and take up the attack again. Although they don't have artillery, the firepower of experienced troops gives them the edge. Even with the shells falling non-stop and exploding on the field of battle, their snipers keep Qi Yuexuan and his men pinned down. Fortunately, the Japanese-built fortifications and blockhouse are well-constructed, and more than a hundred metres of sloping open ground lies between the foot of the mountain and the entrance to the village, with no cover except for a few low bushes. Moreover, the defenders have a plentiful supply of shells that they fire with redoubled vigour. However recklessly the enemy attack, they cannot gain any kind of foothold for the time being.

The Japanese quickly change their tactics. They no longer advance en masse, but split up, rushing a few paces, then crawling a few yards, gradually pressing home their attack until they are right up close. Then they scatter and rush the defences on a broad front. The tactic proves effective, and seven or eight of the devils draw their swords. Yelling their battle cry, they charge into the fray, repeating the close fighting of the early morning with casualties on both sides. Fortunately, they are few in number, and the men behind them are forced to retreat by the machinegun fire from the blockhouse. The space inside the fortifications is very restricted, with no room for the Japanese to wield their swords, so the fighting soon becomes a hand-to-hand affair, which is the speciality of the men of the Left Barracks. The children of the Left Barracks practise martial arts from the time they are in split-leg trousers, and they are only considered grown-up when they can pull a two-dou^2 bow, and wield a broadsword of more than a hundred *jin*. Their martial arts skills are at a level that is seldom seen. In no time at all, they have wiped out those few Japanese, and even Qi Yuexuan tastes blood for the first time. One of the sword-wielding devils charges him and he steps back, drawing his pistol. He is about to pull the trigger when he trips over his own feet and falls, face-up, to the ground. The Japanese can't halt his charge, stumbles, falls forward, lands on top of Qi Yuexuan and the gun goes off. One of his comrades hauls Qi Yuexuan to his feet and exclaims in alarm, seeing the blood all over his body and thinking he has been wounded. He is just pulling open his clothes to take a look, when Qi Yuexuan finally manages to say: "It's alright. I just winded myself on the gun."

Although the Japanese haven't pressed home the attack, the men of the Left Barracks have suffered heavy casualties, with ten dead and six badly wounded. The slightly wounded are too numerous to count, and not a single one of them has escaped completely unscathed. Qi Yuexuan fishes out his pocket watch and sees that, calculating from the first exchange of fire, they have already been holding out for thirty-eight minutes. The men inside the village must have got out by now, so he orders the sergeant: "We'll take advantage of the devils' retreat.

You lead the men away, and don't leave a single one of the badly wounded behind. Just leave me five or six men, and we'll stay here for a short while."

"How can we leave you behind? I'll give you cover, and you lead the withdrawal."

"I've already lived half my life. How old are you? I'm alone without dependants. I've seen everything and done everything I want, and if I were to die today, I would die content. What is there for us to argue about?"

"It won't do."

"A commander in the field can do as he pleases."

"You can shoot me now, but I won't go."

Before they can settle the argument, a voice shouts down from the top of the blockhouse: "Quickly, Mr Qi! Take look and see if the Japanese aren't withdrawing."

"What nonsense!"

"It's true. If you don't believe me, come up here and look for yourself."

Still partly disbelieving, Qi Yuexuan climbs to the roof of the blockhouse, taking his binoculars with him. Sure enough, as if by magic, all the Japanese have turned tail and are running away. Even the mortars and machineguns giving covering fire from the slopes have been abandoned. Looking further into the distance, he can see Japanese soldiers on the southern Incense Road running back at speed along their original route, and the scene gives every appearance of the retreat having been sounded.

"How extraordinary! They came charging in like mad dogs, but they're dropping the bone just as they got their teeth in it!" Qi Yuexuan mutters to himself.

"We scared them off," a man beside him says with pride.

"Let's not get above ourselves," says Qi Yuexuan. "We are quite clear about our own strength, and we could never have frightened the Japanese off. The devils weren't even at full stretch in those exchanges with us. If they had charged us once more, then more than likely we would have found ourselves dying for our country." The he suddenly remembers something, and shouts down to the sergeant: "Do we still have any shells left?"

"Yes, we still have five rounds."

"Any small ones? Fire them off immediately."

"Fire at what? I can't see any target."

"Ha! Fire them at the southern Incense Road so they know we're still here. If you hit something, well and good. If you don't, we'll still be giving them a good send-off."

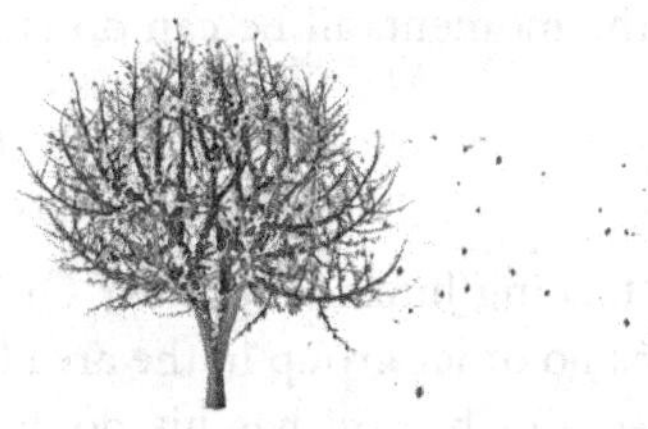

Chapter 40

The sudden retreat of the Japanese reinforcements comes as a shock to everyone, but just as the battlefield goes quiet, they hear the faint sound of gunfire coming from the direction of Junzhuang. It seems to be getting closer and louder all the time. It suddenly dawns on Qi Yuexuan that it must be some of their men clearing the devils out of their lair.

Junzhuang is fourteen *li* from Longjiazhuang. It is bordered to the east by the Fragrant Hills, to the west is Vulture Peak and to the south, the Yongding River. It is an ancient village, and the story is that troops have been stationed there since the Liao and Jin dynasties, which is how it got the name of Junzhuang, or Army Village. After the Japanese occupied Beiping, they too used it as a major military base, garrisoning it with crack troops from the Japanese Army – a brigade formed from various units stationed in northern China. This brigade doesn't just control Junzhuang; their territory includes the area defined by Miaofengshan, Bei'anhe and Wenquan. Therefore, the destruction of the squadron stationed at Longjiazhuang counts as their responsibility. Although the troops are divided across this territory, normally there is a regiment of the Japanese Army stationed in Junzhuang along with another division. When sending reinforcements to Longjiazhuang, the Japanese only leave behind two platoons of the regular army and a squad of military police from the puppet army to take care of the base. The rest of the brigade make up the reinforcements, and in case that isn't a strong enough force in itself, they draft in another platoon and more Japanese soldiers from Bei'anhe. But they do not anticipate losing Longjiazhuang so quickly, nor that they would meet with such a fierce counterattack at the north gate. Even less do they expect that not only would the enemy fight like madmen in the front line, but that things would also erupt in the rear courtyard. So when this information gets to the commander of the reinforcements, after long and careful consideration, he decides to withdraw with all speed. His reasoning is very simple. First, he is afraid that the garrison at Longjiazhuang has already been wiped out, so the reinforcements have lost their main purpose. Second, Junzhuang's strategic importance is too great, and it mustn't be lost. For the moment, all he can do is swallow his pride and look to take revenge later.

So, what force is attacking Junzhuang now? Qi Yuexuan thinks it must be the Eighth Route Army, as no other group in the area has enough strength to take on a major Japanese base. But he still has his doubts. This is the territory of the Ninth Division, so where would the Eighth Route Army have come from? In fact, he is quite right, and it *is* the Eighth Route Army attacking Junzhuang and not the Ninth Division at all, but a detachment from the Second Division, led by Zhang Zhicheng.

Very early that morning, Zhang Zhicheng takes the Second Division on a sneak attack on the power plant on Shijingshan, wiping out the platoon of Japanese Army and puppet army troops who are guarding it. They blow up the plant's furnace with clusters of hand grenades, immediately cutting off the electricity to Beiping and plunging the city into darkness. Although they don't kill many Japanese devils, the overall effect of the attack is enormous. In the past, none of the various resistance forces in the Beiping area have ceased their attacks, but because they have all been at some distance from the city, the Japanese Army and the puppet government have made strenuous efforts to suppress any news of them. So the people in the city haven't heard much at all about the efforts of the anti-Japanese resistance. This time it is different. With all four corners of the city in darkness, the citizens lying on their *kangs* can all hear the sound of gunfire outside the city walls. Recently, the Japanese and the traitor government have been boasting that Beiping is a model of law and order, and that northern China is the bulwark of the holy war in the Far East, but now the lid has been blown off all that, and no one believes them any more. All the consulates and foreign newspapers in Beiping swiftly pass on the news to the outside world. Indeed, the newspaper reporters fall over each other to report it first. But we shall talk more about that later.

After Zhang Zhicheng has led his men in the attack on the power plant, he also checks the advance of the Japanese in the vicinity of Moshikou. After inflicting the inevitable casualties on the enemy there, he stops his mini guerrilla campaign and heads into the mountains, going due south. They cross Cuiweishan, go through Wulituo and bypass Sanjiadian, reckoning to go south from Junzhuang. Then they can head west to cross to the south side of the Yongding River and get back to their base. Although this is a very circuitous route, it avoids the enemy defences on the banks of the Yongding. What they have not reckoned with is that, when they are not long past Sanjiadian and only two *li* from Junzhuang, they discover fierce fighting going on to the southwest. Zhang Zhicheng realises this must be the Ninth Division and the Left Barracks' assault on Longjiazhuang.

During the fighting at the power plant, they captured an enemy walkie-talkie and one of their number understands a bit of Japanese, so as they retreat along the road, they can listen in on the enemy frequency and gather intelligence on their dispositions. From these conversations, they learn that the main Japanese reinforcement expedition has met with no attacks on the road but are facing fierce resistance upon reaching Longjiazhuang. It is not, however, from the Eighth Route Army, but from irregular local militia.

"That's not good," Zhang Zhicheng can't help exclaiming. With such a major engagement in progress, how can he not go to their aid? And if he withdraws, will he not be cutting off the rear defence of the men of the Left Barracks? But if he gives in and meets the enemy head-on, won't that be even more disastrous? Although his own men are already exhausted, and he has no way of contacting HQ for instructions, Zhang Zhicheng doesn't hesitate, and he immediately changes plans. He orders an attack on Junzhuang.

Just as when Sun Bin attacked Wei to save Zhao,[1] this diversionary attack plays out very successfully. When they reach Junzhuang, Zhang Zhicheng detaches a group of men to scatter into the surrounding woods, where they sound bugles, shout, wave flags, fire off machineguns and rifles, and explode grenades, directing it all at the blockhouse. This panics the enemy into tight formation, in the mistaken belief that the main force of the Eighth Route Army is attacking, a whole battalion at the very least. In fact, it is only when the Japanese troops retreating from Longjiazhuang reach Longquanshan, three or four *li* from Junzhuang, that the main attack takes place. Longquanshan is not a high mountain, but it is very steep, with the Incense Road running along its base on one side and the Yongding River on the other. Two detachments of Zhang Zhicheng's men attack ferociously from higher ground and pin the enemy down on the Incense Road. The nerves of the Japanese devils are already drawn as tight as bowstrings, and they are in no state for further battle. Fortunately for them, the Yongding is not deep at this point, and only a dozen or so *zhang* wide, so they manage to wade across and rush in full retreat towards Longquanwu, leaving ten or more bodies on the Incense Road and the banks of the river. Zhang Zhicheng and his men don't pursue them, but hurry down from the mountain to collect the enemy's guns and ammunition, before discontinuing the attack.

It is already after ten in the morning when Qi Yuexuan leads his men back to Jiuwangfen. The fighting has been attritional, and although they managed to kill or wound a good number of the enemy, they only captured ten or twelve rifles. They are unable to haul the mountain gun back with them, and, because they can't bring themselves to destroy it, they make the best of a bad job and bury it in an isolated dip in the ground outside the village, hoping to come back when the opportunity presents itself.

Before they reach the start of the road up the mountain, they are met by the sentries they had put on guard. When they set out, they left behind a platoon of men, most of whom are in the barracks at Qiwangfen, leaving only two sentries at the bottom of the mountain.

"Aiya, Mr Qi, you're back!"

When the sentry sees Qi Yuexuan, his eyes fill with tears.

Initially, Qi Yuexuan pays him little attention and is leading his men up the mountain, when something strikes him as not right, so he looks back and asks: "You're supposed to be on guard, not out for a stroll. Where's your rifle?"

To his surprise, the sentry begins to weep: "They... they took it away."

Qi Yuexuan is startled: "What? Have the Japanese been here?"

"Not the Japanese... the Eighth Route Army."

It turns out that, at just after five that morning, not long after the gunfire at the base at Jiangou had stopped, seven or eight Eighth Route Army men arrived at Jiuwangfen. Seeing they were friends, the two sentries went up to greet them. They had just opened their mouths to ask how the battle was going, when their rifles were suddenly snatched from them. They had seen the leader of the newcomers before: it was the man they had captured the previous night and whose hip they had all but dislocated. He was still limping slightly. Without a word of explanation, they and the grandfather and grandson tomb guardians were locked in a room with a guard set over them, while the rest of the newcomers hurried into the lesser tomb enclosure. It was not long before they heard the sound of explosions outside. Later, another twenty or thirty men arrived, followed by incessant clanging and banging noises that lasted about an hour. The goods excavated from the tombs were loaded onto pack horses, at least seven of eight of them, all laden high with bundles, large and small. Once they were some distance away, the men in the room finally scrambled out through a window. When they looked into the lesser tomb enclosure, they saw that several of the princes' tombs, and those of their wives, have been blown up. The whole place was a mess. Fortunately, their comrades up the mountain stayed where they were inside the temple gates and didn't make any impetuous sortie; this prevented the small incident from snowballing into something much more serious. It was also very lucky that the horses from the grain carts were all stabled up the mountain, and the grain had been unloaded, so down the mountain in the rear courtyard in Jiuwangfen, there were only a few empty carts. Otherwise, the horses would probably have been lost too.

Later on, after midday, when the lunch Qi Yuexuan orders the mess cook to prepare has already gone cold, the main force finally appears on the road at the bottom of the mountain. But this handful of men and their few wagons are moving sluggishly, not looking at all like a victorious army. As he watches them, Qi Yuexuan thinks to himself they resemble frightened sheep and must have been scattered after meeting the Japanese devils on the way. It is only when he welcomes them at the top of the mountain that the light dawns: the men are weighed down with the loot they have seized. Although he himself had expressly urged against this activity, Grandpa Fu has clearly not listened to him. There are several fully-laden carts, and every man is carrying, one way or another, on their backs, shoulders or in their hands, rifles and ammunition, not to mention grain, army uniforms, bedding, boots, helmets, satchels, mess tins, hard tack, tinned food... you name it, they have it, and clearly nothing has been left behind. They are even carrying wooden bathtubs and cast-iron cauldrons. It looks like a household goods store is moving premises. Many of the men are wearing multiple layers of clothing, making them look as round as rubber balls. The steps up the mountain are difficult enough going empty-handed, let alone carrying heavy loads, so it is hard to imagine how they have managed.

Qi Yuexuan takes hold of one of the men and wipes his face, which is running with sweat.

"If you're so hot, why don't you strip off?" he asks with a wry smile.

The man shakes his head vigorously: "That's not it, Mr Qi. I'm not hot, I'm not hot..."

"Strip!" Qi Yuexuan's expression changes in an instant, as he glares and shouts at the man.

The man begins to strip, but he is wearing so many clothes that he has great difficulty stretching and twisting. After an inordinately long time, he manages to remove the Japanese Army uniform he has on, revealing, underneath, a woman's broad-collared embroidered silk jacket. All the men standing around watching him burst into gales of laughter, and the man himself blushes furiously.

Qi Yuexuan just grunts and says to the men standing next to him: "Don't just stand around laughing. Go and help him strip, and don't stop till he's naked. I don't care how humiliated he is, just don't let him get sunstroke."

Before he has finished speaking, and without waiting for further explanation, several men spring into action, and in no time the man is standing there wearing only a pair of long underpants. A large mound of clothes is piled up in front of him: fifteen or sixteen items of military uniform and civilian clothes, both male and female. Among the more everyday items, there is a brilliant blue, shiny silk gown, wide and long, richly embroidered and finely trimmed. One of the men picks it up and says to Qi Yuexuan: "Look – is this a Daoist gown or a stage costume?"

Qi Yuexuan can't help giving a wry laugh as he gestures at the gown: "You'd better put it down quick. It's very bad luck. It's a funeral gown for a corpse."

"What!" the man exclaims in horror, hurling the thing away.

Qi Yuexuan sighs, glares at the half-naked man kneeling in front of him and asks: "Is this what you call booty too? Are we resistance fighters or bandits? Do you think you can do what you like just because you won?"

The man doesn't dare look up, let alone answer. Even the men standing around him are holding their breath, and those with guilty consciences sidle backwards to hide behind their comrades. Grandpa Fu steps forward.

"Ha ha! Don't be cross, Great General, don't be cross. Don't let a little thing like this get to you. Come, come, come. I've brought back several jars of good wine, so shouldn't we celebrate our great victory? Come on now."

Stony-faced, Qi Yuexuan neither speaks nor moves. Grandpa Fu smiles ingratiatingly, trying to make up lost ground: "Ha! I know I didn't listen to you. I'm completely in the wrong. I'm just a country landlord – no great vision and never made serious money. But enough of that. Don't be angry. We all made it back, didn't we?"

"This is no laughing matter. If we hadn't stopped them, you would have been in real trouble."

"Huh! Yes, yes, you deserve a medal! You're not just Zhuge Liang reincarnated, you're also Zhang Fei shouting his challenge at Dangyang Bridge!"[2]

"Ai! To tell the truth, we were lucky. If the Japanese hadn't withdrawn, I doubt we could have stood up to them."

"Withdrawn?"

"That's right."

"Why?"

"There were soldiers about to cut them off from their base."

"Whose soldiers?"

"I don't know yet."

"You were in luck, the luck of the devil."

Grandpa Fu's ingratiating manner has had no effect on Qi Yuexuan's dour expression: "But why am I talking about luck? Go and see for yourself whether there is a single uninjured man among the troops I led. What have our overall losses been? We've taken too many casualties, and our victory is a tragic one. We should not wage this kind of warfare again. It is simply not worth it! Ai!"

Grandpa Fu is about to say something, but his discomfiture prevents him.

When Qi Yuexuan led his men off on their diversionary expedition that morning, Grandpa Fu had been in no particular hurry to organise his retreat, and he had ignored Qi Yuexuan's orders to tell his men to refrain from looting, so they had carried off everything they could lay their hands on. Taking note of how things stood in the north of the village, the men at the south gate followed suit and decided to break ranks. Seeing nothing to prevent it, many of them swarmed into the shops on the streets of the village, stripping bare all the material and clothes stores, including one selling funeral attire. Fearing the attentions of their superiors, they piled the clothes on, piece after piece. When Grandpa Fu gave the order to withdraw, the mob scattered like bolting horses, and just as difficult to round up. What is more, in among the shops and houses were several Japanese snipers taking pot-shots at the retreating figures. This just added to the confusion, and the retreat became a rout, with every man for himself among those at the rear. But bundled up in clothes as they were, round as dumplings, how could they run anywhere? They couldn't take them off on the spot, so many of them became sitting ducks for the Japanese rifles. It was only when they reached Dingjiatan that they were finally able to take breath and re-form. At a quick count, there were anywhere between ten and twenty dead and a further seven or eight wounded.

Grandpa Fu knows this is all going to be rather difficult to explain, so he decides to cover up these losses for the time being. While they are still on the road, he goes round to all the commanders of the various platoons and squads, telling them to instruct their men that none of them are to mention these shameful goings-on in the course of the withdrawal, and to blame all the casualties on the fighting round the blockhouse, and with the Japanese from the barracks. He promises that, however disapproving the authorities might be, no further investigation of the looting would take place, and that everyone could keep whatever they had taken, except for guns and ammunition. Although he has no control over Hao Bingchen, Hao is up in the front cart and not involved in anything that's going on behind him, so when asked, he can't give any account of what has happened. But Grandpa Fu has not expected the appearance of Qi Yuexuan leading his reinforcements, who immediately sees through the whole story. This is why he hurries forward and tries to deflect Qi Yuexuan's attention, fudging matters and buying a little time where he can.

But Qi Yuexuan is nobody's fool, and one look at the appearance of the soldiers tells him most of the story. But he is not willing to speak until he is certain, nor does he rush into interrogating any of the troops. He keeps his peace until they reach the main residence on the second level, where he heads straight to the rear rooms.

Grandpa Fu pulls him back, saying: "Hey! Didn't we say we'd have a few cups of wine to celebrate? You can't go back on that now. Orderly, hurry up and fetch a jar of wine, and then see if Mr Hao is here and invite him too."

The orderly acknowledges his instructions, and seeing Grandpa Fu's flustered and blustering manner, Qi Yuexuan forces a smile and says: "Not just a cup of wine, I think. You go in first and have a good wash. Then wait for me and I'll soon be with you. I'm going to see the wounded. We'll have to send the worst of them back. And we need to think of some way of replenishing our ammunition. Both of these are matters of urgency, and the wine will lose its savour if we don't see to them."

When he returns after half an hour, with a rather amused look on his face, he sees that Grandpa Fu and Hao Bingchen are already seated at the table, on which there is a large jar of wine and several cans with Japanese labels.

Seeing the change in mood, Grandpa Fu perks up a bit and hurriedly pours some wine.

"Aiya, you're back. Our mouths are watering, but we didn't dare start without you."

Qi Yuexuan doesn't reply.

"What's the matter?" Hao Bingchen asks. "Are there many wounded to send back?"

"Ai! One way and another there are twelve of thirteen of them. The doctor says that, if they're not operated on quickly, their fate is a matter of chance. He's afraid none of them will survive."

Hao Bingchen shakes his head with a bitter laugh: "That's not good. How can we send so many back? And where to, anyway? Even if all the Japanese along the way are asleep, won't getting back to the Left Barracks be just as difficult?"

"If we can send them back," Grandpa Fu chips in, "it is better to die at home than in some strange place. That is…"

"Let's have less of such talk," Qi Yuexuan interjects. Then he laughs and says: "Don't worry. I had an idea and I've already acted on it. Go ahead and have your wine."

So saying, he lifts his cup, and seeing this, the others follow suit. The three of them drain their cups.

A little flown with the wine, Grandpa Fu asks: "Are you sure of all this, then."

"I wouldn't say a hundred per cent, but seventy or eighty."

"Ha! Then don't keep me in suspense. I'm still your second-in-command, aren't I? If you're in two minds, I can at least listen to your ideas, can't I?"

Seeing that he is getting worked up, Qi Yuexuan says with a smile: "There's no need to get excited. Some affairs are more important than others, and I'm hoping to use the wine to smooth the way into discussing something important."

"Great affairs can wait, I want to hear about this lesser matter first," Grandpa Fu says forthrightly.

"Alright, alright. Brother Hao was right just now – sending them back is going to be difficult. What with the Japanese checkpoints and all the bumps and jolts on the road, it's by no means certain anyone badly wounded could survive the trip. Even if they do make it back, where are they guaranteed decent treatment? So it's best we don't send them…"

"So that's your idea is it?" Grandpa Fu says, curling his lip. "Just let them wait here to die…"

"Who said anything about waiting to die? I'm not sending them back because I'm going to ask a doctor to come up here."

"You can't even find a butcher up here, so where are you going to find a good one?"

"Don't you know that there's a villa east of Yangtaishan, not far from Wenquan? The people there call it the Bei Family Garden.[3] It's only seven or eight *li* from here. The owner is a Frenchman called Bussiere, and he is a top surgeon."

"Yes, I've heard of this man," says Hao Bingchen. "But he hasn't practised medicine for quite some years. I've heard he is very arrogant and has turned down requests from many important officials. I'm sure he won't come even if you ask him."

Qi Yuexuan shakes his head with a smile: "I'm not so sure. I've heard he's a bit of a knight errant. If I went and explained the whole thing to him, it could be... ha ha, we can always kidnap him if we have to."

Grandpa Fu slaps his thigh. "Now that's an idea I can go along with! And if he comes and isn't any good, then... But it's no use having a doctor without medicines, and the lint and bandages we took from the Japanese have been used up on the urgent cases. It will be like trying to make bricks without straw."

Qi Yuexuan takes another swallow of wine and gives him a crafty look: "And you think we can't ask a Western doctor to use eastern medicine?" When he sees the two others staring at him, he goes on: "I told him to draw up a list and to ask the Japanese devils in Junzhuang for anything we haven't got."

Grandpa Fu gasps in surprise at this, chokes on his mouthful of wine and sets himself off coughing. As soon as he stops, he can't hold back his laughter: "You are a dreamer, aren't you! Is the Japanese commander there your son or something?"

"Ah... no!" Qi Yuexuan stares at him, caught between laughter and anger. "I'm the last in line of the Qi family, and I'm not looking to the Japanese to carry it on. It's just a matter of business with him, an exchange. Do you understand?"

"An exchange? Exchange what?"

"Ah! I'm afraid I can't tell you that. You'll understand when it's over. Don't worry, I'm not going to touch your precious loot. I guarantee it's something you don't want."

"And you think the Japanese prize the stuff that I don't want?"

"I'm not absolutely certain, but pretty sure."

Hao Bingchen has been listening to the two of them, without breathing a word. Then his eyes suddenly light up.

"Ha ha! Now I get it, Yuexuan. It's..."

"Stop!" Qi Yuexuan doesn't let him continue. "I know I can't hide anything from you, Brother Hao. You've got a nose like a bloodhound. But please don't steal my thunder. Remember, a true gentleman watches the chess game in silence. The one who speaks is..."

"Alright, alright, I won't say anything. You can keep your little mystery going."

Hao Bingchen picks up his wine cup and chinks it with Qi Yuexuan's, smiling knowingly. But under Grandpa Fu's penetrating scrutiny, he forgets to drink.

"Drink up! We've already drained ours," Qi Yuexuan urges him, and when he sees he has complied, he continues: "Let's leave all that for now and turn to the far greater matter."

Grandpa Fu pours some more wine and says ill-temperedly: "Go on then. Has the sky fallen down or the Earth caved in?"

Qi Yuexuan's expression loses most of its humour as he says: "Ai, Commander

Fucha! Our casualties are too heavy from this battle – forty-five dead, eighteen seriously wounded and seventy or eighty with light injuries or flesh wounds. This is the count from each of the different divisions, and there could still be some we have missed. The final tally could be as high as forty per cent. It's true that the Japanese casualties are higher, but ours could have been somewhat lower, couldn't they? Some were killed or wounded unnecessarily, weren't they?"

Hearing this, Grandpa Fu realises he has been found out and is feeling rather worried. Qi Yuexuan pauses for a moment before continuing.

"Commander Dong isn't here, so you and I are in charge, and someone has to accept responsibility for those irresponsible actions. And not just for the dead. The living too deserve an explanation."

Grandpa Fu's face flushes, and there is a glint in his narrowed eyes. Observing this, Hao Bingchen hurriedly tries to smooth things over.

"Don't take things so seriously, Yuexuan. It was still a remarkable victory. Didn't you humiliate the government army this morning? It doesn't matter where it is – Beiping, Tianjin, Nanjing. Everywhere they have outnumbered the enemy several-fold, but haven't they always been defeated?"

"That's right," says Grandpa Fu, taking advantage of the diversion. "They were regular troops, and what are we? We don't even have a pretend standard to fight under. But compared with them…"

"Hah!" says Qi Yuexuan, taking an exception to this line of reasoning. "What do you compare to a dwarf for height? What do you compare to a man for contrariness? We are not the only ones resisting the Japanese, and there are certainly others who fight better than us. At Pingxingguan, the Eighth Route Army wiped out more than a thousand Japanese devils, and when they attacked the Japanese airbase at Yangmingbao, they blew up more than twenty enemy aircraft at one go. They were only a few thousand strong when they left Shanxi, and now they number more than a hundred thousand. How do we compare with that? The government army isn't short of heroes and brave warriors either, but their leaders are dull and stupid. Aren't Lao Gao and his men reckoned to be part of the government army? You've seen their courage and ability for yourself, haven't you? Without them, how would our own battle have turned out? If you're going to make comparisons, you have to make them with the best, and even in the north, you won't find any that hasn't won at least one battle. Don't you have any regrets about today's battle when you think about it now? At any rate, what I've heard has sent shivers down my spine. Having won the battle, you didn't withdraw but were tempted by cheap pickings. You couldn't bring yourself to leave any loot behind, and they opened fire on you, so you ended up like a flock of startled birds. Are we soldiers or hoodlums? Are we resistance fighters or bandits? We were lucky today or we could have been wiped out. But luck won't always be on our side. If we don't learn the lesson from today's disastrous casualties, one day it will desert us, and the whole army could be annihilated."

In his anger, these words rattle out of Qi Yuexuan like a burst of rapid fire from a machinegun, as his face grows red and his veins and tendons stand out. Grandpa Fu doesn't say anything, but his cheeks bulge as he clenches his teeth, and his face flushes first red then purple, then almost black with rage. He may not say anything, but it's clear he does not agree with a word of this.

Still hoping to smooth things over, Hao Bingchen stands up and pours the others some more wine. He raises his own cup and invites them to drink. With the wine inside him, Qi Yuexuan says solemnly to Grandpa Fu: "Commander Fucha, I may have been a little harsh, but what I said wasn't directed just at you, it was directed at myself as well. When things like this happen, someone always has to take responsibility, otherwise it is next to impossible to convince the troops..."

"Enough!" Grandpa Fu interrupts him, then grunts with a lop-sided smile. "Pah! There's no need for you to spell it out. You told me what to do, and I didn't listen. You can kill me or just cut off a limb. It's up to you."

"Ha! It's not that serious," Hao Bingchen hurriedly interposes, as he can see the situation is becoming more hostile.

Grandpa Fu smiles coldly. "Then you can stop all this bullshit commander crap, give me eighty strokes of the rod and send me home in disgrace."

Qi Yuexuan is growing more agitated: "Ha! It really isn't my intention to put all the blame on you."

"That's enough. Don't bandy words with me."

"Just let me finish."

"I'm not listening, I can't be bothered to listen. You just do what you want."

Qi Yuexuan sighs deeply and says: "In that case... everyone will be punished according to the army regulations against looting from the people."

Grandpa Fu gives a bark of laughter: "Ha! Alright then, I'll listen. What's the punishment?"

"First, everything that has been taken has to be collected up and taken back. Second, in accordance with army regulations, the punishment will fit the severity of the case."

"Do you know how many men are involved?"

"Sixty or seventy."

"You know that, do you? Then you... Ha! Have you heard of the principle that the law applies to the individual, not the crowd? And there's another saying too – it's officials who drive the people to revolt. Have you heard that one?"

Qi Yuexuan is taken aback at this and asks: "Then how do you say we should handle it?"

Grandpa Fu smiles knowingly. "Handle what? Let's be clear about this. I gave the orders that all the guns and ammunition were to be handed in. As for the other stuff, it's down to the each of the individuals concerned to return whatever they took, and this is not to set any kind of precedent."

"That's not good enough," Qi Yuexuan says.

"Not good enough, eh? Well, then, if what I say doesn't count for anything, you'd better just ignore me and do what you want."

And so saying, Grandpa Fu finishes his wine in one gulp, slams the cup down on the table and turns to go into the inner room.

"Don't be so presumptuous!" Qi Yuexuan is getting really angry now. He bangs the table with his fist and is about to jump to his feet.

Hao Bingchen hurriedly presses him back down in his chair, then pulls Grandpa Fu towards him.

"Ai! If you've got something to say, just say it. Come on now, sit down and have some more wine."

Grandpa Fu stops leaving, but he doesn't sit down. He gives another chilly laugh and says: "Ha! I won't have any wine. I could drink more if I wanted, but I never drink in anger." Then he bows to Qi Yuexuan. "Master Qi, I did wrong today, but we are in the twenty-seventh year of the Republic, not in the Qing empire. The masters are no longer in charge and it's the time of the serfs now. You're outdated. You can't use your status to oppress people any more."

"Who? Who's using their status to oppress you?"

"Well, if you weren't trying to oppress me, what were you doing? Honouring me?"

"I was talking about principles. I may have been harsh, but what did I say that wasn't founded in reason?"

"What do you mean by 'reason'? Being successful is all the reason you need. Nothing else is worth a fart."

Hao Bingchen can see that the two of them are just enraging each other more, so he puts on his most winning smile and intervenes: "You're quite something, you two! You've got more than a hundred years between you, so why are you behaving like two-year-olds? Sit down and give me a chance to set things straight, alright?"

He pushes Grandpa Fu firmly into his chair and continues: "Both of you are resolute, and both of you are justified in what you say. But there are greater and lesser justifications, and the lesser must always defer to the greater. You men of the Left Barracks Army are all farmers, and from a farmer's point of view, getting enough food to keep one's family is fundamental. You don't care where help comes from, east or west, and you will swallow your pride and play along. No one can reproach you. Now you are fighting the Japanese devils, you don't care how the battle is fought. Everything is excusable in the cause of your livelihood as farmers."

Grandpa Fu gives a big thumbs up when he hears this and grunts his approval.

Hao Bingchen now redirects the conversation: "But once you have raised your standard, it doesn't matter whether it is the Heroic Army or a local militia, you are soldiers in an army. Look at it from the farmer's point of view, Commander Fucha. Can you apply farmers' standards to the military? An army must have discipline, for how can it fight effectively without discipline? Thus, Yuexuan has the greater justification on his side, while yours is the lesser. The greater justification makes great things possible, but the lesser reduces things to the small and petty that cannot last. Do you not agree?"

Grandpa Fu remains silent for a while, before saying: "I understand all that, but can it really be applied here? You've only given one side of the story. When troops were being recruited, it was as a regular army. You, Master Qi, were a representative of the government, and you gave me an official commission. Is that not so? But I have only been paid once in all this time. It is clearly written in army regulations that there are rewards and there are punishments. The bounty on a single Japanese head is five silver yuan and one silver yuan for a Chinese traitor. The reward for a captured rifle is two yuan. We have fought quite a few battles now, and we have killed I don't know how many Japanese devils and seized I don't know how many rifles. How many devils have I killed myself? How many have I wounded? And have I seen a red cent? As for those remaining tombs at Jiuwangfen, which the Eighth Route Army blew up, to tell the truth, the thought had crossed my own mind, and if I hadn't had Master Qi watching over me, they might not have had the chance."

Qi Yuexuan has been silent for a long time, but when he hears this, he can't help snorting: "Pah! You dare voice such a thought? How admirable!"

"Driven by necessity and poverty, who wouldn't have eyes on such a prize? Why should I care how admirable you think it is?"

"Then you should lower your flag and not shame the name of the Heroic Army. You could call yourselves the Bandit Tomb-Robbers of Wanping, instead."

"Don't give me that! There's no great distance between bandits and soldiers anyway. If you don't feed your cart horses, are you really going to be surprised if they go foraging?"

"Have I ever said you won't get money, that bereaved families won't receive compensation or that bounties won't be paid? Once we are back at the Left Barracks, I will honour all commitments."

"Whatever's owing? Very well. There are punishments owing too, and the troops will want to see both rewards and penalties if you are going to win them over."

"You..." Qi Yuexuan chokes on this reply from Grandpa Fu. He points a trembling finger at him, but he can't get any words out. Grandpa Fu give him a sidelong look, laughs complacently and pours himself another cup of wine.

Hao Bingchen, too, can't help frowning. He sighs and says: "Ai, Commander Fucha! I think you are going a little far with that. It is the national emergency that comes first at the moment, and the country's resources are stretched very thin. It's not just you, you know. Even the regular troops of the National Army are having great difficulty with supplies. It's not unusual for them to go without pay for several months either. You're demanding pay from Yuexuan here, but where is he going to get it from? It's not..."

At this point, Qi Yuexuan tugs surreptitiously at his jacket, and he doesn't finish what he was going to say. He pauses for a moment, then changes the subject: "That grain I brought didn't come from HQ, you know. I got it by a happy chance and saved you some money bringing it here. You're not in real difficulties, but you are in some trouble. The troops are only held together by army discipline. Once that is relaxed, as it was with today's independent looting, then the army is not far from breaking up completely. Of course, any punishments can take the circumstances into consideration, and can be discussed, but there have to be..."

"I said nothing about no punishments," says Grandpa Fu, giving a wry smile. "Is this what you call setting things straight, Mr Hao? Is it instant justice you want? Or executions? You can start with me. I stand by what I said before, and if you don't agree, go ahead and do what you like. But if you want to butt heads with us of the Left Barracks, there is one thought I want to leave with you – it doesn't matter what flag these men are fighting under, their hearts belong to the Left Barracks. You may think you can gobble us up as an appetiser, but you'll break your teeth on those hearts."

With that he leaves without looking back.

Hao Bingchen curses inwardly at the man's obstinacy and anger flares in his eyes. When he sees Qi Yuexuan sighing helplessly, he suppresses his thoughts and decides to hear what he has to say. But to his surprise, although Qi Yuexuan has given every indication he is about to speak, in fact he stays mum.

"Well, say something," Hao Bingchen exclaims irritably.

"Eh? What do you want me to say?"

"You are a piece of work! Even at this critical moment, you still shilly-shally? Alright then, if you've got no ideas, you just listen to what I have to say."

"Who says I don't have any ideas? But alright, I'll listen to what you have to say first."

"Listen to you! You don't give up, do you? The beak is still hard even when the duck is cooked!" Hao Bingchen laughs, but then he immediately looks serious. "You have three choices in front of you. The first is to leave things as they are, undecided..."

"That won't do. Don't even mention it. It's too close to admitting defeat."

"Then you can try the second way – defeat the enemy by capturing their chief. The first to make a move has the upper hand."

"That's even worse. We haven't reached that point yet. He may be rather narrow-minded, a bit greedy, a bit crabby, but he's not a bad man..."

"Listen to you, sharp-tongued but soft as mush inside. The troops aren't your business partners. If you need to be fierce with them, you must act without hesitation. Of course, you don't have to kill a poisonous snake, but you do have to draw its fangs, or you'll never rest easy."

"That won't do either. Half the troops are from Fucha Village, otherwise he couldn't be so aggressive. If we can't find a compromise to this internal conflict, and split up, that will just be playing into the hands of the Japanese, won't it?"

"Not necessarily. All you have to do is act first, act quickly and act ruthlessly.

If you don't give him time to come out of his daze, the matter will be settled just like that, and where's your internal conflict then? Don't worry about it, I'm your man for urgent action. I may not be good for much else, but this, I can do."

Qi Yuexuan leaps to his feet in agitation, waving his hands.

"No, no, for heaven's sake, stay out of it. When it comes to fighting the Japanese, then of course you should be involved, but I can't let you get involved in internal affairs. I may succeed or I may fail, but there's no way I'm going to allow some kind of secret police murder squad."

Hao Bingchen gives a wry laugh: "Ha! If you can't turn a blind eye and won't bare your fangs, then the only thing left is the third option – fuck off with your tail between your legs."

Qi Yuexuan stares at him blankly, then asks thoughtfully: "Is there really no other way? How about Sunzi's principle of subduing the enemy without fighting?"

"What? You simply don't have the power to do that."

"I'm not so sure. Morality and righteousness have power just as surely as soldiers do."

"Eh? Do you still insist on wasting fine words on philistines?"

"I still have to try."

"Just listen to you! Pah!" Hao Bingchen shakes his head with a sigh, but he can't let go of the matter. "Do you really not want my help? If I raise my standard and stand beside you, won't that strengthen your position?"

"Do you really want to help me?"

"Of course."

"Then when I start my meeting, make sure you and your men are nowhere to be seen. Indeed, it would be best if you simply vanished."

"What?" Hao Bingchen looks at him in astonishment.

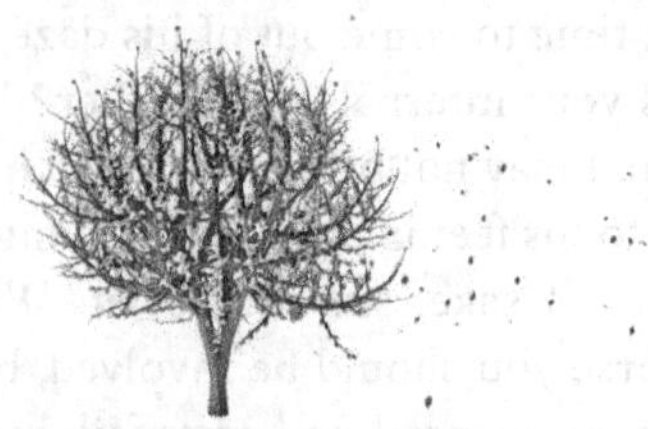

Chapter 41

When Grandpa Fu leaves the building, he hurries into the third inner courtyard. About half of the troops are quartered there, with the second detachment occupying the main hall and the third detachment in the two side buildings. Both the commanders of these two detachments are from Fucha, and both are from the original clan of that village. Most of their non-commissioned officers and men are also from the same place. Since the establishment of the Left Barracks by the Department of the Imperial Household, Fucha has been the biggest of the twelve villages, and apart from Laoqiying and two or three others that sprang up later, it is the largest in area and the most populous.

When the Heroic Anti-Japanese Army was formed, Fucha furnished thirty to forty per cent of the men and rifles. If you except the detachment acting as Second Master Dong's bodyguard, the men of Fucha now account for about half the force. Grandpa Fu is the principal landlord and head of the Fucha clan, so he is confident that blood is thicker than water and that the men will stick with him. It is this confidence that has emboldened him to face off with Qi Yuexuan and challenge him publicly. Indeed, he gathers several of their leaders together, and without exception, they all agree only to listen to their clan chief's orders. This only serves to increase his confidence. His thinking is that, if Qi Yuexuan backs down, then he will be quite content to leave things unresolved as they are; but if Qi Yuexuan rashly decides to make something of it, then he won't hold back and will take the opportunity to cause as much trouble as possible. Since the other detachment is, by good fortune, also made up of fellow locals and relatives, they are not going to side with an outsider against him either. If anyone does dissent, he will have his weapons forcibly confiscated. He does not want to see Qi Yuexuan dead, as he is very much in awe of him as a scholar; he just wants him expelled from the army. The one thing he fears is Hao Bingchen and his men, and if he really does want to act, then he has to get rid of them first.

His plans settled, Grandpa Fu sends out some of his men to keep a surreptitious eye on what is going on across the board, and he also despatches the various group leaders to organise their men. Then he waits for Qi Yuexuan to lay his cards on the table. But to his surprise, there is no sign of movement from the neighbouring courtyard, nor is there any unusual activity from the other detachments. All that happens is that Qi Yuexuan himself makes his way over to Grandpa Zhang's house and buys several of his sheep, which he orders the kitchens to slaughter and cook, saying he wants them for a celebratory feast that evening. A little later, one of Grandpa Fu's men reports to him that tables, chairs and benches have already been laid out in the main courtyard, and firewood has also been assembled. Grandpa Fu smiles to himself, believing that Qi Yuexuan is on the point of giving in and that this feast is his way of climbing down gracefully. Only time will tell whether he is right, however, so he still gives orders for his men to keep their rifles to hand, to stay in their groups, finish their preparations and wait for further orders.

As dusk falls, an orderly comes running in to report that everyone is requested to assemble for a group meal in the front courtyard. The courtyard is soon full, with the various group and squad leaders sitting at several tables specially reserved for them at the front, and the rest of the men taking their places by group in a big circle. Qi Yuexuan makes haste to lead Grandpa Fu to the top table and sits down next to him, along with the four detachment commanders. As soon as they are all seated, Qi Yuexuan looks up and sweeps the assembled company with his gaze. He looks Grandpa Fu up and down, then unexpectedly begins to chuckle.

"What... what's so funny?"

"Well, look for yourself. We're gathered here for a meal and some wine, so why are you all armed to the teeth? Are any of my men carrying their rifles?"

"I expect they are afraid. Afraid the Japanese might..."

"Forget about the Japanese. Do you think they can have regrouped in eight or nine days? You put the fear of God into them in that battle, and there's no way they're going to take the initiative and counterattack. Besides, you've got sentries posted front and rear, and security has been kept tight, so why are you still so nervous? Soldiers have to marshal all their energy when they go into battle, and afterwards they have to know how to relax. How can they do that properly if they're still carrying all their equipment? It just gets in the way. If you make it obvious you're not regular soldiers born and bred, or, at least, this is the first time you've fought an actual battle, then your behaviour will betray you and you're just going to look cocky when other people praise your military skills."

Qi Yuexuan acts out this teasing little speech with broad gestures, drawing a gust of laughter from the assembled company, with even the commanders of the second and third detachments joining in. Only Grandpa Fu's face is mottled with angry embarrassment.

"Ha! Just grin and bear it, if you can." When Grandpa Fu doesn't reply, Qi Yuexuan turns to his bodyguard and says: "You know, those carrying a rifle can't have any wine. We can't have anyone getting tipsy and accidentally shooting someone."

"Stop! Stop!" Grandpa Fu sees his bodyguard about to leave and pulls him back, then turns angrily on two of the commanders from the second and third detachments. "And what do you two think you're doing, letting your men bring their rifles to a banquet? Collect up all the rifles and be quick about it."

The two men are baffled and stare at him blankly: "But..."

"But what? Are you slow-witted or something?"

Grandpa Fu glares at them furiously. Only when he sees them stand up, does he turn to Qi Yuexuan and say with a chilly smile: "They didn't mean anything by it, Master Qi. Please don't give it another thought. Now, if you just change the song you're singing to *The General and the Prime Minister Make Up*, then no one will think the opera is *The Feast at Hongmen*."

Qi Yuexuan laughs. "I think you are being a little over-sensitive and seeing monsters where there are none. I've been singing *The General and the Prime Minister Make Up* all along. It's just your over-thinking things that's turned it into *The Feast at Hongmen*. Why don't you apply some of that over-active imagination to fighting the Japanese?"

Grandpa Fu knows he is being mocked, but he is also desperately trying to work out what exactly is going on behind Qi Yuexuan's words. There is nothing for it but for him to play it by ear. He tries to shift attention from his embarrassment, and asks: "Why can't I see Mr Hao here?"

"He wouldn't be seen dead at a feast celebrating our heroics. In fact, I think it's best he's not here. You may think he's all staid and serious, but actually he's like a powder keg, and who knows what you might say that would strike a spark and set him off."

"Surely he's not as bad as all that..."

"Not that bad? He's not like me. You just don't know what side he is on. Anyone he identifies as a traitor or being hostile to the anti-Japanese resistance, he doesn't simply attack them, he acts on the sly. There was a Chinese traitor who lived in a heavily guarded mansion with large courtyards just inside the Desheng Gate... he even had bodyguards stationed in the courtyards. But it was no use. You won't believe it, but someone climbed the Drum Tower, a good few hundred metres away, with a rifle equipped with a telescopic sight. One shot with a dumdum bullet and half the traitor's head was gone. When he was hit, no one could work out where the shot had come from."

"What? Is he capable of such a thing?"

"Well, that's what I've heard." Qi Yuexuan sees Grandpa Fu staring at him in alarm, and he changes the subject, smiling expansively: "The men and the food are all here, Commander Fucha. Why don't you say a few words?"

Grandpa Fu gestures self-deprecatingly: "No, you're the one who should speak. But let's leave the speechifying in the wine, keep the words to a minimum and concentrate on the drinking. When faces are flushed and eyes are watering, everything else is forgotten."

Qi Yuexuan takes his meaning. He laughs, stands up and calls out: "Settle down, brothers!"

The courtyard, which has been as noisy as a tea garden, quickly quietens down, and everyone turns to look at Qi Yuexuan. The only exception is Grandpa Fu, who huddles close to the two detachment commanders who have just returned and not sat down yet, and whispers in their ears. The two men nod and slip away again.

He hears Qi Yuexuan say: "Brothers, we of the Wanping Regiment of the North China Heroic People's Army of Japanese Resistance are all men of the Left Barracks. A few months ago, you were just ordinary folk. You had fought wolves and leopards, but few of you had engaged in a real battle. As for me, I am just a scholar and have only fought battles with my words – a paper soldier... No, don't laugh, it's all true. It is the Japanese devils who have forced us onto the battlefield, who have forced us to take up arms. In these last few months we have fought well, we have mounted surprise attacks and ambushes, and this time we fought a fine pitched battle. All this is ample proof that the so-called 'Invincible Imperial Army' is just so much bullshit! I am proud of each and every one of you. You are all Chinese to your bones, Beijingers heart and soul, and heroes of the Resistance. I have prepared this humble offering of wine in your honour."

There is an ear-splitting roar of cheering and applause.

The commander of the Third Detachment calls out: "Brothers, we owe our victory to the wisdom of our commanders, so let us drink this first cup in their honour."

So saying, he raises his cup first to Qi Yuexuan and then to Grandpa Fu. All talking at once, the men shout out their approval.

Grandpa Fu laughs rather knowingly but keeps his thoughts to himself. He raises his cup: "Ha ha! We did it together. Here's to all of us!"

"Wait, wait!" Everyone can see that Qi Yuexuan has become more solemn, more serious, even a little angry. The courtyard immediately goes so quiet it is even a little oppressive, as everyone looks at him with a variety of different expressions, waiting to hear what he has to say.

"Brothers, we are standing here alive today, but over the last months, we have lost dozens of our comrades who are no longer with us. What is more, another forty-five of us died in the battle today. They gave their lives for China and for the people. They died bravely, and they died gloriously. But we couldn't even bring their bodies back, and we must bear that shame. It may be that it will be us who sacrifice our lives in the next battle, but today we are alive and we must not forget our brothers who gave their lives to make that possible. We must send men to collect their bodies, every single one of them, and find a way to bring them back home. We must look after their families properly. We must act with filial piety on their behalf and raise their children for them. Once we have chased the Japanese devils out of our country, we must raise a hero's memorial to them, so their memory will live on forever down the generations. No one must claim credit for the deeds of others, of the great and glorious dead, so this first cup must be offered in sacrifice to their martyred spirits. You must forgive me, for this wine today is not enough for everyone to join in, so let us, as your commanders, represent the whole army. Let us represent you, the country and all the people."

With this, he raises his cup above his head in both hands, and sinks to his knees. Grandpa Fu and the detachment commanders hurriedly follow suit and kneel on the ground. They tip the wine from their cups and kowtow three times.

Qi Yuexuan raises his hand. "Now, everybody, drink up. Drink a cup to them." His voice chokes with emotion, and the tears flow down his cheeks. The whole company raise their cups in unison and take a deep draft as the courtyard is filled with a solemn silence.

"Brothers!" Qi Yuexuan raises his cup again. "We also have thirteen badly wounded comrades whose lives hang in the balance, but we have already asked the finest foreign doctor in Beiping to operate on them and have found a way to get hold of the best possible medicines. So, drink again, everyone, drink in prayer that they may be kept safe and sound."

Once again the company's cups are raised in unison, as the men are moved and shaken by Qi Yuexuan's words and actions. The majority of them are descendants of servants of the banner, and are themselves poor farmers, tenant farmers or farm labourers. They seldom find themselves being treated as equals by others, so they cherish the respect they are being shown now and are moved by it, almost overwhelmed by this favour from a superior.

"Vengeance for our comrades who have sacrificed their lives!"

"A blood debt must be played in blood!"

Their shouts ring out like thunderclaps, frightening the birds out of the trees.

This is a situation that Grandpa Fu has not anticipated. He suddenly feels as though, without him quite knowing how, Qi Yuexuan has gained the upper hand, and the ground has given way beneath his feet, so he has to crick his neck to look up. Although they are not at daggers drawn, his self-confidence has been shaken and a degree of timidity is creeping up on him.

Qi Yuexuan gives a signal and waits for the courtyard to settle down before he speaks again: "Brothers, the blood debt must surely be paid in blood, and we must kill even more devils to avenge our heroes. But..." He suddenly falls silent, looks around the courtyard, then continues: "...many of our brothers died in the battle today who should not have done so, whose deaths were pointless sacrifices. They lost their lives because of weak leadership and lax discipline. Does anyone deny it? A victorious army didn't withdraw as ordered but turned into a disorderly mob, like a duck trying to herd sheep. If it hadn't been for a detachment of your brothers risking their lives to hold the enemy at the north gate... if it hadn't been for a friendly force mounting a surprise attack on

Junzhuang and surrounding it, what would the outcome have been? It doesn't bear thinking about."

His relentless rebuke sizzles like a drop of cold water in the bottom of a red-hot pan, momentarily silencing the whole courtyard. Some are alarmed, some suspicious and some afraid, but no one makes a sound, not even a sigh. More than anyone else, Grandpa Fu looks as though he has been slashed by a whip. He had thought Qi Yuexuan was going to be sensible and tactful, and let things go with a nod and a wink. He never expected him to lay hold of his transgression and keep worrying at it, not letting it go. He clenches his teeth, biting back the fury that is rising in him. He wants to hear where Qi Yuexuan is going with this speech, to see just what is going on with him.

At this moment, the commander of the Second Detachment, who has been away from the feast for some time, comes running back and whispers something in Grandpa Fu's ear, which turns his face ashen.

The commander had been instructed discretely to find out Hao Bingchen's whereabouts, and he has come back to tell Grandpa Fu that Hao Bingchen and his men are not in their quarters and have vanished without trace. Grandpa Fu recalls what Qi Yuexuan said at the beginning of the meeting about how the man dealt with Chinese traitors, and he immediately feels there must be a rifle barrel aiming at him out of the darkness. A cold sweat breaks out down his spine.

Qi Yuexuan calls out in a loud voice: "What was this all about, brothers? How could an army not give of its best? How could discipline be so lax? How could a victorious army turn at a stroke into a defeated rabble? Ha! I can tell you in one word – greed! One glimpse of money turns eyes green, and when eyes turn green, there's no holding back. There is an old saying – a greedy official is a traitor, a greedy soldier is a bandit. How true that is. Can such a commander give clear-headed leadership? Can such soldiers strictly obey orders? But in the end, just how much gold and how many precious goods are worth a single life? The dozen or more men who are no longer with us did not die staking their lives against the Japanese devils. They died because of greed. Is it really worth it? Why have we taken up arms? It is to fight the Japanese, to drive them out of Beiping, out of the north, out of China completely. It is not to rake in money and build a family fortune. It is not to play the mountain bandit king. Therefore, we must strictly enforce discipline, we must justify ourselves to our martyred brothers, and we must find men to shoulder the responsibility. When we raised this army, we established its rules and regulations, which everyone accepted. Those rules and regulations are not there just for appearance sake. Hear me well – everyone who took part in today's looting..."

Before he can finish, the man who had been stripped of his clothes that noon kneels down and babbles: "I... I was in the wrong. Next time I won't break ranks... I won't break ranks. Forgive me... forgive me!"

He is just the start, as seven or eight others fall to their knees, also begging for forgiveness.

When the commander of the Second Detachment sees that they are all men from his section, he can't restrain his fury and bares his teeth at them: "You spineless lot! Are you trying to shame Fucha? If you dare to do something, you must accept the consequences. The rules allow for rewards as well as penalties, don't they? First take the beating, then take the money. Isn't that how it is? Pain first, pleasure later."

Qi Yuexuan glares at him and says with a chilly laugh: "Ha! These men are all from your detachment, aren't they? Well it's you who should be beaten first. It's you who most deserves a beating. Once you've been crippled for life by the rod, see how much pleasure you get from holding a gold bar!"

The commander chokes on Qi Yuexuan's words and is temporarily reduced to silence, partly out of anger and partly because he is looking aggrievedly at Grandpa Fu.

"Let him finish, then we'll see!" Grandpa Fu spits out the words.

Qi Yuexuan turns to the crowd and says: "The success or failure of a company of soldiers lies principally with the commander, not with the men. Stand up, stand up, all of you. You've no need to beg forgiveness. I never had any thought of punishing you."

When he sees them get to their feet, he goes on: "Now listen, all of you. Everyone who took part in the looting must hand over everything they took. Then, assign someone from the unit to return it all to its owners. This time, it will be recorded against you as a first offence and will be held on your record for the time being. But if you break army discipline again, you will be punished for both offences. After today, anyone who flouts the rules will be shown no mercy. The punishment may have been suspended, but the rewards will be distributed in accordance with what is laid out in the regulations. I also guarantee that every cent of the pay owing over the last few months will be paid within one week. Do you hear me?"

Perhaps because they haven't yet adjusted to the situation, there is only a muted response from the crowd. Qi Yuexuan frowns and asks again, more loudly: "Do you hear me or not?"

This time the whole crowd reply in unison, loud and clear. Qi Yuexuan smiles faintly and says: "Good. That's more like a real army of resistance. As I just said, the success or failure of a company of soldiers lies principally with the commander, so the faults of their subordinates can be forgiven. But if the commander does not pay sufficient attention to his command, that cannot be forgiven. That is why I want to reprimand your commander today, to cement this in your memories."

Qi Yuexuan's manner through all this, now icy, now fiery, now reprimanding, now rewarding, keeps everyone off balance. The commander of the Second Division thinks that it is being aimed particularly at him, and like an aggrieved child looking to its mother, he says to Grandpa Fu: "These are not the rules we agreed to, Commander."

"Not what you agreed to? Well then, we'll add a new rule, today!" Qi Yuexuan barks emphatically.

"Rules cannot apply only to subordinates and not to superiors. If subordinates have transgressed, then you must look to the responsibility of the superiors. Cao Cao's horse trampled the seedlings and he cut off his own hair[1] to show that he too was subject to military discipline. Should we not be the same?"

When the division commander hears this, he tries to defend himself: "But I... I..."

"Pull your neck back in. You're not important enough to take responsibility for this. Since we have just established the rules today, they must be applied to the full. Twenty strokes of the army rod, with no remission."

To a man, the listening soldiers are stunned by this, especially the men of the Second and Third Divisions, who all look to Grandpa Fu.

"What do you want me to do about it? I'm only the second-in-command." Grandpa Fu's anger rises under their gaze, and he gestures with his chin at Qi Yuexuan: "There's the main man over there."

Qi Yuexuan laughs: "Ha! Am I the main man then?"

"Of course."

"But maybe secretly, you are."

"Not at all."

"But people have to obey the main man, otherwise..."

"Who are you saying won't obey you? Every single one of them will obey you."

"And you? Will you obey me?"

"Ah... yes, yes, I'll obey you."

Qi Yuexuan laughs heartily and says in a loud voice: "Very well then. Since everyone is putting their faith in me, and will obey me, the beating must proceed. I need some volunteers to see military law carried out."

As he speaks, the door to one of the courtyard's side buildings opens, and several men come running out in response, two of them carrying porter's poles. Everyone's gaze turns to them, and they realise they are all Hao Bingchen's men. Qi Yuexuan swiftly takes off his long gown, pulls a bench towards him, lies along it, face down, and calls out: "Come on, start the beating. Twenty strokes. Count them out."

At this, everyone regains their senses, and a buzz of discussion hums round the courtyard like a stirred-up wasps' nest. The man with the pole doesn't dare start. He raises it a couple of times but then drops it, prompting Qi Yuexuan to yell at him angrily: "Get on with it!"

At this point, Hao Bingchen steps forward, close to Qi Yuexuan's ear and whispers: "Alright, you've made your point. You don't really want to take the beating do you?"

"Bullshit, I didn't set out to play games! If I take this beating, then the whole army will recognise the full seriousness of army regulations. It will establish authority and make the troops respect discipline. To that end, I would take forty strokes and think it worth it."

"Can you... can you stand it?"

Qi Yuexuan laughs, a little shrilly: "It's no matter. I... I got the Western doctor to put some anaesthetic cream on my buttocks. You'd better hurry up with the beating, or it will wear off!"

Hao Bingchen keeps a straight face but inwardly is cursing Qi Yuexuan's stupidity: the anaesthetic may numb the pain, but it won't stop the injuries. Equally, however, he can't help secretly admiring the man's quick-witted initiative.

"Go on then," he orders his men, before adding urgently: "But go easy."

Several men hurry to obey. Two of them hold Qi Yuexuan down on the bench, and two of them pick up the pole. With a loud grunt, they raise their poles high in the air but actually bring them down quite gently. Smack, smack. Two blows no heavier than swatting a housefly. The watching crowd, whose hearts have been in their mouths, relax and then burst out laughing.

This time, Qi Yuexuan is really angry: "What do you think you are doing? Who ordered you to play act like that? Do it properly, or when you've finished, I'll personally beat anyone who has been holding back."

When the two men hear this, they have no choice but to set to properly. After the first two heavy blows land on his buttocks, Qi Yuexuan gives a great shout of pain. He realises that the anaesthetic has already begun to wear off, but there's nothing he can do about it now. He'll just have to grin and bear it. He marshals all his resolution and doesn't utter another sound. The whole courtyard falls silent. Hao Bingchen glares at Grandpa Fu but doesn't say anything. Conscious of this, Grandpa Fu moves over to him and whispers: "I know he is taking this beating for me."

"Knowing is all very well, but I'm afraid that, as he's the one being beaten, you won't learn the lesson."

"No, no, I wouldn't dare. I'll obey him, I really will."

At this point, the count reaches twenty blows, and the beating stops. Everyone crowds round the bench, where they see that Qi Yuexuan's head is covered in sweat, his face is ashen, the light trousers he is wearing are beaten to tatters, and his buttocks are a mass of bloody weals. At the sight of him, Grandpa Fu bends down and sobs out: "Aiyo! Master Qi, you mustn't..."

Qi Yuexuan opens his eyes slowly and forces a smile: "I'm not going to die. It's a good thing I'm a few years younger than you. If it had been you, you'd be dead. So you make sure learn from this experience, and don't go headstrong against army discipline again."

"Yes, yes, you're right."

"Come on now, help me up... Aiyo! Slowly does it."

"Hurry up and sit down to catch your breath."

"Fuck that! Do you think I can sit down?" Qi Yuexuan supports himself on the table with both hands and calls out to the company: "Alright, don't crowd me. Just let me stand here, and you all go back to your seats. Bring some torches, light a bonfire and get on with the drinking and feasting."

"Those wounds are quite serious. Hadn't you better get the doctor to treat them?" says a concerned Hao Bingchen.

When Qi Yuexuan doesn't say anything, Grandpa Fu calls out: "I need two men over here to carry Mr Qi back to his quarters. Quick as possible."

But before Qi Yuexuan can leave, the sentry from the bottom of the mountain comes running into the courtyard and pants out: "Permission... to... report. The Japanese... are... coming."

Startled, Grandpa Fu asks: "How many?"

"Just... one, but... it's... an officer."

"If it's only one, can't you handle it? You'll be reporting that you've farted next."

"No... he's brought a... priest... with him... under a... white flag.. He says... he wants to... see the commander."

"That's good timing," Qi Yuexuan says happily. "Bring them up."

"What does a Japanese devil want here?" asks a bemused Grandpa Fu.

"You and your memory! Have you forgotten already? Didn't I say I wanted to do an exchange for medical supplies? I'm sure that's what it's about."

"So what have you actually got to exchange?"

"You'll understand when they get here."

"You really like your little mystery, don't you! But this is..."

"Ha ha, your thinking really is back to front, isn't it!" says Hao Bingchen. "Why are you ignoring the obvious in favour of the obscure? Didn't Yuexuan say at lunchtime, he guaranteed it was something you didn't want? Think about it – what was there in the barracks that you didn't want, that you didn't bring back?"

"What can it be?" Grandpa Fu frowns in concentration. "We even took their boots and uniforms. Apart from their corpses, we... didn't leave anything... behind." Suddenly, the light dawns, and he opens his eyes wide: "You're not... you're going to give them back the bodies are you?"

"That's right. Why not?"

"Isn't that the act of a traitor?"

"Bullshit!" Qi Yuexuan says with a laugh. "How can that be treason? Do you think traitors are so conscientious? We have to observe the decencies even when our two countries are at war. We don't kill soldiers who have surrendered, and the dead should have a proper burial. That is the mark of a wise and benevolent general. Besides, what else do we have to exchange? Do you think we should be handing you over to them?"

Grandpa Fu laughs and mutters to himself: "This is some kind of Japanese trick. The dead are dead..."

"More bullshit!" Qi Yuexuan grunts. "The Japanese are not like you. They have to send home the ashes of any soldier who falls in battle so they can consecrate a shrine and raise a memorial tablet. All you were worried about was collecting as much loot as possible, and you left your own brothers' bodies behind. Don't you get it? Looking after the dead is the responsibility of the living. Who is going to risk their life for you if you're seen to harden your heart against it?"

Grandpa Fu doesn't say a word and hangs his head in shame.

Leaning on the table and using all his strength to stay upright, Qi Yuexuan says in a loud voice: "Brothers, the Japanese are in fear of us and have sent someone to make a formal request. So stop feasting and form up in ranks. Everyone stand to attention, chests out, shoulders back, heads up, so you look like a real Army of Resistance. We don't want the Japanese to look down on us."

"Yessir!" the company responds, and they quickly divide into their respective squads and form up. Although they are wearing all sorts of different uniforms, each presents his own picture of the gallant soldier. With their faces and uniforms reflecting the flickering light of the torches and the bonfire, they look the very image of martial spirit.

Qi Yuexuan points to the general's seat of honour and says to Grandpa Fu: "Sit there. You have to look the part of the commander-in-chief."

"But you should be sitting there!"

"Do you think I can sit down? Alright then, for today you sit there and play the general, and I'll stand beside you as an adjutant." Qi Yuexuan can't help smiling as he says this.

It's not long before the sentry leads the other men into the courtyard, and the priest is revealed as Reverend Sherlock from the church at Longjiazhuang. The Japanese officer behind him is, indeed, carrying a white flag.

When he reaches the front of the crowd, the officer salutes Grandpa Fu as he sits in the seat of honour, and then says, in Chinese: "My is Shoi Hirosato. Is commander of Four Battalion Number Twenty-One Scratch Regiment of Japanese Army of North China at Junzhuang. It is order of Brigadier-General Chiaki to deliver letter to honourable commander. Please to accept."

So saying, he bows from the waist with the utmost respect, holding a letter above his head. Grandpa Fu complacently crosses one leg over the other, and forgetting that it is Qi Yuexuan standing behind him, he waves his hand and orders grandly: "Go and bring me the letter."

Qi Yuexuan is half amused and half angry, but he knows he can't afford to flare up in such a public arena. He does his best to grin and bear it and play the part of an aide-de-camp, but as soon as he moves his leg, an agonising pain shoots through him from his buttocks. Besides, his trousers are all tattered, and he couldn't possibly parade himself in front of the Japanese like that. Fortunately there is someone else, standing beside him, who is sharp-eyed enough to size up the situation and it is he who collects the letter to hand over to Grandpa Fu.

Grandpa Fu takes the letter out of its envelope, but the light is too bad and his old eyes are too weak, so he finds he can't read it. He signals behind him and orders: "Come and read it out for me."

Qi Yuexuan takes the letter and reads aloud: "To the distinguished commander of the North China Heroic Army of Anti-Japanese Resistance at Wanping..."

Having heard this much, Grandpa Fu changes his whole attitude. He quickly turns to look at the Japanese officer and is about to stand up, when Qi Yuexuan pushes him back down and whispers in his ear: "Keep your seat. He's showing you respect, not reprimanding you."

Qi Yuexuan then continues to read: "I have already received the letter you sent by hand with Reverend Sherlock, and I know that your honourable army wishes to return to us the remains of all officers and soldiers who die in battle. To this I say that we have gratitude in the extreme for you to act in accordance with international convention. The medicines that your honourable army requires, my side agrees to provide all of them, except penicillin of which we have short supply and not enough. Everything else we have prepared completely for you. If no impediment, please to make exchange early tomorrow morning at four o'clock at west side of brick kilns two *li* north of Junzhuang. My side guarantee safety. Respectful salutations. Sincerely from Brigadier-General Chiaki."

When he has heard the whole letter, Grandpa Fu asks quietly: "What do you think... is it acceptable?"

"Absolutely. You can agree to it."

"You're not afraid the Japanese are up to something?"

"Don't worry. They wouldn't dare."

Grandpa Fu raises his voice and says to the Japanese officer: "Very well. That is how we will do it. But I am giving you fair warning. We are showing you respect, so don't throw it back in our face. The men you can see here are just one of our plain-clothes squads and you are surrounded on all sides by others. If you don't stick to the agreement, we will not hesitate to fight, so it would be a very bad idea for you not to turn up at the appointed time."

"Yessir, yessir. We won't, we won't," the officer says, nodding and bowing, and waving his hands excitedly.

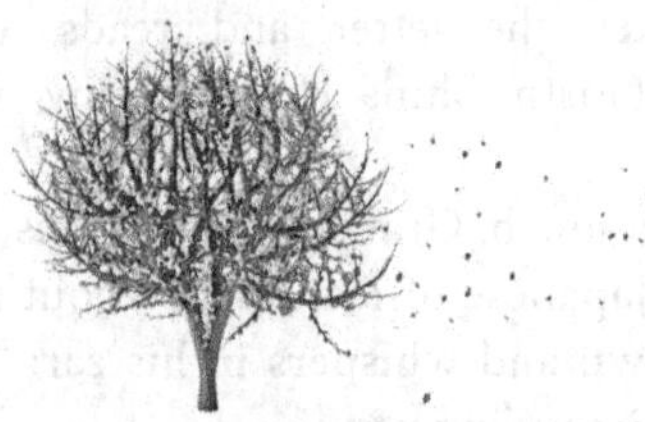

Chapter 42

Yang Zhixing has been worried ever since Wangtian left to get the grain from the family estates, and he has consulted the calendar every day, trying to work out where they should be. Caiping too has been asking for news three times a day, which has only served to increase his anxiety. He only relaxes when, much to his surprise, Wangtian and his companions return, all in one piece and full of vitality.

"So you're back then! How much grain did you bring?" Yang Zhixing asks excitedly.

"Eight big cartloads. Two hundred piculs in all."

"Good, good, excellent. You return in triumph! I've already cleared out the warehouse. You come in and rest, while I get some men to unload the carts."

"There's no need to unload, Uncle. I've got it all here." Wangtian pats the burlap sack under his arm.

Yang Zhixing has spent more than half a lifetime in business, and managed the Qi household for the same period, and what hasn't he seen when it comes to money? How much money has passed through his hands? But this really is the first time he has come across a deal like this and the first time he has seen so much counterfeit currency. He pulls out one of the army banknotes, studies it, feels it, turns it over, puts it down and considers it for a long time before asking: "How did you get so much money into the city? Weren't you searched?"

"Ha! There were some of Chenglong's men at the gates, and they recognised me. Besides, who's going to think there's money in a tatty old sack like this? They didn't even look."

"Well, you really have got some nerve, you young bastard. You're brand new to business and already you dare to risk your life on a deal like this?"

Seeing his stern expression, Wangtian stammers: "I... I know I didn't go through you and did it on my own initiative, but... well, you don't need to worry. I've got a plan for exchanging the fake notes. If it shows a loss, or even if it goes completely wrong, I'll carry the can myself."

"Ha ha, I'm not cross with you. I'm full of admiration. If you're not worried, why should I be? Even if you're risking your life, if it's worth it, then it's a good deal. Still, it would be better if you kept that head on your shoulders, so you need to think it through completely, don't you?"

"Yes, yes, you're right," Wangtian agrees, nodding enthusiastically.

Yang Zhixing continues: "These army notes are government work, much more convincing than the old independently printed fakes. There won't be any problem spending them, but you can't do it in bulk. You'll have to break it down into smaller batches. It goes without saying you don't want anyone taking them to the bank. Get them passing through several hands. Then, even if they get found out, it won't be too much of a problem."

"Yes, that's what I think too. I've given it a lot of thought, actually, and come up with a two-pronged approach – use some of it to buy merchandise and exchange the rest on the black market. Mr Hao thinks it's a good idea."

"Yes, you're right. So you'd better get started right away and concentrate on buying military supplies. I know where the Young Master and his men are at the moment, and one way or another, we've got to get some stuff to them."

"Yes. Mr Hao said that he'll be coming back to the city as soon as he's delivered the grain. When he gets here, we can ask him what they need most, and he can take it back to them without delay."

"Hmm, yes, good idea."

Wangtian suddenly remembers something: "Hey, Uncle Yang, is the Young Master paying those troops he raised?"

"Eh? Of course! Have you heard of a soldier not wanting pay?"

"Then... is it the government paying them?"

"Ha! And where exactly is the government now? They'd be waiting forever. They may call it a national army, but that's just a name. When the army was being formed, everyone pooled their money and weapons, but it was the Residence that led the way."

Wangtian laughs at Yang Zhixing's grumbling and points to the army notes on the *kang*: "Couldn't this be used for their pay? Wouldn't that be another way of getting rid of a large chunk of it?"

"No, no, he can't do that! Just think about it – how could an anti-Japanese resistance army pay its soldiers with Japanese army notes? Wouldn't that be the same as turning them into traitors? Besides, the Young Master and his men have been risking their lives in battle, so how could you dare pay them with counterfeit money? If we're going to use it, we'll have to change it into silver yuan or *fabi* first."

Wangtian flushes with embarrassment and doesn't reply.

Yang Zhixing relents a little and says with a smile: "But this idea of yours about using it as army pay could certainly work if we tweak it a little."

"What do you mean, tweak it?"

"It could be used to pay the CID squad and the puppet army. That would be quite fitting, wouldn't it?"

"You mean, you're thinking of involving Chenglong?"

"Not just Chenglong. We can try it out on anyone who's working for the Japanese and in a position of responsibility."

"Aiyo! That's a bit risky isn't it? Sounds like playing with fire."

"Don't you understand what these people are like? Which of them isn't like a dog drooling at a bone if they see the chance to make some money? If they weren't greedy, they wouldn't have become traitors in the first place. It's because they're greedy that they'll take the bait. Once they've taken it, they won't find it so easy to spit it out."

"Yes, I can see that. But won't you have to get personally involved?"

"Yes indeed. You're new to this kind of underworld business, and I wouldn't be happy leaving it to you. So let's do it this way – we'll split the job so I lead and you follow. How's that?"

"Fine, yes, fine."

Wangtian has just replied when they hear Mother Yan, Yue E and Caiping talking and laughing outside in the courtyard. They try to tidy things away, but half of the army notes are still on the *kang* when the three women come into the room.

Caiping cries out first: "Aiya! You're back!"

But Mother Yan immediately exclaims: "Great Heavens! Did you just rob a bank?"

EVER SINCE military intelligence's Beiping communications network was broken up, there has been no sign of any activity against either the Japanese or those Chinese traitors by the Traitor Elimination Squad. Several city-wide manhunts have had knock-on results so that even the Communist Party underground network has suffered quite a bit of damage. Most Party members and activist students have moved out to the mountains around Beiping, and although the Party's work hasn't ceased entirely, it has become increasingly secretive, so public security in the city appears much more settled. His successes have meant that Chenglong's reputation has grown daily, but after several months, the 'acting' part of the title bestowed on him by his superiors as acting section head of the new government's intelligence bureau has still not been removed. This is causing him some resentment. But he does understand that, as long as he is limited to the muddy waters of Beiping, he'll only ever be a fish that's grown horns, and never a real dragon. The Japanese have been very serious about military intelligence matters around Beiping and the whole of the North China theatre of operations, and they have exercised very strict control over them, so there has been no place for Chenglong. Recently, however, following the increased sphere of activity east and west of Beiping, by the Eighth Route Army and assorted resistance forces against the Japanese and the puppet army, the Japanese Army of North China has become increasingly unsettled and even panicked. A string of defeats has infuriated the army top brass, and they have been raining curses on the staff officers at GHQ and on the Tokko for the incompetence of their intelligence gathering and the opportunities they have let slip. They have, therefore, become increasingly reliant on Matsuzaki Harayama's intelligence work, and his policy of using Chinese against Chinese has gained increasing support. This has naturally presented Chenglong with a number of opportunities. Matsuzaki is not a man to act precipitately, but Yamaguchi has let slip a few things to Chenglong, saying there is a possibility they may extend the scope of his Special Operations Squad, allowing them to participate directly in the work of military intelligence in the environs of Beiping and in special army operations. Although this has not been confirmed, Chenglong is already anxious to get going.

THAT AFTERNOON, Yue E tells Chenglong that Wangtian's grain convoy has returned, and her father has asked him to come to dinner in the western courtyard so he can give him his share of the profits.

Dusk is falling when Chenglong arrives, and as he goes in through the main gate of the Minister's Residence, he is feeling a little out of sorts. Ever since the wall was built to create separate entrances to the western courtyard and the stable yard, he has only been through this gate once, when he came to the opening ceremony of the Yuhua Trading Company. It has also been several months since Yue E took the two children and moved back into her parental home, and although they haven't quarrelled again, he knows that they are just keeping up appearances. Even when the children see him, they greet him very shyly and can't wait to slip away. As for any idea that his mother-in-law might treasure him as a son-in-law, that's just wishful thinking, as she has a face like thunder whenever she sees him. His father-in-law, by contrast, is all smiles; the smiles, however, are somewhat superficial and tend to give Chenglong goosebumps. As for his elder brother, he has been raised to the heavens from the Gao family's broken-down old shack and entered the main courtyard of the Minister's Residence. Noble Red, who he himself had really cared for, is now his sister-in-law, and husband and wife seem very happy. Where isn't his brother doing better than him? The more comparisons Chenglong makes, the angrier he gets. In the outside world he can stamp his foot and the whole city trembles, but inside this courtyard, he always feels ordinary and inadequate. Even though he has only been asked for a bite to eat, he really doesn't want to go, but he has made a big effort and come for his share of the money, so then there'll be no more need for currying his brother's favour. With that thought in his head, he begins to feel a little more comfortable.

. . .

THE TABLE HAS BEEN LAID in the main building of the main courtyard, but Mother Yan, Yue E, Caiping and the two children are not sitting there. They are going to eat separately in the side courtyard, so it is only the three men at the main table.

"Come and eat your fill," Yang Zhixing says with a faint smile. "There are no women and children to get in the way, so the three of us can drink as we please and talk freely. Come now, drink up."

Once he has finished a cup of wine, Wangtian wordlessly hands Chenglong a thick paper package. Chenglong opens it and sees it contains two bundles of Japanese army ten yen notes. He pretends to refuse them: "What's the hurry? We're brothers, after all. Wait till you make the money from selling the goods, and then I'll take it."

Yang Zhixing takes over the conversation: "Grain is in short supply these days. The eight cartloads didn't even reach Beiping but were all sold in Hebei. We got a much better price than here and cleared a healthy profit. Stop being polite and take it."

Chenglong laughs and stuffs the package inside his coat, saying: "Alright, Big Brother. You're the real article, that's for sure. This is a quicker way of making money than bothering with business. These two bundles are more than I get paid in a year. Come on, pick up your cup and we'll have a toast to you, and from now on I'll look to you for any financial support I need."

Wangtian picks up his cup and sighs: "Ai! All you see is the profit, but I'm still uneasy."

"You've sold the goods, cash in hand, so what are you uneasy about?"

"If I'd been paid in silver yuan, I'd be happy enough all right, but I got it all in Japanese army notes, and that's not so good for replenishing my stock."

"Couldn't you have refused the notes? If he didn't have any yuan, then *fabi* would have done. No proper money, no sale. Selling the grain elsewhere wouldn't be a problem."

"I sold it to the Japanese garrison in Jinghai County. I wasn't given any choice. Do you think if I'd asked for silver yuan or *fabi*, they'd have had any?"

Chenglong considers this and responds: "Actually, it doesn't really matter. Now Beiping, Tianjin and the rest of North China are occupied by the Japanese, the army notes have become devalued. They don't even give us all our salary in them, only if they don't have enough yuan. But if you want to get a decent exchange rate for them, you have to do it on the black market."

"That's what I told him," Yang Zhixing interjects, "but he's stubborn and he'll keep on worrying as long as he's holding those Japanese notes."

"Why shouldn't I worry?" Wangtian laughs bitterly. "If it was just a small quantity, that would be different, but I can't exchange all that lot on the black market. And to tell the truth, we're not even sure whether it's genuine or counterfeit. You can tell by the ring of silver yuan, and *fabi* have a watermark, but this rubbish... Ai! I worry every day I still have it."

When Chenglong hears this, he hastily takes out the paper package, extracts a note, feels it, rubs it between his fingers, examines it closely, then laughs: "Don't worry, it's genuine enough. There are counterfeit silver yuan and counterfeit *fabi*, but I've never seen any counterfeit army notes. I haven't even heard of there being any. China can't manufacture this kind of Japanese paper."

"Are you sure about that?"

"Ha! Don't you believe me? What do you think I'm up to? Alright then, suppose it is fake – if I can't spot it, then you'll have no trouble spending it. Aright now, let's drink up."

Wangtian finally takes a sip. Yang Zhixing glances at him and can see he's still not happy.

"Hey you! Stop fretting or you'll spoil the occasion."

"Hey you, yourself! It's fine to say that from where you're standing, but suppose it was your money. You'd be fretting even more than I am."

"Ah! So you're in charge now, are you? Alright then, give it to me at fifty per cent of face value, and I'll take the lot off your hands. How about it?"

"You would say that, wouldn't you, Uncle Yang. Forget about fifty per cent off. If you really want it all, I'll give you a seventy per cent discount."

"For real?"

"Of course! Just tell me when you want to pay for it."

"Ah well, I can't say for certain. I can't use the Residence's money, and I don't have that sort of money to hand myself. If we've got a deal, I'll have to rely on my reputation to borrow it, and then..."

"That's enough, Uncle Yang! Here I am throwing caution to the winds and trying to cut my losses, and all you can do is make fun of me!"

Wangtian has had enough of the subject. He raises his glass and drains it without waiting for the others. Yang Zhixing is not happy about being cut off like this. He looks at Wangtian, grunts and raises his cup, but he only drinks half of it. Meanwhile, Chenglong has been watching the other two bickering and has held his peace, although inwardly he is thinking hard. He takes a sip of wine, looks at the two men and asks with a faint smile: "Just how much of the stuff have you got, Big Brother, if it's making you this anxious?"

"You think I should be less worried? I'm not worried enough! I brought back more than fifty thousand from the sale of my goods on this trip. Ai!" Wangtian sighs, then changes the subject: "Anyway, that's enough of that. Let's drink."

But Chenglong leaves his cup where it is, winks and asks: "How about I help you by taking the whole fifty thousand off your hands?"

"Are you pulling my leg?"

"No, I'm on the up and up."

"Then I accept. When..."

"Don't get ahead of yourself. There are a few things I want to get clear first. When you say seventy per cent off, do you mean from the official rate or the black-market price?"

"Who'd want army notes at the official rate?" Wangtian hesitates, then continues: "If you're really serious about it, I'll give you family rates, and knock seventy per cent off the black-market price. If there was less, I could exchange it all without giving up any profit, but as there's so much of it, I'll have trouble shifting it all in one go if I don't accept some loss of profit. I got a decent price for my stuff this time, and I'd rather take a little less profit and keep things nice and easy."

"Next payday, counting all the offices of the CID squad, I've got several hundred men to pay," Chenglong says. "I can get rid of all of your army notes in one go. I'll use the money HQ sends me to pay you."

"Playing the same old trick, eh? Swapping a potato for a mountain yam?"

"As if I'd dare! I've got an arrangement with some people in my bank, and I can exchange it there without giving the game away. But..."

"But what?"

"The thing is... the price you've given me is fine, but I've got quite a few people to pay off. So what do you say to knocking off another ten per cent? How about it?"

Yang Zhixing doesn't wait for Wangtian to reply before breaking in irritably: "Now you're just kicking a man when he's down!"

"My brother wouldn't say anything as harsh as that. Family understands how these things work. By the time I've paid everyone else off, I'll just be getting a go-between's cut. If you feel you can't agree, then we'll leave the whole thing. What do you say?"

Yang Zhixing spreads his hands wide and shakes his head. He looks at Wangtian and says: "You do what you think best."

Chenglong slaps his chest and says: "Whatever I do or don't do will be open and above board. It's not as though there won't be another time. You've always got to look to the long-term in business, haven't you? However much there is next time, I'll take it. If I don't go through with it this time, there's always the Kempeitai and the puppet army. Don't worry, I've got connections there too."

"If we make a deal, you've got to pay silver yuan. I don't want *fabi*," says Wangtian, breaking his silence.

Chenglong is delighted: "Don't worry. The banks are only taking in *fabi* these days, not paying them out. Even if you wanted them, you couldn't get them."

Wangtian finally nods his head. "Alright, that's how we'll do it. I accept. At least we'll be keeping it in the family."

"Yes, quite right!" Chenglong laughs, and he hurriedly picks up his wine cup, saying: "Drink up!"

Darkness is filling the sky, and the streetlights are lit. Because the Eighth Route Army blew up the power plant on Shijingshan, Beiping has been without electricity for three days, and this evening is the first time since then that the lights have come on. If it hadn't been for the Eighth Route Army's shortage of explosives, and their unfamiliarity with the layout of the plant, the city could have been plunged into darkness for who knows how long.

Clown has just arrived outside the gate of the Lian family's little courtyard, carrying a small sack. The gate is unlocked, but he doesn't go in. He just pushes it open a crack and peers inside. He sees there is no light on in Yuxiang's room on the north side, and Sergeant Lian's western room is also dark. The only light comes from the room on the east side belonging to Yuxiang's three little brothers and sisters. Clown knows that Sergeant Lian can't have come home yet, and he has, in fact, been hurrying to take advantage of his absence. Yuxiang's elder little sister, Yufang, has just turned thirteen and has been ordered by her father to help out in the kitchen at the night soil depot, and they come home together every day, so she is certainly not there either. So at the moment, apart from Yuxiang herself, the only others who should be in are her eleven-year-old little sister, Yufen, and her seven-year-old brother Yuzhu. He can hear Yuzhu in the eastern room crying out that he is hungry, and Yufen shouting back at him, but he can't hear Yuxiang's voice.

After that occasion when Yuxiang threw herself into the Houhai and was most fortuitously rescued by Clown, although the girl's life was saved, she lost her unborn child. After this trauma she lies stiff in a hospital bed for three months, until after the Qingming Festival, when her body gradually relaxes. Chenglong's reaction is pretty hard-hearted. Although he does visit the hospital, he stays only long enough to fart.

"This is a deliberate attempt to smear my good name," Chenglong snarls at Sergeant Lian through gritted teeth. Then he leaves a little money and stalks away haughtily.

After Yuxiang goes home, he visits her a few times but never with any particular good grace. But as Yuxiang returns to her senses, there even seems to be a little warmth from him left in the silver coins and banknotes he hands over to her. Moreover, as her health gradually improves, he becomes gradually more solicitous and often stays overnight in the northern room. Since the disappearance of the Traitor Elimination Squad, he has also become much less neurotic about his safety. When visiting her, he comes alone, without a single bodyguard, but he still keeps his arrivals unpredictable. As far as marrying Yuxiang goes, he has pushed that idea to the back of his mind and not reconsidered it. Seeing that this plan of his has hit a snag, Sergeant Lian doesn't dare pursue it for fear of stirring up a hornets' nest. Fortunately he still has a few strings to his bow. At least he retains his manager's job at the night soil depot, while at home, he can continue to get some money out of the women in his house. Just as before, he can let his wife work as a hooker from home to earn some extra, and he can make additional money by selling his second and third daughters into that brothel. If a man has no shame, anything is possible.

. . .

IF YUXIANG IS SUFFERING, Clown is suffering even more. When they had been on the icy expanse of the Houhai, hovering between life and death, normal restraints were forgotten, and they said things they would not normally dare say, and did things they would not normally dare do. They opened their hearts to each other, so how can they now take it all back and hold back their feelings? While Yuxiang was confined to bed, Clown came to see her almost every day, taking advantage of his roundabout night soil collection route, and of her father's absence. Although neither of them have made their feelings explicit, they both know exactly how things stand. Of course Yuxiang's little brother and sisters are too young to know how to keep quiet, and when Sergeant Lian finds out about the visits, he stamps his foot and tears him off a strip.

"I know you saved our Yuxiang's life, and we owe you a great debt of gratitude. But Yuxiang has a master, and neither of us wants to get on his wrong side, do we? Even if *you* want to get yourself killed, don't drag Yuxiang into it, and don't drag me and my family into it either. Even if Master Liu does give up his claim on her, what makes you think you'd get a look in? What have you got to offer except a quick wit? I'm telling you now, whatever the truth of what's gone before, it's best that everyone forgets about it as if it had never happened. If I catch you here again, I'm sorry, but chucking you out will be the least of it. All I have to do is drop a word in Master Liu's ear, and he won't just kill you, he'll skin you alive."

This speech leaves Clown in a bit of a quandary. On his own account, he'd be happy to risk anything, but he doesn't want to drag Yuxiang into it. Over the last two months, Chenglong has been visiting more frequently, so he hasn't dared go back, but a little voice in his head keeps nagging at him, so he still goes to stand in the doorway snatching a quick glimpse inside. Now he's been back from the grain expedition for ten days or so, a new world has opened up to him, and he has found an additional way of earning money. The first thing he did on getting back was to hand in his notice at the night soil depot and collect what was owing him. Throwing out his chest, he announced to Sergeant Lian that he was leaving the next day and wouldn't be taking orders from him any more. Now he has come to the Lian home to make his feelings properly known to Yuxiang.

As Clown stands distractedly in the doorway, Yuxiang appears from the northeast corner of the courtyard, carrying a tray of cornbread and vegetables. Of course! She's been cooking, and the kitchen is in a narrow passageway between the northern and eastern buildings, so it isn't surprising he couldn't see her before.

Clown hurriedly calls out her name, and when she doesn't hear him, he bends down, picks up a pebble and throws it into the courtyard so it rolls with a clatter under her feet.

Yuxiang turns to look, guessing who it is. She waves hurriedly to him and takes the tray of food into the room.

"Don't eat so fast, Yuzhu! There's no need to act like a hungry ghost!" he hears her say.

"But I'm starving!" Yuzhu says. "The school has ordered everyone to bring in five catties of iron. You didn't give me enough, so I swapped my cornbread with a classmate for some. I only had one left for lunch, so of course I'm hungry."

"That's enough of that. I've already handed over the chains from the gates. Do you think I own an iron factory? Where am I going to get that much?"

"It's no use. There are Japanese inspectors at school, and they say that anyone who doesn't bring in the iron won't be allowed into class. Next they're going to ask for copper as well."

Number three daughter Yufen chips in too: "I heard Headmaster Li say that every household has to contribute, tomorrow and the day after too. Anyone who doesn't will be fined, and if they can't pay, they'll be arrested."

Yuxiang sighs in exasperation: "Ai! That's just plain extortion. Really..." She bites her tongue before turning and pulling open the door.

"Aren't you going to eat, Big Sister?"

"I'm not hungry."

"Where are you going?"

"I'm going to take the knocker off the front door before someone else does."

Yuxiang goes out of the room, shutting the door behind her and hurries over to the front door. She giggles when she sees Clown and whispers: "So you're back from Shandong, Brother Clown."

"Yes." Clown waits outside the door, then pushes it open to step inside. To his surprise, Yuxiang holds the door to.

"No, don't let the little ones see you. They'll just gossip. My father and Yufang will be back soon. He often comes home unexpectedly, and you mustn't bump into him... let's talk here."

Clown grunts in annoyance and then sighs.

"You mustn't think..." Yuxiang says hurriedly. "Ai! I'm not trying to get rid of you. I'm only not letting you in because I don't want you to get into trouble. You've still got to work at that place..."

"Hah! I handed in my notice today. I don't work there any more."

"Then what are you..."

"I'm going to work for Elder Brother Wangtian. It's a much better job."

"Then..." Yuxiang swallows what she's about to say and lowers her voice: "Why don't you go round to the rear wall of the northern building. There's a little window we can talk through."

"Alright," Clown says brightly. He turns and is about to go when he stops and hands Yuxiang the cloth bundle he is carrying through the crack in the door.

"Here, I brought this for you."

Yuxiang takes it and asks: "What's this? It's really heavy."

"Ah! It's copper. Enough for several contributions."

"You've saved the day!" Yuxiang says, taking an object out of the bundle and inspecting it. To her surprise, it's a copper chamber pot. At the sight of it she can't help laughing: "What have you brought this for? Are you sick of the smell of piss? Are you too shy to use it?"

Clown tries hard not to laugh and replies: "The Japanese are forcing us to hand over copper, and this is all I've got. It's made of copper, after all, and they won't know what it's for."

Yuxiang hurries over to the northern room, but she doesn't dare light a lamp, so she stands in the dark on the *kang*, opens the window and looks out of it. After a moment, she sees Clown arrive and stand directly below. The window is high up so she can't see his face, only the top of his shaved head. He doesn't say anything for a long time, so Yuxiang coughs gently, but he only replies with a grunt.

"Say something."

Clown sighs and asks: "So... are you just going to go on living like this?"

"How else am I going to survive?" Yuxiang whispers. "Ai! You... you shouldn't have saved me when I jumped in the lake."

"Can't you make one last effort and come away and find a different life?"

"What's the use? No effort is going to get me out of where I am now. And even if I did get out, how would I be able to live?"

Clown falls silent again, then he suddenly asks: "Do you love me?"

Yuxiang just grunts, before heaving a deep sigh: "What's the use of talking like that?"

"What's the use?" Clown is getting a little agitated, and his voice gets louder. "You love me, and I love you. We..."

"You're wasting your time. I'm... I'm not worthy of you."

"I don't care."

"But I do. I don't even respect myself, and I'll never... I'll never be able to hold my head up again in this lifetime." Yuxiang's voice is becoming a little shrill. After a while she continues: "There's no point in brooding over this. The fact is, there's no hope..." She doesn't finish and closes her mouth, but she can't stop the sound of her tears.

"Aiya! Don't..." Clown stands on tiptoe, straining to stand as tall as possible. Craning his neck upwards, he says: "What do you mean, 'there's no hope'? You have to fight for things in life. I've worked it all out. If you're willing, we can run away together."

"Run away? Run away where?"

"Ha! The world's a big place. I can't believe there's not somewhere we can be safe."

Yuxiang doesn't say anything, and a melancholy silence falls.

Unable to supress his temper, Clown asks: "Well then? Give me a firm answer."

Yuxiang hesitates for a moment, then asks back: "You... you really don't hate me?"

Clown explodes in exasperation: "For heaven's sake, I swear on my life, if..."

"Stop, there's no need. I believe you. Just... just tell me when. I have to get ready."

"There's no need to rush. We'll wait until I've helped Brother Wangtian finish his bit of business, then we'll go. I'll have plenty of money then."

"I've got some money I've put by, too."

"I'm not going to use up *your* money. I'm a proper man. I don't live off women like some pretty-boy gigolo!"

"Then... how long have we got to wait?"

"Around a month at most, ten days or so at best."

"Alright, but I've got to tell you, the sooner the better. I'm going to have a lot of restless nights."

"Don't worry, now I've got your word, I'm not going to mess around, am I? Right, that's it. I'll... I'll be going."

So saying, he leaves with a spring in his step, constantly looking around him, left and right, up and down, until, like a frog in a well looking up at the sky, he gives himself a crick in the neck.

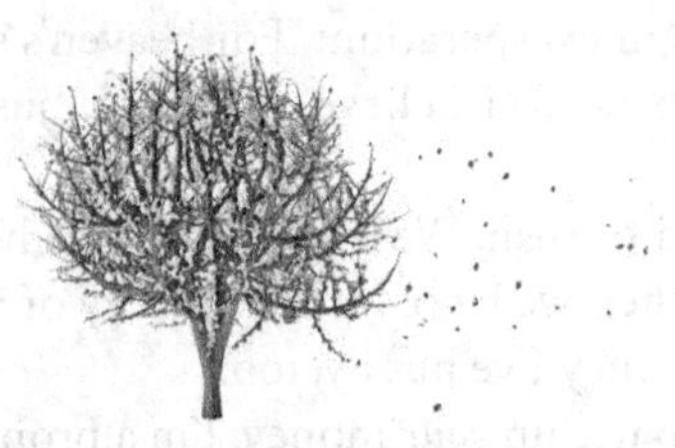

Chapter 43

After Zhang Zhicheng has relieved the encirclement of Longjiazhuang with his tactic of 'laying siege to Wei to help Zhao' by attacking Junzhuang and devising a supporting ambuscade, he then withdraws to his base of operations in the area south of the Yongding River. He has made arrangements to allow the troops a few days to rest and regroup, to report the circumstances of the battle to GHQ and to wait for the next deployment. But after he has only been in Jiuyuancun for one day, he receives company orders to return to Zhaitang in the central area of his base of operations. He is puzzled by this. His original proposal for his detachment was to join with the whole of the First Detachment and with those soldiers of the Ninth Division responsible for works in the area, then to link up with the Left Barracks Heroic Army and other local forces. Then they could strike while the iron is hot and seize back the Japanese bases in the region between Junzhuang and Wenquan, and extend their own base of operations to the south of the Yongding River. By doing this, they could connect the whole mountain region of Wanping and Changping, extend the range of their operations and strengthen the depth of their defences. It would also bring them in line with the military operations in eastern Hebei, allow them to take up encircling positions around Beiping, and undoubtedly improve both their defensive and offensive capabilities. To his surprise, however, he has rolled up his sleeves for action in vain, as he is ordered to retreat immediately. It is only when he leads his troops back to Zhaitang that he understands why.

It is not until the Ninth Brigade returns to base that Instructor Lin is able to inquire into the movements of the various units. Wu Xinmin states that, when he discovered that Japanese troops were on the move from the direction of Yangtaishan, he immediately sent men to alert the defences. The company commander of those men confirms this. Lin still feels there is something fishy going on, and he secretly questions the soldiers themselves. Although many of these men are Wu Xinmin's trusted aides, their wall of secrecy contains a few chinks. Lin's suspicions are confirmed, and by following the trail of clues he is given, he finally arrives at the truth. He immediately goes in person to Zhaitang and makes a report to Divisional Command and the Party Committee. When Wu Xinmin hears of this, he too hurries to Zhaitang. He flatly denies any involvement in the looting of the minor tombs at Jiuwangfen, saying he has no knowledge of it whatsoever. Since it is the irregular Army of the Left Barracks that is stationed there, they must be the ones responsible. He also makes the false counteraccusation that Instructor Lin has fabricated the whole thing in order to push out non-Party members, and that he is illegally encroaching on his, Wu Xinmin's, military authority. With each side insisting on their version of events, it is hard to decide who is telling the truth, and the Party organisation and the various company commanders including Commander Zhao Ran himself, find themselves with divergent opinions. One side wants to suspend Wu Xinmin from duty and send men from the political bureau to investigate; if Instructor Lin's account proves to be true, then there should be no mitigation, and Wu Xinmin should be severely dealt with. The other side is strongly of the opinion that, in the current state of war, they shouldn't listen to rumours, and in the interests of military stability, further investigation should be postponed.

Wu Xinmin is Zhao Ran's aunt's cousin and also his close confidant, and everything has been done under Zhao Ran's orders, without him actually being personally involved. Now the plot has been exposed, Zhao Ran naturally wants to delay any investigation and then gloss things over, so that what starts as an important matter diminishes until it disappears completely. However, the soldiers involved were not originally part of the national anti-Japanese resistance, and although Zhao Ran is a high-ranking officer and an official in the department of military affairs, within the Eighth Route Army forces there is an open Communist Party apparatus. Although they observe the democratic decision-making and collective leadership of the army, in this case there is no way they are going to rely solely on the word of one or two people in this matter. So, despite Zhao Ran's desperate urgings, in the end the majority triumphs over the minority, and a resolution is passed to send men from the political bureau to start an investigation. To placate Zhao Ran, however, Wu Xinmin is not suspended from his duties, but they do order the whole of the Ninth Brigade to return to Zhaitang, at the same time as they order Zhang Zhicheng to bring the Second Division back there too. Although no official explanation is given, everyone there understands why the top brass are taking these precautions, and they also understand that the dilemma their leaders face is like a festering boil about to explode with pus.

ZHAITANG IS AN OLD TOWNSHIP that used to be called Lingguichuan. In the Tang dynasty it was the location for the Lingyue Temple, and the place where the monks and pilgrims took their vegetarian meals later grew into a small village that became known as Zhaitang, meaning 'refectory hall'. Many temples are now located there, not just dating back to the Tang dynasty, but from the Liao, Jin, Yuan, Ming and Qing as well. Moreover, because of its strategic position on a major road, it has always been a magnet for military action. In the Ming dynasty, a defensive stone fortress and several accompanying watchtowers were constructed, making it one of the more important townships in Pingxi.

When the Ninth Brigade returns, it establishes itself in East Zhaitangcun, while the Second Division is quartered in Malancun. These two villages, one east and one west, are both very close to the stone fortress, which is serving as the divisional garrison, and together they form a triangle. In normal circumstances, a divisional garrison would certainly set up sentry posts and send out patrols, but it would usually be some distance away from enemy-held territory and the field of guerrilla operations. If it contained a whole division, it would typically include a command and logistics corps of a couple of hundred men, along with a separate guard company patrolling the entrances to the villages and the main gates of the fortress. But circumstances are different here, and although the two companies have not fallen out, when the Ninth Brigade arrive, they immediately establish twin patrols in the directions of the fortress and of Malancun; they also set up both open and covert sentry posts and place a machinegun on the high ground at the entrance to East Zhaitangcun. Wu Xinmin and his subordinates secretly scope out the dispositions of the divisional offices and the residences of the divisional commanders and the political cadres. These unusual movements are quickly spotted by the Party committee, who immediately instruct Zhang Zhicheng to be on high alert in order to maintain close surveillance and be prepared for all eventualities. They also strengthen the guard over the divisional offices and pay particular attention to the movements of Zhao Ran and his personal bodyguards.

As dusk falls, three men come riding from the direction of Fangshan, skirting Baihuashan to arrive at Zhaitang. One of them announces himself to be Commander Zhao Ran's maternal uncle. He is a man of about fifty, wearing a long gown and with the refined and cultured manner of a scholar. He says he has come from Zhao Ran's mother specifically to visit Zhao Ran and deliver a letter. The sentries lead the three men to the command post, where Zhao Ran shows no sign of recognising them at first sight. Blank-faced, he is about to question them, when the man calling himself his uncle breaks out into laughter.

"Aiyo, so you're my nephew Lian Xiu, are you? We haven't met before, but I heard some time ago that you have been doing important work in the fight against the Japanese. That makes me very proud. My name is Zhou, and I have lived in Hong Kong for many years. My mother and your grandmother are sisters, so I am your mother's first cousin and your maternal uncle. Your mother has gone to Guangzhou and Hong Kong to give lectures and solicit contributions in support of the anti-Japanese resistance. I haven't seen my older sister and younger brother for twenty years, and I've decided to find them again now. I'm here on a buying expedition for mainland goods, so your mother asked me to look you up. Here is a letter she has written you."

Zhao Ran listens to this in some astonishment. He knows there are numerous sisters on his grandmother's side of the family, but he has never heard of any relatives in Hong Kong. However, when he looks at the characters 'To my Son Lian Xiu' written on the envelope, he recognises his mother's handwriting.

When his mother, Hong Wenguo, left Beiping in August the year before, she took her whole family with her to Wuhan in order to promote the resistance movement and solicit contributions to support and supply the troops. Although he hasn't seen her for almost a year, Zhao Ran has received family news from various sources and has heard that they have won support from both the government and society in general in Wuhan, and that his mother has become a figurehead of the resistance movement. She has gained the soubriquet 'Mother of the Guerrillas', and newspapers and periodicals both at home and abroad are carrying stories about her. Wuhan was in a critical situation after the Japanese assault on Nanjing, so she has moved her family to Guangzhou. Zhao Ran himself has longed for government recognition and for his own troops to become part of the regular government army. This would be far better than his current status, following the grassroots Eighth Route Army as an inferior, irregular force. Whether this uncle of his is genuine or not is not important; the important thing is that he has brought exciting news. Laughing genially, he hastens to invite his visitor into his own small courtyard and instructs his subordinates to turn away any other callers, without exception. The two men sit talking and drinking from dusk that day to cockcrow the next. As to what they are talking about, no one knows, but it is quite apparent that the conversation is both congenial and intimate. It is even more apparent that the meeting has acted on Zhao Ran like a huge lungful of opium, so energised and excited has he become.

The next morning, Zhao Ran announces that he wants to summon an immediate meeting of all cadres of divisional commander rank and above, in order to take stock of the current state of the war and to consider a new plan of campaign. Such meetings are not unusual within the military, but at a time when suspicions are rife, it is inevitable that those suspicions increase. The divisional Party committee is in something of a quandary: they have no reason for not agreeing to the meeting, but they are also worried that, with the cadres of all the divisions and brigades assembled, various grievances could come to the boil if there is any kind of dissent. They are also afraid that, with all the important officers absent from their troops, the men themselves might take the opportunity to stir up trouble. After much consideration and discussion, they eventually agree to the meeting, but they request that each division be required to leave behind one senior officer in charge of the troops, and that during the period of the meeting, the troops are to be on standby, in a state of increased readiness and with all leave cancelled; nor are there to be any unauthorised troop movements. When these instructions are passed down the line, some junior cadres can guess something of what is going on, while others remain in ignorance. But everyone notes that the high-ups are getting a little jumpy. However, as subsequent events are to prove, it is fortunate that the Party committee took these precautions and prevented their men becoming involved in a bloody internal massacre.

As it turns out, the meeting passes off without incident, and everything remains calm in East Zhaitangcun. Just after the meeting finishes, Zhao Ran receives a telephone call from Commander Nie, who has charge of the whole military region of Shanxi, Chahar and Rehe, ordering him to leave the next day to attend a meeting in Fuping and then undertake a short training course at the military academy. In his absence, his second-in-command, Gao Peng, is to assume command of his division. Zhao Ran understands immediately that someone has already sent a report of everything that has been going on. He is unsure whether this trip to Fuping augurs success or disaster.

A FORTNIGHT OR SO after the celebration party, the wounds on Qi Yuexuan's buttocks have still not healed properly. Although they are not as bad as on the first day, they still keep him awake at night and prevent him from sitting or lying down. He eats and sleeps lying on his stomach, and if he needs to relieve himself, he has first to lower his legs to the ground from his prone position, and then get help to lift him slowly to his feet and help him shuffle along. If he just needs to urinate, it's no problem, but if he needs to open his bowels, there are inevitable cries of pain.

Grandpa Fu is astounded that Qi Yuexuan didn't cry out during the beating, though of course he has no idea of the trick he played with the anaesthetic cream. But however strange he finds it, there is no denying the reality of the open wounds on Qi Yuexuan's buttocks, and those are enough to convince him. When he looks back on things, that Young Master can't just have been putting on a show, can he? He's not just good with fine words and fancy talk, he has shown he can deploy the troops and lead them into battle, too, hasn't he? Those twenty strokes of the rod have revealed his authenticity and magnanimity; have shown just what kind of man he is. In particular, after Master Qi's respectful and even humble manner when that Japanese came to the camp, which saved his face and diffused his anger, how can he not be convinced? Indeed, when he compares all this with his own petty-mindedness, he can't help but feel ashamed.

So now, after the midnight exchange with the Japanese has been successfully completed, when he sees Hao Bingchen is in a hurry to return to the city on official business, but is worried about Qi Yuexuan, he thumps himself on the chest and says: "You go about your business, Mr Hao, and don't worry about a thing. I'm not going to make the same mistake twice. From now on, as far as Young Master Qi is concerned, if I may use a literary expression, where he leads, I follow, like a fart behind a donkey. Anyone who means him harm will have to get through me first. If I fail, then next time you're back, you can aim that telescopic sight of yours at me, and 'pow'! Alright?"

Stopped in his tracks, Hao Bingchen can't help laughing, and even when he has gone some distance and looks back, he remains smiling.

In FACT, Grandpa Fu is still worried. The troops stationed at Qiwangfen are very exposed now, and he is afraid that the Japanese might mount a retaliatory attack. But according to Qi Yuexuan's analysis, the devils' spirit has been broken, and they are busy enough with their own affairs back at their base with neither the time nor inclination to consider a counterattack. Moreover, troop movements are not something that can be undertaken in just a few hours.

"The more calm and confident you appear," Qi Yuexuan opines, "the more scared the Japanese will be of making a move. We can rest up here for ten days or more, until their reinforcements arrive, and we'll still have plenty of time."

When he hears this, Grandpa Fu details men to arrange daily parades, to raise the colours, to make a show of putting up propaganda posters in all the surrounding villages, appealing for new recruits and soliciting contributions of money and grain. Japanese aircraft fly numerous reconnaissance missions overhead, and the troops on the ground make no effort to hide, but stand in plain view beating drums, banging gongs and blowing trumpets. Just as predicted, after a couple of weeks, there has been no movement from the Japanese in Beiping, or in the bases at Junzhuang and Wenquan. Nor has there been any sign of reinforcements. Meanwhile, the renown of the Wanping Regiment of the Heroic Army of Anti-Japanese Resistance spreads far and wide, and the villagers for many miles around all know that there is an army that has beaten the Japanese devils so badly, all they can do is cower in their camps. In no time, grain is arriving at their gates, along with individual volunteers to enlist and groups of local militia from the villages keen to pledge allegiance. Even some bandit troops from the mountains want to join the roll. Qi Yuexuan is still lying prone in bed, unable to move, so naturally Grandpa Fu basks in the adulation for several days. In fact, there are wheels within wheels of which they are unaware; while they were attacking Longjiazhuang, the eastward advance of the Eighth Route Army had already reached the border area between Rehe, Chahar and eastern Shanxi, and mounted several offensives, first to the south and then to the north. The Japanese in Beiping had already had their claws drawn and were hard put just to defend the city, let alone have time to think about what was going on in the mountains outside the city.

One afternoon, a sentry comes running in to report that Captain Wu of the Eighth Route Army has arrived with an escort for a relative of Qi Yuexuan's, who says he is his brother-in-law. Not knowing exactly what might be going on, Grandpa Fu hurries in to see Qi Yuexuan.

Qi Yuexuan has heard everything from inside his room and doesn't wait for him to ask, but he says irritably: "Pah! That's just nonsense! I've married three times, but I've only got one brother-in-law, and he went to Hong Kong ages ago. This must be some trick that fellow Wu has thought up because he's afraid we'll refuse to see him."

"So you won't see him? Shall I get them to send them away?"

"Don't do that. I still want to hear what he has to say and see who is masquerading as my brother-in-law."

Quite soon, Wu Xinmin leads the way into the outer room, followed by the man who was calling himself Zhao Ran's uncle at Zhaitang. As soon as he enters the room, he looks around him, and without offering any greetings, immediately bursts out laughing and says: "Ai! Yuexuan? You've grown very grand for a Young Master!"

Before Grandpa Fu can say anything, Qi Yuexuan's laughter rings out: "Ha ha! It's you Zhengjie!"

"I know it's me. Why don't you come out?"

On hearing this, Qi Yuexuan hurriedly struggles up, but before he is even out of bed, he groans and lies back down, calling out: "You'd better come in here. I'm stuck in my lair."

Putting aside the question of whether Zhou Zhengjie is Zhao Ran's maternal uncle, he most certainly is Zhou Zhengying's elder brother and Qi Yuexuan's brother-in-law. And like Hao Bingchen, he is a friend of many years standing. When he goes into the bedroom and sees what a sorry state Qi Yuexuan is in, he exclaims: "Aiya! Are you wounded?"

"No."

"Then..."

"Ah! I took twenty strokes of the rod."

"What! Aren't you in charge of this army? Why..."

"A prince who transgresses must be punished the same as a commoner. I ordered my own beating."

"Why did you do that?"

Qi Yuexuan flashes a glacial look at Wu Xinmin: "Ask him. When we attacked Longjiazhuang together, he abandoned us halfway there and ordered our reinforcements to go off and rob some tombs. He caused twenty or thirty of our brothers to lose their lives for nothing. I took this beating because of him."

Zhou Zhengjie grimaces and asks: "Did... did that really happen."

"Yes," Wu Xinmin stammers, "but we didn't intend to drag Mr Qi into it when we planned it. It really..."

"That's enough," Qi Yuexuan interrupts angrily, looking from one to the other. "You don't need to explain. Ai! How did you two get mixed up together?"

"Ha! What kind of talk is that?" says Zhou Zhengjie. "Mixed up together? We have joined forces and travelled together in a great enterprise for the Anti-Japanese Resistance. I don't want to hear about that little affair of yours. It's chicken feed compared with the danger the nation is in."

"So... didn't you go to Hong Kong after all then?" Qi Yuexuan asks.

"The nation's troubles come first. I went, but of course I hurried back."

"For the Resistance? If you wanted to fight the Japanese, why did you go to Hong Kong in the first place? And you struggled through the mountains to join up with the Eighth Route Army? Bah! I don't know what's come over you. Are you really such an altruist!"

Zhou Zhengjie doesn't take any offence: "Ha ha! Sharp as ever! You're half right. I've always been anti-Japanese. I only went to Hong Kong because I was in imminent danger, and now I've come back to really throw myself into things, do you think I'm going to abandon the mainstream and go off with some dissident group? I'm a staunch member of the Kuomintang, so what would I be doing working with the Communists? Let me tell you, I am now a special commissioner of the Central National Government."

It is Qi Yuexuan's turn to laugh now, and he continues until tears come to his eyes.

"Enough! Enough! Spare me! Stop teasing me, I... Aiyo! My arse hurts!"

Zhou Zhengjie is rather put out by this, and he glares at Qi Yuexuan for a moment before giving a chilly laugh and saying: "Listen to you! Next time you get a beating, they should beat that foul mouth out of you. Is our country's distress just a game to you?"

So saying, he takes a document from inside his jacket, along with a certificate of some kind, and hands them to Qi Yuexuan. "Take a good look at these. I think you'll see they trump your paltry former post as a special adviser."

"Ha! I don't need to look at them. I could carve the same seals out of a radish!"

"Pah! You still think I'm trying to trick you? This is my Central Bureau ID and my official letter of appointment from the central government. It's all there in black and white. Do you still doubt me?"

Seeing how insistent he is, Qi Yuexuan takes the papers and looks at them. They are indeed what Zhou Zhengjie claims them to be, and at the top of the government document is written:

'The bearer is special commissioner of the Bureau of Military Affairs of the Central National Government, Zhou Zhengjie, who has permission to travel throughout Beiping and surrounding areas with responsibility for consolidating and reorganising anti-Japanese guerrilla operations behind enemy lines, and re-establishing the National Government in every province. All military and civilian peoples are required to render him assistance wherever he goes. This document serves as official confirmation.'

Below the writing is the official seal of the Bureau of Military Affairs and the signature of the bureau director, Xu Yongchang. It all appears genuine.

When Zhou Zhengjie hears him grunt, he smiles complacently and indicates to Wu Xinmin and Grandpa Fu that he wants to talk to Qi Yuexuan privately. Even when they are alone, Qi Yuexuan is still puzzled, and he doesn't quite know what to say.

"Ai!" Zhou Zhengjie sighs. "I really didn't expect to find you mixed up in rural affairs like this. Is there any of the scholar and the Young Master left in you? I hardly recognised you when I came in just now. With your unkempt appearance and straggly beard, anyone might think you were some mountain bandit chief."

"Bullshit," Qi Yuexuan grunts. "I'm fighting a war, not going out shopping. Just staying alive is enough without worrying about how I look."

"Ai! My heart bleeds for you." Zhou Zhengjie hesitates a moment. "Has... has Zhengying not come back yet?"

"No."

"Have you... had any news?"

He has hit a nerve with this question, as, ever since Zhang Zhicheng brought news of his wife, Qi Yuexuan's heart has boiled over with rage whenever he thinks of her. Moreover, since Zhou Zhengjie has become a government man, even though Nationalists and Communists are working together, he doesn't trust him on this subject, and he just shakes his head.

"Ai! That little sister of mine is..."

"That's enough! Let's not talk about her." Qi Yuexuan doesn't let him finish and changes the subject. "What about you? How has a stumpy-tailed quail like you suddenly sprouted a peacock's fan?"

Zhou Zhengjie doesn't bandy words with him but tucks his documents away again and says: "It's called finding advantage in adversity."

IN ORDER to escape the ravages of war, at the beginning of 1937, Zhou Zhengjie sold up and moved his whole family to Hong Kong. After the Marco Polo Bridge Incident, the Sino-Japanese conflict erupted throughout China, from north to south, but since the United Kingdom was a neutral country, the British colony of Hong Kong was a place of safety. So at the time, all the rich Chinese, especially those who lived on the eastern seaboard, fled there, and almost overnight, Hong Kong became a giant refugee camp. Provisions were in short supply, prices soared and rents increased many times over. There was no way Zhou Zhengjie's slender family resources could survive these turbulent times, and after six months very little was left. Rather than wait and see his family reduced to penury, he went out looking for work wherever he could find it. Although he had been a respected journalist in Beiping, he knows no one in Hong Kong, and no one knows him. He had worn down the doorsteps of the few newspaper houses in Hong Kong before he found a job with a small paper, where he was given a column the size of a square of bean curd. He wrote one piece a day, not covering anything serious, but specialising in celebrity stories and sex scandals. Daily, he haunted the coffee houses and Western dance halls, watching other people enjoy themselves while his own belly groaned with hunger. It was soul-destroying work, and one month's pay only covered half a month's living expenses. In the end, he had to sell a Wang Hui landscape painting that Qi Yuexuan had given him, which raised enough to keep them for several months.

But heaven will always leave a door open, and he bumped into an old friend. This friend was called Xiao Liying, who had been secretary-general of the Town Hall Office in Beiping and who had also held a post in the Central Bureau of Investigations. When Zhou Zhengjie was running his paper *The Truth*, he was a committee member on Xiao's Beiping Press Oversight Committee, and he considered him a good friend. At this time, Xiao Liying's public position was communications director for the National Government in Hong Kong, but secretly he was the overall head of the Central Bureau's Hong Kong Survey and Statistics Office. He had been sent on his own from Chongqing, and his few subordinates were all original local team members, none of whom he particularly trusted, and none of whom spoke decent Mandarin. Running into the down-on-his-luck Zhou Zhengjie, he immediately recruited him. However their friendship and shared language and nationality were not the most important considerations; the most important thing was that Xiao Liying knew that Zhou Zhengjie has a distant uncle called Zhou Fuhai, who was then director of the Kuomintang Central Propaganda Bureau and deputy chairman of Chiang Kai-shek's military sub-committee. Naturally aware of the influence this man wielded within the Kuomintang, he hoped to be able to profit from this connection. He immediately helped Zhou Zhengjie establish contact with his distant relative and formally introduced him onto the staff of the Central Bureau, giving him an assistant's post in the communications department and the Survey and Statistics Office. When Zhao Ran's mother, Hong Wenguo, came to Guangzhou and Hong Kong on her fund-raising tour, Zhou Zhengjie had total responsibility for organising her reception and the rest of her trip.

At the start of summer in 1938, the Central Kuomintang convened its fifth assembly, and after it adopted its policy of restricting and opposing the Communist Party, the Office of the Central Bureau transferred Zhou Zhengjie to a post as a special envoy to Pingxi in northern Hebei, of the National Government's Military Bureau, with the brief to oversee the consolidation of guerrilla warfare behind enemy lines. The plan was to stop the Communist Party and the Eighth Route Army gaining the upper hand in their sphere of operations in North China. It goes without saying that this appointment was the result of the influence of his relative, Zhou Fuhai. Moreover, the main focus of his mission was Zhao Ran and the Fifth Division of the Eighth Route Army he controls in the Hebei, Chahar and Shanxi sphere of military operations. He knew that Hong Wenguo wanted her son to regularise his position and put himself at the disposal of the National Army, so he got her to write him a letter instructing him to leave the Eighth Route Army in favour of the National Army. Then the National Government can appoint him overall commander of anti-Japanese guerrilla operations in North China, with the rank of major-general and the full support of army money and equipment.

Zhou Zhengjie sailed to Tianjin and then went by road to Laishui in northern Hebei and on to Fangshan in Pingxi. After tramping round the dozen or so irregular armies in this area, he finally arrived at Zhaitang in Wanping. Zhao Ran had already decided to leave the Eighth Route Army and make a fresh start, so when he saw his mother's letter, he immediately struck a deal with Zhou Zhengjie. To start with, they planned to use the meeting of cadres to get rid of those who were pro-Communist Party and move the whole division over to the National Army. They hadn't, however, anticipated their opponents' countermeasures, which not only made the use of violence too costly, but also prevented even a single platoon from changing sides. They were obliged to abandon their original plan and conceal their real intentions. Nonetheless, quite a few soldiers in the Eighth Route Army who didn't want to work with the Communist Party were prepared to make a fresh start with the National Army. The dozen or so men Wu Xinmin brought with him first established a forward station, and after a few days men began to drift in to join them.

Surprisingly, when Qi Yuexuan has listened to all this, he shows neither alarm nor pleasure, worry nor anger. Nor does he respond in any way but remains poker-faced, giving nothing away. Seeing his lack of reaction, Zhou Zhengjie laughs and says: "Oh Yuexuan, back when the Twenty-Ninth Army was in Beiping, and you found favour with General Qin, did you use that to help your friends and brothers? There's never been any point in looking to you for favours. I'm not as self-centred as you, and when something good happened to me, I thought of you."

As he is speaking, his manner seems to change, and he pulls out some more documents that he hands to Qi Yuexuan with a broad smile. Qi Yuexuan opens them and looks. They turn out to be several sheets of blank letters of appointment that carry the official seal of the Bureau of Military Affairs of the Central National Government.

"What's the meaning of this? What post are you thinking of appointing me to?"

"Second-in-command of guerrilla operations with a rank no higher than colonel and authority only within the province."

"And you have the power to do this?"

"Of course. My signature is valid anywhere within my sphere of authority. On this trip I travelled from northern Hebei to Fangshan and Wanping, and everywhere I went there were assorted militia, but they all professed allegiance to the National Army. This time, if you and Commander Zhao join forces, you can be second-in-command, special adviser, chief of staff, whatever you want. If you're not willing to take a subordinate role, then we can create a unified county government of Wanping and Changping, and make you its head. The two of you, one military one political, one a scholar one a soldier, will work really well."

"How much can you pay? How many weapons can you provide?"

"Ah well... as far as that goes, let's get the overall plan in place and then we can see about levying taxes."

"Ha! Plenty of noise with nothing to back it up! Do you think all you have to do is run up the flag, and I'll flip a somersault and come running? Even a monkey won't perform unless you feed it. Be off with you and take your letters with you. They mean nothing to me."

"You... Ai! These letters are from the central government. They're not just for show, they're the real deal."

"As far as I'm concerned, fighting the Japanese is the real deal. Forget your 'central government' nonsense. What do you think's so special about that? The people have had a bellyful of it already! Ever since the fighting started, all we've seen is your arses as you run away faster than the bullets can fly. You've lost half of China in a year, and you've still got the nerve to talk about 'the real deal'? Do you think we've shed our blood and sacrificed our lives so you can take all the glory? You can think again!"

Zhou Zhengjie chokes on these words, then says with a bitter laugh: "The people are entitled to be angry that the war has not gone well. The National Army may have suffered more defeats than it has won victories, and lost a lot of territory, but the enemy are stronger than us, and we have put up a desperate fight. In the last year and more, our casualties have numbered more than a hundred thousand, but haven't we succeeded in staving off the Japanese offensive? When they started this war, didn't they say they would obliterate China in three months? At the very least we have stopped them doing that..."

"What a load of nonsense!" Qi Yuexuan is incensed by the words of the Japanese propaganda. "Obliterate China in three months? Even if they didn't have to fight a single battle, fire a single shot, they couldn't cross the whole of China in three months. The Japanese spout this bullshit and you buy into it? Is it something to boast about that they haven't obliterated China in three months? Have you no shame? You're right, the enemy are strong and we are weak, but why don't we learn from this and put our lives on the line and fight more fiercely? Out casualties may be heavy, but how many were shot in the front, and how many shot in the back as they ran away? We have lost so much territory and so many troops, in defeat after defeat, but why don't our leaders accept responsibility for this? You know the old saying – if a general is incompetent, he may lose three armies, but if the ruler is unjust, he will destroy the country and bring suffering to the people!"

"Keep your voice down," Zhou Zhengjie says urgently. "Your big mouth is going to get you in trouble one of these days. What you just said is enough to get you arrested if you weren't on the front line."

"Ha! I forgot that you're a big noise special agent now, aren't you!"

Zhou Zhengjie looks daggers at him but doesn't say anything more.

Reunited with an old friend like this, Qi Yuexuan feels he shouldn't use the nation's woes as an excuse to pick over old times: "I know you are under orders to wave the flag. I'm not having a go at you. But when a general is out on the field, he doesn't have to follow HQ's orders, so why are you gnawing away at this?"

"What do you mean?"

"Do you really not understand, or are you just playing dumb? If the war with the enemy isn't going well, what time do you have to waste on in-fighting? Isn't the Eighth Route Army a unit of the National Army? If you retreat, aren't they allowed to advance? Besides, if you didn't have them at your rear, holding off the Japanese devils, do you think you would have survived until now? As long as they're fighting the Japanese, your forces can increase and improve, so why are you trying to restrict them. Which bit of the territory that you currently occupy did you seize? Why do you think you have to guard against them? Shouldn't you be concentrating all your thoughts on fighting the Japanese? In the north of Hebei and Pingxi you'd be hard put to find a situation where the resistance is going well, and here you are not bringing firewood but taking away the fire and undermining your own troops. When it comes down to it, it's the Chinese against the Japanese now. Surely you don't want to split the Communists and the Kuomintang, and turn this into a three-way war, like in the *Romance of the Three Kingdoms*! What exactly do you think you're doing? Fighting the Japanese or helping them?"

"What I want to know is why you're singing from the same songbook as the Communists. Are you their man now?"

"You're barking up the wrong tree there. My only thought is to fight the Japanese. I stand shoulder to shoulder with anyone who is steadfast against the Japanese, and I'll call out anyone who isn't pulling their weight."

Zhou Zhengjie mutters to himself and then says: "Listen to you! Still the high-handed Young Master and the stubborn scholar, but now you've added the spleen of some ruffian bandit chief. But your politics are too infantile, and you have none of the poise and foresight of a true politician."

Qi Yuexuan tries hard not to laugh. "Alright, alright, I'll wash my ears out and take instruction from you, master politician that you are."

Zhou Zhengjie lowers his voice a little: "Ai! You still don't see the whole picture, do you? There are some things you can't explain with words. You just need to have the feel for them. Let me give you an example. Last year, the central government combined military and civil intelligence bureaux into one entity under the highest committee of military affairs. Each of them still controls their own business, although, nominally, they are no longer separate. The Central Bureau is concerned with monitoring party and government affairs, and it guards against heterodoxy, so their concerns are internal. The Military Bureau controls the military and police, and its responsibility is to monitor Japanese military affairs and operations, so its concerns are external. When these two sister organisations come together, which would you say is the senior?"

"Since resisting the Japanese is of prime importance, it must be the Military Bureau."

"Wrong! The Military Bureau is second in importance to the Central Bureau. Do you understand why?"

Qi Yuexuan sighs and says coldly: "Well... I suppose it is Old Chiang still insisting that 'to resist external aggression requires internal stability'."

"Those are your words not mine," says a smiling Zhou Zhengjie, before going on: "It's probably best not to be explicit about this, as long as you understand it. In fact, anyone in his position would think the same and do the same. When it comes down to it, resisting foreign aggression is a temporary thing, but countering internal division is a fundamental."

"Are you... are you sure that's right?"

"There are no rights and wrongs in politics, only necessities and pros and cons. Even though China and Japan are at war right now, is it certain that it will be fought out to the bitter end? Not at all. In political terms, there is little fundamental difference between the Chinese and Japanese governments, not like between us and the Soviet Union or the Communist Party. The Japanese may be fighting for territory, natural resources and trade, but they're certainly not trying to impose a totally new regime. Assuming there isn't a sudden victory or defeat for either side, but each can take a step back, then some form of agreement is entirely possible."

"Agreement? You are deluded! Haven't you experienced the savagery of the Japanese? They are at fever-pitch at the moment, so just how many Chinese lives do you think it would take to satisfy their hunger before they'll talk peace?"

"There is something in what you say. At the moment, although you still have forces who, outwardly at least, are resisting the Japanese, none of them are really committing themselves to the fight, so you are just suffering defeat after defeat. But looking at it from another point of view, the Japanese have their own pros and cons to consider, and what advantage is there to them in a long occupation of China? If our two countries can unite against the Soviets and the Communists, might they not take a step back? Under the Kuomintang, we just need public opinion to shift away from the past, and there'll be no need to fight. But if we let the Communists seize the opportunity to expand, it would be catastrophic, like cutting our own wrists. Do you understand?"

By the time this speech has finished, Qi Yuexuan's expression has darkened alarmingly. He looks closely at Zhou Zhengjie for a long time, before giving an icy laugh: "Ha! Incisive! How very incisive! Is this your Kuomintang's policy then? Is this what that Chiang fellow calls weighing the pros and cons? But why beat about the bush? It can be said much more simply: for one party's gain, for one man's personal profit, you are willing to surrender the nation's warriors, abandon the ordinary people and sacrifice all honour and dignity. Isn't that it?"

"Keep your voice down!" Zhou Zhengjie is getting very agitated. "Enough! Enough! I thought I could rely on our friendship to... Ai! Me and my big mouth, making the best of intentions sound like evil ones!"

"I'm not arguing with you."

"It doesn't matter if you are or not. Let's just say, each to their own, alright?" Zhou Zhengjie sees him sigh again and laughs. "Look at you, almost sixty and still as perky as a little boy. Ai, these are really muddy waters to wade through, with so many interests at stake. Forget about the Kuomintang and the Communists, there are enough factions within the Kuomintang alone, each with their own objectives. You and I are not movers and shakers. On a chess board, we'd only be pawns. As pawns, we must go with the flow, and..."

"Stop! Stop! I, Qi Yuexuan, am nobody's pawn, and I don't intend to follow anyone, so never talk about me like that again. I can't perform those kinds of contortions." So saying, he hands the blank letters back to Zhou Zhengjie. "You can keep these, I'm not taking up any post, and I don't want any title. Thank you for thinking of me, but I'm not going to accept any favours from the likes of you."

"How can a man like you... Ai!" Zhou Zhengjie can only shake his head, tuck the sheets of paper back inside his jacket and ask: "Are you refusing because of the merger with Commander Zhao and his men?"

"Even without the merger, I wouldn't be joining in with you. But let's leave all that behind us for the time being. I'll give any help I can, and anyone who fights against the Japanese, I count as a friend. As long as they don't snatch the ladder away from under me again, I'm happy to fight alongside them. Is that good enough for you?"

"Alright, let's leave it at that." Zhou Zhengjie nods rather reluctantly. "It wouldn't matter that much if the merger didn't go through, I was just worried there wouldn't be room on the mountain for two tigers..."

"You can stop worrying, I'm very tolerant. But Commander Zhao had better not be harbouring any evil intentions towards us. We're not carrying our rifles just for the fun of it. If he gives us good reason, we'll use them against him. You had better make sure he understands that."

"Yes, yes, that's a given. I'll pass on the message to Colonel Wu, that even if you don't join together, you are still friends. It's a matter of face for me, and even if... Oh, I should have said 'Brigadier Wu', as he is already now a brigade commander in the National Army. I don't know when Commander Zhao is going to get here, and I can't wait for him as I have to go into the city tomorrow."

"You're going into the city?"

"Yes."

"Who are you going to appoint to office there?"

"Ah, no, I'm on a different mission."

Qi Yuexuan knows his place and doesn't try to probe any further. He just advises Zhou Zhengjie: "Be careful when you're in the city. There are a lot of people who know you there. Matsuzaki Harayama is now the most important spymaster in Beiping. Don't let him get his hands on you."

Zhou Zhengjie laughs. "Actually, I'm more afraid that I won't get to see him."

"What do you mean? Are going to... get rid of him?" Qi Yuexuan asks in astonishment.

Zhou Zhengjie just smiles enigmatically.

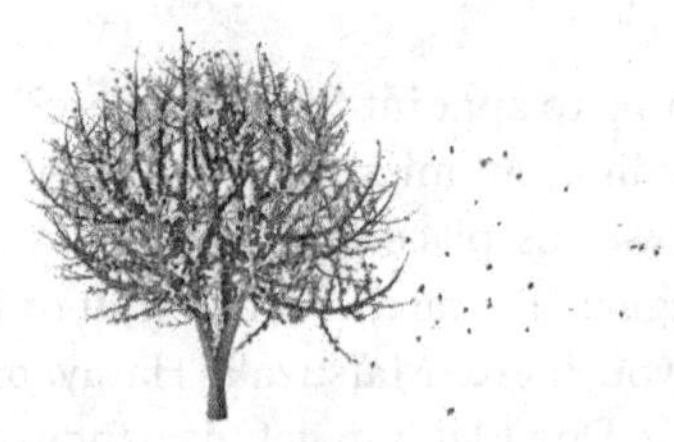

Chapter 44

The Japanese army currency that Chenglong exchanges is only a part of the total, and Wangtian still has to get rid of the rest, bit by bit. Early one morning he brings back a batch of notes and hands it over to the company cashier's office. Because the exchanges have been done piecemeal, the money is in silver yuan, copper and silver coin, and *fabi* all mixed together, and more in loose change than in large coins. Yang Zhixing and two of the cashiers take more than a morning to count it. Just before noon, Lao Zhang returns from Laoqiying to say that Qi Yuexuan wants two thousand silver yuan for the soldiers' pay, and to report that, because of the delay in paying the men, he, Qi Yuexuan, has already ordered himself twenty strokes of the rod that have laid his flesh open and made him miserable. He also says that Qi Yuexuan has told him that, if the required sum isn't sent quickly, he is afraid that he will have to order himself another beating. If the delay is too long, or if funds aren't adequate, then they are not to bother, as the shame would be too great for him to keep living, and they had better just send a donkey cart to fetch his corpse.

The news infuriates Yang Zhixing, and he stamps his foot and shouts: "Is there no justice in this world? He has given his time and money to the cause, and he still gets a beating? Those men aren't Qi family soldiers, nor are they old bodyguards or servants of the Residence, so why are somebody else's troops drawing Qi family blood for nothing? With spending like this, any family fortune, no matter how big, would get frittered away. The Young Master is not being very smart about this. What's the problem with him charging high interest and demanding repayment? Does he think this is a case of 'death before dishonour'?"

Even as he is saying these words, he knows just how stubborn and determined the Young Master is, and he is not prepared to make an issue out of it. He immediately sets about wrapping up the money for him to deliver in person, saying he also wants to have a serious discussion with the men of the Left Barracks and try to talk some sense into them. But before he can even get out of the door, he is seized by a fit of coughing and spits up blood. In fact, Qi Yuexuan has been afraid that Yang Zhixing might deliberately keep him on tenterhooks over withholding the money, but now, as it turns out, in asking for the money, he has almost cost him his life.

When the doctor takes his pulse, he shakes his head and asks why he has not been called in earlier, the illness is so serious. He says that the symptoms – the cough and shortness of breath, the sparse but sticky phlegm, the chest pains and coughing up blood, the red cheeks and hot flushes – indicate tuberculosis, and because Yang Zhixing has dragged his feet in getting treatment, the situation is now critical. He immediately writes a prescription that involves not just the common ingredients of bellflower, rehmannia, dwarf lilyturf, lily, goldthread and silver thorowax, but also the more expensive tortoiseshell, donkey-skin gelatin, Sichuan fritillary bulb, American ginseng, caterpillar fungus and other such things. It also needs a decoction of artemisia carvifolia and several pieces of mountain yam, using pure dew, and the resulting medicine can only be given three times. He makes it clear that, although Chinese medicine can treat tuberculosis, it is a gradual process and cannot be rushed. The patient is already of advanced years and has delayed seeking treatment for too long, so he is afraid he may not survive this acute episode. If there is no improvement after three doses of the medicine, the best thing he can do is go to the main hospital to seek Western treatment.

After three doses of the medicine in the course of the day, there are no visible results, and Yang Zhixing is still coughing, still has chest pains and there is still blood in his phlegm. Everyone wants to send him to the Western hospital. At first, he is unwilling to go, but when he learns that the disease is contagious, he reluctantly agrees. There is strict control of medicines in force in Beiping at this time, and it is the Japanese military hospital that has the best supply of drugs. However, they are not going to accept a Chinese patient. Chenglong makes some telephone calls, asking Matsuzaki Harayama to intervene, and it is finally agreed that an exception will be made to admit Yang Zhixing.

To everyone's surprise, on receipt of this favour, Yang Zhixing explodes with anger: "However good it may be, I'm not going to a Japanese hospital. From ancient times, few people have lived past seventy, and I've already reached that age, so what does it now matter whether I live or die? I have never asked for help in my life, so am I now going to bow my head and beg the Japanese for my life? I don't have it in me! If you force me to go, then I think you should know that I have been prone to sleepwalking, and you shouldn't be surprised if I cause you some headaches by getting up in the middle of the night and throttling a couple of Japanese."

Everyone is well aware of Yang Zhixing's temper, and since he has adopted this attitude, they don't dare take him to the hospital. The best they can do is send him to a local church hospital. In the past, this had been considered one of Beiping's better hospitals, but since Japanese restrictions have tightened, their drugs are in short supply. The doctors there say the illness is very serious and the patient is debilitated by age, so sulphonamide drugs will have little effect. The best hope is that penicillin can act as an antibiotic and reduce the inflammation. Unfortunately, the hospital doesn't have a single injection's-worth, but if the family can use its connections to rustle some up, then there is a chance of a cure.

In modern times, penicillin is a commonplace antibiotic, but in those days, it was a rarity. It was only manufactured in America and a few European countries, and certainly not in China, or even Japan. Before the war, it could only be bought in the biggest hospitals and pharmacies, and it was too expensive for ordinary people to afford. Since the outbreak of hostilities, it has been classified by the Japanese as a military essential not available on the open market, and anyone caught dealing in it faces imprisonment at the very least, and execution at worst. So not only is it no longer seen in hospital pharmacies, it has even disappeared from the black market. In Beiping, it is only available in Japanese hospitals, and even there it is kept in locked drugs cabinets under the supervision of specially appointed staff. It can only be used after a strict process has been observed.

Wangtian has no idea how to go about the business. He scours all four corners of the city without finding a single dose. There's nothing for it but to turn to Chenglong, although he has little hope that he will be able to deliver the goods this time. Chenglong says, since the old man won't go to a Japanese hospital, how can he expect to use Japanese drugs? And if it's a case of expending a lot of money and effort to no good result, then he's disinclined to pursue it. Wangtian suppresses his anger, finds as many honeyed words as he can and also takes out two gold bars. It is only then that Chenglong agrees to try.

But as soon as he has agreed, and taken the gold, his mood shifts, and he suddenly flares up: "Hey! Whose father-in-law is this anyway? Why are you showing more concern than me?"

This infuriates Wangtian again, but all he does is smile coldly and say: "I'm trying to do the decent thing on your behalf."

Wu Xinmin brings a group of men to Qiwangfen, and within three days, a handful of disenchanted Eighth Route Army men have joined them there. These men are mostly from the Ninth Division, but they are not a distinct unit, and the others who come are even more random. On the second evening after Wu Xinmin left the base, one of his company commanders uses the pretext that Commander Wu has not returned and that something might have happened to him; he says he is going to take his own men out to find him. Before any instructions arrive from the top brass, he leads his men out of the camp at the double, but before long, Zhang Zhicheng, as commander of the First Division, leads his men in pursuit. Apart from a few trusted aides, the men in the first group have no idea that they are being led to desert the Eighth Route Army. When they hear the sounds of pursuit, the shouts and warning shots, several of their number understand what is going on. Some of them simply stop in their tracks, some turn round and run back, some scatter to the winds and yet others shoot their rifles wildly to their rear. Fewer than half of them follow their commander into the woods to shake off their pursuers. Later, when they are back on the road, men continue to slip away, so by the time they reach Qiwangfen, there are fewer than thirty left. Counting the men who have come from elsewhere and those who arrived first in the other group, forty-plus men in all, their numbers fall well short of what they originally planned.

News of the mass desertion in Pingxi is swiftly reported back to the Eighth Route Army Shanxi-Chahar-Hebei military headquarters. Commander Nie Rongzhen immediately seeks out Zhao Ran who has just arrived in Fuping. Of course, the news comes as no surprise to Zhao Ran, as this is part of his plan of action, but he is a little put out when he hears that no more than a squadron escaped and that the majority were either chased back to the camp or returned of their own accord. He had been nervous about his recall to headquarters, but now he's there, the top brass haven't treated him differently in any way. Commander Nie even spent half a night in private conversation with him. The commander started by praising him, particularly the success of the Fifth Division and his role as a commander; he encouraged him to continue his good work and to make every effort to become part of the Communist Party apparatus. Of course, he did also advance some criticism of his independent actions and propensity to form cliques and factions. He also mentioned Zhao Ran's antipathy to formal military organisation, his apparent exclusion of political officers, his refusal to enact the policy of presenting a united front and his unauthorised disarming of other anti-Japanese resistance groups. Although the areas of criticism were many, and Commander Nie's language was sharp and incisive, he could tell that the military leadership didn't intend to take any action against him. But now, circumstances have changed: the sword is out of its scabbard and he has no way of putting it back.

Zhao Ran says he is afraid the officers he left in charge will not be able to maintain order, and he anticipates that the emerging chain of events will be tricky to manage. He declares himself willing to gird his loins and return immediately to Pingxi to settle the soldiers' mood. Commander Nie considers this very carefully and agrees the request. Thereupon, Zhao Ran leads his bodyguard out of the county town of Fuping, and they travel the whole route back to Pingxi at a full gallop. On arriving there, they don't return to Zhaitang but veer off to the banks of the Yongding. Once across the river, they skirt Miaofengshan to the west and head towards Yangtaishan. When they reach Qiwangfen, Zhao Ran sends Commander Nie a telegraph message saying that, since he holds the rank of major-general from the Kuomintang Government, and in consequence has that same rank in the National Army, he has been invited to attend the staff officer training behind the lines. From now on, he is withdrawing from the Eighth Route Army, he will no longer take orders from the Shanxi-Chahar-Hebei command centre, and his newly affiliated forces now have equal status in military affairs with everybody else.

Zhou Zhengjie departs, and Qi Yuexuan sets about accomplishing the things he promised. But having two different armed companies in the same camp, with their hackles raised and under separate flags, does indeed present some problems. Originally, he intends to recall the sentries from the bottom of the mountain at Qiwangfen and order them both to Jiuwangfen, with one at the foot of the mountain and one at the top, with each acting independently. Wu Xinmin won't co-operate, saying that the base of the mountain is too exposed and is not safe. The pair discuss the matter at length, and they finally come to an agreement that the two sides will jointly garrison Jiuwangfen, using the Yin and Yang residences as demarcation. The troops from the Left Barracks will remain in the several courtyards of the Yang Residence, while the Yin Residence will be handed over to Wu Xinmin. Each side will have responsibility for security within the walls of their respective residences, but they will share sentry duties at the base of the mountain at Qiwangfen and the temple gates at Jiuwangfen.

WHEN ZHAO RAN ARRIVES, he discovers that the number of men he has managed to abstract falls far short of what he had planned, but he curbs his anger. However, when he sees how the garrisons have been arranged, he explodes and curses Wu Xinmin: "Is that great melon of a head of yours full of beancurd instead of brains? Only tombkeepers live in the Yin Residence and the other side are living in a prince's palace! We're keeping company with dead people, and they are obviously taking the piss out of us. And you agreed to all this? We had everything planned, but you could only bring me this handful of men so that motley crew of misfits can all look down on us. You're not some kind of raw recruit, but they've got more men than us, are better armed, and you've let them occupy the higher ground? If they pluck up the courage to take advantage of this, then you, me and the other twenty or thirty of us will end up buried here."

Wu Xinmin can only listen with bowed head. He doesn't dare try to make any excuses, but when he sees Zhao Ran turn and head for the entrance to the Yang Residence, he follows him and asks: "Do you want me to assemble the men?"

Without breaking step, Zhao Ran grunts icily: "Your head really is full of beancurd, isn't it!"

When the two men reach the entrance to the courtyard of the Yang Residence, before the sentry has a chance to challenge them, Zhao Ran stops and pre-empts him by giving his name to be announced inside. They then wait punctiliously outside. Wu Xinmin is astonished, but Zhao Ran hisses an order at him: "Don't say a word!"

Although Qi Yuexuan's wounds appear to have improved over the last few days, they have only just scabbed over, and he still doesn't dare lie on his back or sit down. When he hears that Zhao Ran has come visiting, he immediately tries to get up.

Grandpa Fu restrains him, saying: "Why should you get up for him? Have you forgotten how crazy he went at Sidixia? It's alright now, though. He's only got a few dozen men, and he'll soon just be a hollow reed with no men to command at all. You wouldn't even accept an appointment in the National Army, so why should you show a man like him any regard? I'll receive him, and that will be enough."

"No! No!" Qi Yuexuan continues to get out of bed and says, as he puts on a gown: "I'm afraid you don't really understand the situation and may say something you shouldn't. These are deep matters, and even *I* can't see the bottom of them, let alone you. I've no intention of joining with him, but if he's got something to say, we should hear it. Even if it's just one side of the story, we might still learn something from it. Besides, what does it matter whether he's with the Eighth Route Army or the National Army, as long as he's fighting the Japanese and hasn't surrendered to them? We have to be tolerant and not look askance at how few men he's got. If we don't make an effort, he'll just think we're snobs. Right, so you just play nice and go out and welcome him all smiles. Here isn't convenient for me, so I'll sit and wait for them in the outer room."

"Are you alright to sit down?"

"Just because I can't sit down doesn't mean I don't have a few tricks up my sleeve."

Grandpa Fu looks where Qi Yuexuan is pointing and almost bursts out laughing. He is indicating a wood-framed commode. It is almost as big as a master armchair, has a backrest, albeit a little low, and a large round hole has been cut into its seat. It is not the most elegant item of furniture, but it's perfect for sitting in if you've got injured buttocks.

After a moment, Grandpa Fu shows Zhao Ran and Wu Xinmin into the room. When Zhao Ran sees Qi Yuexuan trying to get up from where he is sitting to one side, he hurries to stop him: "You're injured, Mr Qi. There's no need to observe the niceties."

Qi Yuexuan doesn't insist and gestures for them to sit down. Forgoing conventional chit-chat, Zhao Ran gets straight to the point: "Mr Qi, I heard Commissioner Zhou say that he is your brother-in-law."

"That's right. He's also a very old friend."

"Well, in that case... I can't understand why you didn't accept the government appointment and agree to join forces with us. Can it really be that, because one of my subordinates made a mistake, you now don't trust me?"

"No, no, no, Commander Zhao. Please don't misjudge me. Neither I nor Commander Fucha are so petty-minded. But since you mention lack of trust, I must be honest with you and say that I certainly do not have a very high opinion of the National Government or the National Army. And that's not just my personal prejudice, the ordinary people feel this way too. After the Mukden Incident, within three months they had lost Rehe and the three eastern provinces, and from the Marco Polo Bridge Incident till now, half of China has gone. A government like that, and an army like that, make it impossible for people to trust them or think they can rely on them. When the foundations and pillars are rotten, even a great mansion may collapse, but I know that even in their weakest state, the people will risk their lives to prop it up. Isn't this how it has been for the last few years, Commander Zhao? What I can't understand is why you don't restring your bow and start over again. Are you unconcerned about the state of the anti-Japanese resistance in Pingxi?"

Zhao Ran has apparently not foreseen that Qi Yuexuan might counter him like this, and he wracks his brain for a reasonable reply.

"Ai! I don't see it like that. To me, it is the Communists who are the real bullies." He slams his fist on the table, making the teacups rattle. Then his words come rushing out like water from a burst dam: from the time he first raised an army of thirty-something men at Baiyangcun in Changping, to his creation of the National Army of Anti-Japanese Resistance, to the time he merged with the Fifth Division of the Eighth Route Army in the north of Hebei and returned to Pingxi, it has been a year of twists and turns and victory after victory, and he has also resolved all kinds of problems within his unit. Of course, he only mentions the successes and doesn't raise the failures. Like a hedgehog that isn't aware of its own spines, he can only see the faults in others. He says that the Communist Party was willing to do anything to spread its power and influence through his troops, and that was what forced him into his rash decision.

"My troops were being subverted from the inside by Communist Party recruiters. If you were in my place, would you stand for it?"

"Commander Zhao," says Qi Yuexuan smiling faintly, "I have never belonged to any party or faction, nor do I wish to engage in politics. But if this is what the people of the twelve villages of the Left Barracks consider important, then I will do it since no one else can. But if I were you, I wouldn't have let it come to this."

"Eh?" Zhao Ran knows that Qi Yuexuan has somewhat unorthodox views. "I'd like to hear more."

Qi Yuexuan considers for a moment, then asks: "Why did you want to raise an army, Commander Zhao?"

"Do you really need to ask? To fight the Japanese, of course."

"Isn't that what the Communists and the Eighth Route Army are doing?"

"Ah... you could say that."

"Just think about it. Was your army more disciplined when it was called the National Army of Japanese Resistance, or when it changed to the Eighth Route Army? Did they fight more bravely as one than as the other? Did they kill more Japanese, occupy more territory, receive more support from the people?"

Zhao Ran can see what lies behind this question, and he dodges it by asking: "So... what exactly is it that you're trying to say?"

"What I'm saying is that, when you raise an army, the reason you take up arms is to fight the Japanese, so the Japanese become the most important thing, and the individual..."

Before he can finish, Wu Xinmin can't restrain himself any longer: "Fighting the Japanese is all very well, but it is quite clear that if you're part of the Eighth Route Army, then it's the Communist Party that is in charge, whatever Commander Zhao may say. He..."

"Shut your mouth!" Zhao Ran glares at him.

"Ha!" Qi Yuexuan laughs. "I can see exactly where your dilemma lies, Commander Zhao. It's in those two little words 'in charge'. You think you're managing affairs, and he thinks he's in charge. That's how it is, isn't it?"

Zhao Ran doesn't reply.

Qi Yuexuan continues: "Then again, if it was me, I'd have put a few words in front of 'in charge' – don't strive to be in charge. Then it wouldn't have come to this."

Zhao Ran takes issue with this: "If you really 'don't strive to be in charge', then why is it our two houses can't come together as one army, and there'd be no need for you to fight under your own flag?"

"Because this isn't my personal army, it is the collective army of the men of the Left Barracks, so I don't have the authority to decide its fate. The way I see it, it's hard to clap with one hand. I'd advocate working more closely together. A crowd is not one person, and a river is not a single drop of water. If it was a case of taking the collective army and making it Zhang's army or Li's army, handing everyone's fate over to one man, although I can't speak for everyone, it is not something I would do."

"Are you saying that ours is a private army? No! We are a properly constituted army and we take our orders direct from central headquarters."

"Don't talk to me about the National Army and even less about central headquarters."

Zhao Ran can see how fixed Qi Yuexuan is in his opinions, and although he inwardly curses him as an old stick-in-the-mud, he keeps his expression solemn and serious: "Surely you are not on the side of the Communists?"

"I don't follow any party or faction."

"Then... why is what you say so favourable to them?"

"Is it? All I'm doing is saying what ordinary people would want to say. What they often do say, in fact. If it fits in with the Communist Party's standpoint, it's not because the people have been influenced by them, it's because the Communists understand what the people think and give a voice to it."

"Ha! That's because the Communists know how to bewitch the masses and manipulate them to their own ends. The ordinary people are ignorant and rely on the leadership to save China from disaster. They rely on the elite. I would never have thought that a scholar such as Qi Yuexuan could hold opinions like these."

"Ha ha... You are a well-read man, Commander Zhao, but you seem not to have understood the books you have read. Throughout Chinese history, the great leaders, the elite, may have saved China, but there have also been traitors among them, and people who have harmed the country. In general, the saviours have come from among the common people, the lower echelons of society, and the traitors, and those who have harmed the country, have come from the ruling classes. There is only a little difference between them, but where does that difference lie? In the end, it lies in public opinion, and whether it is followed or ignored. If you follow public opinion, you are a hero, but if you go against it, your name is mud."

Outraged, Zhao Ran leaps to his feet, but then he thinks better of allowing his anger to explode, and he sits back down, saying: "I am not going to discuss these lofty matters with you, Mr Qi. If you yourself have been exposed to the wiles of the Communist Party and have been beguiled by them, then I'm afraid we may have little in common."

Qi Yuexuan knows that his words have really hit Zhao Ran where it hurts, but he has no intention of letting up: "You're right. I haven't been indoctrinated, but one should always listen to both sides of the story. I have something really important to say to you, Commander Zhao. Will you listen?"

"Of course. Go on."

"Good. You personally raised this army, and you are its leader. If you govern it properly, respect the men and have their loyalty, then no one can beguile and ensnare them. But if all you crave is power and don't respect their wishes, isn't it inevitable that you will find yourself isolated?"

These words hit home with Zhao Ran's keen intellect, and he exclaims shrilly: "Don't you understand? I was a sham. Bit by bit, they turned me into a sham, otherwise I..."

Unexpectedly, Qi Yuexuan leans on a side table and pushes himself up. He stoops and lifts up the blanket from the seat of his chair, revealing the round hole.

"Look! This is what I call a sham. Why? Because my buttocks are covered in scabs, and I can't sit down without it."

Zhao Ran's face blushes the colour of fresh pig's liver in embarrassment. Forcing a smile, Grandpa Fu steps forward, replaces the blanket, and tries to help Qi Yuexuan back into his seat. But Qi Yuexuan shakes his supporting hand off his elbow. He looks at Zhao Ran and continues, relentlessly: "Forgive me for talking bluntly, Commander Zhao. I really don't want to poke at a sore spot, but my motives stem from concern and sympathy for you. As I see it, if those young men of yours are willing to lose their homes and possessions to save the country by fighting the Japanese, then they are showing a hundredfold more strength and determination than me and my generation. This is why I hope you will be able to size up the situation and grasp this opportunity to become a true hero of the people and not simply someone else's puppet."

When Zhao Ran says nothing in reply, he continues: "In the past, there has been bitter rancour between the Nationalists and the Communists, and even now, when they are allies against the Japanese, they cannot completely forget their former enmity. I have no desire to add to the discussion of the merits and demerits of their respective ideologies, or the clarity or muddle-headedness of their politics. Just for now, all that matters, overriding even the most serious politics, is fighting the Japanese. And talking of fighting the Japanese, the Kuomintang has several million men, but it has met with defeat after defeat, with upwards of a million casualties, not to mention the countless ordinary folk who have also been killed or wounded, and has it taken back even a single inch of territory? Whereas the Communist Party, which has only a few tens of thousands of men, and the Eighth Route Army, which keeps ploughing on against the odds, have pushed forward beyond the enemy lines, grown stronger with every battle and opened up a vast new theatre of operations. At the moment, in the war of resistance against the Japanese, the government's National Army is offering only passive resistance and being driven back, step by step, but the newly formed Communist Army is reporting success after success. Surely it is obvious who is the strongest and who the weakest. Aren't we just writing another version of *The Sequel to the Water Margin*?[1] Now, the National Army that ran away so comprehensively have come back here, but have they sent you a single soldier or a single general? Have they provided a single rifle or a single bullet? No! They've come dangling the bait of a fancy piece of paper! They're not serious in their offer of an important position. It's just a ruse to undermine the Eighth Route Army and to circumscribe them. If this is how things go down, then internal strife is inevitable. Commander Zhao, I am afraid that you have been duped and turned into a sacrificial pawn for the Kuomintang to restrict and oppose the Communists, without realising the dangers involved."

Tired from standing up, Qi Yuexuan supports himself on the side table and makes to sit down. Zhao Ran hurries forward and takes him by the arm. He helps him to sit down and asks in a level tone: "With things as they stand, Mr Qi, what do you think I should do?"

Qi Yuexuan sighs gently: "In the end, Commander Zhao, I'm not you. Everyone's disposition is different, and it's hard to generalise."

Zhao Ran's sincerity is even more obvious as he says: "Even so, please be blunt and give me your advice."

"When all else fails, turn to *The Thirty-Six Stratagems*."[2]

"You mean..."

"Essentially, there are three courses of action – retreat, stay put or advance. But I'm afraid now, the only option open to you is to advance. Let's look at 'retreat' first: if you withdraw from the Eighth Route Army, it might not be an impetuous action, but it would deepen your dilemma. The Eighth Route Army is, after all, a Communist army, and it has long been their practice for the Party to command the military. Do you think they are going to change this policy because of you? It's impossible. If you try to contest it, you won't succeed. The Party has always been a collective and more powerful than any individual. You will inevitably lose against the power of the group. You come second both in principle and in practice. The only way is to stop the contest and withdraw, but, in all conscience, do you really think you can do that? And if you can't, what's the advantage? If you try to say one thing and do another, if you try to dissemble, contesting openly and manoeuvring covertly, all you'll succeed in doing is throwing the army into turmoil, and do you think you'll emerge from that unscathed? Whether you act openly or secretly, you can't win. Besides, now we see the National Army trying to buy allegiance with offers of rank and riches, I can't believe you really want to withdraw."

"Alright, we can forget about withdrawing, but why can't I 'stay put' here?"

"Staying put is an even less practical option than withdrawing, and even more dangerous. If the Kuomintang gives you an appointment, it will be to restrict the growth of the Eighth Route Army in Pingxi. In the mountain area west of Beiping, men are few and the terrain hostile and it can't support many troops. If taxes and levies are increased, how are the ordinary people supposed to live? Moreover, the Eighth Route Army are already strong here, and I'm sure you understand the principle of not allowing other people to muscle in on your own territory. If you're only a small force and fall in with them, there is a chance you may survive, but if you are large and obtrusive, conflict is inevitable. When brothers fall out, it is as fierce as beans jumping in a frying pan. Only relatives suffer, the hatred is intense, and that can only serve to help the Japanese. So, only 'advance' remains, to find new territory to exploit. Surely taking ground back from the devils is better than stealing food from your brother's rice bowl. To be quite frank with you, Commander Zhao, these things I'm saying are addressed as much to myself as they are to you. In trying to persuade you, I am trying to persuade myself too, like watching myself in a mirror. This discussion between the two of us has helped me to clarify my own thinking."

Zhao Ran hears him out, then sinks into silence. After a long moment, he forces a smile as he says: "This has been an education for me today, Mr Qi. Please allow me to consider these matters for a while. Goodbye for now."

It is only when he is through the door that Wu Xinmin, who has been standing next to him, listening expressionlessly, finally makes a move to follow him.

"Ha ha! You were quite something there," says Grandpa Fu. "He really ran into a brick wall with you, didn't he!"

But Qi Yuexuan seems not to have heard him. Still looking grave, he mutters to himself: "I hope that some of it sank in."

Grandpa Fu is puzzled: "Eh? What are you worried about him for?"

"When it comes down to it, he genuinely wants to fight the Japanese. But history shows us, great deeds and great misdemeanours are often decided on a whim."

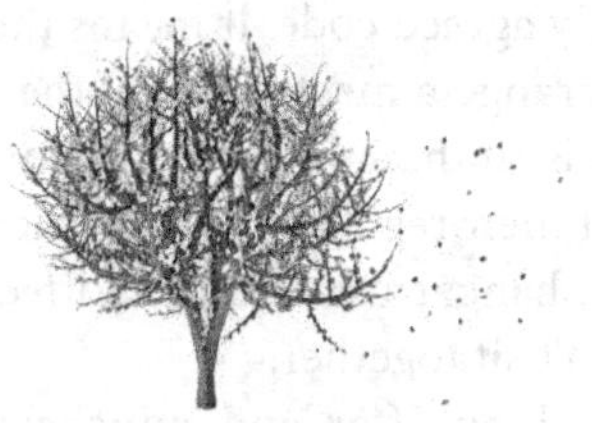

Chapter 45

In Beiping's East Jiaomin Lane, next to the western wall of the US Marine Corps barracks, there is a small, white, three-storey building that houses the offices of the Beiping station of the American-funded Damei Trading Company. When Hao Bingchen and Changzi came to the city a few days ago, they made straight for the building. Some of Hao's men have been living in the company's warehouse, located a few doors down in the same hutong.

Although the Japanese are occupying Beiping, East Jiaomin Lane is in the foreign concession. This area is under the control of the concession's Ministry of Works administrative office, and it is patrolled by Indian policemen. Although the Japanese do send men in to keep an eye on things, they don't dare be too brazen about it, and they are much laxer than they are in other places.

This temporary hideout has been arranged by Mr Charlie. Under continuous pressure from Japanese diplomatic communiqués, Yanjing University has recommenced classes. Although only a few courses are running, more than two hundred students have enrolled, not including the various Japanese secret service agents and informers who have mingled with them. The Japanese have also sent in a resident university inspector who sticks his nose into everything from teaching to administration. CID men guard all the gates, inspecting everything and everyone going in and out, turning the university into something like a prison. Recently, attacks by the Eighth Route Army and other resistance groups in the environs of Beiping have become more frequent, so the Japanese inside the city are on high alert. Not only have they increased security on the city gates, but they have also installed sentry posts at every intersection, and Kempeitai, CID and police patrols are more frequent on the streets than the buses and trams, appearing every few minutes.

Even so, Hao Bingchen's work continues uninterrupted. With the help of Yang Zhixing and Wangtian, he has already got rid of almost half of the army notes, and in another couple of weeks he should have shifted it all. Once Gao Guigeng gets back from Tianjin to join them, they can go home.

One evening, Hao Bingchen takes a telephone call from Mr Charlie, who says: "There is a hurricane at home today, it may reach Victoria early tomorrow."

This is their privately agreed code. It means there is important news from the Americans, and they arrange a meeting early the next day at the Victoria coffee shop. This coffee shop is in the middle section of East Jiaomin Lane. Run by an Englishman, it is one of their regular meeting places.

Hao Bingchen and Changzi arrive at the coffee shop as agreed, but they enter separately, and they don't sit together.

Charlie arrives not long after and nonchalantly sits down opposite Hao Bingchen. He orders a coffee and says in a low voice: "Chongqing has sent a man to Beiping for secret talks with the Japanese. Did you know about this?"

"That's not possible," says a startled Hao Bingchen. "The National Army may have suffered a succession of defeats, but they still hold all the provinces in the southeast and the northwest, and the Eighth Route Army and the local resistance groups are fighting behind enemy lines, so we're still in a strong enough position. There are Japanese sympathisers in the Kuomintang, urging peace negotiations, but they are not in the ascendancy, and Old Chiang still wants to hold the centre ground."

"Ha! And you really have faith in that Chiang fellow? With the example of the three eastern provinces and Rehe to go on, it's not beyond the bounds of possibility that either the Yellow River or the Yangtze could be used as a new border..."

Charlie smiles bitterly and sighs.

Hao Bingchen is even more alarmed, but he still shakes his head, albeit not quite as decisively as before: "Even if Old Chiang does want to hold talks, now is not the time. The Japanese drive hasn't been exhausted yet, and they're not going to take a step back now. Any accord we make at this point will still be signed under duress. And he has to take heed of the other political powers and of popular opinion, doesn't he?"

"The way I see it, it's not that this Chiang fellow doesn't have a plan. I'm afraid he has too many and is going to have to reach a compromise with the foreign powers to realise them." Charlie lowers his voice and continues: "I have heard that the talks with the Japanese have already happened, and the two sides have come to a consensus jointly to oppose the Communists and the Soviets and permitting the Japanese Army to garrison troops here to fight the Communists. It establishes a Sino-Japanese economic agreement, allows the Japanese precedence over exploiting the natural resources of North China, waives any mutual compensation and covers other assorted matters. It hasn't yet been fully agreed because the Chinese side has set the price too high. They want both sides to restore the status quo as it stood before the Marco Polo Bridge Incident, and they also want a separate protocol over the question of Manchukuo. If these further talks can reach a compromise, then it's quite possible that the agreement will be concluded."

"If he's willing to do that, even the half of the country that is left us won't be safe. It won't just be two nations at war, the country will fragment like it did during the Warring States. He's going to have trouble justifying it on the international stage as well. Quite apart from Soviet Russia, and the British and the French, are you Americans going to go along with it? Are they really going to let Japan get the upper hand?"

"Of course not. It's not in my country's interest. So we need to find out whether this is being taken seriously internally and get an accurate picture as quickly as possible."

"Ha! What's this?" says Hao Bingchen. "A high-ranking officer like you still wants to make some extra cash selling information? Can't you at least reveal something? Your predecessor was..."

"Mr Hao," Charlie says solemnly, "I have never asked you about your motives. I don't care about earning any backhanders. I am acting on behalf on my country, and that happens to coincide with China's interests and with what is just and humane."

Seeing that he is getting a little agitated, Hao Bingchen laughs and says: "Alright, alright, I understand. I won't push you. Nonetheless, if you Americans are so keen on upholding righteousness, then you really shouldn't be giving China military supplies on the one hand and selling Japan goods on the other. That's not neutrality, that's profiting from war. I think you should suggest to your government that joining the war sooner rather than later, and helping China fight Japan, will be the most beneficial course of action for your country. Otherwise, the Japanese will just grow even more ambitious and will make a move against America next."

"There is good reason in what you say, and I will do my utmost to bring this about. But... if the secret talks between the government in Chongqing and the Japanese result in an agreement, then there's nothing anyone can do about it."

"Alright then, I'll check what's going on as quickly as possible and give you an answer. But given they are secret talks, the circle of people who are in the know is going to be very small, and I can't guarantee I'll find anything. All I can do is do my best. And then again..." Hao Bingchen hesitates for a moment. "Our Party rules are very strict, and I'm not allowed to be in communication with you without authorisation... so whatever you do, don't give me away."

"Of course not. I understand the rules, but when this is over you may find you are in line for some financial recompense from the American side."

Hao Bingchen looks very serious when he hears this: "If you mention that again, I will ignore it. If you want to play the lord, does that mean I have to become some low fellow only interested in profit? Let's get this clear, the only reason I am agreeing to work with you is to stop our country being sold down the river and to resist the Japanese. Nothing else."

. . .

THE INFORMATION REGARDING the Chongqing government mission to Beiping for secret talks with the Japanese was brought by American secret agents from Hong Kong, and it is no empty rumour. The Chongqing Government representative has already made contact with the Japanese and is staying in the German Embassy in East Jiaomin Lane, only two or three hundred metres from where Hao Bingchen is lodging at the Damei Trading Company. The representative is none other than Zhou Zhengjie. His post as commissioner of the government's Bureau of Military Affairs is just a front, and his mission to consolidate anti-Japanese resistance forces behind enemy lines is equally just a blind, though also a useful bargaining chip. His real mission is to conclude the secret negotiations with the Japanese.

The Japanese negotiating team is made up of two men: the one representing the military is Matsuzaki Harayama, and the one from the Ministry of Foreign Affairs is Iwai Eiichi. Zhou Zhengjie is very familiar with Matsuzaki Harayama and their paths have frequently crossed since the Japanese was undercover in Tianjin and Beiping using the alias Liu Yu. But he knows very little about Iwai Eiichi other than that he is the Japanese deputy consul in Shanghai, and he has flown up specially from there. He also knows that he is a veteran intelligence officer and controller of the Ministry of Foreign Affairs' Special Investigations Office, more generally known as the 'Iwai Mansion'.

As far as the negotiations go, Matsuzaki Harayama isn't too optimistic. The way he sees it, the whole approach is something that the Japanese Government has been urged into by Germany. Their military approach is already settled, and it is not going to be abandoned at the negotiating table. Sitting down there is simply going through the motions and won't produce any practical results. But when he finds out that the representative from Chongqing is Zhou Zhengjie, his attitude changes, and he begins to feel that there is some hope for the talks. This is not just because he knows Zhou Zhengjie himself, but more because he knows something about his background. There are many different factions within the Kuomintang and the government itself, and the fact that a comparative unknown like Zhou Zhengjie has been given this responsibility must have something to do with him being distantly related to Zhou Fohai. According to his information, although Zhou Fohai is one of Chiang Kai-shek's most trusted confidants, privately he has become very close with Wang Jingwei, Chen Gongbo and others, who have formed a low-profile association that has a pessimistic view of the prospects for the anti-Japanese resistance.

Chen Gongbo and his associates find themselves very much at loggerheads with Chiang Kai-shek, and in 1935 at the Kuomintang General Assembly, there was an attempted assassination of Chiang Kai-shek by someone disguised as a journalist. As it turned out, Chiang didn't attend the press call, but Wang Jingwei was shot twice. Wang believed that Chiang was actually behind the assassination attempt, and after that, the rift between the two men grew wider. So even if no agreement could be secured with the Chongqing Government at these talks, if he could reach a mutual understanding and common consensus with the powers behind Zhou Zhengjie, that would be an important prize.

MATSUZAKI IS a highly experienced agent, and his analysis proves entirely correct. The first evening after he left Hong Kong, Zhou Zhengjie received a telephone call from Zhou Fohai in person, which lasted for almost an hour. The most important aspect of the call was to order him not just to represent the government, but also to explore the possibility of, and basic conditions for, discussions with the Wang faction; it would be ideal if he could obtain a written draft agreement from the Japanese. If this can't be accomplished, then he should organise a channel of communications and continue negotiations. So it is quite clear that Zhou Zhengjie's current remit really is like a Russian doll, with many different layers inside it.

Once the upfront talks begin, Zhou Zhengjie's original lofty aspirations become a lot less clear and assured. After a few rounds of discussion, he gives a heartfelt sigh: "Ai! There is no such thing as diplomacy for a weak nation!"

How true that saying is. Before he arrived, he thought his task was quite practicable and that he could advance a more than adequate analysis of China's position: it still has the vast territories of the south and west behind the front lines; it still has an army of many millions; it still has international backing; it still has a broad circle of connections, and if you include the recently incorporated local militia, that adds another string to its bow; and it still has the powerful support of many groups behind enemy lines. But when it comes to the point, all these defences crumble before Matsuzaki's mocking words.

"Your arguments are specious, Mr Zhou. These vast territories you talk about are the provinces of Sichuan, Yunnan and Guizhou which are mostly poor, mountainous terrain, so do you really think you can rely on them to support your front lines? The roads into Sichuan are notoriously hard, but what kind of defence is that against the Imperial Air Force? We wouldn't even have to penetrate very deeply, since we can render the defence of the southwest impossible with siege and bombardment. The Imperial Army already has a strong grip on the Central Plain,[1] so what chance do you have of success when you are fighting with your back to the wall?

"Throughout Chinese history, whoever held the Central Plain won the empire. When Zhuge Liang led six expeditions from the Qi Mountains, and Jiang Wei attacked the Central Plain nine times, the result was always the same: defeat and destruction. Even if it is true that you have several million men, the fighting strength of an army is not decided by its numbers. When you look at your preparations for war, and the fighting spirit of your men, do you really think simple numbers can make up for their inadequacies? Since the war between our two countries started, you have always outnumbered us many times, but have you won a single victory? On the international stage, most of your support is just talk, and you have received only token material aid. Which nation has risked anything concrete for fear of making an enemy out of China or Japan? To be frank, the one real headache I have is the trouble the Communist Party and the Eighth Route Army is causing in our occupied territories. They are taking advantage of the Imperial Army's westward push to establish a broad base of operations, and they are already threatening the safety of our rear. But this doesn't work to the advantage of the Kuomintang. Rather, it is a serpent in your own bosom, is it not? Nor do you have that much available capital, so you shouldn't be over-confident in what it can achieve. You have lost on the battlefield, but your expectation that you can win those losses back at the negotiating table is completely unrealistic."

All Zhou Zhengjie can say is "Not necessarily", but beyond that, he has nothing to offer in reply.

With the official talks broken down, Matsuzaki Harayama's thinking is led down a new path.

"Mr Zhou," he says, "our talks with the current Chinese Government have not prospered, so is there perhaps someone else we should be talking to? If peace is our aim, then we must put peace before everything else. If you could establish communications with an alternative political power, we would welcome it. I am not sure, however, whether you would be willing to change your allegiance."

Of course, Matsuzaki Harayama's hesitancy is just an act, and the result is a foregone conclusion.

The truth is, these secret talks between China and Japan are not just alarming the American and Kuomintang military intelligence bureau's information sections, they are also attracting the attention and interest of the Chinese Communist Party. In fact, the plan was known to the Central Committee of the Communist Party before it was even put into action, and they had full command of all the subsequent events. Security around these secret talks was extremely tight on both sides, with very few people in the know about them, all of whom had received only verbal instructions with no preparatory documents. On the Kuomintang side, they kept things quiet by using relative unknowns such as Zhou Zhengjie, with specially appointed operatives from the Office of Military Affairs providing a smokescreen. The Japanese, on the other hand, relied on the apparatus of the military and the Ministry of Foreign Affairs, and their representatives comprised only a handful of top officials. Germany's only involvement was to offer a venue for the talks and guarantee the safety of the Chinese personnel. From the time he entered the German Embassy, Zhou Zhengjie has been kept isolated from the outside as surely as if he were locked in a safe. There are several levels of security staff within the embassy, and on the outside there is round-the-clock surveillance provided by Japanese plainclothes agents. So how did the Communist Party obtain its detailed intelligence about the secret talks? In fact, it came from a slip-up by the Japanese representative at the talks, Iwai Eiichi.

Iwai Eiichi is much less experienced than Matsuzaki Harayama, but although his post in the Japanese Ministry of Foreign Affairs is not particularly exalted, his influence is considerable as a representative of the new wave in Japanese politics. He considers himself the prime candidate for the post of foreign minister, so he is very autocratic in his actions; he is eager to show off his mettle but tends to overreach himself. Within the Special Investigations Office for which he is responsible, he has set up a number of sub-divisions, into which he has recruited a good few Chinese. Among these, his most valued aide is a middle-aged man called Yuan Shu. He had spent time in Japan as an overseas student and worked as a journalist. He is also a member of the Green Society and has been an officer in the Shanghai branch of the Chinese Civil Intelligence. He is very well-connected, quick-witted and of outstanding ability. Before the war, he hadn't been particularly close to Iwai, but once Iwai recruited him, it was inevitable he would be given an important role. How was Iwai to know that Yuan Shu was also an agent of Chinese military intelligence? In fact, he was personally recruited by the head of military intelligence himself, Dai Li, and is the section leader in charge of undercover operations, holding the rank of major-general. But none of the above are Yuan Shu's real job. Neither Iwai Eiichi nor Dai Li know that, since the Revolution of 1911, Yuan Shu has been a special agent of the Chinese Communist Party, who has made countless major contributions to the underground war. As everyone knows, during the Sino-Japanese War and the War of Liberation, undercover heroes such as Yuan Shu provided enormous amounts of invaluable intelligence, and in a sense, it was they who determined the courses and conclusions of those wars.

Although Yuan Shu can't lay his hands on any written records, he is able to use his exceptional memory to commit to heart the most important areas touched upon. He then transcribes it all when he gets back to his lodgings. Even so, he is still faced with the major difficulty of how to get his report back to his superiors. In Shanghai, he could profit by his post at the Iwai Mansion to find opportunities to contact his superiors directly using the Japanese radio transmitter. This was how he made his report on the imminent commencement of the secret talks, but once in Beiping, this method is no longer open to him. He and Iwai Eiichi are both staying at the Japanese Consulate there, and he has almost no opportunities for going out. Although the Communist Party has an underground network in the city, for security reasons, the underground resistance and the underground

Party have never established lines of communication. But he is afraid of significant consequences if he waits until he returns to Shanghai to make his reports; if this intelligence on the overall state of the anti-Japanese resistance is passed on to his superiors as soon as possible, it may give them the initiative and reduce casualties. In fact, the high-ups have anticipated such a situation, and they informed Yuan Shu before his arrival in Beiping that a comrade would make contact with him. They have not, however, told him the contact's name, only the code-name 'Northern Ice'; nor has a definite time been established, only a password. Yuan Shu has already been in Beiping for several days, but his contact has not yet put in an appearance.

By the sixth day, the talks are approaching their end, and the two sides have reached a general understanding. They take the afternoon off to report back to their respective superiors and make appropriate adjustments to the wording of the agreement so it can be signed off successfully the following day. Zhou Zhengjie immediately uses the radio transmitter in the German Embassy to send a coded report to his uncle Zhou Fohai, and he waits impatiently for a reply. The Japanese, on the other hand, are entirely relaxed about the whole affair and treat the break in negotiations as a holiday. This is because the other side have agreed to everything they want, and they don't need any further instructions. Nor are they the least bit worried about how Wang Jingwei in Chongqing will react. The way Matsuzaki Harayama puts it, a hole has appeared in the trap that their opponents have been caught in for a long time, and if they are allowed through it, they won't bother to check whether there are barbs around that hole.

That afternoon, someone comes to visit Iwai Eiichi. It is a Japanese businessman Shoi Kawa and his wife, Zhou Zhengying, along with a one-year old boy. This isn't the first time this couple have asked for an audience at the Japanese Consulate in Beiping; they also called on the second day after Iwai Eiichi's arrival in the city. Even though the consulate was extremely busy at that time, and despite the need for secrecy over the negotiations, Iwai told his secretary to arrange a time for them to come back. That time was this very afternoon.

Zuo Xichuan's business is doing pretty well at the moment, and with the backing of Shoi Toyoki as a major shareholder, it has quickly become one of the most powerful trading companies in the whole of Rehe. As agreed with the Party apparatus, he has also accepted the request of military intelligence east of the Pass to gather political, economic and military information for them. To facilitate communications, they also laid on a radio transmitter for him, and for this purpose, curtailed Zhou Zhengying's role as his wife so she could become his communications officer. When she was with the Shanxi Anti-Japanese

Resistance Army, she had received special communications training, so she gets her hand in very quickly and is soon fully in command of the task. The Party apparatus place great value on their multi-faceted intelligence outpost, and it orders them to distance themselves completely from the local Party leadership, not just in the north, but in all other areas too, and to communicate directly with the Party's central office. Ten days previously, they received instructions summoning them to Beijing to support Comrade Yuan Shu, codenamed 'South Wind', to receive intelligence reports on the secret talks between the Chinese and Japanese, and to forward them immediately to central office by radio.

There are two reasons they have entrusted this task to Zuo Xichuan. One is that his relative, Shoi Toyoki, was at school with Iwai Eiichi and has been thick with him for many years, which will make it much easier to get close to him. The other is that, because he has a radio transmitter, the chain of communication can be much shorter, benefitting both security and speed. To this end, when Zuo Xichuan takes his leave of Shoi Toyoki, he says he is going to Beiping, on the one hand for business, but also to take his wife back to visit the family she has not seen for a long time. As they are chatting, he makes sure to mention that he is thinking of expanding the business into Shanghai, and asking whether Shoi Toyoki has any reliable contacts there. Of course, Shoi thinks of Iwai Eiichi, and when Zuo Xichuan asks, he immediately agrees to write a letter and tells him to visit Iwai in Beiping so they can discuss, face to face, opportunities for expanding into the Shanghai market. In arranging this meeting, it also gives Zuo Xichuan the opportunity to make contact with Yuan Shu.

AFTER EXCHANGING PLEASANTRIES, Iwai invites Zuo Xichuan into an inner room to discuss things in more detail, since private discussions of schemes to make money are best not done out in the open. He calls Yuan Shu in from the room next door, telling him to look after the wife, as she might find the company of a fellow Chinese more congenial. When he had originally brought the couple in, Yuan Shu noticed that the child in the wife's arms had a large crystal pendant round its neck, which was not very highly worked, but retained its natural form. He recognised it as a coded signal.

"That's a very fine piece of crystal," he says, casually. "Why don't you get someone to carve it?"

Zuo Xichuan replies, equally casually: "Ah, I think it's better as it is, like a piece of ice in the northern sky, natural and brilliant."

This, of course, refers to the pre-arranged password.

Zuo Xichuan and Iwai Eiichi talk for more than half an hour in the inner room, whereas, in the outer room, Yuan Shu and Zhou Zhengying have quickly concluded their business. An outline of the negotiated agreement is already secreted inside little Nan'er's kimono. They have arranged that, if Yuan Shu doesn't make contact by four o'clock in the afternoon the next day, it will be assumed that no significant changes have been made, and the document should immediately be sent to Party headquarters.

When Zuo Xichuan and Zhou Zhengying return to the Japanese Consulate and hastily inspect the draft agreement, they are shocked. They had thought the Chinese side would make some compromises, but they had never expected that the agreement would be an unvarnished, treasonous betrayal of the whole country.

The agreement has seven parts, the content of which is broadly as follows:

1. China and Japan undertake to defend the agreed protocol and recognise that Japanese troops may be stationed in China to defend against the Communists and Soviet Russia.
2. It recognises the legitimate status of Manchukuo.
3. Japanese expatriates have right of residence in China and freedom to do business.
4. China and Japan are to enact economic co-operation; the area of North China is to be established as an autonomous special administrative region, and the Japanese have priority over the use of its natural resources.
5. China agrees to reorganise its National Government, to pursue a policy of goodwill towards the Japanese and jointly promote the prosperity of the whole of East Asia.
6. Neither side is obliged to provide compensation for any losses incurred during the war, or to return any gains made.
7. Beyond the current protocol, after the re-establishment of peace, the Japanese Army will withdraw completely within two years. Troops necessary to maintain defence against the Communists and Soviet Russia are excluded from this provision.

Zhou Zhengying grinds her teeth in fury when she has finished reading the document, but she hides her face in shame at the same time on seeing the name of her older brother, Zhou Zhengjie. Caught between these two emotions, she still sees a thread of hope, that tomorrow this draft agreement may be completely overturned, or, at least, considerably amended. This is her brother who is involved, and she truly does not want to be the hand that carves his name on the stele of shame of those disgraced throughout history. She desperately wants to throw caution to the winds, go and see him and pull him back from the edge of the precipice. But the discipline of undercover work, coupled with the great weight of the trust placed on her shoulders, mean that, in the end, all these emotions can only find expression in a long, deep sigh.

Next afternoon, four o'clock passes and there has been no further contact from Yuan Shu. To be absolutely certain, they wait until five o'clock, but there is still no word, so Zuo Xichuan tells Zhou Zhengying to send the report forthwith.

At midnight that day, the radio station at Yan'an broadcasts the news of the secret negotiations and the contents of the agreement. They use radio on this occasion because it can reach a far wider audience than any form of written communication. On their standard frequency, they send the transmission in Morse code, so it rapidly spreads across the whole country and out into the wider world.

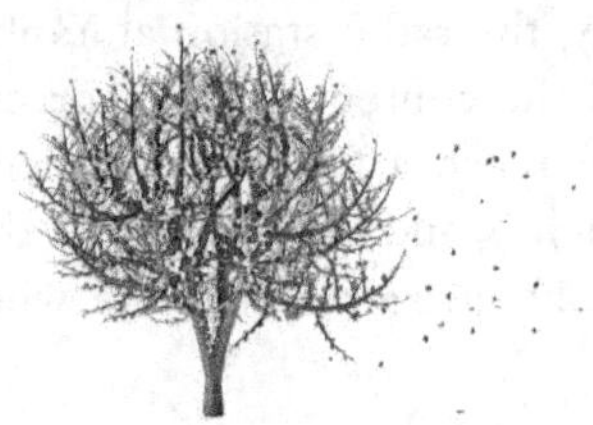

Chapter 46

It really is true that illness 'arrives like a landslide but leaves like a silk thread'. Yang Zhixing has always had the constitution of mule, and no matter how tired or run-down he feels, he has always been able to roll over and regain his energy. But this time he is fighting a losing battle. Since being admitted to the hospital, his health has collapsed. Unable to eat anything for several days, he has been entirely reliant on an intravenous drip. Although his fever isn't excessive, it is proving intractable, and his cough is much worse, often choking him and leaving him unable to draw breath. The phlegm he coughs up is always streaked with red, and sometimes he brings up a whole mouthful of fresh blood. After several days, his naturally lean face has become as drawn as an old loofah, a waxen yellow in colour, wizened and dull, and the skin stretched across his skull is criss-crossed with wrinkles. His eye sockets are sunken, his normally narrowed eyes are much more visible, but there is no sign in them of his habitual vitality.

Fortunately, it is only a few days before the penicillin is obtained. Since Chenglong has been ordered by Matsuzaki to keep watch over East Jiaomin Lane, it is Zhou Si who delivers the two boxes of the drug. The treatment proves efficacious, and after two injections, Yang Zhixing's illness appears to stabilise. Although he still has a low-grade fever, his cough is less severe and his breathing more even. Over the last few days, his intermittent cough has meant that he hasn't been able to get any proper sleep, but now he can.

Wangtian and Yue E, who have been keeping watch over him, can finally draw breath and relax a little. It has all been too much for Mother Yan at her advanced age, and the evening after she escorted her husband to hospital, having tossied and turned all night, she, too, fell ill. Although it is not serious, she can't afford to tire herself out any further. Yue E already has two children getting under her feet, so now she has to look after Mother Yan as well, she is up to her ears in work and can't keep an eye on everything at the same time. Wangtian wants to send her home, but Yang Zhixing's condition is still serious, and if, by any chance, he has something important to impart and there isn't a relative at his side, there will be no one to hear him. All he can do is get

Caiping to make sure the children are fed and to keep an eye on Mother Yan, while he and Yue E keep constant watch at the hospital. Being a man, Wangtian naturally takes on the greater share of the burden of care, massaging Yang Zhixing's chest and back, seeing to his bodily functions and taking care of anything else that is needed. He hasn't slept at all these last few days of looking after him. The doctors, nurses and fellow patients all assume he is Yang Zhixing's son-in-law and say how lucky the old man is, despite not having a son of his own, to have such a good daughter and an even better son-in-law. At first, the two of them try to explain the real situation, but before they can get more than a few sentences out, the questions just increase, until, in the end, they get tired of the endless round of enquiry, and they just smile and let people say what they like.

Seeing that Yang Zhixing is now much more stable, Wangtian whispers to Yue E: "I don't think anything more is going to happen this evening, Yue E. You should go home to see to the kids. Get some sleep and come back in the morning. You've been looking like a ghost these last few days."

"Ha! It's you who's borne the worst of it. I can put up with the discomfort a little longer, but you've been so worried you haven't even closed your eyes..."

"It's not that I can't sleep, it's just that, as soon as I relax and shut my eyes, his face keeps appearing to me."

"That's caused by overheating from stress. It's you who should go home and get some proper rest to calm your nerves. There's nothing to stop you. Even if you're too worried to sleep, at least you can unwind your back and stretch your legs, which has got to be better than being curled up in here."

"Hmm, do you really think you still need to be polite with me? Go on, hurry off home. If you wait any longer, a woman won't be safe in the dark."

"Ai! What a pig-headed man you are! I'll go home tomorrow, but today it's your turn, alright?"

"Alright. I know how brave you are, but are you sure you won't be afraid here overnight on your own?"

"I'm... I'm not afraid."

"You may not be, but I am."

"What's a big strapping fellow like you afraid of?"

"I'm afraid that, when it's so quiet in here at night, if a cat yowls outside, you'll jump out of your skin."

At this, Yue E giggles and slaps him playfully, so that he can't restrain himself and he joins in the laughter. Just at this moment, the door is thrust open, making the two of them jump. When they look to see who it is, there is Chenglong.

"Try and be a bit quieter. This is a sickroom!" Yue E exclaims angrily.

"Oh, so you know it's a sickroom, do you? You were making so much noise with your laughing, I thought I was in a tea house!"

"Ah, Chenglong! Uncle Yang is a bit better today, and I was thinking of sending Yue E home for the night to get some rest..."

"No, don't do that." Chenglong shuts the door and continues: "You two seem to be getting along so well, surely you don't want to stop now."

"You need to clean that dirty mind of yours," says Yue E, glaring at him. "My father's really ill and that's all you can think about?"

"Ai! I don't need to think about it when I'm having my face rubbed in it. I'd just come through the hospital door when a nurse tried to stop me, saying if I'm not family, I can't come visiting in the evening. She only let me in when I told her I was Old Master Yang's son-in-law."

"They let you in eventually, so why are you complaining?" Yue E almost chokes on her words.

"Ha! Well I did get in, and I don't like what I've been hearing!"

"What are you talking about?" Wangtian asks.

"Ha! They said: 'His daughter and number one son-in-law have been looking after him all this time, and I, number two son-in-law, only shows up now, by myself and empty-handed. How do you think that looks?' Alright, I get it, I'm number two in the Gao family, and now I'm number two with my in-laws as well."

"What? Is that all?" Wangtian laughs. "Do you think outsiders have any idea who's who? Are you serious?"

Chenglong stiffens and says: "Why would I be serious about something like that? It's just talk. But I'm afraid my sister-in-law might take it seriously if you leave her at home all by herself, with all her household duties and the kids to look after. Women aren't as forgiving as I am."

Yue E's expression darkens at this and she rebukes him angrily: "Caiping isn't as mean-spirited as you. She is a woman with the heart of a real man, whereas your bitching just makes you sound like a woman. My father is in this condition, and you don't show your face for days on end. Then, when you do come along, you have the nerve to moan about this and bitch about that. What do you think you're up to? I've had enough of you shooting your mouth off."

Chenglong's face flushes scarlet, and he is about to explode with anger, when Wangtian interposes himself: "That's enough. Both of you shut up before you make complete fools of yourselves. Uncle Yang is just beginning to get better, so don't disturb him with your racket."

He can see that Chenglong isn't mollified, so he keeps his temper and goes on: "I let Yue E stay here to keep an eye on things because Uncle Yang's illness is still unresolved, and I was afraid that, just in case anything happened, or his family sent news or had some other errand to him, it wouldn't do if there wasn't a relative here to see to it."

Chenglong grunts and seems to calm down, but his eyes light up at the words 'news' and 'errand'.

"Did... did the Old Master say anything?"

This just annoys Yue E afresh: "Why can't you just wish him well and leave it at that?"

Chenglong doesn't rise to the bait this time, and he moves over next to Yue E: "I'm just afraid in case something unexpected happens." When he sees Yue E glare at him, he hurries on with a conciliatory smile. "Alright, calm down, I was only joking. Don't take me so seriously. You shouldn't blame me too much for not fulfilling my filial duties. I've been crazily busy, and I've come as soon as I've seen to business, haven't I?" Moving even closer, he continues: "Didn't the Old Master entrust the family fortune to you?"

"If that's why you..." snaps Yue E.

Chenglong doesn't wait for her to finish: "I didn't mean anything else by it. I'm only thinking of you. It makes sense for him to make arrangements while he's still lucid. If he dies without saying anything, aren't you afraid there'll be trouble with his widow?"

"Pah! Pah!" Yue E spits out the exclamations before continuing the rebuke: "What kind of negative talk is that? Do you find it impossible to look on the bright side? Doesn't my father seem to be on the mend today?"

Chenglong spreads his hands and sighs. "Ai! I'm just saying 'what if'! Who knows how the old man's illness is going to turn out?"

"Huh! It's so good of you to care!" says Yue E. "There, will that do you? And don't worry, my family all know the score and understand human emotions. Mother Yan may not be my real mother, but she has treated me as her own for the last twenty years, so even if that 'what if' does happen, we're not going to fall out over a little money. Besides, my father has been running the household for others all his life, and tens of thousands of yuan have passed through his hands, but how much of his piddling salary is left? If Mother Yan has a little money, then it's there to look after her in her old age. I'm not giving it a second thought, but is that pittance what you're talking about now?"

"Pittance?" Chenglong stares at her. "You clearly don't think very much of your father, do you? And you don't understand how the world works either. Everyone knows that the Qi family are the bones of the Minister's Residence, but the Yang family is the flesh. What do you think that means? It means that for several generations all the Minister's Residence's property has been earned and hoarded by the Yang family. Forget about the past though, if your father hadn't had a grip on things, that spendthrift of a Young Master would have frittered away everything by now. The family name of the Residence may be Qi not Yang, but your father holds all the power, and the Young Master is just a hollow shell. The same is true of every big residence or mansion. Just a few years ago, the Third Rank Prince of the Qing Mansion was so poor he was reduced to wearing an old sack as a cloak and picking through rubbish, but the former manager of the household opened three antique shops in Liulichang. Where do you think his stock came from? He took it bit by bit from the Prince's Mansion, didn't he! Didn't you yourself say that hundreds of thousands have passed through your father's hands? Don't you think that, over the years, some of it may have stuck there?"

"That's bullshit!" says Wangtian. "Uncle Yang isn't like that."

"Like what?" Chenglong laughs. "I've only ever seen ordinary people, not exceptional ones. People can have a grudge against other people, but they never have a grudge against money. Anything you can squeeze out of your job is just your rightful share. There's nothing shameful about it."

"That's enough!" Yue E cries out, and although she keeps her voice low, there's real power to it. When she sees that Chenglong is remaining silent, she goes on: "You may have no problem with shame and disgrace, and like to act as crazy as you please, but don't drag my father into it. Rich or poor, my family would never get mixed up with you."

Chenglong is silenced by this attack, and it is a while before he can find the words to reply: "Eh? But... but I am mixed up with you, aren't I? You're my wife, and he's my father-in-law. As a son-in-law, how come I don't even have the right to speak out? If I don't, who does?"

"Who's stopping you?" Yue E replies straight away. "Has anyone gagged you? You've said all sorts of things, right and wrong, haven't you?"

"It doesn't make any difference what I say, you don't listen, so it's no use, is it? I'm not bragging if I tell you that, out there, a word from me, and the whole city pricks up their ears. Even the Japanese..."

"I don't care how big a noise you are out there, you're not going to cause trouble in here. Your arrogance won't wash. While my father is still alive, and Mother Yan too, you're not the master in this household. The Yang family are Chinese. Forget about the Japanese, you think it all comes down to money, do you? Well, money just makes everything worse."

Yue E's words sweep away any sense of shame in Chenglong, and he explodes with anger, face flushed and eyes bulging: "So, all my efforts count for nothing, and I'm just a nobody with no standing, am I? If I didn't have some clout with the Japanese, do you think I could have got hold of that penicillin? Would the old man be getting better? It's no use you getting on your high horse with me now. If you really had the courage of your convictions, you wouldn't be in a Japanese hospital using Japanese medicines."

Yue E leaps to her feet at this. She wants to reply but doesn't know what to say. She chokes up, and her eyes redden.

"The more you say, the stupider you sound," Wangtian breaks in, shoving him away. "Get out! Come and shout the odds outside where you won't disturb Uncle Yang."

Chenglong does seem to think he may have gone a little far, and without taking his leave, he just grunts and follows Wangtian towards the door. But just at that moment, an exhausted voice calls out from behind him: "Wait, wait!"

Yang Zhixing has levered himself up on his bed, but he seems to have moved too abruptly, as his arms give way, and he tips towards the edge of the bed. Fortunately, Yue E is close by, and she just manages to catch him. Gasping for breath, the old man begins to cough, and Yue E immediately rubs his chest and pounds him on the back. Wangtian and Chenglong also hurry over to the bedside, plump up his pillows and settle him back in them. Yang Zhixing revives a little and fixes Chenglong with his gaze, smiling faintly. No matter how weak he is, that gaze is still as piercing as a dagger.

"Chenglong!" He beckons him to come closer before going on: "You're worried about this illness of mine."

"And... so I should be, shouldn't I?"

"No, you shouldn't. It's not worth it." Yang Zhixing smiles again and continues: "I know that penicillin is classed as a military necessity, and the Japanese value it like gold. Such a lowly man as me, with such a lowly life, does not deserve to be treated with it."

"You, you mustn't... you mustn't talk like that. I've just..."

"What you just said is right. Yours is a hard and thankless task, isn't it? That's how things are. In fact, you were being too kind to me. I'm really very stupid. Over my lifetime, I've earned many hundreds of thousands of yuan, but not one cent of dirty money has ended up in my pocket. I'm very sorry, but you have been worrying about me for no reason. Ai! Not only can I not offer you any reward, I'm afraid I can't even feel grateful to you. Why not? Do you think, at my age, I care how much longer I live? What I care about is that each day I do live, should be a happy one... that I should be open-hearted and free from worry. I don't want to cause myself any stress, and even less to start criticising anyone else. Even if you were to take my medicine away right now, that would be fine, as I don't want to be beholden to the Japanese, and I don't want to be beholden to you."

Chenglong looks as though he has just had several lumps bitten out of him, and his face flushes scarlet. He does his best to suppress the anger that is surging up inside him. He narrows his eyes, but there is still a dangerous glint to them, and there is a queer expression on his face.

Looking at him, Yang Zhixing laughs and says: "Enough! Be off with you! I've got Wangtian and Yue E here to look after me, and that's quite enough. Whatever you do, don't come back here. You don't want any delay to your master's business – that wouldn't be good for your career prospects. I don't have many days left, so come back when I'm laid out as a corpse, but don't let me see you again while I'm alive. Alright? Don't cause me such distress, or I won't be able to die in peace."

Wangtian follows Chenglong out when he leaves, and it is at that point that Yue E observes twin tracks of tears squeezing their way out of her father's tightly shut eyes.

At noon the next day, Qi Yuexuan comes back to Beiping. On arrival in the city, he and Lao Zhang don't even go home first but make straight for the teaching hospital. Qiwangfen is not very far from Beiping, only seventy or eighty *li*, but Japanese soldiers are stationed everywhere along the way, and you meet many army posts whether you are coming from Changping in the north or Wanping in the south. Fortunately, Lao Zhang knows the area intimately from his frequent bird- and insect-collecting expeditions, and there isn't a mountain that he hasn't climbed. It was only by taking paths that mountain goats would look twice at, and along which he can only lead his donkey, not ride it, that he managed to bring the army pay safely back to Qi Yuexuan. By the end of his journey, he had worn away the soles of his shoes, and his toes were poking out of their uppers. Of course, he gave Qi Yuexuan the letter with the news of Yang Zhixing's serious condition and asking him to return as soon as possible.

When Qi Yuexuan learns of this, all his delight at getting hold of the army pay evaporates, and he wishes he had the powers of Sun Wukong, the Monkey King, so he could get back to Beiping with just one somersault. But as it stands, he has responsibility for two hundred men of the Left Barracks, and he must make arrangements for them before leaving.

Since Zhao Ran's several dozen men took up station at Qiwangfen, Qi Yuexuan has been worried that the Eighth Route Army will follow them into the village. If those two sides were really to go at it with each other, and his men stayed out of it, he's afraid that they would inevitably come out worst from the affair. Fortunately, the Eighth Route Army does not send a body of troops, but just two men. One is the administrator for the unified counties of Wanping from the Anti-Japanese Democratic Government, and the other is Zhang Zhicheng. The two of them arrive alone, on horseback, and totally unarmed. When Qi Yuexuan hears of their arrival, he goes out, intending to give them his support. But to his surprise, before he has even reached the Yin Mansion compound, he meets two of Zhao Ran's men already escorting the visitors away. Zhang Zhicheng is in front with his companion, and Zhao Ran's men are following two paces behind, carrying rifles, to see them out of the main gate and away. Although this procession may have the outward form of a polite, formal escort, it is really an expulsion under armed guard. There is nothing for it but for Qi Yuexuan to escort them down to the foot of the mountain

The fact is, the Eighth Route Army learn of Zhao Ran's withdrawal of his troops almost as soon as it happens. Quite a few of the comrades are in favour of sending a force to wipe them out once and for all, but their commander at HQ doesn't agree. He says that the army and local Party apparatus should work together to consolidate the current situation by, once again, trying to persuade Zhao Ran to join them. If he can be persuaded to bring his troops back, then they will let bygones be bygones, and he can keep his former position. If he is not willing to do this, but just wants to fight the Japanese while not opposing the Eighth Route Army, they can still co-operate peaceably. As long as things don't get taken to extremes, there should be no need for hostilities to break out.

Zhang Zhicheng and his colleague have come bearing this proposal, hoping to talk it over with Zhao Ran. But Zhao stands on his dignity over his official status with the National Army, nor does he trust the sincerity of the offer, so he refuses point-blank. He states, moreover, that he outranks anyone in the Eighth Route Army's Shanxi, Chahar and Hebei military district, and he will not discuss anything with anyone of lesser status than himself. He is going to expand his forces into the areas to the north and west of Beiping, establish his own government and really give them something to look at. If they don't like it, they can just get up and leave. Although Zhang Zhicheng and his colleague are bursting with fury, when Qi Yuexuan hears this, a great weight is taken off his mind. At least for the moment, the two sides aren't fighting, and although they may be at loggerheads, that's still better than any kind of internecine flare-up. When Qi Yuexuan learns that Yang Zhixing is seriously ill, the main reason he dares leave his troops is that he has had this reassuring news.

Even so, before leaving he reminds Grandpa Fu, over and over, that whether the troops are to return to the Left Barracks or to remain on guard at Qiwangfen, will only be decided when he gets back with a clearer picture of the overall situation. While he is away, they are not to pick any kind of fight with Zhao Ran's men, nor are they to undertake any military manoeuvres. Should there be an unforeseen emergency, they must be sure to retreat into the deep mountains south of the Yongding River, where the Eighth Route Army has its base, and whatever they do, not to rush headlong back home. Once he is assured of Grandpa Fu's promise to follow these instructions, Qi Yuexuan relaxes and sets off. The scars on his buttocks still prevent him from riding a horse, so he has to go by donkey cart. Fortunately, both he and Lao Zhang have good citizenship passes and are not carrying much money or many possessions. This means they can take the main route, which, although further, is much quicker than the route across the mountains. Setting out early, they reach the Desheng Gate before noon.

As soon as Qi Yuexuan enters the room, he sees Yang Zhixing propped up in bed, with Yue E feeding him congee from a small bowl. Looking at his haggard face and seeing how listlessly he is eating, Qi Yuexuan's eyes fill with tears. Even though Lao Zhang has warned him of the seriousness of Yang Zhixing's condition, and he has prepared himself for it, his heart still sinks at the sight. As he remembers it, Uncle Yang has hardly aged. Even when he passed sixty and then seventy, he never seemed more than fifty, and a fit fifty at that. Never having seen him looking old and weak like this, Qi Yuexuan had not considered the possibility of him growing old, getting sick and even dying. His heart falls in on itself as suddenly as a house being demolished.

"Manager Yang, the Young Master is here to see you," Lao Zhang says, approaching the bed.

Yue E hurriedly turns to look when she hears this, and for a moment, she doesn't recognise the dust-covered, straggly-bearded figure of Qi Yuexuan. Her mouth opens a couple of times, but no sound emerges.

Yang Zhixing, however, immediately revives and cries out: "Young Master!"

He pushes himself up and pulls back his cover, making to get out of bed. But he swallows his mouthful of congee too quickly, chokes on it and falls into a fit of coughing.

"Don't get up, Uncle Yang!" Qi Yuexuan exclaims, striding over to the bed. Propping him up, he rubs Yang Zhixing's chest and thumps him on the back.

Yang Zhixing lets out a long breath and stops coughing. He grasps Qi Yuexuan's hand, still trembling slightly, and smiles weakly as his eyes fill with tears.

"Aiya, Young Master, this isn't how things should be! It's quite against custom and etiquette!"

"Ai! How can you still think about that kind of thing?" Qi Yuexuan chides him gently. "I lost my father at fourteen and my mother at twenty. I'm over fifty now, and have spent much more time with you than with my parents. You..."

"You mustn't talk like that, Young Master. I know your circumstances, but I wouldn't dare presume upon them. I still remember going as a companion for the Old Master and the Old Mistress to the tomb of one of the Residence's faithful servants. When I meet them again in the other world, they would scold me for not knowing my proper place, and any reputation I have earned for myself in this world would be totally destroyed."

"Oh, listen to you! Who hasn't been ill at some stage? Just because you're sick doesn't mean it's a matter of life or death. How many people are buried in my family graves already? They don't need your company! You just concentrate on getting better so you can keep me company, and your wife and daughter..."

Qi Yuexuan chokes up as he finishes this speech.

"Sit down so you can talk properly, Young Master," Yue E says as she brings over a chair.

Qi Yuexuan nods to her, but after looking at the hard wooden chair, he thinks better of it. After all the shaking and jolting of the journey to Beiping, the wounds on his buttocks have probably opened up again, as they are hurting as though being poked with needles.

Not wanting to reveal the truth, he just grins wryly and says: "Ha! I've been sitting in that cart all morning. I'm more comfortable standing."

Yue E is understandably puzzled as Lao Zhang hurriedly shrugs off his padded jacket, folds it into a cushion which he puts on the chair, then helps Qi Yuexuan slowly to sit down.

Yang Zhixing shoots him a look: "What's the matter? Are your wounds still not healed?"

"Not completely, and after that journey, they're a little... Oh, it's alright, I'll get by," he says with a laugh.

Yang Zhixing looks at him and sighs. "What made you do such a stupid thing?

That official post of yours just isn't worth it. If you wanted to enforce military law, you should have beaten someone else. What reason did you have for inflicting it on yourself? If you go on this way, and the devils don't run away, you'll end up killing yourself."

Qi Yuexuan doesn't try to defend himself. Knowing just how much hurt lies behind Yang Zhixing's words, he lets him grumble on as he always does, actually delighting in it on this occasion.

Yang Zhixing is now smiling too as he talks: "Ha! Well, anyway... for a Young Master like you to go into battle is no easy thing. And to endure suffering, risk your life and stick to your guns, that is truly heroic. I've heard that the war is at a crucial point right now, and I really shouldn't have asked you to come back here, but on this occasion... Ai! I'm afraid I won't be able to hang on much longer. I had to see you face to face to entrust a task to you, and make my funeral arrangements while I'm still lucid. As long as you have everything straight, then when I go, I can go happy..."

"What do you mean, coming out with such talk? Where do you think you are going with it?"

"There's no need to mince your words, my heart can stand it. I'm not afraid to drop down dead right now. I'm just worried that, if I die too suddenly, I won't have time to get things straight, to say everything that needs to be said, and when it happens, I won't die at peace."

"Alright, alright, alright. Go on and say what you have to say."

One by one, Yang Zhixing explains the things he is concerned about: "Young Master, it was my father who handed on to me the position as household manager, more than thirty years ago. Although those have indeed been turbulent years, and we haven't exactly flourished, at least the household has been preserved. Before the Japanese came, I took the proceeds of the sale of several family businesses, along with the money we held in the bank, and turned it all into gold bars, and hid them along with various antiques, paintings and calligraphy. However much you pestered me about this, I never told you anything, and even today..." He hesitates for a moment. "Ai! Even today, I can't tell you where it is all hidden."

Qi Yuexuan has been listening with bated breath, eyes wide, but when he hears this last sentence, he can't help giving a wry laugh: "Ha! Alright, you don't need to go on. If I don't know, no one can force me to tell."

"Now, don't get overwrought. Hear me out, alright?" Yang Zhixing may be telling Qi Yuexuan to stay calm, but he himself is getting so excited, he finds it hard to breathe, and he begins to cough. Yue E hurriedly thumps him on the back a few times, until, at last, he catches his breath and is about to speak again.

Seeing this, Qi Yuexuan cuts him off, smiling: "You just told me not to get overwrought, Uncle Yang, so I won't interrupt this time. Go ahead, and take your time."

Yang Zhixing can't help smiling at this interruption, and he continues: "Ha!

Well, you can't blame me. You're so generous and open-handed. But when you were spending money on birds and insects, and gambling at mahjong and cards, that was just small potatoes. Now you're playing for your life with the Japanese, do you really think you'd be able to keep hold of the family fortune? Once you get your teeth into anything, however unimportant, the family money will be gone in a flash... Don't glare at me. You are a hero for fighting the Japanese, but I'm no traitor either, nor a coward. Resisting the Japanese is no short-term affair, and you need constant running water, not just a basinful to splash around. Why do you think I've gone back into business in a small way, if it's not to put our money to work to finance your service to the country. But I can't afford to fritter away our capital and kill the goose that lays the golden eggs, can I? Supposing you do actually manage to drive the Japanese out after however many years, won't the country be smashed to pieces at the end of it? There will be a thousand things to do, and that is when the money will really be needed, and lots of it. Don't you agree?"

Qi Yuexuan grunts and nods. He is about to say something but then hesitates and thinks better of it. Yang Zhixing knows what he is thinking, and he goes on hurriedly: "Don't worry, Young Master. The only thing I'm taking into my coffin is this one hundred *jin* old body of mine. As well as me, Lao Zhang and Wangtian know where the treasure is buried. So when I'm no longer around and peace comes, you'll still be able to find it."

"What? You know too?" Qi Yuexuan shoots a look at Lao Zhang and gives a grunt of stifled anger.

The look unsettles Lao Zhang, and he hurriedly waves his hand defensively. "Don't be cross, Young Master. It's only with the best intentions that I haven't told you, to protect the family property. The three of us swore a solemn oath, so I really... I really didn't dare tell you."

Qi Yuexuan is bursting with pent-up resentment, but one look at Yang Zhixing's breathless appearance pulls him up, and he just stares blankly.

Yang Zhixing forces a smile: "Although, for the time being, I can't tell you where the treasure is, Young Master, I do have to make sure you get the whole picture. I have already told Wangtian to put together an inventory of the hidden treasure, along with all the household accounts and the title deeds for land and buildings, in order for you to audit when you got back. If there is anything you don't understand, then hurry up and ask me while I still have my full faculties. For thirty years I had control of the family property, and although I had the trust of the Old Mistress and believe that I have acted in good faith, not everyone sees things the same way, and there is bound to be some suspicion. Every single room, every single row of crops I own and everything I have saved from my salary is recorded in the family accounts, and I never salted away anything else. One glance at the accounts will show you everything is in order."

"Ai, Uncle Yang! I've never doubted..."

"It doesn't matter what you may or may not have thought, everything must be done by the book, so you can be reassured and I can go in peace."

"Alright, alright, I'll take a look."

Yang Zhixing smiles weakly and says, as if a great weight has gone from his mind: "Once you have approved the accounts and signed them off, Young Master, then I must hand over as manager of the household."

"You still have time. This illness now shouldn't stop you."

"Ai! I know in my heart... even if Yama doesn't take me this time, I'll still be too weak to shoulder such a heavy burden, so it's for the best that I leave it here."

Qi Yuexuan just grunts and doesn't reply. He knows that, on her deathbed, his mother handed over responsibility for the family property to Yang Zhixing, saying: "You are manager of this household as long as you live, but it is entirely up to you who you pass that job on to."

He knows just how loyal Yang Zhixing has been, but his miserliness, obstinacy and sheer bloody-mindedness have often infuriated him. But because of the instructions his mother had left, he has always had to acquiesce, and he has never been in a position to stand his ground and refuse.

Yang Zhixing sighs again: "Ai! It is really no easy thing, with the world as it is, to find someone to trust. Originally, I had thought to hand on the management of the household to your wife, but I didn't anticipate her getting entangled with the Communists and disappearing without trace. Maybe I should give the job to Lao Zhang..."

"No, no! All I know about is raising crickets. I could never manage the household," says Lao Zhang, shaking his head like a rattle drum.

"Ha! I wasn't really serious," says Yang Zhixing. "Quite apart from whether you're up to the job or not, you're too slippery a customer, and you don't know how to keep your mouth shut about anything. Besides, you're only seven or eight years younger than me, and it won't be long before you're food for the worms too."

"Hey! Just listen to you!" Lao Zhang mutters to himself indignantly. "I'm not even in the market, but you're still running me down!"

Yang Zhixing laughs, then says: "I've already chosen someone for you, Young Master."

"Who?"

"Wangtian."

"Wangtian?" Qi Yuexuan stares at him in amazement.

Thinking he can't remember who that is, Yue E hurriedly interposes: "He's one of the Gao family children, Young Master. Chenglong's elder brother."

"I know." Qi Yuexuan seems to be considering the idea. "The man is honest and sincere, but is he up to taking on the lead role?"

"I've watched Wangtian grow up," Yang Zhixing says with a smile. "He didn't have many years schooling, but he's a natural at business. He may not be that clever, but his hard work makes up for it. You may think he's lacking get-up-and-go, hiding his light, but the most important thing is he has a good heart, knows how to behave, and he's nothing like Chenglong. With the world in such chaos, how much do you expect of him? Just keeping what we've already got is the most important thing. To do that, honesty and sincerity are vital. There's no shortage of smart talkers and slick movers out there, but the stolid and dull are harder to find. Young Master, when it comes to stolidity and dullness, the stolider and duller your manager is, the better. If you get somebody too smart and scheming, he'll have sold off all your antiques within three years."

Everyone begins to laugh, and even Qi Yuexuan can't keep a straight face. "Ha ha, you're right. But if you think about it, if one dull person works with another dull person, wouldn't that just be too dull?"

This provokes even more laughter.

"Young Master." It is Yang Zhixing who breaks in again.

"Alright, let's go with Wangtian. I trust you," Qi Yuexuan says, standing up. "You must rest, Uncle Yang. I..."

"No, wait. I haven't told you the most important thing yet."

"There's something more important? What is it?"

Yang Zhixing doesn't reply, but beckons to Yue E. When she goes over to his side, he caresses her head gently and looks her over in silence.

Yue E is a little nonplussed: "Father, you... what is it you've got to say?"

Yang Zhixing smiles, but there are tears in his eyes: "You're twenty-eight this year, aren't you, Yue E?"

"No, I'll be turning twenty-nine."

"There is something I have been hiding from you for the last twenty-eight years, and today..."

"Uncle Yang!" Qi Yuexuan interrupts him before he can finish. "Let's... let's talk about this later."

Yang Zhixing sighs, and his tears begin to flow. "Ai, Young Master, I know you are thinking of me, but sooner or later, it has to be said. If I drop dead suddenly, then it will never be explained. It's better you let me tell the child. You have the rest of your lives ahead of you, and I would rather break my solemn oath now and take my punishment in the next world."

Qi Yuexuan doesn't say anything but turns his head away.

"What... what are you two... what are you trying to say?" Distressed, Yue E looks first at Yang Zhixing, then at Qi Yuexuan.

"Yue E," Yang Zhixing hesitates a moment, then asks: "Do you... do you know who your mother was?"

"My mother?" Yue E is stunned, but she slowly collects herself. "She... I never saw her, but I heard you and grandfather talking about her. She was called Xiulan, but didn't she die when I was only a month old?"

"No, she didn't die then. She died last year, following in the footsteps of your grandfather, killed by the Japanese for resisting them. She... she was a heroine...

and after she died, she was buried in the family graves. She *was* called Xiulan, but not many people knew that. She was much better-known by her nickname."

"So... what was she called?"

"Flower Branch."

Yue E just stands there, wide-eyed and open-mouthed.

"What? Wasn't he the Junior Master of the Beiyu Lodge, who became Grand Master of the Dragon Gate. Has your illness addled your mind, Father? Can't you tell a man from a woman?"

Yang Zhixing heaves a deep sigh and slowly begins to explain how her mother and the Young Master were lovers, how she fell pregnant and how the Old Mistress forced them to marry. He reveals all the twists and turns of the last twenty-eight years. Yue E dissolves in sobs and tears, as does Yang Zhixing himself. Qi Yuexuan has turned away, hiding his face.

"Yue E!" Yang Zhixing pulls her a little closer and wipes away her tears with his sleeve. At the same time, he opens his eyes wide, afraid his own tears might begin to flow again, and forces a smile.

"Ai! What a business this is, but you mustn't blame either me or the Young Master. It was all forced upon us. Don't cry. This is a good thing, a lucky thing. Come now, and kowtow to your real father. Call him 'Father'. You are the heir of the Qi family of the Minister's Residence, and you must acknowledge your ancestry."

Yue E slowly stands up and timidly turns and looks at Qi Yuexuan in silence. She doesn't make a move but looks at him as though she has never seen him before. There is no joy or celebration in her eyes, only anger and regret.

When Qi Yuexuan sees this, the smile freezes on his lips, and he looks totally put out.

"Yue E! Daughter!"

There is a tremble in his voice, wary and beseeching, and twin tears trickle down his cheeks. Yue E gives a great start at the sound of his voice. She turns to look at Yang Zhixing, and her own tears fall like rain.

"Aiya! What are you crying for? Hurry up and kneel to acknowledge your father," Yang Zhixing says angrily.

Yue E hears him and wipes away her tears. She looks him in the eye and wails: "What are you doing... saying that? You... you are my only father!"

She gives a great gulping sob and runs out of the room, wailing.

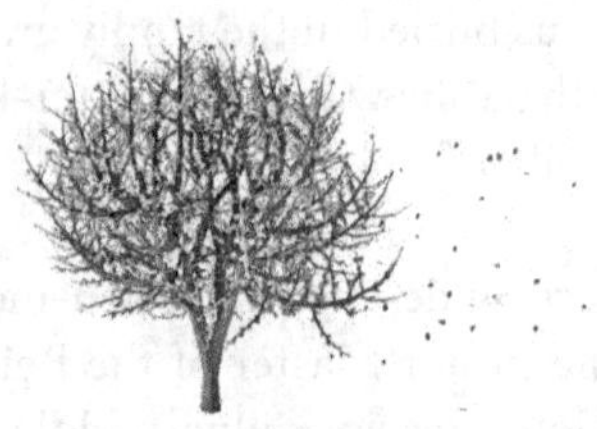

Chapter 47

After Communist Party broadcasts reveal news of the secret talks between the National Government and the Japanese, and of the content of their secret agreement, a storm brews within China and abroad. A chorus of disapproval can be heard across the country. Chongqing is even more in uproar than before. A great crowd of people from all walks of life wanting to see Chiang Kai-shek stack up outside his official residence, and his telephone rings off the hook. Even the ambassadors of the United States, the Soviet Union, the United Kingdom, France and many other countries come in person or telephone, seeking an explanation. In the midst of this crisis, all Chiang can do is order the civil and military committees of the National Government to issue a statement refuting the rumours. They deny that any secret talks have taken place, and furthermore publicly and solemnly declare their determination to see the war of resistance to the Japanese through to the end.

At the same time, secret police agents are dispatched in droves to seize and destroy all remaining copies of newspapers still on the newsstands or in the newspaper offices. But do they really think this is going to be enough to stop the rumours spreading by word of mouth? They are like a prostitute who has failed to hook a client and feels aggrieved at being cursed at with nothing to show for it. It does, however, serve to slow down the rumour mill. When Wang Jingwei, Zhou Fohai, Chen Gongbo and others of the pro-Japanese faction within the Kuomintang see that their secret plan has been exposed, they panic and are at their wits' end. Outwardly, they cease all activities of the Low-Profile Club[1] and cut off, as far as possible, all meetings and telephone communications there. Secretly, however, they sever ties with Chiang Kai-shek and put all their faith in the determination of the Japanese. In the winter of 1938, under cover of making a tour of inspection in Yunnan, they escape to Hanoi, in Vietnam, and then sign the so-called 'Peace Protocol' with the Japanese. After that, they return to Nanjing and form the bogus Reorganised National Government, establishing their reputations, once and for all, as dyed-in-the-wool traitors willing to sell both country and people down the line in the cause of the nation's enemies. But that story is for another time.

. . .

THE JAPANESE ARE SHOCKED by the leak of information about the talks. The revelation of these secret machinations not only hastens the schism within the Kuomintang, it also blocks any pathway to cooperation between the Japanese and Chiang Kai-shek as an effective leader of that party. Moreover, the sudden revelation, within twenty-four hours, of the talks that both sides have been at such pains to conceal, infuriates the Japanese. Because the talks were being led by the Japanese Foreign Ministry, and because all the associated documents and their security were the responsibility of the Office of the Foreign Ministry, Iwai Eiichi is swiftly removed as vice-consul in Shanghai, leaving him only as head of the Investigation Bureau. Whereupon, he returns, crestfallen with his men to Nanjing. Matsuzaki Harayama also receives a severe dressing-down, but he gets away comparatively lightly as he was only an auxiliary to the negotiations. And after the event, he immediately institutes an investigation, which blames the leak on the Germans. He says the most likely explanation is that someone in the German Consulate had installed a secret listening device. He says, specifically, that the German Government have done all this deliberately to prevent the Japanese signing an agreement with Wang Jingwei's faction within the Kuomintang, and that there is a mole in their midst who has to be rooted out. This fabrication is originally just designed to divert attention from his inability to find the source of the leak, but it has the unexpected benefit, beyond absolving himself of any responsibility, of also throwing a lifeline to Iwai Eiichi. Thus, by leaving the matter open-ended, he escapes censure himself and also gains a major bargaining chip. This bargaining chip is none other than the Kuomintang's representative at the secret talks, Zhou Zhengjie.

AFTER THE TALKS BREAK UP, Zhou Zhengjie is in a hurry to go back and take the credit for his achievement and reap its reward. He intends to leave Beiping the next day to go first to Tianjin and then take a ship to the south. But to his surprise, when Matsuzaki's car arrives, as arranged, to collect him, it doesn't take him out of the city. Instead, after taking a circuitous route, it delivers him and his aide to the Japanese Secret Service office, home of the Beiping Special Operations Committee.

As soon as he enters Matsuzaki's office, he explodes: "What do you think you're up to, Lord Matsuzaki? We agreed you'd see me on my way to Tianjin, so why have you dragged me here?"

"Ha! I'm afraid you can't go."

"Eh? Why not?"

"You've got no option but to stay here and co-operate with us."

"When two countries are at war, they don't execute the heralds. Do you really think it will do any good holding me here by force?"

"It's not a question of me forcing you to stay. You've got nowhere else to go now. I'm offering you a way out, out of respect for our friendship."

"What kind of nonsense talk is that? I still need to go back and make my report, so if you do respect our friendship, then send me on my way as soon as possible."

Matsuzaki gives a wry laugh: "Ha ha… calm down Brother Zhengjie and hear me out. If you still want to go when I've finished, I won't stop you. How's that?"

Zhou Zhengjie realises that he must know all about how the content of the secret talks was leaked, and he stares at him wide-eyed and open-mouthed in alarm.

"Brother Zhengjie," Matsuzaki continues with a grin, "are you really of any use now that news of the secret talks is public knowledge? As things stand, you are not only a thorn in the side of the anti-Japanese factions. I'm afraid your own government will want to silence you, to keep public opinion on their side. The people behind you are going to be hard put to save their own skins, let alone have time to think of you. The Kuomintang may be pretty useless as fighting soldiers, but their Special Operations Bureau is not so shoddy. Where do you think you can go? I'm afraid that, as soon as you leave our jurisdiction, you'll be in danger, not knowing when or where you might meet with a hail of bullets or a hand grenade…"

Zhou Zhengjie is sweating profusely as he realises he has gone at a stroke from lead actor to bit part player. He says nothing for a long while, then stammers out: "So… will you… will you let me stay in Beiping… for a while to… to see which way the wind is blowing, then…"

This is just what Matsuzaki wants to hear. "Yes, yes, of course, but as your friend, I should give you some advice: you are going to have to leave sooner or later, and sooner would be best. Your prospects are very different depending on whether you act of your own accord or are forced into it. There are some people in your Kuomintang whom we could work with, but if you wait for all the carriages, horses and cannons to cross the river before you, then a mere pawn like you might get left behind or just discarded. Both the leadership and the rank and file think you are responsible for the leak of the secret talks, with some going as far to say it was deliberate. Even I am under considerable pressure. If you are relying on those rascals, even if you don't end up in a Kempeitai prison, you'll be banished and become a target for your own side. So how about this? I'll find a safe place for you now, to sit and think about your options for a couple of hours. I'll take you to lunch at midday, and then you can decide whether we are drinking a welcome toast or a farewell cup."

"Ai! Here was I thinking I was following in the footsteps of Su Wu.[2] But little did I know that you Japanese are even more merciless than the Mongols…"

"Ha ha! I can turn you into a Su Wu and send you back to Japan for hard labour, if you want. But I'm afraid that may not be what you had in mind. Ah! I've got it! You're an amateur opera singer, aren't you? Isn't there a saying in that profession: 'If you have a minor painted-face military role, don't overplay your part, or you'll make yourself a laughing stock'? That's quite apposite, isn't it?"

Zhou Zhengjie is stunned into silence by his sarcasm and doesn't even have the nerve to meet his eye. He just lowers his head in silence. Finally, he asks in a voice no louder than the buzz of a mosquito: "What... what do you want me to do for you?"

"That's the spirit," Matsuzaki says. "Aren't you still a special commissioner at the Department of Military Affairs? You must know all about the anti-Japanese forces in the environs of Beiping: their numbers, equipment, command structure, the scope of their activities, the locations of their garrisons. I'm really interested in all that. And later on, we could have a place for you here, and, of course, even more opportunities for collaboration."

"But my wife and child are still in Hong Kong..."

"Don't worry, as long as you are genuine in your cooperation, I can move your whole family to Beiping."

At this, Zhou Zhengjie finally nods his agreement.

Qi Yuexuan has already been home for three days, and other than eating and sleeping, all he has done is tell Wangtian and the accountant to go over the books with him. As he surveys the mountain of ledgers piled up in front of them and hears the incessant clatter of the abacus in his ear, he feels both bored to tears and extremely bothered, but he doesn't dare miss a single word, either written or spoken, or be anything but wholehearted in his attention. Because Uncle Yang has demanded a reckoning, and perhaps it may be the last word he utters in this lifetime, even if it is only a 'good' or an 'all correct', that will be enough. But the need for the task is real enough, actual enough, so he can't be cavalier or reckless over it, and even less can there be any kind of funny business.

Finally, the audit is over. Thirty years of accounts, both summaries and details, income and outgoings, invoices and receipts, cash sales and credit are all balanced without a single error. There are just seven accounts receivable that have not been settled, from 1914, 1923, 1931 and 1937, totalling 304 yuan and 75 fen. But Yang Zhixing has marked each of them as settled from his own salary. Indeed he hasn't paid himself a single fen of that salary, but has kept it all on the books and used about half of it to make good that deficit. In prosperous times, the Minister's Residence had a turnover from several hundred thousand up to more than a million yuan per annum; there are a few inactive accounts of uncertain status, amounting to only a few hundred yuan over the thirty years and not enough really to be worth noting. But if anyone did deliberately default on an account, he made a big fuss about it, and for his part, could be very harsh, not to say even a little cruel. Needless to say, Qi Yuexuan and Accountant Lian are both overwhelmed with admiration.

. . .

AFTER THREE DAYS, Yue E has still not acknowledged Qi Yuexuan as her father. They have met again, face to face, but all she has done is nod slightly, then scurry away and hide without even exchanging the time of day. Qi Yuexuan knows that her heart is grieving much more than his. She has been living peacefully for more than twenty years, then, without warning, a father falls from the sky in front of her. No one could be expected to adjust to that immediately. After hiding from her and deceiving her all these years, how could she not be angry and resentful of him? So he repeatedly urges Yang Zhixing not to pressure her; he has already waited more than twenty years, what do a few more days matter?

Chenglong knows all about what is going on too, but his reaction and Yue E's are complete opposites. While she continues to weep, he is so excited he can scarcely stop himself doing handstands and turning cartwheels. He grew up in the Minister's Residence, and its grand buildings and wide courtyards have filled his dreams. It is true he married Yue E and moved into his courtyard there, but, in the end, she was only the manager's daughter, and while he may be able to put on a big show in the outside world, he is not the master inside the Residence. But now, even though he is still in that courtyard and still the same person, his status has changed in a flash. Previously he has been like a monkey staring at the reflection of the moon in the bottom of a well, never thinking that the moon itself would turn out to be his real home. But his attitude is clear and forward-thinking. He doesn't let himself get carried away and start drooling at the mouth like an epileptic. But Yue E remains stubborn and unyielding, and no matter what blandishments or persuasions Chenglong tries, she refuses to accept this change in status.

"I grew up without a mother, but I have never lacked for a father. My name is Yang, not Qi, and my father is still lying sick in hospital. What is a father? Pain, love, nurture, cherishing – that is a father. I don't give a fig what happens to *him*, he has done nothing to deserve the title 'Father'. He could be Marshal Zhao, the God of Wealth himself, and I still wouldn't care about him."

When pressed, she clams up like Xu Shu joining Cao Cao's army[3] and doesn't say another word. Chenglong keeps on at her but without any result, and he is afraid that her stubbornness will provoke Qi Yuexuan into changing his mind and complicating what should be a quite straightforward situation. But if his wife won't recognise her father, as son-in-law there is nothing he can do. Fortunately, however, they have two children, and isn't it only reasonable for grandchildren to recognise their grandfather? With this in mind, Chenglong takes advantage of one of Yue E's visits to the hospital to take his two children over to the main courtyard.

Qi Yuexuan has just finished auditing the accounts and, tired out, is thinking of going to bed for a rest, when he sees the twins, Liangxin and Xinliang. His tiredness evaporates.

"Hello, Grandfather! Hello, Grandfather!" the children cry out for themselves before Chenglong can even say anything.

Chenglong is astonished. How is it that the 'Grandfather' comes so easily to their lips when he has only just taught them it? But while he is puzzled, Qi Yuexuan accepts it quite naturally, and taking one child by each hand, he smiles so broadly his cheeks are in danger of splitting.

The fact of the matter is that, when Chenglong and his family moved into the side courtyard, Qi Yuexuan already knew that Yue E was his daughter, and the twins were his grandchildren, but he had no way of acknowledging it. So he thought up the excuse that he was getting far too old for anyone to be calling him Young Master. How about the children call him Old Master? (In Chinese, Old Master sounds exactly the same as Grandfather.) And from then on, that's just what they did.

"Aiya! How big these children have grown. I expect they're both at school now, aren't they?" Qi Yuexuan asks, looking them over.

"Yes, both in Year Two," Chenglong replies, then adds, with a forced smile: "Father."

Qi Yuexuan stares at him in amazement and immediately looks out of the door. But, on seeing that there is no one else there, he heaves something of a disappointed sigh.

Chenglong continues, hurriedly: "Yue E hasn't come with us, Father. She doesn't really understand this kind of thing, so you really mustn't be angry with her. She won't change her mind for the time being, but I'll work on her gradually and bring her round."

"Good, good." Qi Yuexuan nods eagerly. "I don't blame her. It's Uncle Yang who has raised her by himself all these years. Her mother and I had nothing to do with it. Although there was good reason for her mother and I to deceive Yue E, the end result was that we lost our daughter. It doesn't matter whether she recognises me as her father or not, she is still my daughter. She can't stop my blood flowing in her veins, and I can't push her out of my heart."

Chenglong nods vigorously in agreement and pulls the twins over to him, saying: "Quickly now, kowtow to your grandfather."

The children seem rather uncertain as they go over, but although they don't understand why they should be kowtowing when it's not his birthday or the New Year, they still kneel down properly on the floor and do as they are told, kowtowing formally three times.

Qi Yuexuan hurriedly draws the two children to him with a smile as he scans the room and pats down his body, looking for something he can give them as a greeting gift. He really has to find something to mark their use of the word 'Grandfather', and their kowtows. But he has no money on him, nor can he see any suitable object in the room, so he exclaims: "Aiya! I should have something to give you two little monkeys, shouldn't I!"

"No, no, there's no need, no need. Later..."

But before Chenglong can finish, the little girl Liangxin spies a folding fan on the table, its red silk tassel decorated with a white jade pendant and interwoven with different-sized beads. Grabbing hold of the it, she calls out: "Give me this pendant, Grandpa. That would do."

When Xinliang sees the fan, he calls out excitedly: "You could give me those beads too!"

"Put it down! How can you be so rude?" Chenglong says, pulling them away.

But Qi Yuexuan just laughs: "Ha ha! That's children for you. They just say what they think, eh! Alright, alright, alright, they can have them."

So saying, he detaches the tassel from the fan and removes the jade and the beads. He puts them into the children's hands, saying with a smile: "You two have both got an eye for quality. These are valuable objects. If I hadn't always kept them by me, Uncle Yang would have hidden them away long ago."

He says this carelessly, but Chenglong certainly takes notice and stares at Qi Yuexuan, struggling to contain his anger. But Qi Yuexuan changes tack: "This pendant is fine Hetian mutton fat jade, and the carving shows a gyrfalcon hunting a swan. It's Yuan dynasty work. The beads aren't too bad either – the green ones are *feicui* jade, the red ones are rubies and the blue ones are sapphires. Even the smallest ones aren't glass. They're diamonds..."

"Are they really strong?" asks Xinliang.

"They are the strongest thing in the world," Qi Yuexuan laughs, "so no knife can cut them. Haven't you heard the saying: 'Don't try mending porcelain unless you have a diamond drill'? These are the diamonds it is talking about."

When Xinliang hears this, he blurts out a hasty "Thank you, Grandfather!" and turns and runs out of the room, with Liangxin hot on his heels. Chenglong is about to call them back, but Qi Yuexuan stops him: "It's alright. Let the children go and play. You sit down, I've got something to say to you."

Chenglong does as he is told and waits quietly for Qi Yuexuan to continue.

Of course, Xinliang hasn't understood any of what Qi Yuexuan has been saying and doesn't know the true value of his gift, only that it is the hardest thing in the world. As soon as he is out of the room, he rushes out into the street to find some other children to play marbles with. Even after shattering a dozen or more glass marbles, there's not a mark on his beads.

Qi Yuexuan watches Chenglong sit down, and he stays silent for a moment, before sighing: "Ah, Chenglong. I think you must already know that your master, Flower Branch, was Yue E's mother." When he sees Chenglong nod, he continues: "So, you're not just a son-in-law. There is another layer of connection. The Qi family may not be particularly exalted or wealthy, but we do have something of a scholarly reputation. What a family like ours cherishes is moral values and integrity, not money and power. Although Yue E's mother was lowly born, and became entangled in the underworld, she was principled and a woman of integrity who should be considered a heroine of her sex. In the past, I have not spoken explicitly to Yue E about our relationship as father and daughter. Since you married into the Yang family, there have been a few things I have not felt easy about raising with you directly. But today, since you have chosen to address me as 'Father', I now intend to ask you about them."

"Well then, you must go ahead and ask," Chenglong says hurriedly.

Qi Yuexuan's expression hardens, as he fixes Chenglong with his gaze and asks: "On what basis did you call me 'Father'? And on what basis did you call her mother 'Master'? Given the way you have become a Japanese lickspittle, using your power to oppress others at gunpoint, how can you have the nerve to call me 'Father'?"

Chenglong stands rooted to the spot.

Qi Yuexuan goes on: "You may have married my Yue E, and served her mother, but a son-in-law is not a daughter, and if he is not suited he may just be sent on his way. A disciple is not a son, and he can be as disobedient as he likes once he's finished his apprenticeship. My father and Yue E's mother both died at the hands of the Japanese, and my family's hatred for that country is irreconcilable. So you had better consider carefully just which household you wish to enter and who you want to call 'Father'. These two sides are incompatible, and if you want to be a member of the Qi family, you can't be a traitor reviled and ridiculed by all."

"Father..." Chenglong cries out. But when he sees that Qi Yuexuan is ignoring him, he stammers: "I... that is... I mean, there was no way I could..."

"No way! There was a way alright, but I'm afraid you didn't take it. That way led out of Beiping. The Eighth Route Army took it, the National Army took it, even I took it with my troops. It doesn't matter whether we are official or not, our guns are aimed at the Japanese. If you don't have the skills to fight the Japanese, the least you could do is protect your family and take your wife and children away from here to somewhere safe. Anything would be better than you being a running dog for the Japanese. Surely if you escaped the clutches of those devils, your life would be more comfortable, wouldn't it?"

Chenglong remains silent for a moment, his eyes bulging. Then he stammers out: "But... what about you?"

When Qi Yuexuan hears this, he is even more furious: "What! You think you can make some odious comparison with me? You mean that, when the Japanese offered me an official title in exchange for my support, I agreed? Yes, that's right, I do have a post on a 'preservation committee', but I only took that on for the sake of my fellow countrymen. Do you know what we have been doing over that time? Well, let me tell you! We of Number Twelve Village of the Left Barracks..." He stops suddenly, coughs gently and changes the subject: "Well, whatever we have done, it has been with a clear conscience and without shaming our ancestors."

"And you're saying that's not the case with me?" Chenglong comes back immediately.

Qi Yuexuan gives a bitter laugh and a small sigh. "Alright, let's leave the past alone. What's done is done, and we won't revisit it. But you must remember, there is a reckoning to come."

When Chenglong doesn't reply, he pulls back a bit and says: "Well, Chenglong, leaving aside our relationship as son-in-law and father-in-law, there is a past connection too. But you were very young at the time, and you probably don't remember..."

"No, no, I remember," Chenglong replies excitedly. "That year when you came back to Beiping from the family estates, you protested the injustice done to my father at the *yamen* in Dezhou County."

Qi Yuexuan nods and continues: "Ai! Not only could I not save your father, it also ended up costing the lives of your mother and Old Man Zhang. Even after twenty years, every time I think of it, I cannot help but have the deepest respect for the integrity of your father and Old Man Zhang, and their desire for justice. Ai... ever since you arrived in Beiping and were taken into the Gao family as an adopted son, especially since we have lived in the same hutong for all these years, it may be said that I have watched over you as you grew into an adult. The Gao family did not stint in any way in their care for you. Old Gao was only a night soil collector, toiling away every day, but he would no more have wronged you than he would wrong his own son. Wangtian is only a few years older than you, but he has acted in every way as an older brother should. And why did they do all this? It was because they could not bear the thought of a hero like your father dying without descendants, and also to help you grow into a righteous and honourable man. But you... it was only a few days ago that Old Gao and I were talking about you and expressing our grave disappointment at your failure to meet our expectations or to change your ways..."

"Eh? My father?" Chenglong stares, wide-eyed. "He's really not dead? Where is he now? What is he doing? Why hasn't he... why hasn't he come back?"

In fact, no sooner are the words out of Qi Yuexuan's mouth, than he realises he has spoken out of turn. When he hears Chenglong pursuing the matter, he deeply regrets having said anything, but the words are out there and he can't pull them back in. All he can think of is to say off-handedly: "If a man is dead, how can he come back to life?"

"But you just said..."

"Ah, that was just me dreaming and imagining. I saw your father in my dreams."

But Chenglong's suspicions are aroused, and his brain springs into gear. He remembers the record he found in the files of military intelligence and how evasive Wangtian was when he asked him about it. He is uneasy about probing the matter further, but he stares hard at Qi Yuexuan, as though he might be able to bore out some more information.

Qi Yuexuan hurriedly changes the subject: "Do you remember that time in the tea house, before you and Yue E were married, when Uncle Yang summoned me to meet someone to help him with some plan or other? I asked you if you had read Qu Yuan's *Encountering Sorrow*, and you said you had. I said there was nothing in literature to surpass it for moulding a man, but you disagreed, saying that Qu Yuan's death was wasted, and that if it was you, you would jump into the river taking your enemy with you, so he shared your fate."

"Yes, that's right. I remember," says an embarrassed Chenglong. "I was young then, and that was just ignorant bravado."

"The nation's woes are all that matter now, so there is even a place for the ignorant, and ignorant bravado is still better than cowardice, isn't it?"

"But..." Chenglong begins defensively. "Father, you... I'm afraid you've been listening to too much gossip and idle speculation. You really have to put yourself in my shoes. The Japanese are in the ascendant right now. The Eighth Route Army are too few, the National Army too scared, and my own efforts would never be enough to fill the gaps in the face of the Japanese. Supposing I did go for broke against them. What about my wife and children, my family? Even if I were to put everything into resisting the Japanese, it wouldn't change a thing, and my whole family would lose their lives for nothing. You shouldn't put any faith in what strangers say. I'm not Japanese, so why should I be on their side? If you don't believe me, then just sit back and watch. Wait until they make a mistake and everyone turns on them, and then see what I can do. For the moment, all I can do is bide my time... you might say I am 'sleeping on firewood and eating gall' like King Gou Jian!"[4]

"'Sleeping on firewood and eating gall'?" Qi Yuexuan particularly detests dramatic posturing in men of no real character. "Couldn't you find something a little less hackneyed, rather than hiding behind that tired old nonsense? Ai! I remember the first time you came home after getting married, you were in your cups after the feast and you proclaimed that you knew full well that Shen Peng was responsible for your father's death, and you were just pretending to serve him as you waited for an opportunity to take your revenge. When everyone encouraged you, was that you 'sleeping on firewood and eating gall' too?"

"Ah, yes I remember. But I kept my word then, and I did have my revenge."

"Yes, you did. Not only did you kill him, you took his place too. But what you lost was even greater. And if you persist in your wrong-headed actions now, I'm afraid you will lose yet more."

"What... what will I lose?"

"Well, since you brought up 'sleeping on firewood and eating gall', let me tell you some more of that story. Gou Jian was the ruler of a kingdom, but he still had to walk a thousand *li* and spent more than ten years as a slave in Wu, working in the stables and mending shoes, licking boots and tasting the king's urine. It was only by chance that he was able to overthrow Wu and regain his kingdom. But were it not for that chance, what would he have been? He would have been a degraded man, a traitor who sold out his country! Even if he did have his revenge, could he ever regain ten years of lost dignity, his lost character, his lost humanity, his lost friendships and the lost respect of his subjects and ministers? What kind of man was Gou Jian? After coming to power, he killed his loyal ministers, enacted the cruellest of government, was decadent and dissipated, extorted money from the people through vicious taxes and destroyed Yue completely in three years. It is history's mistake to make that 'sleeping on firewood and eating gall' a model of behaviour, when, in fact, it represents the dregs, the most shameful, most hypocritical of mean-spiritedness. Why does China excel at producing traitors? It is because we are stuck with two thousand years of meaningless moral fig-leaves to hide behind."

Chenglong realises that he has been condemning himself with every word of supposedly erudite history he has been quoting. He feels as uncomfortable as if he was sitting on needles. Qi Yuexuan sees his discomfiture, and knowing that he can't expect to change him in a single day, softens his tone: "I know I have said some things to upset you, but just go away and think about them. You and Yue E have been married for some years now, and you have two children. I hope you grow old together, in wealth and happiness, but you must be sure to cherish them and also allow me my own feelings."

To his surprise, Chenglong shows no inclination to leave. Instead, he suddenly looks up and says: "Father, you have explained things very clearly to me. I will do whatever you tell me."

"You had better first consider the reasons behind all this, and we can talk about it again another time. Alright?"

When Chenglong signifies his agreement, he nods and continues: "Go home now. We just finished auditing the Residence's accounts this afternoon, and we still have to go to the hospital to report back to Uncle Yang. We must make sure we do nothing to worry him."

So saying, he stands up. Chenglong does so too and follows him out. But he doesn't know when to keep quiet: "Father, did you find anything major wrong in the accounts? Just looking at the books isn't really enough. You must physically make sure everything tallies. Didn't he hide away all the best things? Did he tell you where? You must go through it, piece by piece. If you can't bring yourself to do it, then give the task to me, and I..."

Qi Yuexuan ignores him initially, but at this point, he can't stop himself saying in icy tones: "No need."

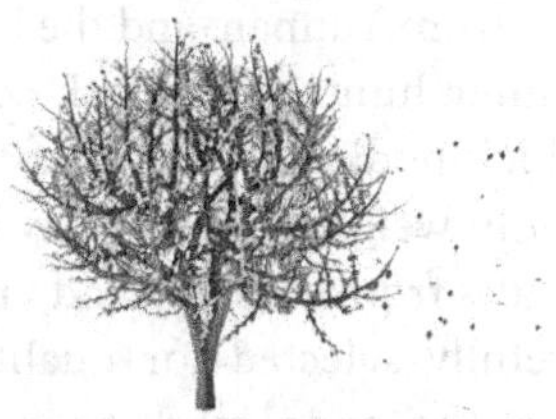

Chapter 48

Over the last few days, Yang Zhixing's condition seems to be improving. Although his cough is still severe, and he is running a fever from morning to night, his underlying constitution is much stronger. He listens to Qi Yuexuan's advice and doesn't raise the question of Yue E acknowledging her birth father again. But, when the occasion arises, he does prop himself up in bed and talk to Yue E about things in her past she is unaware of. Although these are events of more than twenty years ago, when he talks about them, it is as though they are happening before his very eyes. He remembers every little detail and every smile and frown, and it all trickles gently out like the flow of a mountain stream. At first, Yue E is still very angry, pursing her lips and saying she is not listening. But quite soon, she begins to betray just a hint of nervous interest. When he gets to the part where Qi Yuexuan and Xiulan fell in love, Yue E's tears flow alongside Yang Zhixing's. As they talk like this for several days, with Yang Zhixing reminiscing, it seems as though Yue E is growing up rather.

Meantime, Wangtian has been helping check the accounts, busy from dawn to dusk, with no time to consider what else is going on. Fortunately, Mother Yan and Yue E are there to take it in turns to keep Yang Zhixing company. Mother Yan had originally been the junior cook in charge of stewed dishes at the Minister's Residence, and so is a dab hand at medicinal and tonic food. She understands that taking care of the old man's disease requires thirty per cent treatment and seventy per cent nourishment; of the latter seventy per cent, half should be for pleasure and half should be medicinal. So now she is a little better herself, she sets herself to making soup and congee for Yang Zhixing.

In its heyday, the Residence had its own larder of tonic foods and it was as well stocked as any traditional pharmacy. Of course, she could still buy readily available ingredients such as donkey-hide gelatine, goji berries, gingko nuts, fragrant mushrooms, silver fungus and angelica, but in the past, in the rare goods cupboard, there was also real rhinoceros horn and mountain ginseng roots a hand-span and more in length. The birds' nests were sure to be the blood-red nests of the glossy swiftlet from Yunnan, and the bears' paws were all the thickest and biggest from pre-winter hunts. The black sea cucumbers from Bohai Bay were fine-fingered and thick-bodied, while the cordyceps from northern Sichuan were all seven or eight *jin* in weight. These items dated from the time of the Old Master and were mostly gifts from students and visiting officials from all over, so naturally they were carefully selected for quality. It would be impossible to match them shopping on the open market, no matter how much you were willing to spend.

It was said that, in those days, the custodian of these precious commodities was an old eunuch dismissed from imperial service. Before he had even been in the job for two years, he stopped living in the Residence, secretly bought a two-compound courtyard house inside the Desheng Gate and married a young widow with a son from a previous marriage. Later, Yang Zhixing's father, Old Manager Yang, made an inspection of the precious goods larder and discovered the fraud perpetrated by the eunuch, and how he had replaced the real goods with counterfeits. Saffron had been substituted with camel grass stamens, powdered pearls with crushed clam shells, *lingzhi* fungus with common mountain mushrooms, poor man's ginseng for tuber fleeceflower and many other such things. According to family law, the punishment for such a crime was death by beating, but the eunuch was an old man, and a single stroke would have finished him. In the end, Old Manager Yang relented, and after returning some of the stolen goods, the eunuch was expelled from the Residence, and that was that. After the Old Master's death, the standing of the Minister's Residence declined, particularly so after the establishment of the Republic. What is more, Yang Zhixing is even more miserly than his father, and after he became manager, the good things in the larder were only ever taken out and never replenished. Anything that did chance to be brought in was always of mediocre quality, and overall he runs a much tighter ship, with any gifts that are accepted being very distinctly inferior to before. In the end, the post of supervisor of the larder was abolished altogether, leaving the matter entirely in the hands of Yang Zhixing himself. The doors were securely locked, and it has been more than ten years since even Mother Yan went in there, so she has no idea what it might still contain.

She does, however, know where the keys are, but she is also familiar with Yang Zhixing's temper and doesn't dare act without permission. So she goes to find the Young Master, to ask for instructions.

Qi Yuexuan listens to her and says with a smile: "You should do as you think fit. There's no need to ask me. Use whatever there is in the household. A life is worth much more than money. But remember, Uncle Yang has seen pretty much all there is to see in this life, but he isn't much used to fine food, and his weakened stomach may not be up to it. If that's so, you must take it gently. Make sure the food is no warmer than tepid, and not too much at a time. You should increase the quantity gradually and not give it to him all at once, or he won't be able to take it. And whatever you do, if you're giving him something special, don't let him know what it is. Mash it down and stew it to a mush and pretend ginseng is dried radish to get it down him. Otherwise, he'll just fret over eating it for the next few days, and all its goodness will be wasted."

Mother Yan smiles too when she hears this, since although the Young Master is speaking teasingly, there is truth in what he says. As she thinks about it, there is a pained quality to her smile, and she feels rather aggrieved for her old man. But when she goes to open up the larder, she is disappointed. All the locks on the precious goods cupboard are opened, and, inside, it is completely empty. There is no sign of any of the goods it used to be crammed with, and not a single bottle or a jar has been left behind. A few bits and pieces remain in the other cupboards, but they are all ordinary, everyday ingredients. The valuable stuff must have been hidden away by Yang Zhixing. A thief wouldn't have been able to carry everything away, and for the cupboard to be stripped as clean as a cat licking its bowl, there can only be one culprit: the ferocious guardian of the household property himself.

There's nothing for it but to accept the situation and make the best of things. She hasn't lost the skills she has acquired over so many years, so she sets to with a will, and from the ordinary ingredients she is able to conjure up several kinds of restorative and delicious soup and congee. She makes, for example, a five-colour, five-taste, five-fresh phoenix soup using black, white, red, yellow and green beans that she first soaks in warm water, then cooks for fifteen minutes over a medium heat before adding a powder made of five medicinal ingredients comprising Chinese foxglove root, dwarf lilyturf tuber, ladybell root, peony root and fritillary root. She brings the concoction to a low boil for five minutes, then simmers it for two hours. After that, she adds a quantity of chicken stock she has made separately, along with some bits of chicken, shredded ginger, sliced fragrant mushrooms, shredded bamboo shoots and silver fungus. She brings it back to the boil and adds salt, then simmers for another hour. Taking it off the flame, she adds two drops of sesame oil and a pinch of coriander leaves, and it's done. It is deliciously fragrant, sparklingly clear and tastes smooth and rich, melting in the mouth. However, it must be eaten piping hot, so Mother Yan puts a lid on the bowl, wraps it in a padded cover, puts it into a carrying box and rushes over to the hospital.

But all her effort is not rewarded with Yang Zhixing's approval. He wipes his mouth after finishing the soup and doesn't say a word. Unable to contain her annoyance, Mother Yan asks him what he thinks, and only then does he mumble a "not bad". Throughout his life, Yang Zhixing has very seldom vouchsafed a "good" about anyone or anything, so Mother Yan is quite content with "not bad" as not the worst criticism. But what he says next, infuriates her.

"What's this nonsense about five-colour, five-flavour, five-fresh phoenix soup? I couldn't tell what it was. If you spent a whole afternoon on this one small bowl, not to mention all the skill and effort, you must have needed more than one stove. You should just have made a big pot of maize congee if you wanted me to eat something hot. Serve that with a dish of fermented bean paste, wouldn't it be just as good? I've got a stomach like a pig, and everything tastes the same. As long as it's well cooked, I'm happy. It's really not worth spending so much time and trouble."

"Alright, I'll do it differently tomorrow," Mother Yan says through gritted teeth. "I'll give you half a ladle of wine dregs and half a ladle of rice husks, cook it in old cooking water with some tough cabbage leaves and rotten radish skin..."

"Eh? What kind of slop are you cooking?" says Yue E, getting the wrong end of the stick.

"Didn't he just say he's got a stomach like a pig, but even a pig grunts if it eats something good," Mother Yan says. "A pig is more lovable than him."

Yang Zhixing just smiles and nods, uttering "That's right" a few times. He waits until Mother Yan relents, then sighs and says: "Ai! I know you put your heart into making that, but my heart is somewhere else at the moment. Until those accounts are finished, my life is unfinished too, and I'll find no rest. How can any food have savour in those circumstances?"

Mother Yan studies his face and asks, her voice choking with emotion: "Husband, what was your incarnation in your last life that makes you act like this? And in this life... what do you owe the Qi family? Why are you abasing yourself like this? Is it really worth it, putting your life on the line to earn them money and protect their property? I've been married to you for twenty years and... and, however much I study it, I still can't understand why you're like this."

Yue E can't help but sympathise with these sentiments, and her eyes begin to redden with tears.

Yang Zhixing just smiles and says: "That is a good question, and it is one I have often asked myself over the years. I inherited from my own father the belief that a man must show loyalty and righteousness. In the past, that meant loyalty to the emperor and to your master, but if you later left the family roll and changed your name, then you became no more than a menial servant. So I have been loyal to the tasks I agreed to undertake and the promises I made. Sometimes I may have felt myself wronged, but when I unpicked it, I found that that was not the case. However you look at it, on a personal level I found a wife and raised a child, and on a larger scale, I have kept the Residence's property safe, and even increased it since my father's time in charge. In these troubled times, it is not sensible to flaunt one's wealth, but just wait and see once things settle down again. We will be regarded as the number one household in Beiping. Despite everything we have seen, experienced and suffered, we have scrambled our way out of it all. I have not shirked my responsibilities, nor have I coveted what is not mine. I have followed my conscience, incurred no loss or debt and have nothing to fear when I stand before Lord Yama. How many people can say the same? When a man can speak thus with a clear conscience, why should he nurture any grievance?"

Yue E can't help mumbling to herself: "Huh! No grievance! You may have made a mountain of gold and silver, but for the Qi family, not the Yang family."

"Now, now, now..." Yang Zhixing's good humour is completely unruffled. "You are right. The property of the Minister's Residence is not in the name of Yang, but what does a name matter?" He sees Yue E staring at him, and he goes on with a laugh: "When I was young, I wanted to earn some property in the name of the Yang family, but over time, that desire waned, and I didn't think about it any more. It wasn't that I couldn't have done it, I just decided to accept the status quo. A man has to suit his appetite to his stomach. No matter how much wealth and property a man may own, his coffin is still going to be the same size. For a man to prosper, all he needs is food, sleep, his family and happiness. Everything else is nothing to do with you, no matter what your name is."

When she hears this, Mother Yan throws up her hands and replies: "The ways of the world are the ways of the world, and names are names. Is there anything you can do to change that? What I don't believe is that money doesn't have a specific owner or that property is not attached to a particular name. This crazy position you are adopting is just stupid obstinacy, the unrealistic dream of a foolish youth."

"Oh, you really don't get it. Your words are enough to choke a man!" Yang Zhixing thumps his bedcover gently and goes on: "Still, I suppose you can't help seeing it from an old woman's shallow point of view."

"Alright, I'm a shallow old woman, so use your old man's wisdom to explain it to me. If you can, fine. If not, don't be surprised if I scratch your eyes out!"

Yang Zhixing keeps his cool in the face of her anger and just says: "What a shame."

"What do you mean by that?"

"It's a shame that it's not the New Year. If it was, we could be standing together under that old elm tree by the gates of the Minister's Residence, looking at its branches full of seed cases. Then we could strip a couple of strings of them and stuff them in our mouths, chewing them and savouring them. Wouldn't that clear everything up? All the ways of the world are to be found in that elm tree."

"Alright, don't keep us on tenterhooks. Explain!"

Laughing, Yang Zhixing ignores her, and instead turns to Yue E and asks her: "Daughter, do you still remember the story I told you about how the elm tree grew real money?"

"I remember. When I was little, I heard you tell it a thousand times."

"An elm tree growing real money?" Mother Yan interjects. "How can that be?"

"You tell it, Yue E. Supplement your mother's education."

"Yes, you've been talking too much today already, Father. You should take a break. I know it off by heart, and I'll tell it just like you do."

Yue E hesitates a moment, then, with mock solemnity, she coughs gently to clear her throat, just as she has seen Yang Zhixing do so often.

"The story goes that, originally, this elm tree only put forth shoots and leaves, never seeds." Yue E's tone and manner are very like Yang Zhixing's. "In the Ming dynasty, Emperor Zhu Di moved his capital to Beijing and wanted to renovate the city. But where was he to find the money? Well, the imperial court issued a decree, that every family and every household must hand over five strings of copper cash. But the poor of the city did not even have enough to eat, so where were they going to find so much money? If they did not pay up, they would be put in jail or made to do forced labour. When God heard of this, he showed great mercy, and within one night, he made all the elm trees in the city put forth strings of copper cash. The people were delirious with joy as they ran out onto the streets and climbed the trees to gather in the money. Everyone was fighting over the coins, as branches broke and trees fell. When the emperor came to hear of it, he despatched scores of troops to join in. He said that, as everything under heaven belonged to the emperor, the money on the trees must belong to him too. But as soon as the piles of cash entered the Forbidden City, it instantly turned into counterfeit coins. After this, the elm trees of the city never produced real copper cash ever again. Why was this? Because God was angry. He was angry at the people's greed, and he saw no benevolence or righteousness in their rapaciousness. If the trees were always to produce money, then, every day, people would surely die. Even the trees would not survive. So, from that time on, every year, at this time, the elm trees only grow seed cases to fill the stomachs of the poor."

Mother Yan waits to see if Yue E is going to continue, and when she doesn't, she asks: "And so? This is just a story, surely you don't believe it's true! And what do you mean by all the ways of the world are in that elm tree?"

Yang Zhixing opens his eyes wide, smiles and strokes his goatee. Unhurriedly, he says: "I heard that story from my father when I was little. He said he had studied it all his life without fully understanding it. I have done the same and wouldn't dare claim I understand it either. Nevertheless, in the end, I have got something out of it. From ancient times till now, men have always been rapacious, men have always fought and killed each other, all because they want that little bit of money, that little bit of profit for themselves – and the more the better. Some are starving to death, some are fighting for their lives, but those who fight the most fiercely are those who already have more than enough. We Chinese are bad enough for fighting by ourselves, but now we have the devils from the East and the West too, with their rifles and artillery, coming to fight and pillage. Isn't this just the same as the mad scramble for the copper cash in the story? Everyone shouts 'don't fight over it', but they mean other people, while they keep scrabbling away themselves. If you think about it, even the emperor lost his property, so what chance is there for the common folk? They risk their lives for money and break people's heads in the struggle. They live their lives in fear as they try to protect what they seize, but when they die, all they are left with is a funeral feast and some pretty burial clothes. The rest, they can't take with them."

"If you're so clear about all this, why have you spent your whole life being so cautious and stingy? Surely you're not playing the miser for the benefit of others? Clearly you exhausted yourself to the point of coughing up blood for the sake of money, so who do you think you are fooling when you say you don't care about the stuff."

"Ha ha, didn't I say you had a woman's shallow viewpoint? Do you think I would be so high-minded if I was only considering myself and my family? All the money in the world is stained with men's blood and sweat, but those men rely on it to live and support their families. The most important thing is to use it where it should be used, to truly value it, and treat it as you would your mother. In business and manufacturing, the more you make the better, so it can provide even more people with a livelihood. I have never cared whose name money carries, I just made sure that any that passed through my hands was not wasted or abused. If you're not miserly, how can you accumulate? If you're not stingy, how can you grow? If you accumulate and grow, only then can you fill the rice bowls of a thousand families. I'm happy for you to call me a miser, because that is a hundred times better than you cursing me as a profligate."

"So..." Mother Yan is stumped for words.

"Ha! Enough! We're so poor anyway, what's the point in arguing about it?" Yang Zhixing says, teasing her. "However much you debate it, it all comes down to one thing. If a man is too greedy, and thinks that all the money belongs to him, when he does get his hands on it, just like the copper cash on the elm trees, it will turn to dross in the blink of an eye, story or no story, daydream or no daydream. When Pan Gu separated Earth from heaven, did he put anyone in charge of it? When Nüwa created mankind, she only made man and woman, not rich and poor. This is the way of heaven, and the way of heaven is always just. Heaven and earth's riches don't belong to anyone. No one's name goes on forever, and no tyrant reigns indefinitely..."

At this point, a voice interrupts him: "Well said. That is well said. This is what is meant when we say 'Heaven and earth's riches belong to heaven and earth alone'!"

"Aiyo, Young Master!" Yang Zhixing is startled by the arrival of Qi Yuexuan but continues all the same: "Ha! I wasn't speaking with any expertise, just shooting my mouth off. I deserve to be mocked by such a highly educated scholar as yourself."

Qi Yuexuan hurries over to him, takes him by the hand and says with great feeling: "Uncle Yang, you are usually a man of action, not a man of words, but truly you are like a bird that never sings – when it does sing it is worth hearing. I have been pondering this and trying to find the truth for countless years, but even after reading innumerable books and scrolls, that truth has remained shrouded in mystery to me. But your speech just now has thrown the window open wide. When I have the time, I will write a second volume of my book *The*

Elm Tree. Those words of yours will be what make it complete, and you must put your name to it."

Yang Zhixing ignores these words and asks anxiously: "Are the accounts done, Young Master?"

"Done and dusted."

"Everything has been carefully reconciled?"

"It has."

"But…" Yang Zhixing doesn't finish the sentence, but his agitation is clearly unassuaged.

Qi Yuexuan grips his hand tightly: "It's all correct, all correct."

ACCORDING TO THE INSTRUCTIONS of the Department of Communal Affairs, once Zuo Xichuan and Zhou Zhengying have completed their mission, they are to return with all speed to Rehe. Accordingly, Zuo Xichuan hurriedly purchases supplies and orders two trucks, preparatory to leaving for Chengde that afternoon. But after lunch, Zhou Zhengying mentions that she wants to go and have a look around the Longfu Temple market, saying her son has seen some other kids blowing rabbit god[1] whistles, and he's not going to stop pestering until he gets one. Seeing that it is still early, Zuo Xichuan readily agrees.

The Longfu Temple is no more than a couple of hundred metres from where they are staying at the Japanese Consulate, at the other end of the lane. Carrying her child, Zhou Zhengying leaves the guild hall and heads straight for the main gates of the market. She doesn't dawdle, just buys a few toys at a small stall, not really looking what they are and not bothering to bargain. She just pays, picks them up and leaves, quick as a drum roll at the theatre. She is a real Beipinger at heart, but she is still wearing a kimono and has wooden clogs on her feet. Even her son is dressed Japanese-style and is chattering away in Japanese. The stallholder waits until she has gone some distance, then says to some bystanders: "She's certainly not Japanese. She's a Chinese woman who's stayed in the city. If she's not an amah for some Japanese family, then she's married a Japanese and had his little bastard. She's a disgrace to us Beipingers."

Zhou Zhengying hurries out of the market but doesn't go straight back to the guild hall. Instead, she gets into a vacant rickshaw, pulls down the curtain and orders the rickshaw man: "Go to Minister's Residence Hutong in front of the Drum Tower. I'm in a hurry. There's extra money if you go double-quick."

Is Zhou Zhengying going home? Absolutely. And as she sits in the rickshaw, in her heart she is already back in the place she left two years ago, back in the home she has been dreaming of, back beside he man she loves. She is not just going back to look around and see Qi Yuexuan; she is hoping to leave her son there with him. She hasn't breathed a word of this plan to Zuo Xichuan, because she knows he would never agree to it. Children are the best cover in intelligence work behind enemy lines, but Zhou Zhengying doesn't want her son with her when she puts her head into the lion's mouth. She came up with the idea some time ago, but whenever she raised it with Zuo Xichuan, he shot it down every time, so she has no option but to take the initiative and act first, petition later. She is fully aware that this violates every rule of intelligence work and goes entirely against headquarters discipline. But as a mother and a wife, as well as thinking of putting her son in a safe place where he can flourish and be happy, she also hopes to establish an unbreakable bond with her husband. Even if she loses her own life, this little boy will be the proof of that, and a lasting, unforgettable reminder. This is why she is willing to risk everything and endure any punishment.

When they reach the gates of the Minister's Residence, she tells the rickshaw man to wait outside, while she hurries in, carrying her son, and makes straight for the main courtyard.

The auditing of the accounts has left piles of ledgers, receipts and invoices all over the tables in the office and reception room, and the floor is covered in dust and scraps of paper. Qi Yuexuan is on his way to the hospital with Wangtian, and only Lao Zhang is left there, tidying up. When he hears someone come in, he turns to look and stares in surprise. When Qi Yuexuan and Zhou Zhengying got married, Lao Zhang had long since gone to Laoqiying as tomb guardian. He has only had a few chance meetings with her, and there is no way he is going to recognise her, dressed as she is now. He wants to ask who she is, but is afraid she won't understand Chinese, so summons up his courage and speaks in the pidgin Chinese the Japanese use: "Yours what doing?"

"Ha! Do you really think I'm Japanese? Aren't you... didn't you used to be the Residence's insect man, who went off to guard the family tombs? Lao..." Zhou Zhengying remembers the man but can't recall his name.

Lao Zhang replies immediately: "Yes, yes, that's me. My name is Zhang. And you are..."

"My name is Zhou Zhengying. Do you remember me? Qi Yuexuan is my..."

"Ah! You're... you're the Young Mistress?"

"That's me."

"Aiyo! Forgive my old eyes!" Lao Zhang hurriedly wipes down the seat of a chair with his sleeve. "Please sit down and I will bring you some tea."

Seeing he is about to leave the room, Zhou Zhengying stops him: "Please don't worry. Where is Yuexuan?"

"He has gone to the church hospital to visit Manager Yang."

"Is Uncle Yang sick?"

"Yes, he is. He has got tuberculosis, and he looks terrible. The only good thing about it is that it has brought the Young Master back from the mountains."

"Ai!" Zhou Zhengying sighs, then asks: "Then... is Yue E here?"

"She has been looking after her father in hospital."

"What about Mother Yan?"

"She's at the hospital also. She's too busy to think about anything else, and she just said she was taking him some congee."

"Lao Zhang," Zhou Zhengying says, "I can't stay long on this visit. I just came back to see Yuexuan, and to hand our son over to him. Then I was going to leave. I hadn't expected to find no one here, but I must still go at once, so all I can do is give the child to you..."

"No, no, no! Absolutely not!" Lao Zhang exclaims, shaking his head and gesticulating urgently.

Seeing his reaction, Zhou Zhengying grows agitated too, and her head drops: "Oh! I just need you to look after the boy for a short time, and you can hand him over to Yuexuan when he gets back. Then this little matter..."

"Young Mistress, it's not that I want to disobey you," Lao Zhang says, ducking his head and bowing apologetically with hands clasped in front of him. "But just think – it's more than two years since you left this house, and now you suddenly appear, just as suddenly want to leave again and suddenly want to leave a child here. If the Young Master holds me responsible, where am I just as suddenly to find out where you've gone?"

This string of "suddenlys" amuses Zhou Zhengying: "Ai! Why are you making things difficult for me? The child is Yuexuan's son, and he is already one and a half," she says, looking at the child at her bosom.

Up until now all Nan'er has done is look around him and silently exchange meaningful looks with his mother, but now he suddenly breaks into a smile and begins to make a squeaking, gurgling sound. It's not possible to make out what he is saying, but it is definitely not Chinese.

Lao Zhang is even more taken aback: "Aiya, Young Mistress! Where has this little Young Master suddenly appeared from? How did such a thing suddenly come about?"

Zhou Zhengying doesn't offer any further explanation, but just sighs helplessly: "There are some things it is not proper to say just now, but this child is most certainly Yuexuan's flesh and blood. When I left, I was already pregnant with him. At that time, I was going to wait for him to acknowledge Yue E and then tell him, but events overtook me. If Yuexuan doesn't believe it, you can tell him to go and see Dr Zhong, the gynaecologist at the church hospital. She was the one who did the pregnancy test for me. Come now, Lao Zhang, hurry up and take the child. I can't wait any longer now, but I hope I'll be able to come back later on."

She is about to hand the child over, but before Lao Zhang can take him, Nan'er begins to wail. Lao Zhang quickly pulls back his hands and makes to leave the room, saying: "Young Mistress, this is too weighty a matter for me to accept responsibility. You should meet with the Young Master and discuss it. I'll go and fetch him. He's sure to hurry back and not hold you up too long."

Without waiting for Zhou Zhengying to reply, he disappears like a puff of smoke. Once out of the main courtyard, he goes first to the side courtyard to find Caiping and tells her to go and keep the Young Mistress company.

Fortunately, the church hospital is not too far away, less than half an hour round trip by rickshaw, and Qi Yuexuan follows Lao Zhang home. But in the reception room there is no sign of Zhou Zhengying, only Caiping supervising Liangxin and Xinliang as they do their homework.

"Where is the Young Mistress, Ying'er?" Lao Zhang asks hurriedly.

Caiping sighs and says: "I'd only just got over here and exchanged no more than a few words with the Young Mistress, when a Japanese man appeared outside. He was wearing a kimono, not army uniform, but he still looked very fierce. He argued briefly with the Young Mistress, then forcibly pulled her away. I wanted to stop him, but the Young Mistress wouldn't let me. They went out of the main gates, got in a car and drove away."

"What about the child?" Qi Yuexuan asks.

"Ah, the little Japanese boy! The Young Mistress tried to leave him here, but the child didn't want that, and the Japanese man wanted it even less. In the end, he resorted to brute force and snatched the child away and carried it into the car. Young Master, what... what's this all about?"

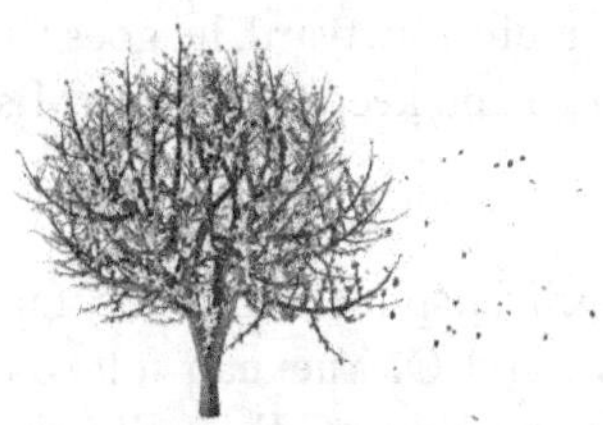

Chapter 49

Matsuzaki Harayama is as good as his word, and on the day Zhou Zhengjie agrees to 'co-operate', he secretly brings his wife, son and daughter out of Hong Kong with the help of the territory's Japanese secret service. Afraid that Zhou Zhengjie won't believe him, he arranges a telephone call between them at the transfer point, assuring him that all is well and that they will soon take an English-registered ship to Tianjin, probably reaching Beiping in a couple of weeks.

Matsuzaki observes with a narrow-eyed grin: "Well, Zhou-san, I have resolved all your family worries. I hope that, before you are reunited, you might resolve some worries of my own, and prove your sincerity and worth at one go. A rare and valuable commodity naturally has a greatly inflated value, but if the reality does not live up to the hype... then the goods may just be dumped. Do you... understand my meaning?"

"I understand, I understand," Zhou Zhengjie replies hastily, pasting a smile on his face. With the situation as it is, of course he understands. Any shreds of self-respect he still cherished have now been reduced to dust. He knows he has no choice but to recognise that the time for prevarication is over, and if he doesn't give the Japanese something of real value first off, not only will he himself not emerge from his current perilous situation, but his family will be in danger too. So he thumps his chest and declares: "Don't worry, Lord Matsuzaki. I will put all my knowledge and abilities at your service to repay you for what you have done, and out of gratitude for saving my life."

The first thing he does is to tell him all he knows about the circumstances of the anti-Japanese resistance forces in northern Hebei and in the area west of Beiping, producing a detailed written account, and marking on a map all their defensive positions and their range of operations. He also lays out, step by step, details of his own military intelligence organisation and every aspect of the internal workings of the Kuomintang. He even goes as far as to make several recommendations to Matsuzaki Harayama on matters such as the concentration of troops, the breaking of encirclement campaigns, the quashing of alliances and, most important, on the Eighth Route Army. He suggests Matsuzaki establish a specialist eavesdropping and code-breaking department to study the secret code patterns used by radio transmitters across China; and that he also set up a special intelligence network, using the publishing of newspapers and periodicals as a cover for their information-gathering activities, while, at the same time, employing them for the dissemination of propaganda to manipulate public opinion.

Zhou Zhengjie has accepted his situation and is putting everything on the line, but is he really still acting under duress while maintaining his loyalties? In fact, he is simply trying to establish a reputation and curry favour, but he is keeping something up his sleeve. All he says about the Army of the Left Barracks is that it is an independent local militia, which has already put itself under Zhao Ran's flag. He doesn't say that it has departed the Left Barracks, nor, more important, does he mention Qi Yuexuan. He is worried about his family relationship with Qi and is also afraid that, if anything happens at the Left Barracks, he may be implicated and punished.

Matsuzaki Harayama attaches great weight to the information given by Zhou Zhengjie and reports it back to his superiors. The commander of the Japanese Army of North China, Hayao Tada, immediately calls a strategy meeting and draws up a plan to clear the enemy out of Pingxi. He decides to pull two units out of the southwest of Hebei and the north of Chahar, and back to reinforce the areas north and west of Beiping and assist the garrisons there in the encirclement and annihilation of anti-Japanese resistance forces. First they are to join forces and quash irregular armies in the mountain lowlands of Fangshan and Changping, and then they are to unite with the main army to execute a pincer attack from north and south to break through the defences in the middle and close in around the Eighth Route Army's main bases in the deep mountains of Wanping and the surrounding area.

The next day, in order to confirm the accuracy of the information, the Japanese Army, following the reported defensive dispositions, send out several aircraft to bomb the Yunju Temple on Xiayun Ridge in Fangshan County. The troops stationed there are irregulars fighting under the second and third divisions of the Allied Anti-Japanese Army, mainly formed of men from bandit troops and local militia, and they number some three or four thousand men. They have been established for more than six months, but apart from gathering contributions of food from the villagers of the area, they have not seen any action against the Japanese. But now, courtesy of Zhou Zhengjie, they have suddenly become part of the National Army's guerrilla campaign. Originally scattered through the local villages, they have assembled at the Yunju Temple, making it their main barracks. As the bombs dropped by the Japanese aircraft explode, one after the other, the area around the temple becomes a seething cauldron. Once the bombardment stops and things start to clear, leaving several hundred dead and wounded, more than half the survivors flee. Afterwards, the commander of the second division simply leads his men down the mountain and puts them in the hands of the Japanese, who form them into the Fangshan County peacekeeping force.

This initial major victory delights Commander Hayao Tada, and he is fulsome in his appreciation of Matsuzaki Harayama's intelligence work and subsequent suggestions. Because Zhou Zhengjie has been responsible for his boss's success and enhanced reputation, he naturally becomes Matsuzaki's blue-eyed boy. He is, indeed, very skilled at intelligence operations, but when it comes to courage and daring, he falls far short of Chenglong. In matters of education, vision and the collation of information, however, he is very much his superior. With the one a scholar and the other a warrior, each has their forte, and they complement each other very well. But Matsuzaki still has some doubts over who to make the leader and who the subordinate.

Zhou Zhengjie only stays in the rear courtyard of the office of the Beiping Special Operations Committee for two nights before being moved into a courtyard house in Meizha Hutong. The house is only two doors down from the Kempeitai, and although it has two courtyards, living conditions are very cramped even for a single family. To ensure his safety, the CID squad are ordered to provide a dozen guards, working in two shifts. The man in charge is Zhou Si.

For the last little while, Zhou Si has been blundering around busily without achieving anything to his advantage. A few months ago, he had come up with a scheme to get the Japanese to arrest Chenglong for smuggling prohibited goods but had not expected to trip himself up. On his return, he doesn't dare make a noise about it, and he tries to look as though he hasn't a care in the world. But he keeps feeling that Chenglong is becoming increasingly cold towards him, and he seems more wary of him. He is certainly not unaware of Chenglong's violent temper. During the time he has worked for him, Zhou Si has always been on his guard against him, and if Chenglong were to get any other kind of hold over him, then it would all be over. Feeling like this, as he does, he is constantly scared and on edge, and consequently is taking extra care. Nor does he quite know whether his feelings are justified, or whether he is just starting at ghosts and frightening himself for no reason.

But recently, since he has been given the task of organising Zhou Zhengjie's bodyguard, he feels that, not only does he now have a way out, but he has also found someone influential he can latch onto. Given Zhou Zhengjie's seniority and the importance Lord Matsuzaki puts on him, Zhou Si is pretty clear about where Zhou Zhengjie is going. What is more, there is only one surname Zhou, so somewhere, five hundred years back, they are related. Making good use of his quick wits, silver tongue and way with words, he very quickly establishes a close relationship with Zhou Zhengjie. He is only a few years younger, but he refers to him as 'Uncle', claiming a family relationship. Although Zhou Zhengjie has no respect for this jumped-up hoodlum, if he is going to find a way out for himself, he needs someone on his side; so he goes along with Zhou Si. As the two men's relationship gets closer and more intimate, their sights naturally become fixed on Chenglong.

Zhou Zhengjie has only met Chenglong once, at Matsuzaki Harayama's celebratory welcome feast. Seven or eight people were there, and among the Japanese special agents, Tokko and Kempeitai men, Chenglong was the only other Chinese person to attend. When Matsuzaki introduced him, he said with a broad smile: "Liu-san, Zhou-san is a distinguished scholar of great standing in both government and literary circles, so your shortcomings are his strengths, eh! I can foresee that, if you two find yourselves singing on the same stage, it will be a very successful double act."

Although Chenglong was smiling as he agreed with this sentiment, there was a glint of jealousy and disdain in his eyes. He raised his cup in a toast, saying: "Mr Zhou's reputation precedes him. Weren't you a famous amateur opera singer? I once saw you playing the part of Jin Wuzhu. Your performance of the 'tumbling warrior' was a triumph."

"What is this 'tumbling warrior'?" asked a confused Yamaguchi.

"It's a non-singing role involving acrobatic stage fighting, where the character takes a beating and falls to the ground after a few rounds," said Chenglong.

This drew a laugh from the assembled company and caused Zhou Zhengjie some embarrassment. However, Chenglong raised his cup to him again and said: "Come now, Mr Zhou, drain a cup with me. Please don't take offence, I just like my little jokes. Drink up, drink up!"

"No offence taken," Zhou Zhengjie replied immediately, and he finished his cup with a smile, but in his heart, his first meeting with this Liu Chenglong fellow had already sown the seeds of resentment and dislike.

Now, Zhou Si's enumeration of his boss's many faults is music to his ears and only serves to increase those feelings.

"These are my innermost thoughts I have been sharing with you, Uncle. That little bastard Chenglong is an intolerable wolf of a man. He keeps everything to himself and is very manipulative as a boss. You really must take extra care. But I'm telling you the truth when I say that I really do want to find a way for you two to get on together. If you want to, that's fine, but you have to look to your status. Whatever you do, don't let him take the lead, or you'll regret it."

Zhou Zhengjie nods and says: "But he's pretty popular with the Japanese by the look of it."

"Not necessarily," Zhou Si says with a wry laugh. "He's pretty well in with Yamaguchi and his Kempeitai buddies, but not so much with rest of them. Even Lord Matsuzaki isn't that comfortable with him, and recently, he has actually asked me to keep a secret eye on him. You don't have to play him false, just protect yourself against his wildness and unpredictability. If you don't, he's bound to get the upper hand, isn't he? Why not make sure he has a 'deputy' added to his title? The way I see it, you're much better placed to be the one calling the shots. When you look at status, education, qualifications, how can he possibly compare to you? In terms of intelligence work, it's determination and ruthlessness that count, not play acting."

"Hah! You're right, but is he going to be willing to play second fiddle to me?"

"If you play on his failings, he'll have to."

"What failings?"

"There are plenty, but you'll only get the better of him if you concentrate on the major ones. Just fiddling around with lesser ones won't work, and he's more than likely to turn the tables on you. You have to be careful. I've tried acting on my own before and it hasn't worked. But if you take over here, you'll have no trouble finding something big to hold over him."

"Then... you'll help me?"

"Of course. It's my duty," Zhou Si replies, his face wreathed with smiles.

IT IS STILL EARLY FOR LUNCH, but Yuerong's Place is already seating customers, and in the main room there are five or six neatly dressed people at one of the tables. It is quite a large table, but the only food in front of them is a platter of leftovers and a basket containing two different sorts of flatbread. Although the food is rather frugal, they are all eating voraciously, and the proprietor, Xiao Yuerong, is sitting at the table too, keeping them company. In fact, these people aren't real customers, but are Xiao Yuerong's fellow actors from the time when he was on the stage and who are now down on their luck and have come for a free feed.

Xiao Yuerong feels all choked up as he watches them eat.

"Brothers," he sighs, "although some of you never had particularly big parts, you were all stars in the Pear Garden Company. Now you are struggling even to find enough to eat, how are you managing in such a 'walk-on' role?"

The third junior who sings the pretty boy parts swallows the food he has just shovelled into his mouth, and is the first to reply: "How are we managing? We're not managing at all. Didn't Lao Chen, the fellow who used to do your hair, just die? In desperation, he went to work as a porter. He fell head over heels and never got up again. I was the one who laid out his body, and under his clothes, he was so thin that his front ribs were sticking to his back ones... Ai! It was hunger that did for him."

Xiao Yuerong sighs: "You need some way to get back on stage..."

"Get back on stage? Huh! Even though the Japanese haven't actually shut down the opera houses, what could we perform?" the third junior asks with a bitter laugh. "Ha! Tragic operas like *Tears on a Barren Hill*, *Mourning at the Funeral Tablet* or *The Battle of Xiaoyaojin* are forbidden because they refer to the rule of a just king. And the Japanese will look askance and stamp their feet at anything to do with injustice of grievance like *Snow in June, Wenzhao Pass* or *The Tragedy of Life and Death*, so they're even less suitable. Anything to do with foreign invaders, no matter whether it's the Jin, the Liao or the Western Liang, will just make them mad. I've got to be careful about any of the pretty young boy parts I perform, because I'll get into trouble if they've got anything to do with rebels and traitors."

The master singer who plays the 'black face' roles joins in: "You're not so badly off with your parts, because there are a lot of comic ones. A 'black face' like me is in the worst position. If I can't sing *The Great Defence of the Nation, The Sin of Lust, The Interlocked Rings* or *Caoqiao Pass*, what *can* I sing? If I can't play loyal ministers or fierce generals, what parts are left me? I can't always play the lucky banner man.[1] If I'm not provocative, who will watch me?"

Xiao Yuerong is doubtful: "Do you think the Japanese... really understand all that? Don't you think you're exaggerating the problem a little?"

The third junior gives a bitter little laugh: "The Japanese can't even tell any of us apart, but you can bet your life there'll be some son of a bitch to tell them. I've been singing these roles half my life, but I've only found out now that even the worst of traitors, the most degenerate of degenerates, are better than a clown like me. Ai!"

His sigh sets everyone else off chattering and moaning.

Xiao Yuerong looks around him and says: "Enough, enough, brothers! Stop now! It's sufficient that you know it, don't say it out loud. Hurry up and eat. Fill your bellies."

The master singer bites into a flatbread.

"We may be full today," he says, "but what about tomorrow? We can't keep bothering you..."

"Ha! We're all old friends here. Just because I've changed professions, that doesn't mean our relationship is any less strong. Whenever this place is open, it doesn't matter what time, as long as you don't come at our peak times, but stagger you arrivals so they're a bit later or a bit earlier, then just come on in. I may not be having the best of years myself, but as long as I can give you a decent meal and you don't call me stingy, that'll do me."

As he is speaking, someone comes in the main door, but as Xiao Yuerong has his back turned, he doesn't see who it is. But the third junior is quick-eyed and quick-witted and shouts out with a laugh: "Hey, how are you? Look, here's a clown who doesn't need make-up!"

Xiao Yuerong looks round hurriedly and sees it is Qi Yuexuan. The two men haven't seen each other since Qi Yuexuan left for the Western Hills, and Xiao Yuerong is overwhelmed by the memory of many years of friendship. Ever since the Japanese forced on Qi Yuexuan the title of honorary president of the New People's Assembly, he has been called every name under the sun and had all manner of insults heaped upon him. But to Xiao Yuerong, he is still Han Shizhong[2] in *Resisting the Jin Army*, unchanged in any way. He has sometimes doubted himself, but these doubts have never extended to his old and trusted friend. The third junior's sarcastic words have no effect on him as he gives a surprised cry of "Aiya!", and he hurries over to the door.

Qi Yuexuan is naturally delighted to see him, but he doesn't immediately take Xiao Yuerong's outstretched hand. Instead, he turns suddenly in a theatrical gesture and says: "Ah! May I ask, elder sister, whether you have a quiet place here where I may wait and rest a while?"

Xiao Yuerong can't restrain a smile and replies, taking on the role of the vivacious young woman: "Ai! Need you ask? How could I, a restaurant owner, not have such a place?"

"And do you have food and good wine?"

"I have leftover rice and rancid vegetables, but the wine is not bad as long as you add enough water."

"From what you say, this must be the kind of place that kills and robs its guests."

"If that is so, with you standing there all alone, you will surely, in a trice, be turned into human dumplings."

"Aiyaya! Now I'm scared..."

Xiao Yuerong can't keep a straight face any longer, and he says: "Enough! Enough! Stop teasing me and come upstairs."

"Wait a moment, wait a moment," Qi Yuexuan replies, turning back to the doorway. He pulls the curtain aside, sticks the top half of his body out of the door and beckons to someone across the street.

"Have you brought some friends?" says Xiao Yuerong who has followed him over.

Qi Yuexuan turns back and nods: "Yes, and you know them both."

"Who is it?" asks Xiao Yuerong, just as the two men come in through the door.

When the first one appears, Xiao Yuerong exclaims: "Aiyo! Mr Hao!"

The second man has his hat pulled down very low, but the half of his face that is visible seems familiar. When the hat comes off, Xiao Yuerong gives a great start as the penny drops: isn't this the hunted assassin of last year who hid out in his restaurant for a while?

Although Xiao Yuerong doesn't know Hao Bingchen's real status, he knows very well what kind of man Gao Guigeng is. So he takes the three men into one of his innermost private rooms that has no other rooms either side and is totally secure once the door is closed. He realises there must be something really important to discuss for these three men to be assembled together, so after a very brief exchange of greetings, he tactfully leaves the room, saying he is going to arrange some food and wine for them. Once he has given the order to one of his waiters, he stations himself in the corridor, keeping watch for them.

. . .

Gao Guigeng has just finished his assignment, and he returned to Beiping from Tianjin the evening before. Previously, Hao Bingchen had told him that, after he had spread the fake army notes around the market, he would let him work on turning Chenglong. If he is successful, he will be brought onto the military intelligence staff; if he is not, then he is to continue his work weeding out traitors, and then withdraw, as previously arranged. But against expectations, the situation has changed, and after the revelation of the secret talks, the Chongqing Government has succumbed to the pressure of public opinion. And when Hao Bingchen informs his superiors of Zhou Zhengjie's defection, it only increases Chongqing's unease. So the head of military intelligence, Dai Li, personally gives them a new assignment to find a way of eliminating Zhou Zhengjie as quickly as possible. This is not only to rid themselves of a lurking danger and to recover their reputation, but it is also designed to stifle the influence of the Civil Intelligence Bureau, thus killing three birds with one stone. The Japanese, however, are maintaining the strictest security around Zhou Zhengjie, to the extent that it is impossible even to be sure where he is actually living.

Hao Bingchen has been giving the matter a great deal of thought, and he finally decides the way forward is to link together the two projects to turn Chenglong and eliminate Zhou Zhengjie. If he can get Chenglong back on board smoothly, and secure his participation and co-operation, the work of weeding out traitors will become much easier. Thus, Hao Bingchen eventually allows Qi Yuexuan to participate in the work of turning Chenglong, greatly strengthening their hand with the combined influence of both father and father-in-law. Afraid there are too many prying eyes in the Minister's Residence, he gets someone to tell Qi Yuexuan to meet at Yuerong's Place.

When Qi Yuexuan hears Hao Bingchen explain the ins and outs of the affair, he is open-mouthed with astonishment. Yesterday, his wife Zhou Zhengying has thrown the household into turmoil by coming home and handing over her son, and today, he learns that her brother, Zhou Zhengjie, has gone over to the enemy. It is unthinkable, inconceivable, it beggars belief. Even though this brother-in-law's moral compass and natural disposition have never been all that they should be, his dramatic transformation first from refugee into government official, and now, in a flash, into a turncoat and a traitor to the nation, is more dizzying than a ride on a roller-coaster, quicker than a stage magician. Who wouldn't be confused by it?

"Are you sure your information is... accurate?"

"Of course! Absolutely accurate," says Hao Bingchen.

"When I saw him a couple of weeks ago, he didn't breathe a word about any secret negotiations."

"Ha! If he had, they wouldn't have been secret, would they! But now the whole affair has been exposed and even the agreement protocols have been revealed. There's a news blackout in Beiping, but outside the capital, especially in the interior, everyone knows about it, and it has rendered the Chongqing Government impotent."

"Supposing the information about him is true, he is still just a mouthpiece. When things went wrong, the people who made the decisions put it all on him and made him their scapegoat... isn't that just typical of their shifty, cloak and dagger evasiveness?"

"You don't understand politics."

"Oh? I don't understand them, and you do? Then please explain to me."

"I do understand," Hao Bingchen says. "Zhengjie is your brother-in-law and a friend of many years..."

"Enough!" Qi Yuexuan interrupts him. "Don't go there. Do you think I'm the kind of man who puts friends above principles? Yes, he's been my friend for many years, but haven't you too?"

"Don't get so worked up..."

"Who's getting worked up?"

Hao Bingchen can't help laughing as he sees Qi Yuexuan's wild-eyed protestation. "Alright, alright, you're not worked up. Just let me finish. After the talks, Zhou Zhengjie stayed on without permission and didn't report back to base, and we have a reliable report that he had already switched sides. Such a seismic change is not something that can be forgiven."

"Are you sure it wasn't that the Japanese detained him?"

"I got the information straight from the Bureau, there's no chance of a mistake."

Hearing the finality of his reply, Qi Yuexuan doesn't pursue the matter.

Hao Bingchen continues: "You're not going to be involved in Zhou Zhengjie's punishment. I'm just giving you a heads-up. But as for the business of turning Chenglong, that is your inescapable responsibility."

Qi Yuexuan gives a wry laugh and stares at Gao Guigeng, saying: "Since Yue E hasn't even acknowledged me as her father, what use is anything I have to say going to be? You should be looking to his real family."

"Ha! What father hasn't had that?" says Gao Guigeng. "Children are allowed to be a little pig-headed from time to time. But Chenglong is your son-in-law, and the responsibility should be shared between us. You're an educated man, not a coarse-mouthed lout like me. So how about this? You use reason and I'll use the rod."

Qi Yuexuan grunts and nods, then says: "If we're going to do it, let's do it soon. Uncle Yang seems to be getting better, and I was originally hoping to go back the day after tomorrow. I'm a little uneasy about leaving Grandpa Fu in charge of the troops."

Hao Bingchen and Qi Yuexuan exchange glances. "Alright, there's no point in delaying, we'll settle it tomorrow evening."

. . .

Seeing how much Yang Zhixing's spirit has improved over the last two days, almost everyone feels that his illness has been cured. Even Mother Yan has mostly relaxed, and she privately jokes that her old man is like a donkey, tough and resilient, and if he takes a tumble he bounces right back up. Only Lao Zhang has a different opinion, as an ominous premonition shivers through his heart when he sees how Yang Zhixing looks. Although he does not understand medical matters, he has been rearing birds and insects for many decades. In his eyes, all living things are the same, regardless of size and lifespan. No matter what the bird, emaciation through illness has never bothered him, and the creature can be limp-winged for two days and not eating a thing, but as long as it is still drinking, there is still a chance of recovery. What he does fear is how it can suddenly revive, hopping around, and fluttering about its cage, bumping into the sides; then, in a very short time, it dies. Insects are the same, no matter whether it is a cricket, a field cricket, a bell-cricket or a katydid. They can start wasting away, then suddenly begin to hop around again, which only means they are very close to death. He feels that Yang Zhixing has undergone a fundamental change over the last two days, from being a stoppered-up gourd to becoming a wide-necked jar. This is not a good thing, as just like a bird or an insect suddenly reviving, it may be the last glimmers of a setting sun. But he doesn't share these thoughts with anyone, for fear of being accused of jinxing the old man's recovery.

That afternoon, Yang Zhixing takes advantage of being alone to call Lao Zhang over to him.

"Tell me the truth now, Lao Zhang," he says. "Do you still want to find a mate and make a real family?"

Lao Zhang is taken aback, and his sun-blackened old face blushes: "You... let's not pick at that pimple."

"Ha! You don't have to hide anything from me. Now you're old, don't you want a companion? And if she already has a son who could look after your funeral rites in the future, wouldn't that be a good thing?"

Lao Zhang doesn't reply, and he lets his head drop.

Yang Zhixing shoots him a look and continues: "I'm not going to beat about the bush with you. I've just got one thing to ask: what do you think of Mother Yan?"

Lao Zhang becomes very agitated at this: "Are you... are you making fun of me?"

Yang Zhixing sighs and says with a wry smile: "You shouldn't mess around with me either. I'm seeing things quite clearly now, and I know I don't have many days left."

"You mustn't talk like that."

"Hah! It's the truth. Who's going to know my body better than me? I just want to get that weight off my chest, and if I say I'm going to die, I'm going to die."

"Enough, I can't take it. Don't frighten me like that." Lao Zhang gesticulates and tries to stand up, but Yang Zhixing holds him back.

"Well, do you agree or not? Say something to encourage me."

Lao Zhang is both agitated and embarrassed, as tears well up in his eyes: "Manager Yang, Master Yang, please forgive me. You know how lowly my status is, and this... this can only embarrass me. For so many years you have helped me protect my privacy and hide my shame, and allowed me to be myself. I will be eternally grateful to you and in your debt. But what you're talking about now, isn't that just hastening my end?"

"So... have you become less interested in looking for someone since you stopped watching over the family tombs?"

"There have been plenty of women, but up to now, none of them have stuck around. Anyway, they've all been strangers, and they didn't make much impression on me whether they stayed with me or left. But Mother Yan's different, she's family, and if the secret gets out one day, you'd never trust me round people again, would you?"

Yang Zhixing can see how desperately worried Lao Zhang is, and he doesn't go on. He just pats his hand, but there is still something he is trying to find a way to say.

Lao Zhang's agitation is not surprising, now he finds the previously kind and generous Yang Zhixing deliberately probing his weak spot. Lao Zhang's name was not originally Zhang, it was Chen. When he was twelve, there was a drought in his home county of Baodi, and in order to find a way for him to survive, his father sent him to be castrated and enter the Imperial Palace to serve as a low-grade eunuch in the Imperial Household Department. He happened to be noticed by an elderly eunuch who raised crickets in the palace, who took him on as an apprentice. From then on, he raised insects and studied every aspect of the art. Later on, in honouring his master as his father, he changed his name to Zhang. In the final years of Emperor Guangxu, at the end of the Qing, the court was in dire financial straits, and staff cuts led to him leaving the palace. Qi Yuexuan was in his playboy phase at that time, when he discovered this insect expert in the insect market at the Longfu Temple, and he took him back to the Residence as his own insect master. Although Lao Zhang is a eunuch, this has not affected his voice or movements, so even Qi Yuexuan was unaware of the fact. Only one man at any level in the Minister's Residence was not deceived, and that was the household manager, Yang Zhixing. He questioned him privately and made sure of his facts. Yang Zhixing didn't expel him from the Residence despite the act of deception, nor did he ever make the information public. Instead, he kept the secret over the decades. So why, now, is Yang Zhixing asking a question to which he already knows the answer?

Yang Zhixing sighs again: "Ai, Lao Zhang, I'm not trying to embarrass you. It's just that, if I die, Mother Yan will be all alone, as you are, and since you already know each other, you would make good companions and be a mutual support for each other. What is more... there are only three of us who know where the family wealth is hidden. If I die, that will be a worry. This way, you can have the best of both worlds, and have Mother Yan for company and guard the Qi family treasure at the same time."

Lao Zhang laughs, but it is a bitter laugh: "Oh! That's what you've been making a fuss about all day, is it? Well, you've certainly given it some thought! So what is it then? You want to tie me up with a wife so she can watch over me while I watch over the tombs? Have you told her yet what to do if I prove treacherous? Is it to be a noose, a knife or poison in my wine?"

"No, no, you mustn't think such nonsense."

"If I'm thinking nonsense, I'm just following your lead, aren't I?"

"It's true I have my concerns, but evil intentions? I..."

"No!" Lao Zhang's tears are spattering his face. "Aren't your intentions evil enough already? Those concerns of yours, aren't they simply that you don't trust me? We have been like brothers for many years, and I've never let you down. So why don't you trust me? Is it because I haven't got that little thing that the rest of you have? There's no point you shaking your head and waving your hands, I know what's going on. Deep down, you've always pitied me. You've never seen me as a real man. I know this. But you've been with Mother Yan all these years too, and you still want to use her as your tool after you're dead. Do you have no shame? You may have that thing that I lack, but does that make you more of a man? Even if I was an insect, I would still have some integrity. Let me tell you this now. I would never dig up anyone else's tomb, but I'll wait to dig up yours. I know how poor you are, but I wouldn't do it for the money. I'd do it to repay your own evil intentions."

While Lao Zhang may have said his fill, Yang Zhixing's face flushes then blanches, blanches then flushes several times. After a while, he opens his mouth to say something, but nothing comes out, and he begins to cough as he chokes on his emotion. Lao Zhang hurries over to rub his chest and thump his back, hoping to restore his composure.

Yang Zhixing stays the old man's hand and says quietly: "It's my fault if I apologise to you and you don't believe me. The truth is, I sacrificed my dignity talking like this today, nine parts out of concern for you, and only one part out of worry. Ai! What nonsense a man can talk when he is close to death..."

"Enough! Enough! Don't go on." Lao Zhang tries to divert the conversation by continuing: "Ha! In all those years, this is the first time you've apologised to me!"

"Ha! And isn't this the first time you've acted like a real man?"

"And do you mean that as praise or an insult?"

"As praise! As praise! Aiyo! I almost forgot something," Yang Zhixing says, taking a small porcelain bottle from his breast and handing it to Lao Zhang.

"What... what is it?"

"Red crane crest arsenic."

When he hears this, Lao Zhang quakes with fear, and the bottle almost slips from his hand.

Yang Zhixing bursts out laughing: "Ha ha, I seem to have been wasting my breath praising you for your manliness if you go weak at the knees at this little thing! I haven't told you to drink it! In the Qing dynasty, only a red-button mandarin was allowed to do that. You're not important enough."

"Then this is your..."

"You must have seen how resolute and unyielding the Young Master is, and how he can't bear to feel wronged. He always carries this with him and often thinks of drinking it. So I..."

"Ah, I understand. You took it away from him. Alright, don't worry, I'll throw it away for you."

"No, don't do that."

"What's the point of keeping it? Even if you hide it, someone might come across it by chance, and that could end in disaster."

"Oh, this isn't the bottle that the Young Master carries, it's the bottle the Old Master drank from all those years ago. I cleaned it out and refilled it with some red-dyed water. I want to swap it for the Young Master's, but if I don't get the chance, you must do it for me."

As Yang Zhixing says this, he grasps Lao Zhang's hand that is holding the bottle. But even as he tries to use all his strength, his hand trembles too much to maintain the grip. Lao Zhang's heart lurches at the hand's icy touch, and he hurriedly places his other hand over the top of it. He knows now that his premonition is not wrong, but he doesn't say anything and just nods seriously as his eyes fill with tears.

But Lao Zhang has not expected his premonition to be realised so quickly. That very evening, Yang Zhixing's condition takes a sudden turn for the worse. A bout of violent coughing leads to him spitting out mouthful after mouthful of blood. By the time everyone hurries back in response to Lao Zhang's report, he can no longer speak and has lost the strength even to cough. He is just lying there, eyes tight shut and mouth half open, gasping for breath.

When Qi Yuexuan sees him like this, he immediately asks the doctor: "Can you... can you still save him, doctor?"

The doctor sighs: "I'm sorry, but we've done all we can. If you have anything to say to him, say it now. I'm afraid the patient won't live through the night."

"Great Heavens!" Mother Yan exclaims, as she throws herself to the ground in front of the bed, wailing.

Yue E grasps Yang Zhixing's hand and sobs: "Father!"

Qi Yuexuan stares with red-rimmed eyes and asks the doctor: "He has seemed so much better recently, after having the penicillin. How can he suddenly..."

The doctor sighs again: "Ai! If we could have continued that treatment, perhaps it might... well, at least it might not have come to this so quickly. It's a pity he only had two injections..."

"What do you mean?" Qi Yuexuan seizes the doctor by the collar and shakes a finger under his nose. "I know we brought two boxes of the drug, so why did he only get two injections? Why?"

The doctor doesn't reply, but a young nurse standing beside him tugs his sleeve and pipes up: "Young Master Qi, it's not Dr Lin's fault. It was the patient himself who forbade the injections."

"What... what's going on?" Qi Yuexuan loosens his grip.

"It... it's like this..." The young nurse is both agitated and scared, but she steels herself and says tearfully: "It's my fault for speaking out of turn. After the first injection, I let slip that the penicillin had come from the Japanese. The Old Master didn't say anything at the time, but after he'd thought about it for a bit, he sent his family away and told me that he was not going to have any more injections, and he wanted to take possession of all the penicillin. I couldn't possibly take such a big decision on my own, so I called Dr Lin over. But even he couldn't dissuade the Old Master, who stuck to his guns and wouldn't budge. He said that, if we gave him another injection, or told the family about the matter, he would immediately kill himself in the hospital. There was nothing else to be done in the end, so Dr Lin gave him the penicillin. After that, all the injections he had were sulphonamide, not penicillin."

Everyone listens blankly to the young nurse.

Half-believing, half-disbelieving, Qi Yuexuan looks at the doctor and sees that he is nodding.

"The old man said he was already seventy years old, and if he died now he would have had his money's worth. He is Chinese and will not be beholden to the Japanese, nor bring down the curses of his ancestors just for the sake of a few more days of life."

Qi Yuexuan's head is in a whirl at this, and when he looks at the dying figure of Yang Zhixing, lying on the bed, he can no longer hold back. He wails: "Uncle Yang! You... How can you be so stubborn?"

"That can't be right," Yue E says, holding back her tears. "Why haven't we seen the drugs? It's not such a big place. Where could he have hidden them?"

Dr Lin and the nurse see that everyone is looking at them, and they hurriedly shake their heads and gesture their ignorance.

Yue E is about to ask again, when she hears Yang Zhixing grunt and sees that his eyes are open. Wangtian sees his trembling hand pointing underneath him, so he immediately feels around there, and does indeed find the two boxes of penicillin, hidden under the mattress. One box is unopened, and the other is missing two doses.

Yang Zhixing opens his mouth wide and moves his head. Although no one can make out any words, everyone can see what he means. Yue E looks at him and nods in reply, at which a faint smile crosses his face. After a while, his mouth opens again, and this time he uses every last ounce of strength to make himself heard. Yue E hears him quite clearly, as he repeats, over and over again, the single word "Father".

Yue E understands his meaning, grasps his hand and sobs: "I understand, Father. I'll do as you say and acknowledge him as my father. But… but you will always be my real father."

So saying she drops to her knees, bows her head to the ground and in heart-rending tones, cries out: "Father!"

Qi Yuexuan hurriedly helps Yue E to her feet and stoops over the bed. He sees Yang Zhixing's eyes slowly close, a contented smile on his face, looking so calm and so much at peace.

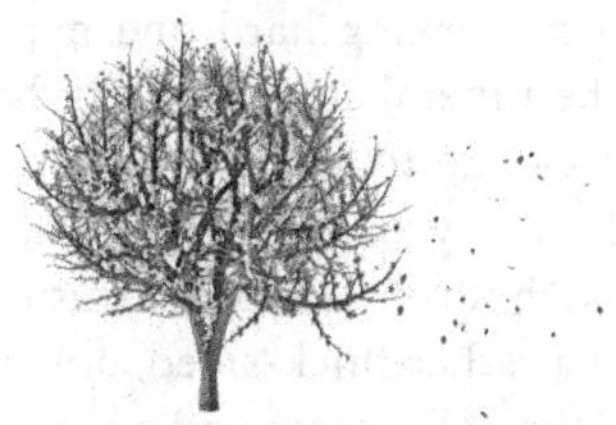

Chapter 50

Yang Zhixing does not last through the night, and he dies just after one in the morning. Lao Zhang washes his body and dresses him in his burial clothes, while Wangtian arranges a hand cart to take him home. When he was still alive, Yang Zhixing had agreed with Mother Yan and Yue E that there would be no laying out of the body, no funeral feast and no procession; he would just be taken straight to the family tombs for the simplest of burials, and that would be that. But of course, Qi Yuexuan takes a different view. He says that Uncle Yang spent his life as a stand-in for the God of Wealth, and he cannot possibly be buried in such a paltry fashion. To have no grand ceremony and no feast is fine, but his body must be laid out, and how could we shovel him straight into his grave without having the feng shui approved? At the very least, it has to last three nights. There must certainly be a procession too, because failing to properly send off a fine man would be like a slap in the face. It is a way of letting everyone know Uncle Yang has died and that China still has men of moral integrity who scorn life to see justice done. That is a slap in the face for the Japanese. With the Young Master talking like this, how can Mother Yan not go along with him?

Qi Yuexuan doesn't allow the body to stay in the side courtyard, and he turns the main hall of the large courtyard into a funeral hall. According to tradition, being laid out in the main hall is the prerogative of the master of the household, and although many funerals from the Minister's Residence have been held over the last few decades, only the Old Master and the Old Mistress have been laid out there. Even Qi Yuexuan's first wife, and Yang Zhixing's father, Old Manager Yang, were not allowed in there. This makes Mother Yan feel very uneasy, and she burns three sets of incense as she mutters: "This is the Young Master's doing. It's not us disregarding the customs. Old Master, Old Mistress, please don't hold it against us."

THE TASK OF MANAGING all this falls to Wangtian, but he is still young and has never organised such a grand occasion before, nor is he familiar with all the old rules and customs. Fortunately, he has Lao Zhang at his side to guide him, and with a dozen or so men working hard one morning, they manage to arrange everything including the funeral apparel, black hangings, incense, paper money and silk flowers. They also go to several major coffin shops but fail to find one that they think suitable. The war has meant that, not only is good rice from the south not getting through, even lacquer furniture is in short supply, and they were lucky to buy even a rather thick-sided, unvarnished, plain elm wood coffin. They fix the time with the pallbearers and pay the deposit. The procession is set for two days' time, with a sixteen-man coffin, the ceremonial weaponry customary for a bannerman, and the drums and horns of both the banners and the Chinese. They still need to buy a complete set of paper men, horses, carts and buildings, and to hire a group of mourners to accompany the relatives, weeping and wailing for the deceased.

But after they have done all this, Qi Yuexuan forbids the pomp and ceremony, saying: "Uncle Yang was frugal and hard-working all his life, so would he really start flaunting his wealth now he is dead? If you were to go ahead, he would surely be stamping his feet in anger and cursing you for wasting the family's money. All that weeping and wailing is just nonsense, and who is it meant to fool anyway? The dead or the living? Don't worry, there will be plenty of people celebrating Uncle Yang for the kind of man he was, and tears of real sadness, real grief and real loss are a hundred times more powerful than the weeping and wailing money buys."

THERE IS NO REST FOR YUE E EITHER, as she hires a rickshaw and rides all over the city giving the news to friends, old and new. According to ancient custom, if the deceased is a man, it should be the son or nephew who announces the death, or if, like Yang Zhixing, the deceased has no male relatives or descendants and the daughter has married, then it is the job of the son-in-law. A woman should not undertake the task. But no one has seen Chenglong from the first evening after Yang Zhixing's death, and no one knows where he has gone. So there is nothing for it but for Yue E to go. But actually this is no bad thing, since everyone knows who Chenglong works for and who pays his wages. His presence might frighten people and lead to curses being heaped on him behind his back.

Chenglong finally deigns to show his face around noon, and although it is only lunchtime, he is already well gone in drink, his face almost purple. When he enters the main courtyard and sees Wangtian busy at his tasks, he feels rather embarrassed. Without waiting to be asked, he launches into his excuses: "I was busy all evening yesterday, Brother, and I've only just heard the news, and then I..."

"And then you poured a stomachful of horse piss cheap wine down your throat, isn't that it?" Wangtian says, choking on his anger.

Chenglong knows he is in the wrong and doesn't reply.

On this day of all days, Wangtian does not want to quarrel with him.

"Alright, enough! Now you're here, hurry up and get dressed, then go and keep vigil in the funeral hall. This afternoon, people are coming to pay their condolences, and it wouldn't do if neither you nor Yue E is there."

"Yue E isn't here?"

"She went out to pass on the news and hasn't come back yet. That was your job as the man of the family, but now you might as well..."

Chenglong's eyes bulge, but he still doesn't say anything. He just gives a boozy belch and heads indoors.

At this point, Qi Yuexuan, who is standing on the threshold of the main room, breaks in: "It wouldn't be auspicious for someone as drunk as you to stand by the coffin. Go home and sober up."

"I'm alright to do it, Father. I really must..."

"Forget it! You won't be missed. Besides, I'm afraid you'll just make our visitors uncomfortable if you're here."

"Then..."

"Just go home!" Qi Yuexuan waves his hand dismissively and goes on: "But you must come back this evening to keep vigil."

"Yes, yes... I'll be here."

"So you say, but this is an absolute duty, and you must be here even if the sky has fallen in."

"Don't worry, I'll be here."

Qi Yuexuan glances at the gun Chenglong is carrying in a shoulder holster, and he asks with a frown: "You're still going about armed on a day like this? Are you showing off, or do you need the reassurance?"

"It's not... it's not... I was so busy I forgot."

"You forgot? Well, don't forget again this evening. And take that bandage off your arm." And without waiting for a reply, Qi Yuexuan goes straight inside.

In fact, the reason Chenglong is so on edge is not because Yang Zhixing's death came on so suddenly and even less is it because of Qi Yuexuan's telling off. He has been holding his anger in all morning.

To co-ordinate with their operations to root out the enemy in the environs of Beiping, the Japanese have instituted sweeping searches across Beiping itself. The evening before, Chenglong received orders to co-operate with the Kempeitai in searching all the hotels, brothels and carters' inns in the south of the city. They went into every place where there were outsiders, checking their IDs one by one and searching their persons and their luggage. It took all night, and although they didn't take any great prizes, they did arrest several dozen people whose IDs were not right or who simply looked suspicious. They were all handed over to the Kempeitai for further investigation.

Just as the operation ends in the morning, Yamaguchi calls him over and asks quietly: "Liu-san, is you know? Your government's deputy department head is promotioned."

Chenglong is delighted: "Ha! How could I know? Are you going to tell me?"

"Department head not you."

Chenglong stares at him: "Then... who is it?"

"Is Zhou-san, Zhou Zhengjie. His is new but his is great merit."

"Then I..."

"Yours is not even deputy."

"Why... why not?"

"Intelligence section and CID is different, understand?"

Chenglong only half understands what is going on and is not going to let the matter drop. He catches hold of Yamaguchi and says: "Come on, let's find somewhere for a quiet drink where we can talk this over."

Yamaguchi shakes his head and hurriedly shoots out some Japanese: "*Yamete, yamete!*"

Chenglong doesn't speak much Japanese , but he does know this: it means 'not want to'. So he asks: "Have you got another job on?"

"Job is not having. Wine in public place is not allow."

"Then... come to my place."

"Your, mine, private all not allow. Senior officer not happy."

"Then..." Chenglong's eyes suddenly light up and he continues: "Ha! I was forgetting. I know somewhere we can be alone. Come on, there's good wine and home-cooked food. Much better than eating out."

"Where?"

"Ha! You wouldn't know it if I told you. We'll take my car. It's only ten minutes away. Let's go. I guarantee you'll be happy."

Yamaguchi doesn't want to keep saying no, so he gets into the car.

"The old place at the Desheng Gate, and put your foot down," Chenglong orders the driver.

It's STILL EARLY, and the roads are clear, so the journey does indeed only take ten minutes. Yuxiang's father, Sergeant Lian, is still working as manager of the Liuji night soil depot. The working day of a night soil collector starts at the fifth watch in the middle of the night, and as manager, he has already left to keep an eye on things. Yuxiang is also up and about, making breakfast for her little brother and sister, so they can be off to school when they've eaten. When she hears the sound of an engine outside, she realises it must be Chenglong. She calls out to the children to hurry up and finish their breakfast and goes out to greet him. To her surprise she sees Chenglong bringing a Japanese man into the courtyard, and when she looks closely at him, she is flabbergasted to discover that it is the same devil officer who raped her all those months ago.

Yamaguchi also recognises her and is equally astounded. Last time, wasn't it because of her that he had almost come to blows with Chenglong, and Matsuzaki Harayama had cursed him out? For Chenglong to bring him here now, breaking all taboos, he finds frankly baffling.

Chenglong laughs offhandedly and draws Yamaguchi into the house: "Ha ha, Lord Yamaguchi, please, please!" And when he sees Yuxiang still rooted to the spot, he orders her: "Hurry up and brew some tea and see what decent dishes you can rustle up. Commander Yamaguchi and I are going to have a few drinks together."

Yamaguchi is looking very awkward, so Chenglong laughs again and says: "Look at you, still worrying about ancient history. I got over it all ages ago."

Yamaguchi doesn't say anything.

"Ha! It's no big deal," Chenglong continues. "Back then, you and I weren't friends, and all we were doing was fighting over a woman. Now we are friends and brothers, and we work together. What does a woman matter? Women are like clothes – if you want to wear them, you wear them, if you want to take them off, you take them off. Isn't that so, Lord Yamaguchi?"

Yamaguchi finally smiles and nods, muttering: "*Yoshi! Yoshi!*"

"Let's not talk any more about that, Lord Yamaguchi. Instead, why don't you tell me exactly what is going on?"

The two men sit down, and Chenglong wastes no time in turning the talk to the real subject at hand.

Matsuzaki Harayama has decided to give Zhou Zhengjie the post of head of the intelligence department in the ad hoc government of North China, but he is afraid that Chenglong will not accept this and may prove disobedient in the future. So now he intends to incorporate the CID into the Kempeitai, so it is totally independent of the government intelligence department. Chenglong is still head of the CID squad but will no longer simultaneously hold a post with the intelligence department. This way the two men go their separate ways, with no connection or interface between them, but it is also, effectively but unofficially, a demotion for Chenglong. Without any duties in the intelligence department, all he can do is flip-flop around in the fishpond of Beiping. But this matter has not yet been finalised, and after Matsuzaki Harayama and Yamaguchi talk it over, they intend to canvass Chenglong's opinion before making a decision.

"Liu-san, this way also better," Yamaguchi says when he sees Chenglong sitting tight-lipped. "Yours being under Zhou, not good like coming to my side. Yours not having friends with Zhou, but yours having big friends with me."

Chenglong is still disdainful: "This Zhou fellow... is Lord Matsuzaki really so well-disposed towards him?"

Yamaguchi laughs and shakes his head: "Ha! Here has superiors' thinking. That's where Lord Matsuzaki is." He makes a thumbs-up and thumbs-down sign. "Your loyalty like this, his useful like this, understand?"

Chenglong nods and asks with a wry smile: "And supposing I'm quite content to work under Zhou as department head?"

"Yours is taking orders?"

"I won't take orders from him, but I will from Lord Matsuzaki. He takes his orders from the Imperial Army, so how could I not obey him? But as for that turncoat Zhou, who is to guarantee he is going to be on the same side tomorrow? I still want to get close to him though, and it doesn't matter if it's not as his deputy, as long as I'm under his command. Why? Because I don't trust him, and I want to help the Imperial Army keep an eye on him."

"Yours truly this intention?"

"Truly."

"I am helping you talk talk, possibly this can be."

"Of course that would be good, but you mustn't say this is my idea. It must..."

"Ah! Understand! Yours is knowing nothing, all is mine opinion."

"That's right, that's right. You're a real brother to me," Chenglong says, clapping Yamaguchi on the shoulder.

Yamaguchi, however, remains impassive and says with a grunt: "Yours is very slippery person, and mine is not yours rival."

Chenglong hurriedly puts on an ingratiating smile: "Aiya! What can you mean by that? I am..."

Before he can finish, Yuxiang comes into the room, carrying a tray, and, without looking up, puts a jar of wine and two dishes of food on the table. She is about to turn and leave, but Chenglong stops her.

"Hey! This is the first time I have invited Commander Yamaguchi as a guest, and I asked you to make some decent food. Is smashed cucumber and stir-fried egg the best you can do?"

Yuxiang keeps a rein on her anger and just says: "It's first thing in the morning. What else do you expect me to have in the house?"

"If you didn't have anything, you could have brought something in from a restaurant."

"What restaurant is open this early?"

When Chenglong sees her turn and leave, he is about to explode with fury. But Yamaguchi stops him: "Liu-san, these is very good. Have wine, dishes is not importance. Make the little lady unhappy, not want."

Ha! So now he decides to play the knight errant, Chenglong curses Yamaguchi internally, but he keeps the smile on his face. "Shall we switch to bigger bowls for the wine, then?"

"*Yoshi!* Big bowls!"

At this, Chenglong fills the big bowls and exchanges toasts with Yamaguchi. After some general conversation, he tries to turn the talk back to the matter in hand. But he has learned from his first attempt, and this time he starts by acting respectfully, then approaching things in a roundabout fashion and not being so explicit about what he wants. But Yamaguchi still refuses to be drawn in, and with three big bowls of wine inside him, just says: "*Yoshi!* My think whatever you say good."

Chenglong is considering how to end the meeting, when the door of the room opens with a crash that makes him jump. Yuxiang comes charging in, carrying a food basket: "You'd better stop drinking and go home at once."

"What's up with you? What's going on?"

"I heard on the street that Manager Yang is dead, and that the white mourning banners are already hanging at the gates of the Minister's Residence."

Chenglong sits up and is about to get down from the *kang*, when he looks at Yamaguchi and feels rather awkward.

This just serves to anger Yuxiang even more: "What's keeping you? This is important. As his son-in-law, how can you want to stay here drinking and not go home? If Aunty Yue E gets to hear about this, she'll be furious with me too. If you make me..."

"Alright, alright, I know. But the man's already dead, and my going won't bring him back to life," Chenglong says impatiently. "I'm lucky Commander Yamaguchi came here today, and we haven't finished drinking yet..."

But Yamaguchi sits up too and says: "Liu-san, yours must go, mine go too. Little lady embarrassed is not wanting."

Chenglong is about to stop him, but then he sees Yamaguchi's drink-reddened eyes looking covetously at Yuxiang. A thought suddenly comes into his head, and he gives a shout of laughter: "Ha! Don't go, Lord Yamaguchi. You can't leave before you've finished your drink. I'll just go and show my face, then come back."

He gets off the *kang*, puts on his shoes and whispers to Yamaguchi: "Lord Yamaguchi, didn't I just say that brothers are comrades in arms and women are just like clothes? I may not have much ability, but you mustn't think of me as ungenerous."

Yuxiang hears Chenglong muttering to Yamaguchi, but she has no idea, for the moment, what he is saying. She just looks blank as Chenglong casually makes her get onto the *kang*.

"You play the hostess, and I'll be back soon. Commander Yamaguchi wants to apologise to you. That's right, isn't it, Commander Yamaguchi?"

"*Yoshi*, mine is... apologise... fault."

Yamaguchi's speech is thickened by the wine, but his evil mind is still agile, and he plays along with Chenglong. He fills his wine bowl and holds it up in front of him. With just a snatch more conversation, Chenglong slips, eel-like, out of the room. His ears are deaf to whatever is going on behind him.

It is past noon, and a constant stream of people are coming to the Minister's Residence to offer their condolences. Yang Zhixing didn't have any close family, and most of these visitors are old family retainers, business acquaintances and neighbours. Everyone has come to give face to the Minister's Residence, but more out of respect for the kind of man Yang Zhixing was. There are, however, some uninvited guests who look disagreeably out of place, and they are the ridiculous figures of Zhou Si and Li Fenggu.

At this time, Li Fenggu is something of a social butterfly on the Beiping scene, and although she is not in the first flush of youth, like an old melon painted with green varnish, she still dresses the part. No one has officially given her the news of Manager Yang's death, but she sticks her nose in everything and has eyes and ears everywhere, so nothing gets past her. And if she has heard the news, then, of course, Zhou Si has too. The way Zhou Si sees it, now he has got his claws into a patron like Zhou Zhengjie, they shouldn't go rushing over to the Residence to curry favour. If Zhou Zhengjie gets to hear of it, he might be angry, and the relationship would be lost. But he can't dissuade Li Fenggu. Like a butterfly after autumn, she has been showing herself off everywhere and going wherever the social buzz is. Although the two of them are living together and have been sharing a bed for quite some time, they have been in no rush to regularise the arrangement and are not officially husband and wife. It is not that Zhou Si doesn't want to get married, but Li Fenggu keeps fobbing him off with all kinds of excuses. Zhou Si understands this; she always has an eye to the future and is aiming high, so she is not really thinking of him as a serious proposition. She has been very busy on the social scene recently, and he has become, even more, just a little light refreshment for her to consume if she's hungry, but not the kind of dish you'd serve at the real feast. But there's no point in him getting upset about it, since however much he hones his toadying technique, he simply can't compete with the effect an eye-fluttering coquette of a woman can have. He really has no choice, so when she says "I'm going whether you want to or not", he doesn't say anything and just meekly follows her.

Li Fenggu's attire is particularly remarkable today, as she has abandoned her *qipao* for a kimono. She has coiled up her hair, put on wooden clogs and walks with quick little steps, so she has a very Japanese air. When she hands over her card at the main gates of the Residence, it is covered in indecipherable Japanese writing. The master-of-ceremony announces in a loud voice: "Miss Mishima Fenggu of the Great Japanese Empire!"

Qi Yuexuan frowns when he hears this: "Aiya! Why are one's worst fears always realised?" As he watches the two of them coming into the inner courtyard, he hurriedly instructs Lao Zhang: "Quick, hurry up and stop them. Don't let them in."

Lao Zhang hurries over to meet them as Li Fenggu approaches the threshold: "Please stop just there, madam."

Li Fenggu stops, standing in the posture of a Japanese woman, bows deeply and says smoothly: "*Konichiwa.*"

Lao Zhang doesn't understand Japanese, and because Li Fenggu's pronunciation isn't very accurate, he thinks she is swearing and saying "Fuck your ma!"

"Ha! Well you're a proper madam who doesn't know what's good for you!"

"She is just saying 'good afternoon' to you," says Zhou Si, coming to her aid.

"She is an expert in Japanese, and when they greet you they make a difference between morning and afternoon. Do you understand?"

When he sees Lao Zhang just standing there, he takes hold of Li Fenggu and says: "Let's go, let's go. There's no point bandying words with him."

"Stay where you are!" Lao Zhang puts out his hand to stop them.

Zhou Si rolls his eyes. "What's this? Do you really not recognise me, or are you just playing dumb?"

"Ha! Of course I know you. You're Master Zhou, aren't you?"

"If you know me, why are you talking such nonsense?"

"I'm not stopping you, I'm stopping that person. Our Young Master has given orders that this is a family funeral. We're not just picking on the Japanese, no foreigners of any kind are allowed. Besides, Manager Yang was a man of such excitable temperament, if you take her in, he might get so angry he'll come back to life."

This infuriates Li Fenggu, but she only knows a few words of Japanese and doesn't have the wherewithal to reply in that language. She is so swept up in her anger, she lapses into Tianjin dialect: "What? What the fuck are you up to? Are you joking us? Aren't you the Residence's insect man? Do you dare say you don't recognise me? I've got some status here. How can I be an outsider to the Minister's Residence when you know my relationship to Third Master Shen?"

"Aiyo!" Lao Zhang chuckles to himself. "You're Third Master Shen's... ah yes, I heard you singing your clapper songs, but how was I supposed to recognise you looking like this and jabbering away in Japanese. What do you think you are you doing all dressed up like this?"

"What are you talking about?" Li Fenggu is beginning to get really angry, and her voice rises: "I'm a real citizen of the Great Japanese Empire. Do you think I'm just shooting my mouth off? I haven't just invented the name Mishima Fenggu. Have you heard of Group Captain Mishima of the Imperial Army. He's my man now. We went through the whole formal thing with the wine, the tea and the bowing. I'm giving you a lot of face coming here today, and you treat me like a bag of dough twists you can break up and munch on as you please!"

With this, she makes to force her way over the threshold, and this time there is nothing Lao Zhang can do to stop her. But fortunately, Caiping, who has been waiting outside, comes over and pulls her back.

"What mischief are you up to today of all days, aunty?"

"Ha! Are you on his side now then, turning on your own people! I came today simply to pay my respects and give the Minister's Residence face, and you still try and lock the door in my face? If you disrespect me, you disrespect the Imperial Army, or is that too rich for you?"

Caiping can't immediately think how to respond, so she just holds on tighter and doesn't let go, which makes Li Fenggu stamp her feet with anger. She shakes herself free and is about to storm inside again, but, thinking on her feet, Caiping doesn't try to stop her this time. Rather, she stands to one side, ushering her in, with a smile.

"Alright, alright. Please go in, aunty. But don't blame me for not warning you if you come to grief."

"Eh? What do you mean?" Li Fenggu stops in her tracks.

Caiping pretends to look very serious and lowers her voice confidentially: "Don't you know how Manager Yang died?"

"He... he died of an illness, didn't he?"

"That's what they're putting out, but secretly there was another reason. I've heard that the illness the old man had wasn't necessarily fatal, and the reason he died was because he refused to go into a Japanese hospital or use Japanese drugs. Of course, the reason he did that is obvious. He hates the devils so much, his dying words were: 'Even when I'm dead, my ghost can still come back to take a Japanese with me.' You haven't seen his body yet. His eyes are wide open and staring, and his mouth is gaping. His arms are outstretched, just as though he is reaching out to grab someone...'"

"Is that... is that true?"

"Would I lie about something like that? If you don't believe me, go right in, and when you have made your kowtows, pull the curtain aside and take a look for yourself."

"Stop! Don't say any more. The more you talk, the more terrified I am." Li Fenggu gives an involuntary shudder, but then says determinedly: "But it's the Japanese he hated, so what's that got to do with me?"

"Oh, I see, you're back to Chinese now, are you? The way you're dressed, if the living can't tell which country you're from, I don't suppose the dead will know either. Of course, I can't be sure. Perhaps there's no fooling the dead, and ghosts have sharp eyes. You'll just have to steel yourself and give it a try. So... please come in."

Li Fenggu has always believed in ghosts and spirits, so when she hears what Caiping is saying, the more she wants to go in and the more scared of doing so she becomes: "That's... that's just crazy talk. I'm... I'm not scared. It's just not worth taking stupid risks. Zhou Si! I'm going home..."

There is no reply, so she turns and looks around, calling his name several times, but still to no avail. There is no sign of him and when she asks, no one else knows where he is.

"Eh? He was here a minute ago. How can he have just disappeared?"

Li Fenggu is baffled. Then she hears Caiping slap her thigh and cry out in alarm: "Damn! Could it be that..." She stops short, a look of indescribable fear on her face.

"Could it... could it be that... what?" There is a tremor in Li Fenggu's voice.

Caiping looks almost as if she has caught a sudden fever, as she wraps her arms around herself and stares at Li Fenggu, stammering and unable to get her words out. Li Fenggu is terrified, her face white as a sheet. Suddenly, she gives a yelp, like a cat that's had its tail trodden on, and she turns and flees. Nor does she try to maintain the quick little steps of a Japanese lady, but kicks her heels up like a little girl. The wooden clogs she is wearing get in her way, and she trips over the threshold. She doesn't actually fall over, just stumbles and breaks the straps on the clogs. In her haste, she doesn't try to fix them but simply takes the shoes off and carries them as she hurtles out of the garlanded gate in her stockinged feet.

Lao Zhang claps his hands to his mouth at the sight of her, makes his way over to Caiping and only then uncovers his mouth. He chokes as his pent-up laughter comes gushing out.

"You... you're quite something... you really are! Like a Buddhist nun scaring off a whore! Brilliant."

"Ha! Catch your breath before you try to say anything more." Caiping laughs and slaps him on the back a few times. Then she thinks of something. "Hey, did you really not see where Zhou Si went?"

"Yes, really... I've no idea."

Lao Zhang feels uneasy as he says this, so he pushes open the door of the porter's lodge to look inside, then does a quick search of the front courtyard, the side courtyard and even the garden at the back. But there is no sign of Zhou Si. He asks the greeter, the man taking the register of guests and the master-of-ceremonies, but none of them have seen him either. In the end, Lao Zhang just puts it down to the number of people and doesn't think much more about it. In fact, Zhou Si hasn't gone home, nor has he left the Minister's Residence at all. He keeps quiet and performs his disappearing act because something has happened that forces him to act very cautiously.

As Li Fenggu and Lao Zhang are arguing, Zhou Si chances to see Qi Yuexuan slipping out of the funeral hall and gesturing in the direction of the gate to the courtyard. Qi Yuexuan doesn't come down the steps from the main hall but follows the veranda round to the west. Zhou Si can't help turning to look, and he sees Wangtian leading two middle-aged men dressed in long robes into the courtyard. They don't go into the middle of the courtyard but also hurry round the veranda to the northwest corner. Qi Yuexuan joins them and then leads them, without ceremony, into the rear garden. Wangtian doesn't follow them but turns and goes back the way he came into the front courtyard.

On a day such as this, there is nothing unusual about greeting some guests, but Zhou Si can't help feeling there is something different about this pair. He also thinks he has seen the older one of the two before. The penny drops when he sees Wangtian coming back. With a body like that, skilled in martial arts and hardened by the labour of years on a night soil route, the man must be Wangtian's father, Old Gao. All those years ago, when Zhou Si was still Third Master Shen's sidekick, he had witnessed Shen Peng's great loss of face outside the main gates of the Minister's Residence. Wasn't Chenglong's *gongfu* all learnt from his father. When Chenglong was still at school, hadn't Old Gao given him,

Zhou Si, a tongue-lashing for helping his son join the Society? He wasn't going to forget those piercing eyes in a hurry. But he was sure that Old Gao had died more than ten years ago, so he must be seeing things or he'd just been dazzled by the sun and got the wrong man. He has to take another look at the figure, but it doesn't help and just leaves him still shaking. As the man walks along, the skirts of his long gown are swept aside, revealing a bulge at his waist. Zhou Si takes him for an old bandit, but he doesn't really have anything else to go on, except that his nose is sharp enough, his eyes wily enough, and he strongly suspects he is carrying a weapon. He is agreeably surprised by this unexpected bonus, as if he can follow it up, he may well have found the weapon he can use against Chenglong. The hook baited and his appetite whetted, Zhou Si, who is normally the timid mouse hiding from the cat, has suddenly become the cat itself. Keen to get to the bottom of the mystery, he silently climbs up onto the veranda and cautiously follows on behind.

Just as Zhou Si suspects, the man who followed Wangtian into the courtyard is indeed Gao Guigeng, and his companion is Hao Bingchen. As they had discussed with Qi Yuexuan two days ago, they are plotting to turn Chenglong. After Yang Zhixing's sudden death, Qi Yuexuan ordered Wangtian to go into the foreign concession to report the news and ask whether they should reschedule. Hao Bingchen decided not to change their original plan, first because his superiors are being very pressing, and second because he felt that Yang Zhixing's death may have affected Chenglong, and their plan might have more chance of success. So now, they have followed Wangtian here and are just waiting for nightfall before going into action. Since Wangtian and his father hadn't seen each other for more than ten years, it goes without saying that all sorts of feelings welled up inside them, as they embraced and their eyes filled with tears. And of course they swapped stories of what has been happening with each of them over the years, all the time they were riding together in the same rickshaw.

Zhou Si follows them into the rear garden, not daring to get too close and using the ornamental rocks and trees as cover, always a dozen or so paces behind them. He sees Qi Yuexuan lead them across the garden along a tree-lined path to the northern range that abuts the back wall. He is about to follow them in when, getting careless in his haste, he trips over a net that is leaning against the wall. This net has a handle more than three metres in length, and the net itself is the size of a wash-basin. In the past it was used for scooping out water fleas from the pond, when goldfish were kept in the garden. As the net falls over, it bangs into an empty flowerpot with a loud crash and a clatter.

Gao Guigeng hears the noise just as he goes into the building, and he rushes back out in the direction of the sound, drawing his pistol as he goes. Zhou Si finds himself rooted to the spot, with nowhere to hide. He tries to draw his own gun to bolster his nerve, but his hand is shaking too much and won't obey him.

He takes a few steps back and, looking round him, sees an isolated building against the south wall. The door is unlocked, so he pushes it open and goes inside. Once there, he discovers it must originally have been a privy but is now empty, with nowhere for a man to hide. He hears footsteps outside getting closer and closer, and with great presence of mind and inventiveness, he grits his teeth, curls into a ball, and disappears into the cesspit. In the past, the Minister's Residence was a well-populated place, and the plants and trees in the garden needed a lot of fertiliser, so the cesspit is considerably larger than average. At the bottom is a brick-faced runnel, the height of a man, which is not blocked off but runs into the cesspool outside. Zhou Si is in luck, as the privy has been out of use for many years, and the leftover shit has all dried up. It trembles slightly as he steps on it, but he doesn't sink in. In the past, if it hadn't covered his head, it would have come up at least to his waist. Even so, after macerating for many years, the smell is almost bad enough to make him faint away. But at a time like this, he is not going to let a little stench get the better of him. He hears the door open up above him and shelters under the plank floor, pressing himself to the wall of the pit, wishing he could disappear into the cracks.

Up above, someone comes in, and soon a stream of piss descends, soaking Zhou Si from head to toe.

A voice asks from outside: "What is it?" The voice belongs to Qi Yuexuan.

"Ha! It's nothing," Gao Guigeng says. "That net just fell over."

"Nothing's good. You and Hao Bingchen rest up in the northern room. There's tea in the pot. I won't stay with you. The viewing is still going on out there."

"That's fine, we're family. There's no need to stand on ceremony. You go and do what you have to."

"I'll bolt the courtyard door from the outside. It'll be safer. You just stay back here, and I'll send Wangtian in with some dinner for you."

"Fine. As for Chenglong..."

"There's plenty of time. He's got to come back here to sleep, and it won't hurt for you to have a bit of dinner."

So saying, Qi Yuexuan hurries out of the courtyard, and even after the sound of the bolt being dropped and the lock turned, the same stream is still falling on Zhou Si's head.

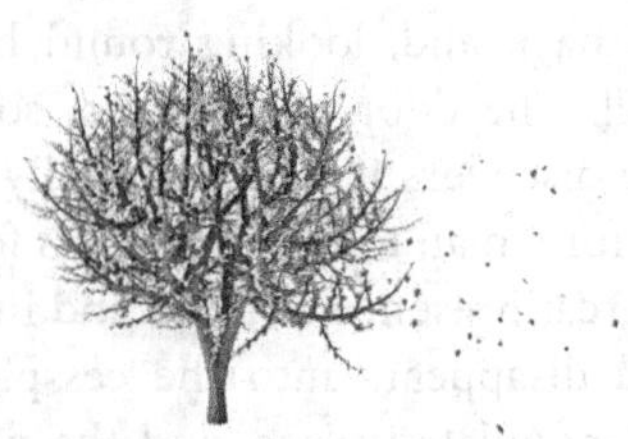

Chapter 51

When Chenglong is ordered by Qi Yuexuan to go home, he walks straight over to his place in the western side courtyard, collapses on his bed and falls sleep. His promise to return to the main courtyard in a while was really just for show, and he actually has no intention of doing so. Based on his knowledge of Yamaguchi's character, he is pretty sure of how that little scene is going to play out. On this occasion, playing dumb and hiding out is an awful lot better than bursting in on whatever is going on back there and delivering himself a slap in the face. But he has only been asleep a couple of hours, when one of his underlings wakes him up.

"I've only just got to sleep. If it's just some pissing little affair, why don't you see to it yourself? I've got to stay awake all night tonight keeping vigil, haven't I!"

"It's not something I can handle, captain. It's the Young Mistress's father who says he's got to see you. He says something big has happened."

Chenglong hasn't had a chance to reply, when Sergeant Lian himself comes running into the room and snuffles out: "It's... it's awful, Master Liu!"

Chenglong sits up and gestures to the original messenger to leave, before asking: "So, what's happened, then?"

Sergeant Lian sighs deeply: "Ai! What do you think has happened after you brought that Japanese back home for a drink, and then left and didn't come back! Yuxiang has been... defiled by him again."

Of course, this is exactly what Chenglong expected, but outwardly he looks shocked and expresses his anger: "What? Is that true? I'd just hurried back home for the funeral. I'd had a lot to drink, and thought I'd have a little rest before going back. This Yamaguchi fellow has really gone too far this time. Fuck it! You go home, I'll go fetch the Kempeitai and you just watch how I deal with him!"

When Sergeant Lian sees Chenglong stand up to go, he says urgently: "That Japanese... he's in hospital at the moment."

"What? Is Yuxiang hurt?"

"Ah, it's not Yuxiang, it's that Japanese fellow. He's... he's had his head broken open."

"Was it... was it Yuxiang who hit him?"

"She's not that fierce!"

"Then was it you?"

"Aiyo! I don't have the nerve. It was me who took him to hospital."

Chenglong is getting really angry and agitated now, as he glares at Sergeant Lian and yells: "Spit it out! Who hit him? What exactly happened?"

It was Clown. Not long after Chenglong left, Yamaguchi's true nature asserted itself, and he started to molest Yuxiang. She resisted, and he tried to rape her. Of course, she was unable to struggle free of him, but by great good chance, before the deed was done, Clown arrived. As soon as he heard Yuxiang's wails, he rushed into the room. Surprised to see a Japanese, he held his hand, not daring to attack him, giving Yamaguchi the chance to deliver a kick to the pit of the stomach that sent him tumbling out of the room and unable to get back to his feet immediately. To Yamaguchi's surprise, however, hearing Yuxiang's piteous screams, Clown found the strength to scramble back up, snatch up a lump of brick, and hurl himself back into the room. Before Yamaguchi could react, the brick smashed into the back of his head. Realising what a disaster this was, Clown fled, no one knows where, taking Yuxiang with him. Yuxiang's little sister fetched Sergeant Lian from the night soil depot, and he took Yamaguchi to the hospital.

Chenglong is somewhat perturbed when he hears all this, and he asks hurriedly: "Is he... is he badly hurt?"

"Not too badly. He's had a belt on the back of the head and has a bit of a cut, but when he came to, there wasn't anything too much wrong with him. I wanted to take him to the Japanese hospital, but he wouldn't go, so I had to take him to a nearby private clinic. He didn't even need an injection. They just put some antiseptic on and bandaged him up. The doctor said there was a chance he might have a slight concussion, and he made him lie down again to keep him under observation. He'd had a lot to drink, and he slept like a pig as soon as his back hit the bed. That's when I came here to see you, to ask you what to do."

Chenglong relaxes when he hears Sergeant Lian's account, but even so, his carefully laid plans have gone awry, and he is annoyed that he has wasted all that effort and still not exacted revenge. He frowns deeply but doesn't say anything.

"What can we do about all this, Master Liu?" Sergeant Lian asks cautiously.

Chenglong considers the matter for a while, then gives a wry laugh: "So what's to be done? You think this is a simple matter? That Yamaguchi fellow is a captain in the Kempeitai, so just you think about that."

"Then..."

"But I'm not saying it's impossible. It's just... a question of what it's worth to you."

"How... how much money will it take?"

"You think this is a matter of money? If you want to square it with him, first you'll have to hand over the attacker. Clown is only a worker at our night soil depot, isn't he? You don't have to worry about him, do you?"

"True, but... the fellow did save Yuxiang's life, and that makes him..."

"Ha! Your daughter's been abducted, and all you can do is make a joke of it. Is your whole family asking for trouble?"

Sergeant Lian doesn't say any more and just gives a hollow little laugh.

Chenglong continues: "Alright, let's forget about the niceties. Why don't you just carry the can, and go and hand yourself in to the Kempeitai?"

Sergeant Lian doesn't dare follow up this suggestion but just mutters cautiously: "But... he's run away. Where... where am I going to find him?"

"Pah! How far can he have got? Do you think he's disappeared off the face of the earth? Security outside the city is really tight now, and you need a pass to leave. Did he just take wing and fly away?"

So saying, Chenglong shouts out "Come here", and one of his underlings enters the room in response. Chenglong whispers something in his ear, and the man nods and hurries out.

Seeing this, Sergeant Lian says in a panic: "Yuxiang is with him. For heaven's sake, don't..."

"Ha! What's your problem? Do you think that little bastard is such a fearsome enemy we're going to need weapons? Don't worry, Yuxiang will be home before dark."

"That's fine, if that's really the case. I'll..."

"What? Do you think that's all there is to it?"

"Well... isn't it? Then..." Sergeant Lian is completely out of his depth.

Chenglong shoots a sidelong look at him and laughs softly: "You've been around long enough, and you still haven't figured this thing out? Yamaguchi isn't going to want this affair made public, as a matter of face. And he's afraid people will find out his weak spot. But if he keeps his fury to himself, and looks for revenge secretly, that will be much worse than if it's all out in the open. You'll never feel safe."

"Aiyo, are you saying if I just hand Clown over, then..."

"Do you think it's that simple? He was attacked in your home, and he knows that Clown is one of my men, so we're both in the same boat. Is he going to believe any explanation you give him? And as for me, he's bound to suspect some kind of behind-the-scenes conspiracy."

"Then," says Sergeant Lian, changing tack, "wasn't he the one who started it, so we've got right on our side?"

"And how far do you think you'll get talking about right and wrong with the Japanese?"

"Then... we've still got you, haven't we? You must..."

"What is it, exactly, you want me to do? Take him to court or fight him to the death? Pah! I've already spent a small fortune keeping you and your family in bed and board, and now she's got herself mixed up with some low-life ruffian who plays the knight errant and elopes with her, cuckolding me, and you still want me to come rushing to the rescue? Think again!"

Sergeant Lian breaks out in a cold sweat.

"So... what are you saying we should do?"

"Well, vegetables are vegetables, whichever way you slice them, but you should try and suit them to his taste."

"I... I don't quite understand."

Chenglong gives a crafty little laugh: "Ha! Surely you don't need me to explain it to you! You're just playing dumb with me, aren't you?"

"No, no, I really don't understand."

"Haven't you considered that, if something is salty, it's because you've added salt, and if something is vinegary, it's because you've added vinegar? Where did all this trouble start."

"Are you talking about Yuxiang?"

"Hmm."

"I should order her to marry that... that Japanese?" Sergeant Lian stares at Chenglong, wide-eyed.

Chenglong gives a little grunt of amusement. "There's no need for marriage, and even if you suggested it, he wouldn't have the balls. No, you just have to turn a blind eye if he comes round to your place from time to time."

Sergeant Lian is dumbfounded, and he stares at Chenglong.

"You... you mean..." He stops short and stays silent for a long time, before choking out: "Isn't that... a bit... generous?"

Chenglong looks sidelong at him and his grin is even more chilling. "Generous? Yes, I think that's the right word, but maybe you'd like me to be a bit meaner? Alright then, when that adulterous pair have been caught and brought back, I'll hand you over to the Kempeitai along with them, for aiding and abetting. If a charge of taking revenge for a little amorous dalliance isn't serious enough for you, perhaps you'd prefer one of organising an anti-Japanese cell..."

"No! No, don't!" Sergeant Lian is panicked, and his voice turns into a wail. "Master Liu, I... I am outraged on your behalf. However you look at it, Yuxiang is your woman, and it's up to you to beat her and curse her as you see fit. I won't say a word. But even though that Japanese is an animal, how can you..."

"Ha! There are things you can't do, and there are things I can't do. Haven't you heard the saying: 'I would betray the nation rather than lose my personal power'? In any case, I never brought your daughter formally into the Liu family, so what obligation do I have to act correctly towards her? For old times' sake, I'll find a way out for you, so once the main problem's disappeared, you won't have to worry. But if I just shrug my shoulders and do as I please, you'll be in a whole heap of trouble, won't you?"

Sergeant Lian stares at him dumbly, the corners of his mouth twitching his cheeks as if in spasm. If it weren't for the twin tears rolling down from his eyes, it might look as though he is sniggering.

"Enough of this! Get over to the hospital, quick as you can, and see what's going on," Chenglong says, fishing out a roll of banknotes and handing it to Sergeant Lian. "I've got to wait here for further news. If he wakes up, tell him what I've said. It will be much better coming from you, rather than me. Do you need me to go over it with you again?"

"No, no. I've got it." The sight of the money has made Sergeant Lian a lot more amenable. With his wits sharpened, he acknowledges the instructions and leaves the room.

THAT EVENING, as night falls, there is still no sign of Chenglong coming back to keep vigil, even when Yue E goes over to the western courtyard to look for him. When asked where he has gone, his men hum and haw and just say he had urgent business, but they don't know what or where. Everyone is furious when they hear the news she brings back, but the sight of Yue E's pent-up emotion and her tearful countenance makes them restrain their curses, and no one utters a single word of censure. To their surprise, this just seems to increase Yue E's misery, and she weeps inconsolably.

Seeing her suffering, Qi Yuexuan hurries over, but before he can open his mouth, she raises her tear-stained face and says: "Father, I can't put up with Chenglong another day. He just gets more and more inhuman. He hasn't even made a single kowtow after my father's death. My father showed him a thousand kindnesses, but none of them are worth as much as a single word from a Japanese. If I have to put up with him a moment more, he will drive me mad. You are my birth father, so you must act for me and make him write a letter of divorce. I don't even care if it has to go to court. All I want is my two children. You… you have to agree…" Before she can finish, the two children at her side begin to wail.

"Yes, yes, I agree," Qi Yuexuan says hurriedly. He bends down and pulls the children into his embrace, one on either side. "Don't worry. The Qi family has a great scholarly reputation and we cannot possibly allow such a disloyal and unfilial fellow to be part of us. Nonetheless, ah…"

He hesitates a moment, then continues: "You are living together as husband and wife, and you have a son and a daughter, and you can only take this step as a last resort if there is absolutely no remedy to the situation. Since he is the children's natural father, it is not just up to you. The whole family must try their best to draw him back in, and give him a chance to change."

"Of course I have given him that chance, Father. I have tried every persuasion I can think of, but he'll have none of it. I am a tolerant woman, but…"

"I understand all that." Qi Yuexuan pats Yue E on the shoulder. "Yue E, although we have only just properly become father and daughter, as a father, I fully understand your suffering, and I feel truly sorry for you. However, although you have been through so much already, you must endure for one last time.

Uncle Yang is still laid out here, and even though you have been further wronged, you must wait, and we will discuss it later."

Yue E doesn't offer any more argument but just weeps incessantly.

Qi Yuexuan turns to the other mourners and says: "Alright, we have been here all day, and everyone must be tired. The night vigil is the job of the menfolk. All the women and children should go home and get some rest."

At this, Caiping helps Mother Yan out of the room, but Yue E has only taken a couple of steps with the children, before she turns and says: "I will come back once the children are asleep, Father."

"No, no. Women can't keep vigil at night. We mustn't break the rules. It doesn't matter whether Chenglong comes or not, I've still got Wangtian to keep me company. Off you go now. Take the children and get some proper sleep."

Wangtian watches Yue E and the children out of the room, then goes over close to Qi Yuexuan and whispers: "Are you still going to keep my father and Mr Hao waiting, Young Master?"

Qi Yuexuan takes out his pocket watch and looks at it.

"It's already ten-thirty. Why should we wait until twelve? Earlier today, Chenglong guaranteed he was going to come and keep vigil. Here, this is the key to the rear garden. All's quiet, so go and ask your father and Hao Bingchen to come over here now. I've only managed to snatch a couple of words with them so far, and now we can sit and talk properly in the study."

Wangtian acknowledges his instructions and leaves the room. He is only just out of the door when he hears a rumble of thunder from the sky, and the rain that has held off all day finally begins to fall. It's only light at first, but it gets harder and harder, so that the water flowing down off the roofs is soon an unbroken curtain, and the floor of the courtyard becomes an expanse of puddles.

When Qi Yuexuan sees the rain, he strolls outside hoping to take advantage of the break in the sultriness of the day. As he stands on the veranda, he sees someone come running in from the front courtyard. Whoever it is doesn't use the shelter of the covered walkways, but runs straight across the courtyard, his feet making 'plopping' sounds in the puddles. It is only when he climbs the steps up onto the veranda, that Qi Yuexuan sees it is Chenglong.

"So... now you come?" Qi Yuexuan says furiously.

Chenglong wipes the rain from his head and face and says: "I... I know... I'm a bit late, but I came as quick as I could. I had urgent business. Something I couldn't get out of. It's really..."

"And just what can be more important than the death of a revered family member? The Japanese have lots of other underlings, but you only had one friend like Uncle Yang. So just ask yourself honestly whether you're proud of your behaviour."

Chenglong ignores the reproach, as he really has been more than busy enough himself. He has waited the whole afternoon in vain for any news from his men, and it is only as night falls that he gets a telephone call from the checkpoint at the

Guang'an Gate informing him that Yuxiang and Clown have been arrested. He orders them to bring Yuxiang home, and puts a sentry at the main gate, in case she tries to run away again. Then he leads some of his men in person, to ingratiate himself by presenting Clown to Yamaguchi. Although Yamaguchi's jaws are clenched in fury, he doesn't want the whole shameful affair made public, and he declines to take Clown to the Kempeitai. It is Chenglong's idea to pretend Clown has cholera and take him to the quarantine unit. The whole of Beiping knows it to be a place you enter alive and come out dead. Although a man may go in hale and hearty, he can scarcely expect ever to emerge from this sinister and vicious building. Chenglong has only come over to the Minister's Residence once he is sure everything has been arranged satisfactorily, but he is hardly going to be willing to talk openly about such a wicked deed.

"So... now you're here, hurry up and put on your mourning clothes and go and kowtow to your father-in-law as custom dictates," Qi Yuexuan orders him.

Chenglong burbles his agreement and follows Qi Yuexuan into the funeral hall. Once he has put on his mourning gown, he kneels in front of the bier and kowtows three times to Yang Zhixing.

Qi Yuexuan watches him stand back up and then points to one side, indicating that Chenglong should stand on the left-hand side of the bier, so that the two of them are facing each other a few paces apart. Chenglong can see that Qi Yuexuan has something to say to him, but no words are spoken. Qi Yuexuan stares at him long and hard, making him as uncomfortable as if little insects were crawling all over his face.

Finally, Qi Yuexuan opens his mouth: "Time passes very quickly. Twenty years have gone by in the twinkling of an eye. When I look at you, I can still see the road in Dezhou Town, with your mother and old Mr Zhang taking you to protest the injustice perpetrated on your father. You must have been, what, ten years old?"

"Yes, that's right. Ten by the old way of reckoning."

When he realises that Qi Yuexuan is no longer admonishing him, but recalling old times, Chenglong begins to relax and says with a smile: "If we hadn't bumped into you then, we wouldn't even have seen the county magistrate, let alone got such a light sentence for my father."

Qi Yuexuan shakes his head. "It was nothing to do with me. It was because your father was innocent. All he did was take the lead in borrowing some grain to save the lives of his fellow countrymen. Where is the crime in that? Even that lenient judgment was an injustice, and he only received it because of the machinations of a petty little man. Ai..."

Qi Yuexuan's words revive a long-dormant grievance in Chenglong's heart, making him frown and lower his head.

Qi Yuexuan continues gently: "Now, more than twenty years on, you are grown up. You have married and set up a business. You are a father too, but how many close family members have you lost? Your father, your mother, your uncle, your cousin, not to mention your master. And now, here is your father-in-law lying in front of you. Ah, Chenglong! You must remember how each of them died."

"You don't have to worry. How could I forget?" Chenglong replies emotionally.

"So, you haven't forgotten?" Qi Yuexuan gives a hollow laugh and stares fixedly at him. "Then why have you not been able to wash away their blood that is still gumming up your eyes?"

Chenglong knows what he is about to say, so he lowers his head and doesn't reply.

Qi Yuexuan sweeps his gaze over him and continues: "Let me tell you something – I didn't ask you here today just to keep vigil. I want a clarification from you."

"What kind of clarification?"

"Who exactly do you recognise as your father?"

"What are you up to? A man can't just randomly acknowledge anyone as their father..."

"I've heard you call me 'Father' only when you're angry, resentful and stressed. If I'm to be that kind of father, it's not worth a Japanese fart. So who really is your father? I am not the only one asking you this. Today, I have brought together several old comrades you have called 'Father'. Here is your birth father."

So saying Qi Yuexuan pulls the black cloth of a memorial tablet on the altar table.

Neatly inscribed on it are the words: 'This tablet is a memorial to the Honoured Liu Kunzhu.' Even in his dreams, Chenglong could not have expected to see his father's memorial tablet in this place, and he drops to his knees with a thud.

Qi Yuexuan points at the bier: "Uncle Yang lies there, I am standing here and your foster-father Gao Guigeng is standing behind you."

Chenglong gives a frightened yelp and turns to look. He sees three men standing in the doorway, just as the one in the middle steps over the threshold and advances towards him. He blinks several times, like a cat that has trodden on its own tail, gives a shout of surprise and is about to jump to his feet. To his surprise, the man is quicker than him, and in one swift stride is standing before him. He pins him, top and bottom, and forces him to keep kneeling.

It is Gao Guigeng.

"Do you truly not recognise me, boy?" he asks, increasing the pressure on Chenglong's shoulder.

"Aiyo! Is it... is it really you, Father? You're not..."

"No, I'm certainly not dead!" Gao Guigeng laughs and relaxes his grip. "Have a proper look, and see whether I'm an imposter or not."

Chenglong scrambles to his feet and scrutinises Gao Guigeng's face. In a moment, his eyes fill with tears, and he cries out: "Father!"

"Come in. We have things to talk about," Qi Yuexuan calls out from beside them, and Hao Bingchen and Wangtian, who are still standing in the doorway, make their way in.

Chenglong doesn't move, his eyes fixed on the sidearm at Gao Guigeng's waist. "Father," he says, "you... are you now..."

Gao Guigeng grins and pats him on the shoulder: "Our paths have crossed before. Have you forgotten that box of pastries?"

"The... the Traitor Elimination Squad?"

"That's right."

Chenglong's face loses all its colour, and his legs go so weak he almost falls to his knees again. There is almost a sob in his voice as he exclaims: "Father, I'm not... I'm not really on the side of the Japanese, I..."

"Enough!" Gao Guigeng interrupts him fiercely. "Show a little backbone. I've come here today to show you the right path, and see whether you take it or not."

"I will, I will! Of course, I'll listen to you."

THE FIRST GLIMMER OF DAWN is showing when the rain finally stops. The small courtyard of Li Fenggu's house is still brightly lit. The lamps are showing not only in the main room; even the ones at the gate, in the yard itself, in the kitchen and the privy are all glowing. A record is playing on the gramophone in Li Fenggu's room in the northern range. It is of songs she herself has recorded, and it has been playing over and over all night. She is not playing it for anyone else, but only because she is afraid. She lit all the lamps to bolster her courage in the dark of the night and is playing the songs to attract company. She hasn't seen Zhou Si since the previous day. She has asked the other members of his team many times, but they all say they haven't seen him. They have searched everywhere he might have gone but found no sign of him. She keeps remembering what Caiping said outside the funeral hall, and the more she thinks about it, the more frightened she becomes. She orders her old servant woman to lock the front gate, bolt the door to her room and light all the lamps. She herself sits next to the gramophone, her eyes wide open. Even in the height of summer she is cold, and she shivers uncontrollably, despite being wrapped in a quilt. If she can get through the night, in the morning she is going to go and lodge a formal complaint.

Suddenly there is a thud from outside, as though a heavy weight has been dropped on the ground. It's so loud that even the gramophone at top volume doesn't drown it out. Mustering her courage, Li Fenggu pulls aside the window curtain to look. Shit! There's a man lying at the bottom of the wall, as though he has just jumped down from on top of it. Her nerves have been stretched taut all night, and this shock is too much for her. She puts her hands over her head and screams like a banshee.

"Don't scream, it's me!" Zhou Si calls out from the courtyard.

When Li Fenggu recovers herself and sees it is indeed Zhou Si, it is like a whirlwind being unleashed.

"What! There's a perfectly good gate, but you have to come over the wall like a thief? Well, fuck you!"

"Stop talking crap." Zhou Si glares and yells back even louder than her. "I've been banging on the gate half the night, but you didn't hear me. You've been making more noise than a broken bass drum. Is someone paying you to sing those songs all evening?"

Li Fenggu almost chokes in amazement at the normally timid mouse, Zhou Si, shouting the odds like this. She gets down from the *kang* and opens the door. She is still in no mood to listen to excuses, but she modifies her tone a little.

"What kind of impudence is this, treating your old lady like that? Where do you think you are? A carters' tavern or a low-grade cathouse? Where the fuck have you been? I've lost a whole night's sleep, worrying that you might be lying dead in a ditch, heaven knows where."

Zhou Si doesn't reply but just limps into the room, his clothes dripping wet. He plonks himself down on a chair by the *kang* and turns off the gramophone.

"That's enough yelling. Hurry up and get me something to eat, I'm starving."

So saying, he picks up a white porcelain teapot from the table and drinks from it as thirstily as an ox at a cattle trough.

"Shit! What have you been up to? Have you been working as a coolie for someone? Even if they didn't feed you, they must at least have given you something to drink!"

Zhou Si puts down the teapot and wipes his mouth. He takes a deep breath and stands tall, slapping his pigeon chest: "Hah! I'll tell you what I've been up to. I've been up to something big, something heroic, all by myself. I've done us a great service. This time, I haven't been hanging on anyone else's coat tails, it's been all my own work, and I've done it fair and square."

Li Fenggu looks at him askance: "Oh yes? And where did you go to sleep it off?"

"What? You don't believe me? Do you really have such a low opinion of me?"

"Oh, it's not that I have a low opinion of you. It's just that you're like a dung beetle on a railway line – you think you've got it made, but you get squashed flat by the train when it passes."

"Eh? You..." Zhou Si's face contorts with anger.

Li Fenggu grunts and is about to say something more, when she suddenly frowns and wrinkles her nose: "Aiyo! Why do you stink like that? Did you fall into a cesspit or something?"

Zhou Si laughs indifferently and makes a show of kicking his shoes off into the doorway. As he strips off the rest of his clothes, he says: "Ha! You've hit the nail on the head. I really did have to hide out in a cess pit for a while. So don't stare at me like that, and it's no use complaining about the smell. If it wasn't for that cess pit, we wouldn't be in the strong position we are now. In fact, I'd be dead. So if I'm smelly now, just live with it. You'll think it's the finest perfume once the Imperial Army have rewarded me with a promotion and great handfuls of silver!"

"Is that... is that all true?" Li Fenggu is beginning to believe him. "Tell me quick, what is this great service you have done?"

"Aiyo!" Zhou Si gives a wry laugh. "Get me something to eat first, alright? I'm so hungry my ribs are sticking to my spine. Where's your reward going to come from if you let me starve to death?"

Li Fenggu takes a tray of pastries out of the cupboard and puts it on the table.

"Get some food inside you and talk as you eat. Don't keep me in suspense, and forget the pregnant pauses if you care anything for me. Tell me quick and tell me the truth. If I like what I hear, I'll take you to a restaurant in a while. But if you're just spouting bullshit, don't be surprised if I strip you naked and throw you out on the street."

Zhou Si is wolfing down the food but clears his mouth long enough to say: "Lord Matsuzaki said that the consequences of this affair are so important, I've got to keep quiet about it. If you know what's good for you, you're better off not hearing about it."

"What? You won't even tell me?" Li Fenggu is so angry, she covers the tray of pastries and takes it away. "Hah! If you're going to mock me by lying to me, you might at least make it convincing!"

"Don't do that!" Zhou Si snatches back the tray of pastries. "Alright, I'll tell you a bit about it, but you've got to keep quiet. If word gets out, it's not just the Japanese who'll never forgive me. Chenglong himself will be the first one after my hide."

"Why does everything seem to come back to him?"

"Ah well, this is all about him. And this time, I think I've really got him where I want him. He's hand in glove with the military intelligence's Traitor Elimination Squad, and they're going to assassinate my new patron, Mr Zhou Zhengjie."

"What? How do you know?"

"Well, I was hiding in the rear yard of the Minister's Residence, and the gate was locked so I couldn't get out. But that worked out really well for me because I could see and hear everything from outside the window. Guess who it was I saw!"

"How should I know?"

"It was Chenglong's foster-father, that Gao Guigeng who used to have a night soil route."

"But he's dead, isn't he?"

"No, he's not. And what's more, he's now the leader of the Traitor Elimination Squad. His elder son and Young Master Qi are mixed up in this too. This time I've got Chenglong's whole family. Once I got out over the wall, I went straight to Lord Matsuzaki to make a report."

"Then why didn't the Japanese go and arrest them immediately?"

"Ah, Lord Matsuzaki is too shrewd to do that. He's biding his time, but I didn't dare try to listen to what he has planned. My guess is he's waiting to scoop the whole lot up together. You see, the day after tomorrow, the Minister's Residence will be holding the funeral. They'll open up the ancestral temple and the place will be heaving."

Li Fenggu laughs delightedly: "Ha ha, I think you've got it. You finish your snack, clean yourself up and have a nap. At lunchtime, I'll stand you a celebratory feast."

"That's fine, but for heaven's sake don't spread it about. Don't get too cocky and lose your head!"

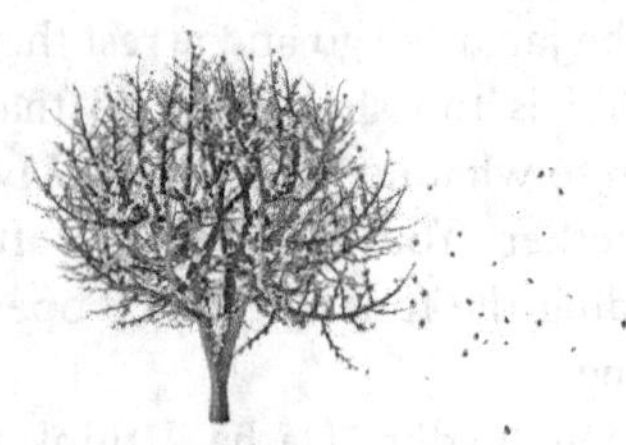

Chapter 52

Before eight o'clock on the morning of the third day, Minister's Residence Hutong is already full of people come for the funeral procession, and they stretch from the front gates of the Residence all the way to the hutong's eastern entrance. Following the rules of the banners, the procession is headed by a sixteen-man banner frame, displaying the Bordered-Yellow Banner of the deceased. They are closely followed by two gate-shaped banners also bearing the Bordered-Yellow Banner. Behind that come: eight 'spear banners'; seven pairs of ceremonial maces; pairs of banners representing the Flying Bear, the Flying Tiger and the Flying Fish; a 'clear-the-road' gong; a large-bodied 'hall drum'; a parasol; a palace fan and a troupe of musicians. Only after that come the palanquin carrying the funeral director and the coffin itself, along with several horse-drawn passenger carts and, finally, the large group of family and friends who are mourning the deceased.

During the Qing dynasty, the requirements for a bannerman's funeral were even more complex, and this procession is missing a number of things: the 'portrait pavilion'; the 'welcoming-the-spirit sedan'; the 'memorial of merit stele'; the broadsword; the spear; the sword; the halberd; the whip; the staff; the rake; two executioners carrying 'ghost-despatching broadswords' and a youth known as the 'Young Bearer' who carries the deceased's personal possessions. It also proves more convenient to omit the hawks on perches, the hunting dogs, the camels and other such beasts, along with the paper models of people, horses and carriages; otherwise the whole procession would be more than doubled in length.

Yue E is standing at the head of the column of mourners, carrying an earthenware basin and a white-shrouded mourning staff. Since the Yang family has no male heir, she has to take the role of the filial son. Behind her are her two children: the deceased's grandson, Xinliang, carries the memorial tablet and his granddaughter, Liangxin, carries Yang Zhixing's portrait. Mother Yan has allowed Caiping to lend her an arm for support, and stands side-by-side with Qi Yuexuan right in the middle of the column. The couplets on the long banners in front of and behind the coffin are written by Qi Yuexuan, and the huge black calligraphy on the white cloth is particularly eye-catching. The front banners read: 'Heaven is blind as the devils come from the east like a terrifying dream. My heart is my memorial tablet as righteous men carry my story west to countless listeners.' The rear banners read: 'In life a servant but never of a servant's nature, he never begged for food when he had none, but his life was not mean and lowly. Although he has no descendants of his own, he has left behind a family flourishing without end. Even in death, his reputation continues.'

As soon as the banners are unfurled, there is a gasp from the waiting crowd, and tongues begin to wag. Yang Zhixing's refusal to enter the Japanese hospital or use Japanese drugs had very quickly ceased to be a secret and soon became common knowledge. Of course, with so many in attendance at the funeral, there are many complete strangers among them, and what has brought them is this unquenchable moral integrity. It also encourages them to bawl and wail to their hearts' content, giving vent to the anger that has been pent up inside them since the occupation of Beiping.

There is no sign of Lao Zhang, Wangtian or Chenglong among the principal family mourners, but the three of them are not idle; they have other arrangements to make. Before the coffin can be buried, the grave has to be dug. Lao Zhang is in charge of this task, and the afternoon of the previous day he has taken some men to Laoqiying. So many strangers line the route of the procession that they have to erect tea stalls along the roadside, and Wangtian has set out in the middle of the night with horse carts full of furniture to get things organised in advance. Chenglong is present when the body is put in the coffin, and still there when the coffin is sealed, but he doesn't join the precession and is nowhere to be seen when the coffin leaves the Residence. This is because, at noon, he will have to be on duty looking after not only the leading members of the Green Society in Beiping, but also the Japanese he feels must be included, whom he has personally invited to attend the celebratory post-funeral feast. It is not usual for the participants in the funeral procession and the guests at the funerary banquet to be split into two groups, but on this occasion, there is no alternative. After all, they cannot simply ignore those VIPs, even including the Japanese, who come to offer gifts and show their respects, but the mourners in the procession are made up of Yang Zhixing's friends and relatives, who all hate the Japanese, and the two groups cannot possibly be brought together. This is why alternative arrangements have been made for the funerary feast.

Right at the auspicious hour of eight o'clock, Qi Yuexuan steps out of the throng and stands on the threshold of the Minister's Residence. In a loud, solemn voice he calls out: "Friends, fellow clansmen, gentlemen!"

Normally, the job of delivering the opening speech belongs to the funeral director, but Qi Yuexuan is worried someone else's words will be too old-fashioned and formulaic, so he has taken it on himself.

"As unexpected as snow in June, or a clap of thunder from a clear sky, our honoured Yang Zhixing has sadly departed this world. The central column of our household has collapsed. Family members have lost a beloved husband and a compassionate father. The world has lost a noble and upright man. Just like the old elm tree at the gates of this Residence, he made money, he managed money, but he did not covet money. It is hard to believe, but although tens of thousands of yuan have passed through his hands, he could walk the street untouched by corruption. He had the chance to save his own life, but he did not wish to live with his name sullied or tarnished. If he had to go, he preferred to go pure and undefiled, calm and at peace with himself. Maybe his death has nothing of the moving and tragic about it, but in my heart I see him as a Qu Yuan to the common people, a Jing Ke[1] to the masses. The noble Yang Zhixing knows the generosity of spirit with which you have all assembled here to send him on his way, and he is grateful for it. Please now accept our kowtows in gratitude for your kind intentions."

So saying, he falls to his knees, his pale, drawn face already streaked with tears. Mother Yan, Yue E and the children immediately kneel down as well, and together, kowtow three times to the assembled company. In doing this, Qi Yuexuan is simply following ancient custom, as this is called 'saluting the coffin and acknowledging grace'. Those at whom it is directed must accept it without response. Even though the mood today is a little unusual, other than the spasmodic sobbing from some of the official mourners, the hutong is completely silent, with scarcely even the sound of breathing to be heard.

Qi Yuexuan slowly gets to his feet, hesitates a moment, then raises his left arm and shouts: "Lift the coffin!"

There follows the combined sound of three strokes on the nine-tone gongs, a roll from the split-stick drum, the sonorous call of the copper horn and the high-pitched wail of the *suona*. At the same time, the sound of weeping and moaning rises from the crowd of mourners: rhythmic sobbing, deep groans and howling wails, first like a solemn, tragic symphony, then a surging tide of unbridled grief. The noise startles the crows in the trees and the pigeons on the rooftops, making them take wing and circle round the empty sky.

"The fares and tolls to the underworld have been paid," calls out the man carrying the pole garlanded with paper money. "Master Qi has given one hundred and twenty strings of cash!"

One voice starts and many others chime in: "Paid! One hundred and twenty strings of cash!"

As they shout, they leap about energetically, throwing sheet after sheet of paper money up into the air, higher and higher. The money flies in all directions, swirling and fluttering, shining white, filling the sky and covering the ground.

The team of pall-bearers proceeds slowly forwards, moving out of the western end of Minister's Residence Hutong, and turning onto Houmen Avenue. They turn west at the Drum Tower and follow Old Drum Tower Avenue towards the Desheng Gate. The cortege stops at every crossroads and proceeds only after the mourners have made offerings. It is only four or five *li* to the city gate, but the procession takes more than an hour to get there. Funerary music plays all the way, and the wailing continues without cease. Passers-by on the street stop and stand around to watch, blocking the avenue so tightly even water couldn't get through. Many of them find their interest aroused, and they join in the procession. The sound of car horns from vehicles stuck on the road only adds to the noise and the general pandemonium. When they reach the Desheng Gate, the Japanese guards at the checkpoint there inspect everyone's passes and even ask to see certificates of good citizenship. But they have only inspected a few of them when they have to give up, as the crowd behind surges forward, swamping the Japanese soldiers and the plain-clothes CID men, and leaving them in a pitiful state.

THE VENUE for the post-funeral feast is none other than Xiao Yuerong's Yuerong's Place. The restaurant is only two storeys, and Xiao Yuerong knows the kind of people who will be turning up that day, so he simply closes the place to passing trade at lunchtime. Swallowing the loss of an empty restaurant is still better than having to bear the consequences of something untoward taking place. Chenglong has arrived early and is waiting at the restaurant. He hasn't seen anyone important arrive yet, but his heart is already pounding. That evening, he had promised his foster father Gao Guigeng that he would renounce the dark and turn to the light. On the spot, he had filled in a form to join the military intelligence apparatus, signed it and applied his thumbprint. He had also agreed to help them eliminate Zhou Zhengjie as an initiation gift to military intelligence. The ad hoc Government of North China have decided to call a meeting at half past ten the next morning, at the Imperial Ancestral Temple, entitled the North China All-Province News Reporting Conference, at which many representatives of newspapers and periodicals are to be present. After the opening of the conference, there will be a welcome lunch. Zhou Zhengjie is there as a representative of the government executive, but the security staff at the venue are organised by Chenglong, and the guards are all members of his Special Operations Squad. Hao Bingchen and Gao Guigeng have arranged a small group from the Traitor Elimination Squad to infiltrate the conference disguised as reporters. Each of the men is to wear a gold badge in the shape of a sailboat on their breast as a distinguishing mark. Gao Guigeng immediately volunteered to lead the group himself. There is no way for Chenglong to participate in the actual assassination, and all he has to do to discharge his responsibility is to arrange for reliable men to allow the group in without inspection. Chenglong readily agrees to this, chooses his most trusted men and puts everything in place. Arranging this funerary feast today has two purposes other than maintaining proper appearances. One is to avoid suspicion, so when such a major event takes place he has the excuse of being elsewhere; the other is to keep several key VIPs busy at the party, so the agents back at the conference will have a greater degree of control. At this time, he has gone over everything in great detail in his head and is sure that he hasn't left any gaps in the arrangements. But his heart isn't going to stop pounding until it is all over.

CAN IT POSSIBLY BE that Chenglong has transformed overnight? Has he really repented and turned against the Japanese? Certainly not entirely. To say that he has set his heart on betraying China, and is completely unmoved by the death of his relatives, by the urgings of his relatives and by his reunion with his relatives, would be to wrong him. But equally, to say that these were sufficient to make him turn over a new leaf, would be to give him too much credit.

He had once privately said to Yue E: "I don't intend to be anybody's dog. I only want to make other people my dogs. But if push comes to shove, and it is all over for me if I don't, then I will be anybody's dog."

He may not normally be a particularly truthful person, but when it comes to this, these are indeed his true feelings. The reason he is so easily persuaded this time has more to do with it fitting in with his own plans, and working things out to his advantage. He knows what would happen if he didn't agree, and with his life in their hands, what else is he going to do? And if he is going to agree, what is the point of not doing so eagerly. Besides, he intends to hedge his bets and keep an escape route open. Doesn't this affair dovetail with his own plans precisely, anyway? Two wheels are always going to be more stable than one, and relying on your father has to be better than relying on a stranger. On top of all this, the Traitor Elimination Squad's assassination of Zhou Zhengjie will take one more obstacle out of his way, so even if it is a little risky, it will be worth it. So, Chenglong's intention is to be as meticulous as possible.

IT IS NOT YET TEN O'CLOCK when Matsuzaki Harayama's car arrives, also carrying Director Imai of the Tokko. What surprises Chenglong is that Zhou Si is in the same vehicle. Even Yamaguchi and various Kempeitai personnel are only riding in motorcycle sidecars, following on behind the limousine, so why has Zhou Si suddenly gone from bit part to leading role? The glint in his eye certainly suggests he is putting on airs rather. But Chenglong has no time to consider the matter more closely, as he hastily smiles and exchanges greetings before leading the group up to a private room on the upper floor. As he pours the tea, he also feels there is something odd about Yamaguchi's expression, but Matsuzaki's face remains unreadable as he chats away as good-humouredly as usual.

"Liu-san," Matsuzaki says as he takes a sip of tea, "I hear that Qi Yuexuan is your wife's natural father."

Chenglong is taken aback, but he smiles and says: "That's right. She only found out as her foster father was on his death bed. The news has certainly travelled fast if you know all about it. Nonetheless, the blessing of birth does not surpass the blessing of nurture, and that filial obligation must be fully acknowledged."

Matsuzaki nods and continues his enquiries: "And don't you yourself have a foster father?"

"Ah... yes, yes, his name is Gao Guigeng. He was a night soil collector, and he fostered me for several years. He died more than ten years ago. But... but you knew that already, didn't you?"

Matsuzaki stares at him, smiling: "Ah, this world is full of extraordinary things, and it could well be that your foster father is not actually dead, but has come back to life!"

Chenglong's heart lurches, but he just smiles more broadly: "If that turns out to be so, and he has clambered out of the grave, then I guarantee I will bring him straight to you. You... you need have no fear of that."

This prompts a burst of laughter, with Matsuzaki joining in as he takes another sip of tea. Chenglong glances sidelong and catches Zhou Si's eye. Zhou Si immediately looks away, his arrogance seeming to waver a little.

"Liu-san," Matsuzaki continues, "Mr Zhou Zhengjie has said he will definitely come, but he may be a little late. He has to wait for the conference to finish first."

"Aiya, I was worried about that. I didn't feel I knew Mr Zhou well enough, so I didn't tell him about this occasion." Chenglong laughs. "Well then... do you think we should wait for him before we start, or..."

"There's no need to wait for him specially," says Matsuzaki, waving his hand. "If everything is ready, then let's start a little early and hope that nothing happens to spoil everyone's enjoyment of the wine."

"Good! Good!" says Chenglong, and he hastily summons the waiters, ordering them to hurry up and pour the wine and lay out the food. As he closes the door, he snatches a look outside and sees that there seem to be several of the Tokko men who have not come in to the feast, but are standing outside on guard. Their eyes fix on him as he pulls the door to.

Chenglong feels even more uneasy, and he tries to use the excuse of his duties as host to go out and see what is going on. Just as he stands up, Matsuzaki seems to guess his intentions and says: "Liu-san, your men can look after the festivities out there. There's no need for you to go. Stay here and play host to this table." Although he is still smiling, there is something chilling about his tone.

Chenglong has no choice but to sit down, and instantly the mood in the room becomes very tense. Fortunately, the food and wine are served. Once the wine has been round a few times, Chenglong steals a look at his watch and sees it is already ten thirty-five. He realises that by now, Gao Guigeng and the others will already be in the conference hall and may be about to make their move. He, however, is in a distinctly ambivalent situation. He doesn't know yet how things will turn out, but he has no way of telling the assassins to stay their hands, even if he wanted to. As he thinks about it, his heart begins to pound even harder, and the sweat breaks out on his forehead. He tells himself to hold his nerve.

Nothing escapes Matsuzaki's shrewd eyes, and he asks with a wintery smile: "You seem a little distracted, Liu-san. Is there something else you need to be doing?"

"No, no, not at all," Chenglong says nervously, then hurriedly finds an excuse. "Ai! Things are a little unsettled outside the city at the moment, and I'm a little worried that the funeral procession..."

"I rather think that is not what you are worried about, is it? But there's no rush. Wipe the sweat off your face first."

Chenglong hastily wipes his face with the end of his sleeve. He forces a laugh, though all he wants to do is wail.

Taking no more notice of him, Matsuzaki raises his cup and turns to the others: "Gentlemen, Liu-san is in the chair today, so please, everyone enjoy yourselves."

When he sees the doubtful looks on their faces, he glances at Chenglong, then says with a smile: "We'll keep the secret a little longer then. That's fine, it will leave you all something to be amazed by. Come on now, drink up everybody!"

Everyone follows his example and drains their cups. Chenglong doesn't dare not join in, but he finds he can barely swallow the wine that he raises so nonchalantly to his lips.

At this moment, shouts can be heard from outside the room, loud and foul-mouthed. Yamaguchi flings open the door to reveal one of Chenglong's underlings, very drunk and determined to crash his way into the room, as the guards try unsuccessfully to restrain him.

"Yours is what's doing? Kill you kill you have!" Yamaguchi yells at the man, grasping his sword.

To his surprise, the man is not intimidated but stands up straight and shouts back: "You... you can't scare... scare me with that. I'm in charge now and I want to... to ask Liu Chenglong... ask him something. When I've finished, you can split me open with your sword... and I won't try and get away... or my name's not Nian!"

While the man is still shouting the odds, Chenglong leaps to his feet and intercepts him: "What drunken nonsense is this, Lao Nian'er? Fuck off, and be quick about it!"

Chenglong is outwardly cursing, but internally he understands only too well what is going on. The man is indeed called Nian, nicknamed Lao Nian'er, and he is a stalwart of the Special Operations Squad. He is also one of Chenglong's close confidants and knows all about the business at the conference. The only reason he can be here now is that he has something urgent to report.

Before Chenglong can get over to him, Matsuzaki calls out from behind: "Let him speak, Liu-san!"

Catching on, the guards let go of Lao Nian'er, who shakes himself free. He advances a few steps and points at Chenglong.

"Tell me... why... why is there good wine... on these tables... when you only... give your own men the... shitty dregs? Aren't I... just as good as... the Japanese?"

"*Baku!*" Yamaguchi curses, seizing Lao Nian'er by the collar, ready to strike. To his surprise, the man's body droops and his legs give way, so that he is sprawled over his attacker. He gives a great, boozy belch as if he is about to throw up. Knowing what's probably coming, Yamaguchi thrusts him violently away so he falls head first into the table. Luckily for him, Chenglong is quick to react, and he steps in. He grabs Lao Nian'er by his belt with his right hand, reaches his left arm round, locking the other man's arms under his own, then, with a twist of the waist and a flick of the hip, he hauls him upright.

"He's had too much to drink. Give him to me, and I'll sober him up," Chenglong says, leading him back out of the room. Lao Nian'er tries to struggle free, but his arms are held tight, and the attempt makes him yelp with pain. By the time the others realise what is going on, Chenglong has already manoeuvred him out of the room. Seeing this, Matsuzaki shoots Zhou Si an urgent look, and Zhou Si hurries out after them, with Yamaguchi and the door guards hot on his heels. But Chenglong quickens his steps, kicks open the door to the toilet and goes in. He pushes one leg back to brace it against the door, so that when Zhou Si tries to follow him in, he bangs his nose against the blockaded door and exclaims in pain. He is so annoyed he is about to kick in the door, but Yamaguchi stops him. There is a crack in the door, and when Zhou Si puts his eye to it, he sees Chenglong thrust Lao Nian'er under the tap and sluice him with cold water. The gurgling of the water is augmented by the sounds of Lao Nian'er squealing like a stuck pig and Chenglong cursing him.

In fact, the two of them are only acting out a pantomime, like Zhou Yu pretending to beat Huang Gai,[2] and under cover of the gurgling and the curses, the two men are conducting the real, stuttering, whispered conversation.

"This situation is all wrong... Aiyo! Aah! They're all breathing down our necks out there... do you have to be so fucking rough!"

"I'm trying to sober you up! So what's going on over there?"

"Aiyo! I'm not really drunk!... I just had a phone call saying the Imperial Ancestral Temple is crawling with Kempeitai... I... is it alright if I just call it a day?"

"Fuck it, no, it's not alright! You have to get the word through to them that they mustn't go in."

"Aiya! They're already in there..."

These whispered words of Lao Nian'er echo like thunder in Chenglong's ears, exploding in his brain, so his mind goes blank.

Seeing him stunned and rooted to the spot, Lao Nian'er spins round, grabs Chenglong by the hair, and thrusts his head under the tap. The shock of the cold water revives him, and he seizes hold of Lao Nian'er's hand in a wrist lock, applying maximum pressure.

"Aah! Aiyo! I've got to get away as quick as possible or I'm done for."

"Hah! Fuck you, are you still trying to fight me?" Chenglong curses him, but his head is spinning. Suddenly, a terrible thought strikes him that freezes him to the marrow. But even in his terror, he grits his teeth and presses close to Lao Nian'er: "Listen to me. You have to make a phone call, and be quick about it. Everyone wearing that badge must be..."

"Arrested?"

"Shit, do I have to fucking spell it out to you?" Chenglong grabs him again and slaps him twice across the face. Then he spits out a single word in his ear: "Killed!"

This time it is Lao Nian'er's turn to be stunned. He has heard the word clearly enough, but he doesn't want to believe it. Chenglong slaps him again and asks: "Got it?"

Lao Nian'er puts on his act again, assumes a piteous expression and pleads with Chenglong: "Master Liu, I really have drunk too much, but now... now I understand, I understand. You think I'm pathetic, so just let me go and be done with it."

Chenglong gives a frosty laugh: "Ha! If you're going to fuck off, be quick about it, and fuck off as far as you can before I change my mind."

At this, Lao Nian'er reaches out and pulls at the door, then pulls again, but it won't budge.

Chenglong reaches across him and unlocks the door, cursing him: "You're still fucking clueless. You need a good beating."

Lao Nian'er grins foolishly, wrenches open the door and hurtles through it. Seeing him dripping water like a drowned rat, Yamaguchi just laughs and lets him go. Lao Nian'er grins ingratiatingly, nodding continuously and makes good his escape with all speed.

Chenglong returns to the private room without bothering to dry off his dripping head, and he hurriedly makes his apologies: "That little bastard really did have too much to drink. Great lords, I've been too lenient with him before, and I've just..."

"That's enough!" Matsuzaki interrupts him coldly. "I admire your nerve, Liu-san, but today you are the lead in the little play I have invited everybody to see. Well, why don't you tell them the title of the play?"

"What title? I... I don't understand what you're talking about."

"You don't understand? Alright, I'll announce the programme. This is a play about the confrontation between civil and military authority called *Disturbance at the Imperial Ancestral Temple*."

Chenglong's heart gives a great lurch when he hears this, but he immediately controls his emotions and laughs in the face of Matsuzaki's icy gaze: "Ha! I know what this is all about! This is why you've been so cross with me. Mr Matsuzaki, I received a report that the Traitor Elimination Squad is going to assassinate Mr Zhou Zhengjie today, so I have already laid a trap for them at the conference."

Matsuzaki is a little taken aback by the reply. He looks Chenglong up and down and asks: "Then why didn't you report this to me?"

"Didn't you once tell me that, in an emergency, the Special Operations Squad can act independently, on its own initiative?"

Matsuzaki stares in amazement for a moment, but then he looks up and slams his fist down on the table.

"Don't talk drivel. Are you saying you wouldn't even have told me if you had already started something?"

"You do me an injustice. It wasn't that I didn't want to tell you, but I was afraid word might leak out and the affair would be bungled, because you have a traitor in your midst."

Before Chenglong has even finished speaking, a shiver runs down everyone's spine.

"And... who do you say this traitor is?" Matsuzaki asks, glaring at him.

"It's him!" Chenglong says, pointing at Zhou Si.

Everyone looks at Zhou Si, making him shiver all over. He leaps from his chair and shouts, face mottled with fury: "Don't... don't listen to his nonsense, great lord! Don't make such bogus accusations, Liu Chenglong! I was listening under the rear window two nights ago, and I heard quite clearly when they persuaded you to change sides. The leader of the Traitor Elimination Squad is... is your father. Not your birth father, your foster father!"

"Ha ha! You mustn't tease people like this," says Chenglong. "My foster father Gao Guigeng has been dead for more than ten years, and he's buried outside the Desheng Gate. The whole street knows that. How can he have leapt from his grave? You're so crap at making up stories, I can't understand why military intelligence use a waste of space like you. It is true, Mr Matsuzaki, that two nights ago, military intelligence did indeed send someone to find me, wanting me to help assassinate Zhou Zhengjie. But I knew they were trying to kill two birds with one stone, because if Zhou Zhengjie was killed, they could throw suspicion on me and get rid of me that way. So I came up with a way to beat them at their own game."

"He's... he's talking rubbish!" Zhou Si stamps his feet with fury.

Chenglong continues unflustered: "It will soon become clear who is talking rubbish, Mr Matsuzaki. If Mr Zhou really does die at the hands of the Traitor Elimination Squad, I'll happily give my own life to make up for it. But if my men scoop up all the assassins, then what more do I need to say?"

Matsuzaki nods. Yamaguchi seems more than half inclined to believe Chenglong; fury is already building in the gaze he fixes on Zhou Si, and he quietly unbuttons his holster.

When Zhou Si secretly laid his information against Chenglong, he also implicated himself. He said that the two of them had worked very closely together, even collaborating in the distribution of fake army notes, for which Matsuzaki tore him off a strip.

At this point, a Japanese special agent comes running into the room and whispers in Matsuzaki's ear. When he has finished, Matsuzaki begins to laugh.

"Well, gentleman, the curtain has already been rung down on our little play *Disturbance at the Imperial Ancestral Temple,* and the ending is that Mr Zhou is safe and well but all five of the military intelligence special agents have been shot dead. However, Liu-san, this is not only your meritorious achievement, it is also your loss, since the Kempeitai will not now be able to wring details of their network out of them."

Chenglong can finally relax and he says with a smile: "I am not looking for any credit for meritorious service, Mr Matsuzaki. If you just clear my name, then I will be satisfied."

Matsuzaki gives a great roar of laughter. "The facts speak for themselves, don't they, Liu-san?"

"So... what about this fellow?" Chenglong asks looking scornfully at the figure of Zhou Si, who is cowering and shivering like a beaten cur. He doesn't dare make a sound but just stares at Matsuzaki, his eyes filled with tears of entreaty.

Matsuzaki claps Chenglong on the shoulder. "I'll leave you to punish your own subordinate."

"Thank you." Chenglong clasps his hands respectfully and bows slightly. Then he says in a loud voice: "I just have this to say to you, lord. Liu Chenglong pledges his life that he will always be there at your command."

With that, he turns and glares at Zhou Si, advancing on him with a cruel smile. Zhou Si's eyes widen in fear, but then he suddenly grits his teeth, springs furiously to his feet and shouts: "I'll get even with you!"

He reaches for his pistol, but before the gun is more than halfway out of its holster, he is hit flush on the hand by a saucer that Chenglong, alert to the danger, has snatched up from the table and flung at him. Zhou Si clutches his hand with a yelp of pain. Before he is fully to his feet, there is a bang from Yamaguchi's pistol, his body sways and then collapses to the ground.

Yamaguchi blows the smoke from the barrel of his gun and slaps Chenglong on the shoulder. But Chenglong just stares dully at the spreading bloodstain on the floor. His elation of a moment ago has only temporarily overridden the fear of losing his life, and when he lets out his breath, his legs go weak, his head spins and his heart empties. In his dazed state, the sound of the gun is not a single report, but something indistinct. The body on the floor is not just one corpse, but has become a pile of corpses. The blood is not a pool but has become a river. He is no longer in Yuerong's Place, but in the Imperial Ancestral Temple...

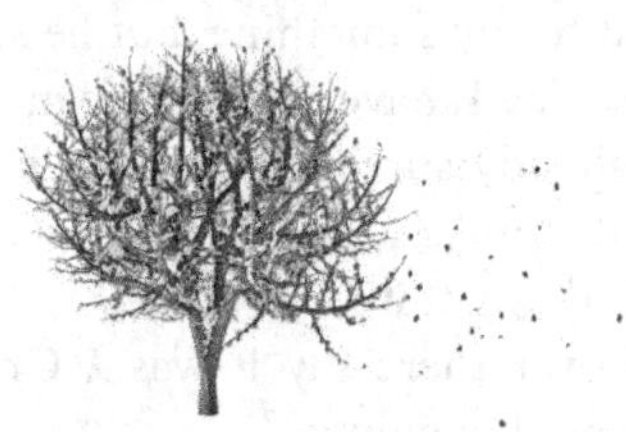

Chapter 53

Yang Zhixing's funeral procession leaves Beiping by the Desheng Gate, follows the moat round to the Xizhi Gate and then heads due west. It could, in fact, have made its way straight through the city, rather than taking this circuitous route, but the Japanese are undertaking military manoeuvres to the west of Beiping, and several of the city gates on that side have been closed to traffic.

It is twenty-something *li* from the Xizhi Gate to Laoqiying, seven or eight *li* of which is along mountain roads. A funeral procession is not like a trip to market, as the blowing of trumpets and beating of gongs makes progress drawn out and slow. So it is almost afternoon before it reaches the bottom of the mountain.

Wangtian, travelling in the lead wagon, has arrived well in advance and set up a stall at the roadside with tea urns, platters of pickled vegetables and baskets of assorted fried doughnuts. The procession makes a short stop here, for a bite to eat and a rest. No one has expected people to arrive in quite such great numbers, however, and there aren't enough tea and snacks to go round. This makes Qi Yuexuan go as red with embarrassment as a Guan Gong opera mask, and he scurries round clasping his hands and bowing to everyone in apology. Fortunately, everyone is there as a genuine mourner, and they know that food is hard to come by this year, so no one is inclined to be annoyed. After a short rest, the procession reassembles, and they are just about to set out along the old Incense Road, when a shout comes from a side road.

"Stop! Stay where you are! Don't go up the mountain!"

Whoever it is, is quite some distance off, but Yue E has sharp eyes and calls out: "Isn't that Lao Zhang?"

"What idiocy is he up to now?" Qi Yuexuan can't help muttering.

Lao Zhang advances on them at a trot, and before he has come to a halt, he manages to pant out: "It's... terrible... Young Master! Don't... don't come up... into the mountains."

"Nonsense! Where are we going to hold the funeral if we don't go into the mountains?" Qi Yuexuan replies irritably.

Lao Zhang is about to say something, but he stops and draws Qi Yuexuan to one side: "The Japanese devils have entered the mountains from the west. When I got there... they had already surrounded the village of Fucha. I could see them clearly... from the family tombs... the two sides were already exchanging fire."

"Why are the devils doing this?"

"I heard someone over there say it was... Grandpa Fu bringing his troops back... that brought them down on us."

Qi Yuexuan swears silently to himself. When he left Qiwangfen, his instructions to Grandpa Fu had been quite clear: if the situation changed at all, he was to stay put if possible, and if he couldn't, he was to retreat south of the Yongding River, back to the Eighth Route Army's base of operations. If he had to deviate from this plan, then whatever else he did, he was not to betray the location of his own lair by returning to the Left Barracks. The Left Barracks are not particularly deep in the mountains, nor are they that far from Beiping, so they could never hold out for very long. Hiding out there is also bound to bring disaster down on the locals. Why didn't that idiot Grandpa Fu listen? Qi Yuexuan has been intending to return to Qiwangfen once he has seen to Yang Zhixing's funeral, and he had no way of anticipating that such trouble would be stirred up before the day was out.

Seeing Qi Yuexuan standing in silence, his brows deeply furrowed, Lao Zhang urges him: "I think we should go back there now, to see which way the wind is blowing, and not..."

"Bullshit! That's a crap idea! Do you think I, Qi Yuexuan, am one of your crickets that jumps at the first breath of wind? I am the leader in all this, and if we pull back there now, if I don't die from the curses heaped on me by the villagers of the Left Barracks, then I will certainly die of shame in any case. Pah! I'm afraid they'd even dig up our family tombs to vent their anger. That would make you happy, wouldn't it, you little bastard, because you wouldn't have any tombs to watch over any more!"

Lao Zhang isn't put out by this little diatribe. After so many years, he is quite immune to Qi Yuexuan's tantrums, and he just says with a wink: "Alright, Young Master. If you have to play the martyr, I'm not going to stop you, but are you really going to take everybody else with you?"

His response takes the wind out of Qi Yuexuan's sails. He considers for a moment, then beckons to the crowd and says in a loud voice: "Listen to me, everybody. I have just heard that the Japanese are in the mountains and have attacked the Left Barracks. You have already shown all the nobility of heart possible, and we are profoundly appreciative and grateful. But now you must accept our apologies. Things are too dangerous up ahead, and you must all halt here and return home as fast as you can."

Even as he is still speaking, the protests begin. The leader of the pallbearers steps forward and says: "Young Master Qi, send your friends and relatives home, by all means, but we pallbearers have our rules, and we cannot turn the cortege around. Whatever fate brings, we have taken your money and must deliver the coffin to its destination. If two or three of us die in the process, we will be doing no more than our duty. Otherwise, our status as pallbearers will be in the mire. Besides, even the Japanese devils have mothers and fathers. Would they really dare attack us when they see we are carrying a coffin? Wouldn't they fear retribution? Don't worry, people like us who carry the dead every day are closer to King Yama than others, and no one will die whose time has not come."

He is quite matter-of-fact about this, and all the other pallbearers chorus their agreement, and even some of the mourners insist on accompanying the coffin to its destination.

Realising they will brook no opposition, Qi Yuexuan relents: "Very well, chief, how about this? We both make a concession – you leave behind several of your brother pallbearers but still follow the chief mourner along Incense Road. The musicians and the ceremonial weapons bearers are quite superfluous, and none of the rest of the procession are allowed either. The Japanese are strangers to decent behaviour, and once their blood is up, there is nothing they won't do. It's not worth the living sacrificing themselves for the dead. Everybody must please do as I say. I'm not worried about the money, as long as nothing happens that will leave us apologising for the rest of our lives. The situation is pressing, and there is no time for discussion. If you agree, we'll proceed like this. If not, then I would rather dig a fresh grave and hold the burial right here."

Seeing his determination, the chief pallbearer has no choice but to agree.

Qi Yuexuan goes over to Mother Yan and says: "You shouldn't be climbing the mountain at your age, Mother Yan."

When Mother Yan doesn't reply, Yue E urges her: "He's right. You take the two children home. It will be enough for me to go on with the coffin."

"Ha! You'll only get in the way," Qi Yuexuan says, waving her away impatiently. "No women or children may continue. If there really is any danger, we won't be able to look after you."

"No... no, that's no good," says an equally stubborn Yue E. "Otherwise, who will represent the filial son?"

Qi Yuexuan is taken aback for a moment, before he bellows: "What? You dare to disobey me? Wretched girl! You are the only heir to two families. You show enough filial piety just by being alive. You're not worried there won't be someone taking the part of the filial son, are you? Won't I do? After all, I've been calling him Uncle Yang all these years, so we'll shuffle families and I'll do it, alright?"

Yue E has never heard him flare up at her like this before, but she knows his harsh words are well intentioned. The next thing she hears is Qi Yuexuan summoning Lao Zhang: "Let's go. Take me by the back roads, and hurry up about it."

Lao Zhang just shakes his head. "You'd better ride the carriage along Incense Road. The back route is very hard going."

"Ha! Hard going or not, that's the way we're taking. There's no point in bandying words when the situation is so urgent."

Qi Yuexuan sets off even as he is still speaking, and Lao Zhang breaks into a brief run to get ahead of him. From behind them can be heard Yue E's plaintive wail: "For heaven's sake be careful, Father!"

IF THERE WAS ANY USE in crying over spilt milk, Grandpa Fu would be in floods of tears at this moment. He has been wounded twice, one shot that breaks his right leg and the other bullet entering his chest and lodging somewhere in his upper torso without emerging the other side. Several of his men carry him out of Fucha the back way, along the mountain ridge to Laoqiying. When he sees Second Master Dong, he begins to howl curses, tears and mucus streaming down his face as he impugns eight generations of ancestors. His curses are not aimed at heaven or Earth though, just at two people: himself and the man who has just pulled out of the Eighth Route Army and become a commander in the National Army, Zhao Ran. And it is no wonder that he does curse him, as only sixty or seventy of his two hundred-strong army have made it back, with the Japanese devils snapping at their heels as the wolf pack descends on their home.

The fact is, not long after Qi Yuexuan returned to Beiping, the Japanese followed up on Zhou Zhengjie's information and began a clean-up operation against the anti-Japanese resistance forces west of the city. They didn't have much intelligence from Zhou regarding the Eighth Route Army, so they didn't dare make any rash move against their base of operations in the area of Wangping, Yanchi and Zhaitang. Instead, they mounted a north-south pincer offensive. In the south, they swept north from Xiayun Ridge on Fangshan, and from the north, they pressed south in a line from Huailai to the Great Wall at Yanqing. The principal force on the southern front was the original Japanese Beiping garrison, but in the south, it was mainly drawn from the local garrison in Zhangjiakou transferred in from Chahar and Suiyuan. Their plan was to purge the surrounding areas, then meet in the middle and mount a combined attack to exterminate the Eighth Route Army.

Yangtaishan at Qiwangfen is not far from either Huailai or Yanqing, and it lies within the scope of the southern front of the Japanese clean-up operation. The brigade dispatched from the Chahar-Suiyaun local garrisons is led by its mechanised unit, backed up with a substantial cavalry force, so it is highly mobile. By the second day of the operation, they have already reached the combat zone. When the two armies garrisoned at Qiwangfen get news of this, the vanguard of the Japanese Army has already joined the base in Junzhuang, further reinforcing the blockade on the main Beiping highway. The main force of the Japanese Army has also already arrived west of Miaofengshan, only twenty *li* from Qiwangfen.

Grandpa Fu has not forgotten Qi Yuexuan's instructions. However, he has no mind to defend his position, but if he withdraws south of the Yongding River, he will put himself into the domain of the Eighth Route Army, and he is not willing to do that either.

After Qi Yuexuan leaves, Zhao Ran and Wu Xinmin become even more attentive, often coming to drink with him and never arriving empty-handed but always with a little present of some kind. Although Grandpa Fu is a local moneybags landlord, when it comes down to it, he is a former bannerman who is not overly concerned with trinkets. Nor is he anybody's fool. He knows quite well that these gifts may not be particularly sizeable, but they are all the kind of thing that could only have belonged to a member of the imperial family. A snuff bottle with a fine Hetian jade body, for example, a gold-inlaid mouth and a carved lapis stopper, clearly palace workmanship and worth ten *mu* of land. How did they come by such things? In his heart, Grandpa Fu knows quite well. Previously, they had laid hands on a lot of stuff from the princes' tombs at Qiwangfen and Jiuwangfen, and they have not been idle recently either, using the cover of night to loot several Ming dynasty tombs as well. These tombs, which are located next to the main tomb enclosure at Qiwangfen, are those of the mother of Emperor Chenghua, the Dowager Empress Xiaosu, and several of his brothers. They are known locally as the Zhou family tombs. So, knowing that the gifts were dishonestly acquired, he is equally sure there will be consequences involved and favours expected. But when it comes to the point, and the two men try to persuade him to join forces with them and throw his hat in with the National Army, he doesn't use the excuse of not being the commander to hide behind. He just says that his men are simple villagers who have come together to protect their homes, and none of them are willing to become official soldiers. Under continuing pressure, he keeps bluffing, saying that they are only going to be there a few days and will be going home as soon as Master Qi gets back. Zhao Ran is unable to get him to move. Nonetheless, their conversations often turns to the Eighth Route Army, about which Zhao Ran had nothing good to say. Whether intentionally or unintentionally, the effect of this constant talk is to reinforce the misgivings Grandpa Fu already has about the Eighth Route Army. So, as the situation becomes more urgent, his doubts and indecision increase proportionately.

Around this time, Zhao Ran comes looking for Grandpa Fu, bringing Wu Xinmin along with him. They say that, if they are going to join forces against the enemy there in front of them, they need to discuss whether to advance or retreat. Grandpa Fu has suffered from their unreliability the last time at Longjiazhuang, so he is quite clear-eyed and does not reply immediately. Seeing his hesitation, Zhao Ran gives a dry cough, and Wu Xinmin goes over to Grandpa Fu, wearing a crafty smile.

"Commander Fucha, I know you probably hold a grudge against me, and I can't blame you. In war, many unfortunate combinations of circumstances can arise." He sees Grandpa Fu looking askance at him and hurriedly continues: "Yes indeed, last time we did have to dig a few graves, but if we aren't willing to make some military sacrifices in our fight against the Japanese, how can we face our bannermen ancestors? The truth is, if we don't have a few valuables to hand, do you think we'd dare act independently? To be precise with you, we can easily turn these trinkets into several thousand rifles."

This catches Grandpa Fu's interest. "What's this? Are you trying to bribe me?"

Before Wu Xinmin can reply, Zhao Ran says with a laugh: "Of course not. I quite understand that you don't want to eat from the same bowl as me. Everyone has their own principles, but we are all fighting the Japanese, and if we co-operate at least, that makes us allies, and friends. Besides, we are already closer than others since haven't we both served under the Eight Banners, and isn't anything we have, yours too? We are with the National Army now, and sooner or later, the government is going to pay us, and we may not have to sell this little treasure we've accumulated. It's just a shame the same doesn't apply to you. But I can promise you that some of that treasure can come your way."

So saying, he takes a sheet of paper out of his pocket and gives it to Grandpa Fu.

"Here, have a look at this list. If you work with us now, then afterwards, I'll hand it all over to you."

Grandpa Fu looks over the list and his heart quickens. After a while, he asks in a hoarse voice: "And... what does Commander Zhao mean by 'work with'?"

Zhao Ran smiles. "The Japanese are coming in force this time, and together we can't muster much more than two hundred men, so there's no point in trying to hold our position here to the last man."

"The thing is, to tell you the truth, when Young Master Qi was about to leave, he left instructions that, if we did have to retreat, then we should make for the deep mountain country south of the Yongding River."

"Ha! That's the Eighth Route Army's base of operations. If you go there, you'll just become another lump of meat on their chopping board."

"You really think so?"

"They pretty much turned my force of three thousand men into a leaderless rabble, and yours won't be any different. Don't you know what the Communist Party is interested in? You know what Communist means? Common property. They might as well have changed their name to the United Front Party. They have nothing of their own to start with, so do you really think they're going to do any sharing with you? Are you happy for them to eat all your rations and use all your equipment, and for you to do everything they say? Once you're there, they'll swallow up everything you've got."

"Pah! They can try to share as much as they like, but if I don't play ball, what are they going to do? They can't swallow what they don't have!"

"Ha! Just listen to you! You don't know the half of it. Communist Party propaganda gets everywhere, and there's nothing you can do about it. Once you come into contact with them, sooner or later you end up in their pocket, and when that happens, do you think you'll be in control of anything? Whether you join them or not, it'll all come to the same thing."

Grandpa Fu is speechless, and after a long moment's thought, he asks: "So... where do you think we should go?"

"Well, Commander Fucha," says Zhao Ran, "haven't you always wanted to take your men back to the Left Barracks?"

"That's true, but..."

"What is there to 'but' about? You have a home of your own, so why go elsewhere to live off someone else's charity? I think the best thing we can do is head southeast and break out of the blockade that way."

"Southeast? Won't that take us straight towards Beiping? We wouldn't be breaking out of the blockade into safety, but breaking out of it straight into the enemy's arms!"

"That's right. It would take them completely by surprise." Zhao Ran rearranges the teapot and cups on the table and points at them: "This is Junzhuang, and we break out from there. It's the devils' most heavily defended base, but once we're through it and head south, there are no major enemy troops within ten *li*, and the mountains are only two *li* to the east. If we go south through Mentougou, then head towards Fangshan, we can join up with the National Army and others there. If you don't want to come with us, you can just head on east back to the Left Barracks. My cavalry can form the vanguard, and you and your men will be the rearguard. Once we've broken through, you just follow us. The enemy's main force will inevitably be sucked in and pinned down by our southern advance, so you'll have no problem getting into the mountains, and then you can follow the valleys back to the Left Barracks, can't you?"

His face is beaming as he talks, but Grandpa Fu remains silent. Seeing this, Wu Xinmin gives a wry little laugh and breaks in harshly: "Well? This time we're taking all the flak and clearing the way for you, so what are you worried about? The only reason we're taking you with us is to create an impression of greater strength. Commander Zhao's obligation to you, regardless of how much extra trouble it entails, stems from the fact that you are both bannermen and both fighting the Japanese – nothing else. If you don't want to play along, we're not going to beg you. We'll just walk away."

Grandpa Fu slaps his thigh and says: "I'll do it! I'll do it! Why wouldn't I?"

That night, they begin the withdrawal. In front are Zhao Ran's troops, only thirty or forty of them, but all mounted. The men of the Left Barracks are more than half a *li* away in the rear, following the path that slants down to Junzhuang.

BY THE THIRD WATCH, the mounted vanguard has reached the army base, and they immediately rush the Japanese checkpoint. At first, the Japanese think they are their own cavalry that has been transferred from Chahar and Suiyuan, and by the time they realise what is actually going on, it's too late. A dozen hand grenades and a burst of machinegun fire later, only a few of the company at the checkpoint are left standing. By the time the machinegun mounted on top of the blockhouse opens up, the cavalry is already past the checkpoint. But the lead horses have stirred up a hornets' nest, and it's those behind who feel the effect. The men of the Left Barracks have just caught up, and they find themselves in the middle of a vicious crossfire. There is nothing for it but for them to put their heads down and rush on as fast as they can.

Only when they are a couple of *li* past the checkpoint are they able to reassemble like a flock of frightened sheep. There's no need to make a proper count, as even a cursory glance shows that no more than half of them have made it through. What is more, many of those that are still standing are wounded. Grandpa Fu has taken a bullet in the leg, but luckily for him he is on horseback, and he sprawls low on the beast's back, hanging onto the reins for dear life. There is no sign of Zhao Ran and his men, who have whipped up their speedy mounts and disappeared completely. Grandpa Fu finally realises that he has been duped. Agitated and angry, he ignores his wound and orders one of his captains to take most of the men into the mountains in the direction of the Left Barracks. He himself leads a handful of men back at the double, to collect their comrades in the rear.

By this time, the Japanese in Junzhuang Township have already come charging out of the gates, hoping to use the beam of the searchlight on the blockhouse to help them outflank the men pinned down by gunfire on either side of the checkpoint. Those men are almost beside themselves with fear, but with their backs to the wall and being unable to escape, when they see Grandpa Fu and his men coming to their rescue, their fighting spirit revives. Just at this moment, vehicle headlights appear in the distance on the highway north of Junzhuang. A patch of deeper black in among the headlights suggests there is also a troop of Japanese cavalry. Of course, these must be the reinforcements transferred in from Suiyuan and Chahar. If the men from the Left Barracks are not to be surrounded and wiped out, they have to stake everything. Grandpa Fu orders them to throw all their grenades in one salvo and then run for their lives, with every man for himself. He has just shouted out these orders when he himself is hit in the chest, and he knows nothing of what ensues. According to the men who get back to the Left Barracks, several of their comrades risk their lives to save him, tying him to his horse and leading him all the way back. The twenty or thirty men who get out with him, other than those who fall on the battlefield or are wounded and captured, all scatter and run. They have just caught up with the troops in front of them, when the Japanese cavalry come charging down on them. By the end of this running battle, there are only seven or eight of them left.

· · ·

IN FACT, once past the checkpoint at Junzhuang, Zhao Ran doesn't make for Fangshan. The supposed plan to link up with the National Army's guerrilla forces was just a pretence. Before even arriving in Mentougou, he sends away the majority of his men. He and the few remaining men, his closest confidants, change into civilian clothes, abandon their horses and head southeast from Pingxi, hastening on foot by back roads to Tianjin. From there, they take a steamship to Hong Kong. This is what he has been planning to do all along: he wants to reunite with his mother and family and then travel together to safety in the hinterland beyond Chongqing. It is quite understandable that there have to be both advances and retreats in warfare, but to abandon not just his allies against the Japanese, but also his own troops when faced by real danger, and to save his own skin, is a despicable act. In fact, not only does Zhao Ran reach Chongqing safely, he is even celebrated by the National Government as a modern-day Yue Fei. He publishes a book, gives lectures and generally rides the crest of public acclaim. At the end of 1939, just as the National Government's Shi Yousan[1] and his colleagues make a major advance against the Eighth Route Army in northern China, under the order to 'advance the guerrilla war', he leads several hundred men back north into the Eighth Route Army's base of operations. There, his force is wiped out in Lingshou County in Hebei, and Zhao Ran himself is killed in the heat of the battle. Later on, after victory in the War of Japanese Resistance, his mother, Hong Wenguo, raises the 'Anti-Communist Restore-the-Nation Army' in Sichuan and enters into a war or resistance against the People's Liberation Army in the greater southwest region, slaughtering several hundred Party cadres and ordinary members of the local populace. But what chance does this 'Mother of Guerrilla Warfare' have when she is finally faced by the real fathers of guerrilla war in the Eighth Route Army? After only one battle, she is defeated and captured. In view of the local fury, she is duly tried and executed. Even though both mother and son end up hitching their wagons to the cause of Chiang Kai-shek, when all is said and done, they did fight the Japanese and take part in the War of Resistance, so many years later, whenever their names and the events surrounding them crop up, Qi Yuexuan finds himself with mixed feelings about them, including both sorrow and regret.

BUT ENOUGH OF FUTURE EVENTS, and let us return to the perilous situation in the Left Barracks.

After following the mountain road for seven or eight *li*, Qi Yuexuan's clothes are wringing with sweat, and his legs are like jelly. It is lucky for him that Lao Zhang is there to help and support him, even dragging him along by his belt sometimes, otherwise he is very much afraid he would be reduced to crawling on hands and knees. Proceeding in this fashion, as soon as they reach their destination, he slumps to the ground and sits down, with Lao Zhang beside him, puffing like a bellows. When he sees Second Master Dong coming out to greet them, he makes a supreme effort and rolls to his feet.

"Aiya, Young Master! I never thought you'd come back, the way things stand," Second Master Dong says, grasping him by the hand as fervently as a drowning man grasps a pole being held out to him from the riverbank.

Withdrawing his painfully crushed hand, Qi Yuexuan says: "Ha! What kind of man do you think I am? We're all under the same sky, so we'll all get hit by the lightning when it strikes."

"It's all Grandpa Fu's fault," Second Master Dongs sighs. "He's too greedy. He was tempted and took the bait, otherwise we wouldn't be in..."

"There's no use dwelling on such things. What matters is what's going on now."

Second Master Dong nods and replies quickly: "There are more than a hundred of the devils here, most of them cavalry. Our men sheltered in Fucha for a while, but they couldn't stay there and had to retreat to Laoqiying. Most of the villagers came with them, but twenty or thirty were left behind when the devils surrounded the place, all old people, women and children. I've already set up a defensive position at the western entrance to the village and ordered some of my men to help move the villagers to the south side of the mountain. We can't have any of them left behind here."

"The devils haven't attacked Laoqiying yet?"

"Not yet. They're probably too busy with Fucha to bother with it for the moment."

"How many men have we got?"

"With the ones you've just brought, sixty something, plus a dozen or so wounded. There are roughly a hundred and thirty in the detachment we left behind, but most of them will have scattered among the villages, and there'll be fewer than fifty in Laoqiying. As for rifles, even counting old blunderbusses, there aren't enough to go round, and I'm afraid we've got even fewer grenades."

When Qi Yuexuan hears this, he says sadly: "But we fought quite a few engagements out there, and captured a whole load of weapons. There were at least a dozen machineguns, several cannons and even a mountain gun."

"Ha! I've seen a few machineguns, but no cannons. We must have lost them all when the devils scattered us like wild ducks. Ai, but lost rifles, cannons and grenades are nothing compared with the loss of fighting spirit. That's why we couldn't even hold on to such a well-situated place as Fucha for longer than it takes to fart."

"Then... have you tried bringing in any of the other villages as reinforcements?"

"I thought about it, but I didn't dare."

"Why not?"

"I reckoned that, even if they all came, there was no hope of success with all their courage gone. Besides, I wasn't at all certain they would come. We'd do better not to drag other villages into it, and only risk our own necks."

"Bullshit!" Qi Yuexuan's eyes bulge with anger. "When we started out, all twelve villages of the Left Barracks took a blood oath, an oath of allegiance, that whatever the risks, we would take them together. If you call on them and they don't come, that will be to their eternal shame. Why wouldn't you call on them? Do you think the Japanese devils are so honourable that they'll leave the other villages alone if they don't join in? Fat chance! Rather than let them be picked off one by one, much better to gather them all together. Fighting spirit can be forced out. Even a rabbit will bite a man when it's in danger, so how much more is that the case with men? When they see the Japanese devils bursting into their homes, do you think their spirit won't be stirred? With their mothers and fathers, wives and children sheltering behind them, won't they become real men again? Pah! Why waste time talking? Let's get on with it and call them together."

Second Master Dong nods, then asks urgently as he sees Qi Yuexuan turn to go: "Are you..."

"I'll wait for you at the entrance to the village," Qi Yuexuan says with a laugh as he walks away.

At this moment, Lao Zhang comes out of the courtyard carrying some water. He calls out "Young Master" several times, to no effect. He puts down the bowl and follows him.

When Qi Yuexuan reaches the entrance to the village, he can see that it is just as Second Master Dong has said, and fighting spirit is as good as non-existent among the troops. The twenty or thirty men who had stayed behind on guard are neatly turned out, but their comrades who have returned higgledy-piggledy from Qiwangfen are all dusty-haired and dirty-faced, their clothes covered in blood stains. Although they are all leaning on the fortifications with rifles in their hands, their heads are down, without a spark of spirit or animation.

"You see, Young Master," Lao Zhang says, "they're just like a cricket that's lost a bout. If you want to get it to fight again, you have to retrain it."

Although this was said half-jokingly, Qi Yuexuan feels there is some truth in it, and after a long pause for thought, he slowly nods his head.

One of the captains catches sight of him and calls out: "Look, brothers, Commissioner Qi has come back!"

Many of the men come clustering round, and at the sight of him, particularly those who have just returned from putting their lives on the line in battle, find their eyes reddening with tears. They may not have had strong feelings about him while he was with the troops before, but after his absence of almost a fortnight, and after they have themselves returned from suffering a devastating defeat, they feel the lack of his firm leadership and calming presence. Qi Yuexuan himself is a man of great empathy, and when he sees his men like this, the tears spring to his own eyes.

At this point, the roar of the signal cannon splits the air, and the great bell of

Laoqiying Village begins to toll, its booming note rolling in waves through the mountains and valleys.

Qi Yuexuan raises his hand and says in clear tones: "Do you hear that, brothers? The cannon and the bell are a call to arms. We are not waging a lone war. Our brothers from all the other villages will come to our aid. One lost battle doesn't matter, we have had our own victories before. To get up after being knocked down is the mark of true heroes. We have nowhere left to retreat to. Behind us are our homes, our families and our ancestors' tombs. Are we going to let the little Japanese devils trample all over them?"

"No!" the men shout back in a ragged chorus.

"I, Qi Yuexuan, may have been late to arrive, but today I am here before you, clad in filial piety. From ancient times it has always been the belief that going into battle clad in filial piety means that you are willing to stake your life. Look!" He points at the freshly dug grave among the Qi family tombs on the mountainside. "This was originally dug for Uncle Yang, the household manager of my Residence, but if I die here today, then that grave will hold two bodies, and I will have a fine companion. If any of you die before me, then as a mark of my filial piety, I will carry the staff of mourning myself and I will personally perform the custom of smashing the flowerpot."

So saying, he gives a shout of laughter, and as everyone else joins in, he raises his hand again. "While life is good, brothers, who wants to die? But if you want to live, you must go into battle willing to die. If anyone is afraid, you can put down your rifle and leave. I will not stop you... but if you stay, then you must dig deep and find your courage again for me. Whether we live or die, we can beat our chests and call ourselves men!"

"You've got that right," someone cries out, and all the others add their assent, one by one. Although the voices may not be in unison, each one rings with determination.

Qi Yuexuan looks around him for a moment, then raises his voice: "Since you are all willing to fight, listen to my orders. Captain of Number Five detachment!"

"Here!"

"You and your men are in charge of the flanks. Send two of your best men secretly back to Fucha to find out what's going on there."

"Yessir!"

"Captain of Number One detachment!"

"Here!"

"All the men who have just returned are under your command, and you are to defend the centre. Re-organise yourselves into four platoons. You choose the sergeants."

"Yessir!"

"Everybody, check your weapons and count your ammunition. Reinforce the defences and prepare for battle!"

"Yessir!"

Having made his arrangements, and seeing that the men are already on the move, Qi Yuexuan climbs to the top of the slope, takes out an antique telescope and gazes into the distance with rapt attention.

Lao Zhang goes up to him, eyes narrowed in a smile, and says with some relish: "Brilliant, Young Master! That little trick I taught you from my expertise in raising crickets really worked out for you."

Qi Yuexuan listens to his nonsense without replying, but that doesn't stop Lao Zhang, who prattles on: "If you want a beaten cricket to go straight back into battle, you have to be quick and fierce about it. The way you lectured them just now, plucking at their emotions, really got through to them. It was spot on. They are too off balance to be afraid, and will surely fight again."

Qi Yuexuan grins in amusement, but then he suddenly looks serious again. "Go and find somewhere quiet to have a little rest, and stop turning serious events into a joke."

"Alright, alright, I've had my say," Lao Zhang says, going off and sitting to one side. But before his buttocks have even touched the rock, he begins to mutter to himself: "Ai! How true it is! War and fighting crickets play by the same rules. Just look at this situation here. There are only two words for it..."

He sees Qi Yuexuan turn his head to look at him, and he shuts up, gesturing with his hands: "Alright, alright, I won't say it, I won't say it."

"Go on, you old rascal," Qi Yuexuan says, wagging his finger playfully at him. "If I don't let you speak, you won't shut up, and if I listen to you now, you'll just start putting on airs. So go on, tell me – what two words?"

Lao Zhang grins with self-satisfaction, and he has just opened his mouth to speak when the sound of fierce gunfire and explosions rolls over from the direction of Fucha.

At first, everyone assumes the Japanese are coming, but when they calm down and look, there is no sign of movement on the ridge. Listening carefully, they realise the sounds are coming from inside their own village. Are the Japanese so exasperated that they have launched an attack on the villagers? But it sounds as though the shooting is coming from the two sides of a firefight. Are their comrades from one of the other villages fighting their way in? But supposing they set out as soon as they heard the signal cannon and the bell, they couldn't have got here so quickly even if they had wings. Are the men who have just been sent out to reconnoitre exchanging fire with the devils? But there are only two of them, and they couldn't possibly make this much noise. Everyone looks at each other in puzzled amazement, and even Qi Yuexuan is unable to make sense of it.

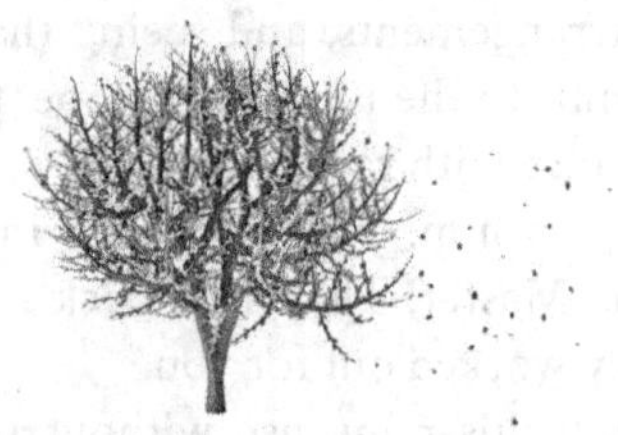

Chapter 54

I n the Qing dynasty, the twelve villages of the Left Barracks were originally barracks under the control of the Department of the Imperial Household and were run along a mutually interconnected system. It didn't matter that they were scattered over an area of several tens of square *li*; those that were close by could hear the signal cannon and the sound of the bell, and those that were more distant could see signal flags and the smoke from beacons. All it took was for Laoqiying to raise the alarm and for it to be heard in one place. The news was then transmitted everywhere else as quickly as any telephone or telegraph. After the establishment of the Republic, respect for these rules weakened, but they have reasserted themselves since the start of the anti-Japanese resistance. In times when nobody believes anything unless they have seen it with their own eyes, this outmoded form of communication can still be of some use.

THE SOUND OF GUNFIRE is still coming from Fucha as Second Master Dong appears carrying water and dry goods. When everyone hears him say that some of the other villages have already responded to the alarm signal, they relax considerably.

"Young Master Qi," says Second Master Dong as he steps forward. "It seems to me that this fighting at Fucha means the devils are afraid of attacking Laoqiying again. Shouldn't we go on the offensive?"

"For heaven's sake, let's not get carried away. We've just suffered a heavy defeat, and we only have these few men and rifles left. We can't afford any more losses. The devils are holding our families, and we've got to think about them. Besides, this terrain makes it difficult for them to attack us, and even more so for us to attack them. Let's wait until we know what's going on and for reinforcements to arrive, and then we'll see."

Second Master Dong doesn't reply. He was born and brought up in this place, and he knows all about its dangers.

. . .

Laoqiying is only a little over four *li* from Fucha, on the same mountain but on separate peaks. From Ming times to the middle of the Qing dynasty, this mountain was called Goat's Horn Mountain, but it is said that, because the Empress Dowager Cixi was born in the Year of the Goat, the name was shortened to Horn Mountain in order to avoid trouble. Three roads connect the two villages, the main one of which is on the northern side of the mountain, and is, in fact, the northern Incense Road used by pilgrims going to Miaofengshan. The secondary road, which is halfway up the slope on the southern side of the mountain, is composed of stone steps and is therefore unusable by vehicles. But there is also an unsurfaced track that follows the ridge of the mountain between the two peaks and is used only by goatherds, hunters and insect collectors. All three of these roads are hazardous attack routes that are easily defended. Although the old Incense Road is broad and even as it winds up around the mountain, its circuitous route adds a good few *li* to the journey and there is no cover on either side. For anyone occupying the higher ground, travellers on this route are sitting ducks from a long distance away. The lesser route on the south side of the mountain is carved out along precipitous cliffs, with vertical drops in many places, and is the kind of path a single man can defend against ten thousand. The track along the ridge is very seldom used, and people say of it that it is 'three steps up and two steps down, and every one of those steps treacherous'. Both sides are lined with waist-high brambles and thorn bushes, along with sour date trees. Branches grow across the path everywhere, and anyone travelling it has to watch out, or their flesh will be cut open as easily as slicing a cucumber. It was along this track that the soldiers and villagers had retreated in the morning, but that choice was only made out of life-or-death necessity.

At this point, one of the men sent out to reconnoitre comes running back, and while he is still quite some distance away, can be heard shouting: "Commissioner Qi!"

Qi Yuexuan hurries towards him, asking: "So, what's going on over there?"

Before he has even caught his breath, the man points behind him: "We've got… the villagers out… but there are Japanese devils… chasing them. Hurry up… hurry up and send some men to… meet them."

"Where to?"

"They've… just come out of… Fucha Village. There are men holding… the rear… but I don't know… how long they'll… last."

"Who rescued them?"

"It's the Eighth Route… Army."

"The Eighth Route Army? Nonsense! There aren't any Eighth Route Army around here."

"It really is… them. They're being led by… that Captain Zhang. I saw him."

Qi Yuexuan's heart lifts at the mention of Captain Zhang, but he has no idea where Zhang Zhicheng can suddenly have materialised from, or how he can have been able to act so easily. He hurriedly begins to organise his men, when a smiling Lao Zhang stops him and asks: "Don't you want to hear the rest of what I have to say, Young Master?"

"Oh!" Qi Yuexuan remembers and shoots a glance at him. "Well you can just stop standing there, grinning like an ape. Just two words, you said previously? Well, go on, spit them out!"

Qi Yuexuan is getting agitated, but Lao Zhang remains quite calm. He clears his throat and says: "You shouldn't mock those two words. If you use them properly, you'll save a lot of weapons. It's a trick I used when I was catching crickets. It really is a lot like fighting a battle."

"Hah! Do you always listen to this fellow's nonsense, whatever else is going on?" says Second Master Dong, stamping his feet in agitation.

By this time, Qi Yuexuan really wants to hear Lao Zhang's idea, so, doing his best to keep his temper, he says: "Cut all the nonsense, and just get on with it. What two words?"

"'Fire' and 'ice'," Lao Zhang says craftily.

Qi Yuexuan and Second Master Dong are hooked now, and they stare at Lao Zhang, waiting for him to explain. Eventually, he continues: "When crickets see fire and smell smoke, most of them are scared back into their burrow. If you block off one entrance to the burrow, and pour water in through the other, where have they got left to run to?"

Qi Yuexuan grunts and nods. But Second Master Dong doesn't get the point.

"And... that's got something to do with the situation we're in now?"

"Of course. Just think about it. The Japanese devils have greater firepower than us, so how many men would we lose if we threw ourselves at them headlong? But if we attack them with fire, and drive them into the ravines, then force a flood like at the Battle of Fancheng, won't they be caught like crickets in a flooded burrow?"

"But how can we attack them with fire? When the devils see it, what's to stop them fleeing elsewhere, not just into the ravines?"

"You've got to prepare the ground first, then adapt as things unfold. The gap between our two peaks here is a wind tunnel, and the prevailing wind at this time of year is from the northwest. If we send smoke down on them from three sides, where else are they going to go?"

Understanding dawns on Second Master Dong, and he slaps his thigh and exclaims: "Ha! You're right!"

"We can manage the fire alright," says Qi Yuexuan, frowning deeply, "but what about the water? Where's that to come from?"

"Ha! Have you forgotten the rockslide at the upper end of Zhangjia Valley and how it formed a giant dam? Didn't you see it last time you went out inspecting the terrain? If that water is released..."

Before Lao Zhang has even finished speaking, Qi Yuexuan is up and off, saying as he goes: "Right, that's what we'll do. I have to admit it, this time you weren't talking nonsense!"

Lao Zhang follows on behind him and calls out: "Young Master, we're going to need a lot of explosives if we're going to burst that dam."

"There's plenty in the workshop store."

"Which road are you thinking of taking?"

"We'll need carriages to transport that much explosive, so it will have to be Incense Road."

"Then we'll have to pass by Fucha, right under the eyes of the Japanese devils."

Qi Yuexuan is nonplussed. He grinds his teeth and finally says: "We'll just have to go for broke and make a dash for it."

"Rather than make a dash for it, we could..."

"We could what?"

Lao Zhang hesitates a moment, then steels himself and forces out the second half of his suggestion: "We could... carry the explosives in the coffin."

Qi Yuexuan's eyes light up briefly, but then his expression hardens. Seeing this, Lao Zhang takes a deep breath and babbles: "Alright, alright, pretend I didn't speak. It's complete nonsense."

ALTHOUGH ZHAO RAN didn't take away that many men when he split off from the Eighth Route Army, the chain reaction from his defection has been considerable. A continuous trickle of mutinies have beset the local militia affiliated with the Eighth Route Army, and a number of attacks have been launched on some of the smaller units of the local government and Eighth Route Army forces. In order to stabilise the army, the Fifth Division has annexed one of Yang Dezhi's districts, amalgamated all combatants into a few main fighting units and focused on consolidating the area between Laiyuan and Fuping. Following the previous advance of the four units of the Eighth Route Army led by Song Shilun and Deng Hua into eastern Hebei, and the break-up and withdrawal of the Fifth Division, this area has been without any regular Eighth Route Army presence. In fact, this region of Pingxi had previously been a fairly solid base for operations, but had changed into an area of guerrilla warfare and a territory constantly changing hands between the two sides. It is only when the Eighth Route Army later returns to Pingxi from eastern Hebei that this situation could be rectified. However, that is several months in the future, and at this time, Pingxi is like a child that has been cut off from its mother's milk, wailing and yelling, not knowing what is going to happen next.

ZHANG ZHICHENG HAS NOT followed his men south, but once again, he has stayed behind to wage a guerrilla campaign. Although his force is still part of the greater army, it has considerable independent standing, and when it acts as a guerrilla unit, Captain Zhang becomes Commander Zhang. His task is to coordinate the local anti-Japanese democratic governments and warlords of Fangshan, Liangxiang, Wanping and several other counties in their opposition to the Japanese, and defend the base of operations in Pingxi. Although he accepts this commission without demur, he knows quite well that, without regular troops to rely on, it is not going to be easy to keep the region stable with only his own three hundred or so men plus the local militia of each district. But he has fought several years of guerrilla war and has perfected the craft. In the end, you make use of the materials to hand, defend what can be defended and don't waste lives on the indefensible. At the very least you should make everything that has been open, secret; you fight not by day but by night and conceal your troops; you don't fight in pitched battles but move around, providing support wherever it is needed; you don't fight an open war but a covert one. All that matters is that you persevere, stay alive and keep the enemy on their toes. Then you can at least say you haven't failed.

Zhang Zhicheng has already received a report from his superiors about the deployment of the main body of the Japanese Army of North China on either side of their base, in preparation for the clean-up operation. He leads a platoon forward to the area around Mentougou in order to make a detailed study of the enemy's dispositions. They hear the sounds of fierce fighting coming from the area of Junzhuang and seize, on the way, several of the men Zhao Ran has set adrift. As a consequence, they discover that the troops at Laoqiying are in a tight spot. It is going to be too late, however fast he hurries, so all he can do is take a shortcut across two mountain ridges to reach the ridge on Horn Mountain not far to the west of Fucha. His vanguard comes back to report that most of the Japanese devils are already up the mountain and into Fucha, and that most of the troops from the Left Barracks have withdrawn, leaving only a few villagers behind. Twenty or thirty Japanese have been left behind in the ravine guarding up to a hundred horses. When Zhang Zhicheng hears how many horses there are, his covetousness almost gets the better of him, but in the end no number of horses is equal to a human life. He immediately leads his men along the ridge, pushing their way through thorn bushes, until they are creeping up on the entrance to the village. After disposing of the Japanese sentries, they steal into the village.

At this time, the majority of the Japanese troops are gathered in the Fucha clan memorial hall. The pigs and goats they have seized have been cooked, and they are just starting to eat. They have locked up the villagers they captured in the animal sheds in the side courtyard and, once they have eaten and drunk their fill, are intending to tie all these elders, women and children together, to use as a human shield in the attack on Laoqiying. Although only two guards have been posted, the prisoners are being held too close to the Japanese soldiers for a secret rescue to be possible.

The best Zhang Zhicheng can do is split his force into two. So he himself leads two platoons in a frontal attack on the memorial hall in order to draw out the enemy, while another platoon goes in over the wall to release the prisoners. At the outset, the results are promising, as the Japanese are taken by surprise and huddle together in confusion. But these are elite troops from the garrisons in Chahar and Suiyuan, and they quickly regroup and begin to counterattack. The houses in Fucha are tightly packed and the roads and alleys between them are very narrow, so the troops have no chance to deploy properly. Moreover, because the village is built on the side of a mountain, you can find yourself below a building one minute, and a few paces later are up above it. Zhang Zhicheng and his men take advantage of the terrain to surround the Japanese, attacking alternately from above and below. When the Japanese try to break out either right or left, they find themselves unable to get to grips with their opponents. Once the rescue party has been successful, they begin to fight their way to the eastern entrance to the village. They are making their way along the ridge between the two peaks, when they meet the reinforcements coming from Laoqiying. These men have the advantage of the higher ground, and they open up with rifles and machineguns, stifling the firepower of the pursuing Japanese and giving support to the rescue party that is halfway up the slope. Zhang Zhicheng reckons that, by this time, the villagers will already have reached Laoqiying, but the reinforcements seem to have no intention of withdrawing.

Zhang Zhicheng is puzzled, and he goes over to one of the captains who is out in front and asks: "Tell me, brother – there's no decent defensive position on this slope, so why don't you withdraw to the entrance to the village where you can engage with the devils properly?"

"You can withdraw if you want to," the captain says, "but my orders are to draw the devils out into the low-lying ground."

"Why do you want to do that?"

The captain immediately whispers a few words in his ear, and Zhang Zhicheng bursts out laughing.

"Ha ha! Excellent, that plan should be called 'cooking the Tokyo goose to make Japanese sausages'! But it's going to take a fierce effort to draw them out, so instead of withdrawing, I need to stay and help you. If the Japanese aren't tempted out, we can still charge in and chivvy them out."

WHILE THE FIGHTING on the ridge is at its height, another scene is playing out elsewhere. Two horse-drawn carts are moving along the old Incense Road. Even though it is a mountain road, the skill of the carters, cracking their whips, and the exertion of the mules and horses between the shafts, mean that they are keeping up a trot. Seven or eight musicians are sitting in the lead cart, and the one behind is pulling the coffin, helped by Lao Zhang, Wangtian and several others, all dressed in mourning clothes. The coffin is indeed the one that contained Yang Zhixing's body, but now it contains explosives rather than a corpse.

Qi Yuexuan has not found it easy to be so callous, and he can't help saying as much when he truncates the funeral procession. He had originally hoped to give Uncle Yang a dignified funeral, never expecting that, after all the formal farewells are over, the very last act would be ruined by the Japanese. When they are still at the foot of the mountain, he has forbidden the formal musicians to accompany them. However, in the past, there was always an annual temple fair at Laoqiying, so it is no problem to find a few drummers and trumpeters. In the end, Qi Yuexuan has allowed Wangtian to take the role of the filial son, and Second Master Dong has provided some explosives experts who are acting as pall-bearers. But Lao Zhang has insisted on coming too, saying that this is all his idea, and he is afraid that, if he doesn't go, things won't be done properly. He is normally such an easy-going fellow, but today he is digging his heels in, and no one can budge him, so Qi Yuexuan has no choice but to agree.

As it turns out, it is a good thing that Lao Zhang has come along, since although the other men going along may be expert at messing around with explosives, and some of them have fought in battle, all of them put together cannot match him in a battle of wits. Once up on the cart, he starts organising everything as he thinks fit. He certainly seems to be right in all his suggestions and to have thought of every eventuality. So much so that even the leader of the other men says: "You tell us what to do when the time comes, master, and we'll do it."

As they arrive beside Fucha, Lao Zhang orders: "Slow down and make the drums and trumpets sound especially plaintive. Whatever you do, don't get excited. If anything happens, the rest of you keep quiet and let me do the talking."

Almost immediately, they do indeed hear the challenge of a Japanese sentry coming from atop a high slope: "*Matte ku desai!*" This means something like: "Stay where you are for me."

Of course, Lao Zhang doesn't understand Japanese, but he catches the tone of voice and sees the accompanying gestures, so can make a good guess. He orders the wagons to halt, jumps down, bows respectfully, straightens up and smiles, before calling out: "We are good citizens, great lord!"

"What is doing?"

"Taking a coffin for burial." Lao Zhang is worried the man won't understand, so he points at the coffin and goes on: "Dead person, we do dead person things."

"Yours is where from?"

"We've come from the city and are going to Zhangjia Valley up ahead. We have certificates of good citizenship and travel passes."

Although Lao Zhang holds up the passes and certificates for the sentry to see, the man still shouts: "Fighting here! *Da-me! Da-me!* [No good! No good!]"

Lao Zhang understands what he means from his gestures, so he replies, adding gestures of his own: "If dead people aren't buried, they get very stinky. Do you understand? Bad stinky to make you sick, very catching... cholera kill everybody."

The Japanese doesn't fully understand, but the word 'cholera' catches his ear. He turns round and begins to shout to his comrades.

At the same time, Lao Zhang throws a package wrapped in oil paper up the slope, scaring the two sentries out of their wits. When they recover themselves, they discover that, inside the package, is an offering of roast chicken and a wad of bank notes.

From the bottom of the slope, Lao Zhang shouts up: "*Misi, misi* [eat, eat], great lord!"

The Japanese soldiers' expressions brighten, and they call out, gesturing: "On your way."

When Lao Zhang hears this, he shouts out a command, and the music and the wailing start up again.

THE DAM IN ZHANGJIA VALLEY is in the ravine between Horn Mountain and Tiantaishan. It is only a dozen or so *zhang* wide. The slopes of the mountains on either side are very steep, especially on the Horn Mountain side where the landslide happened. This isn't one of the main floodwater channels on the mountain, but there has been a lot of rain this year, and it has filled up completely. In the distance you can see some places where the water is already overflowing the dam.

As Lao Zhang and the others reach this place, flames and black smoke can already be seen rising from the direction of Fucha. Very soon, fanned by the wind, the smoke has rolled over the whole area of low-lying ground.

"Come on, brothers, let's get a move on. They're on the second act already up ahead, and we don't want to be late for our star turn."

Lao Zhang hears everyone shout "Yes!" in unison, and the sound of it rouses his spirit and makes the hairs on the back of his neck stand on end. He has spent many decades raising all sorts of insects, but it has been the crickets that saw the action; he has guarded tombs for many decades, but the people he has watched over were no longer breathing; he has won buildings and land; he has had great handfuls of prize money, but none of this has ever earned him respect. Yet today's performance of *Borrowing the East Wind*, with him playing the parts both of Zhuge Liang and Zhao Yun, has really satisfied his craving to take the lead role. He stands there, hand on hip, gesturing and puffing out his pigeon chest, shouting out orders, directing the men, and everyone thinks he is like a man possessed, as his normal, laid-back, tricksy self has disappeared. He may be a bit taller and thinner than your average heavenly general,[1] but he still has a distinct air of command.

But for whatever reason, something always happens at the last moment. Everybody has made a heroic effort to carry the coffin from the roadside to the edge of the ravine, swung it on ropes to the bottom and settled it right in the middle of the dam. Once they have climbed up out of the ravine, the fuse is lit, and the flame sputters forward until it disappears. They cover their ears, waiting on either side, but the expected explosion never comes.

"What's going on?" Lao Zhang asks in agitation.

If he is agitated, the man who set the explosives is even more so. Sweat pours down his face as he blusters: "I expect... it must be... the fuse must be damp."

"Quick! Get down there and take a look."

"Just... just wait a bit... it's too dangerous to... to go down there now."

"Keep waiting? We could be waiting forever!"

Seeing how angry Lao Zhang is getting, the man has no choice but to climb back down into the ravine. He resets the fuse, sees that it is lit, then clambers out. The flame reaches its end again, but there is still no noise or movement from the coffin. Before Lao Zhang can even ask, the man says hurriedly: "There's nothing wrong with the way I set the fuse. That's not the problem. It must be the gunpowder that's damp."

"Does... does that mean it won't go off?"

"Not unless we can light a flame right up against it."

"Well get on and do that!"

The man doesn't say a word but just chokes and goes bright red. The leader of the gang sighs and takes over: "You mustn't blame him, master. None of us checked it after we took it out of the storage shed."

"I haven't got time to blame anyone. Just get on and light it."

"That's easy for you to say, but how? How are we supposed to light it? The powder is wet – too small a flame won't light it, and too big a one will set it all off at once. There'll be no time to take cover even if we had wings. You're just sending him to his death, aren't you!"

"Then who do you suggest does it?"

"Whoever volunteers. But even if someone is willing to take the risk, what about his wife and children? What about his parents? Who would look after them?"

"Then..." But Lao Zhang is stumped for words.

Wangtian has kept quiet because he knows he is no explosives expert, but now he steps forward and says: "A man shouldn't be a soldier if he's afraid of death. I'll do it. When the fart's already in your arsehole, why hold it back? Everybody has a family and livelihood to think of, but in the kind of emergency were in, someone has to do it."

So saying, he ties a rope around his waist.

"You can't go!" Lao Zhang hurriedly pulls him back. "Have you no thought for your wife, for your family? You have just been entrusted with the property of a great household. Who are you going to dump that on so carelessly?"

Before Wangtian can reply, the gang leader gets in first: "Enough, brother. You've shown your worth, and the important thing is you didn't hesitate but were willing to play for real. It's enough that you have volunteered, but it's not your job to perform. I'll go."

He snatches back the rope and ties it round himself, saying: "You go back and help me by having a word with your Young Master on my behalf, and make sure they pay my fee and look after my family if I die." Then he glances at Lao Zhang. "As for you, don't you listen to any more smart-arse, stupid ideas. If the emperor isn't worried, the eunuch should stay out of it."

With that, in two strides he is straddling the side of the ravine, and with a twist of his body he is over and heading down. Qi Yuexuan gets there too late to grab hold of him, but he catches up the rope and doesn't let go.

At the same time, Lao Zhang rushes over like a madman, takes hold of the man's collar and, heedless of anything else, hauls him back up, cursing as he does so: "Don't you have anyone to look after? I'm sure your mother and father didn't raise you to do such shameful things? To lose face by arguing and make others lose face too? To make fun of other people's shortcomings? Even to desecrate the tomb of a poor wretch whose family line has ended when he died childless? Or to harangue a poor widow for her moral failings? I'm older than your father, but you still dare lose your temper with me? What a stupid idea, eh? You're the clever one, I suppose! So what if I'm a eunuch? I may not be a whole man, but I'm still a man, the most wretched and contrary of men. Yes, I'm a servant, but the men I have served have been emperors and princes who wouldn't give you a second glance."

Lao Zhang is jumping up and down, so angry his whole body seems to quiver, and everyone stares at him in amazement, wondering that a few words could have provoked him into such a state.

The gang leader doesn't say any more, but just shoots him a look, mutters the word "Nutjob!" and prepares to go back down into the ravine. But Lao Zhang rushes forward again, seizes hold of the rope around the man's waist and gives it a yank, hard enough to pull him off balance.

"What the fuck do you think you're doing?" the man asks.

Lao Zhang stands with his hands on his hips, his back to the edge of the ravine and says, in a loud voice: "This was my idea, and I'll do it. I don't need you. I am all alone and have no dependents. If I kick the bucket, no one will mourn my loss. You youngsters must leave today's business to me. There'll be no need for payment or recompense for my family, or any nonsense about mourning and funeral processions. If you still have a conscience and want to look good, then just give me your approval."

Everyone stands around looking awkward. Wangtian makes to pull Lao Zhang back, but when he sees how determined he appears, he stops after one step and doesn't dare go any closer.

Noticing this, Lao Zhang beckons to him: "Come over here, Wangtian. I've got something to say to you." He waits until Wangtian is next to him, then whispers: "There is something hidden on top of the ridgepole in the western chamber. It's my genitals. Please have them buried with me so I can be a whole man when I come back in my next life. Please don't forget, but don't show me up either."

"Alright, I'll help you. Let's talk a little further back from the edge, alright? I'm not going to stop you if you want to go down there, but don't you need a rope?" Wangtian says, hoping to trick him.

Lao Zhang just laughs. "That's alright. If you're willing to help me take this load off my mind, then there's nothing more to say. My life has been like a cricket's – pushed around and held in the palms of people's hands, a life of inescapable hardship. But today, it is my own choice to jump into the arena, and baring my fangs and risking my life is for my own satisfaction."

So saying, he shoves Wangtian away, turns on his heel and moves swiftly down the slope and into the ravine. Everyone else rushes down to the edge of the ravine, their hearts in their mouths. Lao Zhang slips easily down five or six *zhang* of slope to the bottom of the ravine. He squirms his way over to the coffin, pries open its lid and, with some considerable effort, scrambles on top of it. He gestures excitedly to the top of the ravine and stretches out inside the coffin. His face disappears. All that can be seen of him are his two hands clutching a box of matches, and all that is heard is a shout of laughter and a loud voice saying: "Ha ha, Yang Zhixing, I've found a use for your coffin. If you're not happy, it just serves you right. Who gave you permission to bad-mouth me? Well, this old man's going to make you eat your words. Look out, here I come!"

As he speaks, he strikes a match, and just after it flares into life, there is a deafening noise and the mountainside trembles. A great spurt of smoke, dust and water leaps into the sky and fills the ravine. Once the smoke and dust have cleared, everyone can see that a gap several *zhang* wide has been ripped in the dam, and a torrent of water is already rushing down the ravine. Everybody standing at the top of the slope falls, as one, to their knees.

"Go in peace, old master!" they cry out.

AN HOUR LATER, the battle is over. Most of the Japanese cavalry from Zhangjiakou, who have just been transferred in from Chahar and Suiyuan, have either burned to death or drowned. Those left in the village have been surrounded by the Eighth Route Army and the reinforcements from the other villages, and not a single one has escaped. They did in fact capture two or three alive, but the villagers were in a killing frenzy, and they shot or cut them down without a second thought. Later they learn that another three or four devils have been very lucky and have been washed down onto the river bank downstream. Twenty or thirty horses that didn't accompany their masters to the grave are rescued by the villagers. But the casualties suffered by the heroic army of the Left Barracks are not inconsiderable either, and not counting previous losses, there are a dozen or so killed and twenty or more wounded. Seven or eight soldiers from the Eighth Route Army also gave up their lives, and half of the rest are wounded. There are ten or twelve wounded or dead among the villagers; half the trees and bushes on the mountainside have burned down; and several dozen houses have been destroyed. If the floodwater hadn't put out the fires, there's no knowing how much higher the cost might have been.

Later on, a number of the men who scattered when they broke out of the encirclement return, one by one. But the peasant army of the Left Barracks, which numbered more than four hundred when it was formed, has now lost more than half its men. Qi Yuexuan and Second Master Dong both feel that, having suffered such a catastrophic defeat, the Japanese are not going to take it lying down and are sure to remount their clean-up operation. In order to protect their remaining forces, they decide to leave behind only the most seriously wounded and to follow the Eighth Route Army, taking their walking wounded with them. So, on the afternoon of the same day, they let Zhang Zhicheng lead them away west along the ridge.

LATER EVENTS PROVE their decision to be the right one. As soon as the section of the Japanese Army charged with the clean-up operation get news of the annihilation of this force, they initiate retaliatory action. It is, however, already the day after by the time they receive this news. One reason for this is that, although the Japanese cavalry had walkie-talkies, they had a very limited range, and the distance was too great for them to connect to their base. So, no matter how fierce the battle, no one outside the mountains got to hear of it. Another reason is that the troops transferred in from Charhar and Suiyuan are newly arrived and still separate from the Japanese Army in Beiping; they have not yet integrated and do not have a coordinated command system. Not only is the enemy's intelligence lagging behind, they are not even clear about exactly who it is they are fighting. According to the reports Zhou Zhengjie gave them, Qiwangfen is in Zhao Ran's territory, and he doesn't mention the local militia of the Left Barracks. Moreover, it happens that a number of the Japanese soldiers who fled the scene report that the enemy was the Eighth Route Army. On top of this, they also have a report saying that, that afternoon, a force of more than a hundred men had headed west out of the Left Barracks and crossed the Yongding River. From all this, they formed the judgment that the attack was the work of guerrilla units of the Eighth Route Army.

SO, ON THE AFTERNOON OF THE FOLLOWING DAY, a squadron of Japanese soldiers goes back into the mountains, accompanied by some other Japanese and Chinese turncoats from Wanping County. Qi Yuexuan has made his preparations the day before, moving the wounded and the supplies into caves at the top of the mountain. He also orders that all the Japanese corpses, and anything else left behind, even including the dead horses, be piled up together. Outwardly, Qi Yuexuan maintains the manner of the chairman of a 'preservation committee' when out and about among the others, yet inwardly he is feeling pretty confident. The troops brought in from Charhar and Suiyuan have no knowledge of what is going on in the area, and the soldiers from Wanping and the Chinese turncoats have no intention of taking responsibility for their own sector. They have swept the area and found not a single Eighth Route Army man, and they have carried out a full inspection and discovered nothing amiss. So in the end, all they can do is carry off some provisions and other portable property before departing.

Whether or not they are really as stupid as they appear, their final report on the matter reads: 'We confirm this attack was the work of the guerrilla forces of the Eighth Route Army who returned to their base after carrying it out. The chance event of a sudden mountain flood caused very heavy casualties on both sides. Our side's casualties number eighty-two, including Colonel Ichiro Harayama, and we calculate the losses of the Eighth Route Army at more than two hundred. The people of the Left Barracks have not, as yet, joined with the Eighth Route Army, and their sterling efforts to gather together the bodies of the soldiers of the Imperial Army and their belongings merit commendation.'

Qi Yuexuan had had to steel himself to go, but when he hears himself praised rather than punished, all kinds of emotions well up inside him.

"Ai!" he cries out. "How Lao Zhang would laugh if he were still with us. They've suffered a great defeat and had their claws snapped off, and they don't know who it was that bit them. What a cave-full of stupid crickets!" Laughing and cursing, the tears roll down his cheeks.

Shortly afterwards, three new graves are dug tight next to one another in the Qi family plot. The large one in the middle is the communal grave for the Eighth Route Army, and the two smaller ones in front of it belong to Yang Zhixing and Lao Zhang. There was no body left to bury for Lao Zhang, so all that is in his grave is the insect-rearing equipment from his room. Wangtian did not forget the task the old man entrusted him with, and he found the cloth bundle hidden on top of the ridgepole. Without telling anyone else, he secretly put it inside a cricket gourd, so it was buried with everything else. They did not dare write any names on the wooden plaque in front of the large grave in the middle, which reads, simply: 'Common grave of righteous warriors'; and underneath that: 'Erected by all the people of the Left Barracks'. The names of the donors on the plaque in front of Yang Zhixing's grave reads: 'Wife of the Yang family from the Yan clan. Daughter Yue E', but in the same space on Lao Zhang's plaque is written the single word 'Sons', and underneath, tightly packed, are more than a dozen names, headed by that of Gao Wangtian, and followed by those of every single person who witnessed Lao Zhang's heroic sacrifice.

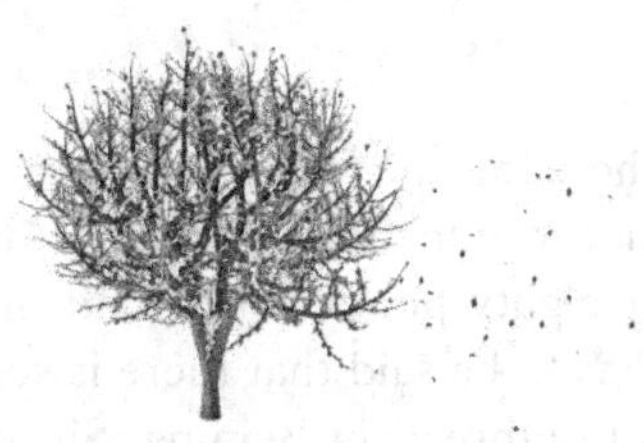

Chapter 55

The quarantine unit to which Clown has been sent is situated outside the Xuanwu Gate, on a dirt road east of Jiaochangkou and west of Xiaxie Street. A length of dilapidated ancient wall there is said to date from the Liao dynasty, so the stretch of road is known as 'Old Wall Base'. In the middle section of the road is the Empty Cloud Daoist Temple, built during the reign of Emperor Qianlong and comprising more than fifty halls and other buildings. The quarantine unit the Japanese opened occupies several of the courtyards of this temple. Of course, this is not the only such unit in Beiping; there is one in Pingfang in the eastern part of the city and another in the Horse God Temple in the west. When Clown was arrested at the Guang'an Gate, he was sent to the Empty Cloud Temple because it was the closest.

Clown already knew this was not the kind of place anyone wanted to find themselves in, but once he is there, he realises that even a devil would want out. There are no beds or *kangs* in the room, just millet straw strewn on the floor. The straw has never been changed since it was first laid, so it is damp, sticky, rancid, smelly, and infested with fleas and bedbugs. There are up to twenty men in the one room, and not only can they not lie down, they can hardly even stretch their feet out when they sit. Prisons have exercise periods, but there's no hope of that here, and the only way out of the room is when you're dead. A small window is opened once a day, and each man gets two cornbread and a ladle of water. The door of the room is also opened daily, and men wearing white gowns and surgical masks come in, take out anyone who has died, order someone to empty the slop buckets, and finally use a spray gun to cover everyone and everything in limewater. The place is called a quarantine unit, but there is no sign of a single doctor, and no injections are ever given or medicines distributed. There is, however, a cremation furnace in the rear courtyard, so when you die out front, you are burned out back. The foul-smelling black smoke that belches out of the chimney envelops the neighbouring households, giving all the residents headaches. Even in the height of summer, they prefer to boil indoors rather than open their doors and windows. This place is no quarantine unit, but a mortuary and crematorium combined.

. . .

THE INMATES are all there for one reason: 'cholera'. Some are genuine cases, some not. Cholera is a highly infectious intestinal disease, and at this time, the mortality rate is over eighty per cent. Its main medium of transmission is the water supply, and it has to be said that there is something a little odd about the existence of a cholera outbreak in Beiping. Since the building of Dadu in the Yuan dynasty, this has been the site of the capital city, and not only has it always been favoured in terms of prevailing wind and of water source, it has also always been meticulously laid out, so there has never been any problem with the water supply. At the end of the Qing and the beginning of the Republic, the city area had running water; even in the smaller hutongs where the supply didn't reach, and the areas just outside the city walls, whether they drew water from a well or had it delivered by water carts, it was as clear and perfectly safe to drink. From ancient times, the people of Beijing have never been troubled by cholera, so now it has appeared, they have taken to saying it is a disease brought in by the Japanese. They have no supporting evidence, and it is just a supposition. Even after the defeat of the Japanese, the matter continued to be something of a mystery. It is only when remains are dug up after the Liberation of 1949 and tested, and the doctored enemy records are set straight, that the answer to this puzzle emerges.

It turns out that the Japanese biological warfare research bases were not just limited to Unit 731[1] in Harbin and Fushun in northeastern China. Similar secret bases were located in Changchun, Beiping, Nanjing, Guangzhou and even in Nanyang and Tokyo itself. The Beiping base was situated just south of the west gate of the Temple of Heaven. In Qing times, the complex was the Office of Divine Music, and after the Revolution, it became the Centre for the Prevention of Infectious Diseases. After the Japanese Army occupied Beiping, they immediately took control of this establishment. At first, it was outwardly called the 'North China Epidemic Prevention and Water Purification Department', which later became 'No. 151 Military Hospital'. Internally it was known as the '1855 Grade One Unit'. They used studies, initially intended for the preparation of vaccines against infectious diseases, for the production of biological weapons that included bubonic plague, cholera and anthrax. As well as breeding large numbers of rats, mosquitoes and fleas to advance their experiments in the cultivation of bacteria, every three months they conducted experiments in infection on live subjects, a hundred people in each batch. Most of them were prisoners of war, but some were beggars taken off the streets. It was in the spring of 1938 that the people began to learn about 'cholera' for the first time, and by August 1943, the epidemic is at its height. At its peak, one thousand eight hundred people die in Beiping in a single month, but the source of the infection remains hidden behind the high walls of the Japanese Army's secret germ warfare base. After the defeat of the Japanese, even though they dispersed all the staff and

552

destroyed all the records, materials and equipment, a lot of evidence remained behind.

OF COURSE, Clown's admission into this living hell is entirely contrived. The fact is that only a few of the people in same room are genuine cholera cases, and the majority are similarly falsely incarcerated. How do the Japanese choose the Chinese to put in here? They just look for anyone who has the runs, is throwing up, running a fever or is generally debilitated by illness. It only takes a couple of weeks in these surroundings for a minor illness to become a major one, or for a healthy person to get sick. Anyone who enters is done for and will end up dead and turned to ashes. Their friends and relatives don't expect to see them again. At this time, many Beipingers who catch cold are too afraid to go to hospital for fear they may be classed as having 'cholera'.

When Clown first enters this establishment, he goes as crazy as a sparrow when it's first put in a cage. All afternoon, he claws repeatedly at the little window, yelling over and over again: "I don't have cholera. I shouldn't be in here. Let me out!"

He yells himself hoarse, but no one outside takes any notice. As evening approaches, the door to the room finally opens, and the men in white gowns come in. Before he can say a word, he is slapped twice around the face and gets a mouthful of limewater. He tries to chat to the other people in the room, but not one of them even opens his eyes. With nowhere to vent his anger and resentment, our five-foot hero is so frustrated, all he can do is howl and wail. When this gives him no relief, he stiffens his resolve and begins to sing comic *ping* opera songs. In Clown's home province of Liaoning, *yangge* folk dance and stilt-walking are very popular. Stilt-walking is called 'ground-bouncing', and the songs that are sung to accompany it are the *ping* opera songs known as 'bouncing songs'. After the Liberation, the name was changed to 'two-man turns'. Men and women, young and old, can all sing this kind of song, and little children still in open-leg trousers can hum a few bars. Even the chants of shamans and the laments of professional mourners have a flavour of it. So it is hardly surprising that, in his misery, Clown turns to these songs, and what he sings is the most mournful of all the operas, *Weeping Through the Five Watches of the Night*. He doesn't sing the first two watches but starts at the most wretched of them all, the third watch. In this, as the crescent moon rises, Lady Meng Jiang[2] goes in search of Fan Lang.

> *My thoughts are sad.*
> *I have travelled a thousand* li *in search of my husband.*
> *I did not expect to find his body lying in the desolation.*
> *Under the bloodstains, I recognise my man.*
> *I cannot hold back my tears.*

Heaven pity me! Earth help me!
My wails have brought down the Great Wall.

Previously, when he spoke, no one replied, and when he wept no one consoled him, but this song makes everyone in the room open their eyes, and some even begin to croon along with him.

To Clown's surprise, one of the Japanese soldiers on duty comes over to him and says, in a mixture of Chinese and Japanese: "*Yoshi*, your *ping ping. Subarashii!* Yours is Manchuria? Mine is Fengtian garrison. Understand?"

Clown understands a little Japanese and knows that '*yoshi*' and '*subarashii*' are both expressions of approval. He also understands that the man has been posted in Fengtian, so has heard 'two-man turns' before. He hurriedly continues in his own mixture of Chinese and Japanese: "*Hai*. I'm Manchuria Railway *shigoto* [worker]. Cholera *chigaimasu* [no/is not]. You must let me go."

Although Clown is talking in a mixture of pidgin Japanese and Chinese, the Japanese soldier seems to understand him. What he has said is that he once worked on the Manchuria Railway, that he doesn't have cholera, and that he has been falsely incarcerated and should be released. The soldier looks him over carefully and smiles without saying anything. Clown still thinks he might be onto something, so he waits, heart in his mouth, for the soldier to speak. The soldier maintains his silence for a long time, then laughs and spits out a stream of Japanese.

Roughly translated, what he says is: "You say you don't have cholera, but what proof do you have? If you're still alive and kicking in a few days' time, we can talk again. Your singing isn't bad, so keep going, loud as you like. But don't sing any more of that sad, moaning stuff. Sing some funny ones about chasing after girls. Understand?"

This just infuriates Clown, and, after huffing and puffing for a bit, he mutters: "Fuck it, you're really taking the piss. I do my best to entertain you, you little devil, and you just laugh while I have to keep singing?"

He doesn't think the soldier will understand and is taken aback when he sees the man's face darken as he brandishes his rifle, saying: "*Baku!* No singing then sure is cholera, soon die, soon die!"

He cocks his rifle.

But Clown doesn't retreat. He considers in silence for a moment, then begins to sing a comic folksong:

Ai! How pretty the girls are beyond the Pass!
They draw the bandits and the wolves.
One day a foolish thief breaks in,
Thinking he knows what he's doing.
He breaks in one evening and sees
A body lying there, all plump and curvy

In black leather gloves and black leather shoes.
Her black hair slick and shiny as oil.
Her black leather cloak is very fine,
Fastened down the front with two rows of bronze buttons.
The foolish thief, his passions roused,
Plans to rape the girl then steal some food.
He puts his arms around her,
Struggling and straining,
When curses erupt from behind him:
"Fool! Do you think you can
Lie in that pigsty and not get filthy?"
Aihai, aihai! Aihaiyeehai!

It sounds just like a sow being mated. And indeed, before he has finished singing, the laughter begins to ripple round, inside and outside the room, and Clown throws all caution to the winds. He doesn't know what this Japanese soldier has in store for him, but even if it's death, he intends to have his fun with him first.

To his surprise, the Japanese soldier laughs harder than anyone else and shouts out: "*Yoshi! Subasashii!* Sing! Go on!"

From this, Clown realises that he has stumbled on someone really dumb, so he stops even bothering to play up to him. He begins to add actions to his singing and puts a bit of everything into the words, sung and spoken. Now blunt, now subtle, now crude, now refined, he mixes it all up together. As he really throws himself into it and his language gets cruder and cruder, the Chinese in the room are panic-stricken, but the Japanese soldier rocks to and fro in amusement. It is not until after midnight, when the soldier goes off duty, that Clown finally stops.

THE NEXT DAY, after such a manic night, Clown is very much on edge. How would you feel, if you'd sung your heart out, wringing your brain empty of ideas, and you just had to grin and bear it when everyone moaned at you and cursed you, and you became the butt of their ridicule, like a little boy pretending to be all grown up? But as it turns out, Clown hasn't been wasting his energies, and in the evening of the third day, some good does come out of it all. The Japanese soldier has changed from the pre-midnight shift to the post-midnight one, and by the time everyone in the room has gone to sleep, there is still no sign of him coming back to demand more songs. Clown was a little troubled by the first night's singing, but it had made him feel more settled, and afterwards, all sweaty from his exertions, he had just collapsed on the ground and gone to sleep. Today, however, the same sleep eludes him, and he might just as well have his eyes wide open. The faces of all the people in his life whom he misses, loves, resents and hates dance before his eyes in never-ending rotation, destroying any chance of sleep. Constantly in the background is also the idiot Japanese soldier.

The soldier can't get Clown out of his head either, and after a while, he comes sidling back. He doesn't say anything, but just unlocks the door to the room and opens it. He beckons to Clown and says: "Yours, come out."

"What... what for?"

"Yours cholera dead. Take dead, take burn."

Clown jumps up and down in agitation, gesturing wildly: "Mine isn't cholera, isn't! *Chigaimasu!*"

The soldier doesn't reply. He pulls Clown out of the room, relocks the door, then smiles and points: "Yours not understand? There is cholera dead. Your burn."

"Aaaah! So someone's dead, and you want me to burn them?"

"*Hai!*"

Clown's spirits rise from the depths to which they had plummeted, and he follows the soldier into the rear courtyard.

There are no proper buildings in the rear courtyard, just two small rooms beside the path. A brick-built cremation furnace is also situated within the courtyard, about the height of a man, behind which is a large chimney. The courtyard is large and filled with heaping piles of coal, firewood, ashes and furnace slag, just leaving space for the narrow path. Two bodies are lying in front of the furnace. A man is in the act of stoking the fire with slag soaked in diesel. The flames in the furnace are leaping and crackling, and the black smoke is streaming out of the chimney. When he gets closer and can see clearly, Clown realises that the 'man' is, in fact, a youth of no more than thirteen or fourteen. The work coat he is wearing is several sizes too big and is threatening to slip off him at any moment, while the surgical mask covering his face just leaves his two eyes staring out.

When he sees Clown about to step closer, he says urgently: "Stay back a bit. Put a coat and mask on first. He's infectious." He has a strong local accent and sounds like a miniature adult.

The soldier takes a work coat and a mask out of one of the rooms, and he gives them to Clown. He watches him put them on, then says something in Japanese, the general import of which is that this is where Clown will work from now on. He is not allowed to leave the courtyard; in fact he is not allowed to many things, on pain of death.

Only pretending to listen, Clown nods his head and agrees promptly. He is beginning to believe there may be some hope, and he can't resist asking: "When can I get out, great lord?"

Either the Japanese doesn't understand, or he is feigning stupidity, and he just grunts in reply. Then he turns to leave the courtyard, but after a couple of steps, he looks back and says with a grin: "Mine is look out front. *Kamate.* Yours is keeping singing songs."

"Ah, then..." Clown is about to follow the soldier and ask again, but he is held back by the young lad. Only when the soldier has left the courtyard does the lad say: "Do you think you can get out if you work here, elder brother? Ha! Not a chance!"

"Why not? I'm fit and active so I can't have cholera, can I?"

"No, you don't. How many people here do you think actually do? I've been here two months, but didn't my workmate, Elder Brother Zhang, die in here?"

"Of cholera?"

"What cholera! He died... Ai!" The youth sighs, bites back what he was going to say and changes the subject. "Keep working while you're talking, or there'll be trouble if they see you."

Clown picks up a spade and shovels some slag, but he still can't resist asking: "So what did he die of?"

"Well, you haven't burned him yet, have you! He's there on the left. Look for yourself."

Clown hurriedly kneels down beside the body and sees that there is a gash about half a *zhang* long, laying open the belly and exposing the intestines. The blood is already clotted, but it is all over the corpse and the ground beside it in clumps and patches. The sight of this throws Clown completely, but he steadies himself and asks: "What... what happened here?"

Exasperated, the youth finally tells the truth.

It's all connected with that Japanese soldier. His name is Kameda, and he's not even a sergeant, just a veteran infantryman. This 'quarantine unit' is only manned by six or seven Japanese soldiers, and since he has the longest service, he has been made head guard. The top brass pays very little attention to this godforsaken place, so this Kameda has the opportunity to run it as he pleases and do whatever he likes. To call him a dirty old man would be being polite. He is quite simply a perverted bastard. Any women who come into the place, no matter how old, become the objects of his evil attentions. If, after three days, they show no signs of cholera, he sends them to live in those two little rooms in the rear courtyard. They work by day, and at night become the sex slaves of Kameda and the other Japanese soldiers. Over the last few months, six or seven women have been admitted to the unit, and, of them, only one has died of cholera; the others have all been tortured to death by the guards. No more women have been admitted for a little while, so Kameda has turned his attentions onto the men, and filled the gap with any good-looking youths who are free from disease. This Elder Brother Zhang was one such. The evening before, Clown had stirred Kameda's lust with his singing, so he had gone to the rear courtyard hoping to slake it on Brother Zhang. But Zhang was not feeling well, and when Kameda shook him awake, he pushed him away and said something uncomplimentary. This offended Kameda, so he snatched up his bayonet and sliced open his belly. Normally, corpses here are cremated during the day, but Kameda was afraid of the affair being bruited abroad, so he ordered Zhang's body to be burnt in the middle of the night.

Clown's first reaction when he hears this story is not anger and even less is it fear. He feels as though his insides have been turned upside-down with disgust. Although the youth has only talked about Elder Brother Zhang, from his humiliated, hangdog look as he is speaking, and the stumbling way he goes about his work, Clown is afraid that he hasn't escaped the clutches of Kameda either. Clown is old enough, and has knocked around the market long enough to have seen all manner of shameful, evil, humiliating things, but he has never heard of anything to rival this. With the youth's help, he puts Elder Brother Zhang's body into the iron drawer of the furnace, pushes it in, and says through gritted teeth: "This can't go on, brother. Let's escape."

"Escape? How? There's electric wire on top of the walls and guards on all the gates inside and out. How's anyone going to get past their guns?"

"Whether we get out or not, it's got to be worth the risk. Even death is better than what's going on here. The two of us..."

Before he can finish, the youth surreptitiously tugs at his sleeve. He stops in surprise, turns to look and sees that Kameda has come into the courtyard. Hastily, he snatches a poker and begins to stir up the coals under the furnace. Kameda walks over to him.

"Yours is rest. Singing opera songs."

When Clown turns and looks into those narrowed, slit-like eyes, his face begins to twitch uncontrollably. He gets a grip on himself and raises a thin smile. "Alright then. Tell me what to sing."

"Flower girls, ha ha!" Kameda unslings his rifle and put it to one side as he sits down on a pile of firewood.

"Right, I'll sing you a bawdy one – *Two Sisters Open a Cathouse*. How about that?"

"Cathouse? Ah, understand. Sing!"

"But..." Clown deliberately keeps him waiting, and he looks around searchingly.

"Yours is what looking?" says Kameda, rolling his eyes.

Clown laughs and gestures. "Ah, I'm looking for something I can ring like a bell in time to the song. It will make it more fun."

"Like a bell? Huh." Kameda looks around too.

Clown looks at him and his eyes light up. "Ha! That will do!"

"What?"

"That bunch of keys with the wooden tag on your belt."

"This?"

Kameda unhooks the keys and Clown snatches them from him. As Kameda glares at him, he is already beginning to hum the tune, and he twists his body and face into an exaggerated theatrical pose. His flashing eyes are riveting.

"Aah! *Yoshi*! Clang clang!" Kameda slaps his thigh, laughing.

"Ai! The spring wind fills the nostrils with its fragrance / As the two sisters primp and preen in their embroidered chamber..."

Clown shakes the keys, beating time on its wooden tag. His hand moves to his throat as he sings and dances, smoothly turning away with neat little stage steps. He sees that Kameda's eyes are fixed on him. At this point, the youth, who has dodged off to one side, sighs, spits slyly and curses vehemently: "Pah, just another fucking show-off! Really..."

Before he can finish, there is a 'clang' as he sees something fly past him, glance off the iron plate at the mouth of the furnace and tumble into the belly of the furnace itself.

"Aiyo!" Clown exclaims, rushing over to the furnace. "That was the key ring!"

"*Baku!*" Kameda panics, as all the keys are on that key ring. Cursing, he runs over to the furnace, pushes Clown aside and looks inside it himself.

The wood-fired furnace has three openings, one above the other, the bottom one of which is for raking out the cinders. It is below ground level and is normally covered with an iron plate. The middle opening is where the fuel goes in and is no more than a foot above the ground. The top one at head height is where the bodies go, and is two-foot square. You just have to lean forward to look in; there's no need to bend down at all.

As Kameda reaches the furnace mouth, beside him, Clown already has the poker in his hand. Before he knows what's happening, the Japanese soldier feels a rush of cold air sweep past his ear, and something thuds into the top of his head. He tries to shout out, but no sound emerges; his legs go weak, and he leans across the opening to the furnace. Clown doesn't let him fall, but throws aside the poker, bends down, clutches him round the legs and shoves them into the furnace opening. In an instant, his head and shoulders are inside, and his hair begins to crackle in the flames. At this point, the pain revives Kameda, and he begins to yell and clutch at the sides of the opening, his legs scrabbling for purchase. Clown doesn't dare let go, but Kameda has the strength of a pack-donkey in his struggles, and he finds he can't hold him. He is about to release his grip, when the youth rushes up with an iron shovel and rams it viciously into Kameda's buttocks. Seeing this, Clown thrusts upwards with desperate strength, and this time, the Japanese can no longer hold on. His grip slips, and he is fully inside the furnace. The furnace cover is slid into place and barred, so it is no use struggling any more. Quite soon, all sounds of movement cease.

"We're in real trouble now, elder brother. How are we going to escape?" the youth asks, his voice trembling.

Clown doesn't reply but just takes something from inside his jacket and hands it to him. When he looks, he sees it is the bunch of keys, which Clown hasn't actually thrown into the furnace but merely concealed with a cunning sleight of hand.

"Go and open all the cell doors, while I find some way of cutting off the electricity," Clown says. "When the lights go out, don't get confused. We'll make a dash for it together, then once we're out, it's every man for himself."

Some seven or eight minutes later, the lights in the courtyards suddenly go out. Since the Japanese occupied Beiping, the power supply has always been inadequate, and localised power cuts are a common occurrence, so the Japanese sentries on duty don't take any notice. It is only when they hear the clamour of raised voices and see a dark mass of people flooding out of the courtyard, that they realise something major is up. But what can they do to stop it? The shouts of the guards and the reports of their rifles ring out. Men fall, one after the other, but those who don't, continue to press forward...

EVEN IN THE SMALL HOURS, Yuerong's Place is still open. In normal times, the last clients have left by ten o'clock, but these are not normal times. There are only a few drunkards around, as everyone else understands that, however tempting the food and wine, if they want to survive, they have no option but to go home in the evening and stay clear of the inns and restaurants. But the people gathered this day in the private room on the second floor are not like this; they are all well-connected, well-protected bigwigs and top brass. The previous day, the interim government has made the formal announcement of Zhou Zhengjie's appointment to the Committee of Government Affairs, responsible for the newspaper industry, and simultaneously, as section chief of the intelligence department. Zhou Zhengjie is playing host today, and he figures that wine will do well to celebrate his appointments, and equally well to thank his patrons; they are, after all, VIPs from all over the government and the army. Even the commander of the Japanese Army of North China, Hayao Tada, has come, although he doesn't stay long before leaving when he feels he has given Zhou Zhengjie sufficient face. In fact, the Japanese are fairly dismissive of Zhou's importance, but they want to use him as part of a strategy to promote the splits within the Kuomintang and win the co-operation of the pro-Japanese factions. Needless to say, this is a fancy-dress rigmarole just for show. Zhou Zhengjie himself is an unwitting player in it, and although he hasn't yet had anything to drink, he is already somewhat intoxicated by the occasion.

He has chosen Yuerong's Place as the venue because, as a consequence of Qi Yuexuan's introduction, he is old friends with Xiao Yuerong. When Xiao first started out on the stage with the Pear Garden Company in Beiping, it was Qi Yuexuan who promoted him as the city's must-see act. At that time, Zhou Zhengjie was very tight with Qi Yuexuan, and as soon as Xiao Yuerong made his mark and Qi Yuexuan began singing his praises, he attached himself to this rising star. Of course, he himself has nothing invested in this burgeoning career, as the money has all come from Qi Yuexuan. Nonetheless, he still attends every performance without paying. Afterwards, when Xiao Yuerong's voice goes and he changes career, from his start with the mixed-meat stall to his current large-scale restaurant, Qi Yuexuan is a frequent visitor; and eighty or ninety per cent of the time, Zhou Zhengjie will be at his side, freeloading on food and wine. Later on, they formed the 'Moonbeam Society' and sang together in amateur performances, but, before the war started, Zhou Zhengjie went to Hong Kong and disappeared from sight for several years.

Regardless of all the changes of time and place, however, his instinct for a free lunch hasn't changed. The previous day, when he went to see Xiao Yuerong, despite his now exalted official status, as soon as the talk turned to money, he immediately reverted to type: at first he wanted to do the banquet on credit, and it was only after Xiao Yuerong had pleaded poverty and insisted that wasn't possible, that he reluctantly agreed to pay cash. Even so, there was still a lengthy discussion of cost, which ended with Zhou Zhengjie doggedly insisting on a fifty per cent discount, with any small change knocked off too. He also demanded that the restaurant should be closed to casual clients. Xiao Yuerong doesn't want to agree to this, but what choice does he have? Zhou's previous freeloading had been part of his strategy of clinging onto the coattails of VIPs in order to claw his way to the top, but now it is different. He has the Japanese solidly behind him, and it is simply a matter of him rolling up his sleeves and bullying you into it, whether you like it or not.

It is certainly true that Xiao Yuerong is upset, but Chenglong is even more so. After the business at the Imperial Ancestral Temple, he has felt a great weight pressing down on his heart. In the circumstances, he reacted with great pragmatism, and at the expense of the assassins and the traitor Zhou Si, a potential disaster has been turned to advantage. Nevertheless, he is still deeply pained that his father, Gao Guigeng, was probably among those assassins. Although he is not his birth father, much as he would like to, he cannot forget how good and charitable his adoptive father has been to him. At the time, he hardened his heart and gave the necessary orders to save his own skin, but afterwards, even allowing himself the necessity of his actions, he still can't calm the turmoil of his emotions. Yamaguchi's efforts on his behalf have not been in vain, and through Matsuzaki Harayama's patronage, he has been appointed deputy head of the intelligence section. But what he hasn't anticipated is that Zhou Zhengjie would be given yet another government post, and one way or another, has got one up on him. Because of his close relationship with Hayao Tada, Zhou Zhengjie is now riding high, while Chenglong has to see to all the security work, on patrol everywhere, and he doesn't dare let anything slide. So now, with all the VIPs gone, he sits in a vacant chair, staring at all the leftover dishes. He is not just angry at missing out on a meal, he is also resentful at Zhou's arrogance in his ill-deserved promotion and his shameless use of his powerful connections. So he ends up heaping his own guilty conscience and self-recriminations on Zhou Zhengjie's head.

Zhou Zhengjie is feeling very pleased with himself, so he is naturally more at ease than Chenglong. On seeing him sitting in despondent silence, he goes over and pours him some wine.

"You've been hard at work, Brother Liu! I'm grateful to you for what happened at the Ancestral Temple a few days ago. I haven't seen you to thank you before, so let me raise a cup in gratitude to you now."

Chenglong manages to dredge up a smile, and he finishes his wine. Zhou Zhengjie pours some more and says: "From now on, Brother Liu, we will be eating from the same bowl and working together in a noble cause, so I will be relying on your help."

"Of course, but surely 'help' isn't the right word. You speak, and I obey, isn't that more like it? Even so..."

Chenglong hesitates a moment, then smiles and shoots a look at him. Finally, he continues: "If you're just an escort and errand boy, then that's fine. But if you've got any big ideas, you'll still have to get the nod from Mr Matsuzaki, so you'd better make sure you don't make a nuisance of yourself with me. You're new to all this, so there are probably a few things you don't fully understand yet. This interim government is like a temple, and no matter how important the official, he's still only a figurehead. Who is in charge of a temple? The older monks. Beneath them are the junior monks, and if this order is kept, there is no call for the Buddha or the Guardian Kings to manifest themselves. So if they want to live a long life, they just tend the incense and don't ask awkward questions. If they keep to this pattern, then all is well, but if not, one day or another, people will come and smash all the statues. Tell me I'm not right."

Normally so ready with his tongue, Zhou Zhengjie is rendered speechless by these remarks.

Chenglong picks up his cup again and continues: "Come now, come now, Committee Member Zhou. I'm just a coarse fellow talking nonsense. Don't take any notice of me. Here, I drink to your promotion and all your future promotions!"

Zhou Zhengjie lifts his cup and takes a sip. He laughs mischievously. "I don't think you are a coarse fellow at all. I would say you are quick-witted, meticulous, sophisticated and exceptionally talented. Ai! It's just a shame..."

Like Chenglong, he keeps the suspense going for a while, then goes on with a broad smile: "The Japanese and Chinese have some attitudes in common. When they employ someone, they consider his family, background, education and his reputation. Why else would they have chosen me? Ai! I know perfectly well that old shit-shoveller Gao is your adoptive father and that you only just got into junior high school. As for the secret societies, as far as I'm concerned, the underworld and the straight world all come down to the same thing. It may be that I am most suited to this position, but I am still outraged by the injustice done you. In due course, I shall make sure that Commander Hayao Tada..."

"There's no need. I really can't expect you to trouble yourself. I know I don't have any prospects, and I don't have any great ambitions, just a full mouth and a full belly. I'm not interested in the kind of job where you only get to smell the incense and not eat the offerings. I can't compare to you. You're a man of culture, slick with words and slick with the pen. People listen to you and respect you, but in the end, what use really are all these abilities? All you have to do is spout the right ideologies and shout the right slogans, and you can be sure you'll be fed and clothed. The Japanese know what they're about, and when they give you this post, it's because they know they got the right man for it. They wouldn't use you if you weren't as good a fit as the boards that make up a coffin."

Zhou Zhengjie doesn't take up the argument again, not because he is afraid of Chenglong, but because he simply doesn't want to get involved in some verbal free-for-all with a ruffian like him, nor to fall out with one of his subordinates when he has only just taken up his position. He considers for a moment, then assumes a more intimate tone: "However you put it, Brother Liu, the two of us are in the same boat now, and we are going to have to pull together. Others can work on their own account, and it's alright for them to plot against each other, but not us two. It's not a question of one of us being the original and the other a copy. Where family is concerned..."

"Hold on a moment," says Chenglong, his eyes narrowing. "Is your ancestral name Liu too?"

"Of course not."

"Then I really don't understand what you mean by 'where family is concerned'."

"Then let me ask you. What is Qi Yuexuan to you?"

"He's my wife's father. We only found out a few days ago. You seem to be very well-informed."

"And do you know what relation Qi Yuexuan is to me?"

"No."

"He's my brother-in-law. He's married to my younger sister."

"Aiyo! I've not... I've not treated you as family before. I should be calling you 'Uncle'!"

"No need for that, no need. We count as one now, not just colleagues, but brothers."

His face dark with suspicion, Chenglong asks: "My father-in-law has married several times. Which one of my step-mothers is your sister?"

"She's his current wife, Zhou Zhengying. Even if you haven't met her, you must have heard of her."

"I've heard of her alright. She's that student at the foreign university who joined the Communists, then ran away."

"That's right, that's her."

"Ha! Well, you've got a nerve, haven't you! You still count her as married after she's been on the run so many years? Once a wife has left home, she can't come back. She's probably married again anyway. Even supposing she does return, do you think my father-in-law will let her back in? Aiya! I would really like to claim this family connection with you. It's just a shame that I am his son-in-law, not a full part of his family, so even if I did want a new stepmother, the idea of you being my uncle is ridiculous."

From this, Zhou Zhengjie realises that Chenglong has just been toying with him all along, and his face flushes with anger. He slams his wine cup down on the table, and smiling icily, spits out through gritted teeth: "You shouldn't be so arrogant, Liu Chenglong. No one wants a dog that doesn't recognise its master. Do you think I don't know about your own murky past?"

Chenglong just grins. "Aiyo, now I'm really scared! Go on, tell me all. I wouldn't want to die in ignorance."

"You wanted to get military intelligence to do away with me, and when that plot was exposed, you mounted a counter-coup. Did you think that, with all the assassins silenced, you could shift the blame onto Zhou Si, and all your troubles would be over? It's a very neat plan."

"Well, if you've got proof, why don't you hand it over to the Japanese and be done with it, instead of standing around here farting aimlessly."

"Of course there's proof. I've just come back from there, and I've got everything I need, so don't think you can bamboozle me. I just don't want to do anything so final just now, so you... you'd better not force my hand by keeping on at me."

Chenglong leaps to his feet. "Well that's just what I am going to do right now, you..."

Zhou Zhengjie just laughs at this display of temper. "Ai! Calm down a bit. Don't let your anger get the better of you. Do you think I'm bluffing? Well, let me just tell you a couple of things."

"Go on then..." Chenglong folds his arms and crosses one leg over the other.

"You searched the files of military intelligence's Beiping station and of the Laiyuan prison, didn't you?"

"That's right. I was researching the origins of the Traitor Elimination Squad. Is that alright?"

"Of course. But one person's file is missing and doesn't tally with the index."

Chenglong's heart lurches but nothing shows in his expression. "So? You'll need something bigger than that!"

"This is quite big enough," Zhou Zhengjie shoots back. "It seems that, out of the seventeen men, the missing file belongs to the bandit chief, Two-Ox Gui. And he is the leader of the Traitor Elimination squad, your adoptive father Gao Guigeng."

"Rubbish! Where's your proof?" Chenglong seems to be losing control of his temper and is about to leap to his feet. The mention of Gao Guigeng at this point fills his heart with fear, worry and sorrow.

"There's no point in getting overwrought. I told you the proof was easy enough to find. All I have to do is put the Japanese on the trail of these clues, and they'll do the investigating."

"Well... your little sister is a member of the Communist Party, isn't she?"

"That's public knowledge, and anyway, it's nothing compared with what you're hiding."

"Pah! The Japanese only trust results, and haven't I done away with the Traitor Elimination Squad?"

Zhou Zhengjie just laughs. "Never mind the Japanese. I don't believe a son has killed his father. I saw the bodies of the assassins before they were buried, and not one of them was old enough to be your father."

Chenglong is shaken to the core by this news. There is a buzzing in his head, his mind goes blank and he falls back into his chair. At the end of the funeral feast, he had gone to the Kempeitai, hoping to view the bodies, but they had already been sent for cremation, and he had no way of knowing if Gao Guigeng's was among them. Over the last two days, he hasn't had any decent sleep, since, as soon as he closes his eyes, all he sees is his adoptive father's bloody form. Even when he forces his eyes open, there is no escape from the torment in his heart. And now, when he hears what Zhou Zhengjie has to say, there is still no rejoicing, as he has sunk into the extremity of fear, and all he can see before him are Gao Guigeng's blood-red eyes and the cold steel of the muzzle of his gun.

When Zhou Zhengjie sees him in this state, he decides not to press him too hard.

"Don't worry," he says. "That's not what I'm going to do. In a while, when you've learned a bit more about human nature and got your priorities sorted, you won't still believe I'm going to make things difficult for you by attacking your father-in-law's reputation. When the world's at war, no one can protect all their friends and family, whichever side they're on, so it's quite understandable for you to have your doubts. But didn't I hide the truth about your father-in-law, Qi Yuexuan's foolishness in leading a force to join the anti-Japanese resistance? Now more than ever, the two of us mustn't fall out, but rely on and help each other, and that's all there is to it. You need to take stock of our circumstances – the interim government may be a temporary phenomenon at the moment, but if in the future it can harness the co-operation between the leadership of the Kuomintang and the Japanese, then it has a chance of bringing the nation together. If the Japanese withdraw their troops, who is going to control the country? You shouldn't consider me a lone wolf. I am a touchstone, an agent provocateur. Have some political savvy and don't see gangsters everywhere. Right, I have things to do, so I can't keep you company, but take your time, eat your fill and have a good think about things."

By the time Chenglong has recovered himself sufficiently, Zhou Zhengjie has already left the room. He needs a drink to settle his nerves, but when he tips up the jug, there are only a few drops left. He stiffens furiously and yells: "Bring more wine!"

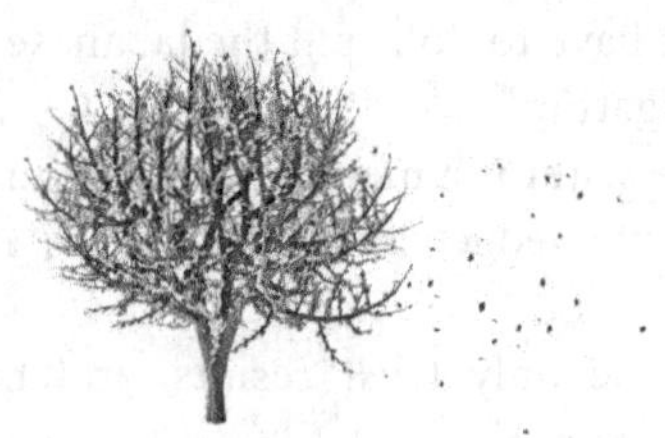

Chapter 56

Caiping wakes up from her sleep, but Wangtian is still not back. She looks at the clock on the table: it's already two o'clock. Wangtian returned from Laoqiying after ten the previous evening, hardly spoke two words to her, other than to tell her to go to sleep, and then he went over to the western side courtyard, saying he had to make his report to Mother Yan and Yue E. Fair enough, but she has seen neither hide nor hair of him since. Although Caiping is always the most tolerant of young women, on this occasion she is finding her patience being tested. When all is said and done, it has hardly been two days since they parted below the Western Hills, but those two days have felt like two months to her, and when she saw her husband safely returned, a great weight was lifted from her heart. But while she was overjoyed, her face wreathed in smiles, he came in sombre-faced and went out again the same. When she didn't ask him what was going on, he was silent as a stoppered gourd, and when she finally did, he just mumbled evasively: "Nothing important... we'll talk about it later."

But whereas he won't talk about whatever it was at home, he seems to have no such inhibition over in the other courtyard, so who can blame her for being unhappy? Though, in fact, this isn't the main reason Caiping is upset with her husband.

Two days ago, halfway back from the Western Hills, Caiping felt a pain in her belly. She tried to vomit, but after a few dry heaves, in the end nothing came up. By evening, however, she finds herself unable to eat anything, and her belly feels unbearably heavy. She is already more than five months gone, and the first two months were trouble-free. Even when Uncle Yang went into hospital, and she had to help with the cooking and childcare, she didn't feel anything wrong. But now there is definitely something amiss, and she is afraid she might be having a miscarriage. She doesn't dare go to the Western hospital, for fear of being diagnosed with 'cholera', so she goes to the traditional Chinese hospital to get a prescription instead. To her surprise and relief, after the doctor there has taken her pulses, he is reassuring.

"You've no need to worry," he says. "It's nothing serious, just fatigue. There's no need for a prescription. All medicines are poisons to some degree, and they are best avoided if possible when you're pregnant. From your pulses, you are carrying a boy, and they are always more troublesome for the mother."

Caiping is twenty-six now, and Wangtian is over thirty. In those days, when people got married younger, it would not be unusual for them to have a child of ten or more already. So when the doctor tells her she is going to have a boy, she is naturally part scared and part delighted. But when she goes home, she doesn't dare share the news, as it wouldn't be fitting since they have only just buried Uncle Yang. However, she is still desperate to share the news with Wangtian so they can celebrate in private. But no sooner does her husband come home than he turns around and leaves again, so she has no chance to pass on the news. Tolerant as she is, she is still a woman and cannot help herself throwing a minor tantrum at her husband on behalf of her unborn son. To her surprise, before she can even begin, she is given the cold shoulder. Now, as she reclines on the *kang*, waiting for sleep, her head is full of dreams. They are not dreams of the dead, but of fighting, and of Wangtian playing Chen Shimei.[1] In that dream, the princess he marries is Yue E, and she herself becomes Qin Xianglian. As he disowns both her and their son, she begins to wail, and she wails herself awake. As she recovers her senses, she laughs at herself, wondering how she could be so foolish. At this moment, she suddenly hears someone outside, tapping very gently on the window.

Thinking it is Wangtian, she calls out: "What's up with you? It's the middle of the night!"

To her surprise, the person doesn't come in, or even speak for that matter. Furious, she throws off her cover, gets down from the *kang* and walks across the room, calling out: "Alright, so don't come in. I'm... I'm going to bolt the door then."

The door opens, and someone puts their head in. Caiping is too quick for him, and he doesn't get across the threshold. But when she sees it isn't Wangtian, she is terrified. She screams, snatches up the long-handled wicker dustpan beside the door and swings it up, ready to hit out.

"Don't hit me, sister. It's me!"

Only then does she realise that person appearing like a moth out of the dark is none other than Clown.

"Ai! How can you be here? You..." But before she can finish, she sees the spreading bloodstain where Clown is wounded in the left shoulder. Once he is inside, she bolts the door tight and offers her shoulder to support him over to a chair. Pulling open his jacket, she can see that it is a serious wound. There is a hole in his shoulder, from which blood is still flowing. Bone is visible through the flesh, and she is afraid he may have a broken collarbone. Caiping has never seen a wound like this, so she doesn't dare move him. She takes some plain white cloth out of the cupboard, wads it up and gives it to him.

"You need to go to hospital with a wound like that. Cover it with this for the time being."

She makes to leave, but Clown exclaims hurriedly: "No, no! I can't go to hospital. They'll see it's a bullet wound and report it to the Japanese."

"What... what have you done?"

"It's all that son-of-a-bitch Chenglong's fault... Ai! It's a long story."

Caiping doesn't press him but makes to leave again.

"Where are you going?"

"Over to the western courtyard to get Wangtian."

Clown claps the wad of cloth to the wound, grits his teeth against the pain, then turns to look at her and says: "If you're going out, sister... aren't you going to put some more clothes on?"

At this, Caiping suddenly realises she is only wearing a pair of under-trousers and a halter-neck bodice. She blushes furiously and rushes over to find her padded trousers beside the *kang*.

"Shut your eyes before they pop out!" she says playfully.

At this moment, they can hear from outside the sound of the bronze handles on the courtyard doors thundering against the door panels, along with several raised voices.

"Kempeitai! Open up! Be quick about it!"

"I'm sorry to refuse you, but this Residence has its rules. No visitors in the middle of the night. If you have business here, come back when it's light." The porter is neither supercilious nor obsequious.

"*Bakayaro*! Insides is anti-Japaneses. You not opens door quick quick, you dead dead!"

Standing right next to the window, Caiping hears all this quite clearly and says reproachfully: "Someone must have seen you come in and called the devils."

"Can't be. I got in over the wall," says Clown as he jumps to his feet. "I must go, sister. That's all there is to it."

Caiping stands in front of him. "Where will you go if you do?"

"If I don't go, I'll drag you all into it." Clown pushes past her.

"Huh! Still intent on playing the martyr, are you?" Caiping glares at him angrily. "For better or worse, you're staying here. Understand? That's the way we have always done things in Beiping." So saying, she pulls the light cord and puts out the light, then reaches over and pushes open the door.

"What are you..."

"The rear courtyards are closed off. There are hiding places there. Hurry up."

"Ah! Alright! Alright!"

Clown is about to follow her out, but she suddenly retreats back into the room and pulls the door to. She sees that Clown is about to ask her what's going on, so she puts her hand over his mouth. Only then does he hear voices and the sound of footsteps already at the gates of the main courtyard. Looking through the window lattice, they see Wangtian leading the way through the flower-garlanded gateway, followed by a Japanese sergeant and two privates. Police Constable Song is there too. The Residence has been on his beat since the beginning of the Republic, and he doesn't care who is in charge, as long as he stays the local policeman. It's already too late to get out of the room, so Clown will have to find a hiding place inside. Fear lends Caiping wings and she drags Clown over to the *kang*. Seeing that he is still not thinking clearly, she whispers urgently to him: "Quick, get on the *kang*!"

Wangtian has stopped under the garlanded gate, blocking the way with outstretched arms. "Just wait a moment and listen to me," he says. "There's only me and my wife in this courtyard. The Young Master isn't here, and he has left me in charge of the household. I can let you look around, that's alright, but I don't want you overturning trunks and pushing over cupboards. I can't afford any losses or breakages. If you agree, you can go in. If not, you can't, unless you give me a gun first."

The Japanese sergeant glares at him angrily. "Yours is arguing with Kempeitai? Whose is you?"

"I'm Chinese," Wangtian replies simply.

"*Baku!*" The sergeant raises his fist, but Constable Song stops him and whispers something in his ear.

Reluctantly, the sergeant says: "*Yoshi!* I is agree yours. Mine is not want make you trouble but your house courtyard has blood signs. Mine is to look look, is also yours safety."

Wangtian changes tack at this and chuckles: "In that case, I must thank you for your consideration. I live in the western courtyard. The rest are all empty, and are locked. Please go ahead and have a look around."

The sergeant gestures to his two men, who acknowledge him and split up, one going into the north courtyard and the other into the east one. He himself leads Constable Song towards the western courtyard. When he sees this, Wangtian hurries forward, forcing his way to the front. He pushes open the door, turns on the lamp and stares in surprise. Despite the disturbance outside, Caiping, normally so lively and active, is still lying indifferently on the *kang*. When she sees the lamplight and people coming into the room, she sits up, flustered, pulling up the quilt to cover her body, and leans against a bedroll in the corner of the *kang*. The strange thing is that, although it is high summer, she doesn't seem be worried about being too hot. Indeed, she is shivering from head to toe, despite being under two thick quilts. When he was here just recently, she only had a single quilt laid over her belly, so he has no idea what sudden illness has prompted her to bring out the thick winter cover and huddle under that as well.

All is well. When the Japanese sergeant comes into the room, he just glances at the *kang* and pays it no more attention. He strolls round the room, inspecting it, and when he sees there is nowhere for a man to hide, he finally turns his eyes onto Caiping. He walks over to the *kang* and asks: "Is this your wife, Gao-san?"

"It is."

"Heehee, you're a lucky man."

Wangtian steps forward so he is standing by the head of the *kang*. "Hurry up and complete your search," he says, "and if you don't find anything, shall I show you the rest of the place? The Residence has a lot of courtyards, and you don't want to miss one."

The sergeant gives a chilly laugh: "Ha! Mine is looking looking on *kang*."

He reaches out a hand to push Wangtian aside and get closer to the *kang*, but although he tries twice, he doesn't budge him.

"What do you think you are doing?" Wangtian glares at him. "Men and women should keep a respectful distance. What do you want to look at a sleeping woman for? If you want to do that, go back to Japan and look at your mother!"

"*Baku!*" The Japanese curses angrily, but he is restrained by Constable Song behind him.

"Don't be angry, great lord. This definitely is his wife. You needn't worry, there's nothing wrong here."

The sergeant shoots him a look. "Yours look, is summer. Hers is sweating big big, why is wanting many covers?"

At this point, Caiping herself pipes up, and although her voice is weak and listless, she is quite coherent: "Aiyo! Have you Japanese never heard of a feverish headache? I've caught a chill and am running a fever, so of course I'm sweating! It's summer, isn't it? You're not ill, and you'd be hot even if you were naked, but here I am, under two quilts and still shivering all over."

Wangtian catches on quickly: "That's right. There's nothing for you to get excited about."

The sergeant stares for a moment, then asks: "You sick, why not go hospital take needle, eat medicine?"

"I don't dare have any injections or take any drugs at the moment," Caiping quickly rejoins.

"Why?"

"All drugs are partly poison. Do you understand? I'm pregnant, and the doctor told me today it's definitely a boy. How can I even think of having any injections or drugs? Otherwise, who's going to take responsibility if things go wrong and I die in childbirth or give birth to a cretin, like you?"

Wangtian is as astonished as anyone when he hears that he is going to have a son. He is just about to say something, but Caiping gives him a surreptitious look, so he stops himself and just keeps muttering: "That's right, that's right."

"Great lord," Constable Song says, looking to find a compromise. "We are very particular about this in Beiping, and we don't go to hospital unless it's really serious."

The sergeant can't find anything to quibble about with this, so he just grunts, and is about to turn and leave, when he notices some red spots on the floor beside the *kang*. He immediately wipes one up with his finger and examines it carefully.

"This is blood, where from?"

Wangtian is taken aback, and he just gapes wordlessly. Without giving him time to recover, the sergeant steps forward and makes to snatch back the quilts. But if Wangtian is slow with words, he is quick with action, and with a twist of the wrist, he pulls the sergeant's hands away before he can even get a grip on the covers.

"*Baku!*" The Sergeant explodes with anger and curses as he grabs Wangtian by the lapel and draws his pistol. But before he can get a firm grip, Wangtian uses a move that his father taught him, and twists the man's arm round into a lock that immobilises him. He also twists the wrist back, so that the muzzle of the pistol is pointing at the sergeant's own chest. The two Japanese soldiers outside hear the commotion and come running into the room. But when they take stock of the situation, they don't dare do anything and just stand there pointing their rifles at Wangtian.

"Aiyo! What's this all about?" Constable Song slaps his thigh with the residents' register he is holding, his head looking from one side to the other like a baby's drum-rattle. "Don't do anything rash. Let's talk this through."

"What talk through? This anti-Japanese faction," the sergeant yells at him. But before he can finish what he is saying, he gives a shout of pain as Wangtian twists his arm even harder.

At this point, Caiping tries to lower the temperature. "Calm down, Wangtian, and let go his hand."

"But he..."

"Just stop fighting with him, and listen to me, alright?"

Wangtian can see Caiping is so agitated she is about to get out of bed, so he grunts and lets go of the sergeant's hand. The sergeant straightens up, ignoring the pain in his wrist, and picks up his pistol. Holding it in both hands, he levels it at Wangtian and Caiping.

"Hah! You Japanese really don't know how to ease up, do you?" Caiping says in a loud voice. "He's just let you go, and you want to attack him again? Why don't you just let me speak? I am his wife, after all."

The sergeant is taken aback by her boldness: "Yours is want say what?"

Instead of replying directly, Caiping asks in return: "Didn't you ask where that blood came from?"

"Hai! Where?"

"I won't hide it from you, the blood is mine."

"Yours? Eh?" The sergeant sounds doubtful.

"What? Don't you believe me?" Caiping laughs, stretches out one of her arms and wiggles five fingers in front of his face. There are needle marks on the tip of each finger, with blood still dripping from some of them.

The sergeant stares at them blankly, and Caiping continues: "Don't you get it yet? I didn't think you were that dumb. It's all part of the same thing as me sweating under the covers. I pricked my fingers with a needle to let out some blood and dispel the fever. Are you so frightened by the sight of a little blood, you think it must mean I'm an anti-Japanese agent? If a woman is having her period, it must drive you crazy!"

Before she has even finished, Wangtian and Constable Song are unable to contain their laughter.

As the sergeant continues to think things through, Constable Song pulls him to one side and whispers to him, gesticulating for quite some time, until, finally, his face splits into a grin. Smiling stupidly, he glances at Caiping, then gestures to his men, shouts the order to be on their way and heads outside.

Constable Song hurries after him, asking: "Do you want to search any of the other courtyards?"

The sergeant doesn't stop or even look back, but he just barks: "Here is not searching, going other places."

When the three Japanese are all out of the room, Constable Song stops in the doorway for a moment and looks back with a chuckle. As he steps over the threshold, he flashes a big thumbs-up sign behind his back.

Once the whole party has left the Minister's Residence, the porter relocks the main gates and Wangtian hurries back to the main courtyard, making sure to lock the gates that are normally left open.

Caiping is still propped up on the *kang*, and when he comes back, she asks urgently: "Have they gone?"

Wangtian only has time to nod before Caiping sits up and throws back the quilts. Wangtian hurriedly covers her back over, saying: "Stay covered, you don't want to freeze again after all that sweating."

"Freeze? I'm about to die from the heat!" Caiping pulls the quilt off again as she speaks. She is indeed dripping with sweat, but she doesn't bother to wipe herself down. Instead, she hurries to put on her pair of padded trousers.

"So... aren't you ill then?"

"It's you who must be ill, unless you're just stupid."

"Then... what you said about having a son... is that..."

"Ha! That bit was true. I saw the doctor today, and it's really true."

Wangtian is elated and folds her in his arms. But she pulls away and says reproachfully: "Have a care for that fellow..."

"What fellow? Who?" Wangtian is taken aback, but then his eyes light up: "Oh! You mean my son!"

Caiping can't help laughing as she puts on her trousers while sitting on the edge of the *kang*. "Yes, that's right. Your grown-up son of twenty-something."

As she's talking, she gets down and hurries over to the rolled-up bedding she was leaning on in the corner of the *kang*.

"Come on out and meet your father," she calls.

But even after she has called out several times, there is no movement from the bed-roll. Worried, she gives the bedding a shove, but still nothing. Really concerned now, she pulls off the quilt that is covering it. Only then does Wangtian see the curled-up figure of Clown, crouching there like a monkey and not moving. He is still breathing but has fainted from his wound and the lack of air. They help him to lie on his back, pinch his upper lip, splash him with cold water, and, quite soon, he revives. His eyes are still filled with fear when he opens them, and he tries to scramble up. The effort makes the wound in his shoulder hurt, and he cries out in pain.

"Aiya! What are you trying to get up for?" says Wangtian, propping him up.

"The devils... have they gone?"

"They're gone. You're quite safe."

Clown relaxes at last. He takes hold of Wangtian's arm and kneels up on the *kang*. Choking with emotion, he says: "Older brother, sister-in-law, you have given me back my life today. The two of you are my mother and father reborn."

He makes to bow to them, but Caiping hurriedly stops him: "No, no, we don't deserve that. 'Brother' is good enough, without getting the generations all mixed up. But if you can promise me one thing, then it will be me kowtowing to you."

"Tell me. My whole life is yours to..."

"I don't need your life, I just need you to keep that mouth of yours under control. No one can gossip about what has gone on here tonight. Do you understand? It's a story best kept to ourselves, alright? You men are thick-skinned enough to take it, but I'd never be able to look anyone in the face again!"

Caiping is already blushing as she speaks, and Clown eagerly nods his agreement, tears running down his cheeks.

Wangtian is discomfited too. He settles Clown back down and takes a small bottle out of the cupboard. Caiping brings over a basin of water, and Wangtian cleans Clown's wound. He tips some black powder from the little bottle onto a folded square of cloth, spits onto it, then lays it on the wound. His touch has been very gentle while dressing the wound, but now he uses a bit more force, pressing down continuously, and Clown yelps in pain.

"You'll have to grin and bear it, otherwise we won't stop the bleeding." He presses down even more firmly.

Clown grits his teeth and doesn't make another sound, but Caiping can't help asking: "What is that black stuff anyway? And doesn't spitting on it make it worse?"

Wangtian smiles broadly and just applies more pressure.

"This is some Golden Wound Powder my father left me, and it acts quicker if you spit on it. It helped heal the wound when Chenglong cut his finger off that time. Now hurry up and get me some more cloth, so I can bandage him up properly."

"If you say so, but what kind of quack are you! If we don't stop the bleeding, he'll die! Is that it?" Mocking as her words are, Caiping doesn't waste any time, but quickly finds some more cloth, tears it into strips and hands it to Wangtian.

As he bandages the wound tight, Wangtian says: "This is just to stop the bleeding and help with the pain. When it's light, I'll find a doctor for you."

Clown comes to life a little, as he smiles and says: "There's no need. If I'm careful, it doesn't hurt that much."

"Who gave you this wound?" Wangtian asks. "What exactly happened?"

Clown sighs and begins to weep again. Finally, he makes a clean breast of it, and he tells the whole story from beginning to end. Wangtian's face goes ashen, and he is silent for a long moment. He is puzzled. That night when he was keeping vigil over Uncle Yang, and Chenglong met his father, it seemed that his brother had listened to the advice he was being given, gone over to his father's side and accepted a mission from him. How then, so soon afterwards, could he have committed such a dreadful deed? For the moment, he really can't get his head round all the twists and turns.

"How could he do this? He's just an..." But seeing Wangtian's expression, Caiping bites back the word "animal" she was about to use.

"Admit it, Clown... aren't you exaggerating a little?"

"Aiyo! Heaven strike me down if there's one word of a lie. If you don't believe me, go and ask Yuxiang. Ask Sergeant Lian."

"Ai! It's not that I don't believe you. It just sounds so improbable."

"Who do you think you're kidding?" Caiping snaps. "What's improbable about it? What isn't he capable of?"

"Ah, there are some things I haven't told you..."

"You don't need to. I know he's just one big pus-filled sore, rotten to the core."

Wangtian is about to reply, but before he can speak, he hears the sound of someone at the gate of the outer courtyard. He looks at Caiping, puts out the light and hurries out of the room. Caiping doesn't dare hesitate either, but quickly helps Clown up and covers him with the quilt again, just as before. This time, Wangtian doesn't open the gates to the main courtyard, but stays behind them looking and listening through the gap between them.

The street gates open, and he hears the porter say: "Ah! It's you, Master Liu. What are you doing here in the middle of the night?"

By the sound of him, Chenglong has had quite a bit to drink, and he is stumbling over his words.

"Whass... whass the matter? I'm the... the son-in-law of the Minister's Residence... my old woman's kids... are here. I can come here... any fucking time I like. Can't I?"

"Aiyo! I wouldn't dare turn you away! I wasn't meaning that you've drunk too much. I was just worried you might bang your head."

"I'm not... I haven't drunk... that much... I'm just all fucking... choked up... and if you... rub me up... the wrong way... I'll go to work on you."

Chenglong comes swaying and stumbling out of the gateway, muttering to himself: "They all fucking think... their old man... is a fucking pushover... bothering me... all the time... I don't care who..."

The porter sees him stop in front of the main courtyard and says hurriedly: "Your wife is in the western side courtyard, Master Liu."

"Did I ask for... for your fucking advice?" Chenglong turns and yells at him. "Are you saying I can't stay in the main courtyard? There's only one... one daughter of the Qi family... and I'm the only... only son-in-law and if... my father-in-law's not here... who's the most important? Me! Do they take me for some kind of bottom-feeder... creeping round the... edges of the pond? Tonight, I'm going to stay in this courtyard... and I'd like to see anyone... try to stop me. Open... open the gates for me."

"Aiyo! Some people are already in there."

"Who... who's getting in my way?"

"Aiyo! Don't you remember. The main courtyard is the company office during the day, and at night your brother and your sister-in-law live there. Wangtian is now..."

"The household manager... isn't that what you were going... to say? So who's he... managing for? I get fucking pushed around out there... and you think I come back here... to get the same fucking treatment? Well, let me tell you... if I'm not happy... no one else's going to be happy... either."

Chenglong has just raised his hand to bang on the gate, when Yue E emerges from the western courtyard, shouting: "What's the matter with you? It's the middle of the night."

Chenglong drops his hand when he sees her. She storms over, grabs him by the arm and begins to drag him home.

"Have you completely lost it this time? We've just had the Japanese in here searching the place, and where were you? So other than throwing your weight around at home, what else is new with you? Now get a move on, and don't embarrass yourself any more here."

Wangtian is finally able to breathe a sigh of relief when he hears them go back into the western side courtyard.

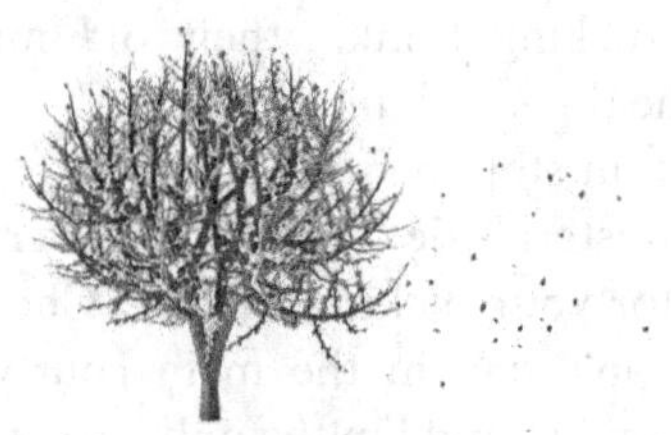

Chapter 57

Yuxiang has had no freedom since she was brought back after being arrested. To stop her running off again, Chenglong assigns two of his men to guard her house at all times. During the day, she is not allowed out of the courtyard, while at night she has to stay in her room. There is no point even contemplating going out onto the street, as the neighbours on either side would stop her.

To curry favour with Yamaguchi, Chenglong has allocated him one of his own two-courtyard houses. He has had an auspicious day chosen, and ordered men to whitewash the walls and set the place in order, promising Yamaguchi that, in two weeks' time, he will allow him to marry Yuxiang. The house may be considered a wedding gift. From Yamaguchi's point of view, although this would be against army rules, when all's said and done, having something like a home to return to is a hundred times better than resorting to the Japanese 'comfort stations'.

Chenglong also has a word with Sergeant Lian, saying: "It was all down to my reputation that nothing happened to Yuxiang this time. If she runs away again, I may not be able to do anything. If she's caught and brought back, it's as a good as certain she'll either be executed or sent to a comfort station. It just depends on what the Japanese decide. And if she escapes and isn't caught, there'll be no question about it – you and your family will be sent to a labour camp beyond the Pass. Because of our long-standing relationship and old obligations, and sparing no money or property, I have found you a Japanese son-in-law to be your protector. You mustn't, at any price, stir up any more trouble."

This really puts the wind up Sergeant Lian, and that evening he drags his youngest children along to kneel in front of Yuxiang, entreating her piteously. They only get up when she grudgingly agrees. Even so, Sergeant Lian is still worried. Whereas previously he would get up early every day to go to work at the night soil depot, and only come home in the evening, now he runs home whenever he has a spare moment. He is even worse when he gets back in the evening, as he sticks to Yuxiang like a leech. Try as she might, she can't shake him off, and he doesn't allow her any more space when she goes to sleep. Afraid to leave her on her own even then, he puts his three youngest children into her room to sleep with her.

In fact, Yuxiang hasn't thought about running away again since she was arrested, not because she is afraid, but out of concern for the other members of her family, young and old. Most important of all, she doesn't know whether Clown is dead or alive, and the only reason she fled before was because Clown was with her. Without him, what is the point, even if she runs to the ends of the earth? She has wept countless tears for him over these last few days, but no amount of crying will save her Clown. The saying goes that 'there is nothing worse than a dead heart', and although Yuxiang has tried to keep her spirits up, her own heart is already as cold as a frozen persimmon in mid-winter.

IT IS ALREADY LATE MORNING when Yuxiang gets up, and she is still sitting on the *kang* staring blankly at the wall when she hears one of the men Chenglong has set to guard the gates.

"Hey there! Why do you girls always poke your noses in where they don't belong? What do you think you're doing barging in here without asking?"

"Ha!" a woman's voice replies. "You can get off my case! Even a dog knows to stand at the gate if it's on guard. What are you doing lounging around in the courtyard?"

"And what's that got to do with you? I do as I please."

"Alright then, you do as you please, and I'll do the same."

"Stay where you are! Who are you looking for?"

"I'm looking for the daughter of the Lian family, Yuxiang."

"What for?"

"Why don't you take your own advice and mind your own business?"

"Ha! You've got quite a mouth on you, haven't you! If you're not careful, I'll forget you're a girl and..."

"Oh yes? What are you going to do? Shoot me? I'd have to lend you the balls! This really is a case of 'like master, like man'. You couldn't expect a useless lump like Liu Chenglong to come up with anyone better. So what else are you good for apart from throwing your weight about in front of ordinary folk? Fuck off out of the road. A good dog knows not to get in the way."

The girl's anger catches the CID man off guard, and by the time he has recovered himself, she is already standing in front of the door of the north range. He has almost caught up with her when Yuxiang opens the door and greets her with a cry of "Aunty Yue E!"

Yuxiang turns to the guard and says: "Don't you know who this is? It's your Commander Liu's wife."

The guard can only stand there, his mouth flapping wordlessly, as his colleague comes hurtling out of the privy, still doing up his trousers and trying to smile ingratiatingly.

"Aiyi! It's you, honoured aunt! Please don't be angry with him. He's a new recruit, and he doesn't know the boss yet. I'd just gone to the privy, and he only started throwing his weight around because he didn't know any..."

Yue E has no desire to listen to his excuses. She just grunts and goes into the room, slamming the door behind her so it only just misses flattening the guard's nose.

"Aunty Yue E, you..." Yuxiang is too surprised to know quite what to say.

Yue E just grins and shouts at the guards outside: "Be off with you! Go and stand at the main gate. Do you think we want you eavesdropping on us?"

They hear the men outside reply and move off. Yue E looks Yuxiang over and heaves a deep sigh. Yuxiang hurriedly pushes the rumpled quilt on the *kang* to one side, deftly clearing a little space.

"Sit down, sit down and let me get you..." She tries to play the hostess at the same time as she runs a comb through her untidy hair, smiling in embarrassment.

Yue E just sits on the edge of the *kang*, not saying anything, looking the other girl up and down.

Yuxiang is more than a little discomfited by this inspection, and she lowers her head, avoiding Yue E's gaze. She hasn't seen her since she took up with Chenglong and left the Minister's Residence. She knows that Yue E must have some reason for this visit today, but for the moment, she can't even guess what it might be. The two of them remain there quietly facing each other, one sitting the other standing, and neither speaking.

Finally, Yue E opens her mouth, but only to say: "You sit down too."

Once Yuxiang has sat down opposite her, she lapses back into silence. Unable to bear the awkwardness of the heavy silence any longer, Yuxiang drops her head and says, as quiet as the buzz of a mosquito: "I must apologise to you, Aunty Yue E. I have been meaning to come and see you, but... but I was too embarrassed..."

Yue E doesn't let her finish, but sighs and smiles bitterly. "You're still just a child. All this is Chenglong's doing. Him and that rotten bastard, money-grubbing father of yours. Now there's that foul Japanese beast too, you're really..." She can't bring herself to complete the sentence, as her eyes fill with tears.

Yuxiang's lips tremble, but no words come out and she begins to weep silently. Yue E pulls her into her arms, and her own tears begin to fall.

IT SO HAPPENS that Yue E is even sadder than Yuxiang. The night before, when Chenglong follows her back to the western side courtyard, he is still well in his cups as he lays down on the *kang*. According to the nonsense he talks, it would seem that the whole world is against him, and he is more wronged than Dou E.[1] After tossing and turning for more than half an hour, he begins to snore, but even in sleep he is restless, crying out suddenly. Although everything he says is clearly fuelled by wine, and by his tormented dreams, two things stick in Yue E's mind. One, said while he is awake, is that he has found a master for Yuxiang, but when she asks him about it, he becomes evasive and changes the subject. The other, uttered in his sleep, he repeats continuously, sounding as though someone has a knife to his throat: "It's not my fault, Father! Don't kill me, Father!"

Yue E slips quietly off the *kang* and sits beside it until dawn. While it is still very early, she goes over to the main courtyard in search of Wangtian, in the hope of sorting out how much of what Chenglong has said is just drunken ramblings and how much is true. To her surprise, Wangtian has already gone out onto the street to fetch a doctor. Caiping knows she can trust Yue E, so she has no qualms about taking her through to the rear courtyard and showing her Clown. When she hears his story, a chill shoots through her.

After a while, Wangtian comes back with the doctor, the same old traditional practitioner who had treated Caiping. He is skilled not just in internal medicine, but also in bone-setting and the treatment of wounds. As soon as he sees that Clown has been shot, he cries out that he has been tricked. The fact is that Wangtian was afraid he wouldn't agree to come, so he had pretended that his wife had had a fall and her belly was hurting badly. This doctor had been very friendly with Uncle Yang when he was alive, and knows Yue E well, so, with her pleadings, he is eventually persuaded to treat Clown's wound and set his broken bone. He doesn't want payment, just their solemn word not to give him away.

At first, it is Wangtian who agrees that Clown should send a letter to Yuxiang, but it is Yue E who insists that she should be the one to take it. In this, she proves quite correct, as it is unlikely that anyone other than her would have got past the front gate.

"Alright now, stop crying." It is Yue E who breaks the silence. "You can cry all day and it will do no good, so settle down and listen to me. I've come here on two missions today. One is to see how you are, and the other is to give you a letter someone has asked me to deliver."

"Clown! Is he still alive? Where... where is he?"

"He's alive. But it's safer you don't know where he is. He's been wounded, but you don't need to worry, it's nothing serious. He'll be fine in a month or so."

"How did he get wounded? What happened?"

"Ah! A lot has gone on in just a few days, too much to tell in a short time. The important thing is that he gave me a three-word message for you – 'Wait for me.'"

When Yuxiang hears this, her tears flow afresh: "Wait for him? How... how can I wait? You must take a message back to him for me. Just one word – 'Forget'. If he has even the slightest chance of getting his life back, then he... he mustn't think about me any more."

Seeing her choking with emotion, Yue E hurriedly takes up the subject: "How can I give him such heartbreaking news? Why don't you show a little more backbone? Women can see things through too. If you don't run this time, what have you got to be afraid of? All you have to do is stay alive..."

"I'm not afraid to die, aunty. I... I really don't want to get Clown involved again. Anyway, what... what would my dad and my brothers and sisters do if I ran off again? I promised my dad on my life that I wouldn't."

"Just listen to yourself! Is it worth it for that money-grubbing dog's turd of a father of yours? Little children shouldn't be dragged into serious stuff like this, so don't let his empty threats scare you into obeying him. Promised on your life, did you? Why? You need to take your life in your own hands. As long as you stay strong, you don't have to worry. Your Uncle Wangtian and I, and your Aunty Ying [Caiping] will help both of you."

Yuxiang laughs bitterly and shakes her head. "But... I'm afraid you'll be too late."

"What do you mean, too late?"

"Don't you know? He's already given me away."

"Truly? Given you away? Who to?"

"To that Japanese, Yamaguchi. He says he is getting a house ready for us over there, and we'll be able to move in in no more than a couple of weeks."

This is the last news Yue E wants to hear, and just for the moment, she is completely at a loss.

Yuxiang falls to her knees in front of Yue E, and she says: "Aunty, if you all just say you can help me, that's enough for me. To tell you the truth, I've already made up my mind that the day I move into that house is the day I die."

Yue E pulls her to her feet. "You mustn't keep thinking of killing yourself, Yuxiang. We'll never let it get that far. But for the moment, you must allow me to go home and discuss the best way forward. What's the matter? Don't you trust me?"

"No, no, I trust you, I trust you." Unable to stop herself, Yuxiang begins to wail again.

SUMMER IN CHENGDE is much cooler and more comfortable than in Beiping, especially in the mornings and evenings, so you have to wear lined clothes when you go out and cover yourself in a quilt at night. The days are sunny and bright, but always with a cool wind off the mountains, so you feel clean and dry. If you leave the old city for the new imperial summer residence, and sit in a covered corridor in the lee of the mountains and next to the water, amid the luxuriant foliage, and watch the southern scenery, drinking a few cups of wine, you are as cool and comfortable as if you were in an earthly version of the Qingliang Palace on the Moon. There is no need to describe how beautiful it is.

But this is not at all how Zhou Zhengying feels about it. She has felt oppressed and impatient since her return from Beiping, with no appetite and unable to sleep, tired when she is on her feet and fretful when she is sitting down. From the time she stepped into that motor car outside the Minister's Residence, she has felt like a prisoner. Although not tied up or in chains, she is always under the stern gaze of Zuo Xichuan. He doesn't show even a flicker of a smile the whole way back to Chengde, and once there, after she has completed all the preparations he has so sternly ordered her to make, she is taken aback by his demands.

"You are not fit to undertake any more intelligence work," he says. "I am going to make a report to our superiors, asking them to send a replacement comrade as soon as possible. From now on, you will stop all work. You are not allowed out, so you can properly examine your own shortcomings while you wait for whatever punishment headquarters see fit."

Zhou Zhengying knows quite well that her recent breach of discipline was very serious, but this speech brings out the contrariness in her, and she determines that she has nothing to lose by doing just as she pleases. She doesn't even leave her room but stays there waging a cold war with Zuo Xichuan, matching his disapproving looks with her own stares, and his frigid indifference with her own lack of interest. But after only a few days, she finds the frustration builds up. Yet since she is not, by nature, someone who loses her temper with others, it is herself she gets angry with. She watches Zuo Xichuan's changing moods as he takes charge of everything, up to his neck in work, and her mood softens, her anger retreats, and she begins to get itchy feet. After all, hasn't she just been participating in the work of the Revolution? What revolutionary principles does she not understand? Alright, so this time she acted on her own initiative in taking her child back to be with Qi Yuexuan, and only when she stopped to think about it afterwards, realised how reckless and impulsive that had been. If only Zuo Xichuan hadn't got in the way, she would have come back and everything would have been just fine. She has already partnered Zuo Xichuan for more than two years, and normally while they were busy about their work, she didn't stop to think about it. But now she has left that job, she feels more bereft than someone who has just lost a lover or a child. Several times she thinks of acknowledging her fault, but the words just won't come out. It has been made quite clear to her that she is unsuited to intelligence work, that the matter has already been reported to headquarters and she must engage in profound self-criticism. Can she really expect to avoid expulsion from the Party? So, although inwardly she nurses her regrets, outwardly she shows no sign.

On this particular day, Zuo Xichuan, who is never normally home before dark, has come back by five o'clock. He looks at her, stony-faced as usual, and says: "Give the child to the servant, and come with me."

"Where to?"

"The west of the old city."

"What... what for?"

"You'll find out when we get there."

Without allowing any further questions, he turns and leaves the room. Zhou Zhengying hurriedly puts her child in the arms of the woman servant and follows him.

They go out of the city gate, through the local market and find themselves on the old trunk road to western Liaoning. In the distance they can see a dark mass of people in a disused brickyard at the side of the road. There are men and women, young and old, all wearing the dress of farmers from within the Pass. There must be more than a thousand of them. They are sitting or squatting on the bare ground, and beside them are large bags and small cloth bundles, all piled up so there isn't an inch of spare space. They are surrounded by armed Japanese guards.

"What's going on there?" Zhou Zhengying asks quietly.

Zuo Xichuan doesn't say anything, but just goes into a nearby tea house. Zhou Zhengying has no idea what he is up to, so all she can do is follow him in. Once the two of them are sat down at a table next to the window on the second floor, Zuo Xichuan looks out of the window and says: "These are all your countryfolk."

"They're from Beiping?"

"That's right, they're villagers from west of the city. Recently, the Japanese have had a crackdown in that area, blockading all the Eighth Route Army men and anti-Japanese resistance fighters. They want to establish a no man's land in the mountains there, so they've forcibly evacuated all the villages. In any places with resistance sympathies, they're sending all the villagers off to labour camps in the northeast. Those people down there are the first batch. More will follow."

"These Japanese are just inhuman," Zhou Zhengying exclaims, then goes on, lowering her voice: "In any case... are we going to rescue them?"

"That's not part of our job. It's already been reported to our superiors, and the local Party organisation will probably deal with it. Our uprising in eastern Hebei is about to break out simultaneously in Luan County and several other locations, and the upheaval that will follow is bound to cut off communications from North China outside the Pass, and could disrupt the whole Japanese military machine in the north. I reckon that, within three months, they won't have time even to think about any 'no man's land'."

"Then... why did you bring me here?"

"I just wanted to show you what's happening to your fellow countrymen."

Zhou Zhengying is incensed and glares at him furiously.

"So you're just putting on a big show, are you? Do you think I'm in any mood right now to watch the fun? Can't you see there are women and small children there? You're unnatural!"

Zuo Xichuan sees she is about to leap to her feet, and he hurriedly holds her back. He growls at her: "Am I supposed to think you're the only one with troubles in the whole of Beiping, and the only woman who has a child? Isn't that it?"

His gaze shifts to the window, and he takes no more notice of her.

Zhou Zhengying finally realises what he is up to, and she blushes furiously.

He glances back at her, and sensing that she is about to say something, he smiles faintly and asks: "You educated folks will go through anything rather than lose face, won't you! Is it really so difficult to admit you were wrong?"

"I... I know... but..." She sobs a little, then mutters: "I was in the wrong, but I don't want to have to explain myself to you."

"Why not?"

"You... once you caught up with me, everything was so cut and dried for you. You reported me to the authorities, and all you wanted was to get shot of me! What's the point in trying to explain to you? If we go back to base..."

Zuo Xichuan smiles bitterly and shakes his head.

"Ai! Do you think things would go better for you there? At the moment, the Party mechanism is concentrating on rooting out traitors, investigating people and re-examining cases, so who can say what label they might pin on a chit of a girl like you if you got sent back now?"

Zhou Zhengying's eyes fill with tears.

"Why... why are you still being so vindictive? It's so horrible, so petty, so inhuman, so..."

Zuo Xichuan remains unmoved in the face of her agitation. He just sips his tea and looks at her, smiling broadly. Then, when he sees her stifle her anger, he asks mischievously: "Anything else? There must be something you'd like to add. Or shall I do it for you? So... autocratic, so dictatorial, so fascist, so worthless..."

Zhou Zhengying finds herself giggling at his teasing, and adds: "So shameless."

"Alright, now you've got that out of your system, let's get down to business."

Zhou Zhengying is all aquiver: "What... what's my punishment? Where are you sending me?"

"How can you be so slow on the uptake?" Zuo Xichuan sighs. "I never did make that report."

"Really?"

"Really."

"Then I should have said 'so wonderful, so...'"

"Alright, that's enough of that!" He clears his throat and looks serious. "Listen up now. Things have changed, and headquarters have come up with a new plan for our team."

On hearing this, Zhou Zhengying suppresses her excitement and nods her head, scarcely daring to breathe.

Zuo Xichuan continues: "After Beiping was occupied, the local Party organisation suffered heavy losses, and the northern bureau and the city committee both moved back to our base. Intelligence gathering in Beiping is currently very weak, so the leadership of our community work department want our small cell to move to Beiping and re-establish the intelligence network with the help of the local Party and the Eighth Route Army."

"When do we leave?"

"Not for a couple of weeks at least. I've got to settle my business here first. I don't want that nephew of mine to feel disrespected. The central organisation has already sent us two comrades to reinforce our team. One's a liaison officer, and the other's an operative."

"Then I..."

"There's more important work for you to do."

"What?"

"Stop asking questions, you'll find out when the time comes. What I can tell you is that, if I can't get away for the moment, I may send you ahead as an advance party to meet up with the two new recruits to set up our cover and find accommodation. But if I do let you fly solo, you mustn't..."

Zhou Zhengying sees him looking at her and recognises what he is worried about. She sits up straight and promises: "You needn't worry, I'm not going to make the same mistake twice and betray the Party's trust." Her gaze shifts out of the window. "Even less am I going to betray these fellow countrymen, these children."

A BLACK LIMOUSINE EMERGES from East Jiaomin Lane in Beiping. The Indian policeman at the mouth of the road has already waved it through, but it is stopped just beyond by a group of Japanese military police and CID men. Although East Jiaomin Lane itself is in the foreign concession, once out of it, you are in Japanese-held territory and subject to vehicle inspections. Usually this has just meant a passport check, but recently they have become much stricter. Now, not only do they want to see documents, when cars that have gone into the lane re-emerge, their registration plates, boots and occupant numbers are also checked. If there are any Chinese, they have to get out of the vehicle for a body search. This is part of the Japanese military intelligence's drive against the Traitor Elimination Squad. According to international convention, no searches can take place in the lane itself, so the best they can do is put guards at either end and make a rigorous inspection of anyone coming and going from it.

When the limousine is stopped, its driver puts his head out of the window with every appearance of irritation.

"We only went in this morning, to the service at the Anglo-American church," he says. "You can't have forgotten us already!"

The Japanese military policeman standing in front of the car just shakes his head, and it is one of the CID men who speaks: "Who do you think you are? You're just a driver for the Brits and the Yanks. It's what the Imperial Japanese Army says that counts now, and if they want to inspect you a hundred times, you'll just have to put up with it. So stop flapping your lips and open up the boot."

The driver is still unhappy, but someone in the back of the car says: "Go on. Let him look."

So saying, he winds down the rear window and continues: "I am Director Charlie of Yanjing University, and these three are all clergy from the church. We did indeed only go in there a little while ago. It was for the baptism of the child of one of our Chinese brethren. Here, these are our documents."

The military policeman looks at Charlie and remembers that, half an hour ago, it was this same car that took this foreigner and three priests into the lane by this entrance. He gives the documents a cursory inspection, hands them back and doesn't make the men get out of the car to be searched. He waits for the inspection of the boot to finish, then waves the car through.

Once the limousine has gone some distance, Charlie speaks to the man next to him.

"You can't come back to the university, Mr Hao. Lectures have started again, and although there are only a few classes, there are many Japanese ears among the students, and there are spies outside the gates too. It's too dangerous for you. I'm really sorry, but you must see..."

Hao Bingchen raises the brim of his black hat and says, with a smile: "I'm already very grateful to you. If you hadn't come to fetch us, I'm afraid we would have had a lot of trouble getting out. We certainly don't want to add to your woes. If you get the car to take us to the pass at Horn Mountain, that will do fine."

"Are you going to Laoqiying? Isn't that... that's a long way from the city, isn't it?"

"We're not even stopping there. We're just passing through. We're moving out of Beiping, and going to the area around Laiyuan and Fuping."

"You're abandoning such an important base as Beiping?"

Hao Bingchen avoids Charlie's gaze, thinks about saying something, but stops himself. Charlie shrugs his shoulders, and says with a wry smile: "I know you've suffered some heavy losses this time, and we don't even know if Captain Gui is alive or dead, but don't you Chinese have a saying that both victory and defeat are commonplace in military affairs?"

"Ai! I don't want to do it, but... these are orders from our leaders."

"And who are these leaders of yours? Their troops give way at the first battle, and even their special agents can't stay behind enemy lines. What are you going to achieve in the rear? Who are you going to spy on? Who are you going to kill?"

Hao Bingchen just shakes his head and laughs bitterly.

"I'm afraid your leaders are even more worried about the Communist Party than they are about the Japanese," Charlie continues. "I don't doubt you and your comrades' commitment to your country, Mr Hao, and I am sure there are many brave resistance fighters in your army and in the Kuomintang. It's just a shame that the leaders of this wolf pack are so weak and feeble, and too busy with in-fighting. If they were like us Americans..."

"Enough!" says Hao Bingchen. "You can stop with all that stuff about how strong and fierce America is. If you're so fired up, why are you still neutral? You're all talk and no action. On the one hand you give us a bit of money, and on the other you sell steel and oil to the Japanese. Pah! Once the Japanese are settled in China, you wait and see if they don't turn on you! I don't doubt you are quite genuine in your support, but as for your leaders, they're no better than anyone else. It's money up front that counts with them."

Charlie knows that there is some truth to this, however roughly put, so he sighs and says: "Of course you're right. None of us have the final word, and lots of constraints have been put on us." He laughs abruptly and continues: "I have to admit, I envy Qi Yuexuan and the way he conducts himself as master of the Qi family. He is more open and free and easy than either of us."

"Have you seen him recently?"

"He came to see me yesterday."

"What for?"

"To buy medicines."

"Yanjing University isn't a pharmacy. Why did he come to you?"

"Any medicines used to treat wounds are banned on the open market in Beiping, aren't they. Not many people know that there are stocks in the university's medicine stores, but my friend Dr Bessiere told him about them. So much as I wanted to, I couldn't pretend I didn't have any. They fought a battle recently at Horn Mountain where they wiped out a Japanese motorised squadron, and suffered heavy casualties themselves."

"How did they manage that, with only a few hundred men?"

"It's true though. You didn't hear about it in the foreign concession, but a villager brought the news. He said it was the Eighth Route Army. According to him, they formed an alliance with the Eighth Route Army."

Hao Bingchen nods slowly when he hears this and asks: "Did you sell them the medicine?"

"Ai! I really didn't want to side with the Eighth Route Army. The ideology of the Communist Party is quite incompatible with my own beliefs, but I couldn't refuse after listening to Qi Yuexuan."

"What did he say that was so persuasive?"

"Hah! He pointed at the cross and asked – 'You Christians believe in Jesus, so why aren't you demonstrating his miraculous powers, and the might of your omnipotent God, instead of just praying to the tortured image of him nailed to the cross?'"

Hao Bingchen is very familiar with the power of Qi Yuexuan's oratory to undermine people's arguments, and, smiling faintly, he waits for Charlie to continue his account of the debate.

"I said that the reason Our Lord Jesus came into the world was to atone for the sins of all mankind. Jesus suffering on the cross is his holiest and most glorious image. Can you guess what he said in reply?"

Hao Bingchen just keeps smiling without replying.

"He laughed and said that Jesus suffered for mankind, and now the people of China are suffering, the Eighth Route Army has taken the place of Jesus in saving the people. They are suffering too, but you, who are God's people, just watch others die without saving them, and watch them being wounded without offering them support. He also said that our Christian teachings need to be adjusted, and that when we claim holiness, righteousness, love and mercy, we need to put the word 'sham' in front of them!"

Hao Bingchen only just manages to suppress a giggle.

"In the face of this kind of opinionated obstinacy, I gave up arguing and just sold him the stuff." Charlie laughs in an exasperated fashion. "No, to be accurate, I should say I gave it to him on credit. More than two hundred yuan-worth of medicines, and he only gave me fifty, with an IOU for the rest."

This time, Hao Bingchen cannot contain himself any longer, and he rocks back and forth with laughter. In the midst of his mirth, he waves his hand and calls out: "We're not going to Horn Mountain any more. Set us down at Xingshi Pass."

"What? You're not going to Laoqiying, then? Qi Yuexuan went back yesterday evening, and he must be in the village by now."

"No," Hao Bingchen says, "we're not going there. Now I've failed in my mission and have to retreat with my tail between my legs, I'd rather stay out of the way. You're all afraid of his eloquence, and I too have no desire to go looking for trouble for myself."

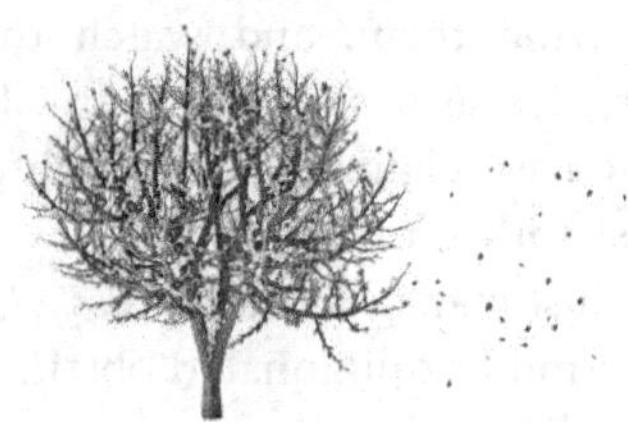

Chapter 58

Within a month, the Japanese Army has swept through Liangxiang, Fangshan, Wanping and the western part of Changping. The multitude of anti-Japanese resistance factions that have sprung up in that area are smashed to pieces by this hurricane assault. In particular, the troops assimilated by the Kuomintang from all over are almost completely scattered. Quite a few simply surrender, while others join the security services. Following the movement of the greater part of the Eighth Route Army, their newly established base for anti-Japanese operations also suffers considerable losses. Most of the major communication routes and the principal settlements fall into Japanese hands.

Ostensibly, these military operations by the Japanese have been highly successful, but in fact, they haven't really damaged the essential infrastructure of the anti-Japanese resistance movement. In Pingxi and the rest of North China, the main protagonist in the war against the Japanese has been the Eighth Route Army, and the majority of the other assorted group forces are simply using the banner of resistance to increase personal fiefdoms, with only a few actively engaging with the enemy. Local militia like those of the Left Barracks that have fought pitched battles with the Japanese are as rare as hen's teeth. The main force of the Eighth Route Army hasn't suffered any significant losses, and it is still there, like an opera troupe that is missing a few bit part players and is short of extras. Although the Japanese have assembled several tens of thousands of men to carry out the clean-up operation, all they can do is sweep through the area and leave it at that. With only a few key places they can actually occupy, they have to leave the vast mountain area ungarrisoned; nor do they dare linger there in any case. Although the main body of the Eighth Route Army has withdrawn, the guerrilla forces they have left behind are still very active, continuing to ambush convoys, dig up roads, attack sentry posts and seize military bases, just as before. The 'preservation committees' the Japanese have set up in every village work day and night shifts. As soon as the devils move out at the end of the day, the guerrillas move in to spend the night there.

· · ·

For their part, the Japanese are actually delighted with the result of the operation. Their rear is secured, and they are sure of victory. Matsuzaki Harayama, however, is less optimistic, as he realised some time ago that the real enemy in North China is not the army of the Kuomintang; it is the Communist Party and the Eighth Route Army that are the hidden danger. A few months before, he submitted a suggestion to the military, urging them to place the Kwantung Army stationed in southern Rehe under the command of the Army of North China, in order to coordinate the response to the Communist Party's integrated command structure in Rehe and Hebei. Only in this way could they consolidate their rear in the area around Beiping. However, his suggestion is not taken up, so when the Fourth Column of the Eighth Route Army first advances into southern Rehe from north of Beiping, and then breaks into eastern Hebei, the Japanese armies in Rehe and eastern Hebei each conduct their own operations. This allows the Eighth Route Army to come and go as they please on incursions deep into enemy territory in counties along the Rehe-Hebei border such as Pinggu and Zunhua, where they fight a number of serious battles. This has been the situation for quite some time. A dozen or so counties in eastern Hebei, including Luanxian, Jixian, Yutian, Qian'an and Leting, raise rebellions one after the other, and they come together to form the United Democratic Anti-Japanese Resistance Army, mustering at least a hundred thousand men. For several weeks they attack many of the county towns and disrupt the Pingshan Railway, which connects northern and northeastern China. Under these circumstances, the high-ups in the Japanese military finally begin to reconsider Matsuzaki's suggestion. But for a variety of reasons, they still do not fully incorporate the army in southern Rehe into the Army of North China. They do, however, follow a compromise plan that allows the special operations sections of the two armies to share intelligence, and to coordinate their responses to the advice and directives that come from the special operations committee in Beiping. All this considerably increases Matsuzaki's influence, and allows him further to advance his ambitions.

Matsuzaki Harayama is certainly much wiser than his army colleagues, mainly because he grew up in China, and his understanding of the country and its people greatly surpasses theirs. It is his tactic of 'using Chinese to govern Chinese' that is his magic talisman. If he is to succeed in his heavy responsibility, he has to keep strict control of those Chinese 'pawns' he has under his control. Under his orders, Zhou Zhengjie is setting up *The North China News*, which is ostensibly a newspaper, but in fact is cover for an intelligence operation gathering and collating information, eavesdropping on radio communications and codebreaking. He plans to use the pretence of news gathering to put feelers out across the whole of North China. It is Zhou Zhengjie who chooses the location of the newspaper in Moxiangzhai. His old newspaper, *The Truth*, was also based there, so he already has a full set of printing equipment in place. Since the Japanese arrival in Beiping, the whole building has been shut down and sealed up, so re-opening it involves breaking those seals. He also has in mind, later on, to find a way to incorporate the rear garden of the Minister's Residence on the other side of the wall. That way they can have all their departments brought together, which will be much more convenient. However, both he and Matsuzaki understand that, no matter whether it is running the newspaper or intelligence gathering, what they lack for both overt and covert operations is talent. So they begin a trawl for just such talent: on the one hand, they search out useful and reliable men from among school-fellows, work colleagues, friends and relatives, and secretly scour every school and institution; and, on the other, they advertise publicly for reporters, editors and additional skilled personnel.

On this particular day, the general manager in charge of the team establishing the newspaper comes hurrying in to see Zhou Zhengjie with some unexpected news. He says that Zhou's younger sister, Zhou Zhengying, is back in town. Zhou Zhengjie is both surprised and delighted, fearful and suspicious, as he asks: "Are you sure about that?"

"Ha! My family lived opposite yours as neighbours for so many years. Of course I'm sure."

"Where did you see her?"

"At the *pailou*[1] in Dongsi. I've got a friend who opened a grocery store over there. His son graduated from Tsinghua University. He speaks fluent English, is a really able fellow and not aligned with any particular cause. I thought he'd be a good recruit for us here. It was when I went over to his house that I bumped into Zhengying. My friend's shop closed down some time ago and is all boarded up. Zhengying had gone to look it over. She said she was going to set up a warehouse."

"So you spoke to her?"

"I did. But I didn't mention anything about you. She didn't ask, and I didn't offer. She didn't seem to know that you are in Beiping."

"Has she gone back to the Minister's Residence?"

"No, no. She said she is staying in the Japanese Guildhall. She has married a Japanese merchant and taken his name. She's called Shoi Zhengying now. They've been doing business in Rehe, but they are thinking of opening up in Beiping."

"Is it just her?"

"She's brought an amah and some servants. She said her husband's still in Rehe waiting for news from her. Once they've found a suitable property, they'll move their stock in. Oh, that's right, she had a young child with her too. She said it was her son. He's called Shoi something or other... I've forgotten what."

When Zhou Zhengjie hears all this, he relaxes a little. Ever since she got into trouble over her membership of the Communist Party and left home, he has been worried about his only sister, but what puzzles him is how such a hard case as her could have abandoned her convictions and her emotional ties like this, and married a Japanese. On the face of it, since she hasn't come on her own, the chances of her being on a mission for the Communists would seem to be reduced, but she still shouldn't be taken at her word, and he needs to be even more careful now he is working for the Japanese. He considers the matter from every angle, and finally decides that the thing to do is to report the whole thing to Matsuzaki Harayama and let the Japanese take up the investigation. If she is acting for the Communists, then he himself won't be implicated, and he can appear at a suitable moment to persuade her to change her allegiance. If she turns out to be on the up-and-up, then he can welcome her back into the family without a qualm. And if she can also ingratiate herself with the Japanese, then their brother-sister relationship can remain intact.

Matsuzaki Harayama is equally surprised when he takes Zhou Zhengjie's telephone call. When he reopened Moxiangzhai before the war, he also later rented the former stableyard of the Minister's Residence, so he had often seen Zhou Zhengying, and was greatly struck by her beauty, grace and intelligence. He immediately orders the Tokko to conduct a secret investigation, and he contacts Rehe as well. On the same evening he gets the results of these enquiries, he wastes no time in calling Zhou Zhengjie.

"I have already carried out enquiries into the circumstances surrounding your sister, Mr Zhou, and there is no problem. She had already left the Communist Party before the war, and is telling the truth about her current circumstances. Her new husband is called Shoi Tanigawa. He is the uncle of Brigade Commander Shoi of the Kwantung Army, works as a merchant and is also an intelligence officer of the Kwantung Army. You can stop worrying and welcome her back into the family as soon as you like. I think you should do your utmost to get her to come and work for us. In China we don't have to be slaves to Japanese conventions, and we mustn't waste her talents. At the moment, we desperately need people with real knowledge and experience of the Communist Party. As soon as your sister's husband gets to Beiping, I'll hold a welcome banquet for them."

Naturally, Zhou Zhengjie is delighted, and he eagerly agrees. Early the next morning, he goes to the Japanese Guildhall for what is, needless to say, a highly emotional reunion between brother and sister, and a first meeting of uncle and nephew. But Zhou Zhengying tactfully declines the invitation to move into her brother's home, saying it wouldn't be very convenient for him if she were to move in with her nanny and all her other servants. Nor does she agree to take up a post at the *North China News*. She says that, although she is interested of course, she has to find out whether her lord and husband approves. This is, in fact, exactly what she has agreed in advance with Zuo Xichuan, on the principle that you do not catch a big fish by being impatient, and rushing into things is no way to do good business.

· · ·

CLOWN'S WOUND HAS HEALED very quickly and is closed over in less than two weeks. His left collarbone is still not fully recovered, so he only really has use of one arm, but he can already dress himself, feed himself, get on and off the *kang* and walk around the room. He is, by nature, as lively as a monkey, and is used to being healthy and active, so he is soon almost tearing his hair out in frustration at being confined. On top of that, he is constantly worried about Yuxiang, so the urge to leave is almost overwhelming. It would be easy enough to get him out of the city by himself, but he wants to take Yuxiang with him, and that is much more problematic. She is being watched so closely, and there is only one of him, with one arm out of action at that, so he is in no position to rescue anyone.

In truth, Clown is not the only one getting agitated. Over the last few days, Wangtian, Caiping and Yue E have been even worse. Chenglong found out the same day about what passed between Yue E and Yuxiang, and although outwardly he gives nothing away, he has already taken preventative measures. He has added two more guards at the gate, and has given explicit instructions that if his wife shows up, she is not to be admitted. So whenever Yue E does now pass by, she finds the gates locked in her face. A fortnight passes in no time, the work on the house earmarked for Yamaguchi is complete, and still none of the conspirators has come up with a plan. Then, quite unexpectedly, it is an outsider who turns the whole situation around.

One morning, Caiping has gone shopping at a fruiterer's on Houmen Avenue. These days she can eat eight meals a day and still feel hungry. She is continually devouring on all kinds of snacks, but she has a particular taste for sour things, so she has just been buying mountain haws, apricot kernels and sour dates. She is about to return home, when she hears someone behind her call out. She turns to look, and sees Li Fenggu standing at the gates of the Tianjiang tea garden. She is not wearing a kimono this time, but has on a white *qipao* embroidered with red flowers. Her eyebrows and temples have been touched up, and her lips and cheeks rouged. Zhou Si's death doesn't seem to have affected her, and she is still putting on a fine show. Inwardly, Caiping has had more than enough of this woman, but outwardly, she has to maintain appearances.

"Ah! It's you, aunty! Are you..."

"I've got nothing much on and I'm full to bursting," Li Fenggu says with a lopsided smile, "so I thought I might pass the time here having a little gossip. But there's absolutely no one to talk to."

"How come such a busy person as you has time on her hands?"

"Ai! Don't talk about it... come on in and we can have a proper catch-up. Come on now, come on."

Caiping wants to refuse, but she can't see any way to get out of it, so allows herself to be drawn into the tea garden. Only a few rickety chairs have been laid out, a far cry from its glory days. And this is considered one of the large, old-established gardens; most of the smaller ones have closed down already.

There can be no doubt that Li Fenggu really is very bored, and as soon as the two of them sit down, the floodgates open. She sighs deeply, pours out her woes, and before she has even finished talking, she dissolves into sobs. According to her, the comfort station she put up the money to establish has been taken over by the Japanese military, leaving her with no commission and a good number of unsettled accounts. As for the society salons that she has forced her way into with such difficulty, invitations have dried up recently, for whatever reason. What is more, the wife of her Japanese sugar daddy group captain has just arrived in Beiping, and she is not inclined to recognise her husband's mistress, or show her any kind of respect. Indeed, her only greeting when they met was a resounding slap in the face. Nor are things any better at home since, in Zhou Si's absence, she only has her old amah for company. Now, she has come out to take a turn around the town, but not found anywhere agreeable. Even in the tea gardens there is an absence of anyone to have a civilised conversation with. She had thought of getting up on the stage to sing a couple of songs, not for money, just for the fun of it, but the proprietor wasn't keen.

"Drink as much tea as you like, on me, great aunt," he said, "but for heaven's sake don't sing. Everyone has seen you wearing your kimono and wooden clogs, and you really don't want to call the wolf pack down on you by singing."

Li Fenggu's eloquent exposition of all her woes sounds more like a comic monologue to Caiping, who has a hard time keeping a straight face. In the end, her only recourse is to open one of her paper bags and stuff a handful of apricot kernels in her mouth to shut herself up.

Observing Caiping's suspect table manners, Li Fenggu's tears turn to smiles as she says: "Aiya! Just the sight of the way you're wolfing those nuts is enough to set my teeth on edge!"

Caiping twists her lips into an answering smile, as she chews hard, then says confidingly: "I've been having cravings for the last few days."

"Aiyo! How lucky you are! Do you know if it's a boy or a girl? I'll bet it's a boy." Li Fenggu sighs. "Ai! I haven't been so lucky. Everyone I have relied on has let me down, and in the end, here I am, alone and with no children. Ai! Life is hard..."

When Caiping sees her eyes filling with tears, she can't help but feel a little sorry for her, and she says encouragingly: "Aunty, we each travel our own road, and we each make our own troubles. Who else do we have to blame? By nature, you are so changeable and quick to react, every time you turn you don't know which way you are facing, so how can you ever have a smooth and easy life? But the way I see it, it's a good thing you're not getting favours from the Japanese any more. This way, you can take a step back, collect yourself and start over again with a new way of life. You could find some docile, biddable man to marry and pass the days peacefully, so the second half of your life is free of worry and rancour. Wouldn't that be good?"

"Yes, it would be good, very good," Li Fenggu says with a bitter laugh. "Ai! But it's too hard. I've thought of getting married since I was in my teens, but up to now what chance have I had for a proper wedding? Do you think a singer like me can marry into a fine family? But if I end up with some second-rater, what does that make me? I'm just a tender young cucumber that's turned into a dried-up old loofah. Hey-ho, maybe in my next life. In this life I'm just left with the dregs. But to get back to what we're really talking about, even if I get a man who's too stupid to count up to one, at least he'd still be a husband. I don't need someone who's going to send electric thrills through me, but they should at least be able to make a light bulb flicker. It's not that relying on someone else is better than relying on yourself alone. If you're alone, you can certainly get by, maybe with a few knocks, but if you don't have money, then you're done for."

The more Li Fenggu talks, the more animated she becomes, until quite soon, her tears have disappeared. Listening to her is making Caiping's head pound, and she doesn't hear any of the last part of what she says. When Li Fenggu still doesn't stop, she can't take any more and says: "I've got things to do at home, aunty. We'll talk again when I've got some time and then I'll..."

Seeing her making to get up and go, Li Fenggu hurriedly holds her back.

"Don't go. Stay a little longer, and I can... there's something important I want to ask you."

Caiping is taken aback. Seeing the other woman's air of mystery and intrigue, she can't imagine where she might be going with this.

Li Fenggu moves a little closer and asks: "Liu Chenglong has a mistress, doesn't he?" When Caiping doesn't reply, she goes on: "He's your brother-in-law, isn't he? As his sister-in-law, you must know."

"Well, yes, it's true. What is it to you?"

"He's going to give his mistress to that Japanese captain, Yamaguchi, isn't he? And he's giving them a house."

"How... how do you know that?"

"Don't you worry about how I know, just tell me whether it's true or not."

All Caiping can do is grunt in reply. All the while her heart is thumping, as she wonders why Li Fenggu is asking her about this. Li Fenggu is getting worked up now.

"Hah! He really has no self-respect. He's all decent and proper to people's faces, but behind their backs he's a real lowlife. Isn't there anyone in your family or your husband's family who can control him, rather than just let him have his way all the time?"

Caiping just sighs and nods, not at all expecting the direction Li Fenggu now takes the conversation.

"This Yamaguchi is a useless scumbag anyway. If he's given a girl just like that, is he going to treasure her as something precious? Is he really going to attach any value to a skinny little thing like that Lian girl? Ha! But then again, maybe she has indeed struck it lucky and she'll be much better off than with Chenglong. Beiping belongs to the Japanese now, and if she finds a patron, who's to say she won't become a naturalised Japanese, and then..."

"You think everybody's like you," Caiping retorts, "but Yuxiang's got no choice, and if she really can't escape, it may well end in her death."

Li Fenggu raises her eyebrows and says, slowly and thoughtfully: "There's no need to jump down my throat. Everyone has their own way of getting by. She may not want him, but someone else might, so why try to force a square peg into a round hole?"

"Who would want this man? You?"

"If I didn't, why would I be asking you about it?"

"But he's Japanese."

"Who cares where he's from. All I'm after is a man."

Caiping almost bursts out laughing and covers her mouth with her hand, before asking: "Surely you're joking, aunty. How old is he? How old are you? Is this all because you want a son? You may want that, but does he?"

"How did you work that out?" Li Fenggu laughs and then continues. "Let me tell you something. Japanese men are base creatures, and their army comfort stations have plenty of older Japanese women. It goes without saying, there are a lot of men who go there after these old ones. Since we've got this far, I won't deceive you. When I ran a comfort station, that fellow Yamaguchi was a frequent visitor, and it wasn't just the girls who were popular with him, the *mamasan* got more than a look in too... now do you understand? The two of us had an affair. We were intimate for long enough. Do you think I don't know what turns him on?"

Li Fenggu moves closer, lowers her voice even further, and what she goes on to say is even coarser. She clears her throat and continues quite matter-of-factly, though her gleeful expression is quite dazzling. What she says, however, turns Caiping bright red with embarrassment, and her stomach turns over.

"Enough, enough! Don't go on! I don't have time to listen to your obscenities," Caiping says, standing up. "You're getting way ahead of yourself. There's nothing you can do about it. You should..."

"Ha! Don't get so agitated. Sit back down and hear me out. It all comes down to the individual, and I'm telling you, I've got a plan."

"What kind of a rancid plan is that?"

"Rancid? It's brilliant! It just needs your help, and we'll be acting out *The Return of the Phoenix.*"

Caiping is so desperate to get Yuxiang out of her current dire straits that she is willing to try anything, so she sits back down again and Li Fenggu murmurs in her ear. She can't help herself 'ah-ing' and 'ah-ha-ing' as the plan unfolds, and she is about to nod in agreement, when her doubts set in again.

"Aunty, are you sure Yamaguchi will just lie back and accept it when he finds out he's been duped?"

"No he won't, but what can he do? Eat me? Don't worry, I'll get that sugar daddy of mine to take a hand, and if he decides just to accept things, that will be that. If he doesn't, then there could be quite a fuss. But this whole thing is against Japanese Army regulations, and if there's too big a fuss, it won't be good for him at all."

"But if he ends up nursing a grudge against you, I'm afraid he'll be plotting his revenge later."

"Don't worry, I can get the better of any man."

"Are you sure your sugar daddy will help you?"

"Ha, he's no newcomer to the shadier side of things, and he understands what it means to be a sugar daddy. I've been dutiful and respectful towards him in the bedroom, so he's bound to help me with things in his sphere of influence. Now his wife's on the scene, I've become an embarrassment to him, so he's not going to pass up on an opportunity to get shot of me."

"What about Chenglong?"

"Pah! He's an irrelevance. As long as Yamaguchi accepts the situation, what can he do about it?"

"You'd better go over it all again, and make sure you've thought of even the remotest possibility."

"I'm the one taking all the risks. What are you worried about?"

Caiping mutters to herself irresolutely, turning the matter over in her head, then finally she nods in agreement.

On the afternoon of the third day following the meeting between Li Fenggu and Caiping, a Japanese Army jeep turns into the hutong and stops in front of the Lian house. The sentries recognise both the figures who get out of the rear doors: one is Yue E, and the other is Caiping.

"Ai! What has brought you two mistresses here? Didn't Master Liu say he was going to send a car so that some of my colleagues and I could escort the bride?"

"When a girl gets married, isn't it the groom's side that collects her? Even if we're not making a big show of it, we still have to stick to the rules, don't we? So now we've got people from the bride's side and the groom's side, we've got both escort and reception committee, haven't we!"

When he hears this, the guard lets the two women through the gates, and they make their way to the middle of the courtyard. Sergeant Lian comes running out of the northern range.

"Senior Mistress, Second Mistress!" he says. "Didn't you say you were coming at four o'clock? It's only..."

Yue E doesn't break stride but heads inside, saying: "Do you think this is a visit to the imperial court, with everything done to the minute?"

Sergeant Lian replies hurriedly in a low voice: "It's Yuxiang. She won't put on her wedding dress at any price. I'm at my wits' end."

"Alright, leave it to me. It's a good thing we came a bit early, isn't it?"

When she gets to the door, she sees that Sergeant Lian is about to follow her in, and she stops him, saying: "You're not to come in and cause mayhem. Go and be nice to the Japanese lords."

With that, she and Caiping disappear inside and shut the door.

Yuxiang is sitting on the *kang*, still dressed in her everyday clothes. With her untidy hair and dirty face, she is even more of a mess than the last time they saw her. When she sees the two of them come into the room, she just glances indifferently at them and doesn't even bother to stand up. Yue E realises that she has misunderstood what is going on and hurries over to whisper to her: "We've come to rescue you. Hurry up and get washed and dressed."

Yuxiang shakes her off and turns away.

Yue E is astounded, and as she desperately tries to think what to say, Caiping steps forward: "Don't you trust even us two, Yuxiang? We're taking huge risks to help you, and we're going to set you free before they can get here to escort the new bride back. So get a move on, or we'll run out of time."

Yuxiang looks at her with astonished delight and asks: "And... and what about Clown?"

"He's waiting for you at the Guang'an Gate."

Yuxiang gives a little yelp of joy and leaps down from the *kang*.

It is not long before Yue E and Caiping are helping a fully dressed and veiled Yuxiang swiftly out of the room, heading for the street. When Sergeant Lian sees the three of them get into the car, he tries to follow them, but Yue E says: "No, you're not coming."

Sergeant Lian pulls a face: "But... but... I'm her father, how can..."

Yue E doesn't let him finish as she shuts the car door.

"You think this is all to your credit, do you?" she says. "You say you're her father, and you'd be happy to make fools of yourselves like this?"

The car pulls up in the north of Dongsi, where Wangtian is waiting beside a rickshaw. Before the car has even come to a halt, Li Fenggu steps out of the rickshaw. She too is dressed as a bride, and it is the work of seconds for her and Yuxiang to swap places in the car. As soon as it sets off again, Wangtian helps Yuxiang into the rickshaw and sets off at a run, heading south towards the Guang'an Gate.

As for Yamaguchi, he is happily waiting in the freshly renovated house, anticipating the happy event. To his surprise, though, it is not his bride-to-be who arrives first, but Captain Mishima. Although Mishima is, indeed, only a captain, he has greater seniority than many generals. He is commander of the Beiping garrison of the Japanese Army, from which most of the Kempeitai has been recruited, so even Yamaguchi was once an officer under his command. Although this is no longer the case, he is still his old commander, and, moreover, the Kempeitai's overall mission is still dependent on the co-operation of the Beiping garrison, so Yamaguchi dares not ignore him. He plasters a smile on his face and goes to greet him, but inside, he is very worried.

Sensing his unease, Mishima immediately reassures him: "You don't need to worry, Lord Yamaguchi. Of course the army has to have rules, but what it values more is fighting spirit. I haven't come to disrupt your wedding, and I'm certainly not going to show you up. I've only come to congratulate you and give you a gift. You are wondering why, perhaps?" He sees Yamaguchi looking at him blankly, and he continues with a smile: "The bride you are welcoming today is my protege, so that makes you my surrogate son-in-law doesn't it?"

This just makes Yamaguchi even more confused. When could Yuxiang have become Mishima's mistress? He has his doubts, but he immediately bows and says "Father-in-law".

IN A SHORT WHILE, the bridal car arrives. Li Fenggu's head and face are covered by her veil, but there's nothing she can do to hide her physique. Yamaguchi gasps when he sees her. How can Yuxiang have blown up like a balloon since their last meeting a few days ago? He wants to take off her veil to have a look, but with Captain Mishima standing there, he doesn't want to break etiquette. Fortunately, this is not a formal wedding and there is no ceremony, so the bride just bows three times to Mishima before being led into the inner chamber. Once Mishima and the bride's escorts, Yue E and Caiping, have left, Yamaguchi remains dumbstruck.

With the door closed, no one can see exactly how this little scene plays out, but by the sound of it, it is a full-scale battle. The banging and crashing and cursing are incredible, and after a while, they are joined by some piteous cries. It goes quiet for a moment, but this is not the end of the show, just the intermission. Quite soon, the racket begins again, but now the action has moved onto the bed. The boards sound as though they are about to crack, the frame about to collapse. The panting sounds like a steam train, and the screams are shriller than its whistle.

By the time Chenglong comes rushing in, the performance is all but over. He calls through the door: "Is... is everything alright, Lord Yamaguchi?"

After a while, the door opens, and Yamaguchi stands there, a coat draped over his bare torso, and his hands still buckling his belt. There are streaks of blood on his face and body. He doesn't come out, but leans on the door frame. He doesn't say a word, but just looks at Chenglong, his eyes gleaming. This gaze disconcerts Chenglong. He pastes a smile on his face and is about to speak, when a voice calls out from behind the bed curtains.

"Liu-san, shouldn't such a fine house have a better bed? This old body of mine can't take the battering any more." Li Fenggu's head and shoulders appear through the curtain, and although she is some distance away, every detail is visible. She has two black eyes, and one side of her face is swollen. Her voice, however, remains coy and girlish: "I'd be really grateful if you could go all the way and get me a spring mattress."

Seeing Chenglong's flabbergasted expression, Yamaguchi gives him a big thumbs-up and says, with a toothy grin: "Yours is done good!"

With that, not waiting for any reply, he steps back into the room and slams the door. Chenglong leaves, puzzled and crestfallen, and it's only when he gets home that he works out exactly what has happened. He storms into the Minister's Residence, bursting with anger. But once he is standing in front of the grinning faces of Yue E and Caiping, he finds himself lost for words. Then, after a long while, he gives a thumbs-up, and just says: "You've done good!"

He turns on his heel and leaves, his words and his expression exactly the same as Yamaguchi's.

WANGTIAN ESCORTS YUXIANG to the Guang'an Gate, and once he has seen she is safely through the checkpoint, he relaxes and turns for home. Outside the city walls, Yuxiang looks all around her and combs the area without seeing any sign of Clown. It is not long before the sun begins to set and the gates are about to close, yet there is still no one to be seen. Her initial elation on escaping the trap fades away, and she leans against a telegraph pole, her eyes full of tears as she stares at the city gate.

In fact, Clown got there some time ago and is squatting down on the street by the walls. He is not just being cautious; he simply can't get out. His own certificate of good citizenship was taken off him when he went into the 'quarantine unit', and the one he now has belongs to Wangtian. Normally, security is tighter coming into the city than leaving it, but today, as luck would have it, it is the other way round. You are in trouble if your face doesn't exactly match the photograph, and even more dangerously for Clown, all men have to undergo a body search, with no exception.

Clown has the bullet wound on his body, and although his arm isn't in a sling, he still has it splinted and bandaged. There's nothing to see as long as he has his coat on, but there's no way of hiding it if he has to take the bandage off. So for the moment, he doesn't dare approach the gate, and he is waiting, at a distance, for some kind of opportunity to present itself. As he listens to the chatter of a roadside cigarette seller, he discovers the reason for the increased security is that, at midday, there was a raid on the Japanese trading company at the entrance to the food market. Apparently, no shots were fired, but the two Japanese who died had their necks broken. Among other things, what was taken was the entire stock of explosives and detonators. Because of this, from midday on, emergency measures have been imposed, including the body searches, and the city gates are locked. It is only after three or four hours that the restrictions begin to relax. Hearing all this, Clown realises how lucky he has been; if he had arrived an hour earlier, he would undoubtedly have been arrested. But now, the city gates will soon be closing, and as he thinks of Yuxiang waiting outside, he is getting more and more agitated.

At this point, in the wake of a noxious smell, two night soil carts appear, each with a man, front and rear, pulling and pushing. They are heading straight for the city gate. When Clown turns to look, his eyes meet with those of the man pulling the lead cart. The cart has passed in an instant, but that is long enough for Clown to realise he knows the fellow. As he watches the retreating form, cudgelling his brains for who it is, the man turns back to look and all becomes clear: it is Zhang Zhicheng. Clown hurries after him.

"Brother Zhicheng, it's me, Clown."

"Ha! I can see it's you, you little wretch!" Zhang Zhicheng says with a broad smile, but not stopping. "We're in a rush to get out of the city now, but later..."

Clown doesn't wait for him to finish: "Later's no good. I've been hoping all along that you might give me your protection, so take me with you today."

"I can't today. It's too dangerous."

"Do you think I'd be asking if I was afraid of danger? Give me that." Clown reaches out to take hold of the handle of the cart, but the movement makes him exclaim with pain.

"Are you wounded?"

"I took a Japanese bullet, but it's almost better now."

"That's enough of that. You shouldn't pretend you're fit when you're not. Besides, you're not filthy enough to look as though you do this for a living."

"Then..."

"Walk along beside the cart. You can make out you're a supervisor. We're going to need your quick tongue in a bit."

Clown grins, then suddenly thinks of something and asks urgently: "Have you all got your good citizenship certificates?"

"Yes, we do. But..." Zhang Zhicheng lowers his voice further. "There's something a bit different about these carts."

Clown gives an amused grunt: "I noticed that. Is it the same as last time? I made the alterations to the carts myself. Did you think you could fool me?"

Zhang Zhicheng laughs, then turns to his companion and orders: "Pass it on to the back – keep the chatter down when we go through the checkpoint, and leave the talking to this supervisor."

"Yessir!" The man acknowledges the instruction and hurries to pass it on.

The carts stop in front of the checkpoint, and Clown hastens to the front and bows, as he hands a bunch of good citizenship certificates over to the Japanese soldier on guard. Because of the stench of the night soil, the man is pinching his nose and holding his breath, and he just glances at the permits before handing them back. He doesn't even say anything, just waves his hand as much as to say: Be on your way, and hurry up about it.

Clown is about to call out to the carts to move on, when a plainclothes CID man steps out in front of the cart and asks: "Hey you! Which night soil yard are you from? I don't recognise any of you."

"Ha! We're from the Liuji depot by the Desheng Gate," says Clown. "Our boss is your captain, isn't he? We don't usually come this way, but the Baituizi vegetable garden needs a load of shit. That garden supplies the Imperial Army, so we didn't dare refuse."

"If you're going to Baituizi, why don't you use the Fucheng Gate, instead of coming all the way round here?"

"Don't you think we would have avoided the detour if we could? Aren't you aware of how things stand today? No one's allowed through the Fucheng Gate, so we've got no choice."

"Hmm... are you carrying anything apart from shit?" The plainclothes CID man points at the carts' wheels. "Does a load of shit always make them sink so low?"

Without batting an eyelid, Clown grins and says: "You don't know? They're all grand houses in the west of the city, and their shit's a lot richer than the stuff from the south. We wouldn't dare send the Imperial Army any old runny stuff. It would be a bit surprising if it wasn't heavier. If you don't believe me, I'll get some out for you to inspect."

So saying, he lifts the leather hose at the back of the cart so its loop is no longer hanging down, and the liquid shit begins to flow out of it.

The plainclothes man doesn't make any reply, but the Japanese Guard rushes forward cursing "*Baku, baku*". Then, holding his nose, he gestures to them to move on as quickly as possible.

Seeing this, Clown doesn't waste any time and shouts: "Get a move on, let's not stink out the Imperial Army."

The other men put their backs into it and haul the carts away at a steady trot.

When they've gone a fair distance, Clown goes over to Zhang Zhicheng and whispers: "Are you the ones who robbed that Japanese firm today, Brother Zhicheng?"

Zhang Zhicheng nods. Clown's interest is even more aroused now, and he slaps his thigh.

"If you set off that many explosives all at once, you could flatten the tower at the Qian Gate. So what are you going to blow up?"

"Keep your voice down!" Zhang Zhicheng glares at him. "This is no place for such talk."

Clown doesn't ask anything else, but the more he thinks about it, the more excited he gets. He even begins to hum a folksong from the northeast.

"Hey! There's a girl calling you, over there at the roadside," Zhang Zhicheng says, nudging him.

Clown turns to look and sees Yuxiang watching him anxiously. He is taken aback that he had almost forgotten about her, and then could have missed her, standing there as large as life.

"Who is she?"

"She's... she's my wife... well, we're not actually married yet."

"Then what are you waiting for? Go to her."

Clown runs over to greet her.

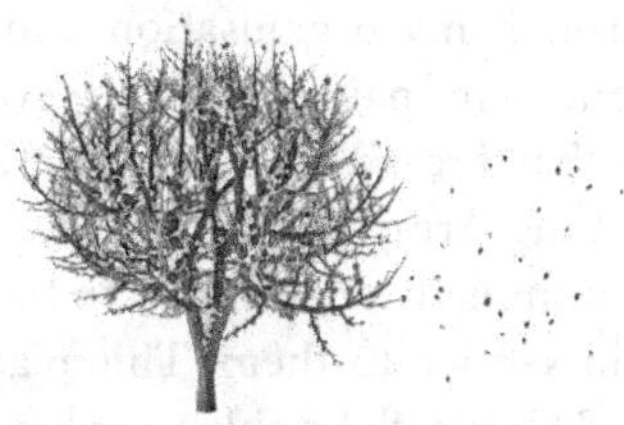

Chapter 59

Ten days later, Zuo Xichuan arrives in Beiping, bringing a lorry crammed with merchandise. Zhou Zhengying has already settled on the shop in Dongsi as their premises. It is situated on a bustling street market and has a generous frontage and a family courtyard in the rear with living space and storerooms. As it was formerly a grocery store, it already has counters and shelves, and even the living quarters in the rear are fully furnished. All it needs is re-stocking and the Julong Mountain Goods Store will be ready to hang up its sign and open for business.

The two comrades sent by headquarters to assist them have already arrived: one man and one woman, both in their twenties. The man, Xiao Zhao, is a communications officer, and the woman, Xiao Xing, is support staff, but outwardly, he is a shop assistant and she is a counter girl. On the evening of Zuo Xichuan's arrival, they send their first telegraphic report, informing headquarters of the Japanese Army troop movements in response to the insurrections in eastern Hebei. So, although it appears the shop has not yet opened, secretly, the intelligence service is already up and running.

Matsuzaki Harayama keeps his word, and when he hears that Zuo Xichuan has arrived, the next evening he insists on holding a welcome dinner for the husband and wife. It will be held in his own area in the building that houses the headquarters of the Beiping Special Operations Committee. He arranges for a chef to prepare Japanese dishes and sends a car for the couple. He hasn't invited any outsiders, so it is just himself, as host, and Zhou Zhengjie and his wife, without their children, as the other guests. Three different parties and two countries are represented by just these five people.

WITH THE POLITE FORMALITIES out of the way, they sip their drinks and swap family gossip. When the wine has been round three times, Matsuzaki Harayama turns the conversation to the main topic.

"Lord Shoi, our military have already issued the authorisation to allow the sharing of intelligence between Manchuria and the neighbouring regions of

North China, and through my organisation and coordination, to counter the anti-Japanese insurgence, in particular, the ever-increasing rapacity of the Communist Party in that area. However, enacting this presents considerable difficulties. The Kwantung Army has previously always provided great support, but although they are nominally answerable to the central military command, in truth they pay only lip service to them. This places me in a difficult situation, which I hope, you, Lord Shoi, will be able to help me with."

"I'm honoured, Lord Matsuzaki," says Zuo Xichuan, "but I am now just a merchant. If it is supplies that you want, then I will do my utmost to help, but when it comes to grand military affairs, I..."

"Come now, Lord Shoi. An intelligent man doesn't resort to subterfuge. If I wasn't sure of my facts, do you think I would be so presumptuous?"

Zuo Xichuan smiles faintly and says: "It is true that, in addition to my business, I have rendered the Kwantung Army some assistance, but you are an old hand at these things, Lord Matsuzaki, and I'm sure you understand the rules."

Zhou Zhengjie sees Matsuzaki debating with himself and not replying, so he hurriedly interjects: "We are family, Lord Shoi, and family doesn't worry about yours or mine. The Kwantung Army and the Army of North China both serve the emperor, don't they? Both in public and in private, they are family too, aren't they? I'm in the same line myself, and I know that everyone has their own constraints, but a general in the field is not bound by the orders of his sovereign. Let's be a bit more open with each other, shall we? Japan and China are at war with each other on all fronts, and Manchuria is just one corner of the whole field, and the heart of China is still the central plain. What is more, Lord Matsuzaki has agreed that we can consolidate all your expenses and pay them out to you from here every month. How does that strike you?"

"That's right," Zhou Zhengying says. "No matter in which direction things develop, we've made the right move in coming to Beiping, as this is more than likely to be the capital city in the future. You really shouldn't be considering returning to Chengde. There's no comparison with Beiping. Lord Matsuzaki is an old friend of my brother's, and when he says he'll give you a hand, that's just him being polite. He doesn't really care about the little stuff. What it comes down to is that he is offering you an opportunity, and you shouldn't be too..."

Before she can finish, she catches a fierce look from Zuo Xichuan. She shuts up abruptly as the atmosphere in the room becomes a little constrained.

Matsuzaki adopts the part of the host: "We should not get overwrought, but let Lord Shoi sleep on it. Come now, don't let this little affair spoil the party mood."

"Absolutely! Absolutely, Lord Shoi. Let's drink up," says Zhou Zhengjie, lending his support.

Zuo Xichuan and the other two men drain their cups together, then he says with a wry smile: "Lord Matsuzaki, I am no innocent in these matters, but I was entrusted this task by my nephew, and if word gets out, it would not be such a good idea for me, as one man, to be seen serving two masters. It would be best if there is no direct contact or agreement between us. See if you think this will work – I will take my wife's advice, and if you intend to invite her to work at the *North China News*, and if she wants to do it, I won't stop her. In China, we don't have to stick meticulously to Japanese conventions, and to keep such an educated and knowledgeable girl at home really would be a waste of talent. If she ends up working for you, gathering intelligence, that would be entirely proper and much better than me coming out into the open."

Matsuzaki finds himself obliged to kill two birds with one stone in this manner, so he nods his agreement, saying: "Hmm, yes, that all sounds quite reasonable, and as to expenses..."

"No need to talk about expenses. They'll balance out on each side anyway, won't they? You can pass on some of your intelligence to me through Zhengying, and I can pass it on to the Kwantung Army. If the secret gets out, there'll be no harm done, as there is nothing unusual about exchanging information. Do you think..."

"I think it's fine. We'll be getting the best of both worlds," Matsuzaki says, smiling broadly. Then he looks at Zhou Zhengying and asks: "Well, madam, you surely must be willing to do this."

"News reporting is work that I love, and I'm keen to get started," Zhou Zhengying replies briskly. "My husband and my lord have both given their approval, so how could I not be willing?"

"Excellent. You should take up your post as soon as possible, then, as we are currently very short-staffed."

"I'll be there tomorrow."

Matsuzaki suddenly thinks of something, and he puts down his wine cup.

"Have you seen Qi Yuexuan since you've been back in Beiping, Madame Shoi?"

"No. I've heard that he is not in the city at the moment."

"That's right. He has been cultivating his soul at Laoqiying in the Western Hills for more than a year now. I think the two of you should meet."

Uncertain of what exactly he means by this, no one says anything. Zhou Zhengying is rather embarrassed and looks at the ground. Zuo Xichuan also lowers his gaze, while Zhou Zhengjie looks at the two of them in bewilderment.

"Aiya!" says Matsuzaki. "I don't have any ulterior motive. I'm a lawyer born and bred, and I just feel there should be a resolution there. Of course it's not just the legal situation, there's the economic aspect too... do you still not get it? You and Qi Yuexuan are legally man and wife, so if you get divorced, you should get your share of his estate. The Minister's Residence is no hovel, so the total amount should be considerable."

Zhou Zhengying doesn't say anything, but Zhou Zhengjie replies with a laugh: "It's true. I thought of that too, but I felt it best to let Mr Matsuzaki speak in such blunt terms. Don't be foolish, Zhengying. There's nothing to be apologetic about, and this year is not the time to be sparing people's sensibilities. Don't you know how deep that family's pockets are? Half the houses on that street, a dozen or more big businesses, more than a thousand *mu* of land in the countryside..."

"That's enough!" says Zhou Zhengying. "I'll look after my own affairs. I don't need your help."

She sees her brother glaring at her and turns back to Matsuzaki. "Lord Matsuzaki, there must be a resolution between myself and Qi Yuexuan, and the best way will be for us to meet to discuss it and come to an amicable separation. Not only must we consider both our reputations, don't we also have to think of Lord Shoi's feelings? I take your goodwill as read, and if there are any problems, I will certainly come to you for help."

There is nothing more Matsuzaki can say, so he just smiles and nods his head.

Zhou Zhengjie steps in to try to smooth things over: "This is of no great importance. We can talk about it again later. For today, our cooperation is the important thing. Let the wine take charge. Come on now, let us fill the cups again."

At this moment, Matsuzaki's secretary comes in and whispers in his ear. Matsuzaki grunts in response several times, then turns and says: "I must apologise, Lord Shoi, but there is some business I have to attend to. Zhou-san must stand in for me as host for a while."

On hearing this, Zuo Xichuan says hurriedly: "Your public duties are very pressing, Lord Matsuzaki. Let us find another day..."

"No, no. We haven't finished today's wine yet. We can't break up the party. It's just a small matter. It won't take long. I'll soon be back."

With this, Matsuzaki hurries out of the room after his secretary.

It's no more than fifteen minutes before he returns, and although he is still smiling, it is clear that the smile is forced and superficial. It cannot completely mask his gloomy expression.

"Have a look at this," he says, sitting down and handing Zhou Zhengjie some sheets of paper. Then he raises his wine cup. "Come now, Lord Shoi, Madame Shoi, let's get back to our wine."

Zhou Zhengying takes a sip of wine and glances at her brother. He is studying the documents with a very ugly expression on his face: "Lord Matsuzaki, I..."

"Don't upset yourself. Think it through and then we'll talk. It's time for wine now. Don't let this little episode spoil the party mood. Pour some more wine."

Zuo Xichuan and Zhou Zhengying can neither probe the matter, nor leave so soon, so they just have to grin and bear it. They drink a few more cups and make small talk until Zhou Zhengying finally uses the pretext of being worried about their son for them to say their farewells and leave.

. . .

THE NEXT DAY, Zhou Zhengying reports for duty at the *North China News*, and it is only then that she learns from Zhou Zhengjie's own mouth what happened the night before. His cover-up of the anti-Japanese resistance activities of the twelve villages of the Left Barracks has been discovered by the Japanese, and not only is Qi Yuexuan implicated, he is at the very centre of the business.

It turns out that, as soon as a report on the battle at Horn Mountain made its way up through the system, it quickly attracted serious questioning from the highest levels of the Japanese Army. Because almost an entire elite squadron of infantry and cavalry had been wiped out in one go, representing the most serious setback to the clean-up operation across the whole region west of Beiping, the central intelligence department has got involved in the investigation. Originally, Matsuzaki Harayama delegates the investigation to the Kempeitai, but after a couple of weeks, all they established was that the fire and flood were both the work of man not nature. They said they believed that the villagers in the area were working with the Eighth Route Army, but they had no proof. It was only a chance discovery by Chenglong's Special Operations Squad that revealed the truth.

BEFORE THREE DAYS HAVE PASSED, the men detailed to keep watch on Yanjing University report that a wounded man was brought into the university in a donkey cart via a side gate. There, he was transferred to an American limousine and taken into the city. Chenglong judges that the wounded man is bound to be a resistance fighter, and the overwhelming likelihood is that he has been taken to the church hospital. As the hospital is on American ground, he can't go in to search openly, so he orders some of his men to disguise themselves as patients, family visitors and water company inspectors and go in undercover. With great difficulty, they finally discover that the hospital authorities have accommodated the wounded man in the rear dormitory block that is closed off to the public. It seems that the patient is an old man with a serious gunshot wound. He has just been operated on, and in addition to the specialist nurses, two family members are constantly in attendance on him, an old woman and a young lad.

Chenglong is desperate to make a name for himself and show off his skills to Matsuzaki Harayama, so he is determined to exploit the opportunity that has presented itself to him. He decides to act first and report later, and he personally leads a group of a dozen men into the hospital under cover of night, and snatches the wounded man and his two family members. The hospital authorities make a complaint to the Japanese through the American Consulate, but in the end there is nothing to be done.

After the successful raid, Chenglong immediately commences interrogation. At first, the old man keeps his mouth firmly shut, just closing his eyes and saying nothing to whatever he is asked. Even after he has been tortured so severely that he twice passes out, he still does not utter a single word. The young lad, however, does not remain quite so tight-lipped, but all he reveals is that his family name is Fucha, and that he comes from Fucha Village in the Left Barracks. The wounded man is his father. He does indeed have a bullet wound, but it was an accidental injury from a stray bullet and he is most certainly not an anti-Japanese resistance fighter. The old lady, however, is much less experienced in such matters and proves very talkative, revealing more and more as she chatters on. Although she is just a woman and doesn't say anything too specific, it is beyond doubt that the resistance forces raised from the twelve villages of the Left Barracks have fought several engagements with the Japanese and that her husband Grandpa Fu is their second-in-command. Armed with this information, it becomes a lot easier to pry open the old man's lips. Even so, he makes three conditions: first, that his wound should be looked after and that he and his family members should not be further maltreated; second, that this is a one-off deal, and he shouldn't be asked to co-operate again; third, that they should pay the cost of his setting up a new home, as he will not be able to show his face in the Left Barracks again and will have to move elsewhere. Of course, Chenglong readily agrees to all this in principle, although he gives no guarantee that he will actually honour his commitment. He wants a full verbal confession first, and then they can discuss it further. But Grandpa Fu refuses to say any more without seeing a senior Japanese official. The best Chenglong can do is ask Yamaguchi to speak to him, and once Grandpa Fu has his word, he finally makes a clean breast of it and explains everything clearly from beginning to end.

How could Yamaguchi have imagined that such a resistance force could be hidden right in front of his very eyes, especially such a well-trained, battle-hardened one as this, which has already inflicted heavy losses on the Imperial Japanese Army time and time again? He doesn't dare believe it, but how can he doubt it when the locations and circumstances of the battles described by Grandpa Fu tally exactly with what they already know? Chenglong is even more shocked. Qi Yuexuan is his father-in-law, after all, and how can he possibly wield the axe without a tremor? Nevertheless, the thought does flit through his head that his father-in-law has just one daughter, and if he should meet with a sudden end, then the Minister's Residence... Although he doesn't dare follow the thought all the way through, he still feels his heart fluttering like the wings of a caged bird.

Chenglong and Yamaguchi hurry over to Matsuzaki's quarters, where their boss interrupts his banquet to go and listen to their report. When he comes back, what he shows Zhou Zhengjie is Grandpa Fu's confession. Zhou Zhengjie is immediately afraid of being implicated as he concealed these circumstances in the information he originally supplied, and after Zuo Xichuan and Zhou Zhengying leave, Matsuzaki does indeed tear him off a strip.

· · ·

When Zhou Zhengying hears the whole story from her brother, her heart constricts, and she fears for the safety of Qi Yuexuan and the people of the Left Barracks. But at the same time, an anger flares within her. She doesn't dare show it, however, and just says tentatively: "Who could have expected that a scholar like Yuexuan would prove such an expert with weapons and cause such a rumpus. I don't suppose the Japanese are going to let matters lie, are they?"

"Your name is Shoi now. Why are you still getting in a state over him?"

"One day as husband and wife creates an unbreakable bond. How could I not still have some feelings for him? What is more, I am under an obligation to him, nor have we ever been officially divorced, so by law, I am still his wife."

"You've never seen Matsuzaki so angry. He looked so fierce I thought he was going to bite me. The Japanese have never suffered such losses at the hands of the National Army or the Eighth Route Army, even though that's regular troops against regular troops. Who are the men of the Left Barracks? A bunch of farmers, not even fighting under anyone's official banner! Do you think the Great Japanese Imperial Army is going to stand for such a humiliation? This is like an eagle being trampled by a rabbit, or a grown man being slapped in the face by a child. It's not how much it hurts that infuriates them. Now it's gone this far, there's nothing anyone can say. Whether I stay clean or not could go either way, but you should stay out of it."

"Is that the best you've got? Why don't you just plead ignorance and be done with it. All I do is ask a simple question, and all you can do is keep parroting 'It's no use' 'It's no use'!"

Zhou Zhengjie can see how angry his sister is getting, so he tries to placate her: "Ai! It's not a question of me not knowing. The main thing is that Matsuzaki himself didn't have a clue. This whole business is a lot more complicated than you think."

"Complicated how?"

"Qi Yuexuan is the honorary chairman of the New People's Assembly, and although he hasn't even taken up the post for a single day, he is a living advertisement of Matsuzaki's influence. If he suddenly becomes an anti-Japanese faction that gives them such a bloody nose, and the high-ups get to hear about it, there's no way out even for Matsuzaki."

"So that's it then, isn't it?"

"That's it? No way! Who is going to leave a thorn like that sticking in him? It's got to be pulled out, and although he hasn't said as much, I'm pretty sure Matsuzaki is going to see to it himself. He can't hand it over to the military to go in banners flying and trumpets blaring and clear the rebels out, so he's bound to have something special up his sleeve."

Zhou Zhengying's heart lurches, as though she's just put her foot down on empty air, and she sways unsteadily.

· · ·

Qi Yuexuan soon receives news of Grandpa Fu's treachery, as Zhang Zhicheng dispatches a man to travel through the night with a letter.

It reads: 'Fucha has been captured and has betrayed us. He has already told everything. The enemy are sure to move against the Left Barracks in the next few days, and it is bound to be something exceptional. Immediately make all necessary defensive preparations.'

Qi Yuexuan doesn't want to believe it at first: "Is this news... certain?"

Zhang Zhicheng's messenger is emphatic: "It has come direct from the underground organisation in the city, so the source is completely reliable."

"Ai! How could he do it? He's spent half a lifetime fighting the Japanese but loses all integrity when the chips are down."

Second Master Dong grinds his teeth in fury: "If it had been up to me, he wouldn't have had the second half of his life. If it hadn't been for his evil actions, we would never have lost half our men like that, the bastard! He brought the devils down on us, and if you hadn't come back when you did, and if we hadn't had the support of the Eighth Route Army, it would have been even worse. But you're so soft-hearted, you didn't just fail to punish him, you even sent him into the city for treatment. And look what's happened, he turns and bites the hand that's feeding him."

Qi Yuexuan is not so harsh and unforgiving, and he just says: "He did, after all, risk his life against the devils. Those bullet holes aren't imaginary. It's just..."

He doesn't finish what he is about to say, but turns to the messenger and asks: "Are things still alright with your lot in the Eighth Route Army?"

"They're not as good as they might be, but still not too bad," the man replies with a display of confidence. "The devils' operation against our base has been fierce, but they've only taken Wangping, Yanchi and Zhaitang. They've not been able to get a foothold in the mountain regions. The losses in our guerrilla forces have been small. Indeed, they've actually been strengthened by those men from the Left Barracks. Now, we've left one part of our forces behind to work with the men in each village to harass and ambush any enemy troops who come into the mountains, but the main body has already withdrawn to our encircling lines, where they've split up to take up positions around Beiping, ready to mount several attacks. Our Commander Zhang says this is known as 'you fight your way, and I'll fight mine'. There's no point in just swatting a handful of wasps, you have to go for the whole nest."

"Quite right," says Qi Yuexuan. "This is rather like the way Cao Cao outwitted the Wuhuan,[1] using a small force to control a larger one, pitting the weak against the strong, avoiding the vanguard and striking at the vital point. Very good. The more battles your Eighth Route Army fights, the more discerning they become."

On hearing this, the messenger becomes even more animated: "The men of the Left Barracks are no slouches either. They joined our guerrillas west of Zhaitang in an attack on a Japanese convoy. They didn't kill many of them, only seven or eight, but they seized one lorryload of ammunition and five of provisions. Our bellies are full now, while the devils at Zhaitang are eating gruel for the next few weeks. Even better, the devils have built a blockhouse at Lizhuang and left a small squad to man it. Everybody wanted to storm the blockhouse, but Commander Zhang wouldn't allow it. Instead, he got hold of a whole load of dead chickens and dead dogs from somewhere and used them to block the water supply. He even dumped several cartloads of night soil all around the blockhouse. The devils came out to clear up the mess, but after we'd picked a few of them off with our snipers, they didn't dare show their faces any more. The stench was so bad, they just couldn't stand it, and after only a few days, they all withdrew back to Zhaitang."

"Ha ha, excellent! But… you're regular army. Aren't you afraid of demeaning yourselves with all these cheap tricks?"

"Our Commander Zhang says 'poor people can't have everything. If you're starving, you don't turn your nose up if the rice is rancid. The Eighth Route is a poor army, so we've got to be cunning when we fight. As long as we kill more devils than we lose ourselves, then it's a good tactic, and a proper tactic. Standing on your dignity when you fight is doubly stupid, and you are just asking for a beating'."

Qi Yuexuan rocks to and fro with laughter, his admiration of the Eighth Route Army increasing several-fold. The more the two men chat, the more friendly they become, and they don't even notice Second Master Dong quietly slip away. It's only when the messenger stands up to take his leave, that Qi Yuexuan realises he is no longer there, and when he asks, all that a farmhand knows is that he has left the compound. He goes back inside to sit and wait, and it is quite a while before Second Master Dong finally returns.

"Where did you get to?"

"Ah, I just went to arrange something. If you have anything to say to me, I'm listening."

Seeing how solemn he is looking, Qi Yuexuan sighs and asks: "Ai, Second Master Dong, what happened with Grandpa Fu is all down to my own thoughtless planning, and I know you are angry. Let's settle about our retreat first, then you can curse me for a while, and we'll be done."

Second Master wags his finger. "How can I blame you? His sins are his own, and no one else is to blame. So why don't you tell me about this retreat of yours?"

"What's your opinion?"

"I can't see we've got any way out. There are only a few dozen rifles among all twelve villages, and if the Japanese really are coming, there's no way we can fight them."

"That's true. But if there really is no way to fight them, then we have to think of something to stop them coming, for the time being at least."

"That's not going to be easy. Do you have any ideas?"

Qi Yuexuan smiles faintly. "At the moment, I think the Japanese are too busy trying to clear out the Eighth Route Army to spare many troops to deal with us. Otherwise, why would they have to think up some clever scheme?"

"What do you mean by 'clever scheme'?"

"Ah, something not out of the army manual, like a sneak attack, an explosion, a poisoning, an assassination or some such."

Second Master Dong purses his lips. "Like that, is it? Then we've nothing to fear. If we pull back into the mountains, we'll be out of their reach."

Qi Yuexuan shakes his head: "It's best if we stop them even thinking about coming up into the mountains."

"Are the Japanese easily scared then?"

"No, they're not, nor are they stupid. The key thing is for us to put on a proper show. Like before, we must install hidden sentry posts at the entrances to the passes, and at the crossroads. Visible ones too. Didn't the wounded Eighth Route Army men change out of their uniforms? Get some of our men to put them on, and make two tours a day round the North Barracks. Make it look as though the Eighth Route Army has come back. The Japanese have only heard Grandpa Fu's version of things, and they don't really know our strength, so they're going to have to give it some thought before they send even a small force into the mountains. Of course, we have to take this very seriously and strengthen our preparations. As soon as the alarm is sounded, the whole Barracks have to respond. If the enemy come in numbers, then we will send the villagers back into the mountains and they have to know in advance how they're going to go and where they're going. If the enemy are few in number, then we just make sure they never go back to their barracks."

Second Master Dong grunts and nods in agreement. "As soon as it's light, we'll ring the meeting bell and gather all the villages here to plan. This time we have to go against the enemy no holds barred, and win or lose, we have to maintain our standards and reputation. I've already singled out some people who deserve to die, to offer as a sacrifice to our victory."

Qi Yuexuan is dumbfounded at this, but before he can speak again, he hears a confusion of voices coming from out on the street. Second Master Dong hurries excitedly outside, with Qi Yuexuan hard on his heels. What they see is a file of people – men, women, young and old – being herded at gunpoint into the courtyard, all of them clearly terrified, scarcely daring to breathe. But as soon as they see Qi Yuexuan, they fall to their knees as one and begin to wail most piteously.

"What are you howling for? The next one to howl will be the first to meet the sword!" Second Master Dong yells, and the courtyard immediately falls silent.

Qi Yuexuan finally sees what is going on. These are all Grandpa Fu's family members. There are his concubines, his eldest son and his wife, his second son and his wife, and several grandsons and granddaughters.

"You... what do you think you are up to?" he demands, glaring at Second Master Dong.

Second Master Dong gives an icy laugh: "Ha! That Fucha fellow sold out all the families of the Left Barracks, so his whole line must be exterminated. His property will go into the common purse, and all our brothers who fell in battle will have their blood vengeance."

"A man answers for his own deeds," says Qi Yuexuan, shaking with fury. "What are you doing dragging women and children into this?"

Second Master Dong raises his eyebrows: "This is the banner law of the Left Barracks, a tradition handed down to us by our forefathers. If we don't pull this evil up by its roots, won't his descendants return later on to seek revenge?"

With an effort, Qi Yuexuan suppresses his anger. He leads Second Master Dong back inside and says in a low voice: "We're in the twenty-seventh year of the Republic now, Second Master Dong. How can you still abide by the rules of the Qing?"

"The Qing may be gone, but our ancestors are all still on this mountain, watching us."

"What? So you insist on following the old rules then?"

"Of course! It is a fundamental rule that under the banner we obey the law of the banner."

"Very well then." Qi Yuexuan can see that he won't budge on this issue, and he laughs coldly. "Under those old rules, while I am here, do you have any right to speak?"

Second Master Dong is choked into stunned silence.

Qi Yuexuan continues more cordially: "Second Master Dong, we have raised an army to fight the Japanese, not to revive the Army of the Eight Banners. Not everything our forefathers left us is necessarily good, or how else could our China find itself in such decline that we are being bullied by a piddling little country like Japan? Now you want these people killed, but not only would that not assuage public anger, or settle their resentments, it would actually be helping the Japanese..."

"Me? Help the Japanese?" Second Master Dong exclaims, slapping his chest. "Even though I, Dong Fuzhong, am not of high birth, when I was young I was a *baturu* of the Banner Army. I am old now, and don't move very well, but my courage is still unyielding. If the Japanese do come, the rest of you can go and leave me with the ammunition store. However many of them there are, I will take them all with me!"

"That I can believe," Qi Yuexuan says with a laugh. "But have you thought this whole business through carefully? Fucha is an important name in the Left Barracks, with many ties of kinship and friendship. How many people are there who share that same ancestry? If you go ahead with this, won't you be driving them into the arms of the Japanese? Once that sword falls, the evil will be unleashed, and the Japanese won't need to attack, as the Left Barracks will already be thrown into turmoil. Besides, although Grandpa Fu may have proved untrustworthy at the end, before that didn't he give meritorious service against the Japanese? Is everything else to be wiped out just because of this one stutter at the end? Is he to be thought no better than those who surrendered right from the start? Even if it is true that one slip may cause a thousand sorrows, this was his deed alone, and if you unleash this mindless massacre, who is going to follow you against the Japanese in the future?"

Second Master Dong just stands there, eyes bulging.

"So," he says eventually, "would that just be that then?"

"You have arrested all these folks, seized all their houses. Do you really think you can settle things quite so simply?"

"Then..."

"What I mean is, why not take this opportunity to let them all leave the mountains? That way, the Japanese will know that we have made preparations. It will show them that we of the Left Barracks have the courage and the strength not to fear them. They will be less ready to make a move against us, and our 'empty city strategy'[2] will be proved successful."

"Ah! Then, if I release the people, what about the property?"

"He is just a local landowner, how much movable property can he have? It will do us no good to make people think we are mean and petty. They can't take the houses and land with them, and I don't think their shame will allow them to come back to claim them. So later on, we can divide them up among their more distant relatives. How will that do?"

Second Master Dong ponders this for a while, then grunts and nods his head.

In the end, things turn out much as Qi Yuexuan predicts. Matsuzaki Harayama has already laid his plans, and he orders a small squad of Kempeitai and Chenglong's CID men to go into the mountains that very evening, to mount a sneak attack. But at noon, Grandpa Fu's relatives arrive in Beiping, and he realises that the Left Barracks have made their preparations. So he puts a temporary halt to the operation and sends out some men to reconnoitre. When this scouting party returns, they tell him that a strict guard is being kept over the crossroads and entrances to the mountain passes, and that the Eighth Route Army is patrolling the mountains. Naturally, Matsuzaki is not anxious to blunt his own strike force against stern resistance, so he has to abandon his original plan and rethink. Moreover, this summer has been particularly wet, with rain falling almost every day, so the beginning of autumn arrives and still no move has been made against the Left Barracks.

When Grandpa Fu sees his family members arrive safely in Beiping, without a hair on their heads harmed and their valuables intact, he feels deeply ashamed. That night, he takes advantage of his son, who is having a doze in the hospital while tending to him, to force open a window and climb down from the fourth floor. He is like a dried radish restored to its former crispness.

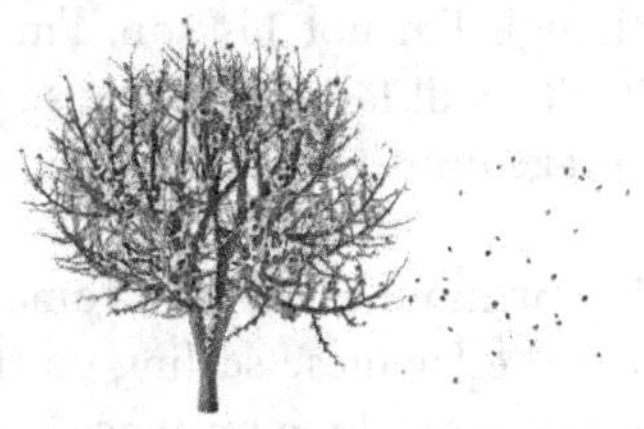

Chapter 60

Although the Left Barracks have a temporary reprieve, the Minister's Residence is in a ton of trouble. First of all, the trading company is forced to close its doors, and its bank accounts, cash holdings and all the goods in its warehouse are confiscated. Then it is Zhou Zhengjie himself who orders that the door between Moxiangzhai and the rear garden of the Residence be reopened, in order to take possession of the full rear courtyard. Wangtian sees that he can't send them away or stop them coming in, so he moves a large wormwood bush across the inner door of the front courtyard to prevent them from bricking it up. Fortunately, Yue E, Caiping and Mother Yan also come bustling over, and in the end, the affair just peters out.

Wangtian has just locked the rear gate and piled some sandbags up in front of it, when he hears a rumbling noise coming from the front courtyard, as though a wall has collapsed. When he runs through to look, he sees that Chenglong has brought some men to topple the locking stones of the moon gate through to the eastern side courtyard.

Mother Yan rushes over and wags her finger under Chenglong's nose, cursing him: "The Japanese have just finished pissing us around, and now you show up? Are you going to profit from our misfortune too? If you raise a dog, it's supposed to guard the household, so what are you doing going against us and helping the enemy?"

Chenglong is unmoved: "Aiya! You really shouldn't mistake my good intentions. If I hadn't got here quickly, the Japanese would have seized this courtyard too, and we have to keep it for my father-in-law and that useless sister-in-law of mine. I've come here to guard the household. If I'm here, whatever happens, the Japanese will have to get past me first."

"This is my family home," Yue E breaks in. "While my real father is still alive, I don't need you to take his place."

"Hah! My father-in-law may still be alive, but do you know what kind of trouble he is in? If it wasn't for my reputation, you lot would be implicated too. At the moment, you all treat me as an outsider, don't you? I know I don't have three wives and four concubines, but you are my wife and my father-in-law's only daughter, so although I'm not his son, I'm halfway there, and husband's family or wife's family, it's still family. So whose place do you say I am taking? Whoever's got the leverage must take charge, and they should be the head of the family."

Wangtian can't take any more of this and comes over to stand in front of him. "Think on! I can accept the Japanese sealing up the doors and confiscating our property, but I can't accept you taking my place."

"We're not talking about the Gao family, Brother, so what right do you have to stick your nose in my family affairs?"

"What right?" shouts Mother Yan. "He's the new manager of the Minister's Residence. My husband entrusted him with the job on his deathbed, and the Young Master voiced his approval too. Just because the Young Master isn't here, doesn't mean you can go over his head in the Residence's affairs."

Chenglong is taken aback: "Alright, I accept that you are my senior, and I have to listen to you, but you still have to be reasonable. So tell me, how can you recognise the Japanese right to occupy the place, but a member of your own family isn't allowed in?"

Wangtian snorts with laughter. "You know as well as anyone else that Beiping doesn't belong to Japan, and sooner or later they're going to have to fuck off out of here. Are they going to be able to take the buildings and land with them? As long as they don't set fire to the place, there's still a hope of getting it back. If you take over this place, it will be like a meat bun jumping into a dog's mouth: does anyone believe you'll spit it out again?"

Chenglong has trouble suppressing his anger, and he glares at his brother.

"So you just want me as a security guard, then? Well, needless to say, that's not what I want, but if I did, it would be quite appropriate. I may just be the son-in-law, but I'm also the master. You are the manager, but you're managing the household on behalf of others, and the property will never come down to your line. When my father-in-law dies, Yue E may be his daughter, but my son can take the Qi family name and continue the line of the Minister's Residence..."

Yue E stamps her foot in anger: "And has my father agreed to this drivel? Have I?"

"You can ask your father whether he agrees or not when he comes back," says Chenglong. "What does it matter whether you do or not? It's never the hen that does the crowing."

Caiping has remained silent until now, but she can't stop herself interjecting: "If you think women don't matter, why are you so obsessed with your wife's property? If you want to line your pockets, go and rob a Japanese bank. How much of a man do you think it makes you, throwing your weight around at home like this?"

Chenglong is taken aback by her vehemence, and he looks at her with a crooked smile. "Aiyo! You really deserve the name 'Noble Red'. That's quite some mouth you've got there. When you flared up like that, you were even more like my cousin Caiping. You're just another one, bullying people with your seniority, now you are my sister-in-law and must act the part. It doesn't matter who you were back in the old Gao family home, you're no big deal in the Minister's Residence."

He waves his hand and calls out: "Some of you men hurry up and hang my name plate in the main gateway. From now on, I'm using the front gate. Take the seals off the main courtyard and pick the locks. Starting from now, the main hall is going to be my office."

Several of his men come running in, and Wangtian immediately stretches out his arms to block their way. The men begin pushing and shoving him, which only serves as further provocation. Striking out with both hands, he gives a convulsive twist of his body and suddenly one man tumbles down in front of him and another behind. Two others are sent reeling back several paces. Infuriated, one of them pulls out his gun and Wangtian stoops swiftly to pick up the bar that locks the gate.

"Put that gun away!" says Chenglong, sensing that things are in danger of getting out of hand. He pastes a smile on his face and calls out: "What do you think you're doing? Trying to start a civil war in the Residence?"

"If you don't want a civil war," Wangtian says, straightening up, "then take your men back to your place in the west courtyard. While the master of the household is still alive, by what right would you occupy the main courtyard and the main hall? The Young Master and Uncle Yang entrusted this place to me, and in accepting, I must be loyal to their interests. If you are intent on going against that, you'll have to come through me first."

Chenglong smiles coldly. "Very well, I'll be equally blunt with you. If you lot are going to make a fuss over me moving in, I'll drop the idea. But when the Kempeitai move their jail and torture chamber here, then it will get really noisy. You'll have to look at the blood and listen to the screams every day. So go ahead and take your chances with the Japanese. Let's go, men!" With a wave of the hand he turns and is about to leave.

"Wait!" Yue E exclaims, and when she sees Chenglong stop, she turns to Wangtian: "Brother Wangtian, it's not worth going against him. Step out of the way and let him in."

"Don't listen to his scaremongering, he..."

"It's just not worth it. If the Japanese can't make off with the land and buildings, nor can he. The property doesn't have his name on the lease, so later on we can certainly find some way of getting it back. Your wife is pregnant. Is it worth risking a miscarriage just for this?"

Caiping softly adds her voice to Yue E's urgings: "Listen to Yue E. You may lose face, but you'll keep the moral high ground. What does him occupying the courtyard matter if you keep your self-respect? Grin and bear it, and don't sacrifice what matters for something so trivial."

Wangtian finally puts down the bar, takes a key off the belt at his waist and throws it to Chenglong. "Enough! I don't care any more. There's no need for you to pick the lock. Just don't wreck everything."

"Ha ha! Now that's more like a family!" says Chenglong, taking the key. "Don't worry, Brother, my father-in-law's not here and you're still the manager. Keep living where you are, and I'll pay you any salary you're owed."

"There's no need," Wangtian says, with a contemptuous look. "I'll move out of here and go back to the old Gao home. You can keep the salary, I'm not going to be a servant to two masters. Hurry up and go pack, Ying'er, so we can hand the place over to them."

But Yue E holds Caiping back and says angrily to Wangtian: "If you're determined not to work with him, why don't you just move into the west courtyard? What's the point of going back to your old place? Won't it need some work before it's fit to live in?"

"No one's lived there for six months or more, but there's nothing major wrong with it. So stop trying to dissuade me, and don't make things difficult. I've got my own reasons for wanting to go back there."

WANGTIAN IS DETERMINED to move back home partly because he doesn't want to have to see Chenglong's face any more, and he is afraid he won't be able to hold himself in and will provoke some major incident. But this is not the main reason, which is his need to deal with the repercussions of the Japanese actions against the Yuhua Trading Company. Their unexpected annexation of the business has caused a lot of headaches. It is a stockholders' company, and although Wangtian's holdings in it are all financed by the Minister's Residence, this is not public knowledge, and to outward appearances, he is himself the majority shareholder. Thus, if Qi Yuexuan gets into trouble, but no one else is implicated, it is only the Minister's Residence's openly held shares that will be forfeit. Yang Zhixing's original appointment of Wangtian as main shareholder is a form of insurance. On this occasion, although the company's bank accounts and cash holdings have been confiscated, Wangtian is quite unperturbed. No discrepancy is obvious in the accounts, and barring anything unforeseen and unreasonable, his own holdings and those of the other minor shareholders can't be seized. So now, he and they have to pull together and make it clear to everyone that they have washed their hands of the Minister's Residence. In addition, in a business, there are always accounts to be settled in either direction, payable and receivable.

In the current circumstances, they can't pester those who owe them money, but their creditors will come swarming round them like flies around a sugar bowl. So his move back home is designed to avoid further disturbance at the Minister's Residence, and to focus the attention on him. He does his best to collect accounts owing and immediately uses any funds collected to settle debts. According to his calculations, it is a very good thing that Caiping has salted away all his salary and dividends over the last few months in a separate account, and has stayed uninvolved, so if he includes his own former savings, he can reckon on having an emergency reserve. The one thing he is unsure of for the moment is how angry his creditors may get when they see him living in this broken-down old shack and how ugly they may turn if they're desperate for their money. He doesn't know either whether his wife will agree or not, as it is, after all, she who has been running the house for the last six months or more, allowing him to ride the rollercoaster and dream so big that his head still hasn't stopped spinning. And he has used up her savings. He gets this far in his thinking, and he begins to feel uncomfortable and full of remorse. It's not just his wife before whom he feels shamed, but his children as well.

THEY SAY IT NEVER RAINS BUT IT POURS, and indeed, before night falls, the rain begins and continues for several hours without showing any sign of stopping. The holes in the roof of the old Gao home mean that, as it pours down outside, a steady rain is also falling inside. Pots, pans and basins to catch the drops cover the floor, and there are even some on the *kang*. The unceasing sound of the rain hitting the pans is like the drum roll announcing the arrival of a performer on stage.

There is a great weight on Wangtian's mind, which he wants to share with Caiping. He has almost raised it several times but always stops at the last minute. There is something Caiping wants to say as well, but she too keeps hesitating.

Finally Wangtian can bear it no longer, so he heaves a deep sigh and says: "Ai! I'm sending you to live with Yue E. You shouldn't come back to the old place with me. You're carrying our child, so why should you suffer like this? It's best that I send you back."

"But... what about you?"

"You look after yourself and our child, and don't worry about me. I have to come back, but there's no reason for you to suffer with me."

"I am your wife, so why should you carry the burden alone when things go wrong? You don't have to tell me. I already know why you have to move back. To outside observers, you're the majority shareholder, and if you're going to shore up the company's reputation, you've got to be seen to be doing something to clear up the mess. That's right, isn't it?"

Wangtian just nods in reply, and Caiping continues: "The way I see it, Young Master Qi isn't here, so we have to lay our cards on the table with Yue E so she can give the property owner's point of view. It's too much for you to take on by yourself."

"We can't do that. She's already had more than enough bad luck. How can we burden her with this as well? And if Chenglong gets to hear about it, everything we've done so far will be in vain. I gave my word to Uncle Shu in the first place, so I have to shoulder responsibility when the going gets difficult."

Caiping sighs, considers things for a moment, then says: "Even so, you can pull your shoulders in a bit. No one can prepare for the unexpected. Everyone has to accept some crap in pursuit of money. Those two lots of people who turned up today were all looking for payment, weren't they? And there'll be more tomorrow. It's fine for us to move back here. Since all we've got is this rickety old shack, we don't have the money to satisfy our creditors when they come asking, and if our lives aren't enough for them, then they can go and ask the Japanese for their money. If you're holding back out of fear of hurting others, then let's hear no more about it. I'm going to help you sort things out."

Wangtian becomes agitated: "No, no, that won't do. That wouldn't be at all seemly. I can't do business like that, and I can't afford to lose those people. Besides, they're all small businesses, and if they don't get their money back, they could all go bust. If any of them kills himself, that's something that can never be recompensed."

Seeing how worried he is, Caiping responds: "I knew that's what you would say, so let's be clear – you're thinking of using my savings, aren't you?"

Wangtian grins sheepishly and doesn't say anything.

"Too embarrassed to say it?" Caiping says with a smile. "Alright, I'm too embarrassed to listen. Let's pretend I don't know anything, then you don't have to worry."

"No, no!" Wangtian says hurriedly. "Let's just... let's just call it a loan, and when the company is released back to us, I'll pay you back immediately."

"Ha ha! A loan? That's a laugh! Alright, how much?"

"I've worked it all out. We've got thirteen outside creditors, with a total of eight hundred and eighty-six yuan and seventy cents. I'm sure you don't have that much, but I'll make do with what you've got, and if it's not enough, I'll think of something else."

"Who says I don't have enough?" Caiping asks, taking a cloth bundle from beneath her. She opens it and takes out a bankbook.

"There's one thousand two hundred in here, so there's no need for you to touch those two gold bars your father gave you."

"Where... where did you get so much?"

"Over the last few days when you've had people exchanging the counterfeit army notes, I put your salary to work to make some money out of the difference in exchange rates. I just changed it to and fro a few times."

"You're quite something!"

"Don't put me on a pedestal. You agreed it was a loan, didn't you? Well, a loan has to be repaid and the interest rate is five per cent, daily and compound. Alright?"

"Aiya, you've turned into a loan shark. That's usury!" Wangtian says, teasing her.

But Caiping isn't amused. She sighs, thinking of her unborn child. "This money I've saved won't last long before it's all gone. We've worked so hard for so long, and we'll end up just as poor as before. It will be like waking up from a dream of wealth to find that, once again, we have nothing at all."

When he hears this, Wangtian hurriedly puts down the bankbook and asks haltingly: "In that case, why don't you... use a little less of it?"

Caiping jabs him in the chest with her finger and says with something between a laugh and a sneer: "How ruthless can you get! You take a slice out of someone and don't let them yell. Am I not even allowed a little moan? Are you trying to suffocate me?"

The two of them bursts out laughing simultaneously. Caiping nestles into Wangtian's chest, picks up a small pan to use as a drum, and begins to sing softly:

The Earth God responds to heaven's call
Hoping henceforth to join the gods,
But to his surprise this is not to be his lot.
With a kick of his foot, God sends him
Tumbling back down to his broken-down temple.
Mother Earth exclaims:
'Ai! You are earth by birth and earth by nature
And earth by nature you are stubborn and obstinate,
Too stupid to understand the ways of the world.
You are stupid and I am none too bright,
Otherwise wouldn't he have expelled you much sooner?
Pah, pah, pah! From now on let's forget these impossible dreams.
If you marry a hen, it will peck the ground like you.
If you marry a dog, it will guard the door like you.
If you marry a fool, then you'll be foolish too
And raise a family of foolish children.
Forget how bright the incense burns,
Just spend the rest of your life in peace and quiet.

DESPITE THE CONTINUING DOWNPOUR, Chenglong is not at home. He has already led his men from the Special Operations Squad over to organise the occupation of every courtyard of the Minister's Residence so now, not only are they established in the front courtyard, they have also taken over the main courtyard, the kitchen yard, the servants yard and the storage yard. Originally, he has ordered Mother Yan, Yue E and the children to move into the main courtyard, but in the end nothing can persuade them, so he has to let them stay in the western side courtyard. The main courtyard is huge, with many buildings, but in the end he finds himself all alone in there with only two sentries and the old wolfdog for company.

Just after he has finished dinner, Matsuzaki Harayama telephones, ordering him to come over immediately. He guesses it must be about his occupation of the Minister's Residence and is fairly certain that Zhou Zhengjie has been sticking his oar in. He knows that Zhou has already gone over his head by taking some men to occupy the rear garden and is, for the time being, operating on his own initiative. He spends the journey over to Matsuzaki's office figuring out how to counter this.

To his surprise, all his preparations are for nought, as Matsuzaki doesn't even mention the subject.

"The reason I've asked you here today, Liu-san, is because I have a very important task to entrust to you. I don't know if you..."

He stops short at this point. There is a faint smile on his lips, but the expression in his eyes is dark and forbidding.

Chenglong immediately snaps to attention. "All you have to do is give the order. As long as you have faith in me, I will go through fire and water for you."

Matsuzaki nods slowly and says: "This is how things stand. The Left Barracks have secretly raised an anti-Japanese militia and linked up with the Eighth Route Army. They have repeatedly inflicted heavy losses on the Imperial Army and have become a serious threat to the peace and stability of Beiping. Originally, I didn't want to enlist the aid of the military at this point, but was intending to send in a crack unit from the Kempeitai to mount a surprise attack. I have, however, discovered that the enemy have got wind of this and have made preparations to counter it. The Eighth Route Army have also sent a unit back to the Left Barracks. A surprise attack is now impossible, so we have to come up with another plan. Fortunately, the Imperial Army want to conduct field trials of a new secret weapon. They have asked us to help select a suitable location, and to assist in the operation. I have naturally settled on the Left Barracks. It was you who started investigations into this whole case, so I am thinking you should be the one to resolve it."

Chenglong doesn't reply immediately but takes some time to think before asking cautiously: "What kind of a secret weapon is it?"

"This is a top-secret Imperial Army project," says Matsuzaki, looking serious, "and I don't have all the details myself. You certainly don't need to know too much. The task for the Special Operations Squad is to thoroughly reconnoitre the upper reaches of all water supplies to the Left Barracks. The implementation will be in the hands of the specialist water supply epidemic prevention team from Unit 1855. Your only responsibility will be to guide the Imperial Air Force from the ground."

This is enough to give Chenglong a general idea of what is intended. He is well aware of the work that is being done at Unit 1855 of the so-called 'Water Supply Epidemic Prevention Department' stationed at the west gate of the Temple of Heaven. Although he is quite inured to the sight of the blood and death of the battlefield, this kind of atrocity makes his heart sink, and it shows on his face.

"What? Is this a problem for Liu-san?" Matsuzaki asks coldly.

"No, no, no problem," Chenglong replies. "It's just that... it's just that I'm afraid I may not be up to such an important responsibility. Don't you think it would be safer to entrust it to the Kempeitai?"

"No, the Kempeitai won't do here," Matsuzaki says. "The reason I'm giving it to you is because your men are Chinese, and all from Beiping. You know the terrain and are better able to reconnoitre in secret. Although, on the face of it, you will only be assisting the army, in fact you will be the key to the success of the whole operation. You may have some qualms, which is quite natural, but this is war, and victory and defeat are all that matter, nothing else. It's not up to you whether you undertake special operations or not. The sooner we put down resistance, the sooner peace will come and the sooner the bloodshed will stop. You have already hitched your wagon to the Imperial Army, so the choice is no longer yours. Now you know the nature of the mission, do you really think you have the option of refusing?"

Chenglong quivers as though he has been stung and immediately defends himself: "Lord Matsuzaki, I..."

"I believe in your loyalty, Liu-san, and I believe in your abilities. If this mission turns out well, you will find you are no longer confined to a small pond but can begin to put your feelers out into the area around Beiping, maybe even the whole of North China. That's what you really want, isn't it?"

"Yes, yes. I'll go back now to start readying my best men..."

"Don't be in too much of a hurry. According to the weather forecast, it's going to be raining for the next few days. Getting the men ready is fine, but you will have to wait a while before you go into action."

"Very well. I'll make my preparations, and when the time comes, I'll lead the operation personally."

"That's probably not going to be possible," Matsuzaki says, smiling and waving a hand in contradiction. "You can get everything set up, but you needn't see it through in person. After all, Qi Yuexuan is your father-in-law, and it is not a pretty thing for family to meet in battle. To be frank with you, I've considered the matter from many angles, and I'm inclined to throw Qi Yuexuan a lifeline. Before the operation starts, I may send someone to invite him down from the mountains. If he is willing to come home, everything that has gone before can be forgiven and forgotten."

"Then... I can send my wife to go in person to persuade him, and if that doesn't work, she can take the children too..."

"No, that won't do. If they go, he might not have any scruples about it, and not only may he not come back, your wife and children may not return either. I... I'd rather find some other suitable person to act as go-between."

"You mean..."

"Don't worry, I'm well aware of who it will most suitable to send," Matsuzaki says, still smiling, as he reminds Chenglong: "I always look at the big picture,

Liu-san. I don't worry about the trifles. I like to use people who are ambitious and rapacious, but I know where to draw the line, and I won't let my choice upset the apple cart."

Chenglong knows immediately where Matsuzaki is going with this, and he hurriedly agrees.

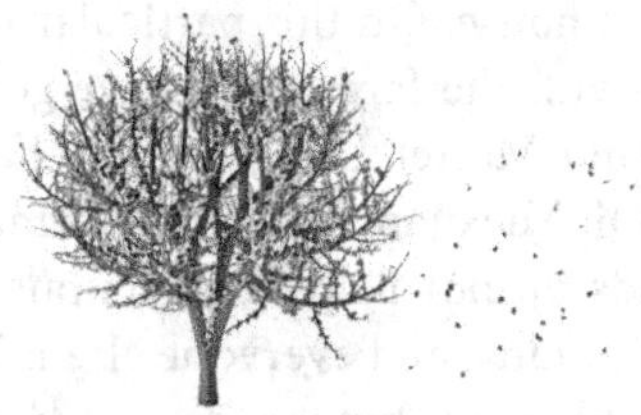

Chapter 61

The summer this year is very wet. From midsummer right through to the beginning of autumn, there are only a few days of watery sunshine. Moderate rain, heavy rain or even torrential thunderstorms occur nearly every day, causing flash floods in the mountain regions north and west of Beiping. This water pours into the Yongding, Juma and Laishui rivers so they overflow their banks. Many places downstream meet with disaster, the low-lying areas being worst affected. The locals say they've never seen rain like it in all their lives, and it must be because the Japanese have disturbed the dragon vein in the Western Hills, and the furious Dragon King is weeping and sneezing.

With the floods happening in a time of war, daily life for the people has become even more difficult. But from another point of view, the conditions have also considerably hampered the Japanese clean-up operations north and west of Beiping. As the flood waters recede, they cause landslides that cover the roads and highways, cutting off lines of communication. As a result, when the Japanese go back into the mountains to continue operations, they find themselves guarding isolated outposts, where they have to tighten their belts and stick it out. Those who can't take it have to wade through water and tramp through mud to get out.

The overcast, rainy weather only ends a little before the Mid-Autumn Festival.

THE TWELVE VILLAGES of the Left Barracks have not escaped the floods. The crops planted at the foot of the gullies are washed away so that not even a root hair is left behind. It is lucky that the villagers here live on the slopes and that what they grow is mainly maize and various beans. So although much of the crop is flattened, when it is swiftly propped back up, the loss to the harvest is only twenty or thirty per cent. As soon as the rain stops, the men and children hurry out to gather the crops, and there are people out on the slopes as far as the eye can see.

Ever since Lao Zhang and Yang Zhixing died, Qi Yuexuan has been living in

Second Master Dong's house. On this particular morning, the young and old of the household along with the farmhands have gone out mob-handed. Even the ageing landlord, Second Master Dong himself, has gone with them, leaning on his walking stick. Qi Yuexuan is also determined to follow them up the mountain, but he ends up not helping at all, but just adding to the chaos. The mountainside is very muddy, and everyone else is barefoot so they can pick their way easily through the mud, but he doesn't dare follow suit. Before he has reached the top of the fields, his shoes are solid clumps of mud. He stops to squat on a rock and clean them, but within a few paces they are just the same. Irritated, he sits back down on the rock and waves his hand.

"That's it. I'll just sit here and supervise the work."

Second Master Dong can't restrain a wry laugh: "Ha! I told you not to come, but you had to follow us. You just sit there, and when the sun comes up it will soon dry you off. Alright, alright, I won't go on up. I'll go back with you to have a cup of tea."

"Huh… alright then, I'll give you my arm to lean on," Qi Yuexuan says none too politely, as he slips and slides down the slope rather too quickly. He said he'd give Second Master Dong an arm, but in fact he should have said he would use him as a crutch.

As the two of them reach the Qi family tomb compound at the west entrance to the village, there is a rumbling sound up in the sky. Soon, an aircraft appears out of the clouds, flying very low, seeming almost to skim the tops of their heads, as it goes on to circle the mountain top.

"Shit!" Second Master Dong exclaims. "It's going to bomb us. We must get back to the village and sound the alarm bell as quick as we can."

Qi Yuexuan is more experienced in this kind of thing, and he remains calmer than Second Master Dong: "No, that's not it. It's just on reconnaissance by the look of it. Nonetheless, we should be very concerned. We must go back and think carefully what to do about this."

Second Master Dong points towards the marshy depression in the direction of Fucha Village and says: "Look, what's that flashing over there?"

Qi Yuexuan turns to look and thinks he sees something reflecting the sun. As the aircraft turns and comes back, he suddenly slaps his thigh and shouts: "Damn! I'm sure someone's spotting for the devils' plane!"

"What should we do?"

"Fuck knows! But just because I can't do anything about the sky, doesn't mean I can't do something about what's going on down here. Quick, you get back up the mountain, and I'll go into the village. We'll gather everyone together, then creep up on them from two sides and do our best to catch them alive."

With that, he reaches down, takes off his shoes and slithers away at a fast trot.

· · ·

IN LESS THAN HALF AN HOUR, the enemy on the mountain sound the retreat. Many villagers are propping up crops all over this part of the mountain, and as soon as they hear the noise, they all rush together towards the spot. In an instant, the mountain resounds with the sound of rallying cries. When the enemy see things turning against them, they begin to run away, opening fire as they go. This just infuriates the villagers further. Those of them carrying weapons return fire, and those without pick up rocks to hurl, or brandish spades and hoes as they charge forward. Before the troops that Qi Yuexuan is leading from the village have even arrived, the battle is already over. There were five Japanese soldiers in total, three of whom escaped down the southern slope of the mountain and disappeared without trace. Of the remaining two, one is shot dead on the spot, and the other is sent sprawling by a rock, and then, as he is still alive, is finished off with several blows from shovels and hoes. Up in the sky, the aircraft has disappeared back into the clouds like a frightened bird.

Qi Yuexuan can't say anything critical, but inside he is bitterly disappointed. After all that effort, no enemy soldier has been caught alive, so he has no idea why they came here in the first place. Fortunately, they find an ID document and a hand-drawn map on the two dead soldiers. The ID is for the 'Beiping Special Operations Committee' which means they are undoubtedly Japanese agents. On the map, the locations of the twelve villages of the Left Barracks are clearly marked, and there are red arrows drawn at several points. The area is clearly the target for an enemy operation, but the nature of that operation remains unclear.

QI YUEXUAN AND SECOND MASTER DONG return to Laoqiying, and it is not long before the village chiefs of the other villages and the clan elders arrive too. They discuss the affair for a long time, and various theories are advanced: some say the Japanese intend to bomb the area; some say they're going to set fire to the mountain; some say they were reconnoitring for an imminent attack; some say it has something to do with a future plan being cooked up by the Japanese. They think of the water supply, and they think of poison, but no one thinks of germ warfare. None of these simple villagers can even imagine the existence of such a thing. With their discussions inconclusive, they are left scratching their heads and stroking their beards. They reinforce the sentries at the heads of the passes, the crossroads and the entrances to the villages. They strengthen the roving patrols, coordinate the system of signal fires, and strengthen and divert the communication routes between the villages. To avoid the risk of poison, they decide that water from the mountain streams and village water storage systems must first be given to animals to drink. If there are no symptoms after half an hour, it is declared fit for human consumption.

There is truth to the old saying that, 'when the knife is about to fall, it is the flash before the eyes that is most to be feared'. They know quite well that the Japanese are going to do something, but not knowing what or when is particularly hard to bear. The whole Left Barracks are on edge, and although the battle has not yet started, their hearts are in their mouths.

WITH THE USE OF HIS WIFE'S SAVINGS, Wangtian reckons he has got past the most difficult obstacle without breaking faith with anyone. After telephoning a few shareholders to re-establish relationships and twist their arms a little, the result is that the Yuhua Trading Company is finally ready to re-open for business. Apart from those held by the Minister's Residence, everybody else's shares are released, and the warehouse also re-opens. In spite of the setback, the shareholders keep faith in Wangtian's honesty and sincerity, and not a single one wants to break up the partnership or withdraw from it. On the contrary, they all offer the money to make up the capital shortfall. But although the equity shares in the company are riding high, they are still a long way from matching Wangtian's holding, so he remains the majority shareholder. He had not originally wanted to agree immediately to all this and would rather make a trip to Laoqiying to consult Qi Yuexuan before making a decision. But when Yue E hears him harping on about this, she soon puts a stop to it. She says that, in the current circumstances, it's best that they don't have anything to do with the Minister's Residence, since they don't want to lose their secret holdings on top of the public ones.

"They gave you this responsibility," she says, "because they have faith in you. And if you're going to safeguard the business, you have to take charge and that's that."

On this basis, Wangtian finally agrees to the shareholders' request, reallocates the shares and continues business as before. Shopkeeper Li also tidies up the back courtyard of his house to rent out, and, as it is not far from the shop front, they now have both an office and a warehouse as well.

THE PLAN IS A SOUND ONE, so, next morning, Wangtian takes some men over to the Minister's Residence. He orders them to start moving the goods out, then heads straight over to the main courtyard with his accountant. Over these last few days, the company's ledgers and the Minister's Residence's old accounts have all been sealed up in the western range by the Japanese, and they need to be retrieved. Just as they enter the courtyard, the wolfdog comes flying out at them. Luckily, Wangtian has some martial arts skills and he dodges out of the way, chopping down with one hand and sending the dog flying with a yelp. It scrambles back up, whimpering, with its tail between its legs, and it doesn't dare remount an attack.

Hearing the noise, Chenglong comes out of the north range, and when he sees it is Wangtian, he swallows the curses he was about to utter, adjusts his expression and finds a smile from somewhere.

"Aiyo, it's you, Big Brother! What's going on? Are you moving back in? That would be the right thing to do. We brothers shouldn't treat each other as outsiders. I stand by what I said, and you..."

"Enough! I won't trouble you. The Yuhua Company is going back into business. I've already found premises away from here, and I've come over today to move our stuff out and free up your space."

"Yes, I know all that. Let me congratulate you. But..." Chenglong deliberately moves up close to his brother, before continuing: "Isn't some of it actually down to me?"

"What? I don't think I ever asked you to get involved, did I?"

"We're brothers, aren't we? It's not a question of asking. If I didn't offer, wouldn't you just throw that back in my face?"

"Alright then, let's say I owe you a favour, and I'll thank you when it's all done."

Wangtian doesn't want to waste any more time talking to him, so he simply turns to head over to the western range.

"There's no need for thanks," Chenglong says as he stops him going. "But there is something you can help me with."

"You want my help?"

"That's right. Come along. Let's sit down in the main hall so I can explain. Let's go."

When Wangtian realises that Chenglong is not going to let go of him, he is too embarrassed to struggle. Besides, he is quite intrigued, so he explains things to the accountant and follows his brother over to the northern range.

Before he can even sit down properly, Chenglong asks him: "Brother, the Residence's holdings in your company haven't been unfrozen, so are you going to have enough capital?"

"The company is muddling along, and we're breaking even. Besides, the other shareholders want to expand their investments, and that will make up the shortfall, so I don't need to trouble you..."

"That's very aloof, Brother. For one thing we're brothers, and for another, I'm here on the spot. If you let outsiders make up the business losses, where does that leave your own people? I've said before, if I'm going to invest in the company, the timing would be just right for me to make up the shortfall from the shares confiscated by the Japanese. If, by any chance, you don't agree to let me in, where are you going to get the money from then?"

Wangtian considers this for a moment before saying: "Listen to you! You only ever consider the profits, not the risks. How can doing business ever compare with your guaranteed income? We may be up and running now, but who knows when the devils might shut us down again. I'm not going to fritter away the family fortune by getting involved with you."

Chenglong grunts in reply, then goes on to say: "If I take over the Minister's Residence's shares, then wouldn't the business become a cast-iron source of income?" Observing Wangtian's silence, he asks grimly: "So you think it will be cheaper to use outsiders, and you don't want to be beholden to me. That's it, isn't it? Is this business of yours on the side of the Nationalists or the Communists?"

"Ha! The more you say, the stupider you sound. The business is neither Nationalist nor Communist. It's not on the side of the Japanese either. It's on the side of making money," Wangtian shoots back irritably, before softening a little: "I just think brothers shouldn't fight over food from the same pot, in case they make fools of themselves in front of others by getting greedy over the profits. If you want to make easy money, then it's best to follow Uncle Yang's plan by which there's no need for you to invest directly in the business, but you just give us a helping hand wherever you can. You'll be recompensed for your help, share for share, so we come out even. How's that?"

Chenglong's expression is even grimmer now: "You may be the majority shareholder of this company, Brother, but where did you get the money from? From selling Noble Red's inheritance? You may fool other people, but you don't fool me. Not by a long way."

"You can think what you like, but it certainly didn't come out of your pocket, did it? So just keep your nose out of other people's business," Wangtian says, standing up to leave.

"Wait, Brother, wait," Chenglong says, holding him back. "Do you think you can slip away when I've just asked you a simple question? Got under your skin, has it?"

"I'm moving house today, and I don't have time to stand around here bandying words with you."

"Don't worry, I haven't got much more to say to you. Just one more question."

"Alright, ask away."

Wangtian sits down again as Chenglong moves a little closer, and asks, in a low voice: "Just tell me the truth for once, Brother – where has all the Minister's Residence's treasure got to?"

Wangtian finally understands Chenglong's real intentions, and he says with a faint smile: "I only took over on Uncle Yang's death. I don't know anything about what went on before. Apart from the confiscated shares in the Yuhua Trading Company, the Minister's Residence still has a few outstanding accounts on the books, but not enough for you to be bothered with."

"Don't talk to me about the books. The stuff I'm interested in is off the books."

"All I know about is what's on the books. I don't know about anything else. You must realise that all this time the Minister's Residence has been eating up its capital with no revenue. There's not much left."

"Impossible!" Chenglong exclaims. "I'll talk to you again tomorrow, and I'll have my people look into this. Before the war started, the Minister's Residence sold off all its businesses, consolidated its bank accounts, liquidated its assets and turned all the resulting funds from these three processes into gold bars. There's no way now of checking the books of the Central Bank, but there are people who have seen them, and they were packed to bursting in a trunk that was so heavy it took four strong men to carry it. And then there's the Residence's paintings and antiques, and all the other portable valuables. Where have they got to? All that money you've got in the company belongs to the Residence too, and that's just a drop in the ocean. So where's the bulk of it hidden?"

Wangtian laughs. "Of course I don't know, and that's all there is to it. What more can I tell you? Everyone loves money, but you have to stick to your own share. This isn't Yue E's dowry, and besides, once a woman's married, she doesn't have anything to do with her parent's affairs, does she? While her father is still alive, there's no point in her asking about this, and even less you, as a mere son-in-law."

Chenglong knows what his brother is like and doesn't respond immediately. After a while, he summons up a smile and says: "We're brothers, aren't we? We should stick together, not favour outsiders. We're just the same, you and I, and given that you rely on your wife for your money, can't you send a little my way and let me benefit from her largesse too? Don't worry, there's enough for both of us. You won't lose out."

"I should be so lucky. You think I know, but truly I don't."

"Then who does?"

"You'll have to ask my employer, your father-in-law."

"That idle layabout? He may not even know himself. But that old insect man, Lao Zhang… he's an old family retainer, perhaps he…"

"If he does, you won't get it out of him."

"You don't think it's likely?"

"It's not a question of likely or not. How much do you think you're going to get out of a dead man?"

"He's… he's dead?"

"It was on the day of Uncle Yang's funeral. After he set off the great flood, there wasn't even a corpse left behind."

Chenglong is appalled and exclaims furiously: "That's not possible!"

"I saw it with my own eyes. His tomb's right there. If you don't believe me, go see for yourself. Enough now, I've got things to do. We'll chat again when we've got time," Wangtian says, getting to his feet.

"A fortune like that can't just disappear without trace," Chenglong says through gritted teeth.

"Alright, take your time and have a proper look if you want," Wangtian says, heading out of the room.

From behind him, comes Chenglong's angry voice: "Don't take me for a simpleton, Brother. I still don't believe you, and if I don't get to the bottom of this, you just wait and see what I'll do!"

· · ·

It is just past midday when a limousine stops at the roadside of the route through the mountain pass of Laoqiying. Xiao Yuerong gets out of the car, but instead of following the main Incense Road to the right, he takes the narrower path to the left. He is closely followed by a man in a Western-style hat and a Sun Yat-sen suit, who has more the appearance of an armed guard from the *yamen* than an attendant. Xiao Yuerong has been drafted in by Zhou Zhengjie as a suitable go-between for Matsuzaki.

That morning, when Zhou Zhengjie arrives at Yuerong's Place, the first thing he says is that he wants to organise a calligraphy symposium on 15 August to which all the civil and military bigwigs will be coming, and it is to be held at Moxiangzhai. He wants Xiao Yuerong to organise the lunchtime and evening meals, and he also asks him to bring along some amateur actors and apprentices to put on a show to liven things up. Xiao Yuerong is delighted to get a catering commission like this. At the moment, he is reliant on passing trade. Japanese and Chinese alike are welcome. They come in as customers, pay when they're full, and there's no real relationship and no need to fawn on them and curry favour. But the amateur theatricals are different. They are not done to provide a living but are just for fun, so that the Japanese and people like Zhou Zhengjie can let off steam together. But to an outsider, they have a rather sordid, corrupt appearance, like flies clustering round rotten meat. Of course, Xiao Yuerong doesn't dare speak his true thoughts, and he looks for some way of getting out of it. He says that the Bright Moon Company has long ago disbanded, and its members scattered. He himself is out of practice and hasn't sung for many years, and would probably stink the place out if he opened his mouth.

Zhou Zhengjie can see he is making excuses, so he tells him what is really going on.

"I'll be frank with you. Brother Yuexuan is in a heap of trouble. He said he was going to the Western Hills to observe the mourning period for his father, but, in fact, he has raised an anti-Japanese army and killed a lot of soldiers of the Imperial Army. The Japanese are mounting a major offensive against him, but I can't bear the thought of more bloodshed, let alone the possibility of Yuexuan dying in battle, so I have implored Lord Matsuzaki to let me stand guarantor for him if he is spared. Lord Matsuzaki has been magnanimous, saying that, if Yuexuan will come back down to the city and renounce his fight against the Imperial Army, then everything will be forgotten and there will be no repercussions. He will still be the honorary chairman of the New Assembly. If he sings a duet with you at this Mid-Autumn Festival calligraphy symposium, then the whole matter will be considered closed. This is a way out of a highly embarrassing situation for both sides, and the Japanese are unanimous that, in this way, the lives of Qi Yuexuan and the men of the Left Barracks can be saved. It's not convenient for me to be seen part of this, so Lord Matsuzaki finally settled on you to take his letter out to present to Yuexuan. You go back a long way with Yuexuan, so conventional formalities can be forgotten. All that matters is that he shakes hands on the deal. Don't worry, all you have to do is deliver the letter and pass on the message. If he comes back, your service will be remembered, and even if he doesn't, there won't be any consequences for you. But if you don't go, I'm afraid Lord Matsuzaki will lose face, and the consequences of that... I leave to your imagination."

This speech leaves Xiao Yuerong on the horns of a dilemma, and he ponders it for a long time before finally, rather reluctantly, he nods his assent.

Zhou Zhengjie immediately organises men and a car to take him on his way, not even bothering about lunch.

Xiao Yuerong has been to the Left Barracks before, after Flower Branch was executed by the Japanese, when he accompanied Qi Yuexuan both to collect the body and to bury it. At that time, he followed the same small mountain path, but today his feet feel as though they are made of lead.

Qi Yuexuan is both surprised and delighted to see Xiao Yuerong, but when he hears the reason for his visit, his face falls.

"Ah, Yuerong! You were born to play the 'virtuous woman' roles, and with a little flexibility, you've got the skills to do the 'coquette' or the 'female warrior'. But today you are out of character. So what part are you playing? Is it the clown or the pantomime dame?"

Xiao Yuerong's face flushes with distress and embarrassment, and he can't find the words to reply, as tears gather in his eyes.

Qi Yuexuan can't bear to see him like this, and he says: "Enough now. I know you are acting under compulsion and had no choice but to come. I'm not going to make things difficult for you. Come and sit down."

Xiao Yuerong hands over Matsuzaki's letter.

It reads:

Brother Yuexuan, take note:

We have not met since you went into the mountains to mourn your father, but I still remember your literary talent, and I hope you are in good health.

I am well aware that the Left Barracks has raised an anti-Japanese army that is already affiliated with the Communist Party. Your leading position therein lays you open to severe punishment. If our main force attacks, I fear for your safety, as gold and dross will burn alike. I cannot bear to see you in such a terrible situation. When the world is in turmoil, brother scholars must look after each other since the common people are foolish and blind, and hard to bear in their stupidity. For this reason, I wish to offer you a way out, to demonstrate the magnanimity of the Great Japanese People. All that is required is that, from now on, you are no longer an enemy to our Japanese nation and that you obey the regional government, in which case, all past circumstances will be forgotten and no repercussions will ensue.

On the occasion of the Mid-Autumn Festival, as a token of our desire for the flourishing of peaceful relations, we plan to convene a grand symposium for practitioners of the calligraphic arts, to be held in the business belonging to your Residence, Moxiangzhai. I have sent the honoured Yuerong to give you my handwritten invitation to this event both to add lustre to the treasures of the ink at this exceptional assembly, and also to demonstrate your conversion from foe to friend in the spirit of true cooperation. How can it not be a fine thing to exchange the weapons of war for gifts of silk and jade? I hope that my brother will remember his friend, have regard to the fate of the people of Laoqiying and carefully consider his request.

Respectfully yours,
  Matsuzaki Harayama

Qi Yuexuan slaps the letter down on the table without a word. After a long pause, he turns his eyes on Xiao Yuerong and asks: "Is there any verbal message to accompany the letter?"

Xiao Yuerong composes himself and says: "Young Master Qi, when Zhou Zhengjie came to me, he said that it was only when he pleaded for clemency and offered himself as guarantor that the Japanese agreed. He tells you not to worry that there may be any danger in returning to the city to attend the meeting. You just have to restrain yourself a little, go with the flow, register your attendance, write a couple of pieces of calligraphy, whatever takes you fancy, and that will be that. Matsuzaki himself doesn't want to make a big thing out of this, or it might cause him some embarrassment. At most, you'll have to spend a few days at the Minister's Residence, until the fuss dies down, and then see how things stand."

"Is… is this what you think too?"

"No, no, no, I…" Xiao Yuerong shakes his head and gestures dismissively with his hand. Then he glances behind him and sees his minder standing outside the door. He lowers his voice and continues: "The way I see it, Young Master, you mustn't take the Japanese at their word. This is undoubtedly a trick."

By this time, Second Master Dong has finished reading the letter too, and he echoes Xiao Yuerong's opinion: "I agree. You can't go back."

Qi Yuexuan sighs. "If I don't go back, then the gloves really will be off."

"So be it then," says Second Master Dong. "If the worst comes to the worst…"

"That's easy enough for you to say," says Qi Yuexuan, "but do you really think you can stop a tiger with a bamboo fence? The worst that can happen is we die, isn't it? You and I can risk our lives together, but can we risk the lives of all the people of the Left Barracks?"

Xiao Yuerong can feel the mood growing very solemn, and he bursts out: "If you don't come back, Young Master, I've got it all worked out for you. In the end, you can't beat 'The Thirty-Six Stratagems'."

So saying, he takes a small cloth bundle from inside his jacket and hands it over. "If you high-profile fellows get a move on and run away now, you can still make it. If you've got nowhere to go, you can make for Tianjin first. There's an old fellow-student of mine who lives in the foreign concession, and you can hide out there for a while. In this bundle are my personal savings. Everything's there. You know what a miser my wife is, but joking apart, she has a good heart and she's happy to give it all for this emergency."

"Take back your money, Yuerong," Qi Yuexuan says, thrusting the bundle back at him, "and listen to what I have to say..."

At this point, Xiao Yuerong can no longer hold back the tears he has been fighting against for so long, and they begin to flow down his cheeks. No longer paying heed to anyone listening outside the door, he continues in a loud voice: "The money is clean, Young Master. It's not reward money from the Japanese. Ai, but what you said before was right. It is only on stage that I dare play a drum-beating Liang Hongyu.[1] Off-stage, I am simply a cowardly, servile clown. But I cherish you as a friend, I admire you, and I respect you for the kind of man you are. If you don't accept this money, how can I have the self-respect to go back home?"

Qi Yuexuan's own eyes fill with tears. He says nothing but just grasps Xiao Yuerong tightly by the hand.

At this moment, a middle-aged man comes running excitedly into the courtyard. It turns out to be the village chief from Majia. Second Master Dong steps forward to greet him, but the man has already come in through the door.

"Second Master Dong, Mr Qi, it's bad. It's very bad. The two of you must come at once... come over to our village."

"What's happened?" asks an alarmed Second Master Dong.

The village chief catches his breath, then says: "I've got a dozen or so households who want to pack up all their belongings and flee the village. They're not from Majia Village, they're all outsiders. I've tried persuading them, and I've tried pressuring them, but it's no good."

"What's their reason?"

"It's obvious! Didn't that Japanese plane circle around us just the other day? They think the Japanese are going to attack for real, and they've panicked."

"What a bunch of fucking cowards. The sooner they fuck off, the better. I'm not going to go and try to persuade them," Second Master Dong fumes.

"If they kick up a fuss as they're leaving, they'll agitate some of our own villagers into going too. The two of you must come at once and help me calm the village down."

"Very well," Qi Yuexuan says, getting to his feet. "The people can see what's going on, and there's no point in trying to reassure them with empty words." When he sees the others looking at him in confusion, he laughs and says to Xiao Yuerong: "I respect your intentions, but keep your money. I have no use for it. I'm coming down from the mountain with you. If I may borrow Second Master Dong's words, the sooner I fuck off, the better."

"What are you playing at, Young Master?" Second Master Dong asks.

"You can't go, Young Master," Xiao Yuerong urges him, clearly agitated.

"Ha! I have to find my own way out of the trouble I have provoked. I can't bring further trouble on the villagers. The people of the Left Barracks have done their utmost not to let down their country, but no more blood must flow."

Qi Yuexuan looks around him, then goes on calmly: "It's alright. It's not as though it's a matter of life or death. All I'm doing is attending a calligraphy symposium, not being taken in chains to Caishikou.[2] Besides, I rather want to see that Matsuzaki fellow again. Ha! I'm sure it will all be very congenial."

When no one speaks, or even makes a move, he falls silent himself and leaves the room alone.

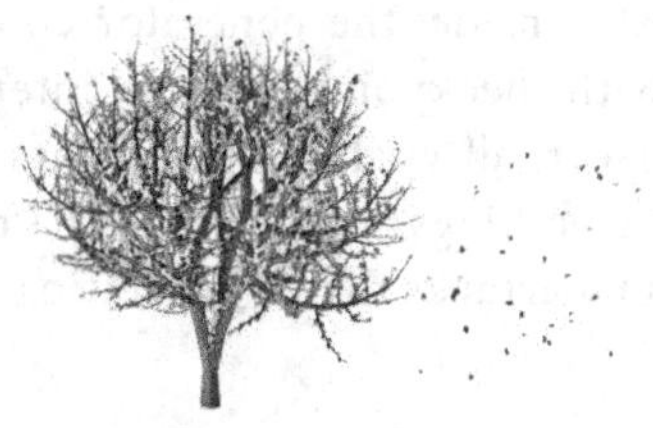

Chapter 62

The Shijingshan power plant, located at the northern foot of Shijingshan in the western part of Beiping, was built during the reign of Emperor Guangxu. At the end of the Qing, its output was very small, supplying only the Forbidden City and the foreign embassies. Later on, it underwent several expansions, and in the tenth year of the Republic it began transmitting electricity across Beiping and became the source of supply for the whole city. For more than a thousand years, generations of Beiping residents had been using pine-pitch and other torches, candles and oil lamps for light, and the advent of electricity was widely ridiculed. Many people said that electric lights were devil's fire, and were afraid to pull the light cord, so they continued to use kerosene lamps. Some reacted in a more extreme manner, and not only were they too scared to use the lights themselves, they were afraid that, if they even looked at one, they might explode or catch fire. Finding themselves unable to sleep for several nights, they just lay there, eyes staring, until they couldn't bear it any longer and had no option but to move out into the countryside. But what can stop the advance of modern civilisation? In just a few days, residents became addicted to this novelty, this new plaything and couldn't leave it alone. In the event of a power cut, even if it lasted only for an hour, they were profoundly inconvenienced and found it almost unbearable. In the summer of this year, the Eighth Route Army blew up the generating station, cutting the power for three days, and for the whole of Beiping it is as though the sky has fallen in. At the time, the Japanese are boasting about 'victory in the holy war' and 'consolidating their rear', but very few people believe them.

Of course, the Japanese are fully aware of the importance of power plants, and right from the start, before they enter Beiping, they send men to occupy the Shijingshan station. As the scope of the war expands, troop transport, railway station equipment, airports, factories and coal mines are all dependent on the supply of electricity. So after the surprise attack by the Eighth Route Army, they strengthen the guard on the power plant. There are three guard patrols outside and body searches for anyone going in. The walls are topped with electric wire, and tall wooden watchtowers stand at each corner, mounted with searchlights and machinegun nests. Inside, the generator compound has been sub-divided into separate areas, with checkpoints at every internal barrier. All the work units have a Japanese overseer, all vital equipment has its own individual guard and teams of soldiers with wolfdogs are on regular patrol, covering the whole area, so it is more like a central barracks than a generating plant.

ON THIS PARTICULAR DAY, Zhou Zhengying doesn't go into the newspaper office. Instead, very early in the morning, a motorcycle and sidecar comes to her house to pick her up and take her to the Shijingshan power station to gather information. This is her own scheme to write a propaganda article on the strength of the defences far behind the front line, the steadiness of industrial development and the diligence and contentment of the local people. As she is using the power station as her focal point, she also wants to have some photographs. The Mid-Autumn Festival will see the official publication of the first issue of *North China News*, and it is still lacking a heavyweight article like this. So Zhou Zhengjie commissions her to gather the information and produce a draft article within the next five days. He is not to know, however, that when his sister makes the trip out to the plant today, she is actually carrying out an assignment for the Communist Party apparatus.

IN FACT, in order to curb the Japanese military operations against their base of operations west of Beiping, and to coordinate with the major offensive being mounted in the east of Hebei, Zhang Zhicheng's guerrilla forces have already moved their elite troops outside the enemy's encirclement, intending to develop a series of surprise attacks in the environs of the city itself. The first blow is to be struck at the Shijingshan plant. Their previous attack was mounted in haste and suffered from a shortage of explosives and a lack of information about the layout of the plant, so after they broke in, all they could do was use clusters of hand grenades to blow up the furnace and gas supply lines. Consequently, the effects were limited, and the plant was back up and running in only a few days. This time, they are determined to blow up the enemy's vital utilities, and they want to put the generator out of action for much longer. Zhang Zhicheng himself leads his men secretly into the city, where they mount the raid on the Japanese company to settle the problem of the explosives. They also have preliminary plans for how to get past the guards and into the generator compound. However, they still don't have details of the precise layout of things inside the compound with which to organise the demolition, so they have no guarantee of success. When the Party's underground organisation hears of this, they obtain some details from contacts in the labour force at the plant, but the enemy have instituted a system of division of labour according to rank, and all the most important posts are held by Japanese. Essentially, no Chinese workers or clerical staff are allowed into the critical areas, so the responsibility for gathering the necessary information is given to Zuo Xichuan's 'Northern Frost' cell and is passed on to Zhou Zhengying.

Although Zhou Zhengying is no newcomer to intelligence work, this is the first time she has gone on a solo reconnaissance mission. She is well aware of the heavy responsibility. The compound is so large, and the equipment so complex, that it is going to be extremely difficult in such a short time to master the overall situation, identify the crucial targets, pinpoint their locations and mark out the best route for the attackers. Despite the size of the site, by keeping her thinking simple and direct, she can see that it is, in fact, fundamentally no different from a smaller generating set-up and merely consists of different sections for power source, electricity generator, power output and power regulation. Since these form a continuous system, destroying any part of it will result in a power cut, the differences lying in the ease of repair, length of outage it will cause and overall damage inflicted. The heart of the power plant is the generating apparatus and it is also the most difficult element to repair. If it is damaged significantly and needs to be replaced entirely, the disruption in terms of time and expense is also the greatest. But it is unwise to put all your eggs in one basket, and if it is possible to obtain a fairly detailed understanding of the whole electricity supply chain, it will give the operation more alternatives and more contingency plans should the need arise.

On the way there, Zhou Zhengying still has a few misgivings. When she reaches the main gate and shows her credentials, she is not immediately allowed in. She has to wait for a phone call to be made to the site management office and is told to wait for someone to escort her before she can be allowed to proceed. After waiting for some considerable time with no sign of anyone, she finds herself becoming even more uneasy. Much to her surprise, after waiting another five or six minutes, the whole mood changes from glacial to warm and welcoming in the extreme.

A limousine hurtles down from the main compound, and before it has even come to a halt inside the main gate, two men leap from it and advance to greet her, faces wreathed in smiles.

"Ah, yours is Mrs Shoi? Welcome, welcome! Mine is plant's manager Noda Jusan. Actually very sorry make you long wait. Please, inside please."

Zhou Zhengying hurriedly exchanges greetings and follows the manager in through the gates. In fact, it is only a short distance to the office building, and they soon arrive. In the reception room there is a table laden with cigarettes, sweets and fruit. This lavish greeting she is being accorded strikes her as a little excessive and puts her on guard.

Zhou Zhengying is the first to speak: "Lord Noda, I have come here today to write a special article on the safety measures at the power plant. I hope that you will facilitate this and give me an introduction to the situation here. Perhaps let me in to have a look around, conduct some interviews and take some photographs. You see..."

"Is not have problem. Ours is certainly to accommodate you. I must have a meeting in little while, cannot escort you, so allow mine assistant escort you round and from him let you make a complete report. You have questions, you must only ask, and his will certainly fulfil them. Please ask that Mrs Shoi goes back and writes many beautiful words."

With this, he looks at his assistant standing beside him, who deferentially hands him a document file. He then continues: "This data information is give you to look at. Is mine little something to you."

At this point, someone comes into the room to tell the manager that everyone has arrived and asking him to come and open the meeting. With many apologies, Director Noda says his farewells and leaves.

Zhou Zhengying quietly opens the folder and stares in astonishment. Where is the promised data? What is actually inside are two thick wads of Japanese army issue banknotes. This bizarre situation is both a fortunate misunderstanding and an excellent joke.

IN THE EIGHTH ROUTE ARMY'S last surprise attack on the power plant, the only thing they blew up was the boiler block, and other than breaking the external supply pipes, the boiler itself suffered little damage except for collapsing some of the internal partitions of the furnace in several places. But when Director Noda took up his post, he not only repaired the damage, he also announced a complete overhaul, scrapping the old equipment. A small portion of the resulting special funding went as a bribe to his own boss, but he had personal control of the remainder, and he even announced an incentive payment dependent on the speed of the work. But recently there has been a rumour that his superiors are suspicions about this incentive payment and might send in spies. This has made him uneasy.

Now the checkpoint at the main gate tells him that a reporter from the *North China News* called Shoi Zhengying wants to come in and inspect the plant. He has never heard of this newspaper, but he remembers the precept that it is inadvisable openly to refuse the demands of influential factions. But still with that in mind, he takes further precautions and telephones his immediate superior, the section chief of the facilities section of the North China Military Supplies Department, who knows the background to the newspaper. This section chief has been transferred in from the Kwantung Army, and although he has never actually met Shoi Tanigawa, he has heard that the man has extensive connections, and many and varied talents. He has even heard that he has married a Chinese woman. When Director Noda hears this, his attitude changes. He doesn't dare decide for sure whether the woman is an investigative reporter or a spy, though he would rather believe in her than not. In any case, there is never any harm in observing the social niceties, and what has just happened is the result of these cogitations.

Although Zhou Zhengying doesn't know about any of these machinations at the time, having got so far in already, all she can do is put her head down and carry on. The director's assistant is even more eagerly attentive than the director, introducing the plant as they walk along and leading her around the whole site, except for the two newly repaired furnaces. Zhou Zhengying takes photographs as she asks questions about this and that, to all of which he replies without hesitation as ordered, explaining everything very clearly. In the end, he takes her to the control room, where he uses the technical plan and operational diagram on the wall to give her a complete account of the site. When the interview is over, Zhou Zhengying says that, by way of thanks, she would like to take a group photograph. A few casual 'clicks', and the plan and diagram on the wall form the background to the photographs. It was, as the old saying goes, a case of finding what you most want where you least expect it.

THAT AFTERNOON, at just after four, two men are already seated at a table in a private room on the second floor. They have arrived for Qi Yuexuan's welcome home feast. Zhou Zhengjie has arranged in advance that the car sent to collect Qi Yuexuan from the mountains should bring him straight there as soon as it gets back to the city. This might be thought a gesture of respect, and an observation of due ceremony, but Zhou Zhengjie is afraid that, if Qi Yuexuan travels directly home to the Minister's Residence, he might refuse the invitation, and he doesn't want to give him that opportunity. He is even more afraid that Qi Yuexuan might be unaware of the real complexities of the situation, and is, by nature, inclined to want to avoid anything troublesome. This is why he is determined to talk to him at the earliest opportunity to explain to him the pros and cons of what is going on, and to establish a few basic understandings.

Zhou Zhengjie is the host, Qi Yuexuan the guest of honour and Xiao Yuerong completes the party of three. Although the parts are few, the play itself is more than enough. The play they are acting out is not *Meeting at the Crossroads*, nor is it the verbal sparring of *Entering the Palace for the Second Time*. Rather, host and guest feel as though they are Zhuge Liang and Zhou Yu in *Borrowing the East Wind*, self-contained, cautious, secretive and suspicious, weighing each other up wordlessly. Of course, Xiao Yuerong is acting out of his normal type of character as Lu Su, smiling and pouring tea for the two others, chatting away for ages, without being able to bring them to the point. He gives Zhou Zhengjie an angry look and secretly kicks him under the table.

Finally, Zhou Zhengjie breaks the stalemate: "What do you think you are up to, Brother Yuexuan, sitting there po-faced as Judge Bao? Here I am, standing as your guarantor, coming to fetch you, giving you a welcome-home banquet. You don't have to thank me, but even a grumble or complaint would be better than nothing. What are you..."

"That's enough," says Qi Yuexuan. "Just listen to you! I don't know what you're doing blowing your own trumpet over this. You're just the messenger boy for your boss's promises. If you handle this affair neatly, that's going to get you into his good books, isn't it? There's no need to stare at me like that, I won't forget you either, it's just that I'm temporarily financially embarrassed and don't have a penny. Don't worry though, I'll make it up to you later. Just tell me how many trips I owe you for."

Xiao Yuerong has trouble suppressing a laugh, but when he sees how red in the face Zhou Zhengjie has gone, he just gives a little cough and swallows his mirth.

Zhou Zhengjie tries to look wise and says, with good humour: "You and your bloody-mindedness! Alright, I won't try to compete with you. We haven't seen each other for ages, so let's just cherish our old friendship and celebrate our long relationship."

"Indeed, let's forget what upsets us, and only talk of what makes us happy," Xiao Yuerong chips in, trying to help smooth things over.

Qi Yuexuan takes a sip of tea and says with a smile: "Very well, but how easy is it going to be to find something that makes us happy? I suppose we have two of the Four Great Happinesses[1] in life remaining to us. With the world in turmoil, brothers can still meet, and even if it is not in a foreign land, it may still be considered 'meeting an old friend'. And you, Zhengjie, must be very pleased to have risen so rapidly to a position of great authority, so that is pretty much the same as 'succeeding in government', isn't it? In the great scheme of things, these are reasons for happiness, I suppose. If the country is one big mooncake, even if someone else has half of it, I guess the other half is still worth having. With such a huge population, what do a million deaths really matter? As for our heroic army who run like rabbits at the first sound of gunfire, thanks to this approach they have been fighting for a year now, and, discounting previous casualties, more and more of them are staying alive. And with our scholars getting smarter and smarter, aligning themselves with whichever side is in power, surely that puts us in what must be considered an invincible position. Pah! In the past, even the antique dealers of Tianqiao weren't this slippery, nor were the performing monkeys of the street entertainers this shameless! Happy, eh? Ha ha, happy or not, who doesn't laugh when he is tickled under the armpits..."

"Enough!" Zhou Zhengjie's anger is evident in his tone, and his expression hardens. "Yuexuan, from your manner and your words, it is hard to tell if there is anything of the scholar left in you. You spill bile from your mouth, espousing everything that is vile and treacherous. It would seem that your year in the mountains has not been wasted, and you've turned into a real country bumpkin. What is the point of just ranting and cursing? You've never really understood what is going on, and politics is even more a closed book to you..."

Qi Yuexuan bursts out laughing, rocking to and fro, the tears coming to his eyes. The laughter scares and upsets Zhou Zhengjie, and he blanches. Even Xiao Yuerong gets to his feet and surreptitiously tugs at Qi Yuexuan's sleeve several times.

Qi Yuexuan forces himself to put on a straight face. "Alright, alright, I admit my ignorance. Let the great political expert have his say."

"It's not a competition, Yuexuan," Xiao Yuerong interjects, afraid that the two men are becoming increasingly at loggerheads. "Let's not go there."

"Don't stop him," says Zhou Zhengjie, waving him away. "Just like you can't get the pus out of a pimple if you don't squeeze it, there's no enlightenment without speech. But he needs to sober up a bit, or he'll be in big trouble."

At this point, a number of waiters file in and put a jar of good wine and eight dishes of assorted cold delicacies on the table. Once they've gone, Xiao Yuerong pours wine for the others.

"Come now," he says, "let's drink slow and talk even slower."

Qi Yuexuan raises his cup. "Drink up, Brother Zhengjie, and then continue. The flush from the wine will give you cover when your face goes red with shame." So saying, he finishes his own cup and holds it up to show it is empty.

Zhou Zhengjie doesn't immediately reply, but drains his own cup before heaving a sigh and saying: "The two of us have been friends for a very long time, Yuexuan, and I am telling you that everything I urge you to do is for your own good. There are only two possibilities for the future of China: one is that Japan will occupy the whole country, and the other is that the country splits east and west with each side governing one part."

"Are you sure two possibilities are enough? Is there not a chance the Japanese are driven out of the country completely?"

Zhou Zhengjie shakes his head with a wry smile: "That hope is dead. It is quite impossible. The Americans, the Soviets, the British and the French won't help, and do you really think Old Man Chiang is going to do anything? In truth, the east-west division doesn't stand a chance, unless there are peace talks and the Japanese get the advantage they want, to allow them to direct all their efforts against the Soviets and the Communists. Then it's a possibility. But Old Chiang is like a man riding a tiger and trying to get off halfway through, so the possibility is very slight. Slice it how you like, it all comes down to one thing – fighting will not succeed, and making peace is the only way to save the nation... there's no point in you glaring at me and grinding your teeth like that. Just hear me out. No matter what the circumstances, China must be governed by Chinese. The old country has gone, so there has to be a new government, and if the country is divided between Chinese and Japanese, there have to be two governments. So what happens if the Japanese put down roots here and don't leave? Without doubt, we'll have to put up with them for a while, but sooner or later they are going to have to let the Chinese take charge..."

"If you rattle the chain and the dog barks, who is controlling who?" Qi Yuexuan mutters.

Zhou Zhengjie frowns and looks keenly at Qi Yuexuan. When he doesn't say any more, Zhou Zhengjie finally continues: "One thing is for sure – whoever takes power now is the person who will control China's future. In short, meeting violence with violence gets no one anywhere. If fighting is out, that leaves only peace. If you can't get somewhere in a straight line, you take the roundabout route, and peace is the roundabout route to saving the nation."

"Good, yes, well said," says Qi Yuexuan, clapping his hands in applause. "Suddenly there is a light in the shithouse…"

Missing the point, Xiao Yuerong corrects him: "You mean 'a light in the darkness'. It's not like you to get your sayings wrong."

"Wrong? Not at all!" Qi Yuexuan says with a smile. "I meant what I said – a shithouse is a filthy place where you fart, shit and piss. It doesn't matter how much perfume you sprinkle around, you can't cover up the stench."

"When did you become so crude?"

This change in his friend is just too much for Zhou Zhengjie, but Qi Yuexuan remains unruffled. He laughs unrestrainedly and fixes Zhou Zhengjie with a look.

"You dislike crudity? Very well then, I'll give you something more elegant… let's see if you remember. Before the war, when Brother Hao was leaving the capital, the three of us wrote a set of matching couplets. You composed the opening line, which was: 'I woke startled from a dream to find I have devils as my neighbours'. Brother Hao replied with: 'Looking towards the ocean, I sigh and sing a song of mourning for my country's dead'. I wrote the linking line, which read: 'Chu Yuan never yielded'."

"Hah, yes, that's right. But…"

"But times change, and things are very different now, is that it?" Qi Yuexuan gives a cold laugh, drains his cup in a single gulp, then goes on in a clear voice: "Today, I'm going to give you a new opening line, so listen carefully: 'Qin Hui cries out his grievance: from ancient times if one bends the knee, all bend their knees. Why should the fault be mine alone? If we kneel, we kneel together.'"

Zhou Zhengjie drains his own cup and says nothing.

"Can't you match it?" Qi Yuexuan laughs. "It doesn't matter. I'll finish it off. The matching line goes: 'When Yue Fei got angry, he saved the nation and upheld righteousness, and no one dared surrender. Those who deserve to be killed were killed'."

"Very good!" says Xiao Yuerong, unable to restrain his admiration.

Zhou Zhengjie glares at him, then tries a new approach: "Good or not, who am I to criticise? All I can say is that it fits very well. But enough of this. Let's not talk about such things while there's wine on the table."

Zhou Zhengjie falls silent, and Qi Yuexuan replies promptly: "Very well, let us keep out lips sealed over the next few days and concentrate on eating and drinking instead. Drink up!"

He downs a cup of wine, picks up some slices of spiced beef in his chopsticks, stuffs them in his mouth so his cheeks bulge and chews vigorously. As soon as he has made room by swallowing that mouthful, he swigs some more wine and plies his chopsticks again. After a while, Zhou Zhengjie's expression calms down a little, and as he watches Qi Yuexuan eating, he laughs and heaves a sigh.

"Ai, Yuexuan! It is as well we don't discuss such great matters of principle, as everyone has their own conscience to follow, and friends should not fall out over such things. From my own point of view, when the world is in turmoil, the crucial thing is to take proper stock of the situation, and, even if it is not possible to turn things round completely, at least to ensure one's own safety. But let's not talk about the future, let's consider your table manners instead. You look as though you haven't eaten rice for three days and all you've had are stale husks and vegetables with no meat. I find it hard to see the master of the Minister's Residence reduced to such a state."

Qi Yuexuan chews his current mouthful and swallows it hurriedly to make room for him to reply.

"Ha! This is the first time since the end of the Qing dynasty that I've actually eaten at your expense, and you have the nerve to talk about my table manners? Is the noise too much for your tender sensibilities? I've spent a lifetime being fastidious, but now I'm a wanted criminal and don't know where my next meal is coming from, I don't give a fart about manners any more. So what if I'm stuffing my face? Would you like to hear me shouting the odds in the street instead?"

"Alright, alright, do what you like. I won't object." Zhou Zhengjie puts on a smile and continues: "But I think you might want to moderate your language a bit. The Japanese might not be so..."

"Ha! Don't worry, they don't want me dead, and I'm not tired of living just yet."

Although he says this lightly, it pulls Zhou Zhengjie up short, and he blurts out instinctively: "What makes you think that? You mustn't take things for granted. You've come back, you've done what you can, so take things as they come and don't get ahead of yourself." He drinks another cup and lets the wine do the talking. "If you want to be proactive, what's the difficulty in letting me use my influence on your behalf? If you're content just to do nothing, then you can be as happy as possible sitting around reciting poetry, writing, eating and drinking tea, can't you? Otherwise, all you have to do is raise your battle cry, and as long as you restrain your natural instincts a little and keep a rein on your tongue, it will be quite straightforward."

Xiao Yuerong joins in too: "Since you have come back, Young Master, you really do have to hold yourself in a bit. If you feel yourself about to burst, then come here to my place. Have a drink and a chat, and if that isn't enough, sing a song or two, and if I'm not too busy, I'll join you."

Qi Yuexuan smiles at him and nods. He takes a sip of tea and gnaws hungrily on a chicken leg he has picked up. Even as fresh, hot dishes are put down on the table, he remains silent, taking long drafts from the wine cup in his left hand, and pecking away like a chicken with the chopsticks in his right, concentrating on keeping his mouth full.

Naturally, Zhou Zhengjie doesn't push him, but keeps quiet himself, slowly sipping his wine. It's only when Qi Yuexuan gives a great belch and exclaims "I think I'm just about full now", that he laughs and takes up the conversation once more.

"Ha ha! Well then, now that you are full, will you let me ask you something?"

Qi Yuexuan knows that this time there is no escape, and he says good humouredly: "Very well, ask away. But hurry up about it. I've had a lot of wine and I'm getting sleepy."

"Now you've come back, you have the Mid-Autumn Calligraphy Symposium as your way out. Once everything is straightened out, you can consider yourself safe, and the past will be expunged. But if you try something foolish, then..."

"Ah yes, what then?" asks Qi Yuexuan, smiling serenely. "Relax. It's a calligraphy symposium, not a martial arts tournament. I'm not going to break any Japanese heads."

"You should wipe that smile off your face. This is no laughing matter. If you can follow my three principles, then fine, but if not, you'd do better to say you are sick and cry off – stroke, epilepsy, an abscess, I don't care what excuse you use."

"Hah! Am I reduced to making up stupid stories for the sake of a mere calligraphy gathering? Alright then, you talk and I'll listen, then I'll tell you whether I can go along with you or not."

"First, you have to keep your mouth shut – more smiles, fewer words, and above all, keep to the mainstream and don't go off on one of your flights of fancy."

"Very well, I can agree to that one. If I'm not allowed to speak, then I'll just stuff my mouth with food and wine. And smiling's easy. All I do is twitch the corners of my mouth upwards, and it looks like I'm smiling even if I'm not."

"Second, you have to watch your hands. Clear, beautiful calligraphy is fine, but absolutely none of your wild, eccentric stuff."

"That, I can agree to as well. I've already got it planned. I'll just do copies of the ancients' work, things that don't reveal my real talent. I'll write a *fu*.[2] Don't worry, it won't be about the current situation, or politics, and I won't even mention the Japanese. I'll call it *A Fu on Characters* and it will be about the history of characters, their form, their meaning, their use, their style and their sound. There's nothing the least bit wild and eccentric about that, is there?"

"Hmm, yes, and the third is that you have to watch your feet. It's still a few days until the symposium, and I need a bit less of your idle wanderings outside the Residence. Most important of all, make sure you can be found when the time comes."

"Well, that's even less of a problem than the others. I don't even think I've got enough time to plan my poem properly, let alone the leisure to go wandering around the place. I may be agreeing to your conditions, but this half-hearted beating the retreat goes against my nature. Still, even if I wanted to run, I couldn't, could I? There's a dog at the gate, isn't there? I've no interest in being bitten by any dog."

Zhou Zhengjie is delighted that Qi Yuexuan has agreed so readily, but he can't help harbouring some suspicions. He probes him further: "Why have changed your tune so quickly?"

"That's a different matter entirely," Qi Yuexuan replies calmly. "It's your dog's fart of a government that dragged me here, but this calligraphy symposium is a cultural event, not a political one, and I don't have any axe to grind there."

"Somehow, I have a little difficulty believing you."

"Difficulty believing me? Alright then, let's get things moving as soon as possible, if we're going to. Either send me back or bring in the Kempeitai. You choose."

Zhou Zhengjie sees that he really is about to get up and go, so he hurriedly restrains him.

"Don't be like that! Can't you take a joke? Alright, alright, alright, I believe you, I believe you. Now sit back down, I've still got something to say to you."

Qi Yuexuan sits back down and says ill-temperedly: "If you've got more crap in you, you'd better let it out."

But if he is getting agitated, Zhou Zhengjie remains calm and says soothingly: "You... you mustn't blame me, Yuexuan. This isn't my idea..."

"Stop beating about the bush, and spit it out."

"Well, here's the thing. Zhengying has come back."

"What? She... When?"

"A few days ago. Originally she was going to go and see you this evening, but something has cropped up, and she's planning to go very early tomorrow."

Qi Yuexuan stares at him wide-eyed. "What's going on? She comes home, and I have to hear about it from her brother?"

Zhou Zhengjie gives a wry laugh and replies somewhat evasively: "No, no... it's not... well, the two of you can talk about it when you meet. It's not really my business."

This news has pierced Qi Yuexuan's heart like a dagger.

EVER SINCE he saved Chenglong's bacon that time at Yuerong's Place, Lao Nian'er has very much become his boss's right-hand man. A few days before, when the Special Operations Squad went to Horn Mountain to spot for the Japanese aeroplane, they didn't complete the mission and had to be rescued. This failure hasn't sat well with Chenglong and he has now given responsibility for the job to Lao Nian'er, who, after several consultations, has changed the timing of the operation from daytime to evening. In addition, he wants part of the team to feign an attack on Laoqiying in order to draw out their main force. As it turns out, the ruse is successful, and in the middle of the night on the third day, Lao Nian'er takes advantage of a burst of machinegun fire to lead a party of men into the pass. When the aeroplane arrives, it zeroes in on the lamps below, swoops down and, in one smooth dive, releases several hundred litres of liquid at three different points. None of the CID men know what it is. It looks just like water, and in the darkness they can't see if it is clean or dirty, but it does have something of a stench to it. Even though they had all been wearing protective clothing, within a few days, four of the six men on the mission are sick with both vomiting and diarrhoea, and a high and intractable fever. Lao Nian'er himself has not escaped. When they are sent to the Japanese Army hospital, they are told they all have 'cholera'. They are secretly sent to the quarantine unit, and within three days, they are all dead.

But we are getting ahead of ourselves. At this point in time, Lao Nian'er has no idea what is in store for him and is delighted with his new situation. The mission has gone well, he will soon be promoted to second-in-command in the CID and has been given a reward of two hundred yuan. So with the money burning a hole in his pocket and the wine strong upon him, that evening he makes his way down the brothels of the Eight Great Hutongs outside the Qian Gate. He goes into one of the larger establishments, chooses a beautiful girl, joins a drinking gathering and passes the night there, partying into the small hours before he finally begins to yawn.

As he is sleeping peacefully, dreaming beautiful dreams, two resounding slaps land across his face, shocking him awake. He is about to shout out, but a knife is held to his throat, its tip under his chin.

"If you want to live, you'd better be honest with me," a low voice rumbles at him.

When he looks, he sees a man standing beside the bed. It's too dark to see his face, but he can feel the eyes boring into him.

In a panic he says: "If you have something to say, brother, say it. What's this all about?"

The man doesn't answer him, but asks: "Are you Lao Nian'er?"

Lao Nian'er realises he is in real trouble. This is not some random robbery; he is being targeted. He knows how this is going to go: if he doesn't admit his identity, he has nowhere to hide. All he can do is say: "Ah... yes... yes, that's me. And you are..."

"Have you heard of the Traitor Elimination Squad?"

Lao Nian'er is shaking with fear now, but he is still alert enough to see that there's no way out. He gathers his courage and says: "If you know I am Lao

Nian'er, then you know what I do. If it's money you're after, take it and go quickly, but you're not going to scare me, waving that name in front of me."

"You don't believe me then?"

"No, I don't."

"Why not?"

"We swept up the core of that organisation in the plot at the Imperial Ancestral Hall. The non-entities left behind wouldn't dare operate in Beiping."

"Are you sure about that?"

"Yes, I am. We've had reports. It's too hot for them here, and they've already left the city to follow the Communists. I can see you've got skill and guts, brother, and are quite a match for me, but is it worth risking your life to steal so little money?"

"Ha! You exemplify your own low opinion of other people. I don't want your money. I want your life."

He increases the pressure of his hand, pushing the tip of the knife a little closer. Lao Nian'er feels a throbbing pain in his neck, and he immediately gives up the pretence and admits defeat.

"Don't, don't! Just take it easy. There isn't any grievance between us that's worth you killing me for, is there?"

"Didn't you just say yourself that you killed many of my brothers at the Imperial Ancestral Hall? Isn't that grievance enough?"

"You really are from the Traitor Elimination Squad?"

"Let me make this clear – I'm not acting on orders from military intelligence, and I don't want to stir up trouble in my own house." The man pauses, then moves a little closer and spits out through clenched teeth: "But I still intend to see the blood debt paid. It's not in my nature to lose face before my dead brothers."

All the fight goes out of Lao Nian'er, and he is trembling so much, he can't speak. It's only when the knife is pushed even tighter to his neck, that he whimpers: "Don't! It wasn't... it wasn't my idea. It was... it was our captain, Liu Chenglong."

The man relaxes the pressure of the knife.

"Very well. If you tell me everything there is to know, and you really weren't part of it, then my knife will spare you as being of no importance. But if you speak one word of a lie, then don't be surprised at the consequences."

"Yes, yes, I wouldn't dare," Lao Nian'er replies, and he goes on to make a clean breast of everything: how he discovered the change in plans that day, how he secretly warned Chenglong, and how Chenglong gave the order to act first and not leave anyone alive to cause trouble later. He makes everything as plain as day from beginning to end.

"And all of that is the truth?" There is a tremble in the man's voice.

Lao Nian'er is even more keyed up than his adversary: "Aiyo! Do you think I'd dare play games with you? I tell you, the man in charge of security at the Imperial

Ancestral Hall that day was Big Zhong. Zhong Yucai is his proper name. You can..."

"Enough. I've already dealt with him." He goes on with a sneer: "That little bastard wasn't as smart as you. He tried to run away before we'd finished our little chat, so I killed him."

At this point, Lao Nian'er begins to weep with fear: "Spare my life, I beg you! Brother... my good man... no, no... dear master! I... I'm not really a traitor to China, I'm... I'm just trying to scrape a living. Please... just give me a chance."

He keeps up his howling for a while, then, getting no reply from the man, pulls himself together and looks around. There is no one there. He turns on a light, and all he sees is a half-open window. It is only then he notices someone huddled under a table, whimpering. When he stoops to look, he sees that it is the girl he picked up, lying on her back, hands and feet tied and her mouth gagged with a towel. He helps untie her, rejoicing in the fact that he has escaped with his life. He is not to know that his reprieve is only temporary.

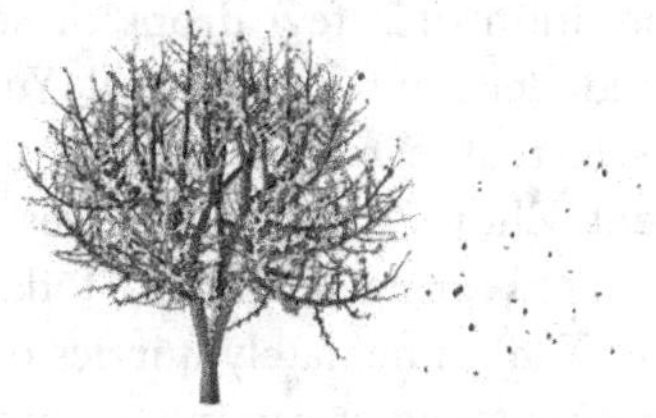

Chapter 63

Day has just dawned, and Qi Yuexuan is taking a turn around the western side courtyard. He hasn't, in fact, just got up; he has been awake all night. When he got back from Yuerong's Place the previous evening, he wasn't sleepy despite the considerable quantity of wine he had drunk. The news of Zhou Zhengying has jumbled his feelings like an overturned spice box, and conflicting emotions are all mixed up together.

He has found nothing to make him feel any more settled at home. He sees the *North China News* sign hanging in the rear courtyard, and the front yards have been turned into the headquarters of the CID squad. He has also learned that the Residence's shares in the company have been confiscated, forcing Wangtian to return to his old lodgings, which is less a case of the turtle dove returning to its old nest, and more the result of introducing a wolf into the house. Although Chenglong moved out of the main building in the central courtyard as soon as he heard the Young Master was back, and set himself up in the western range, Qi Yuexuan has chosen not to take up residence in the main courtyard, preferring, instead, the company of Mother Yan, Yue E and the children in the western side courtyard.

Mother Yan is a light sleeper, and before Qi Yuexuan has even completed one circuit, she has woken up and got out of bed. For more years than she can count, she has made the Young Master his breakfast, and he particularly enjoys this meal. On the streets of Beiping, before the sun is even up, there are breakfast stalls and breakfast shops everywhere, but where among all these merchants of coarse grain can she find the delicacies she loves to prepare? She waits until Qi Yuexuan has finished his stroll, washed his face, brushed his teeth and drunk his tea, before entering his room carrying a large tray. There are two small meat-stuffed buns, two pancakes, two small spring onion fritters and a bowl of rice congee with four dishes of pickles. The pickles are all home-made and are crisp and fresh, and much less harshly salted than store-bought ones. Each pickle is distinct, made with just the right proportions of soy sauce, rice vinegar, yellow wine, sugar, garlic paste, spring onion leaves, ginger slivers, osmanthus flowers, Sichuan pepper and salt mix, chilli oil, sesame seed paste, white pepper... and then the judicious addition of a few drops of sesame oil, all to give each its enticing fragrance and delicious flavour. Qi Yuexuan nibbles on the dishes, extolling their virtues, so that tears of pleasure come to Mother Yan's eyes.

Just at this moment, Zhou Zhengying arrives in the courtyard, carrying her baby. She herself is not wearing a kimono today, but the child is dressed in Japanese style. Mother Yan immediately hurries over to greet her. She heard the day before that Zhou Zhengying was going to come, and she does not consider it a very good idea. She is also annoyed with her for arriving so early and interrupting Qi Yuexuan's peaceful breakfast. Looking stern, she reaches out a hand, stopping Zhou Zhengying before she can go in.

"You're too early. The Young Master is still at his breakfast. Come and sit with me in the side room for a while, so he can finish in peace. Then you two can talk, alright?"

Before Zhou Zhengying can reply, Qi Yuexuan's voice makes itself heard from inside: "Why are you getting in our guest's way, Mother Yan? Hurry up and ask her in."

Mother Yan grudgingly ushers Zhou Zhengying into the main room. When the two of them see each other, they stand stock still, eyes locked, without giving anything away by expression or word. In the end, it is the child who is attracted by the sight and smell of the food on the table. He stretches out a little hand, squeaking and gurgling hungrily.

"Bring some more breakfast, Mother Yan, and another pair of chopsticks," says Qi Yuexuan, smiling faintly.

Mother Yan shoots him a look, then leaves the room to do as she is bidden.

Qi Yuexuan and Zhou Zhengying face each other across the table, still not speaking. Qi Yuexuan picks up a piece of pancake and puts it into the child's hand. He watches him seize it and take a bite, and can't help smiling. He is just about to say something, but thinks better of it.

"Are... are you well, Yuexuan?" It is Zhou Zhengying who breaks the silence.

Qi Yuexuan doesn't look at her, but says, still smiling faintly: "I'm alright. My internal organs are still all there, and I don't have any broken limbs. I can walk and I can eat, and I haven't reached the point when people start asking 'Can he feed himself?' Given the chance, the hand that holds a brush can still pick up a rifle as well."

Zhou Zhengying sighs softly and replies: "I already know your circumstances. I have never doubted your moral integrity, but I didn't think you could lay down the brush, pick up the sword and lead troops into battle. I am not mistaken in you though, Yuexuan. You are a man of indomitable spirit."

Qi Yuexuan can't help looking at her, and as he does so, he sees that her bright eyes are now clouded with tears.

"But Yuexuan..." she says softly, then stops to think for a moment, before continuing: "I know why you have come back. It is not because you are weak but because you have a sense of responsibility. And since you have taken this step, now you have to brace yourself and endure the disgrace. I know what's in your heart, and so do the people of the Left Barracks. History will prove you right. Whatever you do, look out for yourself, and don't lose the big prize for the sake of a smaller one."

"It is hard to believe you still have faith in me."

"I have always kept faith in you."

"Kept faith?" says Qi Yuexuan, giving a wry laugh. "You left home without so much as a word to me. In two years you never sent a single letter. Is that how you keep faith?"

When he sees Zhou Zhengying staring at him in astonishment, his laughter becomes more bitter. "I never sought your faith. Whether you wanted to give it or not was your choice. I know my own heart, and that is enough."

Zhou Zhengying is becoming upset: "Yuexuan, I..."

"Let's not talk about this nonsense now." Qi Yuexuan clearly doesn't want to get drawn into this discussion. "Tell me the truth. Why have you come here today?"

Zhou Zhengying looks at him and hardens her heart. She is about to say something, but the words won't come out.

Qi Yuexuan sighs gently: "Ai! You really are Zhou Zhengjie's little sister. The two of you are cut from the same block."

"How am I like him?"

"How are you not!"

Zhou Zhengying glances quickly outside the door, then says in a low voice: "There are some things I have to tell you, Yuexuan, but you have to believe that my feelings for my country, for my Party and for my husband have never changed, and never will change. I... ach, in the future I... my..."

"Enough!" Qi Yuexuan cuts her off short. "Don't talk about the future. I may not live to see it. So give me the truth now, what business has really brought you here today?"

Zhou Zhengying makes a little humming noise, then says: "I... I came today... to talk about formalising our divorce..."

"Ha! I thought as much! So you want to marry that Japanese fellow properly, do you?"

"His name is Shoi Tanigawa, and he is also..." Zhou Zhengying's words die on her lips.

"A comrade? Is that it? And just what kind of comrades are we talking about? I'm not listening, and I'm not going to listen. Nor am I going to have the divorce published in the newspapers. I'm not going to lose face to a man like him."

So saying, he takes a sheet of paper from inside his jacket and slaps it down on the table. "I've already prepared the divorce letter. You have broken the seven conditions of marriage, and we are going to follow the proper Chinese way of doing things."

Zhou Zhengying is getting annoyed, but she drops her voice even lower:

"Don't insult my dignity, Yuexuan. Shoi and I are not really man and wife, and I'm only divorcing you because there is no other option. It is because..."

"Don't try to explain," Qi Yuexuan interrupts again. He points at the child she is carrying. "Look how old the child is, and you're still trying to tell me what's true and what isn't."

The tears he has bullied out of her gather in the corners of her eyes, but she forces her eyes wide open so they don't fall. She meets his imperious, unrelenting gaze and says: "Take a proper look, Yuexuan. Don't you think this child looks like you?"

He looks up. "Like me? Impossible."

"He is your flesh and blood, so why shouldn't he look like you?" Her voice rises with her anger. "Look at pictures of you when you were little and you'll see that you're carved from the same block. I was pregnant already when I left home. I didn't tell you when I got the news at the hospital because I was trying to persuade you to acknowledge Yue E. If you don't believe me, you can go and ask the doctor at the church hospital."

Qi Yuexuan is thunderstruck, and he just stands there in amazement for a moment. Then he leaps from his seat, takes a giant stride over towards her, takes hold of the child's tiny hand and looks carefully into its chubby face. The child is not the least bit shy with him and gurgles happily.

Zhou Zhengying sighs, and her tone softens: "I didn't give him a proper name when he was born. I just called him Nan'er, like in the word for suffering, *ku'nan*. A while ago, I came here without permission, to hand him over to you. I thought that, if I couldn't be with you, you might like to have your own flesh and blood..."

With tears in his eyes, Qi Yuexuan smiles and stammers: "Yes, yes... leave him here, leave him here. That will be fine. The little fellow is so adorable, I don't care if he's mine or not. Leave him here and I'll raise him as my son."

He cradles the child in his arms, then lifts him up high.

Zhou Zhengying's heart is filled to bursting at the sight of father and son so happy together, but she can't break discipline now, so she hardens her heart again and says: "I can't leave him with you this time."

"Why not?"

Zhou Zhengying lowers her voice again: "The demands of my work. My superiors won't let me leave him. I've already been criticised and disciplined for acting without permission last time."

"Then why did you bring him here today?"

"I just wanted you to see him, to let you know that you do have a son and to prove that my feelings haven't changed. I'm only leaving you now for a short time. It won't be long. And Nan'er and I will surely come back to you."

Qi Yuexuan feels as though a bucket of cold water has been emptied over his head, and he just stands there staring at Nan'er in silence for a long time. Suddenly he thrusts the child into Zhou Zhengying's arms, apparently unable to control his anger.

"Go then! If you're going to go, do it quickly, and don't come back. The Qi household isn't a cupboard that you can just put things into and take out as you like."

Maybe because his voice has got louder, and his manner has changed, Nan'er begins to wail and won't stop, no matter how Zhou Zhengying tries to distract him. The tears she has been holding back finally begin to flow, and her voice cracks: "What I have said today, Yuexuan, has already gone against my superiors' orders. All I am seeking is your understanding. Are you saying that..."

"Stop!" Qi Yuexuan waves his hands. "I don't want to listen to any more of your explanations. I'm not part of any organisation of yours, and I don't follow anyone's rules. If you really do still love me, and this child really is mine, then stay here and don't leave. If you can't do that... then don't promise me things I have desired for so long. I don't believe you. I don't believe a word you have said."

And with that, he turns his head away.

Zhou Zhengying has no option but to leave the room, carrying the still crying Nan'er in her arms, and she almost barges headlong into Mother Yan who is on her way in, bearing a tray. When Mother Yan sees Zhou Zhengying heading purposefully outside, and Qi Yuexuan sitting there rigid and then standing up to give chase, she hastily puts down the tray and calls out: "Do you really still want a woman like her as your wife? I've got ears too. Is that child yours? She's obviously using it to try and get more money out of you. What are you doing losing face by chasing after her. The quicker she fucks off, the better."

Qi Yuexuan doesn't reply. He still wants to go after her but can't think of an excuse to do so. He looks down at the letter on the table and finds one.

"Hey! She hasn't taken the divorce letter I wrote for her."

Mother Yan is quicker than him, and she snatches up the letter.

"You don't need to bother with this. I'll go. You just finish your breakfast in peace."

At the foot of the mountain, forty-five *li* south of the Shijingshan power plant, there is a village called Xishanhui, where Zhang Zhicheng and a column of his men are hiding out. Although the village isn't large, with only thirty or forty households and a hundred or so people, it is one of the first villages in Wanping County to have set up a Communist Party organisation. It has about a dozen Party members and a reliable core of villagers. Five or six of them have joined the Eighth Route Army, two of whom are in the company Zhang Zhicheng has brought back with him. The chairman of the village's 'preservation committee', Grandpa Lin, is also a Party member of eight years' standing, and the Party branch secretary. This makes him a real roseheart radish: white on the outside and red all the way through. It would not be possible to hide out so successfully in the environs of Beiping, under the very eyes of the Japanese devils, if it weren't for the help of this Party organisation and the strength of popular support.

The young men of the village all work in the limestone quarries, leaving the women, old people and children to toil in the fields. The village has just harvested its wheat a few days before, and also gathered in its winter vegetables, so the extra thirty or forty Eighth Route Army men have been an enormous help. The villagers are delighted, of course, but privately, the soldiers are grumbling among themselves, saying they've been taken off the front line and aren't fighting, but planting and harvesting crops instead, and doesn't that just make them seasonal workers for the villagers? Commander Zhang always used to be a real firebrand, so why has he suddenly turned into a wet blanket? Little do they know that Zhang Zhicheng is even more annoyed than they are, but is acting like a dog facing a hedgehog: he doesn't know where to bite.

Until around noon on this particular day, that is, when he receives a letter from the Party's underground communications officer that contains a detailed ground plan of the Shijingshan power plant. The plan shows, in precise detail, the plant's facilities, transport routes and defences. There are also separate plans of the areas they particularly want to target, with notes highlighting key demolition information. Zhang Zhicheng's mood brightens considerably. He immediately convenes a meeting of his officers to share the plans for an attack on the power plant. He also sends messengers to inform his other two columns who are lying low elsewhere, that coordinated attacks will take place at nine o'clock in the evening of the day after tomorrow, on the Japanese base at Zhaoxinzhuang and the railway station at Changxindian.

The plan of action has been clear to Zhang Zhicheng for some time. An all-out attack would incur unacceptable losses, so he prefers to smuggle in the explosives in the specially adapted night soil carts and coordinate outside and inside offensives. Although this ploy has been used twice before, the enemy have not seen through it yet, and so it is still ripe for use. Several days before the attack, he has already given Clown his instructions, but this time, getting past the barrier is a different matter. They need to get empty carts into the plant, so the plan needs further study and modification. After the meeting with his officers is over, Zhang Zhicheng hurries into the rear courtyard looking for Clown, to see how he is getting on.

On entering the courtyard, he looks around for Clown and finds him huddled in a corner of the walls with Yuxiang, cheek to cheek and arms around each other, all very cosy. Quite unabashed, Clown lets go of Yuxiang, and looks up with a smile.

"I've done what you told me, Brother Zhicheng. Come over and see if you think it will do."

Zhang Zhicheng is delighted, as this is just what he wanted to hear, and his eyes fix on the newly adapted night soil carts in the middle of the courtyard. Meanwhile, Yuxiang flees back inside, red-faced with embarrassment.

"You see," Clown says in explanation, "previously, the secret compartments were in the bottom of the cart, and well-disguised by the load of shit, but, if you want empty carts, the space will obviously look too shallow. So this time, I've distributed the secret compartments all around the tank, so they are better disguised than before. Unless they actually take a ruler to it, it won't be obvious to the devils."

Zhang Zhicheng carefully inspects the cart all over, tapping here, peering in there, and finally he is satisfied.

"If it's alright," says Clown, "shall I do the same to the other one too?"

"Sure, and get a move on. You'll need to have it done by tomorrow afternoon, and leave a bit of time to fix them up with full loads of real shit. We must be set to go by the evening of the day after tomorrow."

When Clown hears this, he moves closer to Zhang Zhicheng and asks: "Is there really no part for me to play in the rest of this, Brother Zhicheng?"

"Ha! Haven't I already told you? You're not part of the army and you can't go into battle with us."

"Then... why don't you recruit me now, in which case I can, can't I!"

Zhang Zhicheng glances towards the building and smiles. "You've got a family to think of now," he says. "What will Yuxiang do if I recruit you? This is a very dangerous mission, and if anything happened to you, who would she have to turn to?" When he sees Clown's dejected expression, he pats him on the shoulder and continues: "You've done a fine job adapting the carts, and that certainly counts as meritorious service. I'll tell you what – wait until the mission is over and we're back at base. You get Yuxiang nicely settled in, then come and talk to me again, alright?"

Clown doesn't say anything for a while, then suddenly bursts out: "The way I see it, Brother Zhicheng, if you leave me behind, then the whole plan is bound to fail."

"Now you're just blowing your own trumpet," Zhang Zhicheng laughs. "Go on, blow some more."

"It's not an idle boast," Clown says, getting a little annoyed. "Just think about it. Once you're inside and messing around with the shit carts, if you don't have someone who knows the business, what's going to happen when one of the guards sticks their nose in? They'd only have to ask a couple of questions, and they'll see right through you. Perhaps you won't even make it through the gates, and once you have to open fire, your whole plan to let off the explosives secretly will backfire."

"That... that won't happen. I'm going myself."

"Ah, so the general takes charge of everything! How often has that strategy worked out for you?"

Zhang Zhicheng is rather put out by this, and he doesn't reply.

Clown starts to perk up, and he chuckles and clasps his hands in mock supplication: "So? What do you think? You're going to have to let me go, aren't you?"

"Well..." Zhang Zhicheng hesitates, then asks quietly: "Have you talked to Yuxiang about going?"

"A real man like me doesn't..."

Before he can finish, there is a 'thud' as a rice bowl lands in the doorway, and a cornbread rolls across the ground and stops at Clown's feet. He picks it up, turns to look and suddenly stands stock still. Yuxiang is standing in the doorway, her eyes filled with tears as she seems to sway on her feet. Clown stares at her for a moment, then runs over and crouches in front of her. He is about to start picking up the bowl and its pickles, but before he even touches them, Yuxiang has squatted down too, and delivered him a great slap around the face.

As she begins tidy up, she whispers: "Do you... do you really want to go?"

Clown doesn't reply but just nods his head, and she says, even more agitated: "We only just escaped by the skin of our teeth... please don't go."

"Alright, alright, I won't go anywhere." Clown helps her to her feet and continues: "Let the Japanese kill who they like, seize who they like, take any family's daughter they take a fancy to. The two of us got out by the skin of our teeth, so why bother about anyone else? As long as we're alive, what does it matter to us how many other Chinese die?"

This earnest counter-argument greatly amuses Zhang Zhicheng: "Forget all that nonsense, and don't worry, Yuxiang. I'm not going to let him go. But that's enough. I've disturbed you, so I'll go now and leave you two get back to what you were doing."

Seeing him about to leave, Yuxiang blurts out: "Uncle Zhang, I... I don't really want to stop him going." Her tears begin to flow. "I... I'm not the kind of person who can't tell good from bad. I have lived a life of pure misery, and it has all been at the hands of the Japanese devils and Chinese traitors. I'd like to see them all skinned alive. It's just that... Ai!"

Clown can see that she is too overwrought to speak, but he just laughs and says: "So... so do you agree then?"

Yuxiang looks at him, sighs deeply and says: "What does it matter whether I agree or not? Haven't you told everyone that I'm your wife, but what ceremony have we been through? What rituals have we observed? So what's the point in you asking me, anyway?"

She turns and is about to go, but Clown stops her: "Yuxiang! Listen to me..."

"I won't!" Yuxiang pushes him away furiously and glares at him, before launching a veritable hurricane of words: "What was I thinking of when I ran away with you, Brother Clown? I was thinking that you loved me! But now we've reached this crucial moment, what is it you find lacking in me? Even if I never sat in a wedding sedan or went through any ceremony, is it so hard for us to be man and wife? If I was your wife, I would look after you if you were injured, I would bury you if you died. I would do everything right and proper and just as it should be. Even if I spent my whole life cradling your spirit tablet, I would endure it, counting it my honour to have married a real man. But now... Ha! You just do as you please, and if you are injured and have to beg for food, or die and are eaten by wild dogs, I simply won't care!"

Even as she is still speaking, she rushes back inside and slams the door, leaving the two men staring at each other in astonishment.

"Well, brother, now do you understand?" Zhang Zhicheng says.

"Ai! It really is a tough job trying to guess what is in a woman's heart, isn't it?"

"Are you really that stupid, or are you just pretending? Everything she just said comes down to one thing. If you want it in two words – 'marry me'! Or if you'd like it in four words: 'marry me or else'!"

"Oh!... Ah!... But..."

"Enough! Enough! Not another word! Come with me, and I'll fix things up for you."

So saying, Zhang Zhicheng drags Clown away with him.

That same evening, a wedding ceremony is held in the small courtyard. Although it is simple, all the proper rites and traditions are observed: a three-gun salute, firecrackers, a veiled bride, garlands of flowers, stepping over the brazier, worshipping heaven and earth, filial piety tea. Everything is done properly and in due order. Zhang Zhicheng and Grandpa Lin stand in as heads of the two families, and a hundred or more soldiers and villagers join in the party. If two catties of sugar are not enough for everyone to have a lump each, at least they can get a lick and share in the sweetness. And if three catties of strong wine can be watered down to fill a big jar, when that's finished you just keep on adding water. They'll get just as merry on that as if they were drinking wine.

THE SECOND DAY after the attack on the Left Barracks, people begin to fall ill in the villages downstream. It starts with a stomach ache, then vomiting and diarrhoea, followed swiftly by an intractable fever. At first no one thinks there is anything particularly odd about it, putting it down to eating food that has gone off in the height of summer. There's nothing unusual in a bit of a stomach upset, and a little medicine will quickly cure it. Even Second Master Dong doesn't make any connection between the illness and the Japanese. As time goes on, more and more people fall sick, and the increasingly severe diarrhoea and exceptionally high fever prove too much for some of the elderly and children, who begin to die. At this point, alarm starts to build.

There is a doctor named Tong in Laoqiying, who is held in high regard throughout all the villages. When the first sick villagers come to consult him, he takes their pulses and diagnoses a form of cholera brought on by excess heat and moisture. He writes out several prescriptions involving blue liquorice, dried orange peel, china root, magnolia bark, goldthread and so on. He also advises isolation of the patients to prevent contagion. Since a large-scale cholera outbreak has never occurred in Beiping before, he believes this to be an isolated case. It never crosses his mind that it could be the result of germ warfare, nor that it could spread as quickly as it does. Once realisation dawns, it is already too late, and the illness has reached six of the villages of the Left Barracks. At a rough count, there are more than thirty cases, several of whom have died. His own supply of medicine is quite inadequate, and in consternation, he goes to see if Second Master Dong has any ideas.

Second Master Dong immediately realises the severity of the situation, but he also thinks there is something odd about it.

"It shouldn't be happening. How has a disease from the south suddenly broken out here in the north?"

"From the way it looks, it has something to do with the water supply," Dr Tong replies.

"It can't be. We've followed all Young Master Qi's instructions. We've given the water to animals to drink before humans use it, so how come not a single horse or mule has fallen ill?"

"Ah, you probably don't know that the medical textbooks say that cholera is 'only for man'. That is to say, domestic poultry and livestock are not affected. It is only transmitted through humans and only harms humans."

"So what do you think we should do?"

"First, we can't drink the water any more. Second, all the people infected must be quarantined together, and their eliminations kept separate. Third, someone must go to the city to buy medicines. My own supply is exhausted. Fourth, this illness is too serious for me to cure. If these people are to survive, they must be sent to the big hospital."

Second Master Dong considers these recommendations, then says: "I agree with you over the first three, and we'll put them into action immediately. The fourth is impossible."

"Why is that?"

"Ha! Well, you may be better than me at diagnosing illness, but you are far less well-informed than me on the current news. The Japanese are keeping a tight rein on so-called 'cholera' in the city. You just have to display the symptoms, and you are carted off to the quarantine unit. These people who really do have the disease would be being sent to a certain death. Besides, if news of all this gets out, this whole area will be designated an epidemic area, and the Japanese will have an even better opportunity to come into the mountains and wipe us out."

"So... we just wait to die?"

"There's no other way. We have to sacrifice the few for the many."

Dr Tong is not at all happy with this suggestion, but however long he thinks, he can't see any alternative. So in the end, he just nods.

Second Master Dong doesn't dare delay any longer, and he hurriedly tells the doctor to make a list of medicines, and then he summons his son. He orders him to go into the city the next night and find Qi Yuexuan at the Minister's Residence to help him buy medical supplies. Second Master Dong and Dr Tong leave the house together, intending to go and ring the alarm bell, to summon a meeting of all the villages. But on their way, they hear a hubbub coming from outside the village gates. When they listen carefully, it seems to them to be the sound of shamans' drums and the chanting of sutras with massed accompaniment. They remain puzzled until someone informs them that it is a crowd of people from Guojia Village carrying iron spades and hoes. They are saying that the spirit summoned by the Buddhist master has told them that the source of the epidemic is an evil spirit from the southwest, and its lair is in the Qi family tombs to the west of Laoqiying. The Buddhist master is going to summon the spirit again to show where the evil spirit's physical body is buried so they can destroy its lair and get rid of the source of the curse forever. Furious, Second Master Dong tells his son to summon his men as quickly as possible, while he himself and Dr Tong hurry off to the entrance to the village.

THE LONG ESTABLISHED TRADITION in Beiping of summoning spirits and exorcising them has its origins in the shamanic ancestor worship of ancient nomadic tribes. The Khitan, Jurchen and Mongols of the Liao, Jin and Yuan dynasties brought these shamanic traditions to the city. Before the foundation of the Qing, the Manchus were also nomadic hunter-gatherers, whose original name for their dynasty was the Later Jin, and their beliefs followed those of the Jurchen, so naturally they were shamanic in nature. However, just as with the Liao, Jin and Yuan, once they entered the Central Plain and came into contact with the more advanced Han civilisation, shamanism quickly lost its influence, disappearing from the mainstream and remaining only in the ancestral sacrifices of the banner clans. Latterly, the prevalent open religions across the country were Buddhism and Daoism, and this applied also to the emperors and empresses of the Qing court. By the end of the Qing and the beginning of the Republic, shamanism had declined even more, and it was only at temple fairs, weddings and funerals that the shamans' drums were still heard, and the dances to summon spirits were still seen. But even there, they had lost any religious significance and were just part of the merriment.

In recent times, such activities have only been performed in rural areas. They have no connection with religious beliefs and are simply a way of making a living. The form and content have become entirely Chinese and secular, and are known as spirit dances in the folk culture, and the shamans are called spirit men and spirit women. They are no longer fluent in the Manchu language, and simply speak Chinese. The songs they sing are clapper songs and funeral dirges. Even the spirits they summon are those of popular culture, such as Rulai, Guanyin, the Jade Emperor, the Empress Mother, Guan Yu, Bao Gong and even the King of the Ox Devils and the Monkey King. This hodgepodge of folk belief and charlatanism doesn't normally attract much credence even among the old bannermen in a place like Laoqiying, and it would seem that the current crowd of people are simply clutching at straws and trying anything in panic over the spread of the disease.

On reaching the entrance to the village, Second Master Dong catches a glimpse of flames. He can make out that several dozen men carrying torches and implements have already entered the Qi family tomb compound. Hampered by age and infirmity, he hobbles as fast as he can towards them, shouting: "Stop what you're doing!"

When they see Second Master Dong, most of the crowd are rather cowed, and they shuffle backwards, making a path for him. But the spirit woman, who is already in the grip of shamanic possession, is sitting on the memorial stele under the ceremonial gate, her body trembling, her voice chirruping and chattering, as her spirit interpreter beats his drum and chants, relaying and translating her messages: "The Jade Emperor has arrived with the Empress Mother, with seven princesses in their train. The heavenly kings are standing around them in support, and here too are the Metal God and the Wood God, all their brother gods..."

Second Master Dong fixes one of the elders of the Guojia clan with a glare, and he asks coldly: "What do you think you are doing here?"

The man, who is in his seventies and bent with age, replies: "It... that is... seven or eight of our villagers are sick already. My little grandson is one... and, ah, the best thing is to ask for the help of the immortals. The Mountain God has said that the evil is in the southwest, so where other than here does that road lead? The Earth God has also said that there are too many new devils in the Qi family tombs, and it is they who have summoned the evil. This is the source of all our trouble, so we must..."

"Nonsense!" Second Master Dong interrupts him fiercely. "You know quite well that the Qi family are the lords of Laoqiying. All those members newly buried here were interred with due ceremony and died as heroes. Not all of those buried here are from the Minister's Residence. There are also those soldiers of the Eighth Route Army who gave their lives in defence of Laoqiying. Mark my words, anyone who moves a single stone, a single branch, a single blade of grass will lose all ties of friendship with me."

"Ai, Second Master! Do you... do you really mean that?" the old man says. "Not all the Qi family have been such heroes. Hasn't the Young Master left the mountain and gone over to the Japanese? If there is no harm in the devils of the dead, there is still harm in the living ones!"

Second Master Dong grows even more angry and shakes his fist under the man's nose, cursing him: "How lucky you are that, in your great age, your mouth has connected itself to your arsehole! The Young Master is risking his life for the sake of Laoqiying. You have no work or family ties here, yet you curse him for risking his life and his fortune? Have you no conscience? Curse me as a traitor if you want, but not him! If I hear you utter one more word against him, then everything is over between us."

The old man doesn't dare say anything in reply, and the men around him all look at each other, clearly unhappy with developments, but no one daring to take the initiative.

At this moment, the spirit woman makes a noise like the sounding of a ram's horn, and she begins to tremble even more violently. Her assistant beats his drum, twists around and begins to chant: "The evildoer is under the second ceremonial arch. If you want peace to return, topple it over. A thousand years of my arts are all used up and the spirit remains unbound. If you do not destroy it now, no man will live for a hundred *li* around."

The crowd of onlookers is stirred into a commotion.

An old woman begins to wail: "Aiya! How terrible! What are you waiting for? It's just an archway, isn't it? Destroy it if you value our lives."

A number of voices in the crowd take up the cry, and the men begin to push forward. Dr Tong tries to stop them, but no one takes any notice. Instead, they push him back a few paces so he almost slips and falls. In an instant, the crowd charges forward and are standing in front of the second ceremonial arch, ready to act.

But to everyone's surprise, the interpreter suddenly straightens up and chants in a shrill voice: "It's not to be destroyed, it's not to be pulled down."

When the crowd hears this, they stop what they are doing and turn to look. What they see is the spirit woman staring blankly as a plank of wood, her tendons standing out and thrumming like bowstrings. Her interpreter looks even more alarmed, his drum silenced. Second Master Dong stands behind him, his hands thrust in his sleeves, his belly stuck out and his face expressionless.

Then the interpreter begins to chant again: "It seems... it turns out that the flood washed away the Dragon King's home and the immortals have taken note of this wrong. This is... this is... this is the stone left over after Nüwa repaired the heavens, but the lesser spirits had not the eyes to recognise it."

On hearing this, the elder of the Guojia clan exclaims: "How wonderful this is!"

When he hears Second Master Dong's wry laugh, the interpreter hurriedly begins to chant again: "Hurry up and leave the mountain. Hurry home and lock your doors. Bow towards the southwest, and pray to the gods not to unleash their fire. Everybody's life and death is ordained, but do not dare, do not dare continue this disturbance."

He is about to turn tail and leave, when Second Master Dong fixes him with a glare and he hurriedly continues, not so much chanting as yelling: "Why haven't you gone? If you don't go now, the sky will fall and the thunder will rend asunder..."

At this, the crowd, which has been standing in stunned silence, comes back to life and scatters like a nest of ants, disappearing far quicker than they had arrived. Just as they have left the tomb compound, Second Master Dong's son arrives with his men and block the road, levelling the rifles they are carrying.

"Don't stop them," says Second Master Dong. "Let them go!"

Once the crowd of people is a good distance away, Second Master Dong turns to the interpreter and says with a laugh: "Ha! It would seem the spirits are afraid of real weapons, wouldn't it! Now you two can fuck off too!"

With that, he takes his hands from his sleeves, revealing the grenade in his right hand, its pin hooked onto his little finger.

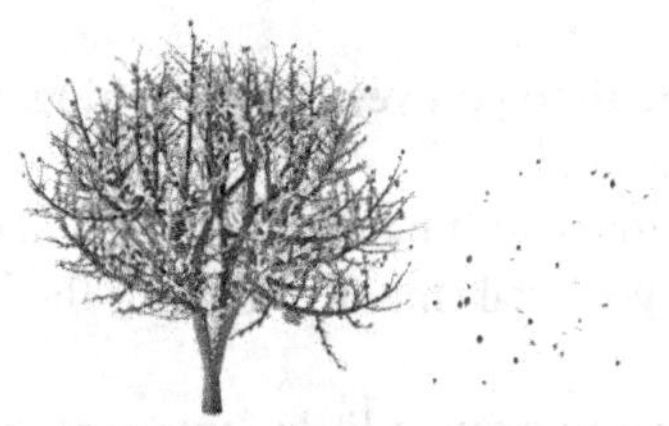

Chapter 64

Qi Yuexuan hasn't encountered a single happy event since his return to Beiping, and his meeting with Zhou Zhengying has stressed him even more. Although he has long had the framework of his poetic essay in his head, he hasn't yet written a single character. It's not down to a lack of desire, he just can't get the words out. There is an old saying that 'anger brings out the poet in a man', but on this occasion it is not anger that is working on Qi Yuexuan. A hundred different emotions have all welled up together and he can't grasp them properly, he can't see them clearly, he can't guess their true nature and he can't let them go. The past, the present and the future crowd into his head one after the other, scrambling over each other in a tumultuous rush. It is hardly surprising that the verse won't come out, and if he were to try to force it, the results would surely be scatterbrained and nonsensical. Come evening, he has calmed down a little, but as he sits at his desk, having ground his ink and is poised to pick up his brush, someone calls him from outside his door.

"Still not sleeping, Father?" It is Chenglong's voice.

When Qi Yuexuan realises who it is, he says, without looking up: "I'm busy writing. If it isn't urgent, then…"

Chenglong pushes open the door without waiting for him to finish, and he comes in carrying two bundles and wearing an ingratiating smile on his face.

"Good timing, Father. I've sprung a yuan or two and bought some decent tea for you. There's more than three catties of this year's new Longjing tea. I wrapped it up myself."

He puts the bundles down on the desk and continues: "There are some sweet cakes from Dashunzhai too, and soy sauce tripe from Tianfuhao, barbeque pork from Puwufang and some assorted fried vegetables. I've heard you're fond of these things, so I've tramped halfway across Beiping to find them for you. Once your writing has made you hungry, you can brew yourself a pot of good tea. It's bound to help you sleep well."

"Yes, yes, good… now what do you want?"

Chenglong doesn't reply immediately, but sighs gently then says: "Why don't you move into the main courtyard, Father?"

"No need."

"But I explained it all to you yesterday evening. Everything is…"

"I know, I understand."

"Then you… Ai! How can it be right for the elder of the family to be living in a side courtyard? If you tell me to live in the main courtyard, I won't be comfortable there."

Qi Yuexuan begins to grow a little impatient, but he still manages to contain himself: "Ha! A man only has one body, and he can sleep wherever he lays it down. I'm really not bothered about all this. You go back and sleep in peace. I still want…"

"Alright, alright. I won't get in the way of your writing," Chenglong says. But his actions don't match his words, as he stays where he is and says with a smile: "Just watch out what comes out of that brush of yours, and don't give the Japanese anything to use against you."

Qi Yuexuan nods perfunctorily and doesn't reply, so Chenglong continues: "This isn't just my idle talk, Father. I've discussed it all with Matsuzaki. Unless you actually commit some crime, I won't have to quit my job. So…"

"Ha! Enough! If so many different people have put themselves out to do me favours, and everyone is now coming to seek my blessing in return, who exactly is it I am beholden to?"

Chenglong chokes on this reply, and when he gets his breath back, he says: "Outsiders may all talk nonsense, but surely you can trust what your own flesh and blood tells you. Besides, the Japanese are very simple and straightforward, and always do what they say they will. You need to be a bit more careful and leave yourself a little room for manoeuvre."

"Ah, and just what kind of room for manoeuvre do you have in mind?" Qi Yuexuan asks, fixing him with a stare.

"That's not really for me to say, but actually I feel I have to…"

Seeing that Chenglong is looking at him expectantly, Qi Yuexuan gestures to him and says: "Go on, say whatever you have to say."

So, Chenglong continues: "The Minister's Residence has flourished for more than a hundred years, so how can you consider leaving it as just an empty shell? You surely have to leave it as a solid foundation for the next generation, just in case anything terrible happens."

"Ha! That's like going to the Earth God to pray for rain. You're asking the wrong god. Since my youth, I've had no truck with wealth and property. I spent what I had but never bothered to ask about where it came from. So if you come asking me, you can have the two-word, three-word or four-word answer: 'don't know', 'I don't know' or 'I really don't know'."

This answer annoys Chenglong: "We're talking about something handed down over the generations here, so don't tell me you don't give a damn about such a great family fortune. This is…"

"So, you think these buildings, this land, this wealth all belong to the Qi family, do you?"

"If it doesn't belong to them, who else can it belong to?"

"Ha! Well, maybe Uncle Yang was right – a man can only eat so much and spend so much in a lifetime, and whoever inherits a family's fortune really has it in name only. They can't spend it when they're dead, and, in truth, it belongs to the whole nation. Spending and saving, saving and spending, it's all part of the same perpetual cycle. So when you come down to it, if it belongs to the nation, shouldn't it be used by the nation?"

"You mean... you mean," Chenglong chokes on his words, before finally managing to force them out. "You mean you're not leaving it to the next generation?"

Qi Yuexuan stops smiling, and looks solemn.

"What will be left is enough to live on, but don't expect too much. Money can be a good thing, but good for what? If it is used, it must only be used where it is genuinely of use. If it is not used, that is an indication of the vices of miserliness, acquisitiveness and tyranny, and then it becomes a scourge."

Chenglong remains silent, but his expression is one of disbelief and rejection. After a while, he says haltingly: "You... you haven't said who will inherit the estate, but you must have thought about it. You must see what you should do."

"That was Uncle Yang's concern for many years. Do you really think he didn't leave a trustee after he died?"

"Then... then who is it?"

"It had to be someone honest and reliable, of course."

"Is it..."

"Enough! There's no point in foolish guesses." Qi Yuexuan puts an end to the subject. He suppresses his feelings of distaste and continues: "As for you, you should have a long hard think about what kind of man you are, and about the choices you have made, rather than keep worrying about things that don't concern you. So, be off with you! I must burn the midnight oil."

"But Father, aren't you... that is, what about the small matter of Yue E and me? Doesn't that make it my business? I've been doing some thinking for you about the problem of the Qi family having no heir, and as long as you agree, my son and I, and any future generations will change our family name to Qi. Surely it will be better for you to rely on your own flesh and blood, rather than an outsider. If you agree to this now..."

"Stop there!" Qi Yuexuan doesn't want to hear any more. "I understand your intentions, but it's no use. I am quite clear about this. Wen Tianxiang[1] and his whole family were killed by Mongol soldiers, yet he is still remembered and celebrated. Did not Qin Hui[2] have many sons and heirs, and yet today do they not kneel in temples to Yue Fei, and which of them would dare change his kneeling statue for a standing one? I had not even reckoned to allow Yue E to change her name. Grace and virtue come from upbringing much more than just by chance of birth. If you are not afraid of offending your birth father, then it would be fitting to change the name of your descendants to Yang. But you would have to be sure that you live up to that name, lest you provoke Uncle Yang into snatching up the sword of Yang Jiye[3] and rising from the grave to come after you."

This speech would be enough to choke anyone, and Chenglong goes purple in the face with bottled rage. Abruptly, he gives a dismissive grunt, takes a newspaper out of his pocket and puts it down on the desk.

"Very well then, I'll go and leave you to your composing. This is today's newspaper. Have a read of it when you've finished."

Qi Yuexuan glances at the paper and suddenly understands the reason Chenglong has sounded so amused. The two-column headline splashed across the front page in large characters reads:

'Rear defences consolidated in glorious Holy War; Host of VIPs and scholars to attend calligraphy symposium; Returning to the fold with a great future ahead of him, the master of the Minister's Residence once again writes in celebration of Sino-Japanese friendship.'

There is a crash as Qi Yuexuan seizes a plate from the desk and hurls it to the floor, where it shatters into a dozen pieces.

THE NEXT MORNING, several heavily laden trucks drive into the courtyard of the Yuhua Company's warehouse. Wangtian jumps down from the first of them and shouts to the warehouse manager, who has come scurrying out to greet them: "Hurry up and unload these trucks into the warehouse, but you can stack the soy sauce and peanut oil up outside. There'll be another truck along in a while to take them away."

"Yessir," the manager replies hastily. "Don't worry about it. Just go inside and have a rest. Catch up on your sleep. A big boss like you should leave this kind of thing to his workers. You shouldn't have to bother with it. If you keep going like this, even if you're made of steel, you're going to end up exhausted."

"Ha! This is the first time we've done this round trip out of Beiping. I would only have worried if I hadn't come along."

"Aiya! I almost forgot," the manager continues. "Your wife came looking for you in the middle of the night."

"Oh! What did she say?"

"When she saw you weren't back yet, she left a message that you weren't to waste any time and get yourself straight back to the Minister's Residence."

Wangtian is taken aback. He had gone to see Qi Yuexuan the evening he returned, and he fully understood the dangers of his current situation. He himself hadn't intended to go anywhere and decided to stay on guard throughout the night. It was the Young Master himself who had said, when he heard about the goods convoy, that the Japanese weren't going to make any move against him before the Mid-Autumn Festival, and that Wangtian should go to supervise things to avoid any delays or hold-ups for the business. But now, having been away less than a day, here is his heavily pregnant wife coming out looking for him in the middle of the night. Something unforeseen must have happened, and now isn't the time to dwell on what it might be. He must get home as quickly as possible. Luckily, it isn't far. He slips past the Drum Tower to the west, and through the hutongs at a fast trot, and within ten minutes he is there. It is only when he goes into the main room of the western side courtyard, and sees Qi Yuexuan at his desk entertaining a guest, that he calms down a little.

The guest is none other than the son of Second Master Dong. Qi Yuexuan has heard him tell the story of the 'cholera outbreak' at Laoqiying, and he is all afire to help buy the necessary medical supplies. This is why he has summoned Wangtian.

Wangtian has heard Clown's story of what happened in the quarantine unit, and he is well aware of the dangers of this disease, so when he hears what Qi Yuexuan has to say about the situation, he is full of concern: "This is a very serious illness. I'm afraid that Chinese medicine alone can't cure it."

"Yes, I think so too," Qi Yuexuan sighs, "but where can we find any Western drugs? We can't go to any of the city hospitals, and we can't condemn them to an even quicker death in the quarantine unit either."

"That's not what I meant, Young Master," Wangtian counters. "As a child, I once heard my father say that, when the White Horse Barracks went to exterminate the Nian rebels, the same disease sprang up in their army, and he got it too. There were no Western medicines then, and they got better using traditional medicines and *guasha*,[4] and relying on the resilience of youth."

"So why did you say Chinese medicine won't work?"

"Well, the disease is transmitted so quickly, you can't get on top of it by trying to cure it. My father said they stopped it in its tracks by paying particular attention to two orifices: the mouth and the anus."

"What do you mean 'the mouth and the anus'?" Qi Yuexuan asks, frowning.

Wangtian grins and goes on: "Paying attention to the anus means that you mustn't shit and piss where you please and pollute the water supply. Paying attention to the mouth means not drinking polluted water."

As he finishes speaking, Second Master Dong's son chimes in: "What you say is all very well, Brother Gao, and it's easy enough to control the bottom bit. But what can we do about the mouth? The water for the Left Barracks all comes from one source, and if we don't drink from that, we have to bring water in from twenty or thirty *li* away. So if we don't die of the disease, we'll die of thirst and exhaustion. The only useful thing you can do is help us buy the medicines on this list."

"I think there is something in what Wangtian says," Qi Yuexuan says thoughtfully. He turns to Wangtian and asks: "Was that all your father said?

Think carefully, was there anything else apart from paying attention to the two orifices?"

Wangtian considers this and says: "My father said that, when the spread of the disease was at its height, there was a real downpour, so heavy you couldn't see through it. It lasted for an hour, then stopped. The amazing thing was that the infection rate dropped after that. Everyone said the rain was a blessing from heaven."

At this point, he sees Second Master Dong's son curl his lip in disbelief, so he stops and then continues in embarrassed tones: "But this is just an old wives' tale. I don't really believe it."

To his surprise, Qi Yuexuan slaps his thigh and exclaims: "Ha! *You* may not, but *I* do!"

"You actually believe it?" Second Master Dong's son says disdainfully. "So there's no need to go and buy the medicines? We just go to the Dragon King Temple and pray for rain, is that it?"

Without replying, Qi Yuexuan goes into the inner room and comes out with a newspaper. He points to the weather forecast and says: "The forecast here says that there are going to be severe thunderstorms today, from afternoon to early evening in the northwest mountain regions. If it's accurate, this could be our salvation. This isn't just superstition, there's a scientific basis to it. After heavy rain, there are flash floods in the mountains. Might that not be Nature's way of washing away the poison? Old Dong's son, you mustn't explain it like that when you go back. You must dress it up as an unexpected intervention from the gods."

"Do... do you think the weather forecast is accurate?"

"Aiya, I wouldn't dare say. But heaven helps those who help themselves, so you two hurry off and buy those medicines. Buy more than you think we need, so you don't have to waste time coming back. Get some disinfectant spray and quicklime too."

"But I've only brought the money for..."

"Ha! Saving lives is more important than money. If he doesn't have enough, Wangtian, make it up yourself. Our fellow countrymen have put their trust in us by coming here, and I rely on them to look after my family tombs, so we mustn't let people die because we delay."

Wangtian acknowledges his orders without question, and he leaves the room with Second Master Dong's son.

Luckily, most of the items on the prescription are commonly-used ingredients to be found in any old pharmacy. The only problem is that the quantities are very large, so the two of them ride across half the city in a rickshaw, visiting a dozen or more pharmacies before they finally have everything. The disinfectant spray and quicklime are easy enough to buy if you have the money, so, before noon, two lorries leave the city, fully laden with all the medical supplies.

Later in the day, as it turns out, just as the lorries arrive at the village, the heavens open and the rain pours down. After it has stopped, it seems that the spread of the disease has indeed also been contained. However, a few days later, the disease breaks out again in the area downstream around Shijingshan, especially in the shantytown, where it spreads particularly quickly due to the overcrowded living conditions. The Japanese end up by pushing even living sufferers into big pits, setting fire to them and then filling the pits in. But even this doesn't stop the fatalities. Even today, if this subject is mentioned, the elderly inhabitants of Shijingshan still grind their teeth in anger.

By nightfall, Qi Yuexuan has been sitting at his desk for the entire day, apart from a two-hour nap in the afternoon. However, just like the previous evening, he still hasn't written a single character. After dinner, he returns to his desk and watches the darkness grow deeper outside and listens to the thunder rolling away to the northwest. The black expression on his face that has been there all day gradually begins to lighten. Like a sculpture coming to life, although his face is stern, his lips begin to move, and his expression shifts between grief and happiness, now scowling coldly, now filled with righteous indignation. He gesticulates occasionally, almost striking a theatrical pose, and most alarmingly, he suddenly strikes the desk.

Mother Yan doesn't dare take in his tea. Instead, she retreats to the side room and calls to Yue E, saying she doesn't know what devil has got into the Young Master. Yue E tiptoes into the room with the tea, quietly puts it down and withdraws without Qi Yuexuan even noticing her.

Yue E draws Mother Yan to one side and says with a smile: "You shouldn't make a fuss about nothing. When the Young Master is writing an essay, he's like you steaming *mantou*. He's a pressure cooker."

But it seems he's lacking a little heat, as several times he picks up his brush, only to put it down again, and other than a few ink spots that spatter like black measles, the paper remains blank.

At this point, a noise like thunder comes from the southwest, and suddenly, all the lights, inside and out, are extinguished. As Qi Yuexuan gropes his way through the darkness into the courtyard, Mother Yan and Yue E come running out too, carrying the children. The outer courtyard and the side courtyard are both in a hubbub, with people milling around in confusion. The noise from the southwest hasn't stopped, with a series of rumbling sounds coming in rapid succession. Now he can hear it properly, Qi Yuexuan realises that it is the sound of explosions, not thunder. The dark of the moonless, starless sky is suffused with red light in one corner. He is about to go out of the Residence to see what is going on and has just reached the gate, when the porter sends someone to stop him, as this is where the guard dog has been specially posted.

"Have a look from here, Master Qi. Don't go outside. It's chaos out there and not safe."

"Where are the explosions coming from?"

"The power plant at Shijingshan by the look at it. In any case, power to the whole city has been cut off."

"Quite some explosion then. Who has that kind of nerve?"

"Aiyo, I think you already know the answer to that. Who else but the Eighth Route Army could do something that big?"

Qi Yuexuan looks up at the sky and laughs loudly, scaring the sentry at the gates into exclaiming and clasping his hands. Before he can say anything, Qi Yuexuan has turned around and is striding towards the main room.

As he goes, he says to Yue E: "Hurry up and light some candles. I'm afraid the power is going to be out for quite some time. Go back and settle the children, then get Wangtian and Caiping. You and Mother Yan come along too, there's something I have to tell you."

WHAT IS THE MOST difficult flame of all to extinguish? I am sorry to say it is the flame of hope. Once it has flared up, trying to damp it down is like trying to hold back the wind – there is no way.

Even though Chenglong has received an early and thorough rebuff from Qi Yuexuan, that rebuff seems to have served only to stoke his fire. It has added fuel and fanned the flames, so the fire that has been hidden in his heart suddenly bursts into open flame. He has already determined that whether Yue E calls herself Qi or Yang is of no concern. What matters is that she is his father-in-law's only daughter. Whether she likes him or is indifferent to him is also unimportant; he has a son and a daughter, and there is no getting away from the fact that she is his wife. A woman follows the man she marries no matter what happens to him. She belongs to her husband, and so does her money. So it is only right and proper that the estate of the Minister's Residence should be under his control. But this is just a pipe dream at the moment. In his eyes, the whole family are not being straight with him. Indeed, they seem to be doing everything they can to pull the rug from under him. Once a man enters a blind alley, his vision is limited, and even the shrewdest can lose the bigger picture, seeing only the immediate advantage.

In fact, Chenglong has been busy ever since he took over the Minister's Residence and he has ordered his men to search every inch of the courtyards and buildings. He has even ransacked the rear courtyard occupied by Zhou Zhengjie, using the excuse of security precautions. They have searched high and low, and he has even borrowed a metal detector and swept the place as though looking for mines, but he has found nothing, and all he has done is leave the place looking as though it is infested with giant mice. This morning, on his return from the western side courtyard, he has made yet another search and come up empty-handed again. He is far from happy, but in the end he has no idea who holds the key to all this. If it's not in this courtyard, then searching by himself is like looking for a needle in the ocean. The way he sees it, his brother Wangtian is the most likely person to know the secret, but he has no proof. The fact is he simply doesn't know, and, for the moment, there is nothing he can do about it.

THAT EVENING, after the blowing up of the Shijingshan power plant, and fearing an attack on the city itself, Matsuzaki Harayama sends out orders mobilising the Kempeitai, the CID squad and the police onto the streets to impose martial law across Beiping. Chenglong is just about to set out after receiving orders by phone, when his man watching the gate of the western side courtyard comes running over and whispers in his ear. He has overheard what Qi Yuexuan just said to Yue E, and has come to report it, as well as to ask whether, this late into the evening and with everything in darkness because of the power cut, he should let anyone in.

"My old father-in-law has invited my elder brother and his wife over," says Chenglong. "They're all family, so how could I not let them in? However..." He lowers his voice and whispers some more instructions.

The man listens carefully and nods. "Yessir. Don't worry, I won't miss a word."

HEARTS THUMPING, the group gather to meet with Qi Yuexuan, none of them knowing the reason why he has summoned them with such urgency in the pitch darkness. When he sees that they are all there, Qi Yuexuan addresses them in measured tones.

"The reason I have called you here so urgently is that I have something of great importance to tell you." He pauses and picks up some newspapers from his desk. "Look at this. I haven't even got my make-up on, and the Japanese are already starting the performance. This sets the tone, forcing me tomorrow to follow their instructions and play the clown, like a performing monkey, so everyone can see how I, Qi Yuexuan, am disgracing myself in front of my ancestors."

He stops and surveys the room. Seeing that everyone is looking at him in open-mouthed astonishment, he gives a wry laugh and continues: "Ha! Well, that is all wishful thinking on their part. Eight generations of the Qi family have never acted like that, and nor can I, even if they break every bone in my body. So today, there is something I have to tell you..."

"Why can't you just not go tomorrow?" says Yue E, unable to stop herself interrupting.

"That's right," Mother Yan joins in, "just fail to show up. Pretend you're ill, then..."

"Ha! So you are agreeing with Zhou Zhengjie now, are you? Well, if I don't go, I'm afraid the Japanese will just send men to take me there in chains. And if I don't go, won't that just give the Japanese a reason to make up their own cock and bull story? They'll just say 'thank you very much' and do anything they please. Suppose they get someone in as a ghostwriter to put my name to whatever they want to say? Won't that just make matters worse? I had a visitor from Laoqiying today who told me that the commemorative stele at my family tombs was almost demolished recently, on the pretext that I had come down from the mountains to join the Japanese. For that reason alone, I have to attend tomorrow."

"Young Master, aren't you... aren't you taking an unnecessary risk by going?" There is a tremor in Mother Yan's voice.

"Ha! I'm going to a calligraphy symposium, not some kind of free-for-all. I'm going to write a calligraphy scroll with a poetic essay, and when I've finished, I'll leave."

This reassures Mother Yan a little, but Wangtian, who has remained silent until now, finally opens his mouth: "Young Master, how about you show us this essay before you write it at the symposium?"

"Ha! I haven't finished it yet," Qi Yuexuan laughs, and then he goes on to ask: "What? Isn't it enough that you have the whole household to manage, but you have to inspect everything I write too? Alright, alright. I'm well aware of the situation, and my mind is made up, so let's not squabble over this matter any more. Still, the unexpected can always happen, so it's best I pass a few things on."

He stops and turns his gaze onto Yue E with a faint but penetrating smile. "Ah, Yue E! There are two people in my life I feel I have failed: you and your mother. If, by any chance... Ai! There are two things I can't leave be. The first is the family property, and although there is no need to make invidious comparisons, it is certainly more than some others. The house and land are no problem, but there are the gold ingots and antiques that Uncle Yang hid, which are worth more than ten Minister's Residences could ever use up. I have done very little for you, and in normal circumstance I would make it up to you, but I cannot. You all heard what Uncle Yang said when he died, and he was quite right. In the past, I couldn't understand why he expended so much effort over this treasure, but now I find that incomprehension quite laughable. You were raised by him, so you will understand his arrangements better than me. A person only needs what they can spend in a lifetime. There is no point worrying about anything beyond that. Uncle Yang handed everything over to Wangtian, so that, in future, the money will be used where it ought to be used. When you recognised me as your father, you became the daughter of a great family, and as a woman you also have to be a real grown-up woman, and not one of those twittering little girls who values money above everything. I don't know if..."

"Don't worry, Father, I've already thought of all that," Yue E chimes in, as the tears she has been holding back now come flooding out. "I don't care about the money. Having a father like you is enough."

Qi Yuexuan's eyes also fill with tears, as he nods gratefully. "There is one other thing I can't ignore," he continues, "and that is the question of your marriage. It is my fault, and Uncle Yang's, that we two fathers of yours did not help you to set things straight. Several times you made it very clear you wanted to separate, but every time I stopped you. This time I won't get in your way. It is right that you should, and you will be able to take advantage of the fact that you are still young to find yourself a man you can love. I have already written..."

As he is speaking, he takes out a sheet and slaps it down on the desk. In the dim light, the small characters on the paper are hard to read, but the words 'letter of divorce' are clear enough.

The others don't dare, but Mother Yan bursts out laughing: "Aiya Young Master! I realise you know how to play the game, but where in the old rules does it say a woman can leave her master?"

Caiping has remained silent up to this point, but now she chips in: "Isn't this how it stands? If Yue E wants a divorce, can't she just go to court?"

Qi Yuexuan doesn't answer, but Wangtian takes over: "You've all misunderstood what the Young Master means. You say 'go to court', but who's running the courts at the moment? If Chenglong refuses to play ball, do you really think this marriage will be dissolved?"

"I've looked at this over and over from every angle," Qi Yuexuan says, "and if you want to separate from him, the only way is for you to leave and go as far away as possible. For heaven's sake, don't try to match wits with him. Just leave the divorce letter behind and go as quietly as you can. I'll leave this in your hands, Wangtian. You need to find an opportunity to get Mother Yan, Yue E and the two children, even your own wife as well, away to the family estates. I know it's the countryside, but there are no guard dogs or thieving wolves there, and they'll be able to live happily enough. When the Japanese devils finally fuck off out of here, then they can come back."

"That's no good," says Mother Yan, shaking her head vigorously. "How's that ever going to work? If everyone goes to the countryside, with none of us left to watch over this place, then won't that little bastard Chenglong just get even bolder and do whatever he likes?"

"You'll have to give up whatever has to be given up. We mustn't lose sight of the main target for the sake of trivialities. Whatever happens, we mustn't let my daughter live out her life sullen and resentful. Besides, I have the land deeds to this place, so I'll get it back sooner or later. Do you think you can steel yourself to do this, Yue E?"

Yue E thinks about it, then nods slowly and seriously. "Yes, I'll do as my father says."

"Good," says a smiling Qi Yuexuan. "Now I've said everything I had to say, and I feel unburdened. You all go home and get some rest. I have to go to the calligraphy symposium tomorrow, and I haven't written a word of my *fu* yet. I'll have to use up a few candles to get it done. Off you go, all of you. I'm feeling inspired at the moment, so don't make me lose it."

For the whole night, right through until dawn, the northern rooms and the side range of the western courtyard are aglow with candlelight.

When Wangtian and Caiping get home, they discover there is only a dribble of oil left in their lamp. They have a hasty wash, get onto the *kang* and put the lamp out before it burns dry. Caiping clearly remains both excited and worried, and is not the least bit sleepy. She nestles her pillow into the crook of her husband's arm, restlessly chattering away, sighing and asking about this and that. Wangtian, however, is not really interested.

"Go to sleep," he says, "I have to get up early tomorrow." Then he rolls onto his other side.

In fact, Wangtian can't get to sleep either as his heart is weighed down with worry. Indeed, the importance of the task he has been entrusted with has made it difficult for him even to talk about it. Qi Yuexuan has already had a long conversation with him, including about what he told Yue E today, and has thoroughly canvassed his opinion. Telling Yue E to leave without goodbyes, and sending them all back to the family estates, are Wangtian's ideas. So although he has not been surprised by what Qi Yuexuan had to say, it all became very real and urgent today, and this is what has got him worried. Not only is he concerned for Qi Yuexuan's safety, he is also worried whether such a heavy responsibility may not prove too much for one man to bear. In particular, the secret of the gold ingots and antiques is almost crushing the breath out of him. With all this going on, Wangtian lies awake all night, not even closing his eyes.

The fish-belly silver of pre-dawn is just beginning to show when Wangtian sits up and gets down from the *kang*. When he told Caiping last night that he needed to get up early, it was not just an excuse to shut her up. He really does need to leave the city this morning to take delivery of some goods, and he wants to get out as soon as the city gates open. He had hoped to have a few words with his wife before leaving, but when he sees she is fast asleep, he says nothing and carefully tiptoes out of the room. It is only when the sky is fully light, and there is an urgent knocking at the door, that Caiping is finally startled awake.

"Mistress, mistress, there's trouble!"

Caiping sits up, wrapping her clothes around her and calls out: "Who's there? What is it?"

"I'm from the shop. Boss Gao has... he's been kidnapped."

When she hears this, forgetting her pregnancy, Caiping slips down from the *kang*, puts on some shoes and goes over to open the door.

It turns out that this shop boy had gone with Wangtian to take delivery of the goods, so along with the cart driver, there were three of them altogether. The sky was still barely light, and the curfew was just over, so the streets were empty.

They were quite some way beyond the Xizhi Gate, when suddenly four or five strapping fellows appeared from nowhere and stopped the cart. Before Wangtian could say anything, the leader of the gang came up to him, a false smile on his face, and whispered something in his ear. The driver and the shop boy couldn't hear what was said, but they guessed he was identifying himself and telling Wangtian to step down so they could talk. Without taking any great precautions, Wangtian got down from the truck and went with the man a few paces into a nearby hutong. As the man was talking to him, two more men appeared in the hutong. One of them hit Wangtian with a blackjack, while the other threw a sack over his head. Several other of the men piled in, trussed him up and dragged him off down the hutong. Another man held the driver and the shop boy at gunpoint and told them this was a kidnapping. Then he blindfolded the two of them and tied them up, back to back. But they weren't taken away, nor was the cart stolen. All they heard from the hutong was the sound of an engine disappearing into the distance. The two of them managed to struggle free of their bonds and ran back to the city to report what had happened.

"Did the men say how much ransom they wanted?" Caiping asks.

"No, no they didn't."

"And they didn't say how it is to be paid? Or where?"

"No."

"Did you recognise any of them?"

"No. It was dark, and we couldn't see their faces clearly. But..."

The shop boy had clearly thought of something, but stopped himself from saying it. Caiping pounces on the hesitation: "But what? If you saw something, tell me."

"I didn't see anything clearly," the shop boy says, "but right at the end, I heard one of the men ask in a whisper 'Did the captain say where to take him?', and one of the others said 'Don't ask so many questions.'"

As soon as she hears this, Caiping realises what is going on, and she grinds her teeth in fury.

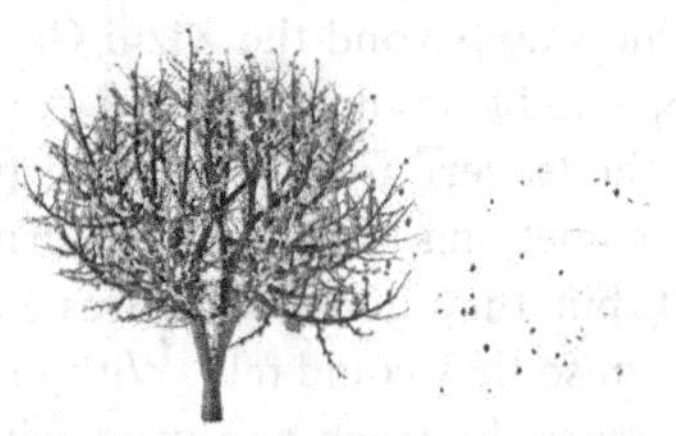

Chapter 65

The next day, the Mid-Autumn Calligraphy Symposium is held as scheduled. It is due to begin at ten o'clock. Many of the Japanese military and political leaders in Beiping, along with senior members of the interim government, are due to be there. Even the commander of the Japanese Army of North China, Hayao Tada, has agreed to attend and make the opening address. But as a result of the continuous state of emergency in eastern Hebei over the last two days, the Eighth Route Army's four-pronged advance eastwards and the Communist Party's own launch of armed insurrection in eastern Hebei, a dozen or more counties have been engulfed by conflict. The evening before, the power plant at Shijingshan, the railway station at Changxindian and several other locations came under simultaneous attack. The best the top brass of the Japanese Army of North China can do is convene an emergency meeting to discuss new military dispositions and plan a counterstrategy. Of course, the calligraphy symposium is really just a show event and is of no great importance. With none of the VIPs able to attend, the only thing to do is change the day's programme, so the delegates are given a welcome meal, and are then to left write, view the exhibition and wait. The opening ceremony will take place some time that afternoon, whenever the VIPs actually arrive. Zhou Zhengjie does his best to adapt to the new situation by throwing the whole of Yuerong's Place into confusion and filling the attendees so full of tea their stomachs are about to burst, as they wonder anxiously when they are going to get something to eat.

Qi Yuexuan has arrived at the appointed time and the appointed place, and he has also made a special effort for the occasion. He has shaved his face, blow dried his hair, put on a long blue gown with a dark green jacket, complete with gold watch chain, and his collar, cuffs and even his stockings are all brilliant white. As he strides into the venue, he is ostentatiously carrying a sandalwood and ivory fan with a foot-long handle. When Zhou Zhengjie sees him appear, he half relaxes, feeling that he has clearly come to make a good showing and is not likely to cause any trouble. After he has exchanged a few conventional greetings and sat down, Zhou Zhengjie fully relaxes. Qi Yuexuan is sitting at a table, sipping tea in silence, occasionally nodding and smiling, and if anyone proves too persistent, he fobs them off with an "Ah", an "Oh", a "That's right" or a "Very good". When the food and wine finally arrive, he lapses even deeper into silence, drinking moodily.

Zhou Zhengjie comes over to him and says, with a smile: "Well, it looks like you have taken my advice today, brother. The less you say, the better."

Qi Yuexuan returns the smile and says: "Ha! So, are the actors all raring to go behind the scenes? I'll see you on stage, shall I?"

"Ah, yes, see you on stage," Zhou Zhengjie replies automatically, not really understanding what he means.

When he sees delegates gradually leaving the banquet, Qi Yuexuan follows them out. It is only a few steps from Yuerong's Place to Moxiangzhai, and once in through the main door with its horizontal banner, Qi Yuexuan suddenly comes to life, as though he has just stepped out on stage.

Seven or eight desks and painting tables of different sizes are laid out on the ground floor, and people are already standing and sitting at them writing. A small stage is set up on the left, next to the wall, on which an opera set has been erected. Xiao Yuerong is also on stage, in full make-up, singing the *kunqu Awaking from a Dream*.

Not worried about putting him off his performance, Qi Yuexuan calls out cheerfully: "Hey there! Stop singing *kunqu*, why don't you? It's far too boring for this occasion!"

"So what *should* he be singing?" a man standing next to him asks.

"Well," Qi Yuexuan snorts, "if it's not *Resisting the Jin Army*, then it should be *The Fury of the Empress Dowager*. These days, even if you're not fighting, aren't you betraying your country if you don't at least curse our foreign enemies?"

No one else dares agree with this sentiment, and those standing near him slip away, pretending not to have heard. Unconcerned, Qi Yuexuan flicks open his fan and moves swiftly over to the tables on the right-hand side of the room, looking at the calligraphy, before stopping behind one particular old man. He knows him as a former Chinese teacher at the women's college who now holds a position in the secretariat of the interim government. He has already completed a four-character inscription in clerical script on a handscroll. It reads: 'The nation of the Rising Sun'. Qi Yuexuan doesn't actually say anything as he looks at it, but he does make a 'tut-tutting' noise.

The old man turns in annoyance, but when he sees who it is, he fishes up a smile: "Ah, Young Master Qi! Could it be the sentiment is wrong, or are the characters badly written?"

Qi Yuexuan sucks in his breath: "It's just I don't understand it. Could you explain it to me?"

"What is there not to understand?" the old man asks, as he points at the scroll with a shake of his head. "Why is Japan called Japan?[1] It is because it is the origin of the sun, the country that gives birth to the sun, so I have written 'The nation of the Rising Sun.'"

Qi Yuexuan laughs. "If you present this scroll in the symposium, it's bound to backfire on you. If the Japanese stop to think about it carefully, they'll see it is both a coded and an open insult."

The old man is astonished, and he hurriedly asks: "How... how do you make that out?"

Putting on a mock earnest expression, Qi Yuexuan says: "Chinese characters were originally pictograms, weren't they? So look at this character 本 in 日本. The horizontal stroke at the top is like the horizon, and with a 人 [rén – person] transecting it, it looks like a tomb mound. Then, underneath, there is the character 十, meaning 'ten'. Can you tell me this isn't a hidden curse?"

"But, the Japanese... don't the Japanese write it the same way?"

"Ha! Even if the Japanese don't understand, you're Chinese aren't you? Now, as for the character 日 [rì – sun]..."

"How... how should that be written?"

"You shouldn't write it at all, just draw the Japanese flag, and you can be sure of not causing any problems. Forget about hidden curses, 日 is one of the filthiest words in the Chinese language. Don't some of our worst curses like 日你娘的 [motherfucker] start with it? You can't deny that is an open insult, can you?"

Qi Yuexuan begins to laugh as he says this, but the old man doesn't join in.

The Young Master turns away and goes over to another table, where an officer of the puppet army has just finished writing another handscroll with a four-character inscription that reads 'Continued luck in the fortunes of war' in a bold hand.

Qi Yuexuan looks it over and asks: "How can you be so opposed to the Japanese and the war if you've taken the Japanese's salt?"

The officer is so startled, he drips ink onto the scroll. He is about to burst out angrily, when he looks up and sees who it is. He stifles the furious comment he is about to make and says more temperately: "You shouldn't startle me like that, Young Master Qi. I don't see how anyone can take this the wrong way. It's a phrase the Japanese themselves use. You can see it everywhere."

Qi Yuexuan gives a wry laugh: "Ah, don't doubt it! Let me explain. If you break down the character 武 [wǔ – martial/military], on the bottom you have 止 [zhǐ – stop] and on top you have 戈 [gē – halberd]. What does 'stop halberd' mean? What else but 'halt the war' or 'surrender'. The character 運 [yùn – luck] has a form of 军 [jūn – army], and underneath, the short form of 走 [zǒu – go], and when you put those together what else is it saying other than that the Imperial Army is defeated and must soon retreat. To put it politely, 'be off with you', or less politely, 'fuck off'."

The officer's face goes pale with alarm, and he hurriedly begins to roll up the scroll, attracting laughter from those around him.

Half talking to himself, half apparently addressing the company, Qi Yuexuan observes: "We Chinese have been writing poetry for several thousand years, but from the Japanese point of view, you seem to be creating some unfortunate lines.

When the blow lands, you'll discover the true ineffectiveness of your brown-nosing."

The bystanders all look at each other, but no one dares take up the subject.

At this point, Zhou Zhengjie passes by and observes: "Less of this idle chatter, Brother Yuexuan, and get on with writing your own piece."

Qi Yuexuan closes his fan with a flick of his wrist and says with a laugh: "Alright, there's no need for you to keep guard over me. But my piece is a very long one, and I need three eight-*chi* scrolls, laid out on a long table, to enable the freedom and abandon of my calligraphy to be accommodated."

"Alright, alright," Zhou Zhengjie replies brusquely, beckoning to some attendants. "Hurry up and bring brushes and ink."

AT THE SAME TIME, over at the Minister's Residence, a scene is playing out in the main courtyard. Caiping is sitting opposite Chenglong at a square table in the central room of the northern range. One is looking stony-faced, and the other is smiling craftily.

Ever since the shop boy had told his story, she has known there is something fishy going on. The words the shop boy overheard have made her quite certain that this is no real kidnapping, but Chenglong's work and no one else's. So, once the boy has left, she makes straight for the Minister's Residence. But Chenglong is not there, and the only thing that meets her in the main courtyard is the wolfdog, barking at her. When she asks Chenglong's men in the front courtyard, all they can tell her is that he went out last evening to supervise the imposition of martial law, and he hasn't returned. Caiping makes her way over to the western courtyard, but since she doesn't dare tell Qi Yuexuan what has happened, she only has a quiet word with Yue E. Yue E is outraged, but she too can only wait for Chenglong's return to challenge him. But midday passes, and there is still no sign of him. Because she is concerned for her father's safety, she tells Caiping to keep waiting at the Residence, and she herself goes over to Moxiangzhai to see what is going on. It is shortly afterwards that Chenglong finally shows up.

CHENGLONG IS NOT HAPPY when he sees Caiping there.

"What are you doing here with a face like thunder, Sister-in-Law? Why are you here by yourself? Where's my brother?"

Caiping gives a cold laugh: "Don't play dumb with me, Liu Chenglong. You know quite well what I want from you."

"Aiya! I've only just got back, and here you are, putting on airs and talking nonsense."

"I want you to sort things out and get your brother back."

"You've lost your man, and you want me to find him for you?"

"I've told you what I want from you, and if there's no sign of him, I'll just wait here. I'll follow you wherever you go. You won't have a moment's peace."

"Well, I don't know where he is." Chenglong looks at her and shakes his head. "How did someone like Noble Red learn to act so shamelessly and make such an unreasonable scene? So my brother's been kidnapped. Why should I be bothered? What's it got to do..."

"What's it got to do with you? I'll tell you what. I didn't say a word about what was bothering me when I arrived, so how did you know he has been kidnapped?"

Chenglong realises he has blundered, and he hurriedly tries to cover it up: "Ah, well... what else was I to think when I saw you so flushed and anxious?"

"It's no good pretending. The secret's out and there's no use trying to stuff it back in again."

"Pah! You can say what you like. It's got nothing to do with me," Chenglong says.

"What kind of man are you, not taking responsibility for your own actions?" says Caiping, glaring at him.

"I'm not as well informed as you. Why should I believe what you say? However much we've drifted apart, he's still my older brother..."

"Ha! So you still remember he's your brother, do you? Look me in the eye, if you don't have a guilty conscience."

"Why should I look at you? Are you going to eat me or something?"

Chenglong looks up, but when he meets Caiping's blazing eyes, he can't stop himself looking away again. Caiping's laugh makes his cheeks flush the colour of pig's liver, as she goes on to say: "I know what's behind this brutishness of yours. You want to find out where the treasure of the Minister's Residence is hidden, don't you? I can tell you, you're not going to get a word out of him with this disgraceful behaviour. It's as much use as a blind man lighting a lamp. I was going to cut you some slack, but no chance now, if you won't own up to anything."

So saying, she stands up and continues: "I'm going now. You keep your brother wherever you've got him, and beat him to a pulp or slice him into pieces if you dare."

These words really get under Chenglong's skin. Just as Caiping has said, his pretend kidnappers have been interrogating Wangtian all morning without getting anything out of him. From what she says, she knows exactly what is going on, so Chenglong hurriedly changes tack. He strides over to her and stops her leaving.

"Don't go, Sister-in-Law. You haven't let me finish."

Caiping just spits out one word: "Speak!"

"It's not easy to explain in just a sentence or two. Let's sit down and talk."

Before he can say any more, the wolfdog in the courtyard begins to bark, and he looks outside, searching for the right approach.

"Look, the food I ordered from the restaurant has arrived. Have something to eat and drink with me, and then we'll talk. How about it?"

She sees one of his men acting as waiter and carrying a large steamer basket in over the threshold, so she smiles and says: "Ha! That's more like it. I'm eating for two at the moment, and I won't have to listen to your nonsense on an empty stomach!"

With that, she makes her way rather grandly back to the table and sits down.

With Chenglong's approval, the waiter hurriedly lays out the food, and without waiting to ask, Caiping begins to eat, saying, as she chews away: "Go on, I'm listening."

Sounding as though he is summoning all his courage, Chenglong says: "Sister-in-Law... my brother is indeed here."

He hesitates, steals a glance at Caiping and sees her still eating away, apparently unruffled. A little put out, he gives a dry cough and then goes on: "But you mustn't worry, I haven't laid a finger on him, and he has had the best of food and drink. I just want him to let me in on the secret."

Caiping keeps on eating. She makes no reply and doesn't even look up.

Seeing this, Chenglong sighs and says: "I didn't have a choice. The Qi family want to kick me out, but is that something they can just do with impunity? How can I stand for them leaving me empty-handed after so many years of Uncle Shu and Master Qi using me and making me venerate them as if they were my father? What I can't understand is how my brother can't tell the difference between close family and distant relatives. Even though he's been made manager, isn't it still a case of 'I'm the master, you're the slave'? Yang Zhixing was manager for a whole lifetime, but apart from pity, what did he ever get out of it? If my brother won't think of himself, shouldn't he at least be thinking of his wife and children? Surely he must stand by me too! If it was me who came into the property, wouldn't I give him a share, as my elder brother? I..."

Caiping doesn't let him finish, but cuts him short with a gesture. "There's no point you trying to explain all this to me," she says icily. "If my husband is still shutting you out, I've no interest in hearing about it. Give me some good news instead, like when are you going to let him go?"

"Ha! Well that will just take a telephone call, but..." Chenglong stops deliberately and fixes her with a smile.

"Ha! So, all you want to know is where the treasure is hidden? Ai! You must know what kind of man your brother is! You could lock him up for the rest of his life, or offer him a mountain of gold and silver, and he still wouldn't tell you. But if you let him go at once, I'll tell you everything."

Chenglong looks at her, half believing, half suspicious. "This is so secret, even Yue E doesn't know about it. How can you..."

"You really don't get it, do you?" Caiping grins. "It's always been the case that the man is in charge outside, and the woman at home. Your brother may outwardly be running things, but I'm the money box and the safe. Don't forget, I married into the Minister's Residence too. Just think why, on my wedding day, Uncle Yang made sure so many witnesses heard him say I was mistress of the household."

Chenglong considers this, then grunts and says: "Well then... are we still playing by the standard rule s– cash on delivery?"

The smile leaves Caiping's face and she fixes him with a stare, her eyes like daggers. "So it really is just a bandit kidnapping, then? If I don't tell you, you'll kill the hostage? Very well, let's not waste words. I won't pay the ransom if you demand it, and you can do what you like."

"And if I let him go, and you don't pay up, what then?"

"If you let him go, I'll still be here won't I? That's two for the price of one, and you'll be in an even stronger position, won't you? We're just little people and don't pose any threat to you. You'll always find a way, so what are you afraid of?"

Chenglong thinks about this for a moment, then laughs. "Alright, so you're saying I don't need to worry about being stood up because you're family. Is that it?"

With that, he gets to his feet and goes into the inner room, where he picks up the telephone and orders in a loud voice: "Is that Lao Nian'er? This is Liu Chenglong. Let the man go. Don't let him see you and don't ask any questions, just get on with it."

Caiping is finally able to relax and smile.

Qi Yuexuan's long inscription is almost finished, and his cursive script does indeed look like 'flying dragons and dancing wind'. Yet even amid such vigour and boldness, purity and clarity are not forfeited; heaviness and lightness of touch complement each other; there is a picturesque disorder, full and flowing. In a single burst of creativity, the large-brush characters fill all three eight-*chi* scrolls. Even though he has taken off his buttoned jacket and long gown, and stands in his shirt sleeves, he is drenched in sweat, drops of which are dripping from his face and making splash marks on the paper. In some places they even blur the ink, but this only serves to increase the feeling of naturalness and spontaneity. A crowd six-deep are gathered around him, watching. Some are calling out their approval, some are gasping, some discussing the work in low voices, some just watching in silence, even though only a few of them can actually read the work in its entirety.

Zhou Zhengying has been there for some time with her camera. Although she too does not fully understand this work, *A Fu on Characters*, she can tell from his manner and bearing that there is good reason to be worried. She stealthily hands him a handkerchief to wipe away the sweat and whispers: "Gently does it. Don't stir things up."

But when Qi Yuexuan sees it is her, he deliberately lets the handkerchief drop to the ground. Embarrassed and red-faced, Zhou Zhengying retreats from the crowd of onlookers.

Even from a distance, Xiao Yuerong can see that something's not right, and he whispers to the Second Lead who is standing next to him: "Just what part do you think Young Master Qi is playing today?"

"I can't tell for sure, but if he's playing the clown, why does he keep trying to provoke the musicians?"

"Eh? What do you mean by that? It looks to me as though he's about to sing *Ramming the Stele!*"[2]

"Aiya! That would be terrible."

At this moment, Matsuzaki Harayama arrives with Yamaguchi in tow. He doesn't come in right away, but stops in the doorway and looks around him. The whole room falls quiet, and the crowd of onlookers in the middle begins to disperse.

Zhou Zhengjie hurries up to greet him, smiling fit to split his face: "Mr Matsuzaki! I was hoping you would come."

Matsuzaki nods but doesn't reply. He smiles thinly. Zhou Zhengjie looks beyond him and asks cautiously: "Has... er... has Hayao Tada not come with you?"

"He may not be able to make it. We'll know in half an hour or so," Matsuzaki replies offhandedly, making straight for the long table in the middle of the room.

Qi Yuexuan has already written his signature and applied his seal, but when he sees Matsuzaki walking over, he dips a 'scholar's seal'[3] into his pot of red ink, pretending not to have noticed him.

"Mr Qi!" Matsuzaki greets him, smiling.

"Ah! If it isn't Mr Matsuzaki!" Qi Yuexuan replies dryly, but he doesn't stop what he is doing until the new seal is properly applied. When he sees Matsuzaki scrutinising the characters, he says: "Ha! So, what do you think, Mr Matsuzaki?"

Matsuzaki nods his head, making approving noises: "It's good, well-written, lots of spirit. But I can't read that much of it."

Qi Yuexuan laughs and looks at Zhou Zhengjie: "Why don't you read it aloud for him?"

Zhou Zhengjie hurriedly declines with a wave of his hand. "No, no. The cursive script you've used is so wild, I can't read it all either."

"In that case," Matsuzaki grins, "can we trouble Mr Qi to read it through himself, so we can all benefit?"

"Alright then, I suppose just writing it is not enough, and I'll have to do everything for you."

He pauses for a moment, considering carefully, and is just about to start, when Xiao Yuerong stops him: "What's the need to read it out? Everyone can study it for themselves, whether they understand it or not. Now, I bet you're itching to sing, so why not perform a number with me?"

So saying, he makes to roll up the scrolls on the table.

This annoys Zhou Zhengjie, who exclaims: "What are you sticking your oar in for? Lord Matsuzaki is here..."

Qi Yuexuan glares at him, then grins at Xiao Yuerong and says: "Ah, Yuerong, I've been practising calligraphy for many years, but this is the largest piece I have ever written, so please don't steal my thunder and spoil my pleasure."

Xiao Yuerong is about to say something, but Qi Yuexuan is already smoothing down the paper as he begins to read, in a loud voice: "*A Fu on Characters*: characters have ancient origins and were created by Cangjie. They developed in the area of central China between the Two Rivers before being transmitted on to the oceans in the east, the open plains in the west, the far borders of the south and the lands of the north. Characters are imbued with the quickness of the heavens and the strength of the Earth. They have the solidity of stone and the fluidity of water. They are the conduit of man's vital energy."

Having heard this much, Matsuzaki Harayama and Zhou Zhengjie exchange satisfied looks, as the rest of the audience whisper to each other.

Qi Yuexuan continues: "Characters are said to be square in form. Their vertical strokes must be straight, their horizontal strokes must be level, and neither should lean or slope. Their dots must be small and their hooks must be short. If a dot is too big, it is like a guest taking advantage of his host. If a hook is too long, it seems to be harbouring ominous motives. How can a left-slanting stroke or a down-curving right-slanted stroke be allowed to extend too far? They would be like a hand thrust into someone else's pocket or a foot stretching out over the threshold. If it is not your rightful position, how can you be allowed to usurp it?"

Matsuzaki seems to detect a discordant note, and he frowns slightly. Zhou Zhengjie's heart contracts, and he avoids Matsuzaki's eye. There is absolute silence in the room.

With single-minded determination, Qi Yuexuan continues: "There is logic to a character's meaning. That meaning may be deep or shallow, noble or commonplace, but it cannot be fabricated or dressed up. It cannot be absurd or deranged. If you point to a horse and call it a deer, point to blood and call it water, point to evil and call it good, point to the strange and call it familiar, point to a man and call him a mustard plant, that is to show no discrimination. How can it be consistent with the logic of characters? How can it tally with the nature of Man or the way of heaven? The usefulness of characters is wide indeed. They can compose poetry, write a treatise, record history or keep accounts. The names of countries, classifications of land, the taxonomy of creatures and the names of men are all dependent on characters. They make a hundred ventures flourish, and they advance the ages. If the world is without writing, then the blazing sun at noon becomes like a night of evil dreams. If the world has characters, then the cramped space of a thatched hut can become as boundless as the wide seas and the open skies. Characters are by nature vehicles of good, but if they are used for evil, they can slander, they can wound, they can defame and they can kill!"

Qi Yuexuan looks around and sees that the expression on Matsuzaki's face has become ugly. He smiles faintly and continues: "There are four categories of character. The lowest category has no bones to support it. Its body cannot stand up straight and is bloated and decaying. We call it an 'ink pig' and it is despised by all. The middle category has no suppleness. Its frame is rigid and has no grace, like an undernourished colt unsuitable to ride across the open plains. The top category has suppleness and rigidity that support each other, with firmness at the heart of its softness, and it has inner strength within its smoothness and suavity. It is not reliant on single strokes in single characters, but embodies the grandeur of the whole. It is known as the 'spirited serpent'. The cutting edge is free and unconstrained in its fluency. But if a character can cast aside all ambition, stand outside considerations of life and death, be without desire, without demand, without jealousy and without fear, and become a single unbroken outpouring of meaning, then that is known as a 'spirit dragon'. It is like the flood of a river that has broken its dike, sweeping away all that is dried up and rotten, and encompassing all the grandeur of the mountains and rivers. That then is the ultimate form of the character."

At this point, many of the onlookers seemed to forget their inhibitions, and they start to discuss Qi Yuexuan's words in low voices, exclaiming in admiration.

Qi Yuexuan pauses just for a moment, then goes on: "A thousand years pass in the twinkling of an eye. Ten thousand characters are hard to write with a stroke of the brush. There are many instances in history of the atrocity of burning books, when literature was falsely accused. The list of those who have tarnished the name of characters include men with no knowledge of characters themselves and who simply bared the fangs of wild beasts. But they are outnumbered by high officials of good education. Because they feared the power and might of characters, they wished to burn them and destroy them. They wanted to cause all citizens to descend into ignorance and stupidity, and bend willingly to tyranny. This made them worse than dumb beasts, as they became wolves and tigers among men. But where are we today with regard to the burning of books and the repression of the people? We are already deep in the dunghill. But characters are still with us, and brute force will not suppress them. Characters are here in our nation and are preserved within its people. Good and evil in mankind, beauty and ugliness, truth and falseness can all be found in the annals of history, and on both steles of celebration and pillars of disgrace."

At this point, he suddenly raises his voice, heaving his shoulders to put all his might into his words as he shouts: "How wondrous! How strong! How mighty! Chinese characters! The Chinese people! Chiiiiina!"

Silence. Not even a whisper. As though everyone has been frozen. Then suddenly the crowd bursts into cries of approval and applause. Furious, Yamaguchi pounds his fist on a table and shouts in Japanese. In an instant, several Japanese military policemen come running in, and the room falls silent again.

Qi Yuexuan lets out a long sigh, but his expression remains calm and relaxed. He laughs coldly. It is a laugh of pure satisfaction: haughty, unconstrained and disdainful. Matsuzaki's face is ashen as he waves the military policemen away, and only when they have left the room does he turn to Qi Yuexuan with a wry smile.

"Qi Yuexuan, Mr Qi, you have proved yourself a true scholar. That is a fine piece of writing, uninhibited and incisive. Truly an essay in veiled criticism. To me, however, you were shouting yourself hoarse in what will prove to be your swan song."

Qi Yuexuan stares at Matsuzaki, and says evenly: "A true scholar? I thank you for such unmerited praise. But as for a swansong, you are right. I came here today to establish a true reputation for myself and to raise a standard for the scholars of China."

Matsuzaki gives a nasty laugh, and says, making each word distinct: "Ha! Isn't trying to buy your name with empty bravado like an ant trying to shake a tree?"

Qi Yuexuan realises that Matsuzaki is showing off his knowledge of Chinese idiom, partly as a way of venting his anger, partly out of vanity and partly to gain face: three birds with one arrow. Forgetting all restraint, he continues: "Pah! And isn't occupying a country solely through force of arms just asking for trouble?"

When Matsuzaki doesn't reply, Qi Yuexuan goes on: "You like word play, don't you? Well, here's another one for you: 'The tyrant who would wear the emperor's crown, only likes men whose noses are brown!' Ha ha." His great burst of laughter gives everyone in the audience goose bumps.

"Do you really want to die?" Matsuzaki snarls.

"Ha! I didn't come here today expecting to live!"

With that, he takes out a small bottle, uncorks it and swallows the contents.

"What is that?" Matsuzaki asks.

Qi Yuexuan laughs and hands him the bottle: "Red crane crest arsenic. Do you want to try some?"

The crowd suck in their breath, and Xiao Yuerong rushes forward and catches hold of Qi Yuexuan, his eyes filled with tears.

"What... what have you done, Young Master?"

"Didn't you once say to me, Yuerong, that I wanted a little in boldness and rectitude. Well, will today's little performance do for you?"

"Yes! Yes..." says Xiao Yuerong, choking on his own voice.

Qi Yuexuan laughs boisterously as he makes for the door, head held high. Yamaguchi goes to stop him, but is held back by Matsuzaki, who smiles at the crowd. He is hoping to project an impression of insouciance, but the smile is forced and looks more like a grimace.

"Let's go, brothers!" Following Xiao Yuerong's cry, Wen Wuchang sets up an insistent drumbeat and a high-pitched chant. There is a dramatic contrast between the bright sunshine outside and the gloom inside the hall. The sun's backlighting makes Qi Yuexuan's tall, frail silhouette look particularly upright and imposing.

CHENGLONG IS GETTING IMPATIENT, as Caiping's attitude has changed since he made the telephone call ordering the release of the captive. She is now saying that, even if she tells him where the treasure is located, he has no chance of finding it alone. If he waits for her to finish eating and drinking, she will take him herself. Although Chenglong is suspicious, he doesn't want to fall out with her just yet, so he decides to put up with it for the moment. He watches as she eats with relish, but he takes no food himself and just matches her wine bowl for rice bowl, drowning his worries with wine. As Caiping eats three bowls of rice, Chenglong soon sees the bottom of a bottle of wine.

Finally, Caiping puts down her chopsticks, slaps her belly and says with a grin: "A full stomach always makes me sleepy. How about I take a little nap first, and then we'll see about things? Alright?"

"No! Not alright!" Chenglong slams his wine cup down on the table and glares at her. "Stop treating me like a child!"

"Why the rush? I'm eating for two at the moment, and if you don't let me digest it properly, I'm not going to be able to walk anywhere."

"Then..." Chenglong suppresses his anger and then continues: "Why not just tell me where it is, and I'll go by myself."

"Alright, but don't blame me if you still can't find it even after I've told you."

"Come off it! If I can't find it, you're not going anywhere."

Caiping looks at Chenglong's face, flushed with wine and anger, and gives a harsh and bitter laugh: "Can't you rein yourself in a bit, Chenglong?"

"You've all ganged up on me and backed me into this corner, and you want me to rein myself in!"

"Alright then, pin back your ears and listen," Caiping says, picking up a chopstick and striking the pose of a drummer.

Chenglong stares at her: "What are you doing?"

Caiping grins. "I'm going to sing it to you as a drum-song. Singing sounds so much prettier than talking. You can keep drinking while I fill you in. How's that?"

There once was a general, I don't know his name,
Who fought many battles and gained much fame.
He suffered great wrong in the people's cause back home,
And his life was cut short when he borrowed some grain.
The people now praise his cruel death in jail,
Who would not call him a hero staunch and true?"

At this break in the song, Chenglong sneers: "Well, that's a bit of a stretch, but since the song seems to be about my natural father, I'll hear you out. Keep on singing."

Mother and son seek family in Beiping,
She dies on the road and the wretched son weeps and wails.
In the city his uncle disowns him,
In the depths of winter life on the street is harsh,
But heaven looks down and sends a night soil man to save him.
He becomes an adopted son but does not change his name.
The father treats him like his own flesh and blood,
The brother takes him to his heart the same way.
Although they are all just men of the people,
True steel will always show through.

Although Caiping is not singing in a loud voice, it is full of emotion, plaintive and mournful, and Chenglong can't help but be plunged into memories of former times. Suddenly, Caiping changes style and introduces some Peking opera style commentary: "This poor suffering boy – quick and smart by nature, fierce and determined, full of ambition – was drawn into the underworld, joined the secret societies, rose to be boss, flourished in business, became king of the night soil carts and changed from small-town boy to city slicker."

Then, at the end of this narrative, she burst back into song: "Truly a life of ruthlessness and ambition!"

Chenglong laughs: "Not bad, not too shabby at all as a thumbnail sketch."

Caiping continues singing:

Who could have foretold that,
Once the poor suffering child had made his mark,
He would forget his roots,
Forget his poverty,
Forget the charity he received,
Forget his emotions,
Forget his country and his ancestors?
He sold himself to the enemy, a running dog to the Japanese,
He threw his weight around before his own family.

"Stop singing!" Chenglong yells, but Caiping takes no notice and begins to sing louder:

If heaven has eyes, it will punish him,
If Earth is awake, it will bring about his ruin.
An evil bastard may live a long life
But all the people will remember is your infamy!

When Chenglong sees that she has finished singing, he pretends to be quite unaffected, rolls his eyes and says: "Don't stop. Keep singing! Keep cursing!"

When he sees that Caiping is still catching her breath and unable to reply, he asks: "Hmm, yes... but shouldn't you be singing about the important stuff?"

Noting his manner, Caiping laughs coldly. "Cursing you is the important stuff, nothing else. I tell you clearly now, I've never been told where the treasure is hidden. I simply have no idea. Even if I did, I would never breathe a single word of it to you."

This time, Chenglong explodes like a firecracker. He slams his fist on the table and leaps to his feet. An evil grin transforms his face.

"Just because I let you off easy, don't think I'm some kind of pushover. Let me make it clear to you – I've never thought much of you as a sister-in-law. The only reason I have held you in any regard is because you are so like my cousin Caiping, to whom I was betrothed when I was little. How dare a smelly little sing-song girl like you challenge me? Not breathe a single word, eh? Do you really think I'm bothered?"

He grabs Caiping's arm and shoves her towards the inner room.

"What are you going to do to me?" Caiping cries out, struggling with all her might to get free.

Chenglong twists her arm, applying a little force and lifting her off the ground as he strides inside. But before they reach the door to the inner room, he suddenly cries out and lets go of her. Caiping staggers back a couple of paces and leans against the partition wall to steady herself. She is holding a razor-sharp knife in her hand. Chenglong feels under his ribs, withdraws his hand and sees that it is covered in blood.

"Fuck you! Do you think you can play games with me?" he moves towards her with a curse.

"Don't come any closer, or I'll..."

Before she can finish, he is beside her. He evades the thrust of her knife, grabs her wrist and twists it round and back on itself so it sticks the knife into her own breast. The blood spurts out, and when Chenglong lets go of her, she slumps to the ground.

In a rage, Chenglong grunts and is about to turn away when he is stunned into immobility. Caiping is supporting herself on the wall, swaying to her feet. The knife is still sticking in her chest, and blood is still flowing from the wound, soaking her bodice. She fixes Chenglong with a deathly stare and manages a stern and mournful laugh.

"You can... you can still laugh?" Chenglong tries to sound fierce but the sound comes out shaky and timid.

Caiping stops laughing. "Pah! Of course I can laugh. I am laughing because, from now on, your heart can never be clean again."

"What... what do you mean?"

"Do you not still hold in your heart the memory of that cousin of yours? And yet you now snuff out that memory... with your own hand."

"What... what is it that you are saying?" Chenglong cries out.

Caiping looks at him and laughs again, but the laugh is full of tears. With a great effort, she says slowly, pausing between words: "Because I... I am... I am the very same... Caiping... you were betrothed to!"

On hearing this, a tremor passes through Chenglong, and his face goes as blank as a clay statue. Slowly, life returns to him, and his eyes sweep over Caiping as he exclaims: "Caiping, is it really you? Why... why didn't you tell me before?"

"Ha! I would rather... die in front of you... than acknowledge a brute like you. From now on... all your dreams... will be nightmares."

She draws from her breast a blood-soaked envelope. It contains the elm seeds that Chenglong gave her twenty years before: the treasured keepsake she has kept all this time. She opens the envelope and throws it into the air. As the blood-stained elm seeds flutter to the ground, her legs go weak and she falls. Chenglong comes back to his senses.

"Help! We must get her to hospital immediately!" he cries as he hurries over to support her.

One of his men comes running at his cry and is about to help lift Caiping up, when Wangtian appears in the doorway. As soon as he sees what is going on, he rushes over, sending the man flying with a kick. Chenglong turns to run, but Wangtian stops him too, with a fierce punch to the chin. Chenglong stumbles back several paces, until he bumps into the table that he uses to steady himself. The underling pulls out a gun, but Chenglong stops him, and cringing like a cur, leads him out of the room.

Wangtian doesn't bother to follow them, but cradles Caiping in his arms, his tears flowing freely. He shakes her, crying out: "Ying'er! Ying'er!"

Caiping opens her eyes, nestles into his chest and smiles.

"Brother Wangtian, I should have told you before, I... my name isn't Ying'er, I... I am Dong Caiping."

"Pah! I don't care what your name is. You are my wife and the mother of my child. You've got to hang on!" Wangtian says, holding her tight in his arms. She nestles in even closer and tries to speak, but no longer has the breath to do so.

As Qi Yuexuan leaves Moxiangzhai, none of the many sentries try to stop him. After he has gone twenty or thirty yards, Yue E, who has been waiting for him all this time, comes up to meet him. She has not seen what has been going on inside and supposes that all is well with her father. Laughing and crying, she takes him by the arm and heads for home. Qi Yuexuan wants to tell her what he has done, but the words won't come. He is enjoying her warmth as she snuggles close to him, afraid of introducing a chill into her heart with what he has to say.

Moreover, he is assailed by doubts as to why he is feeling no pain, no fever, no nausea, no anything, even though he has just drunk a bottle of red crane crest arsenic. He has no way of knowing that what he actually drank was the bottle of red-dyed water that Yang Zhixing and Lao Zhang had substituted. With Qi Yuexuan still puzzling over what is going on, the two of them reach the old elm tree outside the Minister's Residence without noticing that they are being closely tailed by two plainclothes agents. At this moment, Wangtian comes running out of the Residence with Caiping in his arms and meets them head on. Yue E gives a shrill cry of alarm at the sight of the blood on Caiping body.

"What... what has happened?" Qi Yuexuan asks urgently.

"Ha! This is that bastard Chenglong's work!" Wangtian curses, not stopping at all.

Yue E comes back to her senses and runs after him. By good luck she is able to hail a passing rickshaw. She helps Wangtian put Caiping into it, then follows on behind at a fast trot. Qi Yuexuan watches their progress for quite a way before running furiously up the steps. He sees the Minister's Residence name plaque hanging over the doorway, and suddenly, as though seized by madness, he hurls himself through the gates. He snatches up one of the bars used to lock the gates and slams it into the name plaque with all his strength. The plaque falls heavily to the ground with a crashing noise.

"There is no Minister's Residence any more. From now on, this place is a witch's cave and a nest of evil." Qi Yuexuan yells with an ear-splitting, tragic howl of laughter. He staggers over to the old elm tree and looks up into its spreading canopy, weeping. He leans against its trunk, supporting the weight of his body as he feels himself go weak. The sky seems to swim, and his body feels lighter and lighter, as though he is about to fly up past the tips of the branches and into the atmosphere. From the midst of a dazzling light, countless figures and countless images swarm around him. They are swift and indistinct, but ringing crisp and clear in his ears is the old nursery rhyme:

Hot steamed elm seed cakes,
Happy do the poor man make.
The elm tree coins won't fill our purse
But save our bellies from hunger and thirst.

Chenglong is kneeling in the middle of the courtyard, grasping a handful of blood-stained elm seeds. Two tracks of tears are running down his face. The wolfdog barks twice, then gives a blood-curdling screech and collapses to the ground, its legs outstretched. Chenglong gets up to look and sees a throwing knife sticking out of the dog's belly. Terrified, he hears a sound behind him, but when he turns round, he just stands there, eyes staring and mouth agape. His face goes ashen, and his legs turn to jelly. He falls to his knees and sobs out the single word: "Father!"

The sound of a shot rings out, a single gunshot, but it throws the whole Minister's Residence, inside and out, into chaos.

OUTSIDE THE COURTYARD, Qi Yuexuan is slowly recovering from the shock of the sound of the gunshot and the ensuing hubbub. He has no idea what is going on and is just about to go and find out, when one of the plainclothes agents who has been following him all this time suddenly appears behind him, sets him on his feet and leads him away. Before they have gone more than a few paces, a white canvas-covered truck with the sign 'Disease prevention' on both sides comes flying up and skids to a halt in front of them. Four or five people wearing white gowns and white face masks jump out, and they wordlessly bundle Qi Yuexuan and the two plainclothes men into the truck. Before they can find their feet, the truck roars off again. Qi Yuexuan bangs his head on the roof and falls flat on his back. It is only when he has been helped up that he discovers the two plainclothes men have been tied up together.

He looks at the person who has helped him up and asks: "Where are you taking me?"

"Out of the city." It is a woman's voice. He can't see her face clearly behind the large white mask, but the two big bright eyes look very familiar.

Qi Yuexuan persists: "Who are you all?"

The eyes sparkle, and although the woman doesn't say anything, he recognises her. It is Zhou Zhengying. In that moment, Qi Yuexuan's mind begins to whirl, and he can no longer tell whether he is dead or alive, awake or dreaming.

NOTES

CHAPTER 76

1. Ren'e and E'ren mean 'hated' and 'hatred', respectively.

CHAPTER 77

1. Huaiyang is one of the Four Great Traditions in Chinese cuisine. It is derived from the native cooking styles of the region around the lower reaches of the Huai and Yangtze rivers, and centred on the cities of Huai'an, Yangzhou and Zhenjiang in Jiangsu Province.

CHAPTER 78

1. A *baturu* is an official title of the Qing dynasty, awarded to commanders and soldiers who fought bravely on the battlefield. In Manchu, *baturu* means 'warrior' or 'brave'. The name derives from the Mongolian word *bayatur*, which has the same meaning.

CHAPTER 84

1. Li Zicheng, born Li Hongji and also known by the nickname The Dashing King, was a Chinese rebel leader who overthrew the Ming dynasty in 1644. He ruled over northern China briefly as emperor of the short-lived Shun dynasty before its defeat by the invading Qing.
2. Qin Hui (1090-1155 AD) was a Song dynasty official said to have betrayed General Yue Fei.

CHAPTER 85

1. The Kwantung Army was a Japanese army unit stationed in Manchuria. It became the largest and most prestigious command in the Imperial Japanese Army, and was responsible for many of the worst Japanese war crimes in the Second World War.

CHAPTER 86

1. Shao Piaoping (1884-1926), pioneer of journalism and founder of the newspaper *Beijing Press*, was executed in 1926 by the warlord Zhang Zuolin.
2. The Three Realms are the Underworld, the World of Men and the Land of the Immortals.
3. The *Investiture of the Gods* or *The Creation of the Gods*, also known by its Chinese names *Fengshen Yanyi* and *Fengshen Bang*, is a 16th-century Chinese novel and one of the major vernacular Chinese works in the gods-and-demons genre written during the Ming dynasty.

CHAPTER 88

1. Frogbit is a type of water weed.
2. A *yamen* was the administrative office or residence of a local bureaucrat or Mandarin in imperial China.

<h1 style="text-align:center">CHAPTER 90</h1>

1. Xiao Yuerong is actually the stage name of Wang Qingsheng.
2. Mei Lan (1894-1961), better known by his stage name Mei Lanfang, was a notable Peking opera artist, famous for his female lead roles. Mei was the first artist to spread Peking Opera to foreign countries. He toured the world, forming friendships with the Western contemporaries of his day, including Charlie Chaplin.
3. At the end of the 19th century, the Empress Dowager Cixi, effective ruler of China for fifty years, was particularly fond of Peking opera, and acting at court was seen as a route to both financial reward and elevation to official rank.

<h1 style="text-align:center">CHAPTER 92</h1>

1. 'Clearing the countryside' was a tactic developed by the Japanese to counter resistance movements. It involved cutting off all lines of communication and preventing food production in rural areas likely to foster any form of resistance.
2. The *baojia* system was an invention of Wang Anshi in the Song dynasty. He created this community-based system of law enforcement and civil control that was included in his major reform of Chinese Government from 1069 to 1076. It was expanded under the Qing and then borrowed by the occupying Japanese.
3. *Bao* and *jia* were units of the *baojia* system by which population was measured. Ten family units = one *jia*; ten *jia* = one *bao*.

<h1 style="text-align:center">CHAPTER 93</h1>

1. Tokko is short for Tokubetsu Kōtō Keisatsu (literally 'Special Higher Police'), the Japanese secret police that existed from 1911 to 1945.
2. Yuan Chonghuan (1584-1630) was a politician, military general and writer who served under the Ming dynasty. He is best known for defending Liaoning from the Jurchens during the Later Jin invasion of the Ming. He was resented by the court eunuchs who plotted against him and falsely accused him of conspiring with the enemy. After his execution, his body was displayed at the flower market outside the inner city walls. His reputation was later restored, and he is still revered as a great patriot.

<h1 style="text-align:center">CHAPTER 96</h1>

1. Zhao-Hong Wenguo was a heroine of the Sino-Japanese War who joined the resistance along with her husband and children. At the age of sixty, when her husband and elder children had been killed, she continued to fight battle after battle, charging into combat with a gun in each hand. At the end of the war, she sided with the Nationalists. She was eventually executed by the Communists.

<h1 style="text-align:center">CHAPTER 98</h1>

1. The drowning of the seven armies refers to an episode in *Romance of the Three Kingdoms*, when the River Han flooded during the Battle of Fancheng.

<h1 style="text-align:center">CHAPTER 99</h1>

1. '*Baka*' and '*surasura*' mean 'idiot' and 'quickly' respectively.
2. This is a reference to the novel *Romance of the Three Kingdoms*. Guan Yu, sworn brother of Liu Bei, last scion of the Han dynasty and founder of the kingdom of Shu, was captured by Cao Cao, founder of the kingdom of Wei. However, Guan Yu continued to profess his loyalty to Liu Bei.

CHAPTER 100

1. Cai Jing (1047-1126) was a government official and calligrapher who lived during the Northern Song dynasty. He is also fictionalised as one of the primary antagonists in *Water Margin*, one of the four great classical novels in Chinese literature.

CHAPTER 101

1. Zhuang Shidun is the Chinese name of Sir Reginald Fleming Johnston (1874-1938), a Scottish diplomat who served as tutor and advisor to Puyi, the last emperor of China.
2. 'Red and blue armbands' is a reference to the anti-Japanese resistance led by the local villager Tang Wanning in Baiyangcheng Village in Changping District outside Beiping.
3. Stupas are miniature pagodas built to house the remains of past abbots and monks.

CHAPTER 102

1. This is a reference to a famous episode in 206 BCE when future Han emperor Liu Bang escaped attempted murder by his rival Xiang Yu.
2. The explanation is necessary because the Chinese for 'second in command' is *fusiling*, so Grandpa Fu's title is 'Fufusiling'. The double 'fu' is confusing, as *siling* by itself means 'commander', so Qi Yuexuan might be saying "Commander Fu Fu", not "Second-in-Command Fu".

CHAPTER 103

1. This is another reference to the occasion when Xiang Yu invited Liu Bang to a feast with the intention of murdering him. Fan Kuai defended Liu Bang.
2. This is a quotation from the Southern Song dynasty author Zhao Yushi, writing when China was being invaded by the Jurchen Tartars.
3. This refers to the Jingkang Incident, which took place in 1127 during the Jin-Song Wars when the forces of the Jurchen-led Jin dynasty besieged and sacked Bianjing.

CHAPTER 104

1. Zhao Zilong was a famous general under Liu Bei in the Three Kingdoms period.
2. The Manchu Restoration of July 1917 was an attempt to restore monarchy in China by General Zhang Xun, whose army seized Beijing and briefly reinstalled the last emperor of the Qing dynasty, Puyi, to the throne.

CHAPTER 105

1. The Ruifuxiang Silk Store is a chain of silk stores in eastern China. It was founded by Meng Hongsheng, a descendant of the Confucian philosopher Mencius.
2. Tongshenghe is a famous chain of shoe stores founded in Tianjin in 1902.
3. The Chinese *taijun* is a transliteration of the Japanese honorific *taijin*, used for addressing senior officials.
4. The *Generals of the Yang Family* is a collection of Chinese folklore, plays and novels on a military family from the earlier years of imperial China's Song dynasty.

CHAPTER 106

1. Prince Fu of the Second Rank, or simply Prince Fu, was the title of a princely peerage used in China during the Qing dynasty.
2. The Western Empress Dowager Cixi and the Eastern Empress Dowager Ci'an got their titles because Cixi lived in the eastern Zhongcui Palace, while Ci'an lived in the western Chuxiu Palace.

CHAPTER 107

1. *Fabi* was the first currency issued by the Kuomintang in 1935, in use until 1948.

CHAPTER 108

1. Maize with giant kernels typifies food from the northeast.

CHAPTER 110

1. Mountain guns are artillery pieces designed for use in mountain warfare and areas where wheeled transport is not possible. They are similar to infantry support guns and are generally capable of being broken down into smaller loads.
2. A *dou* is a measurement of weight for dry grain equivalent to about ten litres.

CHAPTER 111

1. In 354 BC, the state of Wei attacked Zhao and laid siege to its capital Handan. Zhao turned to Qi for help, but the Qi general Sun Bin determined it would be unwise to meet the army of Wei head on, so he instead attacked their capital at Daliang. When the Wei general Pang Juan heard that the capital was being attacked, he rushed his army back to defend it. The army of Wei retreated in haste, and the tired troops were ambushed and defeated at the Battle of Guiling. Zhao was thus rescued while Pang Juan barely escaped back to Wei to recoup his losses.
2. Zhuge Liang and Zhang Fei were both great generals who fought for Liu Bei of the Eastern Han in the Three Kingdoms period. At the battle of Changban (208 CE), fighting a rear-guard action, Zhang Fei stood in front of the bridge at Changban in Dangyang County and shouted out a challenge. The enemy were too intimidated to advance, so Zhang Fei and his men had time to cross the bridge and destroy it.
3. The Bei Family Garden, also known as the Bussiere Garden, is located in the north of Sujiaguo Town, in Beijing's Haidian District. It was constructed by Dr Jean-Augustin Bussiere of Peking Union Medical College during the years of the Republic of China. It was once one of the Communist Party's underground intelligence interface locations for Pingxi. Before the Japanese invasion, Bussiere's British friends delivered two high-power telegraph transmitters to Yan'an through the Bussiere Garden. The Party's headquarter of guerrilla forces in Mount Miaofeng was located less than 100 metres from the garden.

CHAPTER 112

1. This relates to an episode from *Romance of the Three Kingdoms*, when Cao Cao ordered that his troops were not to touch the crops of the local people after a victorious battle, on pain of execution. His horse bolted and trampled a field of seedling crops, and having been dissuaded from taking his own life, Cao Cao publicly cut off his own hair as a symbolic punishment.

698

CHAPTER 115

1. In *The Sequel to the Water Margin*, written in the seventeenth century by Chen Chen, the author picks up on the stories of some of the heroes of the original Ming dynasty novel. These men are waging a war of resistance against the invading Jin (Jurchen Tartars), but the reigning Song dynasty treat them as outlaws and traitors. The analogy is with the way the Kuomintang are now treating the Communist Party.
2. The *Thirty-Six Stratagems* is a Chinese essay used to illustrate a series of stratagems deployed in politics, war and in civil interaction. The prevailing view is that the *Thirty-Six Stratagems* may have originated in both written and oral history, with many different versions compiled by different authors throughout Chinese history.

CHAPTER 116

1. The Central Plain covers the middle and lower regions of the Yellow River, including Henan, western Shandong, southern Shanxi and Hebei.

CHAPTER 118

1. The Low-Profile Club was an unofficial group of pro-Japanese Kuomintang colleagues who met in the basement bomb shelter of the Western-style villa built by Zhou Fohai at No. 8 Xiliuwan in Nanjing.
2. A Chinese diplomat and statesman of the Han dynasty, Su Wu is known in Chinese history for making the best of his mission into foreign territory. During his mission, he was captured and then detained for nineteen years, enduring particular hardship in the early years of his captivity.
3. In the Three Kingdoms Period, Xu Shu was an adviser to Liu Bei, ruler of Shu Han. He was tricked into changing sides and serving Cao Cao, but he swore never to give his new ruler any practical advice.
4. Gou Jian, King of Yue, was a ruler in the late Spring and Autumn Period who never relished kingly riches, but instead ate food suited for peasants. He also forced himself to taste bile in order to remember his humiliations while serving as a vassal under the State of Wu. Here, it means Chenglong is suffering patiently, firmly resolved on revenge.

CHAPTER 119

1. The Rabbit God is a deity of Chinese folk religion unique to Beijing, where his sculptures are traditionally crafted. He is related with moon worship as he is considered the moon rabbit of the goddess Chang'e.

CHAPTER 120

1. The lucky banner man is an extra who appears on stage at the beginning of a performance, or when a particularly important character arrives, dressed in a red costume and carrying red banners with auspicious inscriptions.
2. Han Shizhong was a Chinese military general, poet and politician of the late Northern Song dynasty and the early Southern Song dynasty. He dedicated his whole life to serving the Song dynasty and performed many legendary deeds.

CHAPTER 123

1. Jing Ke was one of the several heroes who attempted to assassinate King Ying Zheng of Qin, before he conquered the rest of China to become Qin Shi Huangdi, the first emperor.

2. This refers to an incident from *Romance of the Three Kingdoms* and the subject of a popular Peking opera. Huang Gai was a subordinate of the Wu general Zhou Yu. Before the Battle of the Red Cliffs in 208 CE, they feigned a disagreement in order to deceive the enemy Cao Cao into believing there was dissention in their ranks.

CHAPTER 124

1. Shi Yousan was a serial traitor and defector, also responsible for burning down the Shaolin Monastery in 1928, destroying most of its library. He is known in China as the 'Defector General' and 'Three-Times Turncoat Shi'.

CHAPTER 125

1. This refers to the stocky, burly statues of the Guardians of the Four Directions found in the entrance hall of a Buddhist temple.

CHAPTER 126

1. Unit 731 was a covert biological and chemical warfare research and development unit of the Imperial Japanese Army that undertook lethal human experiments during the Second Sino-Japanese War (1937-45). It was responsible for some of the most notorious war crimes carried out by Imperial Japan. Unit 731 was based in the Pingfang District of Harbin, the largest city in the Japanese puppet state of Manchukuo, and it had active branch offices throughout China and Southeast Asia.
2. The story of Lady Meng Jiang is counted as one of the four great folktales of China. It is set in the Qin dynasty, when Lady Meng Jiang's husband was pressed into service by imperial officials and sent as corvee labour to build the Great Wall. Lady Meng Jiang heard nothing after his departure, so she set out to bring him winter clothes. Unfortunately, by the time she reached the Great Wall, her husband had already died. Hearing the bad news, she wept so bitterly that a part of the Great Wall collapsed, revealing his bones.

CHAPTER 127

1. Chen Shimei is a Chinese opera character and a byword in China for a heartless and unfaithful man. He was a poor scholar studying for the imperial examinations. He was married to Qin Xianglian, who took care of him, his parents and their children, so Chen Shimei had time to study. When he came first in the examinations, the emperor offered him his daughter's hand in marriage. Chen kept quiet about his existing marriage and accepted.

CHAPTER 128

1. *The Injustice to Dou E* is a Yuan dynasty play written by Guan Hanqing (c. 1241-1320). The story follows a child bride turned widow, Dou E, who is wrongly convicted of crimes by a corrupt court official for actions perpetrated by a rejected suitor. After her execution, three prophesied phenomena occur to prove her innocence: blood raining from the sky, snow in June and a three-year drought. After a visit from the ghost of Dou E, her father eventually brings the corrupt court official, a doctor and the suitor to justice.

CHAPTER 129

1. A *pailou* is a decorated ceremonial gateway.

CHAPTER 130

1. The Wuhuan is a nomadic tribe from the north that was defeated by Cao Cao at the Battle of White Wolf Mountain in 207 CE.
2. The empty city strategy was deployed by the military strategist Zhuge Liang, who made himself appear unperturbed while making it evident that his city was undefended, hoping his adversary would suspect an ambush.

CHAPTER 132

1. Liang Hongyu was a Chinese general of the Song dynasty. She became famous during the Jin-Song wars against the Jurchen-led Jin dynasty.
2. Caishikou was the principal execution ground in Qing dynasty Beijing.

CHAPTER 133

1. According to the Song dynasty academician, Zhu Wang, the Four Great Happinesses are: to encounter a sweet shower after a long drought; to run across an old friend in a distant land; to spend your wedding night with bright candles; and to succeed in government.
2. *Fu*, often translated as 'rhapsody' or 'poetic exposition', is a form of Chinese rhymed prose that was the dominant literary form during the Han dynasty.

CHAPTER 135

1. Wen Tianxiang (1236-1283) was a Song dynasty politician, poet and folk hero celebrated for his resistance to the Mongol invasion in Jiangxi in 1275.
2. Qin Hui was a Song dynasty politician. During his chancellorship, he was responsible for the arrest, torture and execution of the great folk hero General Yue Fei. Subsequently, kneeling statues of Qin Hui and his wife, who was complicit in the plot against Yue Fei, were placed in front of Yue Fei's tomb, where they were spat on by visitors to the tomb, leading to statues being put behind barriers and protected as cultural relics.
3. Yang Jiye was a general serving first the Northern Han state during the last years of the Five Dynasties and Ten Kingdoms period, and later the Song dynasty when it annexed the Northern Han in 979 AD.
4. *Guasha*, or body-scraping, is a therapy in traditional Chinese medicine that uses a massage tool to stimulate the circulation.

CHAPTER 136

1. The characters for Japan in both Chinese and Japanese are 日本, which mean 'sun' and 'root' or 'origin' respectively.
2. *Ramming the Stele* is a reference to the Peking opera *Yang Ye Rams the Stele* or *Twin Wolf Mountain*. Yang Ye was a famous general in the period known as the Five Dynasties and Ten Kingdoms in the tenth century. During the battle of Twin Wolf Mountain, he was surrounded by enemies. His eldest three sons had already died and his fourth and fifth sons were missing. His sixth son Yang Yanzhao asked the seventh son to seek aid while he tried to fight a way out for his father. Feeling hopeless, Yang Ye saw in the distance a commemorative stele. The name on it was Li Ling, a famous Han dynasty general who in 99 BCE was forced to lead an army of 5,000 to attack the 80,000-strong Xiongnu Army forces from the north. Fighting valiantly for more than ten days and killing over 10,000 Xiongnu soldiers, Li received no reinforcement and eventually defected to the enemy, resulting in the execution of his entire family back home. Refusing to become another Li Ling, Yang Ye decided to commit suicide by ramming his head on the stele.
3. A scholar's seal is a seal that doesn't bear the owner's name but a well-known verse or suchlike. It is used for artistic purposes on paintings and other artworks.

ABOUT THE AUTHOR

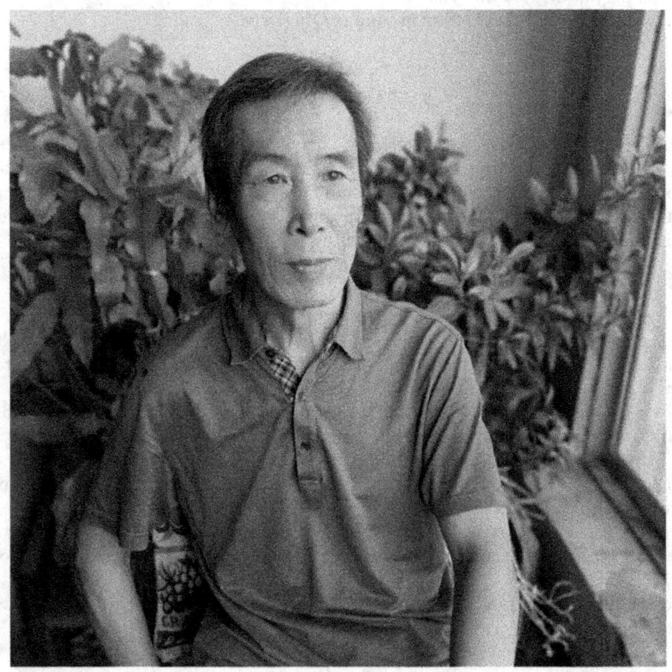

Ma Pinglai was born in Beijing in 1953. At the age of sixteen his education was disrupted by the Cultural Revolution, and he spent the next six years in Inner Mongolia serving in the People's Liberation Army.

He returned to Beijing in 1975, where he worked in a factory and then took on various teaching jobs. During the market reforms of the 1980s he set up his own business, and in 2003 he devoted himself to writing. In 2014 he won the Lao She Literary Award for Outstanding Long-Form Novels, and two years later *The Elm Tree* won the inaugural Haoran Literature Prize.